Religion
in America

AMERICAN EXPERIENCE

Religion in America

Timothy L. Hall

Facts On File
An imprint of Infobase Publishing

Facts On File, Inc.
An imprint of Infobase Publishing
132 West 31st Street
New York NY 10001

Library of Congress Cataloging-in-Publication Data

Hall, Timothy L., 1955–
Religion in America / Timothy L. Hall.
p. cm. — (American experience)
Includes bibliographical references (p.   ).
ISBN-10: 0-8160-6198-X (alk. paper)
ISBN-13: 978-0-8160-6198-3
1. United States—Religion. 2. United States—Church history. I. Title. II. Series: American
experience (Facts On File, Inc.)
BL2525.H345 2007
200.973—dc22   2006013945

Facts On File books are available at special discounts when purchased in bulk quantities for
businesses, associations, institutions or sales promotions. Please call our Special Sales Department
in New York at (212) 967-8800 or (800) 322-8755.

You can find Facts On File on the World Wide Web at http://www.factsonfile.com

Text design by Joan M. McEvoy
Cover design by Dorothy Preston
Maps and graphs by Dale Williams

Printed in the United States of America

VB FOF 10 9 8 7 6 5 4 3 2 1

This book is printed on acid-free paper.

For my sister Sherry and my brother Dan

Contents

Acknowledgments

While writing this book, I had the privilege of working in the office of the provost at the University of Mississippi. My former secretary and partner in academic administration, Martha Bowles, helped me immensely, especially in the selection of photographs and the copying of original sources. Shirley Pegues and I have formed a new partnership after Martha's retirement. Shirley managed the administrative work that crosses our desks so ably that I was able to find odd moments here and there for final editing of this book. Samantha Rayburn, a graduate student in accounting, made constant trips to the main campus library for sources, copied sources, and proofed quotations in the manuscript, for all of which I am extremely grateful. Provost Carolyn Ellis Staton graciously tolerated my attempt to continue the work of a scholar even as I joined her in the work of academic administration. And finally, my children, Ben and Amy, and wife, Lee, endured my evenings and weekends of work on this project. Lee, especially, supported me with encouragement and, most of all, love. She makes everything possible.

Introduction

The history of religion and America stretches from the precolonial period, when hundreds of American Indian groups with a wide variety of religious traditions shared the continent, to the 21st century, when America is home to every major religion of the planet. Some of the religious groups in this history have wielded more influence than others, of course. The many subdivisions of Protestantism, for example, have collectively outnumbered any other single religious tradition in members. Earlier in the nation's history, in fact, Protestants enjoyed such a cultural influence in the United States that some observers were prepared to call America a Protestant nation. Moreover, for much of this history, Protestant Christianity has enjoyed the privileges of a majority faith in America, if it is even fair to characterize the jostling assortment of denominations and sects housed within Protestantism as a "faith." By the middle of the 20th century, though, Catholics and Jews had become prominent enough participants in America's religious life that sociologist Will Herberg could write an influential description of the American religious landscape titled, simply, *Protestant, Catholic, Jew*,[1] but 50 years later the book's title seemed hopelessly underinclusive. At the beginning of the 21st century, when Muslims outnumber Episcopalians, mainline Presbyterians, and Jews in the United States, calling America a Protestant or Christian or even Judaeo-Christian nation seems not very helpful.[2]

The champions of religious homogeneity have never had an easy time of it in America. Diversity and disagreement are written large across the chapters of American religious history. Before the first European settlers arrived, religious diversity had already taken root on American soil, in the varied beliefs and practices of Native Americans already present. Although the Europeans who began arriving in America in the 16th century generally brought with them the expectation that stable government required a measure of religious uniformity, they proved incapable of barricading themselves against the incursions of religious difference. Catholics erected a colony in Maryland, Jews arrived in New Amsterdam (present-day New York) and planted themselves there, and Quakers found refuge in the Providence Colony (present-day Rhode Island) and later in Pennsylvania, established by Quaker leader William Penn. In New England Puritans worked diligently to impose a quarantine against religious views they thought erroneous and dangerous. But Baptists and Quakers, pronounced unwelcome by the Puritans, refused to stay away. Before the 17th century had ended, whatever dreams of religious uniformity New England Puritans or southern Anglicans had cherished were irrevocably shattered. Colonies and later states had to abandon their established churches during the 18th and early 19th centuries in the face of religious pluralism that could not be tamed.

The attempt to claim America for one religious tradition or another is at odds with the very character of American religion, which has, at least since the Revolutionary period, resisted the recognition of any religious tradition as the "official" religion of America. At first colonial America assumed the centuries-old axiom that government and religion must necessarily be allied. Colonial America was spacious enough for such alliances to exist: those between Congregationalism and the New England colonies, for example, and between Anglicanism and the southern colonies. But these differences assumed a common frame of reference inherited from Europe: government needed the support of religion, and religion needed the assistance of government. More than a millennium of Western history seemed to prove this axiom, and early American colonists, whether Puritan or Anglican or Catholic, saw no reason to doubt its veracity. Civil stability required the support of religious uniformity, and the early colonies promptly set out to nurture and defend this uniformity. Consequently, no one could have been remotely surprised that Virginia Anglicans would assume that the Church of England ought to be established in their corner of the American wilderness or that Massachusetts Puritans would labor to give civil expression to their own alliance between church and state. It would be some time before either colony imagined it appropriate to tolerate the presence of religious dissent. Thus, one after another colonial government set out to establish its own particular religious orthodoxy as a foundation for civil life.

During the later part of the 17th century, though, the traditional wisdom about the connection between church and state came to be called into question. A sudden surge in religious diversity in England prompted the first revisions. Toward the end of the 17th century, England adopted the Act of Toleration, intended to grant religious dissenters a measure of freedom to pursue the dictates of their various consciences. Civilization, though sometimes made unruly by the cacophony of religious disagreement, did not collapse. Even before the adoption of the act, England had demonstrated that a fair measure of religious dissent did not seriously threaten civil peace. Consequently, the Puritans of the mid-17th century, who went so far as to execute four Quakers on the Boston commons, seemed increasingly to be following an antiquated vision of church-state relations.

By the end of the 18th century, when Americans recently victorious in the war of independence from Britain turned to the task of drafting the Constitution, the framers of that document made an extraordinary decision. Though the men who met in Philadelphia were no strangers to religious faith and devotion, they crafted the formative political document of "We the people" without reference to God, thus producing what may be fairly termed a "godless Constitution."[3] Unlike most of the important political documents of the time, the Constitution did not invoke either the blessings or superintendence of God. It simply stated tersely that religious tests for political offices were forbidden and, when later amended, added a prohibition against laws abridging the free exercise of religion or respecting an establishment of religion. These later provisions applied initially only to the federal government, leaving states free to chart their own arrangements with respect to religious liberty and the relationship between church and state. By the 1830s, however, every state had followed the same course—providing for the protection of religious liberty and forswearing state religious establishments. These legal developments did not settle at once the question of how a nation of many faiths would conduct its affairs. Even after the end of colonial and revolutionary era religious establishments, minority religious groups had good reason to complain of mistreatment and neglect within American society, some of it officially sponsored by law, other aspects embedded in a dominant Protestant culture. During the 20th century, especially, the

U.S. Supreme Court wrestled with what the first amendment's prohibition against laws "abridging free exercise of religion or respecting an establishment of religion" meant in a society as religiously diverse as America's.

America's encounter with religious diversity has been an enduring part of the nation's history. An equally prominent aspect of this history has been the encounter between faith and modernity. Since at least the early 19th century, new developments in philosophy and scientific discovery have repeatedly challenged traditional religious understandings. Champions of modernity have frequently predicted that religious faith and practice must inevitably decline. Toward the dawn of the 20th century, some influential social observers began to announce the expected demise of religious faith. These announcements accelerated during the 1960s, when Harvard professor Harvey Cox wondered in *The Secular City* what forms religion might take in a culture increasingly dominated by secularism.[4] Sociologist Peter Berger suggested that the 21st century would see American religious believers "found only in small sects, huddled together to resist a worldwide secular culture."[5] By the dawn of the 21st century, however, these visions of an anticipated secular future seemed out of touch with an America that had become home to lively faiths of every imaginable variety.

Even if America's religions have not been vanquished by modernity, however, they have been forced to confront it. During the 20th century some religious traditions tried to make their peace with modern science, for example, even as others continued to war against its dominant ways of thinking. Liberal Protestant theologians quickly absorbed Charles Darwin's evolutionary theory into their vision of how the spiritual world manifested itself. More conservative Christians, though, concluded that evolution was merely the sacred scripture of godlessness and determined that they would war against this false canon. The Scopes "monkey trial," conducted across a few scorching days in the Tennessee summer of 1923, was an early battle in this war, pitting noted attorney Clarence Darrow against fundamentalist political leader William Jennings Bryan. But the war itself has stretched on into the 21st century, as public school authorities continue to battle over the teaching of evolution and its conservative Christian alternatives—Creation Science and, more recently, Intelligent Design.

Modernity, especially in the form of industrialization, also introduced new social problems to the world that religious believers inhabited. Some believers insisted that their faith had something to say about the relationship between workers and corporate management or about the increasingly stark disparities in wealth produced by industrialism. Proponents of the Social Gospel would, beginning in the late 19th century, argue that religious faith must address the needs of modern industrial society and that believers must ask themselves, in the words of Charles Sheldon's best-selling book *In His Steps*,[6] what would Jesus do? Other believers, though, confronted modernity by wondering whether it were merely a sign that history had run its course. American Indians dislocated from traditional patterns of life participated in the rituals of the Ghost Dance religion, expecting that they might help inaugurate a new world in which the tragedies of their circumstances were undone. Premillennialist Christians looked into the face of modernity and saw the leering visage of the Antichrist, who would soon be revealed and war unsuccessfully against the armies of God. Other religious believers found refuge from modernity not in an anticipated future but in an ecstatic present. Beginning with San Francisco's Azusa Street Revival in the early 20th century, Pentecostalism and still later the charismatic movement emphasized the present experience of God's indwelling and supernatural gifts that leaped past the secular certainties of science to demonstrate God's miraculous power in the present.

But even the most ardent opponents of modern challenges to religious belief were happy to take advantage of modern technology, especially modern media of communication such as radio and television. The "electric church" became in many Americans' lives a surrogate for traditional forms of religious community. The biggest churches ceased to be housed within the walls of a religious sanctuary and came to be represented by viewers lodged in their various living rooms. Religious leaders who became adept at using the new technology found it a fertile source of financial resources and sometimes even, as in the case of television personality Pat Robertson, an entree into the world of politics.

Viewed from the vantage of the 21st century, then, American religious experience is both more diverse and more vital than many observers are prepared to admit. No single religious orthodoxy has been able to subdue the many alternative spiritual visions that find their home in America. The axioms of modernity have been alternately absorbed or rejected, but they have not presided over the extinction of either religious faiths or religious practices. These contentions, though, need not be accepted uncritically. The chapters that follow collect eyewitness accounts of American religious experience from the precolonial era through the present, accompanied by a narrative introduction to the main issues, events, and personalities present in each period and a chronology of the events from each period.

Author's Note

Sources from the colonial period often use older or idiosyncratic spelling, punctuation, and capitalization conventions that may make reading these sources difficult. Morever, modern books quoting or reprinting these sources do not follow any uniform convention as to correcting archaic spelling, punctuation, or capitalization. In the face of the many possible variations, I have adopted the following practice on these issues. When quoting reprinted sources whose spelling, punctuation, and capitalization have already been adjusted to follow modern conventions, I have accepted these adjustments without change. In cases, though, of colonial sources with archaic spelling, I have modernized the spelling to make these sources more comprehensible to contemporary readers. So that readers, however, will have some flavor of older specimens of writing, I have retained the original punctuation and capitalization of passages as they appear in whatever source is relied upon. Because the difficulties with archaic spelling are most acute for sources drawn before the 18th century, I have corrected spelling in passages included through chapter three of this book. Thereafter, I have retained the original spelling, punctuation, and capitalization of all sources quoted. Unless otherwise indicated, I have removed footnotes from all original sources.

CHAPTER ONE

Migrations and Meetings
(1400–1620)

On October 12, 1492, Christopher Columbus came ashore on an island in the Caribbean he named San Salvador, thus stumbling upon the Americas while searching for a direct sea route to the Far East. He discovered a land already peopled, since European immigrations to the New World were themselves preceded by other immigrations, but he assumed that he had arrived in "the Indies," the name Europeans gave to the part of Asia east of the Indus River. Accordingly, he named the inhabitants he found in the New World *los indios,* or "Indians." Though spectacularly wrong about the identity of the land he had come upon, Columbus was closer to the truth about the identity of the land's inhabitants. Thousands of years before English colonists planted a fragile settlement in Jamestown or the Pilgrims

Columbus landed on the island of San Salvador on October 12, 1492. *(Library of Congress, Prints and Photographs Division LC-USZ62-105062)*

landed at Plymouth Rock, America was inhabited by the descendants of people who had migrated here centuries before from northeastern Asia, which Europeans of Columbus's age included as part of "the Indies." In search of game, these first Americans followed a land bridge, now referred to by geographers as Beringia, then existing between Asia and Alaska, and arrived in North America between 12,000 and 20,000 years ago. Some historians wonder whether the earliest inhabitants of America might not have also included adventurers who reached the shores of the continent by boat. In any event, these peoples brought religious beliefs and practices of their own to the American continent, and these were the first American religions.

European explorers and settlers arriving in the Americas beginning in the late 15th century determined that God intended them to spread the light of Christian truth to regions darkened by religious superstition and idolatry. Starting with Columbus's second voyage, priests and members of religious orders became regular participants in the various exploratory missions sent to the New World. Pope Alexander VI, in fact, conferred the lands "discovered" there to Spain and stipulated that Spanish explorations should assume responsibility for seeing that Native inhabitants of the new lands be converted to Christianity. American Indians responded to the subsequent missionary activity with curiosity, occasional conversions—either real or feigned—and sometimes determined hostility. Europeans, for their part, were curious about the religious traditions they encountered among American Indians, but this curiosity did not blunt their missionary zeal or immunize them from practicing cruelty as readily as compassion. Furthermore, their presence among American Indians, even when it took benevolent forms, introduced diseases to Indian populations, who lacked immunity to many of the sicknesses that Europeans imported along with their religious beliefs. The pre-Columbian Americas were home to tens of millions of inhabitants. Over the initial decades following European arrival to the New World, however, the conquerers' cruelty, invisibly allied with diseases such as smallpox, influenza, cholera, and measles, reduced this population by as much as 90 percent. Thus, the initial century of European exploration of and immigration to the New World witnessed both discovery and holocaust, and it was in this context that different spiritual visions encountered one another for the first time.

The American Indian Preface to European Colonization

Precision regarding the nature of precolonial American Indian religion is difficult to achieve since literary sources for Indian religious beliefs and practices are few. Instead of the sacred writings common in many traditions, American Indian cultural groups communicated their sacred stories orally, passing them from one generation to another. Moreover, archaeological discoveries have not always been sufficient to provide a detailed picture of America's earliest religious traditions. Nevertheless, some features of these religions can be established from archaeological evidence and others inferred from oral traditions carried across the centuries from the world of the first Americans to the present.

It is clear, for example, that the earliest inhabitants of America shared a diversity of religious beliefs and practices not unlike the diversity present in contemporary America. This religious diversity sprang from extensive cultural diversity among the Americas' indigenous peoples. Modern estimates suggest that at least 500 different Indian cultures existed in the New World in the period just prior to the first European arrivals and that these various cultural groups spoke some 300 different languages.[1] Thus, to the extent that the designation of pre-Columbian inhabitants of the Americas as "Indians" suggests that the various peoples so referred to were culturally indistinguishable from one another, then the term is grossly misleading. It collapses the cultural differences among groups that ranged from the Inuit of present-day Alaska, the Plains Indians of the continental United States, the Aztec (who called themselves "Mexica") of Mexico, and the Inca of Peru, to name only a few of the hundreds of groups. Present-day scholars do, however, identify three broad types of precolonial American Indian cultures. The lives of the first—and the earliest—group of Americans were centered around the activities of hunting and gathering. In fact, the pursuit of game probably drew the first Indians to North America as they followed herds of migrating game animals across a land mass then connecting Asia and present-day Alaska and thus became immigrants themselves. Over time, some of the cultural groups that arrived in the Americas devoted more attention to agricultural cultivation as a source of livelihood. These groups formed the second major type of American Indian culture, sometimes referred to as Woodland peoples. Finally, a third group of cultures consisted of those who joined together to create urban settlements not wholly different from contemporary cities.

Hunter-gatherers, who represented the earliest American Indian cultural groups, sustained themselves by hunting game for meat and gathering nuts, berries, and other food from the land. Their religious beliefs centered around reverence for the natural environment and attempts to maintain harmony with this environment. Thus, their religious rituals observed the changing seasons and marked the great passages of life, such as birth and death. They told one another stories about how the world came to be and how they came to occupy a place in it. Hunter-gatherers looked to shamans whose spiritual insights could help them find game or understand and deal with the causes of sickness and who served as intermediaries between particular clans or tribes and the natural and supernatural forces that surrounded them on every side.

Some subsequent American Indian cultures crafted for themselves a more durable bond with the natural environment by cultivating a variety of domesticated crops. This work and the associated need to store the produce of their labors made these groups more sedentary. A more permanent attachment to specific land yielded religious beliefs and practices similarly attached more closely to the land. Archaeological discoveries relating to agricultural cultures have thus discovered, for example, more elaborate burial arrangements. Perhaps the most famous example of these arrangements is the Fairgrounds Circle, located in Newark, Ohio, and thought to have been erected 2,000 years ago by an American Indian group referred to as Hopewellians. The Fairgrounds Circle appears to have been built across several generations more than 1,500 years before the first Puritan church appeared in New England. A structure some three stories tall and 400 yards across, with a massive outer wall, the Fairgrounds Circle had as its center a burial house with a stone altar. Here, archaeologists have found evidence of cremation, suggesting that the religious beliefs and practices of the Hopewellians devoted considerable attention to navigating the intersection between life and death. In addition to elaborate burial structures, Woodland people also erected effigy mounds shaped like animals such as eagles and snakes. These mounds appear to have had religious significance, representing forces of the natural world that their builders revered.[2]

The last major cultural group of American Indians were urban dwellers. It is a mistake to think of American Indian groups before Columbus as consisting of scattered bands that wandered across the face of the North and South American continents. Though some pre-Columbian Americans were nomadic, the New World was also home to great cities. Cahokia in modern-day Illinois, near the Mississippi River across from present-day St. Louis, Missouri, flourished some 2,000 years ago and was home to more than 40,000 people. Some 1,800 years before this, El Paraíso on the coast of central Peru boasted an equally impressive urban culture.[3] Perhaps the most famous urban dwellers were the Aztec of Mexico. They inhabited a number of cities, most importantly the city of Tenochtitlán (meaning "the place where the gods meet"), home of some 250,000 residents at the end of the 15th century, when Christopher Columbus "discovered" the New World. Among their religious rituals were those involving human sacrifices in the city's many temples. Their chief god, Huitzilopochtli, to whom a temple was built at the center of the city, fed on human hearts, and at the temple's dedication in 1487, thousands of victims were sacrificed.[4] The inhabitants of Tenochtitlán sacrificed enemy captives and their neighbors as well sometimes, but all these sacrifices eventually came to an end with the arrival of Spanish military forces led by Hernán Cortés. Allied with enemies of the Aztec, Cortés sacked the city in 1521, and in the years following the destruction of Tenochtitlán Catholic churches rose up in the place of Aztec temples in what is present-day Mexico City.

American Indian religion prior to European colonization was anything but a monolithic, unified system of beliefs and practices. There were, though, common features in the various sacred stories and practices of American Indians. The monotheisms of Judaism, Christianity, and Islam tend to organize their experience in terms of great events—the Exodus from Egypt of the Jews, for example, or the death and resurrection of Jesus for Christians. But for American Indians, the most important sacred stories placed less emphasis on time and more emphasis on

This engraving pictures the first Catholic mass conducted in the temples of Yucatán, Mexico. *(Library of Congress, Prints and Photographs Division LC-USZ62-101696)*

space. "What is this place, and how did we come to be here?" are the questions that dominated their religious understandings of the world. Moreover, like most other religious traditions, those lived and practiced by America's first inhabitants told stories to explain the origins of their world and their place in it. These are richly varied and cannot be cataloged here. Native American groups at different times and in different places have often told similar sacred stories, though. Many groups, for example, told an account of the world's beginning involving an earth-diver who plunges beneath the watery surface of the world to find earth beneath the waters with which to establish dry land. For the Yokut, who lived in the San Joaquin Valley in present-day California, Earth-Diver was a duck who died trying to bring dirt back to the surface but whose fingernails contained enough earth for Eagle to fashion dry land. For the Creek of the Southeast, Earth-Diver was a crawfish.[5] Other American Indian groups—the various clans of the Hopi nation, for example—located themselves in the world through sacred stories centered around the discovery of a *sipapuni,* or opening, through which the world's various peoples had climbed up out of the underworld.[6] This account parallels one told by the Jicarilla Apache, according to which the world was initially "covered with water, and all living things were below in the underworld."[7]

A great scholar of religion, Mircea Eliade, maintained that the distinction between the sacred and the profane is a core feature of religious experience.[8] For American Indians generally, this distinction was not perceived in sharp terms. Many contemporary Western believers, for example, draw a fairly sharp line between their religious experience and the other experiences of their lives. Faith is segregated, cabined in special days and special places. American Indian religious perspectives are not completely oblivious to this kind of segregation, but they generally possess an even more fundamental sense that the sacred lies always and everywhere close at hand. Although some places, activities, and rituals possess special sacred meanings, American Indian religious traditions also tend to cloak all sorts of everyday activities in sacred garb, possessed of sacred significance. Instead of a fracture between the sacred and the profane, these traditions emphasize wholeness and harmony. This recognition of desegregated sacredness is certainly not unusual among the religious traditions of the world, including some of the Christian traditions that would eventually join American Indian traditions in the New World. But the copious space Native Americans saw the sacred occupying stands in sharp distinction to religious beliefs that accord to the sacred only a minor corner of the everyday world.

Spanish Missions in the New World

For the first century of European presence in the New World, Spain was the dominant colonial force. Portugese explorations arrived somewhat later than those launched by Spain, and these mainly focused around present-day Brazil. French colonial efforts also trailed those of Spain and focused in the north, beginning with explorations undertaken by Jacques Cartier of the Gulf of St. Lawrence and the St. Lawrence River in 1534. France, less religiously stable than Spain in the 16th century, made less headway in its missionary activities and did not make significant gains until the early decades of the 17th century. English colonial efforts in North America, at least, proved to be more durable overall than those of the other European powers. But these also took place much later than their Spanish counterparts.

Only toward the very end of the 1620s did England at last establish a permanent presence in North America, first in Virginia and then shortly afterward in New England. This presence, which introduced Protestantism to the Americas, is explored below. But during the 16th century at least, the story of religion in America is primarily the story of the encounter between American Indian religion and the Catholic faith brought to the New World by Catholic explorers and settlers.

When Columbus made landfall in 1492 in the Caribbean, he christened the island San Salvador, or "holy Savior," thus tethering his mission to an acknowledgment of religious faith. Though no missionary himself, Columbus brought to his ambitions of exploration and conquest a confidence that his mission had God's blessing and that it included responsibility for carrying the Christian gospel to regions where it had not previously been known. He observed that the island's inhabitants were "very ripe to be converted to our Holy Catholic Faith" and "cognizant that there is a God in the sky . . . and any prayers that we tell them they repeat and make the sign of the cross."[9] Subsequent explorations of the New World would continue to ally themselves with a religious mission, especially with respect to the prospect of spreading Christian faith to the peoples encountered. For example, following Ponce de León's arrival in Florida in 1513, Spain's King Ferdinand appointed him governor the following year of what was then thought to be an island, with instructions that de León be industrious in devising means to introduce Native inhabitants to "Our Catholic Faith."[10]

Spain's emissaries to America could not always agree on the spirit with which they would encounter the inhabitants they found there. Conquering zeal traveled hand in hand with missionary enthusiasm, and this enthusiasm itself had acquired a militant edge from Spain's embrace of the Inquisition, its final defeat of the Moors of Grenada, and the expulsion of Jews in 1492. Europe's most vigorously Catholic power thus arrived in the New World animated by visions of both material and spiritual conquest.

Spanish missionary activity in America initially centered around the *encomienda* system, a feudal arrangement in which a Spanish settler, who occupied the role of *encomendero*, was given the right to compel the labor of and receive tribute from Native Americans in a particular geographic area in return for the pledge of the *encomendero* of loyalty and service to the Spanish Crown. In addition, the *encomendero* was expected to provide a living wage to his Indian workers and agreed to see to the spiritual instruction of the Indians of the *encomienda*. In theory, the system of *encomienda* envisioned the American Indians as free people entitled to the protections of liberty. In practice, though, the coerced labor to which Indians were subjected was often brutal and—in the case of work in gold and silver mines especially—deadly. Though justified as necessary to cultivate the potential of conversions among America's indigenous peoples, *encomienda* amounted principally to the gross exploitation of Indian populations, whose numbers were decimated by the lethal combination of inhuman abuse, on the one hand, and the diseases brought to Indian populations by Europeans, on the other hand.

A related Spanish strategy for securing a colonial workforce did not even pretend to preserve the idea of Native American liberty. Traditional Catholic thinking did not generally condone the practice of enslavement, though an exception to this rule applied with respect to conquered people upon whom a "just war" had been waged. According to at least one school of thought at the time, a just war might be waged upon people who obstinately refused to hear the preaching of the Christian gospel. Reasoning in this vein led to the creation of an influential document called the Requerimiento (the "Requirement"), thought to have been drawn up by the Spanish jurist Juan López de Palacios Rubios for Pedrarias Dávila's 1513 expedition to the Americas. The Requerimiento called upon American Indians to recognize the authority of the pope and the Spanish monarchs and to submit to having the Christian gospel preached to them. Failure to comply with these conditions, the Requerimiento warned, would authorize Spanish conquistadores to make war against the Indians and seize them as slaves. In theory, at least, the Requerimiento was intended to be read to Native Americans in their own languages with the assistance of interpreters. In practice, however, it was not uncommon for American Indians to experience having the document read to them in Spanish, not responding at all to the incomprehensible announcement, and then being set upon by Spanish conquistadores, who enslaved them for their supposed belligerence.

The most famous critic of the abuses associated with the Requerimiento and the system of *encomienda* was Bartolomé de Las Casas, a Spanish priest and an important advocate of American Indian rights. After a short tenure as an *encomendero* himself, Las Casas became an implacable foe of the exploitation of American Indian labor and the attitude, widespread in some quarters, that Indians were less than fully human. His long crusade against Spanish cruelty toward these indigenous inhabitants of the New World was not entirely successful, though it did help persuade Pope Paul III to issue the papal bull *Sublimis Deus* ("The Sublime God") in 1537, which agreed that Indians were fully human and were to be evangelized in this light.[11] The campaign of Las Casas and others against the practice of *encomienda* also persuaded Spain to pass the New Laws of 1542, which outlawed further enslavement of American Indians, prohibited the creation of any new *encomienda*, and provided that existing *encomienda* would revert to the Spanish Crown upon the death of their holders. Partially in response to Las Casas's apologetic on behalf of Indian rights, Charles I of Spain also convened the Junta of Valladolid in 1550, at which a panel of judges listened to a debate between Las Casas and Juan Ginés de Sepúlveda. Sepúlveda argued that the practice of human sacrifice by Native Americans or their refusal to recognize the authority of the pope were sufficient reasons to prosecute a "just war" against them and to enslave them. Although Las Cases presented a point-by-point rebuttal of Sepúlveda's arguments, the judges failed to reach any decision on the matter. The provision in the New Laws of 1542 calling for the reversion of *encomienda* to the Spanish Crown attracted such opposition that it was not subsequently enforced. Nevertheless, the system of *encomienda* gradually waned in the second half of the 16th century, both as a result of the continued protests of critics such as Las Casas and of the reality that Native American populations had been so decimated by the combination of forced labor and disease that the system could no longer operate effectively. Consequently, Spanish settlers resorted to the importation of slaves from Africa to replace the Indian workers once provided by *encomienda*.

Spanish attempts to plant the flag of Catholic faith were mostly unsuccessful in southeast North America. One exception was the mission at St. Augustine, established in Florida in 1563 by Pedro Menendez and subsequently directed by Franciscans who took control of the mission in 1573. But in the Southwest matters were different. There Spanish Catholicism left an enduring legacy. Again, the legacy was of cruelty as often as it was of faith, as in the case of Don Juan de Oñate, who visited robbery and death upon New Mexico Pueblo Indians on his first expedition in

1595. But in spite of this cruelty, Catholic missionaries from Spain remained active in the Southwest into the 19th century.

English Protestantism Transplanted to the New World

The American colonies inherited from England its Protestant bent. Catholics could be found, but they were a minority even in Maryland, where they mostly clustered. A Jewish presence in America dates to the last few decades of the 17th century, but this presence could be measured in terms of only a few scattered congregations. Protestantism, consequently, loomed like a jealous parent over its children, ensuring a variety of legal and political preferences for itself and discouraging its religious competitors.

Of the many colonies that England planted in the New World, Virginia is the oldest. History tends to remember its northern neighbors, especially the Puritans of Massachusetts Bay, as having been animated by more visible religious devotion. But the establishment of Virginia and its oldest settlement, Jamestown, was in no sense a secular adventure. The Virginia charter, granted to the London Company in 1606, gave central place to evangelistic aspirations of bringing the truth of Christianity to those who "as yet live in darkness and miserable ignorance of the true knowledge and worship of God."[12] This aspiration found perhaps its most celebrated fulfillment in the marriage in 1614 between John Rolfe and Pocahontas. To observers curious about the origins of this unlikely romance, Rolfe insisted that he acted in his courtship of Pocahontas "for the good of this plantation, for the honor of our country, for the glory of God, for my own salvation, and for converting to the true knowledge of God and Jesus Christ an unbelieving creature: namely Pocahontas."[13] It was clear from the beginning that the "true knowledge of God" given such prominence in the royal charter and in the remarks of Rolfe was the truth as understood by the Church of England. For more than a century and a half, Virginia would remain closely moored to Anglicanism, until the rise of dis-

Pocahontas is pictured here at the court of King James I. *(Library of Congress, Prints and Photographs Division LC-USZ62-71915)*

In this illustration the Pilgrims are pictured landing at Plymouth. *(Library of Congress, Prints and Photographs Division LC-USZ62-113229)*

senting Protestant groups after the Great Awakening and the Revolutionary War with England finally loosened the grasp of the Church of England on Virginia's religious life. In fact, apart from pockets of Protestant dissent, Quakerism, and Catholicism, which took root in Rhode Island, Pennsylvania, and Maryland, respectively, the Church of England could claim to be the spiritual parent for most of the early American colonists. Even the Puritans of Massachusetts Bay, dissenters who adhered to religious beliefs and practices ever more distinct from Anglicanism, remained at least formally attached to the Church of England during the earliest years of that colony's history.

At the conclusion of the first two decades of the 17th century, the first religious dissenters arrived in New England. History names these dissenters Pilgrims for the restlessness of the spiritual journey that eventually cast them on the shore of the New World. Part of that larger body of Protestant dissenters known as Puritans, the Pilgrims too believed that the reforms under England's various 16th- and early 17th-century Protestant monarchs had not sufficiently purified Anglican practices and principles of their lingering Catholic vestiges. They opposed ritual practices such as making the sign of the cross or bowing when Jesus' name was spoken, and they looked with dismay on the encroachments of Arminian theology within the Church of England, which they claimed placed too much confidence in human spiritual capacity and not enough in God's sovereign grace. The Pilgrims differed from the more numerous main body of Puritans is being separatists. This is to say that the Pilgrims believed the Church of England to be so contaminated with spiritual error that it had ceased to be a true church. Consequently, they thought, it was the obligation of true believers to separate themselves from this pseudo-church and establish new congregations. They furthermore rejected the hierarchical structure of the Anglican Church, which placed the various congregations under the spiritual authority of bishops and archbishops. Pilgrims thought each congregation of Christian believers should be autonomous, needing the supervision of no higher authority than Christ.

The separatist Congregationalists known today as the Pilgrims did not arrive in New England by a direct route. They had begun as a small community of believers meeting in the home of William Brewster in the village of Scrooby in England.

Their dissenting religious views made England a dangerous place for them to stay, and they accordingly elected to relocate to the Netherlands, first to Amsterdam and then to Leiden. Neither of these Dutch cities proved attractive to the Pilgrims, though. They feared especially that their children were being tempted to spiritual ruin by what they considered the immoral youth of Holland. Consequently, they eventually secured the right to relocate to the Virginia colony in America, and in summer 1620 a group from the Leiden church returned to England long enough to ready two ships for passage across the Atlantic. Only one ship, the *Mayflower*, proved seaworthy, however. After arriving in Plymouth, England, from Southampton, the *Mayflower* set sail with 102 passengers on September 6. After sailing for more than two months, the Pilgrims arrived in the portion of the Virginia colony now known as New England. Before disembarking they entered into a covenant known as the Mayflower Compact, according to which they "solemnly and mutually in the presence of God and one of another, Covenant[ed] and Combine[d] [themselves] together into a Civil Body Politic." After initially landing on Cape Cod at a location that is now Provincetown, the Pilgrims finally chose to settle at Plymouth. There they established a fragile colony governed by William Bradford for its first three decades and ably chronicled by him in his journal *Of Plymouth Plantation*. Death stalked the Plymouth colony in its first year, and the survivors who celebrated Thanksgiving in the fall of 1621 did so under the long shadow of loss.

Chronicle of Events

1492

- Historians estimate that at the time of the arrival of the first Europeans in the New World approximately 500 different Native American cultural groups, speaking some 300 different languages, are present in the New World.

1500

- The constitution of the five nations of the Iroquois Federation is adopted at approximately this time.

1501

- Pope Alexander VI issues the papal bull *Eximiae Devotionis,* which permits the Spanish monarchs to collect tithes in the New World.

1504

- Queen Isabella of Spain, who had helped support and finance Christopher Columbus's expeditions to the New World, dies.

1508

- After King Ferdinand of Spain refuses to accept bishops appointed for the New World by Pope Julius II without consultation with the Spanish monarch, the pope issues the papal bull *Universalis Ecclesiae,* which gives the Spanish monarchy the right to present names to the pope for the various ecclesiastical offices in the New World.

1509

- Henry VIII becomes the king of England and marries his dead brother's widow, Catherine of Aragon.
- Protestant reformer John Calvin is born.

1511

- *November 30:* The Dominican friar Antonio de Montesinos delivers a sermon in Santo Domingo complaining of atrocities committed against the indigenous peoples of the island.

1512

- *December 27:* Ferdinand II of Aragon issues the Laws of Burgos, which regulate Spanish treatment of American Indians and establish for them some protections against the cruelty of Spanish explorers and settlers.

1513

- The famous jurist Juan López de Palacios Rubios draws up a document known as the Requerimiento for Pedrarias Dávila's 1513 expedition to the Americas. The Requerimiento requires Native inhabitants of the Americas to recognize the authority of the pope over the whole world and his delegation of part of that authority to the Spanish monarchs and to submit to having the Christian gospel preached them. Failure of Native Americans to comply with these conditions means that Spanish explorers may rightfully make war against them and seize them as slaves.
- Vasco Núñez de Balboa crosses the Isthmus of Panama and becomes the first European to see the Pacific from the New World.
- *April 2:* Ponce de León arrives in Florida and claims it on behalf of Spain.

1514

- King Ferdinand of Spain appoints Ponce de León governor of Florida with instructions that he make efforts to spread "Our Catholic Faith" among the Native Americans encountered there.

1517

- Francisco Fernández de Córdoba discovers the Yucatán Peninsula in Mexico.
- *October 31:* Martin Luther posts his 95 Theses on the door of the Palast Church in Wittenberg.

1519

- Hernán Cortés arrives on the coast of central Mexico.

1520

- Martin Luther is excommunicated by the Catholic Church.

1521

- *August 13:* The Aztec city of Tenochtitlán (present-day Mexico City) falls to Hernán Cortés.

1526

- The first bishopric in New Spain (present-day Mexico) is established in Tlaxcala, home of the Aztec's chief enemies, who allied with Spanish forces to defeat the Aztec.

1528

- Pánfilo de Narváez arrives near Tampa Bay, Florida. A few survivors of his ill-fated expedition are shipwrecked off the coast of Texas and eventually make their way to Mexico. One of these, Alvar Núñez Cabeza de Vaca, will subsequently publish an account of this journey (referred to in Spanish as *La relación*), which will include information about American Indian religious practices observed by de Vaca.

1531

- Henry VIII is recognized as the head of the Church of England.

1533

- After Thomas Cranmer, Archbishop of Canterbury, declares the marriage between Henry VIII and Catherine of Aragon void and his previous secret marriage to Anne Boleyn lawful, Henry is excommunicated from the Catholic Church by the pope.

1534

- Jacques Cartier explores the Gulf of St. Lawrence and the St. Lawrence River on behalf of France.
- Ignatius of Loyola founds the Society of Jesus (the Jesuits) in Paris, France. This religious order will play a prominent role in missionary efforts in the New World.

1537

- Pope Paul III issues the papal bull *Sublimis Deus* ("The Sublime God"), which declares that Native Americans in the New World are fully human and should be evangelized in a manner consistent with this fact.

1538

- Viceroy Antonio de Mendoza in Mexico City dispatches the Franciscan Fry Marcos de Niza to lead a small party of explorers north of Mexico City in search of the legendary cities of Cibola. Niza will eventually return with tales of having seen these cities and will accompany a subsequent reconnaissance mission led by Francisco Vasquez de Coronado. Niza will be discredited, though, by the failure of Coronado's mission to duplicate the Franciscan's alleged discoveries.

1541

- After landing in Florida two years previously accompanied by eight priests and four friars, Hernando de Soto discovers the Mississippi River and calls it Río Espíritu Santo ("River of the Holy Spirit").

1542

- Spain enacts the New Laws, which prohibit further enslavement of Native Americans and the grant of any new *encomienda*. Existing *encomienda* are to revert to the Spanish Crown on the death of their holders.
- Juan Rodriguez Cabrillo leads a Spanish expedition that explores the California coast.

1545

- The first session of the Council of Trent begins, in which the Catholic Church responds to the Protestant Reformation.
- Beginning in approximately this year, Catholic priests and members of religious orders—in particular the Franciscans—arrive in Yucatán with the mission of evangelization. They will build a network of monasteries, sometimes on the foundations of former Mayan temples.

1547

- The diocese of New Spain becomes an archdiocese, thus becoming independent from the archdiocese of Seville.

1550

- Charles I convenes the Junta of Valladolid, at which judges hear the arguments of Juan Ginés de Sepúlveda justifying war against Native Americans who engage in human sacrifice or refuse to recognize the spiritual authority of the pope, and Bartolomé de Las Casas's rebuttal of these arguments. The judges eventually fail to produce a decision on the issues presented.

1552

- Bartolomé de Las Casas publishes *The Very Brief Account of the Destruction of the Indies*, which depicts Spanish cruelty and exploitation of Indians in the New World.

1553

- Mary I becomes queen of England. Her persecution of English Protestants results in many of them fleeing to Switzerland, where they come in contact with the views of John Calvin. When they return to England after the death of Mary in 1558, they will possess an enthusiasm for reforming the Church of England that will win for them the name *Puritans*. Eventually thousands of Puritans will migrate to New England during the fourth decade of the 17th century.

1555

- The enactment of the Peace of Augsburg creates religious freedom for Lutherans in Lutheran European states under the principle of *cuius regio, eius religio* (that is, the religion of the sovereign is to be the religion of the nation).

1558

- Elizabeth I becomes queen of England after the death of Mary I. Many Protestants exiled during the reign of Mary begin to return to England with Calvinist views acquired on the Continent.

1562

- In approximately this year, Franciscan friar Diego de Landa burns many Mayan hieroglyphic books in the town of Maní, in northern Yucatán, in an effort to destroy lingering vestiges of idolatry.

1563

- The settlement of San Agustín (present-day St. Augustine) is established in Florida, and the first mass in the present-day continental United States is celebrated there on August 25.

1573

- Franciscans take over the missionary work previously conducted by Jesuits in Florida.

1577

- In about this year Fray Bernardino de Sahagún completes a compilation of narratives about Mayan life referred to as the Florentine Codex.

1583

- The ordination of Native Americans is prohibited by Roman Catholic bishops of New Spain.

1584

- Sir Walter Raleigh attempts to establish an English colony in Virginia.

1585

- The Jewish metallurgist and mining engineer Joachim Gaunse works for the colony on Roanoke Island, founded by Sir Walter Raleigh, in what is now North Carolina before the colony fails the following year and he returns to England.

1586

- *July:* Puritan minister Thomas Hooker is born in Marfield, England.

1587

- John Winthrop, the first governor of the Massachusetts Bay Colony, is born in Suffolk, England.

1591

- *July:* Anne Marbury Hutchinson is born in Alford, England.

1595

- Don Juan de Oñate makes his first expedition, characterized by extreme cruelty to the Pueblo Indians, into territory that includes present-day New Mexico.

1597

- Guale Indians in present-day Georgia revolt against Franciscan missionary activity there, killing some of the missionaries.

1598

- The Edict of Nantes grants French Huguenots (Calvinist Protestants) freedom of religion.
- Ricardo Artur, the first Italian priest to serve in the present-day United States, becomes pastor of the church in San Agustín.

1601

- The Franciscan friar Juan de Escalona writes the Spanish viceroy complaining about the mistreatment of American Indians carried out under the direction of Don Juan de Oñate, who is serving as governor of what is now known as New Mexico.

1603

- James VI of Scotland ascends the throne of England as James I. He is not sympathetic to the attempts of Puritans to reform the Church of England.

1606

- King James grants a royal charter to the London Company to establish a colony in Virginia.

1607

- Colonists arrive in Virginia and establish the first permanent English settlement at Jamestown. They are accompanied by Robert Hunt, a vicar in the Church of England and the first Protestant minister assigned

James I, for whom the King James version of the Bible was named, ruled England and Ireland from 1603 until his death in 1625. *(Library of Congress, Prints and Photographs Division LC-USZ62-105812)*

to serve in the New World. The Jamestown settlement will suffer severe hardships in its early years. By the end of the first year alone, almost two thirds of the original settlers will have died.

- Settlers in Virginia establish the first Anglican church in the colonies, and Reverend Robert Hunt conducts the first Communion service on May 14.

1608

- A group of Puritan separatists who established a community in the village of Scrooby, England, decide to seek a haven in Holland and immigrate first to Amsterdam and later to Leiden. Part of this group will eventually immigrate to New England and be known as the Pilgrims.

1611

- The King James version of the Bible is published.
- After the earlier death of Richard Hunt, the Anglican minister at Jamestown, a new minister, Alexander Whitaker, arrives and attempts to establish a mission to the Native Americans at Henrico, a fort about 70 miles from Jamestown. A new deputy governor, Thomas Dale, also arrives in the colony. He enforces worship on the Sabbath and vigorously punishes other offenses, such as speaking ill of God.

1614

- John Rolfe and Pocahontas marry, and their marriage is claimed by some observers to provide an incentive for the conversion of other Native Americans.

1619

- Virginia makes the Church of England the established church of the colony.
- According to the diary of John Rolfe, a Dutch ship arrives in the Jamestown colony in August bearing 20 black slaves who are sold to colonists.

1620

- Pilgrims on the *Mayflower* set sail from Plymouth, England, on a voyage to North America "for the Glory of God and advancement of the Christian Faith and Honor of our King and Country." Upon their arrival at Plymouth they create and sign the Mayflower Compact, by which they "Covenant and Combine [themselves] together into a Civil Body Politic."

Eyewitness Testimony

The gods Quetzalcoatl and Tezcatlipoca brought the earth goddess Tlalteuctli down from on high. All the joints of her body were filled with eyes and mouths biting like wild beasts. Before they got down, there was water already below, upon which the goddess then moved back and forth. They did not know who had created it.

They said to each other, "We must make the earth." So saying, they changed themselves into two great serpents, one of whom seized the goddess from the right hand down to the left foot, the other from the left hand down to the right foot. As they tightened their grip, she broke at the middle. The half with the shoulders became the earth. The remaining half they brought to the sky—which greatly displeased the other gods.

Afterward, to compensate the earth goddess for the damage those two had inflicted upon her, all the gods came down to console her, ordaining that all the produce required for human life would issue from her. From her hair they made trees, flowers, and grasses; from her skin, very fine grasses and tiny flowers; from her eyes, wells and fountains, and small caves; from her mouth, rivers and large caves; from her nose, valleys and mountains; from her shoulders, mountains.

Sometimes at night this goddess wails, thirsting for human hearts. She will not be silent until she receives them. Nor will she bear fruit unless she is watered with human blood.

Aztec myth that explains, in part, the practice of human sacrifice, in Bierhorst, Myths and Tales of the American Indian, *pp. 50–51.*

In the beginning there was endless space in which nothing existed but Tawa, the sun spirit, who gathered the elements of space and added some of his own substance, thereby creating the First World. This world was inhabited by insect like creatures who lived in caves and squabbled with one another ceaselessly. Dissatisfied, Tawa sent a new spirit, Spider Grandmother, to lead them on a long journey, during which they changed form and grew fur like dogs, wolves, and bears.

They arrived in the Second World but still didn't understand the meaning of life, so Tawa created a Third World, lighter and moist, and sent Spider Grandmother again to lead them. By the time they arrived in the Third World, they had become people, and Spider Grandmother told them to renounce evil and live harmoniously with one another. They built villages and planted corn, and Spider Grandmother taught them to weave and make pots. But it was cold in the Third World: the pots didn't bake and the corn didn't grow.

Sometime later, a Hummingbird arrived, telling of yet another world, above the sky, ruled by Masauwu, who was owner of fire and caretaker of the place of the dead. The Hummingbird taught the people to make fire with a drill, and left. The people learned to bake pottery in the fire and warmed their cornfields with fires.

Things went well in the Third World until sorcerers began turning the people's minds from virtue. Men gambled, women revolted, rains failed, and so did the corn. Again Spider Grandmother arrived, saying that it was time to leave this world and go forth to the Upper World. The chief and some wise men sent a Sparrow up into the sky, and he found an opening there but was blown away by the winds. . . . But how were they supposed to reach the hole in the sky? Spider Grandmother again intervened, reminding them that Chipmunk planted seeds that grew into trees. So they enlisted Chipmunk, who planted several different trees that didn't grow tall enough, and finally he tried a bamboo reed, which reached through the hole. . . . Then led by Spider Grandmother and her twin sons, the people climbed up the reed into the upper world. . . .

Hopi story about how the world came to be inhabited, in Page, In the Hands of the Great Spirit: The 20,000 Year History of American Indians, *pp. 16–17.*

Old-One, or Chief, made the earth out of a woman, and said she would be the mother of all the people. Thus the earth was once a human being, and she is alive yet; but she had been transformed, and we cannot see her in the same way we can see a person. Nevertheless, she has legs, arms, head, heart, flesh, bones, and blood.

The soil is her flesh; the trees and vegetation are her hair; the rocks, her bones; and the wind is her breath.

She lies spread out, and we live on her. She shivers and contracts when cold, and expands and perspires when hot. When she moves, we have an earthquake. Old-One, after transforming her, took some of her flesh and rolled it into balls, as people do with mud or clay. These he transformed into the beings of the ancient world.

Okanagon account of the creation of earth and people, in Bierhorst, Myths and Tales of the American Indian, *p. 55.*

This is wisdom and justice on the part of the Great Spirit to create and raise chiefs, give and establish unchangeable

This figure of an Aztec sacrificial stone includes a representation of an Aztec god. *(Library of Congress, Prints and Photographs Division LC-D428-244)*

laws, rules and customs between the Five Nation Indians, viz the Mohawks, Oneidas, Onondagas, Cayugas and Senecas and the other nations of Indians here in North America. The object of these laws is to establish peace between the numeras [sic] nations of Indians, hostility will be done away with, for the preservation and protection of life, property and liberty.

. . . . .

And when the Five Nation Indians confederation chiefs assemble to hold a council, the council shall be duly opened and closed by the Onondaga chiefs, the Firekeepers. They will offer thanks to the Great Spirit that dwells in heaven above: the source and ruler of our lives, and it is him that sends daily blessings upon us, our daily wants and daily health, and they will then declare the council open for the transaction of business, and give decisions of all that is done in the council.

From the Constitution of the Iroquois Federation, adopted around 1500, and later reduced to writing in the second half of the 19th century, in Moquin, Great Documents in American Indian History, *pp. 20–21.*

In order to make this known to you, I have come up here, for I am the voice of Christ crying in the wilderness of this island, and therefore you had better listen to me, not with indifference but with all your heart and with all your senses. For this voice will be the strangest you have ever heard, the harshest and the hardest, the most terrifying that you ever thought that you would hear. . . . This voice says that you are in mortal sin and live and die in it because of the cruelty and tyranny that you use against these innocent peoples. Tell me, by what right or justice do you hold these Indians in such cruel and horrible slavery? By what authority do you wage such detestable wars on these peoples, who lived mildly and peacefully in their own lands, in which you have destroyed countless numbers of them with unheard-of murders and ruin. . . . Are they not men? Do they not have rational souls? Are you not bound to love yourselves? Don't you understand this? Don't you feel this? . . . Be sure that in your present state you can no more be saved than the Moors or Turks, who do not have and do not want the faith of Jesus Christ.

The Dominican friar Antonio de Montesinos in a sermon delivered in Santo Domingo, November 30, 1511, in Lippy, et al., Christianity Comes to the Americas, 1492–1776, *p. 79.*

On the part of the King, don Fernando, and of doña Juana, his daughter, Queen of Castille and León, subduers of the barbarous nations, we their servants notify and make known to you, as best we can, that the Lord our God, Living and Eternal, created the Heaven and the Earth, and one man and one woman, of whom you and I, and all the men of the world, were and are descendants, and all those who came after us. But, on account of the multitude which has sprung from this man and woman in the five thousand years since the world was created, it was necessary that some men should go one way and some another, and that they should be divided into many kingdoms and provinces, for in one alone they could not be sustained.

Of all these nations God our Lord gave charge to one man, called St. Peter, that he should be Lord and Superior of all the men in the world, that all should obey him, and that he should be the head of the whole human race, wherever men should live, and under whatever law, sect, or belief they should be; and he gave him the world for his kingdom and jurisdiction.

And he commanded him to place his seat in Rome, as the spot most fitting to rule the world from; but also he permitted him to have his seat in any other part of the world, and to judge and govern all Christians, Moors, Jews, Gentiles, and all other sects. This man was called Pope, as if to say, Admirable Great Father and Governor of men. The men who lived in that time obeyed that St. Peter, and took him for Lord, King, and Superior of the universe; so also they have regarded the others who after him have been elected to the Pontificate, and so has it been continued even till now, and will continue till the end of the world.

One of these Pontiffs, who succeeded that St. Peter as Lord of the world, in the dignity and seat which I have before mentioned, made donation of these isles and Terra-firme to the aforesaid King and Queen and to their successors, our lords, with all that there are in these territories, as is contained in certain writings which passed upon the subject as aforesaid, which you can see if you wish.

So their Highnesses are kings and lords of these islands and land of Terra-firme by virtue of this donation; and some islands, and indeed almost all those to whom this has been notified, have received and served their Highnesses, as lords and kings, in the way that subjects ought to do, with good will, without any resistance, immediately, without delay, when they were informed of the aforesaid facts. And also they received and obeyed the priests whom their Highnesses sent to preach to them and to teach them our Holy Faith; and all these, of their own free will, without any reward or condition, have become Christians, and are so, and their Highnesses have joyfully and benignantly received them, and also have commanded them to be treated as their subjects and vassals; and you too are held and obliged to do the same. Wherefore, as best we can, we ask and require you that you consider what we have said to you, and that you take the time that shall be necessary to understand and deliberate upon it, and that you acknowledge the Church as the Ruler and Superior of the whole world and the high priest called Pope, and in his name the King and Queen doña Juana our lords, in his place, as superiors and lords and kings of these islands and this Terra-firme by virtue of the said donation, and that you consent and give place that these religious fathers should declare and preach to you the aforesaid.

If you do so, you will do well, and that which you are obliged to do to their Highnesses, and we in their name shall receive you in all love and charity, and shall leave you your wives, and your children, and your lands, free without servitude, that you may do with them and with yourselves freely that which you like and think best, and they shall not compel you to turn Christians, unless you yourselves, when informed of the truth, should wish to be converted to our Holy Catholic Faith, as almost all the inhabitants of the rest of the islands have done. And besides this, their Highnesses award you many privileges and exceptions and will grant you many benefits.

But if you do not do this, and wickedly and intentionally delay to do so, I certify to you that, with the help of God, we shall forcibly enter into your country and shall make war against you in all ways and manners that we can, and shall subject you to the yoke and obedience of the Church and of their Highnesses; we shall take you and your wives and your children, and shall make slaves of them, and as such shall sell and dispose of them as their Highnesses may command; and we shall take away your goods, and shall do all the harm and damage that we can, as to vassals who do not obey, and refuse to receive their lord, and resist and contradict him; and we protest that the deaths and losses which shall accrue from this are your fault, and not that of their Highnesses, or ours, nor of these cavaliers who come with us. And that we have said this to you and made this Requirement, we request the notary here present to give us his testimony in writing, and we ask the rest who are present that they should be witnesses of this Requirement.

The Requerimiento, 1512, thought to have been drafted by the Spanish jurist Juan López de Palacios Rubios for Pedrarias Dávila's 1513 expedition to the Americas, requiring American Indians either to submit to Christian preaching or be enslaved, in Hanke, History of Latin American Civilization: Sources and Interpretations, *vol. 1, pp. 123–125.*

[A]s soon as you embark . . . you may summon the chiefs and Indians . . . by the best device or devices there can be given them, to understand what should be said to them, conformably to a summons that has been drawn up by several learned men . . . by all the ways and means you may be able to devise, that they should come into the knowledge of Our Catholic Faith and should obey and serve as they are bound to do; and you will take down in signed form before two or three notaries, if such there be, and before as many witnesses and these the most creditable, as may be found there, in order that it may serve for Our justification, and you will send the said document; and the summons must be made once, twice, thrice.

And if after the aforesaid they do not wish to obey what is contained in the said summons, you can make war and seize them and carry them away for slaves; but if they do obey, give them the best treatment you can and endeavor, as is stated, by all the means at your disposal, to convert them to Our Holy Catholic Faith; and if by chance, after having once obeyed the said summons, they again rebel, I command that you again make the said summons before making war or doing harm or damage.

Instruction given by King Ferdinand of Spain to Ponce de León upon de León's appointment as governor of Florida, September 26 or 27, 1514, in Quinn, New American World, *vol. 1, pp. 238–239.*

If we have bishops and other dignities, they will only follow the customs which, for our sins, they pursue these days, of squandering the goods of the Church on pomp and ceremony, and other vices, and leaving entailed estates to their sons or kinsmen. And the evil here would be still greater, for the natives of these parts had in their time religious persons administering their rites and ceremonies who were so severe in the observance of both chastity and honesty that if any one of them was held by anyone to have transgressed he was put to death. If these people were now to see the affairs of the Church and the service of God in the hands of canons or other dignitaries, and saw them indulge in the vices and profanities now common in Spain, knowing that such men were the ministers of God, it would bring our Faith into much contempt, and they would hold it a mockery; this would cause such harm that I believe any further preaching would be of no avail.

Hernán Cortés in a letter to Charles I, October 15, 1524, in Lippy, et al., Christianity Comes to the Americas, *1492–1776, p. 31.*

[W]e had a cross made thirty feet high, which was put together in the presence of a number of the Indians on the point at the entrance to this harbor, under the cross-bar of which we fixed a shield with three fleur-de-lys in relief, and above it a wooden board engraved in large Gothic characters, where was written LONG LIVE THE KING OF FRANCE [Vive Le Roy de France]. We erected this cross on the point in their presence and they watched it being put together and set up. And when it had been raised in the air, we all knelt down with our hands joined, worshiping it before them; and made signs to them, looking up and pointing towards heaven, that by means of this we had our redemption, at which they showed many marks of admiration, at the same time turning and looking at the cross.

When we had returned to our ships, the chief, dressed in an old black bear-skin, arrived in a canoe with three of his sons and his brother; but they did not come so close to the ships as they had usually done. And pointing to the cross he [the chief] made us a long harangue, making the sign of the cross with two of his fingers; and then he pointed to the land all around about, as if he wished to say that all this region belonged to him, and that we ought not to have set up this cross without his permission.

Jacques Cartier, 1534, from his account of his voyage to the Strait of Belle Isle and the Gulf of St. Lawrence, in Quinn, New American World, *vol. 1, p. 302.*

I should have preferred to have the requirement explained to the Indians first, but no effort was made to do so, apparently because it was considered superfluous or inappropriate. And just as our general on this expedition failed to carry out this pious proceeding with the Indians, as he was supposed to do before attacking them, the captains of many later expeditions also neglected the procedure and did even worse things. . . . Later, in 1516, I asked Doctor Palacios Rubios . . . if the consciences of the Christians were satisfied with the requirement and he said yes, if it were done as the proclamation required. But I recall that he often laughed when I told him of that campaign and of others that various captains later made.

Gonzalo Fernández de Oviedo y Valdéz, Historia general y natural de las Indias, *1535, full posthumous edition published in 1851, in Lippy, et al.,* Christianity Comes to the Americas, *1492–1776, p. 81.*

Melchor Diaz told the interpreter to speak to the Indians in our name and say that he came in the name of God, who is in Heaven, and that we had traveled the world over nine years, telling all the people we met to believe in God and serve him, for he was the Lord of everything upon earth, who rewarded the good, whereas he meted out eternal punishment of fire to the bad. That when the good ones died he took them up to heaven, where everyone lived forever and there was neither hunger nor thirst, nor any other wants—only the greatest imaginable glory. But that those who would not believe in him nor obey his commandments he thrust into a huge fire beneath the earth and into the company of demons, where the fire never went out, but tormented them forever. Moreover, he said that if they became Christians and served God in the manner we directed, the Christians would look upon them as brethren and treat them very well, while we would command that no harm should be done to them; nor should they be taken out of their country, and the Christians would become their great friends. If they refused to do so, then the Christians would treat them badly and carry them off to another country as slaves.

To this they replied, through the interpreter, that they would be very good Christians and serve God.

Upon being asked whom they worshiped and to whom they offered sacrifices, to whom they prayed for health and water for the fields of corn, they said, to a man in Heaven. We asked what was his name, and they said Aguar, and that they believed he had created the world and everything in it.

We again asked how they came to know this, and they said their fathers and grandfathers had told them and they had known it for a very long time, that water and all good things came from him. We explained that this being of whom they spoke was the same one we called God and that thereafter they should give him that name and worship and serve him as we commanded, when they would fare very well.

Alvar Nuñez Cabeza De Vaca in an account of how he and several companions from the ill-fated Narváez expedition made their way from Florida to Mexico, 1542, after a shipwreck left them stranded in North America, in De Vaca, Chronicle of the Narváez Expedition, *pp. 99–100.*

And they named the hearts of the captives "precious eagle-cactus fruit." They lifted them up to the sun, the turquoise prince, the soaring eagle. They offered it to him, they nourished him with it.

This was called "the sending upward of the eagle man"; because he who died in war went into the presence of [the sun]; he went before and rested in the presence of the sun. That is, he did not go to the land of the dead.

Thus the captive's valor would not in vain perish; thus he took from the captive his renown.

From the Florentine Codex, Book II: The Ceremonies, ca. 1550, a collection of narratives about Mayan culture compiled by Fray Bernardino de Sahagún, in Thomas, The Native Americans: An Illustrated History, *p. 54.*

Thus mankind is one, and all men are alike in that which concerns their creation and all natural things, and no one is born enlightened. From this it follows that all of us must be guided and aided at first by those who were born before us. And the savage peoples of the earth may be compared to uncultivated soil that readily brings forth weeds and useless thorns, but has within itself such natural virtue that by labor and cultivation it may be made to yield sound and beneficial fruits.

Bartolomé de Las Casas, 1550, Apologetica Historia, in Moquin, Great Documents in American Indian History, *p. 4.*

On one hand I was delighted to see how well Our Lord the King helped us, and on the other I felt upset and thwarted to see that nobody of the Company was coming, nor even a learned man of religion; for in view of the many chiefs we have as friends, and the good understanding and sense of the natives of these provinces, and the great desire they have to be Christians and know the Law of Jesus Christ, six such men of religion will do more in a month than many thousands of us laymen will achieve in many years: for we needed them to explain the doctrine to ourselves. It is just a waste of time in a place like this to think of establishing the Holy Gospels here with soldiers alone. Your Honour should be sure that, unless I am much mistaken, the Word of Our Lord will spread in these areas.

. . . . .

They ask me to make them Christians as we are, and I have told them that I am waiting for Your Honours, so you can make wordlists, and quickly learn their language, and then tell them how they are to be Christians, and enlighten them that if they are not they are serving and having as their Lord the most evil creature in the world, which is the devil, who is deceiving them,

and that if they are Christian, they will be enlightened and serve Our Lord, who is Chief of Heaven and earth; and then, being happy and content, they will be our true brothers, and we will give them whatever we may have.

. . . . .

It has done a great deal of damage that there have not come any of Your Honours nor other learned men of religion to explain the doctrine to these people; for as they are highly treacherous and unreliable, if with time and firm foundations the peace I have made with them is not strengthened, to open the door to the Holy Gospels being preached, and to what the men of Religion have to say making sure of the chiefs, then we will be too late and achieve nothing, if they think we are deceiving them. May Our Lord encourage that good Company of Jesus to send to these parts up to six Companions, and may they be such, because they will be bound to achieve very much.

Pedro Menéndez de Avilés, founder of St. Augustine in Florida, to a Jesuit, 1566, in Gaustad, A Documentary History of Religion in America to the Civil War, *pp. 67–68.*

Now the friar is dead. This would not have happened if he had allowed us to live according to our pre-Christian manner. Let us return to our ancient customs. Let us provide for our defense against the punishment which the governor of Florida will mete out; if he succeeds in punishing us, he will be as rigorous in avenging the death of this single friar, as for the death of all.

. . . . .

Well, then, if the retribution inflicted for one will not be less than for all of them, let us take back the liberty these friars steal from us with their promises of treasures they have never seen—in expectation of which they assume that those of us who call ourselves Christian will put up with this mischief and grief now.

They take away our women, leaving us only the one and perpetual, forbidding us to exchange her; they prevent our dancing, banquets, feasts, celebrations, games, and warfare, so that by disuse we shall lose our ancient courage and skill inherited from our ancestors. They persecute our old folks, calling them witches. Even our work annoys them and they want us to cease on certain days. When we are disposed to do all they ask, still they are not satisfied. It is all a matter of scolding us, abusing us, oppressing us, preaching to us, calling us bad Christians, and taking away from us all the joy that our forefathers got for themselves—all in the hope that we will attain heaven. But these are delusions, to subjugate us by having us disposed to their ends. What can we hope for, unless to be slaves? If we kill them all now, we shake off the heavy yoke from that moment. Our courage will cause the governor to treat us well; in case, that is, he doesn't come off badly beforehand.

A speech made by a Gualean leader, called "Juanillo" by the Spaniards, who led a revolt against Spanish authority in the town of Tolomato, Florida, in September 1597, in which the friar Pedro de Corpa was killed by Gualean Indians, in Mann, Native American Speakers of the Eastern Woodlands, *pp. 16–17.*

[T]he governor does not have the resources to carry out the discovery of these lands. I do not hesitate to say that even if he were to stay here for twenty thousand years, he could never discover what there is to be discovered in this land, unless his majesty should aid him or take over the whole project. Moreover, the governor has oppressed his people so that they are all discontented and anxious to get away, both on account of the sterility of the land and of his harsh conduct toward them. I do not hesitate to say that his majesty could have discovered this land with fifty well-armed Christian men, giving them the necessary things for this purpose, and that what these fifty men might discover could be placed under the royal crown and the conquest effected in a Christian manner without outraging and killing these poor Indians, who think that we are all evil and that the king who sent us here is ineffective and a tyrant. By doing so we would satisfy the wishes of our mother church, which, not without long consideration and forethought and illuminated by the Holy Spirit, entrusted these conquests and the conversions of souls to the kings of Castile, our lords, acknowledging in them the means, Christianity, and holiness for an undertaking as heroic as is that of winning souls for God.

Because of these matters (and others that I am not telling), we cannot preach the gospel now, for it is despised by these people on account of our great offenses and the harm we have done them. At the same time it is not desirable to abandon this land, either for the service of God or the conscience of his majesty since many souls have already been baptized. Besides, this place where we are now established is a good stepping stone and site from which to explore this whole land.

Juan de Escalona, a Franciscan friar, writing to the Spanish viceroy, 1601, concerning the misconduct of Don Juan de Oñate, who was serving as governor of the territory now known

as New Mexico, in Gaustad, A Documentary History of Religion in America to the Civil War, *p. 72.*

James, by the grace of God, King of England, Scotland, France, and Ireland, Defender of the Faith, etc. Whereas our loving and well-disposed subjects, Sir Thomas Gates, and Sir George Somers, Knights; Richard Hackluit, Clerk, Prebendary of Westminster, and Edward-Maria Wingfield, Thomas Hanham, and Ralegh Gilbert, Esqrs William Parker, and George Popham, gentlemen, and divers others of our loving subjects, have been humble suitors unto us, that we would vouchsafe unto them our licence, to make habitation, plantation, and to deduce a colony of sundry of our people into that part of America, commonly called Virginia, and other parts and territories in America, either appertaining unto us, or which are not now actually possessed by any christian prince or people.

. . . . .

We greatly commending, and graciously accepting of, their desires for the furtherance of so noble a work, which may, by the providence of Almighty God, hereafter tend to the glory of his divine Majesty, in propagating of Christian religion to such people, as yet live in darkness and miserable ignorance of the true knowledge and worship of God, and may in time bring the infidels and savages, living in those parts, to human civility, and to a settled and quiet government; Do by these our letters patents, graciously accept of, and agree to, their humble and well intended desires.

The First Virginia Charter, April 10, 1606, in Hening, The Statutes at Large: Being a Collection of All the Laws of Virginia, from the First Session of the Legislature, in the Year 1619, *vol. 1, pp. 57–58.*

We whose names are underwritten, the loyal subjects of our dread Sovereign Lord King James, by the Grace of God of Great Britain, France and Ireland King, Defender of the Faith, etc.

Having undertaken, for the Glory of God and advancement of the Christian Faith and Honour of our King and Country, a Voyage to plant the First Colony in the Northern Parts of Virginia, do by these presents solemnly and mutually in the presence of God and one of another, Covenant and Combine ourselves together into a Civil Body Politic, for our better ordering and preservation and furtherance of the ends aforesaid; and by virtue hereof to enact, constitute and frame such just and equal Laws, Ordinances, Acts, Constitutions and Offices, from time to time, as shall be thought most meet and convenient for the general good of the Colony, unto which we promise all due submission and obedience. In witness whereof we have hereunder subscribed our names at Cape Cod, the 11th of November, in the year of the reign of our Sovereign Lord King James, of England, France and Ireland the eighteenth, and of Scotland the fifty-fourth. Anno Domini 1620.

Mayflower Compact, November 11, 1620, in Bradford, Of Plymouth Plantation, pp. 75–76.

CHAPTER TWO

The City on a Hill and Its Detractors and Alternatives (1621–1659)

From 1553 to 1558 English Protestants endured the zealous attempts of Queen Mary to restore Catholicism as the nation's official faith, after Henry VIII had previously severed the nation's ecclesiastical relationship with Rome and established the Church of England. So bitter did Mary make life for Protestants during this period that many of them fled to the European continent to havens such as Geneva, more amenable to their faith. While abroad, these English exiles discovered that the Protestantism of the Church of England was—at least in their view—more Protestant in name than in substance, a kind of veneer that overlay beliefs and rituals little different from those held and practiced by Catholics. In places such as John Calvin's Geneva, they came into contact with a far more vigorous Protestantism, one that had purged itself of lingering vestiges of "popery." Consequently, when these exiled English Protestants returned home after the ascension of Elizabeth I to the throne in 1558, they brought with them renewed enthusiasm for purifying the Church of England. They began to complain about practices, such as making the sign of the cross and bowing when the name of Jesus was spoken, that seemed to them vestiges of Catholicism. And they railed, especially, against an ascendant Arminian theology that placed too much emphasis on human merit and too little on God's grace. Opponents of these reformers dubbed them *Puritans*, little suspecting how profoundly their reformist zeal would influence the course of English history and, even more importantly, the history of religion in the New World.

Puritan New England

England of the late 16th and early 17th centuries looked with little favor on the Puritans. Its monarchs—first Elizabeth, then James, and finally Charles I—were impatient with the Puritans' increasingly shrill demands for reform in the Church of England. Moreover, when Charles I appointed William Laud archbishop of Canterbury, life for the Puritans in England, especially Puritan ministers, became not only vexatious but downright dangerous. Laud harried Puritan ministers with the threat of imprisonment and death. As a result, waves of Puritans sought refuge from persecution in North America. The movement of the Puritans who braved the Atlantic passage during the decade of the 1630s, especially, became known as the Great Migration. An earlier group of Puritan exiles from England, the Pilgrims, had landed at Plymouth in 1620 and established a colony there. But the main body of Puritans began arriving in 1630, including an important group aboard the *Arabella* led by John Winthrop, a politician with the soul of a preacher, who would be a prominent force in the early life of the Massachusetts Bay Colony, established a short time before. Even before his company arrived in New England, Winthrop preached a sermon on board the *Arabella* that summed up the colonists' aspirations to establish a godly community in which church and state—thought of as "two twins"—labored together to see that the affairs of the colony brought glory to God. Unlike a good many other early settlers of the New World, the Puritans of Massachusetts Bay embarked on what a later minister referred to as an "errand into the wilderness" less out of a desire to find riches than to build a holy commonwealth. And Winthrop's sermon insisted that the world would be watching their experiment: "we must consider that we shall be as a city upon a hill, the eyes of all people are upon us."[1] Unlike the Pilgrims, who had abandoned the Church of England as a spiritual wreck, the Massachusetts Puritans held out hope in their earliest years in America that they would be able to set an example to the Anglican Church at home. They aspired to provide a model of what godly churches and a godly commonwealth might look like, believing that God might use their example to purify church and state in England.

The Spanish explorers of the 15th and 16th centuries had transported to the New World a relatively homogenous Catholic faith. But English settlers, who began arriving in North America in significant numbers during the third decade of the 17th century brought with them a measure of the religious diversity already prominent in England. There Archbishop Laud's attempts to enforce religious uniformity had made life difficult for a variety of Protestant dissenters but had failed to subdue the fractiousness inherent within Protestantism to a single spiritual vision. Congregationalists, Presbyterians, Baptists, and later Quakers jostled side by side with Anglicans in England and imported the same religious diversity into the New World. At first, though, the Massachusetts Bay Colony, under Winthrop's leadership, attempted to discourage dissent. This fact has prompted some contemporary observers to chastize the Puritans for hypocrisy, noting that they fled England in search of religious liberty for themselves but failed to accord similar freedom to the variety of religious dissenters who soon began to arrive among them. But the Puritans were hardly alone in believing that civil society required religious uniformity. More than a thousand years of history in the West had seemed to establish the necessity of religious uniformity as an axiom of social life, an axiom recognized in England, on the Continent, and, with significant precedent, in the New World. Before the 17th century ended this axiom would be called into question both in England and in isolated colonies within the New World, such as Providence, Maryland, and Pennsylvania. During the middle decades of the 17th century, however, the Puritans insisted that the only freedom of religion protected in the Massachusetts Bay Colony was the freedom either to believe as they did or leave the colony. As Nathaniel Ward, an influential lawyer in the colony, put it, those who did not agree with the reigning Puritan orthodoxy in Massachusetts had free liberty "to keep away from us."[2]

While the Puritans of the Massachusetts Bay Colony fended off challenges from religious dissenters, they also labored to articulate their own civil and spiritual vision. Although officially they did not attempt to separate themselves from the Church of England, in reality they were able to practice a form of church government radically different from the Anglican Church establishment. In the first place, membership in one of the colony's churches was not automatic in the way membership in the Church of England had been. Anyone who lived in England became a member of the Church of England essentially by being born there. But the New England Puritans believed that church membership should be reserved for those who gave evidence of being visible saints, that is, among the elect chosen by God to receive the gift of salvation. In the second place, the Puritans rejected the hierarchical form of church government practiced by the Church of England and the Puritans' close spiritual kin, the Presbyterians. Instead, they believed that each individual church was an autonomous spiritual body, not under the control of any higher ecclesiastical authority. New churches were created as a result of a covenant entered into between a minimum of at least seven visible saints and God. The New England Puritans eventually articulated this congregational vision of church structure in a formal statement adopted in 1648 and referred to as the Cambridge Platform. The heirs of these Puritans would be known as Congregationalists.

Though sometimes declared a theocracy, the Massachusetts Bay Colony actually believed that church and state were distinct and ought not to meddle improperly in the affairs of each other. The influential preacher John Cotton emphasized the duty of both civil and ecclesiastical officials to recognize the limits of their power: "It is therefore fit for every man to be studious of the bounds which the Lord hath set. . . . And it is meet that magistrates in the Commonwealth, and so officers in churches should desire to know the utmost bounds of their own power, and it is safe for both."[3] New England clergy, for example, were disqualified from serving as magistrates for fear that allowing the same individual to hold both civil and ecclesiastical positions would confound what the Puritans believed should remain distinct. Nevertheless, the colony clearly envisioned that civil affairs would be conducted along lines pleasing to God. The right to vote was restricted to male church members, for example. And the influential code of laws adopted by the colony in 1648, *The Laws and Liberties of Massachusetts*, contained not only laws drawn from English legal principles but provisions copied virtually verbatim from the Old Testament of the Bible. Finally, as the cases of Roger Williams and Anne Hutchinson would reveal, the civil authorities of the Massachusetts Bay Colony determined that it was within their province to punish outspoken religious dissenters. They reasoned that religious dissent threatened the public peace and was therefore not simply a private matter. Furthermore, they were convinced that religious error was the spiritual equivalent of an infectious disease. Just as the civil government might act to prevent the spread of a contagious illness, Puritans believed government might act to prevent the spread of infectious spiritual error.

Orthodoxy's Critics

Contrary to the wishes of Nathaniel Ward and the other Puritans in Massachusetts, dissenters would not keep away. As early as 1631, for example, one Philip Ratcliff had his ears cut off in addition to being whipped and fined and then banished from the colony for criticizing the colonial government and one of its churches.[4] The same year a young minister named Roger Williams found his way to Massachusetts and almost immediately began to voice opinions deeply offensive to the colony's officials. He denied, for example, that the king of England had any right to hand out land in New England to ventures such as the Massachusetts Bay Colony. To the contrary, he insisted that if the Puritans wished to settle in Massachusetts Bay, they should have purchased land from American Indians in the area. Even more importantly, he leveled a complaint against the close fraternity between church and state in the colony, declaring that the civil government had no business attending to the spiritual affairs of its citizens. Massachusetts, for its part, was not inclined to endure Williams's critique. Four years after Williams arrived in New England, the Massachusetts authorities banished him from the colony and tried to ship him back to England. In support of this action, the general court announced its judgment that Williams had "broached and divulged diverse new opinions against the authority of the magistrates, [and] also wrote letters of defamation, both of the magistrates and churches here."[5] Looking back from his perch at the beginning of the next century, Puritan minister and historian Cotton Mather expressed orthodoxy's relief that Williams's radicalism had been extinguished before it blazed out of control, since "there was a whole country in America like to be set on fire by the rapid motion of a windmill in the head of one particular man."[6] Williams, though, refused to be shipped back to England and fled to what is today Rhode Island, purchasing land from American Indians there and assisting in the establishment of the Providence Colony. Along the way Williams also helped to organize the first Baptist church in the New World, although he eventually parted ways with the Baptists after he became convinced that no true churches existed any longer in the world.

Although Roger Williams served for a time as minister at the church in Salem, his radical views never commanded much of a following in the Massachusetts Bay Colony, and so his dissent remained relatively isolated. The year before authorities exiled him in 1635, however, a woman named Anne Hutchinson arrived with her family in Massachusetts. Hutchinson and her husband were Puritans and migrated to the New World partially because their favorite preacher in England, John Cotton, had done so previously himself. Cotton had assumed the role of teacher in the church at Boston alongside the senior minister there, John Wilson. Soon after she arrived, Anne Hutchinson began holding meetings in her home at which she commented on the sermons being preached at the church in Boston. She was a gifted teacher in her own right and argued that John Cotton's preaching emphasized a "covenant of grace," unlike the "covenant of works" embodied in the preaching of John Wilson. Hutchinson, for her part, made no secret of her belief that Cotton's emphasis on the "covenant of grace" was superior to Wilson's preoccupation with a "covenant of works."

At the root of Hutchinson's dissatisfaction with Wilson's preaching was a question that continually occupied the Puritan mind. They shared a belief that only some individuals—"the elect"—would receive salvation. But they differed over the immensely practical question of how one knew whether one was among the elect. Hutchinson argued that a person knew she was a member of God's elect through an inner confidence provided by God's spirit and not by her adherence to any particular standards of conduct. Many of the colonists found Hutchinson's teaching attractive, but most of the colony's civil and spiritual leaders saw great danger in her views. They branded her an antinomian, that is, one opposed to law, for her impatience with external standards of conduct as evidence of salvation. For

Anne Hutchinson is pictured here preaching in her house. *(Library of Congress, Prints and Photographs Division LC-USZ62-53343)*

communities trying to carve order out of the disorder of the New World, this was a weighty condemnation. Accordingly, the church at Boston found Hutchinson's views dangerous enough to excommunicate her, and the colony's highest court thought her spiritual errors infectious enough to justify banishment.

Other religious dissenters followed Williams and Hutchinson. In the early 1650s Baptists began to venture into the Massachusetts Bay Colony from the security of the Providence Colony (present-day Rhode Island), where the first Baptist church in America had been established. These were fined or whipped and expelled from Massachusetts. That same decade Quakers began to arrive from England, settling in Providence—where their views were tolerated even if opposed—and then venturing into Massachusetts. Puritan authorities in Massachusetts thought the Baptists were dangerous but that the Quakers were even more so, since they seemed to place more emphasis on the experience of the "inner light" than on careful study of Scripture. Consequently, Massachusetts Puritans soon began to pass laws to keep the Quakers away. They threatened to cut off the ears of Quaker men who refused to stay out of the colony once banished, and, when this did not deter the Quakers, Massachusetts passed a new law stipulating that Quakers who returned to the colony after being banished would be executed. In 1659 three Quakers, two men and a woman, defied this law. The men were hanged on the Boston commons that year. The woman, Mary Dyer, though released and warned not to return, came back to Massachusetts the following year and was also executed on the Boston commons.

Providence—Alternative to Holy Commonwealth

While the Puritans of the Massachusetts Bay Colony were busy framing and defending their City Upon a Hill, other visions of religious life took root in the New World. Roger Williams, for example, had defied his Puritan judges and fled into the wilderness of Narragansett Bay rather than be exported back to England. Once there, he did what he had counseled the Puritans themselves to do and purchased land on which to settle from local American Indians. Williams soon attracted other spiritual dissenters with whom he established the Providence Colony in what is present-day Rhode Island. In 1638 Williams and the other Providence settlers entered into a compact to decide their collective affairs by majority rule, with one notable exception: they agreed to be bound by collective decisions "only in civil things."[7] Not even a democratic majority could pass laws intended to tell people what to believe or how to practice those beliefs. Because of Providence's early commitment to the ideal of religious liberty, other dissenters from Puritan orthodoxy tended to be attracted to the colony. Anne Hutchinson and her family, for example, settled on the island of Aquidneck and helped establish the town that would eventually be known as Portsmouth. For his part, Williams played an active role in the colony's affairs. In particular, he traveled twice to England to obtain charters for the colony. He made his first return to his native country in 1643 and successfully secured a charter for the Providence Colony from Parliament. After the restoration of the English monarchy two decades later, he returned again to England and with the assistance of the Baptist John Clarke secured a new charter. This legal document included an early American guarantee of religious liberty:

> No person within said colony, at any time hereafter, shall be any wise molested, punished, disquieted, or called in question, for any differences in opinion in matters of religion, and do not actually disturb the civil peace of our said colony; but that every person and persons may . . . freely and fully have and enjoy his and their own judgments and consciences, in matters of religious concernments . . . they behaving themselves peaceably and quietly, and not using this liberty to licentiousness and profaneness, nor to the civil injury or outward disturbance of others.[8]

When he was not busy tending the affairs of the Providence Colony or his own modest trading operation, Roger Williams devoted himself to a running debate with the Massachusetts Puritans about religious liberty. He never forgot the cold of the winter in which he had been banished from the Bay Colony, and he devoted nearly half a century to an ongoing critique of the Puritans' much vaunted City upon a Hill. His most famous book, *The Bloudy Tenent, of Persecution for Cause of Conscience, discussed in a Conference between Truth and Peace,* published in 1644 while he was in England, argued that religious persecution was contrary to biblical teaching and offensive to the character of Christ. The Massachusetts Puritans did not bear these attacks in silence, though. John Cotton, one of the colony's most famous ministers, responded to Williams in 1647 with *The Bloudy Tenent, Washed, and made White in the Bloud of the Lambe: Being Discussed and Discharged of Bloud-Guiltiness by Just Defence.* Williams, who never met a debate he could not keep going, managed one more salvo against the Massachusetts way of church and state before Cotton, his rhetorical adversary, died in 1652. Williams titled his rejoinder to Cotton *The Bloudy Tenent Yet More Bloudy: By Mr Cottons Endevour To Wash it White in the Blood of the Lambe; of Whose Precious Blood, Spilt in the Blood of His Servants; and of the Blood of Millions Spilt in Former and Later Wars for Conscience Sake, That Most Bloudy Tenent of Persecution for Cause of Conscience Sake, Upon a Second trial, is Found Now More Apparently and More Notoriously Guilty.* In this book Williams chastised the Puritans for their allegiance to "the bloody Tenet of Persecution for cause of Conscience: (a notorious and common Pirate, that takes and robs, that fires and sinks the Spiritual Ships and Vessels) the consciences of all men, of all sorts, of all Religions and Persuasions whatsoever."[9]

Though eloquent, if not sometimes tedious, Roger Williams had little impact on the Massachusetts Puritans. America would eventually catch up to the Providence Colony in terms of its respect for religious freedom, but for most of the colonial period the colony had few admirers. The New England Puritans, especially, scorned the hospitality accorded to religious dissenters in Providence. Their attitude found reflection in the nickname given to Providence during colonial times as the "latrine of New England." History today reveres Williams as one of the architects of the idea of religious liberty, but during most of the colonial period he was ignored while he was alive and, after he died in 1683, promptly forgotten.

Catholic and Jewish Communities

Protestant Christianity assumed center stage in the early American colonies, and Protestants frequently buttressed their social prominence with laws reinforcing their legal preeminence as well. But in spite of the frequent legal disabilities they suffered, Catholic and Jewish communities also found their place in the New World. Spanish explorers had originally planted Catholic missions in the New World during the 16th century, and at least some of these extended into locations within the present-day United States, such as Florida and New Mexico. But the importance of this Spanish Catholic presence diminished during the 17th century as Protestantism—especially its English variants such as Anglicanism and Congregationalism—claimed a more dominant foothold in North America. Farther north, however, in New France (present-day Canada), Catholic faith also took root. Jacques Cartier explored the St. Lawrence valley in 1534 and 1535, but it was not until the early decades of the next century that a significant Catholic missionary presence arrived. Jesuit missionaries such as Jean de Brébeuf attempted to evangelize American Indians such as the Huron in New France, although the ravages visited upon these peoples by diseases carried by Europeans eventually dulled their enthusiasm for hearing the Christian message. Brébeuf was himself tortured and killed in 1649, not by the Huron of present-day Ontario, with whom he labored for more than a decade, but after he and another missionary were captured by an Iroquois war party. The Iroquois were enemies of the Huron and, having allied themselves with Dutch trading interests, enemies of the French as well. Brébeuf's martyrdom for the cause of Catholic missions inspired others to follow his example. In particular, female religious orders also joined missionary efforts in New France. Of the members of these orders, the most famous is Marie Guyart Martin, a member of the Ursuline order, who established a school in 1642 for French and American Indian girls in Quebec and who was a contemporary of Brébeuf. Martin, known also as Marie de l'Incarnation, or Marie of the Incarnation, joined the Ursuline order in Tours, France, in 1631 after the death of her husband, leaving her young son to be raised by her sister. She subsequently had a dream that convinced her that God wished her to become a missionary to New France and immigrated there in 1639. Shielded from public life in the convent in Quebec, she nevertheless had a significant missionary impact especially through the lives of young American Indian girls. Moreover, she was an avid correspondent, and her more than 270 surviving letters, including those to her son, are an important chronicle of Catholic New France during the 17th century.

Farther south, in Maryland (named for King Charles I's Catholic queen, Henrietta Maria), Cecil Calvert, the second lord Baltimore, established a colony based on a charter granted to him by Charles I in 1632. The foundation for receiving this patent had actually been laid by Cecil's father, George Calvert, the first lord Baltimore, who converted to Catholicism in 1625. Upon the senior Calvert's death in 1632, the patent went to his son Cecil, who appointed his brother, Leonard, governor of the colony. The first settlers in Maryland arrived by two ships, the *Ark* and the *Dove*, in 1634. The colony's Catholic proprietor took pains to encourage the minority of Catholics aboard these two ships, whose number included two Jesuit priests, to practice their religion discretely, so as not to offend Protestants, who remained a majority both onboard these two ships and in the colony's subsequent life. Lord Baltimore's appeal for discretion from his Catholic colonists was not entirely effective. Upon their arrival one of the Jesuits, Andrew White, had a large cross carved out of a tree and led the Catholic minority in the celebration of the first Mass in Maryland on March 25, 1634.

Since discretion could not always be counted upon to shield Maryland's

George Calvert was the first Lord Baltimore. *(Library of Congress, Prints and Photographs Division LC-UCSZ62-102742)*

Cecil Calvert, son of George Calvert, was the second Lord Baltimore. *(Library of Congress, Prints and Photographs Division LC-UCSZ62-102742)*

Catholic minority from the religious prejudices of a Protestant majority, the colonial government took steps to enact a public commitment to the idea of religious liberty. Significantly, in 1639 the Maryland legislature adopted a law that secured a measure of religious freedom for inhabitants of the colony. Even this legal protection did not prevent Protestants from seizing control of the colonial government in the early 1640s. But Lord Baltimore resumed his authority in 1646, and three years later Maryland passed a landmark guaranty of religious freedom called the Act Concerning Religion, which stipulated that "no person . . . professing to believe in Jesus Christ, shall from henceforth be any ways troubled . . . for . . . his or her religion nor in the free exercise thereof . . . nor any way [be] compelled to the belief or exercise of any other Religion against his or her consent."[10] Non-Christians, however, or even Christians who denied the doctrine of the Trinity, did not enjoy the free exercise of religion guaranteed to orthodox Christians under the act. This legislation also made an attempt to secure civil relations among the various religions of its citizens by banning religious name-calling. It was worth a fine of 10 shillings for anyone to refer to another lawful inhabitant of the colony as "heretic, Schismatic, Idolater, puritan, Independent, Presbyterian, popish priest, Jesuit, Jesuited papist, Lutheran, Calvinist, Anabaptist, Brownist, Antinomian, Barrowist, Roundhead, Separatist," or other such derogatory references.[11] During the 1650s, after Parliament had deposed and executed Charles I, Protestants, led by William Claiborne, were again able to seize control of Maryland's colonial government and bar Catholics from holding office or practicing their faith publicly. But with the restoration of the English monarchy in 1660, Lord Baltimore once again regained control of the Maryland colony and was able to provide a measure of security to Catholics there.

While Catholics established a presence in the North American colonies, Jews also began to arrive in the New World. As early as 1585, Joachim Gaunse accompanied English colonists who attempted to establish a settlement on Roanoke Island (in present-day North Carolina) sponsored by Walter Raleigh. The venture failed, however, and Gaunse, who worked as a metallurgist and mining engineer for the colony, returned to England in 1586. Other Jewish visitors to the New World followed Gaunse, but the first permanent Jewish settlers arrived in 1654. In September of that year, a small group of Jewish refugees who had been expelled from Recife, Brazil, arrived by ship in the port city of New Amsterdam (today New York City) in New Netherland. The Jews from Recife had been encouraged to settle there by the Dutch West India Company after Holland seized the colony of Pernambuco in

This engraving celebrates the establishment of religious liberty in Maryland. *(Library of Congress, Prints and Photographs Division LC-USZ62-51766)*

Brazil from the Portuguese. But when Portuguese forces retook the colony in January of 1654, they expelled both Jews and Protestants who had taken up residence there. Consequently, a small contingent of the banished Jewish community made its way to New Amsterdam later that year. However, neither the director general of New Netherland, Peter Stuyvesant, himself an elder in the Dutch Reformed

Church, nor the colony's Dutch Reformed minister, Johannes Megapolensis, welcomed the Jewish arrivals. Megapolensis declared that "as we have here Papists, Mennonites and Lutherans among the Dutch; also many Puritans or Independents, and many atheists and various other servants of Baal among the English under his government, who conceal themselves under the name of Christians; it would create still greater confusion, if the obstinate and immovable Jews came to settle here."[12] Stuyvesant wrote to the Dutch West India Company seeking permission to expel the exiles from Recife, protesting that they were "deceitful," "very repugnant," and "hateful enemies and blasphemers of the name of Christ."[13] But Stuyvesant was not the only person writing the company. Jewish merchants in Amsterdam, aware of the plight of the exiles from Recife, also petitioned the Dutch West India Company, and they proved to be more persuasive than Stuyvesant. The company, apparently motivated by a desire to encourage immigration to New Amsterdam and thus enhance the possibilities for profit in the colony, instructed the governor to permit the Jews to remain there. For the time at least, the Jews in New Amsterdam had to content themselves with private worship—a restriction they shared with the colony's Lutherans—but they had at least secured the right to belong in the New World.

Stuyvesant's attempt to bar the Jewish arrivals to New Amsterdam mirrored his general enthusiasm for enforcing Dutch Reformed orthodoxy in theology and morals. When he had initially arrived as director general of the colony in 1647, he set out to punish Sabbath-breakers, compel church attendance, and close down the taverns and brothels. But New Amsterdam possessed the morals typical of a port city, and Stuyvesant's successes as an enforcer of Christian morals were modest. He was even less successful, as his experience with the Jewish arrivals of 1654 demonstrated, with attempts to enforce religious uniformity. He was able to convince the Dutch West India Company to refuse a request by Lutherans to import a minister to the colony and to insist that Lutherans practice their faith in private. But he could not ultimately prevent the steady influx of various believers and unbelievers into New Amsterdam. Consequently, over the first decades after its initial founding, New Amsterdam and the associated forts and trading outposts that grew to be New Netherland soon attracted believers from a variety of religious traditions. Dutch Calvinists lived and traded alongside Puritans, Lutherans, Catholics, and Anabaptists. The lay residents of the colony were happy to concentrate on trading possibilities and thus little inclined to let religious differences stand in the way of economic success. The colony's governing corporation, the Dutch West India Company, generally shared the same view. Consequently, New Amsterdam and New Netherland boasted a religious diversity unusual for their time. The modest religious liberty that flourished in association with this diversity was more a matter of pragmatism than of principle, born more of a desire for profit than of ecumenical fraternity. Nevertheless, New Amsterdam's relative tolerance in religious matters became an important model for advocates of religious freedom.

Chronicle of Events

1621

- The Wampanoag Indians share an annual harvest ceremony in October with Plymouth Plantation settlers, inaugurating what will eventually become the Thanksgiving holiday.

1624

- *July:* George Fox, founder of the Quakers, is born in Leicestershire, England.

1625

- After the death of King James, the ascension of Charles I to the throne results in increased persecution against Puritans in England.
- The Catholic priest (and later Jesuit) Jean de Brébeuf arrives in Quebec from France and subsequently undertakes missionary activity among Native Americans, chiefly the Huron Indians.

1626

- The Dutch establish New Amsterdam as a trading post on Manhattan Island after the director general of the colony, Peter Minuit, purchases the island from American Indians.
- Around this year Salem (in present-day Massachusetts) is established by fishermen led by Roger Conant. The town will soon be absorbed into the Massachusetts Bay Colony.

1628

- John Endicott and other Puritan settlers arrive in Salem, and Endicott serves as governor of the newly formed Massachusetts Bay Colony.
- The first Dutch Reformed clergyman, Jonas Michaelius, arrives in New Amsterdam (present-day New York City), and the first Dutch Reformed congregation in North America is established there.

1629

- Puritans in Salem, lead by pastor Samuel Skelton, create a church covenant and thus form the first Congregationalist church in North America.
- Charles I dissolves Parliament.
- The Dutch Reformed Church becomes the established church of the New Netherland colony.

- *March 4:* The Massachusetts Bay Company obtains a royal charter from Charles I.
- *April:* A group of 400 colonists, mostly Puritans, who intend to settle in Massachusetts Bay depart from England. William Laud, bishop of London, has increased pressure for Puritan ministers to conform to Anglican doctrine and practice.

1630

- This year dates the beginning of a decade of immigration by Puritans from England to the New World, referred to as the Great Migration.
- The First Church in Boston is established.
- Holland captures the colony of Pernambuco in Brazil from the Portuguese and encourages Jewish settlement in the colony.
- William Bradford, governor of the Plymouth Colony, begins writing his famous history of the colony and the Pilgrims who settled there, *Of Plymouth Plantation.*
- *March:* John Winthrop and a group of about 700 Puritan colonists depart from England for the Massachusetts Bay Colony. The Puritan minister John Cotton preaches a sermon on the occasion of their departure. While aboard ship en route to America, Winthrop himself preaches a lay sermon titled "A Modell of Christian Charity," which attempts to articulate the principles by which the colony should live.

1631

- Roger Williams arrives in the Massachusetts Bay Colony and declines the opportunity to serve as minister of the Boston church because its members have not decisively separated themselves from the Church of England, which he views as corrupt.
- The Puritan minister John Eliot arrives in the Massachusetts Bay Colony, where he briefly serves as minister of the church in Boston until its senior minister, John Wilson, returns from England. Afterward Eliot relocates to Roxbury, where he becomes teacher of the church there.
- *May 16:* The general court of the Massachusetts Bay Colony restricts the right to vote to church members.

1632

- John Eliot begins missionary activities to Native American tribes in the Massachusetts area.
- Cecil Calvert, the second lord Baltimore, obtains a charter from King Charles I for the colony of Maryland, named in honor of the king's consort, Henrietta

John Endicott served as first governor of the Massachusetts Bay Colony. *(Library of Congress, Prints and Photographs Division LC-USZ62-38669)*

Maria. Charles expects the colony to serve as a buffer between Virginia and New Netherland.

1633

- Charles I appoints William Laud archbishop of Canterbury, and Laud institutes even more vigorous persecutions of Puritans.
- The Puritan preacher John Cotton, having been twice suspended from his pulpit at St. Botolph's Church in Boston, Lincolnshire, immigrates to the Massachusetts Bay Colony and becomes teacher of the church at Boston.
- Thomas Hooker arrives in Boston and soon becomes senior minister of the church in New Towne (present-day Cambridge).

1634

- The first colonists, both Catholics and Protestants, arrive in Maryland. The Catholics celebrate Mass for the first time on March 25, led by one of the two Jesuit priests who arrived with them.
- Roger Williams becomes pastor of the church at Salem, Massachusetts.
- Anne Marbury Hutchinson and her family immigrate to Boston, following their favorite preacher, John Cotton, who had immigrated to the Massachusetts Bay Colony the previous year.

1635

- The Massachusetts Bay Colony banishes Roger Williams for various doctrinal offenses, including his suggestion that church and state were too closely entangled in the Massachusetts Bay Colony and his insistence that England had no right to grant a patent to lands in New England and that colonists, instead, should have purchased land from the Indians.
- Having returned to Canada from France, the Jesuit Jean de Brébeuf establishes a series of mission posts among the Huron Indians. Contact between Europeans and the Huron eventually facilitates the spread of disease to the Huron and contributes to rising hostility of the Huron against French missionary activity.
- Richard Mather, a famous New England preacher whose son (Increase) and grandson (Cotton) will become equally famous Puritan preachers, arrives in Boston from England.
- Jesuits in Quebec found the Collège des Jésuites.
- Mary Dyer, who will eventually be martyred as a Quaker, migrates with her family from England to Boston.

1636

- When Massachusetts Bay authorities attempt to ship Roger Williams back to England, he flees to Providence (present-day Rhode Island).
- Harvard College is founded at New Towne (present-day Cambridge) in the Massachusetts Bay Colony to train ministers.
- The conflict between Massachusetts colonists and Pequot Indians in 1636 and 1637 ends with the virtual destruction of the Pequot as a tribe.

1637

- A synod is convened in Massachusetts to consider the antinomian heresy.
- The general court of the Massachusetts Bay Colony tries Anne Marbury Hutchinson for heresy.
- John Clarke arrives in Boston from England but soon relocates to the Providence Colony.

1638

- Found guilty of heresy by Massachusetts authorities, Anne Hutchinson is banished from the Massachusetts Bay Colony and relocates to Aquidneck Island in the Providence colony.
- John Clarke helps to buy the island of Aquidneck from neighboring Indians and to found the town of Portsmouth there.
- Roger Williams and other Providence settlers sign a social compact that restricts the power of government to "civil things" only.
- Thomas Hooker, Puritan minister in Hartford, preaches a sermon that influences the adoption the following year of Connecticut's Fundamental Orders, the earliest written constitution in America.

1639

- Roger Williams helps to establish the first Baptist church in America. He subsequently leaves this church after determining that no true churches exist any longer in the world.
- The Maryland assembly passes a law stipulating that "Holy Churches within [the] province shall have all her rights and liberties."
- *June 4:* The colony of New Haven, influenced by the advice of Puritan minister John Davenport, establishes a constitution with the purpose of "settling civil government, according to God."

1640

- Richard Mather, John Eliot, and Thomas Weld publish *The Whole Book of Psalms Faithfully Translated into English Metre*, known as the Bay Psalm Book, the first book published in the American colonies.
- Henry Dunster becomes the president of Harvard College.

1641

- John Winthrop in the Massachusetts Bay Colony records in his journal the first known baptism of an African-American slave.
- John Eliot becomes senior minister of the church in Roxbury, Massachusetts, and he soon begins studying the Algonquian language so that he can engage in missionary activities among the Algonquian Indians.
- John Clarke helps establish a Baptist church in Newport, one of the towns that will eventually make up the Providence Colony (present-day Rhode Island).
- More than 70 Virginians sign a letter to Puritan minister John Davenport of New Haven pleading for Puritan clergy to move to Virginia. Although three Puritan ministers accept this call, they will leave Virginia by the end of the decade.

1642

- French Jesuits establish a mission in Quebec that will eventually become Montreal.
- Marie Guyart (Marie of the Incarnation) founds a school for French and American-Indian girls in New France.
- In England Civil War erupts between Charles I and Parliament, and Charles is eventually arrested and executed.

1643

- Roger Williams publishes *A Key into the Language of America*, a sympathetic portrayal of American Indian life.
- After relocating from Providence to the Dutch colony of New Netherland in Long Island, Anne Marbury Hutchinson and five of her children are killed in an Indian massacre.
- The New Haven Colony is established under the leadership of Theophilus Eaton and John Davenport.

1644

- The general court of the Massachusetts Bay Colony enacts a law banishing Baptists (or Anabaptists, as it refers to them) from the colony.

- The first American Presbyterian church is established in Long Island, New York.

1645

- Eusebio Kino, a Jesuit missionary to what is today the southwestern United States, is born in Austria.

1644

- Roger Williams obtains a charter for the Providence Colony while in England and publishes *The Bloudy Tenent, of Persecution for Cause of Conscience, discussed in a Conference between Truth and Peace*, a critique of religious persecution in the Massachusetts Bay Colony.
- *October 14:* William Penn is born in London, England.

1645

- Puritan minister John Cotton publishes *The Way of the Churches of Christ in New-England*, which attempts to justify the Congregational structure of New England churches.

1646

- The Cambridge Synod convenes in Massachusetts and establishes a form of government for the Congregational churches in New England.
- In England the Westminster Confession of Faith is produced. It will become an important statement of faith for American Congregationalists and Presbyterians.
- John Eliot delivers the first Puritan sermon in an Indian language.

1647

- John Cotton, a teacher at the church in Boston, defends the Massachusetts arrangement between church and state from the attacks of Roger Williams by publishing *The Bloudy Tenent, Washed, and made White in the Bloud of the Lambe: Being Discussed and Discharged of Bloud-Guiltiness by Just Defence*.
- Leonard Calvert, first governor of the Maryland Colony and brother of the second lord Baltimore, Cecil Calvert, the colony's proprietor, dies. Lord Baltimore appoints the Protestant William Stone to serve as the colony's next governor.
- Peter Stuyvesant arrives as director general of New Netherland and attempts to enforce Sabbath-keeping and church attendance, close taverns and brothels,

and otherwise enforce Dutch Reformed orthodoxy against its various Christian and (later) non-Christian alternatives.

1648

- Congregational churches in New England meet and subsequently adopt the Cambridge Platform, a statement of doctrinal principles.
- The Puritan minister Thomas Hooker publishes a defense of New England Congregationalism titled *A Survey of the Summe of Church-Discipline.*
- Margaret Jones becomes the first person executed for witchcraft in the Massachusetts Bay Colony.
- George Fox begins a preaching ministry in England that leads to the formation of the Society of Friends, commonly known as the Quakers.
- John Clarke in the Providence Colony becomes convinced that infant baptism is unscriptural, and he leads his church to become a Baptist congregation.
- *October 27:* The Massachusetts Bay Colony enacts *The Book of the General Lawes and Libertyes Concerning the Inhabitants of the Massachusetts* (the *Laws and Liberties*), the first codification of law in North America. Its provisions include some laws drawn directly from the Old Testament.

1649

- The Maryland assembly passes the Act Concerning Religion, which provides a measure of religious freedom to all inhabitants by stipulating that "no person . . . professing to believe in Jesus Christ, shall from henceforth be any ways troubled . . . for . . . his or her religion nor in the free exercise thereof . . . nor any way [be] compelled to the belief or exercise of any other Religion against his or her consent."
- Parliament establishes the Society for the Propagation of the Gospel in New England.
- Iroquois Indians attack Huronia in New France, and they torture and kill Jesuit missionaries Jean de Brébeuf and Gabriel Lallemant.
- *January 30:* Charles I is executed in England.

1650

- Jonathan Mitchell becomes the minister of the church in Cambridge.

1651

- Three Baptists from Providence, including John Clarke and Obadiah Holmes, are arrested for venturing into the Massachusetts Bay Colony to hold private religious services. Clarke is fined, and Holmes, who refuses to pay a fine, is whipped.
- Puritan missionary John Eliot establishes the first of a number of villages for American Indian converts to Christianity. Converts are called Praying Indians.
- Following the victory of Parliamentary forces in England over Charles I, a commission is appointed to make sure the British colonies in North America are loyal to the new government. One of the commissioners, William Claiborne, eventually gains control of Maryland's government for several years and restricts the right of Catholics there to practice their faith openly.

1652

- John Clarke, a Baptist minister in the Providence Colony, publishes an attack on Puritan treatment of religious dissenters in New England called *Ill News from New England.*
- Mary Dyer and her family return to England from America for five years, and, while there, she becomes a Quaker.

1654

- Henry Dunster resigns as president of Harvard College after his opposition to infant baptism places him at odds with Congregationalists in Massachusetts.
- The first Jews arrive in New Amsterdam (later New York) and establish the congregation of Shearith Israel. They had been part of a significant Jewish community established in Recife but were expelled when Portugal reacquired control of Brazil in 1654.
- Edward Johnson publishes his important chronicle of the first generation of the Massachusetts Bay Colony, *The Wonder-Working Providence of Sion's Saviour.*

1655

- The Protestant William Claiborne, acting on the authority of the English Parliament, assumes full control of the Maryland Colony and bars Catholics from holding public office or from worshiping publicly.
- Jews begin to settle in Newport, Rhode Island.
- Jews in New Amsterdam are successful in acquiring a separate cemetery for their burials, an acquisition that helps to maintain their separate religious and cultural identity. The same year the Jewish community receives a copy of the Torah on loan from Amsterdam, but the subsequent return of this copy

around 1663 reflects the decline in numbers of the community.

- The first Quaker in the New World, Elizabeth Harris, travels in the Chesapeake area.

1656

- Quakers Mary Fisher and Ann Austin arrive in Boston by way of Barbados and are arrested, examined for signs of witchcraft, and subsequently deported to England.
- French Jesuits establish a mission to the Onondaga Iroquois in what is now New York.

1657

- While returning via Boston to Providence, Mary Dyer is arrested as a Quaker and released only after her husband posts bond.
- Massachusetts enacts a law that makes Quaker males who return to the colony after banishment subject to having their ears cropped and, for further returns, their tongues bored with a hot iron.
- The first Quakers arrive in New Amsterdam.

1658

- Massachusetts enacts a law that provides for the execution of Quakers who return to the colony after being banished.
- Dr. Jacob Lumbrozo, a Jewish inhabitant of Maryland who had immigrated to the New World from Portugal, is charged with blasphemy, but he ultimately escapes prosecution after the governor of the colony issues a general pardon for various criminal defendants.
- English Congregationalists adopt the Savoy Declaration, a Congregational version of the predominantly Presbyterian Westminister Confession.

1659

- The Massachusetts Bay Colony executes two Quaker men who returned to the colony after being banished. Quaker Mary Dyer is reprieved on the scaffold and warned not to return. She will return the next year and be arrested and executed.
- François de Laval is consecrated the first bishop of New France.

Eyewitness Testimony

A long time ago, when there was no such thing known to the Indians as people with a *white skin* (their expression), some Indians who had been out a-fishing, and where the sea widens, espied at a great distance something remarkably large swimming, or floating on the water, and such as they had never seen before. They immediately returning to the shore apprised their countrymen of what they had seen, and pressed them to go out with them and discover what it might be. . . . It was at length agreed among those who were spectators, that as this phenomenon moved towards the land, whether or not it was an animal, or anything that had life in it, it would be well to inform all the Indians on the inhabited islands of what they had seen, and put them on their guard. Accordingly, they sent runners and watermen off to carry the news to their scattered chiefs, that these might send off in every direction for the warriors to come in. These arriving in numbers, and themselves viewing the strange appearance, and that it was actually moving towards them, (the entrance of the river or bay,) concluded it to be a large canoe or house, in which the great Mannitto (great or Supreme Being) *himself* was, and that he probably was coming to visit them. By this time the chiefs of the different tribes were assembled on York Island, and were counseling (or deliberating) on the manner they should receive their Mannitto on his arrival. Every step had been taken to be well provided with a plenty of meat for a sacrifice; the women were required to prepare the best of victuals; idols or images were examined and put in order; and a grand dance was supposed not only to be an agreeable entertainment for the Mannitto, but might, with the addition of a sacrifice, contribute towards appeasing him, in case he was angry with them. . . . It now appears to be certain that it is the great Mannitto bringing them some kind of game, such as they had not before; but other runners soon after arriving, declare it a large house of various colors, full of people, yet of quite a different color than they (the Indians) are of; that they were also dressed in a different manner from them, and that one in particular appeared altogether red, which must be the *Mannitto* himself. They are soon hailed from the vessel, though in a language they do not understand; yet they shout (or yell) in their way. . . . The chiefs and wise men (or councillors) had composed a large circle, unto which the red-clothed man with two others approach. He salutes them with friendly countenance, and they return the salute after their manner. They are lost in admiration, both as to the color of the skin (of these whites) as also to their manner of dress, yet most as to the habit of him who wore the red clothes, which shone with something they could not account for. He *must* be the great Mannitto (Supreme Being,) they think, but why should he have a *white skin?* . . . After this . . . the man with the red clothes returned again to them, and distributed presents among them. . . . They say that they had become familiar to each other, and were made to understand by signs; that they now would return home, but would visit them next year again, when they would bring them more presents, and stay with them awhile; but that, as they could not live without eating, they should then want a little land of them to sow some seeds in order to raise herbs to put in their broth.

An account concerning an early meeting between Dutch traders and Native Americans in the first part of the 17th century, as communicated to the Reverend John Heckwelder, a Moravian missionary in the Ohio Valley, who recorded the narrative in the 1760s, available online at URL: http://historymatters.gmu.edu/d/5829. Accessed on August 29, 2005.

We will not say as the Separatists are wont to say at their leaving England, "Farewell Babylon, Farewell Rome" but we will say, "Farewell dear England, Farewell the Church of God in England and all the Christian friends there." We do not go to New England as Separatist from the Church of England, though we cannot be separate from the corruptions in it.

The Puritan Francis Higginson at his departure for New England, 1629, in Corrigan and Hudson, Religion in America, *p. 67.*

Thus stands the cause between God and us. We are entered into covenant with Him for this work. We have taken out a commission, the Lord hath given us leave to draw our own articles. We have professed to enterprise these actions, upon these and those ends, we have hereupon besought Him of favor and blessing. Now if the Lord shall please to hear us, and bring us in peace to the place we desire, then hath He ratified this covenant and sealed our commission, [and] will expect a strict performance of the articles contained in it; but if we shall neglect the observation of these articles which are the ends we have propounded, and, dissembling with our God, shall fall to embrace this present world and prosecute our carnal intentions, seeking great things for ourselves and our posterity, the Lord will surely break out in wrath against us;

be revenged of such a perjured people and make us know the price of the breach of such a covenant.

Now the only way to avoid this shipwreck, and to provide for our posterity, is to follow the counsel of Micah, to do justly, to love mercy, to walk humbly with our God. For this end, we must be knit together in this work as one man. We must entertain each other in brotherly affection, we must be willing to abridge ourselves of our superfluities, for the supply of other's necessities. We must uphold a familiar commerce together in all meekness, gentleness, patience and liberality. We must delight in each other, make other's conditions our own, rejoice together, mourn together, labor and suffer together, always having before our eyes our commission and community in the work, our community as members of the same body. So shall we keep the unity of the spirit in the bond of peace. The Lord will be our God, and delight to dwell among us as His own people, and will command a blessing upon us in all our ways, so that we shall see much more of His wisdom, power, goodness and truth, than formerly we have been acquainted with. We shall find that the God of Israel is among us, when ten of us shall be able to resist a thousand of our enemies; when He shall make us a praise and glory that men shall say of succeeding plantations, "the Lord make it like that of New England." For we must consider that we shall be as a city upon a hill. The eyes of all people are upon us, so that if we shall deal falsely with our God in this work we have undertaken, and so cause Him to withdraw His present help from us, we shall be made a story and a by-word through the world. We shall open the mouths of enemies to speak evil of the ways of God, and all professors for God's sake. We shall shame the faces of many of God's worthy servants, and cause their prayers to be turned into curses upon us till we be consumed out of the good land whither we are agoing.

Massachusetts Bay leader John Winthrop, from a sermon titled "A Modell of Christian Charity," 1630, delivered onboard the ship Arabella *prior to the arrival of Winthrop and his companions in Massachusetts, in Mulford,* Early American Writings, *pp. 244–245.*

And now the new-come Soldiers of *Christ* strengthen themselves in him, and gather a Church at *Charles* Town, whose extent at present did reach to both sides of the River, and in very little time after was divided into two Churches, the Reverend and judicious Mr. *John Wilson* was called to be pastor thereof, a Man full of Faith, Courage and Zeal, for the truth of *Christ* persecuted, and hunted after by the usurping Prelates (and forced for present

John Winthrop preached a sermon titled "A Modell of Christian Charity" onboard the *Arabella. (Library of Congress, Prints and Photographs Division LC-USZ62-124240)*

to part from his endeared Wife) yet honored by *Christ,* and made a powerful instrument in his hands for the cutting down of Error, and Schism, as in the sequel of this History will appear, in whose weakness *Christ's* power hath appeared.

The Grave and Reverend Mr. John Wilson, New England, now Pastor of the Church of Christ at Boston, in

John Wilson will, to Christ's will submit,
In Wilderness, where thou hast Trials found,
Christ in new making did compose thee fit,
And made thy Love zeal, for his truth abound.
Then it's not Wilson, but Christ by him hath,
Error cut down when it o're topping stood,
Thou then 'Gainst it didst shew an holy wrath;
Saving men's souls from this o're-flowing flood.
They thee deprave, thy Ministry despise,
By thy thick utterance seek to call Men back,
From hearing thee, but Christ for thee did rise.
And turned the wheel-right over them to crack.
Yea, caused thee with length of days to stand,
Steadfast in's house in old Age fruit to bring.
I and thy seed raise up by his command;

His Flock to feed, rejoice my Muse and sing.
That Christ doth, dust regard so plenteously,
Rich gifts to give, and heart to give him his,
Estate and person thou spends liberally;
Christ thee, and thine will Crown with lasting
Bliss.

This, as the other Churches of *Christ*, began with a small number in a desolate and barren Wilderness, which the Lord in his wonderful mercy hath turned to fruitful Fields. Wherefore behold the present condition of these Churches compared with their beginnings; as they sowed in tears, so also have they Reaped in joy, and shall still so go on if plenty and liberty mar not their prosperity.

Historian Edward Johnson describing the establishment of the church at Boston in 1631, and its first pastor, John Wilson, in 1650, The Wonder-Working Providence of Sion's Saviour, *pp. 39–40.*

[T]he people of the plantation began to grow in their outward estates, by reason of the flowing of many people into the country, especially into the Bay of the Massachusetts; by which means corn & cattle rose to a great price, by which many were much enriched, and commodities grew plentiful; and yet in other regards this benefit turned to their hurt, and this accession of strength to their weakness. For now as their stocks increased, and the increase vendible, there was no longer any holding them together, but now they must of necessity go to their great lots, they could not otherwise keep their cattle; and having oxen grown, they must have land for plowing & tillage. And no man now thought he could live, except he had cattle and a great deal of ground to keep them, all striving to increase their stocks. By which means they were scattered all over the bay, quickly, and the town, in which they lived compactly till now, was left very thin, and in a short time almost desolate. And if this had been all, it had been less, though too much; but the church must also be divided, and those that had lived so long together in Christian & comfortable fellowship must now part and suffer many divisions.

Pilgrim leader William Bradford, 1632, Of Plymouth Plantation, *pp. 164–165.*

The governor & Assistants met at *Boston,* and took into consideration a treatise which mr. *Williams* (then of *Salem*) had sent to them, & which he had formerly written to the Governor & Council of *Plymouth* wherein among other things, he <questions> disputes their right to the lands they possessed here: & concluded that claiming by the king's grant they could have no title: nor otherwise except they compounded with the natives: for this taking advice with some of the most judicious ministers (who much condemned mr william's error & our presumption) they gave Order that he should be convented at the next Court, to be Censured etc.: There were 3: passages chiefly whereat they were much offended. 1: for that he Charged King James to have told a solemn public lie: because in his Patent he blessed God that he was the first Christian Prince that had discovered this land. 2: for that he charged him & others with blasphemy for calling Europe Christendom or the Christian world: 3: for that he did personally apply to our present King Charles these 3: places in Revelation viz:

mr Endecott being absent the Governor wrote to him to let him know what was done, & withal added diverse Arguments to confute the said errors. <when> wishing him to deal with mr wms. to retract the same & whereunto he returned a very modest & discreet answer: mr wms. also wrote to the Governor & also to him & the rest of the Council, very submissively: professing his intent to have been only to have written for the private satisfaction of the Governor &c. of Plymouth: without any purpose to have stirred any further in it, if the Governor here had not required a Copy of him. withal offering his book or any part of it to be burnt &c: At the next Court he appeared privately & gave satisfaction of his intention [and] his loyalty. so it was left & nothing done in it. . . .

. . . . .

mr *Williams* of *Salem* was summoned & did appear. it was laid to his Charge that being under Question before the magistrates & Churches for diverse dangerous opinions viz. 1: that the magistrate ought not to punish the breach of the first table, otherwise than in such Cases as did disturb the Civil peace. 2: that he ought not to tender an oath to an unregener[ate] man. 3: that a man ought not to pray with such though wife child, etc. 4: that a man ought not to give thanks after the Sacrament nor after meat. etc.: that the other Churches were about to write to the Church of Salem to admonished him of these errors: notwithstanding the Church had since called him to [the] office of a Teacher. Much debate was about these things the said opinions were judged by all magistrates & ministers (who were desired to be present) to be erroneous & very dangerous: & the Calling of him to office at that time was judged a great Contempt of authority: so in fine time was given to him & the Church of Salem to consider of these things till the next general Court,

& then either to give satisfaction to the Court, or else to expect the sentence.

Puritan leader John Winthrop, December 27, 1633, and August 5, 1638, concerning the objectionable opinions of Roger Williams that would ultimately prompt his banishment from the Massachusetts Bay Colony, The Journal of John Winthrop, *pp. 107–108, 149–150.*

It is very suitable to Gods all-sufficient wisdom, and to the fulness and perfection of Holy Scriptures, not only to prescribe perfect rules for the right ordering of a private mans soul to everlasting blessedness with himself, but also for the right ordering of a mans family, yea, of the commonwealth too, so far as both of them are subordinate to spiritual ends, and yet avoid both the churches usurpation upon civil jurisdictions . . . and the commonwealths invasion upon ecclesiastical administrations. . . . Gods institutions (such as the government of church and of commonwealth be) may be close and compact, and co-ordinate one to another, and yet not confounded. . . . [N]o man fashions his house to his hangings, but his hangings to his house. It is better that the commonwealth be fashioned to the setting forth of Gods house, which is his church: than to accommodate the church frame to the civil state.

John Cotton, Puritan teacher in Boston, in a letter to Lord Say and Seal, 1636, in Miller and Johnson, The Puritans, *vol. 1, p. 209.*

The Examination of November 1637 of Mrs Anne Hutchinson at the court at Newton.

Mr. Winthrop, governor. Mrs. Hutchinson, you are called here as one of those that have troubled the peace of the commonwealth and the churches here; you are known to be a woman that hath had a great share in the promoting and divulging of those opinions that are causes of this trouble, and to be nearly joined not only in affinity and affection with some of those the court had taken notice of and passed censure upon, but you have spoken divers things, as we have been informed very prejudicial to the honour of the churches and ministers thereof, and you have maintained a meeting and an assembly in your house that hath been condemned by the general assembly as a thing not tolerable nor comely in the sight of God nor fitting for your sex, and notwithstanding that was cried down you have continued the same.

. . . . .

Mrs. Hutchinson. I am called here to answer before you but I hear no things laid to my charge.

Gov. I have told you some already and more I can tell you.

(Mrs. H.) Name one, Sir.

Gov. Have I not named some already?

Mrs. H. What have I said or done? . . .

Gov. Why do you keep such a meeting at your house as you do every week upon a set day?

Mrs. H. It is lawful for me to do so, as it is all your practices and can you find a warrant for yourself and condemn me for the same thing? . . .

Gov. . . . by what warrant do you continue such a course?

Mrs. H. I conceive there lies a clear rule in Titus, that the elder women should instruct the younger and then I must have a time wherein I must do it.

Gov. All this I grant you, I grant you a time for it, but what is this to the purpose that you Mrs. Hutchinson must call a company together from their callings to come to be taught of you?

Mrs. H. Will it please you to answer me this and to give me a rule for then I will willingly submit to any truth. If any come to my house to be instructed in the ways of God what rule have I to put them away? . . . Do you think it not lawful for me to teach women and why do you call me to teach the court?

Gov.: We do not call you to teach the court but to lay open yourself. . . .

Mrs. H. . . . if you look upon the rule in Titus it is a rule to me. If you convince me that it is no rule I shall yield.

Gov. You know that there is no rule that crosses another, but this rule crosses that in the Corinthians. But you must take it in this sense that elder women must instruct the younger about their business, and to love their husbands and not to make them to clash. . . .

Gov. Your course is not to be suffered for, besides that we find such a course as this to be greatly prejudicial to the state, besides the occasion that it is to seduce many honest persons that are called to those meetings and your opinions and your opinions being known to be different from the word of God may seduce many simple souls that resort unto you. . . . And besides that it will not well stand with the commonwealth that families should be neglected for so many neighbors and dames and so much time spent. . . .

Mrs. H. Sir I do not believe that to be so.

Gov. Well, we see how it is we must therefore put it away from you, or restrain you from maintaining this course.

Mrs H. If you have a rule for it from God's word you may.

Gov. We are your judges, and not you ours and we must compel you to it.

Governor John Winthrop and religious dissenter Anne Hutchinson, 1636, from the transcript of Hutchinson's trial before the general court of the Massachusetts Bay Colony, in Hall, The Antinomian Controversy, *pp. 312, 314–316.*

During the present year, eighty-six [Huron Indians] have been baptized, and, adding to these the fourteen of last year, there are a hundred souls in all who, we believe, have been rescued from the service of the devil in this country since our return. Of this number God has called ten to Heaven,—six while they were young, and four more advanced in age. One of these, named François *Sangwati*, was Captain of our village. He had a naturally good disposition, and consented very willingly to be instructed and to receive Holy Baptism, a course he had previously praised and approved in others. I admired the tender Providence of God in the conversion of a woman, who is one of the four deceased. I baptized her this Autumn at the village of *Scanonaenrat*, when returning from the house of Louys de saincte Foy, where we had gone to instruct his parents. The deafness of this sick woman, and the depths of the mysteries I brought to her notice, prevented her from sufficiently understanding me. . . . My own imperfect acquaintance with the language rendered me still less intelligible, and increased my difficulties. But Our Lord, who willed to save this soul, immediately sent us a young man, who served us as interpreter. He had been with us in the Cabin of Louys, and had heard us talking of our mysteries, so that he already knew a considerable part of them, and understood very well what I said. It is said that this woman, who was named Marie, in the midst of her greatest weakness foretold that she would not die for eight days; and so it happened.

Jean de Brébeuf, Jesuit missionary to the Huron in Canada, 1636, from Relation of What Occurred in the Country of the Hurons in the Year 1636, *in Mulford,* Early American Writings, *p. 431.*

You must have sincere affection for the Savages, looking upon them as ransomed by the blood of the son of God, and as our Brethren with whom we are to pass the rest of our lives. . . . You should try to eat their sagamite or salmagundi in the way they prepare it, although it may be dirty, half-cooked, and very tasteless. As to the other numerous things which may be unpleasant, they must be endured for the love of God, without saying anything or appearing to notice them.

Jean de Brébeuf, Jesuit missionary to the Huron in Canada, 1637, in Noll, A History of Christianity in the United States and Canada, *p. 19.*

Adulteries, Murders, Robberies, Thefts,
Wild Indians punish these!
And hold the Scales of Justice so,
That no man farthing less.
When Indians hear the horrid filths,
Of Irish, English Men,
The horrid Oaths and Murders late,
Thus say these Indians then.
We wear no Clothes, have many Gods,
And yet our sins are less:
You are Barbarians, Pagans wild,
Your land's the Wilderness.

Roger Williams, 1643, A Key to the Language of America, The Complete Writings of Roger Williams, *vol. 1, p. 227.*

After God had carried us safe to New England, and we had built our houses, provided necessaries for our livelihood, reared convenient places for God's worship, and settled the civil government, one of the next things we longed for and looked after was to advance Learning and perpetuate it to posterity, dreading to leave an illiterate ministry to the churches when our present ministers shall lie in the dust. And as we were thinking and consulting how to effect this great work, it pleased God to stir up the heart of one Mr. Harvard (a godly gentleman, and a lover of learning, there living amongst us) to give the one half of his estate (it being in all about 1700 £.) towards the erecting of a college, and all his library. After him another gave 300 £., others after them cast in more, and the public hand of the state added the rest. The college was, by common consent, appointed to be at Cambridge (a place very pleasant and accommodate) and is called (according to the name of the first founder) Harvard College.

From a promotional pamphlet titled New England's First Fruits, *1643, in* America's Religions: From Their Origins to the Twenty-First Century, *pp. 112–113.*

[S]uch as have given or taken any unfriendly reports of us *New English*, should do well to recollect themselves. We have been reputed . . . wild Opinionists, swarmed into a remote wilderness to find elbow-room for our fanatic Doctrines and practices: I trust our diligence past, and constant credulity against such persons and courses, will plead better things for us. I dare take upon me, to be the Herald of *New-England* so far, as to proclaim to the world, in the name of our Colony, that all Familists, Antinomians, Anabaptists, and other Enthusiasts, shall have free Liberty to keep away from us, and such as will come to be gone as fast as they can, the sooner the better. . . .

. . . . .

If the devil might have his free option, I believe he would ask nothing else, but liberty to enfranchise all other Religions, and to embondage the true; nor should he need: It is much to be feared, that lax Tolerations upon State-pretenses and planting necessities, will be the next subtle Stratagem he will spread. . . . Tolerations in things tolerable, exquisitely drawn out by the line of the Scripture, and pencil of the Spirit, are the sacred favors of Truth, the due latitudes of Love, the fair Compartments of Christian fraternity: but irregular dispensations, dealt forth by the facilities of men, are the frontiers of error, the redoubts of Schism, the perilous irritants of carnal enmity.

Nathaniel Ward, a minister and lawyer in the Massachusetts Bay Colony, in 1647, The Simple Cobler of Aggawam in America, *in Miller and Johnson,* The Puritans: A Sourcebook of Their Writings, *pp. 227–228.*

TO OUR BELOVED BRETHREN AND NEIGHBORS the Inhabitants of the Massachusetts, the Governor, Assistants and Deputies assembled in the General Court of that Jurisdiction with grace and peace in our Lord Jesus Christ.

So soon as God had set up Political Government among his people Israel he gave them a body of laws for judgement both in civil and criminal causes. These were brief and fundamental principles, yet withal so full and comprehensive as out of them clear deductions were to be drawn to all particular cases in future times. For a Common-wealth without laws is like a Ship without rigging and steerage. Nor is it sufficient to have principles or fundamentals, but these are to be drawn out into so many of their deductions as the time and condition of that people may have use of. And it is very unsafe & injurious to the body of the people to put them to learn their duty and liberate from general rules, nor is it enough to have laws except they be also just. Therefore among other privileges which the Lord bestowed upon his peculiar people, these he calls them specially to consider of, that God was nearer to them and their laws were more righteous than other nations. God was said to be amongst them or near to them because of his Ordinance established by himself, and their laws righteous because himself was their Law-giver: yet in the comparison are implied two things, first that other nations had something of God's presence amongst them. Secondly that there was also some what of equity in their laws, for it pleased the Father (upon the Covenant of Redemption with his Son) to restore so much of his Image to lost man as whereby all nations are disposed to worship God, and to advance righteousness. . . . But the nations corrupting his Ordinances (both of Religion, and Justice) God withdrew his presence from them proportionably whereby they were given up to abominable lusts. . . . Whereas if they had walked according to the light & law of nature they might have been preserved from such moral evils and might have enjoyed a common blessing in all their natural and civil Ordinances: now, if it might have been so with the nations who were so much strangers to the Covenant of Grace, what advantage have they who have interest in this Covenant, and may enjoy the special presence of God in the purity and native simplicity of all his Ordinances by which he is so near to his own people. This hath been no small privilege, and advantage to us in New England that our Churches, and civil State have been planted, and grown up (like two twins) together like that of Israel in the wilderness by which we were put in mind (and had opportunity put into our hands) not only to gather our Churches, and set up the Ordinances of Christ Jesus in them according to the Apostolic pattern by such light as the Lord graciously afforded us: but also withal to frame our civil Polity, and laws according to the rules of his most holy word whereby each do help and strengthen other (the Churches the civil Authority, and the civil Authority the Churches) and so both prosper the better without such emulation, and contention for privileges or priority as have proved the misery (if not ruin) of both in some other places.

The Laws and Liberties of Massachusetts, 1648, *the first codification of laws in America, adopted by the Massachusetts Bay Colony, p. A2.*

My very dear and well-loved son:
The life and love of Jesus be your life and love for eternity.

[S]ince I told you something of the great and extraordinary persecution of the Iroquois, there has been yet another great clash between the French and those barbarians in an encounter near Trois-Rivières, when our men went in search of nine Frenchmen that the Iroquois had captured and carried off.

. . . . .

They are resolved (so we are told) to come, after they have taken Trois-Rivières, to attack us. Although in appearance there is not so much reason for fear in our houses, which are strong, still what has happened in all the Huron villages, which were laid waste by fire and arms (for assuredly they are powerful), should make the French apprehend a like disaster if prompt help does not come to us.

. . . . .

This help can only come to us from France, for there are not enough forces in all the country to resist them. If France fails us, then, we must shortly either leave or die. But because all the French, who are to the number of more than two thousand, will not be able to find means to withdraw, they will be forced to perish, either through poverty or through the cruelty of their enemies.

. . . . .

We ourselves have other motives, through the mercy of Our Lord. It is not worldly goods that keep us here but rather the remnant of our good Christians, with whom we should deem ourselves happy to die a million times if it were possible. These are our treasures, our brothers, our spiritual children, whom we cherish more than our lives and all the worldly goods under heaven. Rejoice, then, if we die and if news is brought to you that our blood and ashes are mingled with theirs. There is likelihood that this will happen if the thousand Iroquois that have separated to go to the Neutral nation rejoin those that are at our gates.

Marie Juyart Martin, an Ursuline nun who helped establish and became the superior of a school for converted Native American girls in Quebec, to her son, Claude Martin, August 30, 1650, in Mulford, Early American Writings, *p. 444.*

There goes many a Ship to Sea, with many a Hundred Souls in one Ship, whose Weal and Woe is common; and is a true Picture of a Common-Wealth, or a human Combination, or Society. It hath fallen out sometimes, that both Papists and Protestants, Jews, and Turks, may be embarked into one Ship. Upon which Supposal, I do affirm, that all the Liberty of Conscience, that ever I pleaded for, turns upon these two Hinges—that none of the Papists, Protestants, Jews, or Turks, be forced to come to the Ships Prayers or Worship; nor, secondly, compelled from their own particular Prayers or Worship, if they practice any. I further add, that I never denied, that notwithstanding this Liberty, the Commander of this Ship ought to command the Ship's Course; yea, and also command to that Justice, Peace, and Sobriety, be kept and practiced, both among the Seamen and all the Passengers. If any of the Seamen refuse to perform their Service, or Passengers to pay their Freight;—if any refuse to help in Person or Purse, towards the Common Charges, or Defense;—if any refuse to obey the common Laws and Orders of the Ship, concerning their common Peace or Preservation;—if any shall mutiny and rise up against their Commanders, and Officers;—if any shall preach or write, that there ought to be no Commanders, nor Officers, because all are equal in CHRIST, therefore no Masters, nor Officers, no Laws, nor Orders, no Corrections nor Punishments—I say, I never denied, but in such Cases, whatever is pretended, the Commander or Commanders may judge, resist, compel, and punish such Transgressors, according to their Deserts and Merits.

Roger Williams, founder of the Providence Colony and staunch advocate of religious liberty. ca. Jan. 1654/55, Letter to the Town of Providence, *in* The Correspondence of Roger Williams, *vol. 2, pp. 423–424.*

CHAPTER THREE

New Anxieties
(1660–1699)

As Puritan New England passed through its second and third generations, some observers wondered whether spiritual laxity had overtaken its inhabitants. The "city upon a hill" seemed not so brightly lit as in the days of New England's infancy, and the children and grandchildren of believing parents did not appear to believe so fervently as had previous generations. Churches could no longer expect as much of their members, and the number of members in churches fell. Decline seemed to be the order of the day. William Bradford, governor of Plymouth, captured the sense of the period when he complained that the churches in the Plymouth Colony were like an "ancient mother grown old and forsaken of her children."[1] Moreover, New England orthodoxy had to contend with a flood of spiritual error that threatened to sweep up into its meetinghouses. First came the Baptists, "incendiaries of commonwealths," Massachusetts called them. Baptists—unlike Catholics and most other Protestants of the time—believed that baptism was not appropriate for infants, but only for those old enough to experience conversion themselves. Authorities tried to whip the Baptists back to the Providence Colony, from which they spread initially, but with little success. In fact, Massachusetts had to endure the indignity of seeing the president of its most illustrious center of learning, Harvard College, resign from his post in 1654 because he had become a Baptist. But the Baptists, alarming enough, were followed by the even more dangerous Quakers. These spiritual radicals, by their reliance on an inner spiritual voice, threatened the very foundations of the holy commonwealth. And what was worse, nothing seemed to keep the religious dissenters away, not fines or whippings or ear croppings or even hangings. They continued to flow into the colony, and their religious ideas and practices could not be contained. New England's ministers constantly warned their congregations that God would not tolerate sin among his people, and current events eventually gave them proof that their jeremiads were right. In the last half of the 17th century, when a vicious war erupted between American Indians and colonists of New England, many Puritan ministers saw the troubled times as evidence that God was judging the people for their individual and collective sins. New England suffered because it had turned away from the Lord, and unless it repented and turned back it could expect still greater judgment.

To punctuate the sense that New England had lost its way, the devil himself seemed prepared to establish an outpost in the very heart of the holy commonwealth. In the last decade of 17th-century New England, witches, it seemed, suddenly appeared in Salem, one of the colony's oldest towns. In the frenzy that followed 20 souls were executed before Massachusetts realized that it had new sins to confess, namely, the innocents killed and imprisoned in Salem. Satan, it seemed, could be even more devilish than New England imagined and could summon ministers and judges to his work as readily as witches.

But while New England was growing old, other parts of America were still inventing themselves. Dutch New Netherland resigned itself to British control in 1664 but maintained something of the pragmatic appreciation for religious diversity that had characterized its first generation. Although British oversight strengthened the position of the Anglican Church in the colony, other religious traditions continued to find in New Netherland more room to practice their faiths than in many other parts of America. New colonies also were planted in the last half of the 17th century. In 1663 Charles II, recently crowned king of England, granted a charter to new land in North America that would eventually become North and South Carolina. Anglicanism became the predominant religious tradition in the early years of the Carolina colony, though events in Europe made the colony home to other strains of Protestantism. One such event was the revocation of the Edict of Nantes in 1685. This edict had served mainly to protect the religious freedom of French Calvinists, known as Huguenots. With this protection eliminated, many French Huguenots made their way to North America, and not a few settled in the Carolina colony. In addition to these developments, the Quaker William Penn established a new colony named Pennsylvania whose appreciation for religious freedom would contribute greatly to the diversity of America's religious experience during the colonial period.

Quaker Arrivals and Departures

In the late 1640s George Fox began a preaching ministry in England that eventually produced one of the most controversial religious groups of the 17th century—the Society of Friends, also known as the Quakers. They earned this nickname for claiming to "tremble at the Word of the Lord" and for sometimes shaking or dancing at their meetings. The core of Quaker belief was the insistence that true worship centered in the experience of the "inward Christ" or the "inner" light of Christ, rather than in conformity to external norms of conduct or belief. Furthermore, Quakers maintained that this inner light was available to every person, not just a privileged group of elect. Both propositions alarmed the Puritans. Quaker enthusiasm for the inner light seemed to undermine the authority of Scripture and lent itself to an impatience with external forms of conduct reminiscent of antinomianism. Quaker pursuit of an inward Christ available to all people both threatened the Reformed doctrine that only the elect are saved and seemed to diminish the historical gift of Christ's sacrifice on the cross. Consequently, when Quakers began to arrive in New England in the 1650s, the Puritans greeted them with all the enthusiasm that healthy people have for the prospect of being exposed to a deadly disease. The Puritan minister John Cotton had died by the time the first Quakers appeared in New England, but while alive he had helped to provide the justification for the banishments promptly visited upon the Quakers.

> If [those holding false beliefs] be infectious, and leprous, and have plague sores running upon them, and think it their glory to infect others, it is no want of mercy, and charity, to set such at a distance. It is a merciless mercy, to pity such as are incurably contagious, and mischievous, and not to pity many scores or hundreds of souls of such as will be infected and destroyed by the toleration of the other.[2]

Cotton summed up the Puritans' perception of the Quaker arrivals: it was as though plague personified had stepped off the wharf in Boston and hurried to infect the town.

Not everyone shared the view that Quakers represented something like a spiritual virus from which the colonists of the New World needed to be quarantined. When Peter Stuyvesant, director general of New Netherland, acted on this view and tried to prevent Quakers from settling in the colony, his superiors at the Dutch West India Company reproved him. The colony needed settlers, they warned Stuyvesant in 1663, and he would be well served to think of New Netherland as a haven for religious dissent and to refrain from "vigorous proceedings" against the Quakers. Roger Williams, from his perch in the Providence Colony, did not doubt that the Quakers deserved the protections of religious liberty, and Providence, already home to a variety of spiritual misfits, generally practiced toleration toward the Quakers. In particular, Williams did not think Quakers posed any threat as a kind of spiritual virus. His conclusion in this regard, though, did not proceed from a benevolent regard for the views of Quakers; he thought their theology was a gross distortion of biblical truth and was happy to rail against it. When he was in his 70s, Williams thought it important enough to combat Quaker errors that he rowed three days to participate in a debate with three Quakers. But as wrong as the Quakers were—and Williams thought they were very wrong—they posed no risk of spiritual infection in his mind. Williams concluded that most people were already spiritually dead anyway and thus were as immune to infection by such as the Quakers as a corpse was immune to the possibility of catching a cold.

Roger Williams and the Dutch West India Company, though, held the minority view when it came to tolerating the Quakers. Elsewhere in the North American colonies, Quakers could count on far more inhospitable treatment. The speed with which Massachusetts Puritans reacted to the new Quaker presence in New England is some measure of the spiritual peril they associated with this presence. The first Quakers in Massachusetts, Mary Fisher and Ann Austin, arrived via Barbados in 1656 and were promptly exiled to England. Three years later two Quaker men, Marmaduke Stephenson and William Robinson, were executed by hanging. In 1660 Mary Dyer and William Leddra were added to the list of Quaker martyrs.

Present-day Rhode Island, New York, and New Jersey served as tolerable havens for Quakers, and when George Fox himself visited America in 1672 and 1673, he helped to establish Quaker meetings in Maryland, Virginia, and North Carolina as well. But an even more secure harbor for Quakers in America was provided by the founding of Pennsylvania by William Penn. The son of a wealthy English military hero, Penn earned his father's displeasure but an important place in American history when he became a Quaker in 1667. Prior to this conversion he had been trained as a lawyer in London, and he subsequently became a vigorous advocate for Quakers—so vigorous, in fact, that he shared the fate common to many Quakers of spending significant time in jail. He was thus well equipped to write one of the

The Quaker William Penn founded the colony of Pennsylvania. *(Library of Congress, Prints and Photographs Division LC-USZ62-106735)*

17th century's important arguments for religious freedom: *The Great Case for Liberty of Conscience,* published in 1670. But William Penn was able to provide an even more tangible assistance to Quakerism when in 1681 Charles II repaid a debt he owed to Penn's father by making William Penn the proprietor of a new colony in America, Pennsylvania.

Like Providence and Maryland, the colony of Pennsylvania had as one of its foundations a significant devotion to religious liberty. The Frame of Government, enacted in 1682, provided that "All persons who profess to believe in Jesus Christ the saviour of the World, shall be capable to serve this government in any capacity, both legislatively and executively."[3] Non-Christians, according to this language, could be excluded from participating in civic affairs but were not excluded from the colony itself. Though stunted by the standard of today's liberties, this restriction to the general principle of religious freedom was modest for its time. Its inclusion of Catholics and Quakers within the shelter of religious freedom was in advance of the more limited versions of this freedom recognized in most of the other American colonies. As a consequence, thousands of Quakers fled from England to enjoy the liberty granted to them in Pennsylvania, so many, in fact, that English Quakers complained that Penn's colony was stripping their meetings of members.

William Penn himself spent two years in Pennsylvania beginning in 1682, but dwindling fortunes and mounting debt eventually cast him ignominiously into debtor's prison for a time. His return to England did not radically improve the state of his financial affairs, and for most of the rest of his life, apart from a brief return visit to Pennsylvania in 1699, Penn had to content himself with overseeing the colony from a distance while he struggled with financial and political problems of his own. Not the least of the controversies he had to endure remotely was the schism that developed among Pennsylvania Quakers in the early 1690s, shortly after the death of Quaker founder George Fox in 1691. Prominent Philadelphia Quakers accused Quaker leader George Keith of various spiritual errors, and he responded with his own counteraccusations, which split Pennsylvania Quakers between the followers of Keith, known as "Christian Quakers" or "Keithites," and more mainstream Quakers. In spite of these disappointments, William Penn was able to witness the steady growth of a colony where Quakers, notoriously despised elsewhere in the American colonies, were able not only to practice their religion freely but maintain political and economic control of the colony's affairs until well into the 18th century.

Puritanism and Decline

By the beginning of the 1660s, the first generation of New England Puritans had made way for the second. Two events, especially, during the second half of the 17th century highlighted the general sense of decline that troubled many Puritans. These events revolved around controversies involving the two ordinances the Puritans recognized as central to Christian faith and practice: baptism and the celebration of the Lord's Supper. Controversy concerning baptism arrived in New England first. According to the original practice of Puritan churches, baptism was an ordinance administered only to the children of church members. To be a church member one had to give testimony to having been converted or regenerated. This testimony, if satisfactory, meant that one was recognized as being among the visible saints, those who were parties to God's covenant of grace. The children of church members were also thought to be members of covenant families and fit objects for baptism, which was understood as a sign of covenant membership. Children, though, once baptized, were not thought of as full church members in their own right. Becoming so required that they eventually experience God's saving grace themselves and give public testimony to this experience. Until then, they could not participate in the other central Christian ordinance, the Lord's Supper. By New England's second generation, however, it was clear that many of the children of believing parents who had been baptized as infants never became church members themselves as they grew older. They did, though, have children of their own and wished to see these children baptized. Accordingly, Puritan New England had to struggle with whether baptism was appropriate for the children of non–church members who had themselves been baptized as infants.

In 1662 New England's Congregational churches convened a synod to consider the issue of baptism. The issue created tensions among different churches and ministers and even, in one famous instance, between members of the same influential family. Two of Massachusetts's most prominent ministers were father and son, Richard and Increase Mather, and these two ministers, bound by ties of kinship, nevertheless found themselves divided for a time over the issue of baptism. The son, Increase Mather, believed at this time—though he later swung round to his father's views—that baptism should be reserved for the children of full communing church members. His father, Richard, however, sided with a majority of ministers who proposed what came to be known as the Half-Way Covenant. This doctrinal compromise permitted the baptism of children whose parents had themselves been baptized but had never subsequently testified to a conversion experience that would have qualified them to become full church members. Like their non-church member parents, however, children baptized under the terms of the Half-Way Covenant were not full church members. They were excluded from the church's most importance ordinance, the celebration of the Lord's Supper, until they could give satisfactory proof that they had been regenerated themselves. Although adoption of the Half-Way Covenant offered some relief against the spiritual decline that seemed prevalent in New England, it had a limited long-term impact. It served only to help incorporate into the life of churches colonists whose parents or grandparents had participated in this life. But it had no application to the many new settlers who arrived in New England during the second and third generations

The Massachusetts minister Increase Mather is pictured here. *(Library of Congress, Prints and Photographs Division LC-USZ62-75070)*

of European colonization. An alarming number of these new arrivals failed to become members of any church.

A further controversy centered around the ordinance of the Lord's Supper followed two decades later. In 1679 Puritan churches convened the Reforming Synod to discuss the general decline in spiritual purity and devotion that seemed to characterize New England's churches. At this synod Solomon Stoddard, the minister of the church in Northampton, Massachusetts, revealed that he had adopted ecclesiastical innovations a good deal more radical than even the innovation ratified by the Half-Way Covenant. The Half-Way Covenant retained the traditional practice of limiting church membership and participation in the ordinance of the Lord's Supper to believers who gave evidence of having been converted, not simply baptized as infants. But Stoddard threw open the doors of church membership both to those who had given evidence of conversion and to those who had received baptism as infants. Even more significantly, he applied the same standard to allow members who had not given proof of conversion to participate in the Lord's Supper if they had been baptized as infants. In fact, Stoddard argued that the Lord's Supper should be understood as a "converting ordinance." When participated in by those who formally assented to the truths of Christian doctrine and led moral lives, he insisted, the ordinance had the power to produce the inward acceptance of the Christian gospel necessary for true conversion. Unlike the synod that produced the Half-Way Covenant, the Reforming Synod of 1679 produced no clear consensus concerning Stoddard's innovations. Stoddard's views were vigorously opposed by Increase Mather, another influential Puritan minister. Nevertheless, Stoddard's liberalization of the requirements for church membership and participation in the Lord's Supper became especially influential in western Massachusetts and Connecticut.

Witnessing to and Warring against Native Americans

During the 17th century evangelistic activity by Europeans among American Indian tribes continued, especially among Spanish and French missionaries. The most famous Native American convert to Christianity during the colonial period was Kateri Tekakwitha, who was baptized into the Catholic faith in 1676. Jesuit priests had visited Tekakwitha's Mohawk village when she was an adolescent, and this initial contact appears to have paved the way for her subsequent conversion when another Catholic priest returned to the village. Afterward, she remained for a time in her village, where she suffered significant persecution for being known as "the Christian." Eventually, she made the 200-mile journey to the French mission of St. Francis Xavier at Sault St. Louis on the St. Lawrence River, near Montreal, Canada. Here she took a vow of chastity and poverty, and her pious example led to her becoming known as "the Lily of the Mohawks" and, sadly, to her early death as a result of the severity of her ascetic practices. In the 20th century she became the first American Indian proposed for sainthood within the Catholic Church. The late 17th century also saw the beginning of the long missionary career of the Jesuit priest Eusebio Francisco Kino, who labored across three decades to plant the Catholic faith in what is now the southwestern part of the United States. He established the first Catholic mission in California in 1683 at San Bruno, near present-day Loreto and in the decades after this event founded scores of missions across the Southwest.

Puritan missionary activity among the American Indians of the northeast proceeded along more modest lines. In theory, the Puritans were not insensible to the need for evangelistic efforts directed toward Native Americans. John Winthrop, governor of the Massachusetts Bay Colony during most of its first generation, had sworn upon his first appointment to this position that he would "draw . . . the natives of this country . . . to the knowledge of the true God."[4] The colony's charter stated that one of its principal aims was to "win and incite the natives of [the] country to . . . the Christian faith."[5] In practice, however, Winthrop and the other New England Puritans focused their energies primarily on building and sustaining a godly commonwealth. Unlike the Spanish in Mexico and South America, the Puritans saw no place for the use of force in planting Christianity among American Indian populations. Thus, preoccupied with the work of colonization and fettered in their evangelistic efforts by language barriers, the Puritans did not place a priority on missionary activity among American Indians.

The Puritan minister John Eliot was a prominent exception to the general arrangement of priorities. Soon after his arrival in New England in 1631, he assumed a position as junior minister of the church at Roxbury. But history remembers him less for his pastoral work in this church than for his determined efforts to bring the Christian gospel to American Indians living in New England. Upon his appointment as the senior minister of the Roxbury church in 1641, he began to devote substantial energy to the study of the Algonquian language to facilitate his missionary efforts. He subsequently preached the first Puritan sermon in this language in 1646, and in later years his preaching yielded a number of American Indian converts. These he began to settle in separate villages as early as 1651, where they became known as "Praying Indians." The benevolent regard Eliot earns from many historians for his humane treatment of American Indians is tarnished somewhat by his willingness to encourage converts to adopt not only the teachings of Christianity, but to assume the cultural habits and mannerisms of Europeans. In addition to his founding of villages for American Indian converts, John Eliot's other important contribution was a translation of the Bible he prepared in the Algonquian language. The New Testament of this translation, published in 1661, was the first Bible printed in America. Eliot published a translation of the Old Testament as well two years later.

John Eliot's missionary efforts among the American Indians of Massachusetts suffered a sharp setback during King Philip's War. This conflict between the New England colonists and Native Americans led by Metacom (called King Philip by New Englanders), son of Massasoit and chief of the Wampanoag, raged from 1675 to 1676. Although Massasoit had enjoyed friendly relations with European settlers in New England, Metacom eventually bristled at the steady expansion of colonial settlements and forged an alliance with other tribes, including the Naragansett, to attack the colonists. All-out war between the colonists and Metacom and his allies erupted after Native Americans massacred several hundred settlers. Eventually, Metacom himself was killed in August 1676, and the main body of Native American military strength was defeated by the colonists. The end of King Philip's War brought with it the destruction of American Indian tribal life in southern New England. In the course of the war, the Indians who had been converted to Christianity under the ministry of John Eliot were driven from the villages in which he had settled them and dispersed. Although Eliot continued evangelistic efforts after King Philip's War, the success of these efforts was only a shadow of what they had been before the war.

The Devil and Salem

By the final decade of the 17th century, John Winthrop's vision 60 years earlier of establishing a city on a hill seemed to many New Englanders long ago and very far away. New England had lost the battle to keep religious diversity at bay, suffering the incursions of Baptists and Quakers and Catholics and even Jews. And the piety of second- and third-generation Puritans seemed not so fervent as that practiced by the original Puritan generation in New England. King Philip's War had appeared to many as God's judgment on a holy commonwealth that was no longer holy, but even this judgment did not rekindle Christian devotion or restrain the Babel of religious diversity. As they witnessed the decline of religious devotion and orthodoxy, many Puritans found it convenient to blame Satan and to look for his agents among them. In any event, from 1640 to 1690, the number of prosecutions for witchcraft climbed drastically. Before the 17th century ended these prosecutions culminated in one final burst of zeal for revealing the devil's nefarious schemes. It occurred in Salem Village in 1692.

What climaxed in the execution of 20 people convicted of witchcraft and the imprisonment of scores of other Salem inhabitants began in January 1692 with a strange illness suffered by two young girls, the daughter and niece of the local minister, Samuel Parris: nine-year-old Elizabeth Parris and 11-year-old Abigail Williams. When a local physician concluded that their malady had a supernatural source, some inhabitants of Salem began to suspect that devilry was afoot. In fact, a neighbor suggested that Parris's two slaves, one of them the West Indian woman Tituba, prepare a witch's cake—made out of rye and containing the urine of the afflicted girls—to be fed to a hound that might then lead to the identification of a witch. Inspired by this environment of suspicion, no doubt, Elizabeth Parris and

The trial of George Jacobs of Salem for witchcraft is pictured here. *(Library of Congress, Prints and Photographs Division LC-USZ62-94432)*

Abigail Williams claimed in late February that three women, including Tituba, had practiced witchcraft against them. This was a crime punishable by death under the codification of law adopted in 1648 in Massachusetts called the *Book of the Laws and Liberties*. It prescribed that "[i]f any man or woman be a WITCH, that is, has or consults with a familiar spirit, they shall be put to death."[6] Salem authorities responded to the allegations of the girls by arresting the three women and interrogating them. Although two of the accused denied that they had participated in witchcraft, Tituba confessed to being a witch. Intuitively, she grasped the perverse truth that ruled subsequent proceedings: citizens who admitted that they had sold themselves in servitude to Satan fared better than those who steadfastly affirmed their innocence in the face of witchcraft accusations. All those who confessed to witchcraft escaped the gallows; only those who insisted on their innocence were hung.

From this beginning accusations of witchcraft spiraled upward in number as other young girls and later other residents of the village leveled charges of witchcraft against their neighbors. At first, only individuals on the margins of Salem society were accused, but eventually more prominent citizens were also accused of having done the devil's bidding. At the end of May newly appointed colonial governor William Phips created a special court to preside over the witchcraft cases. The court heard evidence regarding various unusual occurrences alleged to have been caused by the activity, but it also considered "spectral evidence." This latter evidence included testimony from the girls and others to the effect that they had seen one person or another in the presence of Satan or that they had been invisibly tormented by the spectral, that is, invisible, forms of persons accused of witchcraft. The girls, for example, might claim to be pinched or pricked with pins by the specters of those appearing in court; they might appear struck dumb by an alleged witch whom they subsequently claimed stopped their tongues. The use of this evidence was the most controversial aspect of the Salem trials and ultimately sparked a disagreement between two prominent Puritan ministers who were father and son: Increase Mather and his son, Cotton Mather. Increase publicly opposed the use of spectral evidence in witchcraft prosecutions, while his son Cotton supported the admissibility and probity of this evidence.

Those who met their deaths at the hands of the Salem inquisition died, except in one instance, by hanging. One defendant, Giles Corey, was accused of witchcraft but refused to participate in the trial against him. For this act of insubordination he was found in contempt of court and sentenced to be pressed by large stones until he either renounced his contempt or died. He refused to accept the court's authority to the very end, when, after two long days of suffering, tradition records his last words as being "more weight." Henry Wadsworth Longfellow more than 150 years after the event gave poetic expression to Corey's death in his drama *Giles Corey of Salem Farms*. In Longfellow's version, Corey declares before he dies

I will not plead. If I deny, I am condemned already, in courts where ghosts appear as witnesses, and swear men's lives away. If I confess, then I confess to a lie, to buy a life which is not a life, but only death in life. I will not bear false witness against any, Not even against myself, whom I count least . . . I come! Here is my body; ye may torture it, but the immortal soul ye cannot crush![7]

After the final glut of executions on September 22, the tide of opinion in Salem began to change. The proceedings still had their defenders, not the least of whom was the Puritan minister Cotton Mather, who was given access to court records and eventually published a defense of the witchcraft proceedings titled *The Wonders of the Invisible World.* But Cotton's father, Increase Mather, published a critique of the Salem affair in early October—*Cases of Conscience Concerning Evil Spirits.* In this work Increase Mather subjected to particular criticism the use of spectral evidence at Salem. After publication of this work, Massachusetts governor William Phips received a copy of it and, convinced by its indictment of spectral evidence, forbade any further use of this form of evidence in subsequent witchcraft trials. Proceedings continued into the first part of 1693 under a new court. But either because general sentiment had turned decisively against the witchcraft allegations or because convictions were rarely possible without the use of now forbidden spectral evidence, most of those accused were acquitted of charges. Of more than 50 indictments for witchcraft, only three further convictions resulted. By May 1693 the colonial governor had pardoned and released all those in jail as a result of the witchcraft proceedings, thus officially closing the sordid affair.

The governor's pardons, however, could not close the wounds inflicted by the witchcraft trials. Surviving victims and family members of those who had been executed began to seek and were generally granted reparations. But the mere payment of money could not assuage the losses. In hindsight, it appeared that key participants in the madness had been motivated less by holy zeal than by mundane sinful desires: a weak minister desiring to halt the decline in his power and authority, accusers anxious to acquire the property of those they accused, a village tired of having to live side by side with strange or disagreeable neighbors. Participants in the Salem proceedings responded with varying degrees of remorse for their roles. Five years after the original trials, the Massachusetts general court appointed a day of fasting and prayer concerning the Salem incident, and in response one of the judges, Samuel Sewell, confessed to his church the sinfulness of his own judgments concerning the witchcraft allegations. His signed confession accepted responsibility for the part he played:

> Samuel Sewall, sensible of the reiterated stroke of God upon himself and family; and being sensible, that as to the Guilt contracted, upon the opening of the late [witchcraft proceedings] . . . he is, upon many accounts, more concerned than any that he knows of, Desires to take the Blame and Shame of it, Asking pardon of men.[8]

But even as the Salem participants scrutinized their own conduct, they did not wholly absolve Satan for his role in the affair. Satan may not have sent his agents to pinch and poke the upright citizens of Salem, as the girls had alleged, but, at least according to Salem's minister, Samuel Parris, the devil had surely been present in the village. God, he insisted, had "suffered the evil angels to delude us."[9]

Chronicle of Events

1660

- The Quaker Mary Dyer, previously banished on pain of death from the Massachusetts Bay Colony, returns to the colony and on June 1 is executed by hanging in Boston.
- The Virginia House of Burgesses forbids ship captains from bringing Quakers to the colony.
- In England the monarchy is restored under Charles II.

1661

- Samuel Green publishes Puritan minister John Eliot's translation of the New Testament into Massachusett, an Algonquian dialect, the first Bible printed in America. Eliot's translation of the Old Testament into Massachusett will be published two years later.
- The English government bans any further executions of Quakers in New England.

1662

- A synod is convened in Massachusetts that produces the Half-Way Covenant, an agreement among Puritan churches that children might be baptized whose parents had themselves been baptized even if these parents had not given evidence of conversion and thus had never become full church members.
- Massachusetts enacts the "cart and whip" law, providing for Quakers to be transported to Rhode Island and publicly whipped in each village along the way.
- The Virginia assembly passes legislation prohibiting ministers in the colony who had not received episcopal ordination.
- William Penn, future founder of Pennsylvania, is expelled from Oxford University in England for complaining against compulsory chapel attendance at services of the Church of England.
- In England Parliament passes the Quaker Act, which prohibits Quaker meetings.

1663

- John Clarke, assisted initially by Roger Williams, obtains a new charter for the Providence Colony after the Restoration, in which Charles II assumes the British Crown.
- A Baptist church is established in Swansea, Massachusetts.
- A Catholic seminary is established in Quebec.

Cotton Mather defended the Salem witchcraft trials. *(Library of Congress, Prints and Photographs Division LC-USZ62-92308)*

- The directors of the Dutch West India Company instruct Peter Stuyvesant, director general of New Netherland, to be more tolerant of the diverse religious faiths there.
- Charles II grants a charter for territory in America that will eventually be divided into North and South Carolina.
- A Torah loaned to Jews in New Amsterdam by the synagogue in Amsterdam in 1655 is returned to Amsterdam around this date, suggesting that the *minyan,* or prayer quorum of 10 males over age 13 required for worship, could no longer be maintained in New Amsterdam.
- *February 12:* Cotton Mather, later a prominent Puritan minister, is born in Boston.

1664

- After the British take control of New Netherland from the Dutch, they rename it New York. According to the Articles of Capitulation providing for transfer of authority, freedom of worship is guaranteed to the inhabitants of New York.
- Charles II sends four commissioners to New England with the mission, among others, of securing religious freedom for Anglicans and public support for Anglican ministers.
- Increase Mather assumes the position of teacher in Boston's Second Church, where he will serve for nearly 60 years.

1667

- William Penn becomes a Quaker while on a business trip to Ireland.
- Virginia enacts a law that provides that the baptism of a slave does not entitle the slave to freedom.
- Jesuit priests visit the village of Kateri Tekakwitha, an American Indian girl who will subsequently be converted to Catholicism and in the 20th century be declared a Catholic saint.

1669

- Solomon Stoddard becomes the minister of the church in Northampton, Massachusetts, where he will ignite controversy by liberalizing the requirements for church membership and participation in the sacrament of the Lord's Supper and where his preaching will serve as a precursor for the Great Awakening in the 18th century.

1670

- William Penn is arrested in England for inciting a riot but is acquitted of this charge by a jury. He publishes *The Great Case of Liberty of Conscience.*

1672

- George Fox, founder of the Quakers, visits the American colonies, stopping in Maryland, Virginia, and North Carolina. Roger Williams challenges him to a public debate.

1673

- *August:* Roger Williams participates in a public debate with three Quakers.

1674

- Pope Clement X appoints François-Xavier de Montmorency Laval the first bishop of Quebec.

1675

- Massachusetts passes a law requiring church doors to be locked during services (to prevent attenders from departing early).
- Connecticut suspends a law that had fined Quakers for not attending Sunday services in local Congregational churches.
- King Philip's War, a bloody conflict in New England between colonists and Native Americans, rages from 1675 to 1676.
- During the course of King Phillip's War, colonists grow distrustful of the "Praying Indians" who inhabit towns for converted Native Americans established by John Eliot. They drive these converts out of the towns.

1676

- Native American convert Kateri Tekakwitha is baptized into the Catholic faith.
- In England Robert Barclay publishes an influential statement of Quaker belief titled *An Apology for the True Christian Divinity.*
- *February 10:* Wampanoag Indians attack the village of Lancaster, taking Mary Rowlandson captive. When she is ultimately freed, she will write an account of her captivity titled *The Narrative of the Captivity and Restoration of Mrs. Mary Rowlandson.* This account will be published posthumously in 1682 and widely read both in England and in the colonies.

1677

- John Rogers, a Puritan dissenter, attracts followers who form the Rogerenes in Connecticut and Rhode Island.
- Massachusetts ends the practice of publicly whipping Quakers.
- *November 5:* Solomon Stoddard, minister of the church at Northampton, stops recording whether members of the church are full, as opposed to half-way, members (under the Half-Way Covenant).

1678

- In England John Bunyan publishes *Pilgrim's Progress.*
- Jews in Rhode Island establish a cemetery in Newport.

1679

- At the request of Solomon Stoddard and others, the Reforming Synod meets in Massachusetts this year and the next to consider reasons for the general decline in New England's religious faith. At this synod Stoddard defends his view that the ordinance of the Lord's Supper should be made available even to the unconverted, so long as they lead morally upright lives and are sufficiently knowledgeable about the Christian faith.

1680

- *August 10:* Pueblo Indians, led by a medicine man named Popé, who was punished for adhering to Native American beliefs rather than converting to Christianity, kill hundreds of Spanish settlers and drive those remaining from Taos.

1681

- William Penn obtains a charter from Charles II for the colony of Pennsylvania.

- The first sessions of the Philadelphia Yearly Meeting of Quakers are held.
- The Plymouth Colony begins to allow Quakers to participate in civic affairs.
- The Jesuit priest Eusebio Francisco Kino arrives in Veracruz and makes his way to Mexico City with the object of engaging in missionary activities in Mexico. He will eventually establish missions in the present-day United States.

1682

- William Penn spends two years in Pennsylvania, but financial difficulties lead him to debt and to a nine-month stay in debtor's prison.
- The Frame of Government for the colony of Pennsylvania guarantees religious liberty to all those who believe in God but restricts office-holding to Christians.
- Joseph Bueno de Mesquita purchases a burial site "for the Jewish nation in New York."

1683

- Jesuit missionary Eusebio Francisco Kino establishes the first mission in California at San Bruno, near present-day Loreto.
- Francis Makemie, known as the father of American Presbyterianism, arrives in America from Ireland and begins an itinerant preaching career in Maryland, Virginia, and North Carolina.
- Dutch Mennonites establish Germantown in Pennsylvania.
- Increase Mather helps found the Boston Philosophical Society, modeled after the Royal Society of London.

1684

- The Quaker George Keith immigrates to East Jersey, where he becomes surveyor general.
- William Penn returns to England from Pennsylvania.
- The Plymouth Colony is absorbed into the Massachusetts Bay Colony.

1685

- Cotton Mather is ordained a minister in Old North Church, where he will serve with his father, Increase Mather, until his father's death 40 years later.
- In France Louis XIV revokes the Edict of Nantes, enacted in 1598, which had granted religious freedom to French Calvinists, and prompts the migration of many French Huguenots to North America.
- Jewish families in New York petition to be allowed to worship in public but are informed that the right of public worship is granted only to Christians.

1686

- Sir Edmund Andros, an Anglican, becomes governor of the Massachusetts Bay Colony.

1687

- Massachusetts colonial governor Edmund Andros compels the Congregationalists in Boston to allow the Old South Meetinghouse to be used for Anglican services.

1688

- In England the Glorious Revolution sees the Catholic monarch James deposed and his Protestant daughter Mary and her husband, William of Orange, assume his place. This event sparks a rise in anti-Catholic feeling in England and the colonies.
- A resolution of Germantown Mennonites condemns slavery.

1689

- The Toleration Act is passed in England and influences the development of religious liberty in the American colonies. The terms of the act are generally applied to the colonies.
- In England John Locke publishes *A Letter Concerning Toleration*, a defense of religious liberty that will greatly influence the debate on this subject in the American colonies. Locke, however, implicitly excludes Catholics from the protections of religious liberty.
- A group of Massachusetts ministers and merchants remove Edmund Andros from his position as colonial governor and imprison him.
- King's Chapel is completed in Boston and becomes home to the first Anglican congregation in New England. Slightly less than a century later, in 1785, King's Chapel will become the first Unitarian congregation in America.

1690

- Solomon Stoddard, minister of the church at Northampton, announces to his congregation his belief that the ordinance of the Lord's Supper is a "converting" ordinance, that is, appropriate even for those who have not previously been converted.

1691

- After George Fox, the founder of the Quakers, dies this year, a schism develops between George Keith and his followers, referred to as "Christian Quakers" or "Keithites," and the main body of American Quakers.

- The Massachusetts Charter of 1691 requires that "a liberty of Conscience" be allowed "in the Worship of God to all Christians (Except Papists)."

1692

- Massachusetts receives a new charter as a royal colony.
- Maryland loses its status as a proprietary colony, under which a measure of protection for Catholics had been accorded, and becomes instead a royal colony under the control of Protestant England.
- After William Penn falls out of favor with the British government, he temporarily loses control of the Pennsylvania colony until 1694.
- *January:* Eleven-year-old Abigail Williams and nine-year-old Elizabeth Parris, residents of Salem, fall ill and begin to exhibit signs of strange behavior.
- *February:* A local physician declares that the illness suffered by Abigail Williams and Elizabeth Parris has a supernatural origin. Tituba feeds witchcake to a dog as a means of discovering who afflicted the girls. Elizabeth Parris identifies Tituba as the source of her affliction. She and Abigail Williams subsequently accuse Sarah Good and Sarah Osborne of witchcraft as well. Arrest warrants are issued for Tituba, Sarah Good, and Sarah Osborne.
- *March 1:* Tituba, Sarah Good, and Sarah Osborne are questioned. Tituba confesses to being a witch. Subsequently, further accusations of witchcraft are leveled by Williams, Parris, and others. Various citizens so accused are arrested and examined.
- *May 27:* William Phips, newly appointed governor of Massachusetts, appoints a court to hear the Salem witchcraft cases. None of the accused has legal representation.
- *June 2:* Bridget Bishop becomes the first person tried for witchcraft at Salem. She is convicted and sentenced to die.
- *June 10:* Bridget Bishop is executed by hanging for witchcraft.
- *July:* Abigail Williams and other Salem accusers are invited to Andover, where they accuse numerous townspeople of witchcraft.
- *July 19:* Five more Salem residents are executed by hanging for witchcraft. Rebecca Nurse, a woman of some standing in the community and greatly admired before the witchcraft proceedings, is among those executed. She dies with such dignity that some observers doubt the legitimacy of her conviction.

- *August 19:* An additional five Salem residents are executed for witchcraft.
- *September 19:* Giles Corey, a Salem resident who refuses to accept the authority of the court, is pressed to death.
- *September 22:* Nine more Salem residents, including Martha Corey, whose husband Giles had been pressed to death three days earlier, are executed for witchcraft. The judges meet with Puritan minister Cotton Mather and arrange for him to have access to court records so that he can compose a defense of the witchcraft proceedings. He eventually publishes this work under the title of *The Wonders of the Invisible World.*
- *October 3:* The Puritan minister Increase Mather, father of Cotton Mather, publishes *Cases of Conscience Concerning Evil Spirits,* criticizing the witchcraft prosecutions at Salem, in particular the use of spectral evidence. Later in the same month the governor of Massachusetts, having read Increase Mather's work, will forbid further use of spectral evidence in the Salem witchcraft trials. Toward the middle of October he will dissolve the initial court he appointed to hear the Salem witchcraft accusations. Late in the same year the colony will establish a new superior court of judicature, and this court will be given jurisdiction over crimes involving "life and limb," including witchcraft.

1693

- The Quaker George Keith publishes the first American antislavery tract, titled *An Exhortation to Friends Concerning Buying or Keeping Negroes.*
- New York passes the Ministry Act, providing for tax support of ministers in every town, though New York citizens at the time and historians since debate whether the Ministry Act established the Church of England in New York.
- The College of William and Mary is chartered to provide a pious education to Virginia students, train future Anglican ministers, and encourage missionary efforts among "Western Indians."
- *January:* The Salem witchcraft trials resume before the newly constituted superior court of judicature, though spectral evidence is not admitted. Of 56 individuals indicted for witchcraft, only three are convicted. Subsequent trials in the spring will produce no convictions, and in May the governor of Massachusetts will pardon all those previously convicted, including those scheduled for execution.

1696

- North Carolina enacts a law guaranteeing religious liberty for "all Christians (Papists only excepted)."
- New York City's first Anglican church, Trinity, is established.
- In England John Toland publishes *Christianity Not Mysterious,* an influential apologetic for deism.

1697

- After the general court of Massachusetts orders a day of fasting and prayer concerning the Salem witchcraft trials, one of the judges in the trials, Samuel Sewall, confesses to his church that his role in the trials was sinful.

1698

- A South Carolina law provides tax support for the minister of the Anglican church (St. Philip's Episcopal Church) in Charleston.

1699

- Thomas Bray in England establishes the Society for Promoting Christian Knowledge, intended to publish Anglican literature for use in the colonies.
- East Jersey passes legislation prohibiting Catholics from holding public office.
- William Penn visits Pennsylvania again for two years.

Eyewitness Testimony

To the General Court now in Boston:

Whereas I am by many charged with the guiltiness of my own Blood; if you mean in my coming to Boston, I am therein clear, and justified by the Lord, in whose Will I came, who will require my Blood of you be sure; who have made a Law to take away the Lives of the innocent Servants of God, if they come among you, who are called by you, Cursed Quakers; although I say, and am a living Witness for them and the Lord, that he hath blessed them, and sent them unto you: therefore be not found fighters against God, but let my Counsel and Request be accepted with you, To repeal all such Laws, that the Truth and Servants of the Lord may have free passage among you, and you kept from shedding Innocent Blood, which I know there are many among you would not do, if they knew it so to be: nor can the Enemy that stirs you up thus to destroy this holy Seed, in any measure countervail the great Damage that you will by thus doing procure: Therefore, seeing the Lord hath not hid it from me, it lies upon me, in love to your Souls, thus to persuade you: I have no self-ends, the Lord knows, for if my Life were freely granted by you, it would not avail me, nor could I expect it of you, so long as I should daily hear or see the Sufferings of these People, my dear Brethren, and Seed, with whom my Life is bound up, as I have done these two years; and now it is like to increase, even unto death, for no evil doing, but coming among you: Was ever the like Laws heard of among a People that profess Christ come in the flesh? And have such no other weapons but such Laws, to fight against Spiritual Wickedness withal, as you call it? . . . Therefore I leave these Lines with you, appealing to the faithful and true Witness of God, which is One in all Consciences, before whom we must all appear; you will hear or forbear: with Him is my Reward, with whom to live is my Joy, and to die is my Gain, though I had not had your forty eight hours warning, for the preparation to the Death of Mary Dyer. And know this also, That if through the Enmity you shall . . . confirm your Law, though it were but by taking away the Life of one of us, That the Lord will overthrow both your Law and you, by his Righteous Judgements. . . . If you neither hear nor obey the Lord nor his Servants, yet will he send more of his Servants among you, so that your end shall be frustrated, that think to restrain them, you call Cursed Quakers, from coming among you by any thing you can do to them. . . . In Love and in the Spirit of Meekness I again beseech you, for I have no Enmity to the Persons of any; but you shall know, That God will not be mocked, but what you sow, that shall ye reap from him, that will render to every one according to the deeds done in the body, whether good or evil; Even so be it, saith.

Quaker Mary Dyer, 1660, address to the general court of the Massachusetts Bay Colony, after the court had pronounced her sentence of execution for venturing back into the colony after having been banished the previous year, in Hart, American History Told by Contemporaries, *vol. 1, pp. 479–481.*

ANNO 1661. At the said next General-Court, *Wenlock Christison* was again brought to the Bar.

The Governor asked him, *What he had to say for himself, why he should not die?*

Wenlock. I have done nothing worthy of Death; if I had, I refuse not to die.

Governor. *Thou art come in among us in Rebellion, which is as the Sin of Witchcraft, and ought to be punished.*

Wenlock. I came not in among you in Rebellion, but in Obedience to the God of Heaven; not in Contempt to any of you, but in Love to your Souls and Bodies; and that you shall know one Day, when you and all Men must give an Account of your Deeds done in the Body. Take heed, for you cannot escape the righteous Judgments of God.

Major-General *Adderton. You pronounce Woes and Judgments, and those that are gone before you pronounced Woes and Judgments; but the Judgments of the Lord God are not come upon us yet.*

Wenlock. Be not proud, neither let your Spirits be lifted up; God doth but wait till the Measure of your Iniquity be filled up, and that you have seen your ungodly Race, then will the Wrath of God come upon you to the uttermost; And as for thy part, it hangs over thy Head, and is near to be poured down upon thee, and shall come as a Thief in the Night suddenly, when thou thinkest not of it. By what Law will ye put me to Death?

Court. *We have a Law, and by our Law you are to die.*

Wenlock. So said the *Jews* of Christ, *We have a Law, and by our Law he ought to die.*

. . . . .

Court. *You are in our Hand, and have broken our Laws, and we will try you.*

Wenlock. Your Will is your Law, and what you have Power to do, that you will do: And seeing that the Jury must go forth on my Life, this I have to say to you in the Fear of the Living God: Jury, take heed what you do, for you swear by the Living God, *That you will true Trial make, and just Verdict give, according to the Evidence.* Jury, look for your

Evidence: What have I done to deserve Death? Keep your Hands out of innocent Blood.

A Juryman. *It is good Counsel.*

The Jury went out, but having received their Lesson, soon returned, and brought in their Verdict *Guilty.*

[After the Court sentenced Wenlock to death, he responded.]

Wenlock. The Will of the Lord be done: In whose Will I came amongst you, and in his Counsel I stand, feeling his Eternal Power, that will uphold me unto the last Gasp, I do not question it. . . . Do not think to weary out the Living God by taking away the Lives of his Servants: What do you gain by it? For the last Man you put to Death, here are *five* come in his Room. And if you have Power to take my Life from me, God can raise up the same Principle of Life in *ten* of his Servants, and send them among you in my Room, that you may have Torment upon Torment, which is your Portion: *For there is no Peace to the Wicked,* saith my God.

Governor. *Take him away.*

From the trial of a Quaker in Massachusetts, 1661, in Hart, American History Told by Contemporaries, *vol. 1, pp. 481–484.*

We very much doubt if vigorous proceedings against them [the Quakers] ought not to be discontinued except you intend to check and destroy your populations, which, however, in the youth of your existence ought rather to be encouraged by all possible means. . . . The consciences of men, at least, ought ever to remain free and unshackled. Let every one be unmolested as long as he is modest; as long as his conduct in a political sense is irreproachable; as long as he does not disturb others or oppose the government. This maxim of moderation has always been the guide of the magistrates of this city, and the consequence has been that, from every land, people have flocked to this asylum. Tread thus in their steps, and, we doubt not, you will be blessed.

The Dutch West India Company to Peter Stuyvesant, director general of New Netherland, April 16, 1663, in Stokes, Church and State in the United States, *vol. 1, p. 152.*

He that desires to see the real Platform of a quiet and sober Government extant, Superiority with a meek and yet commanding power sitting at the Helm, steering the actions of State quietly, through the multitude and diversity of Opinionous waves that diversely meet, let him look on *Mary-Land* with eyes admiring, and he'll then judge her, *The Miracle of this Age.*

Here the *Roman Catholic,* and the *Protestant Episcopal,* (whom the world would persuade have proclaimed open Wars irrevocably against each other) contrary-wise concur in an unanimous parallel of friendship, and inseparable love entailed onto one another: All Inquisitions, Martyrdom, and Banishments are not so much as named, but inexpressibly abhorred by each other.

George Alsop, an indentured servant for a time in Maryland, who returned to England and wrote "A Character of the Province of Mary-Land," 1666, in Hart, American History Told by Contemporaries, *vol. 1, p. 268.*

[I]mposition, restraint, and persecution for matters relating to conscience directly invade divine prerogative and divest the Almighty of a due, proper to none besides Himself.

. . . . .

First . . . whoever shall interpose their authority to enact faith and worship in a way that seems not to us congruous with what He has discovered to us to be faith and worship (Whose alone property it is to do it) or to restrain us from what we are persuaded is our indispensable duty, they evidently usurp this authority and invade His incommunicable right of government over conscience.

. . . . .

Secondly, such magisterial determinations carry an evident claim to that infallibility which Protestants have been hitherto so jealous of owning that, to avoid the Papists, they have denied it to all but God Himself.

. . . . .

Thirdly, it enthrones man as king over conscience, the alone just claim and privilege of his Creator, Whose thoughts are not as men's thoughts but [Who] has reserved to Himself that empire from all the Caesars on earth.

. . . . .

Fourthly, it defeats the work of His grace and the invisible operation of His eternal Spirit, which can alone beget faith and is only to be obeyed in and about religion and worship, and attributes men's conformity to outward force and corporal punishments—a faith subject to as many revolutions as the powers that enact it.

Fifthly and lastly, such persons assume the judgment of the great tribunal unto themselves; for to whomsoever men are imposedly or restrictively subject and accountable in matters of faith, worship, and conscience, in them alone must the power of judgment reside; but it is equally true that God shall judge all by Jesus Christ and that no man is so accountable to his fellow creatures as to be imposed upon, restrained, or persecuted for any matter of conscience whatever.

Quaker leader William Penn, 1670, from The Great Case of Liberty of Conscience in The Witness of William Penn, *pp. 70–71.*

I must change my ditty now. I have much to write of lamentation over the work of Christ among our praying Indians, of which God hath called you to be nursing Fathers. The work (in our Patent) is under great sufferings. It is killed (in words, wishes & expression) but not in deeds as yet. It is (as it were) dead, but not buried, nor (I believe) shall be. . . . We needed through our corruptions & infirmities all that is come upon us & which the Lord hath performed all his work, his purging work upon us; he can easily and will lay by the rod. When the house is swept, he will lay away the broom. . . . I complain not of our sufferings, but meekly praise the Lord that they be now worse. Yet I cannot but say, they are greater than I can or in modesty & meekness is not for me to express. Be it so. It is the Lord that hath done it, & shall living man complain?

. . . . .

There be 350 souls or thereabout put upon a bleak bare Island, the fittest we have, where they suffer hunger & cold. There is neither food nor competent fuel to be had, & they are bare in clothing because they cannot be received to work for clothing, as they were wont to do. Our rulers are careful to order them food, but it is so hard to be performed that they suffer much. I beg your prayers, that the Lord would take care of them & provide for them. I cannot without difficulty, hardship & peril get unto them. I have been but twice with them, yet I praise God that they be put out of the way of greater perils, dangers & temptations.

. . . . .

At another place there were a company making ready to go to the Island, but were surprised by the Enemy & carried away captive & we cannot hear anything of them. What is become of them, whether any of them be martyred we cannot tell. We cannot say how many there be of them, but more than an hundred, & sundry of them right Godly, both men and women. . . . All in Plymouth Patent are still in quiet & so are all our [Martha's Vineyard] Indians & all the Nantucket Indians. I beg prayers that they may be still preserved.

John Eliot, 1675, letter to the New England Company in London regarding the effects of King Philip's War on his missionary activity among the American Indians of New England, in Gaustad, A Documentary History of Religion in America to the Civil War, *pp. 122–123.*

We are not insensible that your ears are daily filled with the cries of many people in this day of calamity, through all parts of the Country, & are loth to add unto your affliction, by bringing any unnecessary trouble upon you; yet we do no other in faithfulness unto ourselves & the Country, than present briefly our condition before you. We dare not entertain any thoughts of deserting this plantation. The Lord has wonderfully appeared of late for our preservation, & we fear it would be displeasing unto him if we should give up into the hands of our enemies, by running away, that which the Lord has so eminently delivered out of their hands, when they did so violently assault us. If we should desert a town of such considerable strength, it may so animate the enemy & discourage other plantations as may prove no small prejudice unto the Country.

Minister Solomon Stoddard and other citizens of Northampton, Massachusetts, March 28, 1676, petition to Boston authorities

This engraving pictures settlers preparing for an Indian attack during King Philip's War. *(Library of Congress, Prints and Photographs Division LC-USZ62-75122)*

for military protection for the town during King Philip's War, in Coffman, Solomon Stoddard, pp. 65–66.

As weary pilgrim, now at rest,
Hugs with delight his silent nest,
His wasted limbs now lie full soft
That mirey steps have trodden oft,
Blesses himself to think upon
His dangers past, and travails done.
The burning sun no more shall heat,
Nor stormy rains on him shall beat.
The briars and thorns no more shall scratch,
Nor hungry wolves at him shall catch.
He erring paths no more shall tread,
Nor wild fruits eat instead of bread.
For waters cold he doth not long
For thirst no more shall parch his tongue.
No rugged stones his feet shall gall,
Nor stumps nor rocks cause him to fall.
All cares and fears he bids farewell
And means in safety now to dwell.
A pilgrim I, on earth perplexed
With Sins, with cares and sorrows vext,
By age and pains brought to decay,
And my clay house mold'ring away.
Oh, how I long to be at rest
And soar on high among the blest.
This body shall in silence sleep,
Mine eyes no more shall ever weep,
No fainting fits shall me assail,
Nor grinding pains my body frail,
With cares and fears ne'er cumb'red be
Nor losses know, nor sorrows see.
What though my flesh shall there consume,
It is the bed Christ did perfume,
And when a few years shall be gone,
This mortal shall be clothed upon.
A corrupt carcass down it lies,
A glorious body it shall rise.
In weakness and dishonor sown,
In power 'tis raised by Christ alone.
Then soul and body shall unite
And of their Maker have the sight.
Such lasting joys shall there behold
As ear ne'er heard nor tongue e'er told.
Lord make me ready for that day,
Then come, dear Bridegroom, come away.

New England poet Anne Bradstreet, 1678, "As Weary Pilgrim, Now at Rest," in Lundin and Noll, Voices from the Heart, *pp. 58–59.*

As it was Sunday, in order to avoid scandal and for other reasons, we did not wish to absent ourselves from church. We therefore went, and found there truly a wild worldly world. I say wild, not only because the people are wild, as they call it in Europe, but because most of the people who go there to live, or who are born there, partake somewhat of the nature of the country, that is, peculiar to the land where they live. We heard a minister preach, who had come from the up-river country, from Fort Orange, where his residence is, an old man, named Domine Schaats, of Amsterdam. As it is not strange in these countries to have men as ministers who drink, we could imagine nothing else than that he had been drinking a little this morning. His text was, Come unto me all ye, etc., but he was so rough that even the roughest and most godless of our sailors were astonished.

Jaspar Dankers and Peter Sluyter, two Dutch Protestants who visited New York to find a site for a colony for their religious group, ultimately established in Maryland, 1679, Journal of a Voyage to New York, 1679–1680, *in Colbert,* Eyewitness to America, *pp. 35–36.*

Forasmuch as the . . . General Court at their session of the 13 Oct. 1675 were moved under a deep and humbling sense of divine wrath that is broken out upon us and like to burn into a general consumption to make a strict inquisition after those provoking evils which had been the procuring cause of that displeasure and to take into their serious consideration the great business of reformation . . . for the glory of God and the salvation of this perishing people . . . upon our own utmost peril in case of unfaithfulness. . . . That the churches may concur (and) . . . discharge ourselves faithfully in all duty unto the children of the covenant, which is a principle part of the work of reformation as being the only way of the propagation of religion to the rising generation of the neglect and defect of which we are the more sadly sensible.

Minister Solomon Stoddard and others, May 28, 1679, petition to the general court in Boston to convene a synod to discuss the reasons for the decline in piety, in Coffman, Solomon Stoddard, *p. 70.*

When first thou on me Lord wrought'st thy Sweet
Print
My heart was made thy tinder box.
My 'ffections were thy tinder in't.
Where fell thy Sparks by drops.

Those holy Sparks of Heavenly Fire that came
Did ever catch and often out would flame.

But now my heart is made thy Censer trim,
Full of thy golden Altar's fire,
To offer up Sweet Incense in
Unto thyself entire:

I find my tinder scarce thy sparks can feeL
That drop out from thy Holy flint and Steel.

Hence doubts out bud for fear thy fire in me
'S a mocking Ignis Fatuus,
Or lest thine Altar's fire out be,
It's hid in ashes thus.

Yet when the bellows of thy Spirit blow

Away mine ashes, then thy fire doth glow.
New England poet Edward Taylor, "The Ebb and Flow,"
undated but probably composed during the last two decades of
the 17th century, in Mulford, Early American Writings,
p. 303.

Before I knew what affliction meant, I was ready sometimes to wish for it. When I lived in prosperity, having the comforts of the world about me, my relations by me, my heart cheerful, and taking little care for anything, and yet seeing many, whom I preferred before myself, under many trials and afflictions, in sickness, weakness, poverty, losses, crosses, and cares of the world, I should be sometimes jealous least I should have my portion in this life, and that scripture would come to my mind, "For whom the Lord loveth he chasteneth, and scourgeth every Son whom he receiveth" (Hebrews 12.6). But now I see the Lord had His time to scourge and chasten me. The portion of some is to have their afflictions by drops, now one drop and then another; but the dregs of the cup, the wine of astonishment, like a sweeping rain that leaveth no food, did the Lord prepare to be my portion. Affliction I wanted, and affliction I had, full measure (I thought), pressed down and running over. Yet I see, when God calls a person to anything, and through never so many difficulties, yet He is fully able to carry them through and make them see, and say they have been gainers thereby. And I hope I can say in some measure, as David did, "It is good for me that I have been afflicted." The Lord hath showed me the vanity of these outward things. That they are the vanity of vanities, and vexation of spirit, that they are but a shadow, a blast, a bubble, and things of no continuance. That we

Mary Rowlandson is pictured here captive in a canoe. *(Library of Congress, Prints and Photographs Division LC-USZ62-113682)*

must rely on God Himself, and our whole dependance must be upon Him. If trouble from smaller matters begin to arise in me, I have something at hand to check myself with, and say, why am I troubled? It was but the other day that if I had had the world, I would have given it for my freedom, or to have been a servant to a Christian. I have learned to look beyond present and smaller troubles, and to be quieted under them. As Moses said, "Stand still and see the salvation of the Lord" (Exodus 14.13).

> *Mary Rowlandson, concluding observation concerning her captivity during King Philip's War with the Wampanoag Indians, 1682,* The Narrative of the Captivity and Restoration of Mrs. Mary Rowlandson, *in Lundin and Noll,* Voices from the Heart, *p. 64.*

You shall permit all persons of what Religion soever quietly to inhabit within your Government without giving them any disturbance or disquiet whatsoever for or by reason of their differing Opinions in matters of Religion, Provided they give no disturbance to ye public peace, nor do molest or disquiet others in ye free Exercise of their Religion.

> *Instructions of King James II to Thomas Dongan, governor of New York, 1682, in Stokes,* Church and State in the United States, *vol. 1, p. 166.*

New York has first a chaplain belonging to the Fort, of the Church of England; secondly, a Dutch Calvinist; thirdly a French Calvinist; fourthly, a Dutch Lutheran. Here be not many of the Church of England; few Roman Catholics; abundance of Quaker preachers, men, and women especially; Singing Quakers; Ranter Quakers; Sabbatarians; Anti-Sabbatarians; some Anabaptists; some Jews; in short of all sorts of opinion there are some, and the most part none at all.

> *Report by Thomas Dungan, governor of New York, concerning the religion of its inhabitants, 1687, in Stokes,* Church and State in the United States, *vol. 1, p. 167.*

These are the reasons why we are against the traffic of men-body, as followeth: Is there any that would be done or handled at this manner? viz., to be sold or made a slave for all the time of his life? How fearful and faint-hearted are many at sea, when they see a strange vessel, being afraid it should be a Turk, and they should be taken, and sold for slaves into Turkey. Now, what is *this* better done, than Turks do? Yea, rather it is worse for them, which say they are Christians; for we hear that the most part of such niggers are brought hither against

their will and consent, and that many of them are stolen. Now, though they are black, we cannot conceive there is more liberty to have them slaves, as it is to have other white ones. There is a saying, that we should do to all men like as we will be done ourselves; making no difference of what generation, descent, or color they are. And those who steal or rob men, and those who buy or purchase them, are they not all alike? Here is liberty of conscience, which is right and reasonable; here ought to be likewise liberty of the body, except of evil-doers, which is another case. But to bring men hither, or to rob and sell them against their will, we stand against. In Europe there are many oppressed for conscience-sake; and here there are those oppressed which are of a black color. And we who know that men must not commit adultery—some do commit adultery *in* others, separating wives from their husbands, and giving them to others: and some sell the children of these poor creatures to other men. Ah! do consider well this thing, you who do it, if you would be done at this manner—and if it is done according to Christianity!

> *Resolution of the Germantown Mennonites against slavery, February 18, 1688, in Commager,* Documents of American History, *p. 37.*

The examination of Sarah Good before the worshipful Assistants John Harthorn Jonathan Curran

(H.)   Sarah Good what evil Spirit have you familiarity with.

(S.G.)   None.

(H)   Have you made no contract with the devil.

Good answered no.

(H)   Why do you hurt these children.

(g)   I do not hurt them. I scorn it.

(H)   Who do you employ then to do it.

(g)   I employ no body.

(H)   What creature do you employ then.

(g)   No creature but I am falsely accused.

(H)   Why did you go away muttering from Mr. Parris his house.

(g)   I did not mutter but I thanked him for what he gave my child.

(H)   Have you made no contract with the devil.

(g)   No.

(H)   Desired the children all of them to look upon her and see if this were the person that had hurt them and so they all did look upon her, and said this was one of the persons that did torment them—presently they were all tormented.

A woman accused of being a witch is pictured here before a court. *(Library of Congress, Prints and Photographs Division LC-USZ62-475)*

(H)   Sarah Good do you not see now what you have done, why do you not tell us the truth, why do you thus torment these poor children.

(g)   I do not torment them.

(H)   Who do you employ then.

(G)   I employ nobody I scorn it.

(H)   How came they thus tormented.

(g)   What do I know you bring others here and now you charge me with it.

(H)   Why who was it.

(g)   I do not know but it was some you brought into the meeting house with you.

(H)   We brought you into the meeting house.

(g)   But you brought in two more.

(H)   Who was it then that tormented the children.

(g)   It was osburn.

(H)   What is it that you say when you go muttering away from persons' houses.

(g)   If I must tell I will tell.

(H)   Do tell us then.

(g)   If I must tell, I will tell, it is the commandments. I may say my commandments I hope.

(H)   What commandment is it.

(g)   If I must tell I will tell, it is a psalm.

(H)   What psalm.

(g)   After a long time she muttered over some part of a psalm.

(H)   Who do you serve.

(g)   I serve God.

(H)   What God do you serve.

(g)   The God that made heaven and earth. Though she was not willing to mention the word God. her answers were in a very wicked spiteful manner. reflecting and retorting against the authority with base and abusive words and many lies she was taken in. it was here said that her husband had said that he was afraid that she either was a witch or would be one very quickly. the worthy Mr. Harthon asked him his reason why he said so of her, whether he had ever seen any thing by her, he answered no, not in this nature, but it was her bad carriage to him, and indeed said he I may say with tears that she is an enemy to all good.

Salem Village March the 1st 1691/2
Written by Ezekiell Chevers

The examination of Sarah Good for witchcraft before Salem judges, March 1, 1692, in Records of Salem Witchcraft, *vol. 1, pp. 17–21.*

I found the Devil had taken upon him the name and shape of several persons who were doubtless innocent and to my certain knowledge of good reputation for which cause I have now forbidden the committing [to jail] of any more that shall be accused without unavoidable necessity, and those that have been committed I would shelter from any Proceedings against them wherein there may be the least suspicion of any wrong to be done unto the Innocent.

William Phips, governor of Massachusetts, 1692, to British authorities concerning the Salem witchcraft trials, in Hoffer, The Salem Witchcraft Trials, *p. 132.*

Seeing our Lord Jesus Christ hath tasted Death for every Man, and given himself a Ransom for all, to be testified in due time, and that his Gospel of Peace, Liberty and Redemption from Sin, Bondage and all Oppression, is freely to be preached unto all, without Exception, and that *Negroes, Blacks,* and *Tawnies* are a real part of Mankind, for whom Christ hath shed his precious Blood, and are capable of Salvation, as well as *White Men;* and Christ the Light of the World hath (in measure) enlightened them, and every Man that cometh into the World; and that all such who are sincere *Christians* and true Believers in Christ Jesus, and Followers of him, bear his Image, and are made conformable unto him in Love, Mercy, Goodness and Compassion, who came not to destroy men's Lives, but to save them, nor to bring any part of Mankind into outward Bondage, Slavery or Misery, nor yet to detain them, or hold them therein, but to ease and deliver the Oppressed and Distressed, and bring into Liberty both inward and outward.

Therefore we judge it necessary that all faithful Friends should discover themselves to be true Christians by having the Fruits of the Spirit of Christ, which are *Love, Mercy, Goodness, and Compassion* towards all in Misery, and that suffer Oppression and severe Usage, so far as in them is possible to ease and relieve them, and set them free of their hard Bondage, whereby it may be hoped, that many of them will be gained by their beholding these good Works of sincere *Christians,* and prepared thereby, through the Preaching the Gospel of Christ, to embrace the true Faith of Christ. And for this cause it is, as we judge, that in some places in *Europe* Negroes cannot be bought and sold for Money, or detained to be Slaves, because it suits not with the Mercy, Love & Clem-ency that is essential to *Christianity,* nor to the Doctrine of Christ, nor to the Liberty the Gospel calls all men unto, to whom it is preached. And to buy Souls and Bodies of men for Money, to enslave them and their Posterity to the end of the World, we judge is a great hindrance to the spreading of the Gospel, and is occasion of much War, Violence, Cruelty and Oppression, and Theft & Robbery of the highest Nature; for commonly the Negroes that are sold to white Men, are either stolen away or robbed from their kindred, and to buy such is the way to continue these evil Practices of Man-stealing, and transgresseth that Golden Rule and Law, *To do to others what we would have others do to us.*

Therefore, in true Christian Love, we earnestly recommend it to all our Friends and Brethren, Not to buy any Negroes, unless it were on purpose to set them free, and that such who have bought any, and have them at present, after some reasonable time of moderate Service they have had of them, or may have of them, that may reasonably answer to the Charge of what they have laid out, especially in keeping Negroes Children born in their House, or taken into their House, when under Age, that after a reasonable time of service to answer that Charge, they may set them at Liberty, and during the time they have them, to teach them to read, and give them a Christian Education.

Quaker George Keith, 1693, An Exhortation & Caution to Friends Concerning Buying or Keeping of Negroes, *available online at http://www.qhpress. org/quakerpages/qwhp/gk-as1693.htm. Accessed January 10, 2006.*

Whosoever travels over this Wilderness, will see it richly bespangled with Evangelical Churches, whose Pastors are holy, able, and painful Overseers of their Flocks, lively Preachers, and virtuous Livers. . . . We are still so happy, that I suppose there is no Land in the Universe more free from the debauching, and the debasing Vices of Ungodliness. The Body of the People are hitherto so disposed, that *Swearing, Sabbath-breaking, Whoring, Drunkenness,* and the like, do not make a Gentleman, but a Monster, or a Goblin, in the vulgar Estimation. All this notwithstanding, we must humbly confess to our God, that we are miserably degenerated from the first Love of our Predecessors. . . . The first Planters of these Colonies were a chosen Generation of Men, who were first so pure, as to disrelish many things which they thought wanted Reformation elsewhere; and yet withal so peaceable, that they embraced a voluntary Exile in a squalid, horrid, *Ameri-*

can Desert, rather than to live in Contentions with their Brethren. . . . [T]hose Interests of the Gospel, which were the Errand of our Fathers into these Ends of the Earth, have been too much neglected and postponed, and the Attainments of an handsome Education, have been too much undervalued, by Multitudes that have not fallen into Exorbitances of Wickedness; and some, especially of our young Ones, when they have got abroad from under the Restraints here laid upon them, have become extravagantly and abominably Vicious. . . . A Variety of Calamity has long follow'd this Plantation; and we have all the Reason imaginable to ascribe it unto the Rebuke of Heaven upon us for our manifold *Apostasies.*

. . . . .

The *New-Englanders* are a People of God settled in those, which were once the *Devil's* Territories; and it may easily be supposed that the *Devil* was exceedingly disturbed. . . . Wherefore the Devil is now making one Attempt more upon us; an Attempt more Difficult, more Surprising, more snarl'd with unintelligible Circumstances than any that we have hitherto Encountered. . . . An Army of *Devils* is horribly broke in upon the place [i.e., Salem] which is the *Center,* and after a sort, the *First-born* of our *English* Settlements: and the Houses of the Good People there are fill'd with the doleful Shrieks of their Children and Servants, Tormented by Invisible Hands, with Tortures altogether preternatural. . . . '[T]is Agreed, *That* the Devil has made a dreadful Knot of *Witches* in the Country, and by the help of *Witches* has dreadfully increased that Knot: *That* these *Witches* have driven a Trade of Commissioning their *Confederate Spirits,* to do all sorts of Mischiefs to the Neighbors, whereupon there have ensued such Mischievous consequences upon the Bodies and Estates of the Neighborhood, as could not otherwise be accounted for: yea, *That* at prodigious *Witch-Meetings,* the Wretches have proceeded so far, as to Concert and Consult the Methods of Rooting out the Christian Religion from this Country, and setting up instead of it, perhaps a more gross *Diabolism,* than ever the World saw before.

Puritan minister Cotton Mather, concluding that witches were active in Salem, 1693, The Wonders of the Invisible World, *pp. 10–16.*

CHAPTER FOUR

Awakenings
(1700–1740)

By the beginning of the 18th century, religion in the American colonies might be separated into three predominant strands. In New England a Congregational establishment occupied the center stage of colonial life, though this establishment had been forced to accept the presence of a variety of other religious groups. In the southern colonies the Church of England had been established, and this Anglican establishment was vigorous enough to discourage any significant competition from other religious groups until the middle of the 18th century. In the middle colonies a robust religious pluralism inherited from the previous century allowed Baptists, Quakers, Presbyterians, and various denominations from continental Europe to live side by side in relative peace. Even Catholics and Jews, though generally denied a variety of civil rights, could at least engage in private worship according to the dictates of their consciences.

The 18th century witnessed a dramatic increase in religious pluralism in the American colonies, as the kind of diversity common in the middle colonies gradually infiltrated New England and the southern colonies. Older established faiths reluctantly learned to tolerate the presence of religious dissenters while grappling to maintain their own social prerogatives. Dissent arrived on American shores partially as a result of immigrations—those of Scots-Irish Presbyterians, for example, and of French Huguenots after the Edict of Nantes was revoked at the end of the previous century. But an internal force of division and diversity also presented itself during this century, and the force was revival. During the 1730s the American colonies began to experience a profound and widespread spiritual awakening, so profound and so widespread, in fact, that history names the episode the Great Awakening. It was a period in which a religion of the heart came to supercede notions of faith centered primarily in the intellectual assent to particular doctrines or in adherence to patterns of religious or moral conduct. The surge of religious piety ignited by the Great Awakening was above all personal, even though it might be experienced in a congregation of thousands of others assembled, say, in a field listening to a revival preacher. For those touched by the hand of this awakening, the faith of parents or community or church became secondary to the faith experienced by the individual, stripped, as it were, of social connections and naked before the presence of God.

The Great Awakening thus introduced a renewed element of voluntarism into American religion, the idea that faith is something that one chooses rather than inherits. Religious voluntarism may be contrasted with religious understandings that emphasize the inheritedness of religious belief and practice on the basis of either geographic location or familial ties. Within the Anglican Church, for example, one belonged to the Church of England essentially by virtue of being an inhabitant of England. Individual religious identity derived from national religious identity. Similarly, among other religious traditions the religious faith and practice of an individual descended primarily from parents. But religious voluntarism emphasizes the degree to which the individual chooses—or is divinely chosen—to experience faith. Among New England Puritans, at least, this focus on religious voluntarism was not entirely novel. Although the Puritans emphasized the interconnectedness of families and communities in matters of faith, they also recognized a personal dimension to religious belief and practice. Thus, for the first half century of Puritan presence in New England, church membership, for example, was still rooted in evidence given by applicants for membership that they, individually, had experienced religious conversion. Developments such as the Half-Way Covenant and Stoddardism had a tendency to blur the importance of this individualized faith but did not wholly eradicate it from Puritan consciousness. The Great Awakening, however, reintroduced the necessity of individual conversion and suggested that what was necessary was also possible—that individual souls, aware of their sinfulness and of God's merciful provision for salvation, could turn toward God and experience conversion.

Like many cultural movements, though, the birth of the Great Awakening is not easy to identify with precision. This awakening's most significant event occurred when the Anglican revivalist George Whitefield conducted a preaching tour along the eastern seaboard of the American colonies in 1740. Whitefield's preaching, though the primary catalyst of the Great Awakening, had itself been preceded by earlier murmurs of religious revival stretching back to the previous century when Solomon Stoddard's liberalization of the requirements for partaking of the Lord's Supper had sparked a series of revivals in his church at Northampton, in western Massachusetts. In the period immediately preceding Whitefield's influential preaching tour, other ministers had begun to emphasize the need for a personal religious experience, an emphasis that would become one of the Great Awakening's central tenets. This revival emphasis crossed denominational boundaries with ease. Whitefield himself was a minister in the Church of England with close ties to the Methodist movement led by John and Charles Wesley. Once Whitefield arrived in America, he discovered that the spiritual ground he planted had already been tilled by preachers such as the Dutch Reformed minister Theodorus Frelinghuysen and the Presbyterian minister Gilbert Tennent. Perhaps most importantly, the awakening leaned on the intellectual support of one of America's most brilliant theologians, the Congregationalist minister Jonathan Edwards.

The Blossoming of Religious Diversity

Prior to the last decade of the 17th century, the overwhelming majority of immigrants to the North American colonies were either Congregationalists who settled mainly in the North or Anglicans who settled in the South. From 1690 until the Revolutionary War, however, new waves of immigrants arrived on the American shore, and they brought with them a rich variety of religious faiths. The strength of Congregationalist dominance in New England and Anglican establishments in the southern colonies tended to make the middle colonies more attractive to these later arrivals, but virtually every colony witnessed the growth in the kind of religious diversity that England had experienced since the middle of the 17th century. For example, after the Edict of Nantes was revoked in 1685, French Protestants, mainly Calvinistic believers referred to as Huguenots, were stripped of the toleration they had enjoyed in Catholic France since the original enactment of the edict in 1598. As a consequence, many French Huguenots made their way to New York, one of the more religiously diverse colonies since the days of its original Dutch founders. Some French Calvinists settled in Boston and South Carolina as well. German-speaking immigrants introduced their own varieties of religious experience as groups including Lutherans, German Reformed, Mennonites, Moravians, and German Baptists settled in the North American colonies. Jews, mostly of the Sephardic tradition—though some Ashkenazic Jews also made their way to the New World—continued to arrive in North America in limited numbers. By 1730, for example, the congregation Shearith Israel in New York City was able to move out of the rented quarters it had occupied for years into a synagogue built on Mill Street. Even before the beginning of the 18th century, Quakers had immigrated to the colonies in significant numbers, settling especially in Pennsylvania, New York, New Jersey, and Rhode Island.

During this period Baptists also arrived from England and Wales, soon eclipsing in numbers the older congregations of Baptists that had been established during the middle years of the 17th century. These older congregations themselves had already suffered significant divisions, particularly when a group of Rhode Island Baptists who were followers of John Rogers broke apart from existing Baptist churches in the 1670s to form new Rogerene congregations, characterized by Sabbatarian worship and religious convictions against the use of medicine. After the Great Awakening the numbers of Baptists swelled even more as those converted during this period left established Congregational and Anglican churches and frequently found their way into new Baptist congregations. These Baptists, driven to separate from their existing congregations, are often referred to as Separate Baptists, and they were not always on friendly terms with the Baptist congregations that predated the Great Awakening. Nevertheless, American Baptists enjoyed sufficient numbers and possessed enough cooperative regard to establish the first association of Baptist churches in 1707.

The early decades of the 18th century also saw significant growth among Presbyterian congregations in America. Presbyterianism is a hierarchical form of church government within the Reformed tradition of Protestant Christianity. Inherited primarily from Scotland, this form of church polity emphasizes shared authority between clergy and lay leaders at several levels of church government: the individual congregation, the presbytery, the synod, and the general assembly. Early in the 18th century North America received a wave of Scots-Irish immigrants (sometimes referred to colloquially as Scotch-Irish). These new arrivals were the legacy of James I's policy of settling Scottish Protestants in Ireland. After later British developments made the situation of the Scots-Irish settlers less comfortable, many of them left Ireland for America. The most prominent minister among these Scots-Irish immigrants was Francis Makemie, often referred to as the father of American Presbyterianism. He migrated to America from Ireland in 1683 and for the next two decades practiced an itinerant preaching ministry in Maryland, Virginia, North Carolina, and Barbados. By the beginning of the 1700s, Makemie had settled in Virginia, where the established Anglican church and the energetic activities of the newly established Society for the Propagation of the Gospel in Foreign Parts made his preaching career difficult. Seeking solidarity in numbers, Makemie encouraged a number of other Presbyterian ministers from Maryland, Virginia, Delaware, and Pennsylvania to form the first American presbytery in 1706.

The Growth of Religious Toleration

At the end of the 18th century, the American people ratified an amendment to the U.S. Constitution that protected the free exercise of religion and prohibited laws "respecting" an establishment of religion by the federal government. This provision was not applicable to state governments, but the political developments that gave birth to the First Amendment's religion clauses would ultimately secure religious liberty in the states and topple those few state establishments of religion that survived the First Amendment's ratification. At the beginning of the 18th century, these developments were still distant, though a trend toward greater toleration of religious diversity was clearly at work. Partially this trend sprang from the passage in 1689 in England of the Act of Toleration and the publication in the same year of John Locke's *A Letter Concerning Toleration*. Both events, while occurring in England, had profound impacts on subsequent developments in the colonies. In the early years after the Act of Toleration became effective, it was not immediately clear whether its terms applied automatically to the American colonies or only insofar as royal instructions to colonial governors included the protections of the act in those instructions. Thus, for example, the Presbyterian minister Francis Makemie famously clashed with New York governor Edward Cornbury over this issue in 1707. Makemie was arrested for preaching without a license in New York but appealed to the terms of the Act of Toleration in his defense. Although Governor Cornbury refused to acknowledge the applicability of the act to New York, a jury ultimately acquitted Makemie of the criminal charges against him. A Connecticut law of 1702 attempted to prohibit citizens from demonstrating hospitality toward Quakers and certain other religious minorities. British authorities explained, however, that this form of legislation violated the rights accorded to religious dissenters under English law, rights applicable to residents of Connecticut as well. In general, the protections granted to religious minorities in England under the Act of Toleration came to be enforced in the American colonies as well during the course of the 18th century. And the arguments that John Locke made in support of religious toleration informed further debates on this subject in North America.

The advantages secured to religious minorities by the Act of Toleration were, of course, quite limited. In the first place, the Act of Toleration did not eliminate colonial religious establishments. The presence of these continued establishments offended the consciences of religious minorities because these minorities generally had to contribute tax support to faiths they did not share. In the New England colonies, especially Massachusetts and Connecticut, Congregationalism remained the established religion, even if Quakers, Baptists, and other religious minorities at least won the right to worship in public according to the dictates of their consciences. In the southern colonies the Church of England was established by law, although the strength of this establishment was considerably less than that enjoyed

British philosopher John Locke's theories had a significant influence in the American religious community. *(Library of Congress, Prints and Photographs Division LC-USZ62-59655)*

by Congregationalism in New England. In the second place, the Act of Toleration did not secure religious liberty for either Jews or Catholics equal to that possessed by Protestant Christians.

The 1701 Charter of Privileges of Pennsylvania, established by the colony's Quaker proprietor, William Penn, expressed the outer limits of toleration for Jews in colonial America: it secured their freedom from being "molested or prejudiced" because of their beliefs and prevented their being compelled to attend or support the religious worship of others. Only Christians, though, were permitted to hold colonial offices in Pennsylvania. The Delaware charter of the same year contained similar provisions. Although Jews in America labored under these sorts of civic disabilities, several new Jewish communities were established in the 18th century. After the British Crown chartered its final royal colony, Georgia, Jewish settlers arrived there in the summer of 1733 and promptly established a community in Savannah. Two years later they opened a synagogue. In 1740, however, the threat of a Spanish invasion that might be launched from St. Augustine, Florida, led most of the Savannah Jews to relocate. But while Savannah's Jewish community dissolved after a few brief years, similar communities sprang up during the 1740s in Charleston and Philadelphia. The following decade Newport, Rhode Island, became the home of an important colonial Jewish community.

Catholics fared in some ways worse than Jews, since they were widely thought to practice an allegiance to the pope that was superior to their allegiances to the various civil governments where they lived. John Locke implicitly denied them religious liberty on this account in his *Letter Concerning Toleration*. Moreover, virtually all Protestants of the day believed that the Catholic Church was the anti-Christ referred to in the New Testament and, influenced by English experience with Catholic rulers, tended to equate Catholicism with tyranny. Consequently, colonial governments practiced a variety of discriminations against Catholics. Most significantly, perhaps, these governments administered loyalty oaths incompatible with Catholic reverence for papal authority and visited punishments on those who declined to make the oaths. As a corollary, in most colonial jurisdictions Catholics were thought to lie outside the boundaries of the religious toleration increasingly afforded the variety of Protestant faiths in the 18th century. The Massachusetts Charter of 1691 made clear the distinctions concerning Catholics in a climate otherwise respectful of religious differences. It guaranteed "liberty of Conscience" in the "Worship of God" to all Christians, "Except Papists."[1]

Catholic fortunes in Maryland were a barometer of the times. The colony had originally been established by the Catholic Lord Baltimore and partially designed as a colonial haven for fellow Catholics. By the beginning of the 18th century, however, Lord Baltimore's vision of a Catholic Maryland had been supplanted by a new political reality. The colony had lost its proprietary status in 1692, and the British Crown transformed it into a royal colony under the control of a very Protestant Parliament. Maryland's laws promptly began to reflect this Protestant reorientation. By 1702 the colony had established Anglicanism as its official church. Two years later the first of a stream of anti-Catholic legislation appeared. The 1704 Act to Prevent the Growth of Popery banned Catholic worship and proselytizing by Catholic priests, including the baptism of converts to Catholicism. Although Maryland soon amended the act to permit private Catholic worship, it also strengthened Protestant political power in the colony in 1718 by denying Catholics the right to vote. In all, the experience of Catholics in Maryland mirrored the difficulties they faced in most parts of colonial America during the early decades of the 18th century.

Preface to Awakening

There were murmurs of revival in the decades before the arrival of George Whitefield ignited the Great Awakening. Solomon Stoddard, famous for his belief that participation in the ordinance of the Lord's Supper might inspire conversions among the participants, had himself witnessed five periods of revival at his church in Northampton. In 1726 Stoddard's grandson, Jonathan Edwards, became junior minister at the Northampton church and senior minister after his grandfather died three years later. In the following decade Edwards himself presided over a period of religious awakening in his church. After Whitefield's preaching sparked a more widespread and sustained revival, Edwards became an important defender and theologian of the Great Awakening. But Edwards, certainly the most renowned of the American ministers whose preaching contributed to the Great Awakening, was joined by others. These included the Dutch Reformed minister Theodorus Jacobus Frelinghuysen and an influential Presbyterian father and son, William and Gilbert Tennent.

Frelinghuysen migrated from Germany to America in 1719, where he assumed pastoral oversight of several Dutch Reformed congregations in New Jersey's Raritan Valley. Here he warred against religious formalism and complacency, insisting that true Christian faith was more than a matter of mere doctrinal orthodoxy or moral living; it required a personal piety born of religious conversion. Lively faith, as Frelinghuysen understood it, expressed itself through lively worship. He opposed the use of the Lord's Prayer in Christian worship as overly formalistic, and his extemporaneous public prayers were animated enough to be characterized as "howling prayers" by more traditional ministers.[2] Criticism about his form of public devotion, however, was minor compared to the opposition he generated from insisting that church membership and participation in the ordinance of the Lord's Supper were not to be had simply on the basis of orthodox beliefs and a generally upright life. Frelinghuysen required proof of a religious conversion from those who wished to become church members and, more controversially, from those existing church members who wished to participate in the Lord's Supper. He barred several prominent church members from the Lord's Supper because of their lack of satisfactory responses to his pointed interrogations concerning their spiritual conditions. Public reaction to these pastoral practices included enough criticism that Frelinghuysen composed a rebuttal which he displayed on the back of his sleigh:

> No one's tongue, or no one's pen,
> Makes me other than I am.
> Speak, sland'rous speakers, speak on end.
> With words you no one here can rend.[3]

Criticism, though, was not the only fruit of Frelinghuysen's ministry. By the last half of the 1720s, his preaching had sparked revival not only in the churches under his care but in others nearby, so much so that George Whitefield called him the "beginner of the great work . . . in these parts."[4]

At roughly the same time a Presbyterian minister named William Tennent was also developing styles of preaching and education that would preface developments during the Great Awakening. His preaching attempted to speak not only to the minds of his hearers but to their hearts as well. This would be a central feature of George Whitefield's own preaching and of the other ministers who labored with him across the American colonies to awake slumbering souls. But William Tennent is even more famous for having turned his attention to the education of ministers sympathetic to revival. In 1735 he purchased land in the Warminster Township of Pennsylvania, where he established in Neshaminy an academy in a log house, promptly dubbed by his critics the Log College. Here he championed evangelical learning hospitable to revival for future ministers, including his sons, and his academy became a model for other Presbyterian institutions in the future, including the College of New Jersey (now Princeton University), established a little more than a decade after Tennent opened his Log College to students. Most of Tennent's students went on to become Presbyterian revival preachers during the Great Awakening.

The most famous of William Tennent's sons, Gilbert, benefited from his father's educational methods and subsequently engaged in a preaching ministry that first anticipated and then supported the Great Awakening. After graduating with an M.A. from Yale in 1725, the younger Tennent was licensed to preach by the Philadelphia presbytery and soon was ordained as the pastor of a church in New Brunswick, New Jersey. There he became friends with Frelinghuysen, the minister of a nearby Dutch Reformed congregation, whose congregation was already experiencing revival. Encouraged by Frelinghuysen, Gilbert Tennent preached the necessity of personal holiness and piety and the necessity of conversion as the source of both. In fact, when George Whitefield began his preaching tour through the American colonies in 1739, Gilbert Tennent accompanied him. The next year Tennent published one of the Great Awakening's important tracts, *The Danger of an Unconverted Ministry.* Here again he emphasized the necessity of personal conversion, even among ministers. The willingness of Tennent to question the spiritual credentials of more established ministers became one of the characteristic themes of preaching during the Great Awakening and one of the sources of divisions that would spring up in churches and denominations in the wake of revival.

The preaching ministries of Frelinghuysen and the Tennents are well known to students of the Great Awakening. Their support of revival was joined by another minister who became one of the most important figures in American religious and intellectual history, Jonathan Edwards. In 1726 Edwards was called to assume the position of junior minister in the church where his grandfather, Solomon Stoddard, served as senior minister. After Stoddard died in 1729 and Edwards became senior minister, he developed a revivalist style of preaching and witnessed revival again in the Northampton church in 1734 and 1735. Edwards's preaching was distant in many ways from the kind of revival preaching that would become prominent in the 19th and 20th centuries. Instead of delivering his sermons extemporaneously, he read them in his early days as a preacher, and the sermons themselves were closely reasoned discourses characteristic of a mind that was as academic as it was practical. But Edwards's sermons, which painted vivid pictures of both the judgment of God on sin and his loving mercy toward sinners, pricked his listeners and prompted many of them to experience religious conversions. In 1737 he published an account of the Northampton revival called *A Faithful Narrative of the Surprising Work of God in the Conversion of Many Hundred Souls in Northampton, and the Surrounding Towns and Villages.* A young Anglican minister named George Whitefield who visited America for the first time in 1738 read this work and was profoundly moved by it. After Whitefield returned to America the following year and began a preaching tour that ignited revival all up and down the Atlantic seaboard, Edwards became an important ally of the revival spirit. He used his copious intellectual gifts to defend the role of "affections," or emotions, in religious experience and thus helped to authenticate what was to become an enduring aspect of American religious experience.

The Great Awakening

George Whitefield himself experienced a religious conversion in 1735 while a student at Oxford and was ordained an Anglican minister the following year. At Oxford he also became friends with John and Charles Wesley and was a member of the Holy Club that became the seed of the subsequent Methodist movement. At the urging of the Wesleys, Whitefield visited Georgia in 1738, where he conceived the plan of establishing an orphanage. When he returned to England to raise money for this project, he began the practice of preaching outdoors, a practice that allowed him to reach larger audiences than he would have otherwise had and that created opportunities for preaching that did not require invitations from ministers willing to open their churches to him. He returned to America in November 1739 and the following year began the preaching tour that ignited the Great Awakening. Like Edwards, Frelinghuysen, and the Tennents, he stressed the necessity of personal conversion, urging his hearers to abandon their refuge in doctrinal correctness and moral propriety in favor of heartfelt piety. He sought to infuse faith with feeling, and in this he was extraordinarily successful. It was said that he could bring an audience to tears merely by enunciating the word *Mesopotamia*. Preaching to audiences of thousands at a time, he pricked the consciences of those who heard him and fanned a revival that subsequently swept across the American colonies.

If Whitefield and the other new revivalists differed from their predecessors in any regard, it was in their general sense that those who experienced regeneration would be aware of this fact. They quoted Romans 8:16 from the New Testament where the apostle Paul indicates that God's Spirit testifies to the spirits of those who have experienced conversion that they belong to him. Thus, for Whitefield and other revival preachers, conversion came to be understood as a spiritual awakening that could be typically identified as a moment in time when the soul received God's gracious offer of salvation. John Wesley, the founder of Methodism, who would spend nearly two years in Georgia as an Anglican missionary, described his own conversion in this vein in his journal:

> In the evening I went very unwillingly to a society in Aldersgate Street, where one was reading Luther's preface to St. Paul's Epistle to the Romans. At about a quarter to nine, while he was describing the change which God works in the heart through faith in Christ, I felt my heart strangely warmed. I felt I did trust in Christ, Christ alone for salvation; and an assurance was given to me that He had taken away my sins, even mine.[5]

The idea that one might be immediately aware of salvation was at odds with the more traditional view that the best evidence of salvation was a holy life. Critics of the Great Awakening not infrequently suggested that revivalism tended to duplicate the twin errors of enthusiasm and antinomianism. By *enthusiasm*, these critics meant an improper confidence in individual intuition in spiritual matters that weakened reverence for the revealed word of God—the Bible—and for the ministers who had been trained to interpret the Bible properly. The focus on inner assurance of salvation seemed to critics to inspire antinomianism, since this focus tended to sidestep the sustained pattern of moral living that earlier generations had seen as the surest evidence that a particular individual had been converted.

The preaching that ignited the Great Awakening in the American colonies generally sprang from the Reformed tradition, which emphasized the utter sinfulness of men and women and their absolute need for God's gracious salvation. Later in the century Methodism arrived on American soil and presented a more optimistic account of human ability to participate in the drama of salvation. In fact, George Whitefield, the dean of preachers during the awakening, disagreed sharply with John Wesley over the relative prominence to be accorded God's sovereign grace. Whitefield, a Calvinistic Anglican, was theologically distant from the Arminian Wesley. And the primary voice heard in the American colonies during the Great Awakening was that of Whitefield rather than Wesley. A characteristic of Reformed theology and, through men such as Whitefield and Edwards, the theology that fueled the Great Awakening was an emphasis on the sinfulness of human nature. A recognition of one's own sinful condition was often thought of as a prerequisite for salvation, and preachers such as Gilbert Tennent made an emphasis on sinful humanity and the nearness of God's judgment on this sinfulness a prominent part of their sermons. In the ministerial language of the day, this rhetorical emphasis on sin and the nearness of divine judgment was referred to as "preaching of the terrors."[6] And no preacher offered a more vivid and enduring description of sin and judgment than Jonathan Edwards. He delivered perhaps the most well-known sermon in American history on July 8, 1741, in Enfield, Connecticut, titled "Sinners in the Hands of an Angry God." For Edwards the judgment of hell against sin loomed behind every human moment, near as tomorrow, inevitable, inexorable. "[T]hus it is that natural men are held in the hand of God, over the pit of hell; they have deserved the fiery pit, and are already sentenced to it; and God is dreadfully provoked, his anger is as great towards them as to those that are actually suffering the executions of the fierceness of his wrath in hell, and they have done nothing in the least to appease or abate that anger."[7] Though contemporary readers might imagine this judgment arbitrary and capricious, Edwards insisted that it was the appropriate fate for a race that had forgotten God.

> The God that holds you over the Pit of Hell, much as one holds a Spider, or some loathsome Insect, over the Fire, abhors you, and is dreadfully provoked; his Wrath towards you burns like Fire; he is of purer Eyes than to bear to have you in his Sight, you are ten thousand Times so abominable in his Eyes as the most hateful venomous Serpent is in ours. You have offended him infinitely more than ever a stubborn Rebel did his Prince: and yet 'tis nothing but his Hand that holds you from falling into the Fire every Moment.[8]

The judgment Edwards pronounced, though, was not simply an abstract one, applicable to unknown sinners out of the range of his voice. It was, rather, a judgment directed to many of those in the very audience to whom he thundered. "There is reason to think," he warned his listeners, "that there are many in this Congregation now hearing this discourse, that will actually be subjects of . . . Misery to all Eternity."[9] Nevertheless, the sinners Edwards sought to awaken from their spiritual slumber were not without hope. "[Y]ou have an extraordinary Opportunity," he assured them, "a Day wherein CHRIST has flung the Door of Mercy wide open, and stands in the Door calling and crying with a loud Voice to poor Sinners, a Day wherein many are flocking to him, and pressing into the Kingdom of God. . . ."[10] The words of Jonathan Edwards dissolved many in the congregation that heard him to tears. One observer noted that there was "such a breathing of distress and weeping" among the listeners that Edwards had to stop his sermon and ask for silence.[11]

The Great Awakening was quickened by the eloquence of preachers such as Whitefield and Edwards, but it reached far past the limits of their particular voices. An entire American generation witnessed a religious revival, even if many did not experience it or even agree upon its worth. The revival split churches and denominations, creating new congregations even as it sundered older ones. So pervasive was its impact that it became not simply an awakening itself, but a model for future awakenings, a memory of experiences—longed for by some and abhorred by others—that would pass on into the future and become the pattern for a climate of revivalism that has never disappeared from the American religious scene. The heirs of the Great Awakening would themselves become household names in the history of American religion—Charles Finney, Dwight L. Moody, Aimee Semple McPherson, Billy Sunday, and Billy Graham. These and other voices would see that the legacy of the Great Awakening passed on across the generations into the 21st century.

Chronicle of Events

1700

- New York enacts legislation banishing Catholic priests and missionaries of various Catholic orders from the colony.
- After Quakers in England disavow George Keith, he is ordained an Anglican priest.
- Boston merchant Robert Calef publishes his book *More Wonders of the Invisible World*, which criticizes New England ministers who supported the Salem witch trials.
- Puritan judge Samuel Sewell publishes *The Selling of Joseph*, the first colonial antislavery tract.

1701

- Thomas Bray establishes the Society for the Propagation of the Gospel in Foreign Parts for the purpose of strengthening the influence of Anglicanism in the American colonies.
- William Penn establishes a new constitution for the Pennsylvania colony called the Charter of Privileges, according to which Christians of any denomination are eligible to hold government office and in which monotheists willing "to live quietly under the Civil Government" are never to be "molested or prejudiced" for their religious beliefs or practices, nor are they to be "compelled to frequent or maintain any Religious Worship place or Ministry contrary to his or their mind."
- The Delaware Charter of 1701 grants a measure of religious liberty to all monotheists but restricts office-holding to Christians.
- Increase Mather, a symbol of Congregational orthodoxy, is forced from his position as president of Harvard.
- The Collegiate School (present-day Yale University) is established at Saybrook, Connecticut, for the purpose of seeing to "the liberal and religious education of suitable youth . . . under the blessing of God." In 1716 the institution will be relocated to New Haven. The institution is founded, in part, out of concerns about more liberal theological tendencies thought to be at work at Harvard.
- North Carolina makes the Anglican Church the colony's officially established religion.

1702

- Cotton Mather publishes a history of New England Puritanism titled *Magnalia Christi Americana*.

- The Massachusetts general court declares that the Salem witchcraft trials were unlawful.
- Maryland passes legislation making the Church of England the established church in the colony.
- South Carolina passes legislation making the Church of England the established church in the colony and requiring legislators to swear an oath of loyalty to this church, thus precluding religious dissenters from serving in the colonial legislature. Parliament will subsequently disallow the test oath, but the colonial legislature will reaffirm the Church of England as the colony's established church in 1706.
- The British Crown merges East and West Jersey into a single colony and excludes Catholics from the protections of religious liberty in the colony.
- George Keith, previously a leader of American Quakers, after being ordained an Anglican priest in 1700, returns to America as an agent for the Society for the Propagation of the Gospel in Foreign Parts.
- Connecticut attempts to prohibit its citizens from entertaining Quakers or other "heretics" but is forced by British authorities to repeal this legislation because it is inconsistent with the rights guaranteed to dissenters under English law.

1703

- *October 5:* Jonathan Edwards, Congregationalist minister and theologian, is born in East Windsor, Connecticut.

1704

- At approximately this time (although some scholars place the date closer to 1695) the Jewish community in New York begins to worship publicly in a rented house on Mill Street (today South William Street). This congregation will become known as Shearith Israel (meaning Holy Congregation Remnant of Israel).
- Maryland passes the Act to Prevent the Growth of Popery, which bans Catholic worship, prohibits proselytizing by priests, and forbids priests to baptize any but the children of Catholic parents. An exception is soon added that allows Catholics to worship in private homes.
- Anglicans establish a congregation in Newport, Rhode Island.
- South Carolina makes the Anglican Church its officially established religion.

1706

- In Philadelphia Francis Makemie and six other Presbyterian ministers form the first American presbytery, and Makemie is chosen its first moderator.

- *August 25:* Ann Putnam is received into communion in the Salem Village Church and confesses to having been deluded by Satan in connection with her role as an accuser in the Salem witchcraft trials.

1707

- Francis Makemie and John Hampton are arrested for preaching in New York without a license under orders of New York governor Edward Cornbury. When Makemie attempts to assert the protections of England's 1689 Toleration Act, Cornbury informs him that the terms of the act do not apply to New York. Nevertheless, a jury acquits Makemie.
- The Philadelphia Association of Baptists is formed, the first cooperative association of Baptist churches in America.
- In England Isaac Watts publishes *Hymns and Spiritual Songs,* and hymns such as he composed begin to be used in America in Protestant family worship at first and then still later in church services. Prior to this only Psalms were sung in worship services.

1708

- Connecticut Congregationalists adopt the Saybrook Platform, which establishes a hierarchical form of church government similar to Presbyterianism.

1710

- In Germany Gottfried Wilhelm Leibniz publishes *Theodicy,* which argues that God is just because he has created the best of all possible worlds.

1711

- Massachusetts passes legislation exonerating the victims of the Salem witchcraft prosecutions and granting restitution to their heirs.

1714

- *December 16:* Revivalist George Whitefield is born in Gloucester, England.

1715

- North Carolina makes the Church of England the established church of the colony.

1716

- The Philadelphia Synod, the first Presbyterian synod in America, is formed.

1718

- Catholics are disenfranchised in Maryland.
- William Tennent immigrates to America from Ireland and is admitted as a minister in the Philadelphia Presbyterian synod.
- *April 20:* David Brainerd, a Presbyterian missionary to Native Americans, is born in Haddam, Connecticut.

1719

- Dutch Reformed minister Theodorus Jacobus Frelinghuysen immigrates from East Friesland to central New Jersey's Raritan Valley, where he accepts a call to serve as minister to several Dutch Reformed congregations. He begins a preaching career emphasizing the need for individual conversion and personal holiness and piety.

1720

- Samuel Johnson is ordained a Congregational minister, although he will subsequently convert to Anglicanism and serve as the president of King's College (present-day Columbia University) in New York.
- Johann Conrad Beissel, later founder and leader of the Ephrata commune of Seventh Day Baptists, immigrates from Germany to Pennsylvania.

1723

- Samuel Johnson, previously ordained a Congregational minister, converts to Anglicanism, is ordained a priest in England, and returns to America as an Anglican missionary under the auspices of the Society for the Propagation of the Gospel in Foreign Parts. In Stratford he organizes the first Anglican congregation in Connecticut.
- At the Yale commencement for this year, the college rector, the Reverend Timothy Culter, concludes the ceremonies with a prayer that borrows from the Anglican Book of Common Prayer. The event becomes known among Congregationalists as the great "apostasy." Cutler subsequently becomes an Anglican minister in Boston and an influential opponent of the Great Awakening.

  Solomon Stoddard, the Congregationalist minister of the church in Northampton, Massachusetts, publishes a tract titled *Question Whether God is not Angry with the Country for Doing so Little Towards the Conversion of the Indians.*

1724

- *January 9:* Isaac Backus, later an influential Baptist minister and advocate of religious liberty, is born in Norwich, Connecticut.

1725

- John Philip Boehm, though not ordained, begins to minister as pastor of several German Reformed congregations in Pennsylvania. He will subsequently be ordained in 1729 by two Reformed ministers in New York.

1726

- Jonathan Edwards is called to serve as junior minister in the Northampton church in Massachusetts, where his grandfather, Solomon Stoddard, is senior minister. Edwards will be ordained February 15, 1727.

1727

- Charles Chauncy, known as the Great Opposer of the Great Awakening, becomes assistant pastor of Boston's First Church, where he will minister for 60 years.

1728

- Johann Conrad Beissel publishes *Mysterium Anomias,* "The Mystery of Lawlessness," which defends his belief that Saturday is the appropriate day for Christian worship.

1729

- The Irish clergyman and philosopher George Berkeley arrives in America and takes up residence near Newport, Rhode Island, for three years.
- The Philadelphia synod of the Presbyterian Church adopts the Westminster Confession, with limited exceptions, as its official statement of faith and requires that ministerial candidates signify their assent to the key elements of the confession as a condition of ordination.
- In England John Wesley, a fellow of Lincoln College at Oxford University, joins his brother Charles, an undergraduate at Oxford, in meetings they call the Holy Club. These meetings will form the basis for the birth of Methodism.
- Upon the death of his grandfather, Solomon Stoddard, Jonathan Edwards becomes the senior minister at the church in Northampton, Massachusetts.

1730

- The first Jewish synagogue in America is built by the congregation Shearith Israel in New York City on Mill Street.

1731

- The first Masonic lodge in the American colonies is established in Philadelphia.

John Wesley, pictured here, was the founder of Methodism. *(Library of Congress, Prints and Photographs Division LC-USZ62-5824)*

1732

- Johann Conrad Beissel establishes the Ephrata commune of Seventh Day Baptists along Cocalico Creek in Pennsylvania.
- The colony of Georgia is chartered, with a provision for religious liberty to all but Catholics, insofar as they are "contented with the quiet and peaceable enjoyment of the same, not giving offence or scandal to the government."

1733

- *July 11:* 42 Jewish settlers arrive in Georgia from England and establish a community in Savannah.

1734

- A spiritual awakening begins in Jonathan Edwards's church in Northampton, Massachusetts, and eventually spreads across the Connecticut Valley. Edwards's account of this awakening, published in 1737 as *A Faithful Narrative of the Surprising Work of God,* will focus international attention on the subject of revival.

1735

- The Presbyterian William Tennent establishes a school in his home for training ministers, referred to by detractors as the Log College, which will become a model for subsequent educational institutions, including the College of New Jersey (later Princeton University), founded in 1746.
- Seneca prophet and founder of the Longhouse religion Handsome Lake is born around this date.
- Jewish residents of Savannah open the K.-K. Mikveh Israel Synagogue.

1736

- *January 8:* John Carroll, first Catholic bishop in the United States, is born in Upper Marlboro, Maryland.
- *February 5:* John and Charles Wesley arrive in Georgia as missionaries on behalf of the Church of England's Society for the Propagation of the Gospel in Foreign Parts. Charles leaves to return to England in July. John will remain in Georgia 20 months, until December 1737.
- *February 29:* Ann Lee, founder of the Shakers, is born in Manchester, England.

1737

- Jonathan Edwards earns international fame as a revivalist after publishing *A Faithful Narrative of the Surprising Work of God,* which describes the experience of revival in his church.

1738

- Revivalist George Whitefield visits the American colonies for the first time. He returns to England to raise funds for an orphanage he will later establish in Georgia.

1739

- *October:* George Whitefield returns to America and conducts an initial preaching tour.

1740

- George Whitefield embarks on a second preaching tour of the colonies, which is a defining event in the Great Awakening. The same year he establishes an orphanage named Bethesda near Savannah, Georgia.
- Gilbert Tennent publishes *The Danger of an Unconverted Ministry,* a tract supportive of the Great Awakening and critical of ministers who have not experienced a personal conversion themselves.
- Most of the Jewish residents of Savannah, Georgia, fearful of a possible invasion of Georgia by Spanish forces in St. Augustine, Florida, leave Savannah and relocate elsewhere.

Eyewitness Testimony

The numerousness of slaves at this day in the province, and the uneasiness of them in their slavery has put many upon thinking whether the foundation of it be firmly and well laid, so as to sustain the vast weight that is built upon it. It is most certain that all men, as they are the sons of Adam, are coheirs and have equal right unto liberty, and all other outward comforts of life. "God hath given the Earth [with all its commodities] unto the Sons of Adam" (Psalm 115:16), "And hath made of one blood all nations of men, for to dwell on all the face of the earth, and hath determined the times before appointed, and the bounds of their habitation: that they should seek the Lord. Forasmuch then as we are the offspring of God," etc. (Acts 17:26, 27, 29). Now, although the title given by the last Adam does infinitely better men's estates, respecting God and themselves, and grants them a most beneficial and inviolable lease under the broad seal of heaven, who were before only tenants at will. Yet through the indulgence of God to our first parents after the fall, the outward estate of all and every of their children remains the same as to one another. So that originally and naturally, there is no such thing as slavery. Joseph was rightfully no more a slave to his brethren than they were to him; and they had no more authority to sell him than they had to slay him. And if they had nothing to do to sell him, the Ishmaelites, bargaining with them and paying down twenty pieces of silver, could not make a title. Neither could Potiphar have any interest in him than the Ishmaelites had. (Gen. 37: 20, 27, 28) For he that shall in this case plead alteration of property seems to have forfeited a great part of his own claim to humanity. There is no proportion between twenty pieces of silver and liberty. The commodity itself is the claimer. If Arabian Gold be imported in any quantities, most are afraid to meddle with it, though they might have it at easy rates; unless it should have been wrongfully taken from the owners, it should kindle a fire to the consumption of their whole estate. It is a pity there should be more caution used in buying a horse or a little lifeless dust than there is in purchasing men and women: Whereas they are the offspring of God, and their liberty is *Auro pretiosior omni* [more precious than gold].

And seeing God has said, "He that stealeth a man and selleth him, or if he be found in his hand, he shall surely be put to death." (Exod. 12:16) This law being of everlasting equity, wherein man-stealing is ranked among the most atrocious of capital crimes: What louder cry can there be made of the celebrated warning, *Caveat emptor!* [Let the buyer beware.]

Massachusetts judge Samuel Sewall, 1700, "The Selling of Joseph," in Blaustein and Zangrando, Civil Rights and African Americans, *pp. 13–14.*

PROPOSALS for the Propagation of the Christian Religion in the several Provinces, on the Continent of *North-America.*

WHEREAS it has pleased God of late to stir up the hearts of many People in the American Plantations, who seemed formerly to have forgot Religion, now to be very solicitous, and earnest for Instruction, so as of themselves to call for those Helps, which in Duty they ought to have been prevented in, by us, from the beginning: And whereas, to our shame, we must own, that no Nation has been so guilty of this neglect as ours: The Papists, of all Countries, having been most careful to support their Superstitions where-ever they have planted: The Dutch with great care allowing an Honorable Maintenance, with all other Encouragements, for Ministers in their Factories and Plantations: The Swedes, the Danes, and other small Colonies, being seldom, or never deficient in this Particular; and we of the English Nation only being wanting in this Point: And lastly, Whereas though it be true that some of our most considerable Plantations have set out Parishes, and Allowances for Ministers, yet it is not so in all; and where some Provision is made, it is as yet far short of being sufficient to maintain a Minister: And there is a total Neglect of informing the poor Natives. Out of all these Considerations, we do not think a more charitable Work can be carried on, than as much as in us lies, to contribute towards the Redress of these great Failures.

Thomas Bray, 1700, from A Memorial Representing the Present State of Religion, on the Continent of North-America, *in* Rev. Thomas Bray: His Life and Selected Works Relating to Maryland, *pp. 172–173.*

Whereas divers Jesuits priests and popish missionaries have of late, come and for Some time have had their residence in the remote parts of this Province and other his majesty's adjacent Colonies, who by their wicked and Subtle Insinuations Industriously Labor to Debauch Seduce and withdraw the Indians from their due obedience unto his most Sacred majesty and to Excite and Stir them up to Sedition Rebellion and open Hostility against his majesty's Government for prevention whereof Be it Enacted by his Excellency the Governor Council and Representatives Convened in General Assembly and it is hereby

Enacted by the Authority of the Same, That all and every Jesuit and Seminary Priest missionary or other Spiritual or Ecclesiastical person made or ordained by any Authority power or Jurisdiction derived Challenged or pretended from the Pope or See of Rome now residing within this province or any part thereof shall depart from and out of the Same at or before the first day of November next in this present year Seventeen hundred.

New York law, enacted August 9, 1700, in Gaustad, A Documentary History of Religion in America to the Civil War, p. 148.

I desire to be humbled before God for that sad and humbling providence that befell my father's family in the year about '92; that I, then being in my childhood, should, by such a providence of God, be made an instrument for the accusing of several persons of a grievous crime, whereby their lives were taken away from them, whom now I have just grounds and good reason to believe they were innocent persons; and that it was a great delusion of Satan that deceived me in that sad time, whereby I justly fear I have been instrumental, with others, though ignorantly and unwittingly, to bring upon myself and this land the guilt of innocent blood; though what was said or done by me against any person I can truly and uprightly say, before God and man, I did it not out of any anger, malice, or ill-will to any person, for I had no such thing against one of them; but what I did was ignorantly, being deluded by Satan. And particularly, as I was a chief instrument of accusing of Goodwife Nurse and her two sisters, I desire to lie in the dust, and to be humbled for it, in that I was a cause, with others, of so sad a calamity to them and their families; for which cause I desire to lie in the dust, and earnestly beg forgiveness of God, and from all those unto whom I have given just cause of sorrow and offence, whose relations were taken away or accused.

Ann Putnam, one of the original accusers in the Salem witchcraft trials, confessing to her church her role in the affair, August 25, 1706, in Upham, Salem Witchcraft, vol. 2, p. 510.

Lord Cornbury. How dare you take upon you to Preach in my Government, without my Licence?

Mr. Makemie. We have Liberty from an Act of Parliament, made the First Year of the Reign of King William and Queen Mary [the Toleration Act of 1689], which gave us Liberty, with which Law we have complied.

Ld. C. None shall Preach in my Government without my License.

F. M. If the Law for Liberty, my Lord, had directed us to any particular persons in Authority for License, we would readily have observed the same; but we cannot find any directions in said Act of Parliament, therefore could not take notice thereof.

Ld. C. That Law does not extend to the American Plantations, but only to England.

F. M. My Lord, I humbly conceive, it is not a limited nor Local Act, and am well assured, it extends to other Plantations of the Queen's Dominions, which is evident from Certificates from Courts of Record of Virginia, and Maryland, certifying we have complied with said Law.

Both Certificates were produced and read by Lord Cornbury, who was pleased to say, these Certificates extended not to New-York.

Ld. C. I know it is local and limited, for I was at making thereof.

F. M. Your Excellency might be at making thereof, but we are well assured, there is no such limiting clause therein, as is in Local Acts, and desire the Law may be produced to determine this point.

Ld. C. Turning to Mr. Attorney, Mr. Bekely, who was present, asked him, Is it not so, Mr. Attorney?

Mr. Attorney. Yes, it is Local, my Lord, and producing an Argument for it, further said, that all the Penal Laws were Local, and limited, and did not extend to the Plantations, and the Act of Toleration being made to take off the edge of the Penal Laws; therefore the Act of toleration does not extend to any Plantations.

F. M. I desire the Law may be produced; for I am morally persuaded there is no limitation or restriction in the Law to England, Wales, and Berwick on Tweed; for it extends to sundry Plantations of the Queen's Dominions, as Barbados, Virginia, and Maryland; which was evident from the Certificates produced, which we could not have obtained, if the Act of Parliament had not extended to the Plantations.

And Mr. Makemie further said, that he presumed New-York was a part of Her Majesty's Dominions also; and that sundry Ministers on the East-end of Long-Island, had complied with said Law, and qualified themselves at Court, by complying with the directions of said Law, and have no License from your Lordship.

Ld. C. Yes, New-York is of Her Majesty's Dominions; but the Act of Toleration does not extend to the Plantations by its own intrinsic virtue, or any intention of the Legislators, but only by her Majesty's Royal Instructions signified unto me, and that is from Her Prerogative and

Clemency. And the Courts which have qualified those men, are in error, and I shall check them for it.

F. M. If the Law extends to the Plantations any manner of way, whether by the Queen's Prerogative, Clemency, or otherwise, our Certificates were a demonstration we have complied therewith.

. . . . .

Ld. C. That act of Parliament was made against Strolling Preachers, and you are such, and shall not Preach in my Government.

F. M. There is not one word, my Lord, mentioned in any part of the Law, against Traveling or Strolling Preachers, as Your Excellency is pleased to call them; and we are to judge that to be the true end of the Law, which is specified in the Preamble thereof, which is for the satisfaction of Scrupulous Consciences, and Uniting the Subjects of England, in interest and affection. And it is well known, my Lord, to all, that Quakers, who also have Liberty by this Law, have few or no fixed Teachers, but chiefly taught by such as Travel; and it is known to all such are sent forth by the Yearly Meeting at London, and Travel and Teach over the Plantations, and are not molested.

Ld. C. I have troubled some of them, and will trouble them more.

Interrogation of the Presbyterian minister Francis Makemie after his arrest for preaching without a license by New York governor Edward Cornbury, 1707, in Gaustad, A Documentary History of Religion in America to the Civil War, *pp. 150–151.*

[February 8, 1709]. I rose at 5 o'clock this morning and read a chapter in Hebrew and 200 verses in Homer's *Odyssey.* I ate milk for breakfast. I said my prayers. Jenny and Eugene were whipped. I danced my dance. I read law in the morning and Italian in the afternoon. I ate tough chicken for dinner. The boat came with the pork from Appomattox and was cut. In the evening I walked about the plantation. I said my prayers. I had good thoughts, good health, and good humor this day, thanks be to God Almighty.

. . . . .

[February 22, 1709]. I rose at 7 o'clock and read a chapter in Hebrew and 200 verses in Homer's *Odyssey.* I said my prayers and ate milk for breakfast. I threatened Anaka with a whipping if she did not confess the intrigues between Daniel and Nurse, but she prevented by a confession. I chided Nurse severely about it, but she denied, with an impudent face, protesting that Daniel only lay on the bed for the sake of the child. I ate nothing but beef for dinner. . . . I had good thoughts, good health, thanks be to God Almighty.

. . . .

[June 10, 1709]. I rose at 5 o'clock this morning but could not read anything because of Captain Keeling, but I played at billiards with him and won half a crown of him and the Doctor. George B-th brought home my boy Eugene. . . . In the evening I took a walk about the plantation. Eugene was whipped for running away and had the [*bit* or *boot*] put on him. I said my prayers and had good health, good thought, and good humor, thanks be to God Almighty.

. . . .

[December 1, 1709]. I rose at 4 o'clock and read two chapters in Hebrew and some Greek in Cassius. I said my prayers and ate milk for breakfast. I danced my dance. Eugene was whipped again for pissing in bed and Jenny for concealing it.

. . . .

[February 27, 1711]. I rose at 6 o'clock and read two chapters in Hebrew and some Greek in Lucian. I said my prayers and ate boiled milk for breakfast. I danced my dance and then went to the brick house to see my people pile the planks and found them all idle for which I threatened them soundly but did not whip them. . . . In the afternoon Mr. Dunn and I played at billiards. Then we took a long walk about the plantation and looked over all my business. In the evening my wife and little Jenny had a great quarrel in which my wife got the worst but at last by the help of the family Jenny was overcome and soundly whipped. At night I ate some bread and cheese. I said my prayers and had good health, good thoughts, and good humor, thank God Almighty.

Virginia plantation owner William Byrd, describing everyday events in his life, 1709–11, in The Secret Diary of William Byrd of Westover, 1709–1712, *pp. 1–2, 46, 113, 307.*

In these twenty-one years, after having been missionary of California. . . . I have baptized here in these new conquests and new conversions about four thousand five hundred souls, and could have baptized twelve or fifteen thousand if we had not suspended further baptisms until our Lord should bring us missionary fathers to aid us in instructing and ministering to so many new subjects of your Majesty and parishioners of our Holy Mother Church.

Catholic missionary and explorer Eusebio Kino, 1711, in Kino's Historical Memoir of Pimería Alta, vol. 1, pp. 88–89.

The Five Nations are a poor and, generally called, barbarous People, bred under the darkest Ignorance; and yet a bright and noble Genius shines through these black Clouds. None of the greatest Roman Heroes have discovered a greater Love to their Country, or a greater Contempt of Death, than these People called Barbarians have done, when Liberty came in Competition. Indeed, I think our Indians have outdone the Romans in this Particular; some of the greatest of those have we know murdered themselves to avoid Shame or Torments; but our Indians have refused to die meanly, or with but a little Pain, when they thought their Country's Honour would be at Stake by it; but have given their Bodies, willingly, to the most cruel Torments of their Enemies, to shew, as they said, that the Five Nations consisted of Men, whose Courage and Resolution could not be shaken. They greatly sully, however, those noble Virtues, by that cruel Passion, Revenge; this they think it not only lawful, but honorable, to exert without Mercy on their Country's Enemies, and for this only it is that they can deserve the Name of Barbarians.

But what, alas! Sir, have we Christians done to make them better? We have indeed Reason to be ashamed, that these Infidels, by our Conversation and Neighbourhood, are become worse than they were before they knew us. Instead of Virtues we have only taught them Vices, that they were intirely free from before that Time. The narrow Views of private Interest have occasioned this, and will occasion greater, even publick Mischiefs, if the Governors of the People do not, like true Patriots, exert themselves, and put a Stop to these growing Evils. If these Practices be winked at, instead of faithful Friends, that have manfully fought our Battles for us, the Five Nations will become faithless Thieves and Robbers, and join with every Enemy that can give them any Hopes of Plunder.

Cadwallader Colden, 1727, The History of the Five Indian Nations of Canada which are Dependent on the Province of New York, and Are a Barrier Between the English and the French in that Part of the World, vol. 1, pp. x–xii.

As to Religion in general & the state of our respective Churches, it is certain that in many places thro' the prevailing of the Gospel there is a great reformation in life & manners, & vice and immorality, rampant heretofore, do now begin to disappear, the Lord's Day free from former profanations is now observed with commendable strictness, and Swearing, Drinking, and Debauchery are put under proper restraints, more from the awe of Religion than the Laws of Government, and that these things are owing to the settlement of the Church in these parts, is not only with joy acknowledged by her friends but is plainly allowed by her Enemies both in principles and morals in their grief, envy and united opposition to it. But this brings us to the cause of it.

. . . . .

As for Rhode Island, that fertile soil of Heresy & Schism, tho' in the main the Church doth triumph over those prostrate Enemies, yet still they endeavor to recover fresh strength & again finding encouragement from the commander in chief, an Anabaptist, & his Deputy, a Quaker, who, howfarsoever they disagree in principle, yet strenuously endeavor to promote what they have peculiarly espoused & if in nothing else concur in this to treat the Church with united indignities.

. . . . .

And it moreover appearing to us by the frame of our Constitution impossible in the nature of the thing to observe our Rubrick or obey our Canons without a Bishop to whom we may have immediate recourse & whose frequent visitations of us is by them supposed, we pray to be heard, when we beg that without which our ministerial functions cannot be regularly discharged, namely, the presence of a Bishop amongst us, for tho' no person can be more if so vigilant over us at the vast distance we have the unhappiness to be from him, than our Right Reverend & extremely beloved Diocesan, yet it being without the power & bounds of any mortal to make us capable of discharging our duties according to our Offices, our Orders & our Oaths, whilst he is so inaccessible to us, we would humbly represent the absolute necessity of being blessed with the favor we so earnestly pray for.

Letter from Timothy Cutler, Samuel Johnson, and other Anglican ministers of New England to the Society for the Propagation of the Gospel, July 20, 1727, in Gaustad, A Documentary History of Religion in America to the Civil War, pp. 158–159.

My very dear father,

Our Reverend Father carefully sees to it that we are provided with food. We are better off than we would ever have believed, but this is neither the intention nor the wish of our enterprise. Our principal aim is to attract souls to the Lord and He accords us graces so that we can perform this duty. Our Reverend Father aids us well in this. He says Mass for us daily and gives public conferences. If we had the misfortune of losing him, either by illness or otherwise, we would be much saddened and greatly to be pitied.

. . . . .

[O]ur Reverend Father is of such an admirable zeal it seems that he has taken it upon himself to convert everyone here and is determined to accomplish his goal. But I assure you, my dear Father, that he will have a lot of work to do before he succeeds because not only do debauchery, lack of faith and all other vices reign here more than elsewhere, but they reign with an unmeasurable abundance!

. . . . .

Our little Community increases each day. We have twenty boarders, eight of whom make their first Communion today, three ladies who are also boarders and three orphan girls whom we took in out of charity. We also have seven slave boarders to instruct for Baptism and first Communion, a large number of day students and Negresses and Indian girls who come two hours each day for instruction.

Letter of Marie Madelein Hachard (Sister St. Stanislaus), an Ursuline novitiate in New Orleans, to her father, April 24, 1728, in Mulford, Early American Writings, *pp. 457–460.*

One day, perceiving an uncommon drought and a disagreeable clamminess in my mouth and using things to ally my thirst, but in vain, it was suggested to me, that when Jesus Christ cried out, "I thirst," His sufferings were near at an end. Upon which I cast myself down on the Bed, crying out, "I thirst! I thirst!" Soon after this, I found and felt in myself that I was delivered from the burden that had so heavily oppressed me. The spirit of mourning was taken from me, and I knew what it was truly to rejoice in God my Saviour: and, for some time, could not avoid singing psalms wherever I was; but my joy gradually became more settled, and, blessed be God, has abode and increased in my soul, saving a few casual intermissions, ever since.

Thus were the days of my mourning ended. After a long night of desertion and temptation, the Star, which I had seen at a distance before, began to appear again, and the Day Star arose in my heart. Now did the Spirit of God take possession of my soul, and, as I humbly hope, seal me unto the day of redemption.

George Whitefield, 1735, in George Whitfield's Journals, *pp. 48–49.*

I was surprised with the relation of a young woman, who had been one of the greatest company-keepers in the whole town. When she came to me, I had never heard that she was become in any wise serious, but by the conversation I then had with her, it appeared to me, that what she gave an account of, was a glorious work of God's infinite power and sovereign grace; and that God had given her a new heart, truly broken and sanctified.

. . . . .

Though the work was glorious, yet I was filled with concern about the effect it might have upon others. I was ready to conclude, (though too rashly) that some would be hardened by it, in carelessness and looseness of life; and would take occasion from it to open their mouths in reproaches of religion. But the event was the reverse, to a wonderful degree. God made it, I suppose, the greatest occasion of awakening to others, of any thing that ever came to pass in the town. I have had abundant opportunity to know the effect it had, by my private conversation with many. The news of it seemed to be almost like a flash of lightning, upon the hearts of young people, all over the town, and upon many others. Those persons amongst us, who used to be farthest from seriousness, and that I most feared would make an ill improvement of it, seemed greatly to be awakened with it. Many went to talk with her, concerning what she had met with; and what appeared in her seemed to be to the satisfaction of all that did so.

Presently upon this, a great and earnest concern about the great things of religion, and the eternal world, became universal in all parts of the town, and among persons of all degrees, and all ages. The noise amongst the dry bones waxed louder and louder; all other talk but about spiritual and eternal things, was soon thrown by; all the conversation, in all companies and upon all occasions, was upon these things only, unless so much as was necessary for people carrying on their ordinary secular business. Other discourse than of the things of religion, would scarcely be tolerated in any company. The minds of people were wonderfully taken off from the world, it was treated amongst us as a thing of very little consequence. They seemed to follow their worldly business, more as a part of their duty, than from any disposition they had to it; the temptation now seemed to lie on that hand, to neglect worldly affairs too much, and to spend too much time in the immediate exercise of religion.

. . . . .

But although people did not ordinarily neglect their worldly business; yet Religion was with all sorts the great concern, and the world was a thing only by the bye. The only thing in their view was to get the kingdom of heaven, and every one appeared pressing into it. . . . All would eagerly lay hold of opportunities for their souls; and were wont very often to meet together in private houses, for religious purposes: and such meetings when appointed were greatly thronged.

There was scarcely a single person in the town, old or young, left unconcerned about the great things of the eternal world. Those who were wont to be the vainest, and loosest; and those who bad been most disposed to think, and speak slightly of vital and experimental religion, were now generally subject to great awakenings. And the work of conversion was carried on in a most astonishing manner, and increased more and more; souls did as it were come by flocks to Jesus Christ. From day to day, for many months together, might be seen evident instances of sinners brought out of darkness into marvelous light, and delivered out of an horrible pit, and from the miry clay, and set upon a rock with a new song of praise to God in their mouths.

Jonathan Edwards, 1735, "A Faithful Narrative of the Surprising Work of God," in The Works of Jonathan Edwards, *vol. 1, p. 348.*

[A]s I was walking in a dark thick grove, "unspeakable glory" [I Pet. 1:8] seemed to open to the view and apprehension of my soul. By the glory I saw I don't mean any external brightness, for I saw no such thing, nor do I intend any imagination of a body of light or splendor somewhere away in the third heaven, or anything of that nature. But it was a new inward apprehension or view that I had of God; such as I never had before, nor anything which had the least remembrance of it. . . . My soul was so captivated and delighted with the excellency, the loveliness and the greatness and other perfections of God that I was even swallowed up in him.

. . . . .

Thus the Lord, I trust, brought me to a hearty desire to exalt him, to set him on the throne and to "seek first his Kingdom," i.e. principally and ultimately to aim at his honor and glory as King and sovereign of the universe.

. . . . .

If I could have been saved by my own duties or any other way that I had formerly contrived, my whole soul would have refused. I wondered all the world did not see and comply with this way of salvation entirely by the "righteousness of Christ" [I Cor. 1:30].

David Brainerd, recounting his conversion on July 12, 1739, in The Life of David Brainerd, *pp. 138–140.*

In this journey, traveling in Talbot County, an elderly man asked us if we saw some posts to which he pointed, and added, the first meeting George Fox had on this side of the Chesapeake bay, was held in a tobacco house there, which was then new, and those posts were part of it. John Browning rode to them, and sat on his horse very quiet; and returning to us again with more speed than he went, I asked him what he saw amongst those old posts; and he answer, "I would not have missed what I saw for five pounds, for I saw the root and ground of idolatry. Before I went, I thought perhaps I might have felt some secret virtue in the place where George Fox had stood and preached, whom I believe to have been a good man; but whilst I stood there, I was secretly informed, that if George was a good man, he was in heaven, and not there, and virtue is not to be communicated by dead things, whether posts, earth, or curious pictures, but by the power of God, who is the fountain of living virtue." A lesson, which if rightly learned would wean from the worship of images and adoration of relicks.

John Churchman, a Maryland Quaker, 1740, in Trueblood, The People Called Quakers, *p. 214.*

George Fox was the founder of the Quakers. *(Library of Congress, Prints and Photographs Division LC-USZ62-5790)*

Rode last night after sermon about eight miles. Lay at a friend's house, and preached this morning to near three or four thousand people at Abingdon, a district under the care of Mr. Treat, a Dissenting minister, to whom God has been pleased lately to shew mercy. He has been a preacher of the doctrines of grace for some years; but was deeply convinced, when I was here last, that he had not experienced them in his heart. Soon after I went away, he attempted to preach, but could not; he therefore told his congregation, how miserably he had deceived both himself and them, and desired those who were gifted, to pray for him. Ever since, he has continued to seek Jesus Christ sorrowing and is now under deep convictions, and a very humbling sense of sin. He preaches as usual, though he has not a full assurance of faith; because he said it was best to be found in the way of duty. I believe God is preparing him for great services, and I hope he will also be a means of awakening some dead, false-hearted preachers among the Dissenters, who hold the form of sound words, but have never felt the power of them in their own souls. When I had done, I took a little refreshment, baptized a child, and hastened to Philadelphia, where I preached to upwards of ten thousand people, upon the woman who was cured of her bloody issue. Hundreds were graciously melted; and, many, I hope, not only thronged round, but also touched the Lord Jesus Christ by faith. About ten came to me after sermon, under deep convictions, and told me the time when, and manner how, the Lord Jesus made Himself manifest to their souls. What gives me greater hope that this work is of God, is, because these convictions have remained on many since I was here last. Blessed be God, there is a most glorious work begun in this province. The Word of God every day mightily prevails, and Satan loses ground apace. Lord Jesus, stretch out Thy arm, and let not this work be stopped till we see that new Heaven and new Earth wherein dwelleth righteousness.

George Whitefield, April 17, 1740, in George Whitfield's Journals, *pp. 405–406.*

The Session, viz. The minister & Elders of ye Presbyterian congregation of New-Londonderry, being sensible yt the coming of godly men into ye ministry, such as are experimentally acquainted wt the renewing & sanctifying grace of God in their own souls, has ye most hopeful aspect upon ye interests of Christ's Kingdom & true vital godliness amonst us; and that upon ye other hand, the receiving men of a contrary character into that sacred office is ye great Bane of ye Church of Christ, and ye

great reason of ye sad Decay of true lively experimental Religion, and being apprized that there are several very promising & hopeful youths under ye care & instruction of the Rev Mr. Tennent at Neshaminey, in order to their being educated & trained up for ye service of ye church in ye gospel-ministry, some of whom have not a sufficiency of their own to support them in ye course of their preparatory studies, We think the yielding them our Assistance by contributing to their support for their carrying on & obtaining their pious, and so very needful as well as useful Design, one of the best ways in wt our charity can be bestowed; and therefore, being ready to contribute our own mite, we heartily recommend it to all such of our christian Brethren to whom these may come, to join us in ye same, promising, yt upon their giving what they allow this way, to any of us, it shall be appl'd to the aforesd purpose. And in so doing we hope ye Blessing of many souls ready to perish will come upon the givers, and ye interest of our Glorious Redeemer be promoted in ye world.

"The Session of the Fagg's Manor Congregation Recommends a Contribution for the 'Log College,'" December 8, 1740, in Pears, Documentary History of William Tennent and The Log College, *p. 125.*

The whole Church in this Town and the adjacent parts, with all the Church both at home and abroad, hath felt the ill effects of Mr. Whitefield's visits. Our sufferings here are very particular, being but an handful to the dissenters, who of all orders and degrees were highly fond of his coming, and gave him a most hearty and distinguishing welcome, and strived to excell one another in it, and to be cold or differently effected is with them a pretty strong mark of reprobation. The clergy of this Town never invited him into their Pulpits, nor did he ask them, nor ever attended anyone of our Churches, saving one Friday at Prayers, upon his first entrance, to make himself known to us, tho' he tarried over three Sundays in Town, daily preaching in our Meeting Houses, and in open places, and was an hearer among the Dissenters on one part of two Sundays. Bishops, Divines, Churchmen and Christians are with us, good or bad, as he describes them, and nothing but a conformity to his notions and rules will give us a shining character. The Idea he gives us of the present Church (and too many receive it) is Heterodoxy, Falsehood to our articles and rules, Persecution, and never more so. The principals, and books and practices of this Country are applauded and preferred to everything now in the Church, and People are exhorted to adhere to their Dissenting Pastors.

Too many unhappy Feuds and Debates are owing to Mr. Whitefield's being among us; and we have even disobliged the Dissenters in suffering them to engross him, but I hope the Fury and Ferment is subsiding, and that we shall at length be tolerably sweetened towards one another. What may hinder it are the enthusiastic Notions very much kindled among us and like to be propagated by his Writings, dispersed every where, with Antinomianism revived, and I fear also, Infidel and Libertine Principles, which some express a particular fondness for at this time. Our labours among our people would be very much assisted by suitable Books on these subjects, and the Society's bounty in this kind never wants good effects, tho' not so large as good men wish.

Anglican rector Timothy Cutler, December 11, 1740, letter to the Secretary of the Society for the Propogation of the Gospel, concerning the unhappy spiritual effects of George Whitefield's preaching, in Gaustad, A Documentary History of Religion in America to the Civil War, *pp. 199–200.*

CHAPTER FIVE

Revolutionary Religion
(1741–1780)

British journalist G. K. Chesterton once famously referred to America as a "nation with the soul of a church."[1] It was, perhaps, inevitable that the birth of such a nation would intersect both the political and the religious lives of the American people. Religious impulses had animated many of the migrations that colonized North America, and the revolutionary generation still felt the effects of the Great Awakening, which had reinvigorated a sense that America held a special place in God's plans. Even though the awakening itself had generally subsided by the conclusion of the 1740s, its effects were enduring. In particular, the sense that God had ordained an exemplary role for America, widely shared during the 18th century, contributed to a growing national consciousness. But even for those who did not share these theological views, the Great Awakening helped to incubate a national consciousness simply by virtue of its being the first prominent intercolonial cultural event. The shared experience of the awakening was not always characterized by harmony, however. The awakening fueled the splintering impulse long latent within Protestantism. The colonial revival touched Congregational and Presbyterian churches most significantly, and in both denominations it drove wedges between those who supported the revival and those who opposed it. Congregationalists fractured between New Lights and Old Lights; Presbyterians divided themselves into the New Side and the Old Side. Yet these divisions were themselves part of a larger, *American* experience. A new national consciousness increasingly nourished a spirit of independence as residents of the various colonies began to see themselves not simply as inhabitants of a particular colony but as constituent members of a larger American people.

The Great Awakening was the American expression of an international spiritual renewal that occurred during the 18th century. This renewal would see the birth of Methodism in England beginning in 1729 with the formation of the Holy Club at Oxford by John and Charles Wesley. The Wesleys briefly visited Georgia the following decade as Anglican missionaries under the auspices of the Society for the Propagation of the Gospel, in Foreign Parts, but the first Methodist congregations in America were not established until 1766. Another prominent strand of Protestant renewal during the 18th century expressed itself in the form of German Pietism, a reform movement within German Lutheranism that emphasized the importance of personal holiness rather than mere assent to Lutheran doctrine or participation in the sacraments. The most important expression of German Pietism was the Church of the Brethren, or renewed Moravian Church, established in 1727 under the patronage of Count Nicolaus Ludwig von Zinzendorf on his estate in Saxony. Like Methodism, the Moravian Church also made its way to America after Zinzendorf was exiled from Saxony and visited Pennsylvania for 18 months beginning in 1741. There he made an unsuccessful attempt to consolidate various German Protestant groups into a single ecclesiastical structure but left an enduring mark on evangelical piety in America by helping to establish a Moravian community in Bethlehem, Pennsylvania.

In all, the Great Awakening launched a surge of evangelical piety whose current flows into present-day America. Evangelicalism is not confined to any particular denomination. It constitutes a breed of Christian experience located primarily though not exclusively within the Protestant tradition that emphasizes a personal religious conversion experience, heart-felt devotion to Christ, and personal holiness. It tends to scoff at excessive formalism in religious worship and practice and to insist that mere intellectual assent to particular tenets of Christian doctrine is not a sufficient basis upon which to erect a spiritual life. Beginning toward the end of the 18th century, the Second Great Awakening reinvigorated evangelical piety. In the next two centuries evangelical revival, through the careers of ministers such as Charles Finney, Dwight L. Moody, and Aimee Semple McPherson, became a permanent fixture of American religious experience.

Awakening's Divisions

Viewed from one perspective, the Great Awakening introduced an ecumenical impulse to American religion. Revival preachers such as George Whitefield frequently downplayed the doctrinal differences among various Protestant denominations in favor of a focus on religious conversion. Thus, the Anglican Whitefield might find himself closely aligned with the Methodists John and Charles Wesley in England, accompanied on an American preaching tour by the Presbyterian Gilbert Tennent, and defended by the Congregationalist theologian Jonathan Edwards. A religion of the heart had the effect of blunting lines of divisions generated by religions of the head, which magnified the significance of doctrinal distinctions. But this very demarcation between heart and head inspired its own new divisions, since not all observers of the changes in the colonial religious climate occasioned by the Great Awakening were pleased with these changes. Some established ministers bristled at the suggestion made by revival preachers such as Gilbert Tennent that they were unconverted and a hindrance to the work of God's grace. According to Tennent, unconverted ministers were "like a man who would learn others to swim before he has learned it himself, and so is drowned in the act and dies like a fool."[2] This was a judgment not calculated to inspire ecumenical fraternity. Other established preachers, such as Boston's Charles Chauncy, minister at the city's historic First Church and nicknamed the Great Opposer of the Great Awakening, believed the focus by revival preachers on appeals to the "affections," or emotions, of their listeners was dangerous to real spiritual health. He published an influential tract in 1743 titled *Seasonable Thoughts on the State of Religion in New England.* In the early 1740s Chauncy could claim as allies leaders at Harvard and Yale, who published their own critiques of Whitefield and revivalism. Consequently, the Great Awakening inspired new divisions among Protestants that generated new churches and denominations. It became an engine of religious pluralism.

Prior to the Great Awakening religious pluralism in America had been fueled predominately by the immigration of those who brought with them different religious traditions and practices to the New World. The Atlantic was a wide corridor through which Congregationalists and Anglicans, Presbyterians and Baptists, Dutch Reformed and Quakers, Catholics and Lutherans and Jews all made their way to the new continent. Old World pluralism, transplanted to America, became New World pluralism. But America, thus populated by religious faith, rapidly became a laboratory for its own indigenous religious fractures, and the Great Awakening was the most important source of these fractures during the 18th century.

No less a luminary than Jonathan Edwards himself experienced the kinds of division that the Great Awakening sowed. Scarcely a decade after the height of the Great Awakening, Edwards found himself at odds with his congregation at Northampton. His grandfather, Solomon Stoddard, had famously liberalized the requirements for membership and for participation in the Lord's Supper at the church by abolishing sharp distinctions between those who had experienced conversion and those who had not. But Edwards attempted to overturn his grandfather's practices and restore conversion as the sine qua non of both church membership and participation in the ordinance of the Lord's Supper. These changes reflected Edwards's commitment to the necessity of conversion and of evangelical piety as the foundations of church fellowship, touchstones of the Great Awakening itself. Edwards's attempt to restructure core features of his church's life and his willingness to denounce specific sins committed by some of the members of his congregation ultimately alienated him from a majority of the members of his church. In one particular instance Edwards learned that some young men in his congregation were using lorid details from books on midwifery and popular medicine to taunt young women. His attempts to investigate this incident and to censure participants earned him prominent enemies within his church. Ultimately, in 1750 a council of ministers from nearby congregations recommended that Edwards be dismissed, and the Northampton church after a bitter controversy sided with the council and removed Edwards from his position as pastor. He was forced to accept a far less prestigious ministerial post at the church in Stockbridge, Massachusetts, where he remained until the College of New Jersey (later Princeton University) made him president in 1758. His tenure in this position, though, was tragically brief, and he died little more than a month later of complications from a smallpox inoculation.

Divisions between New Lights and Old, New Siders and Old Siders, were not the only fractures produced by the Great Awakening. Among the Congregational churches of New England, especially, many of the members touched by the current of revival were convinced that their churches were not only wayward but dead. They saw no point in struggling over the control of these dead congregations and believed, instead, that the appropriate spiritual response was to separate themselves from the congregations to which they had previously been joined. They thus formed new "Separate" congregations. In the wake of the Great Awakening, many of these Separate congregations became convinced that the practice of infant baptism so central to the covenantal theology of their former Congregational churches was unscriptural. Determined that baptism was an ordinance properly reserved for those who had been personally converted, many of these Separate believers and their new congregations began to think of themselves as Baptists. To distinguish these congregations from the older Baptist congregations that had been present since the 17th century in North America, located primarily in Providence and Newport, Rhode Island, and in other scattered places across New England, history sometimes refers to them as Separate Baptists. Among the Separate Baptists one prominent minister was Isaac Backus, who was converted during the Great Awakening and subsequently became a minister for a Separate congregation in 1748. He subsequently came to hold Baptist beliefs and reorganized his church as the First Baptist Church of Middleborough in 1756. In the decades before and after the Revolutionary War, Backus became one of America's most prominent advocates of religious liberty and disestablishment. As a historian of Baptists in America, Backus also made the important contribution to American religious history of rediscovering an even more important advocate of religious freedom who had been briefly a Baptist himself, Roger Williams.

Awakening, American Identity, and Independence

The Great Awakening sparked by the preaching of George Whitefield and other evangelical ministers in the 1730s and 1740s was part of an international religious renewal. In England Methodism would be the chief fruit of this renewal. On the European continent German Pietism would become the most important expression of this wider current of renewal. But the American colonies experienced the Great Awakening not so much as an international religious revival but as a peculiarly *American* one. The awakening recaptured a sense of American exceptionalism that early colonists in the 17th century had brought with them to the shores of the New World. Colonial leaders such as John Winthrop had seen their migration to North America not simply as a relocation to a new geographical place, but as inaugurating a new chapter in sacred history, a chapter in which the New World would be at the center of God's sovereign plan. This sense of being exceptional in the divine plan had been strained and even blunted in the latter decades of the 17th century. But the Great Awakening helped to rekindle this sense. Ministers such as Jonathan Edwards saw in the awakening evidence that God was busy in America laying the stage for the end of times. Not surprisingly, Christians in other countries who experienced aspects of the general, international religious revival during the 18th century did not always accept the notion that America lay at the center of God's plans. Admirers of the Great Awakening in Scotland, for example, where revival also occurred in the 1740s, tended not to share this sense of American exceptionalism. Moreover, as revival in America cooled toward the end of the 1740s, even Edwards had to reconsider his original confidence that happenings in America might preface the end of times. But perhaps because the Awakening nurtured a venerable conviction, reaching back to the earliest days of Puritan New England, that America was in some sense a City upon a Hill, even the gradual cooling of revivalistic fervor did not invalidate this conviction.

The Great Awakening also assisted the colonies in seeing themselves not simply as separate outposts of the British empire but as sharing a collective life. It was ironic that an Anglican minister, George Whitefield, helped to create this vision, but his preaching tours and the news of their results connected colonists in a way that had not been experienced on the same scale before. Even when colonists disagreed about the value or legitimacy of revival, they found themselves commenting upon

The preaching of Anglican evangelist George Whitefield has been credited with beginning the Great Awakening. *(Library of Congress, Prints and Photographs Division LC-USZ62-075073)*

a shared experience that had irrevocably altered the landscape of American religion. This did not mean, of course, that church membership, which had swelled during the Great Awakening, would not suffer subsequent decline or that revival, once ignited, would continue unabated. The awakening, nevertheless, had touched lives and restructured religious institutions across the American colonies and given these separate colonies reason to think of themselves as "we." The political and social sources of the American Revolution were many and varied, but the sense of national identity aroused by the Great Awakening must be counted as one of the Revolution's midwives.

A new sense of national identity allied itself with an older tradition of political dissent to strengthen revolutionary currents in the middle years of the 18th century. Revolutionary era America inherited from the Puritans of the previous century a keen awareness of the potential for human power to assert itself in the form of tyranny. "[W]hat ever transcendent power is given," Puritan minister John Cotton had insisted a century before, "will certainly over-run those that give it, and those that receive it. There is a strain in a man's heart that will sometime or other run out to excess, unless the Lord restrain it, but it is not good to venture it."[3] Men and women who believed in the inherent sinfulness of human nature had no difficulty imaging the "excesses" to which that nature might run if left unchecked. Moreover, theological reflection found itself buttressed by actual experience. The first generation of Puritans in America had themselves suffered harrying at the hands of Charles I and his ecclesiastical henchman, Archbishop William Laud, and they had been distant spectators of the war between Charles and Parliament that had ultimately thrown off the perceived yoke of royal tyranny. They had also heard stories of the persecutions visited upon Protestants by Mary Tudor during the 16th century. Thus, both current and remote history joined to offer the Puritans examples of the kind of mischief into which an excess of human power might run. Moreover, the so-called wall of separation between church and state did not exist in New England in anything like its present form, and Puritan ministers demonstrated no reluctance about instructing their congregations on biblical principles they thought pertinent to political life. Consequently, Puritans of the 17th century were nurtured on a steady diet of election-day sermons that emphasized both the obligations and the limitations of rulers. However autocratic the New England governments of the 17th century appear to observers today, they were erected on a foundation of suspicion of human power and a conviction that such power must necessarily be limited.

The Great Awakening also amplified latent Puritan suspicions of human power by creating a climate in which the laity felt free to challenge the authority of the clergy. In the 17th century Puritans were familiar with the form of sermon referred to as the jeremiad, in which a preacher chastised a congregation for its spiritual decline in a style reminiscent of the Jewish prophet Jeremiah. But during the Great Awakening George Whitefield and others began to preach what has been referred to as an "inverted jeremiad."[4] In this form of sermon, the preacher lamented the spiritual decline not of laity, but of ministers. The Presbyterian Gilbert Tennent published one of the awakening's most famous tracts, *The Dangers of an Unconverted Ministry*, and the title of this work captured one of the common themes of revival preaching during the Great Awakening and the essence of the inverted jeremiad. Tennent's tract, along with other sermons following its mold, gave currency to the possibility that the spiritual authority in which some ministers cloaked themselves was illegitimate, since these ministers were not true Christians. Tennent was thus tutoring his hearers in the vocabulary of revolution. If spiritual authority might be misused, then so might political authority. It required no great transformation of thinking to move from religious insubordination to political revolution.

Americans disposed to be suspicious of human power eventually perceived grievances against British authority sufficient to inspire the struggle for independence. In the decades leading up to the Revolutionary War, one persistent source of suspicion against British encroachment on colonial liberties was the prospect of a bishop being appointed for the Anglican Church in America. In the late 17th and early 18th centuries, the fortunes of Anglicanism in America had prospered. The Church of England, initially established by law only in Virginia, subsequently acquired this preferential status in Maryland, the Carolinas, and Georgia. In these colonies and elsewhere, missionaries for the Society for the Propagation of the Gospel, established in 1701, labored to see Anglican faith flourish. During the 18th century these missionaries regularly petitioned British authorities to appoint a bishop for the Anglican Church in America. They supported this request partially with arguments about the ecclesiastical convenience of having an American bishop. But they also suggested that an American bishop would help to inspire greater loyalty among the colonies to England itself and counter the effects of ministers from other faiths, who, they suggested, were no friends of British rule. Not surprisingly, these suggestions had the effect of inspiring further suspicion toward Anglican authority as well as British political authority.

As suspicion accelerated toward rebellion, friends of Anglican authority in America found themselves increasingly isolated. Even as revolution disrupted formal political ties with England, it also disturbed ecclesiastical ties with England's established church. The ordination vows of Anglican priests, including those who served in the American colonies, included a pledge of allegiance to the British throne. Not infrequently, as in the case of the Anglican minister Samuel Seabury, this pledge of allegiance was buttressed by an affinity for Britain itself as well as its government. The combination of formal pledge and informal affinity tended to make Anglican clergy in America opponents of independence. Seabury, for example, who later became the first Episcopal bishop in America in 1784, served the cause of British Loyalists by writing several influential tracts under the name A. W.

Samuel Seabury, pictured here, was the first Episcopalian bishop ordained to serve in America. *(Library of Congress, Prints and Photographs Division LC-USZ62-86077)*

Farmer, in which he argued the case against American independence from Great Britain. "[I]f I must be enslaved," he fumed in one tract, "let it be by a King at least, and not by a parcel of upstart, lawless Committee-men. If I must be devoured, let me be devoured by the Jaws of a lion, and not *gnawed* to death by rats and vermin!"[5] Not surprisingly, with sentiments such as these, Seabury found himself in an uncomfortable position after war with England erupted. For the sake of safety he had to withdraw to Long Island, New York, behind British lines.

After the Revolutionary War it became even more apparent that Anglicanism in America could no longer exist simply as an outpost of the Church of England. In recognition of this religious—and political—reality, Samuel Seabury was eventually commissioned to seek ordination as a bishop. Since Seabury was no longer in a position to swear fealty to the English Crown, authorities of the Church of England refused to ordain him as a bishop. Eventually, Seabury was consecrated bishop of Connecticut by Anglican bishops in Scotland, referred to as "non-juring" bishops because their predecessors had refused to take the oath of allegiance to William and Mary the previous century after they had already sworn allegiance to King James II. Only late in the 18th century did the Church of England finally recognize Seabury's ordination. But under his spiritual leadership American Episcopalianism, the successor to the Church of England in America, had already taken root in the new nation.

Early Methodist ministers in America experienced some of the same tensions as did Seabury and other Anglicans. John Wesley, Methodism's founder and early leader, insisted throughout his life that Methodists were loyal members of the Church of England. Many of Methodism's early itinerant ministers, unlike Wesley himself, had not been formally ordained in the Church of England and had thus not sworn the formal oath of allegiance to the British Crown. Nevertheless, most of these ministers counted themselves loyal subjects of British rule. Consequently, when the Revolutionary War began many of the Methodist itinerants previously dispatched to the American colonies retreated back to England. Francis Asbury was a conspicuous exception to the general pattern. He arrived in Philadelphia in 1771 after having accepted the call of John Wesley for volunteers to preach in America. Thereafter, Asbury settled first in New York, which became the center of his itinerant preaching ministry; by the beginning of the Revolutionary War he had migrated to Maryland. Although most of the other Methodist ministers in America decided to return to England once war began, Asbury determined to stay. He was unwilling to forswear allegiance to the British Crown, however, as Maryland law soon required, and had to relocate to Delaware for two years, where such an oath was not required. Following the war in 1784, John Wesley recognized that formal ties between British and American Methodism were no longer tenable, and he ordained Asbury and Thomas Coke as joint superintendents of the Methodist Church in America. Coke, however, did not permanently remain in America. Consequently, Asbury became Methodism's first permanent bishop in America and earned the nickname the Father of American Methodism.

Religion and the State Constitutions

After the American colonies declared their independence from Britain, the Continental Congress urged them to draft state constitutions to organize their new political lives. These constitutions commonly included provisions relating to re-

Francis Asbury is often referred to as the father of American Methodism. *(Library of Congress, Prints and Photographs Division LC-USZC4-6153)*

ligious liberty, provisions that formed the chief framework for relations between government and religion at the state level. Although the U.S. Constitution, when subsequently ratified and amended, contained its own provisions relating to religious liberty and disestablishment, these initially governed only the relationship between religion and the federal government. It was only in the 20th century, after the Fourteenth Amendment to the Constitution was ratified, that this amendment's due process clause was interpreted to make provisions of the First Amendment applicable to state and local governments. Consequently, the state constitutions are the best source for understanding the nature of religious liberty as experienced in the states at the end of the 18th and the beginning of the 19th centuries.

The revolutionary generation conceived that all men were "created equal" and believed as a corollary to this proposition that religious liberty was among those inalienable rights with which a beneficent creator had endowed each individual in equal measure. The Virginia Declaration of Rights, for example, adopted in 1776, proclaimed both that "all men are by nature equally free and independent" and that "all men are equally entitled to the free exercise of religion, according to the dictates of conscience."[6] But states at the time of the Revolution had generally not yet understood the reach of their stated constitutional principles. The "all men" considered "equally free and independent" under the Virginia Declaration of Rights were, in fact, men rather than women, and most definitely white men rather than black. Similarly, with some exceptions, the "all men" recognized as entitled to equal religious liberty in the various state constitutions were generally Christians and, in a some cases, Protestants. New York had since the late 17th century enjoyed a measure of religious diversity and toleration unusual among most of the American colonies. Consequently, it was no surprise that its revolutionary constitution guaranteed religious free exercise "without discrimination of preference" to "all mankind."[7] But the other states generally defined religious liberty more narrowly. Delaware and Maryland guaranteed religious freedom to all those who professed "the Christian religion,"[8] Massachusetts and New Hampshire to "every denomination of Christian,"[9] and Connecticut to "any Christian sect or mode of worship."[10] Not every state was prepared to abandon the long respectable legal preference for Protestants. South Carolina envisioned a religious equality to be enjoyed only by "Christian Protestants."[11] As time passed, though, these explicit constitutional discriminations in favor of Christianity, or even Protestantism, were gradually replaced with more expansive guarantees of religious liberty. In 1792, for example, Delaware eliminated its restriction of religious liberty to Christians by enacting a new constitutional provision.

> Although it is the duty of all men frequently to assemble together for the public worship of the Author of the universe, and piety and morality, on which the prosperity of communities depends, are thereby promoted; yet no man shall or ought to be compelled to attend any religious worship, to contribute to the erection or support of any place of worship, or to the maintenance of any ministry against his own free will and consent; and no power shall in any case interfere with, or in any manner control, the rights of conscience, in the free exercise of religious worship, nor a preference be given by law to any religious societies, denominations, or modes of worship.[12]

Similarly, in 1790 South Carolina exchanged its original guarantee of equality to Christian Protestants for one that guaranteed free exercise "without discrimination or preference" to "all mankind."[13] These revisions reflected the growing awareness that religious liberty was not simply a Christian right, but a human right. The consensus around this principle was not unanimous, of course. The 19th century would witness efforts to add an amendment to the U.S. Constitution that would explicitly characterize America as a Christian nation. But this effort eventually failed, and both Catholics and Jews and still later believers from other religious traditions gradually earned the liberty of conscience recognized in the early state constitutions.

Reasonable Religion

Opponents of the Great Awakening scoffed at the unlearned preachers who sprang up in its wake, uneducated and unmannerly. But the current of revival, in spite of the claims of its detractors, had significant room for reason. William Tennent's Log Cabin school was undoubtedly plain and unfinished, but the learning Tennent dispensed to his students was substantial. Its combination of intellectual vigor and heart-felt piety would become a model for subsequent institutions, not the least of which was the College of New Jersey, later Princeton University. And the Great Awakening's great defender, Jonathan Edwards, is perhaps the most brilliant theologian ever nurtured on American soil. Nevertheless, the evangelical reasoning championed by men such as Jonathan Edwards remained firmly tethered to orthodox Christianity in general and Reformed Protestantism in particular.

The adversaries of revivalism, however, Charles Chauncy most specifically, emphasized a reasonable religion that began to drift down less orthodox pathways. Chauncy, together with men such as Jonathan Mayhew and Ebenezer Gray, began a spiritual migration that would ultimately contribute to the birth of Unitarianism in America. But well before Unitarianism took root in American soil, the reasonable religion of deism flourished, especially among the upper stations of society in colonial America. It had its genesis in two related intellectual currents. The first of these was the religious latitudinarianism that began to appear in England during the late 17th century. A group of Anglican theologians, generally hostile to the Calvinism of the Puritans and impatient with narrow arguments about specific Christian doctrines, preferred to emphasize instead a few key religious beliefs, such as the existence of God and the reality of future rewards and punishments. They were also confident that reason was capable of elaborating these essential truths and that religious knowledge need not be tethered to the truths revealed in the Bible. The confidence of these latitudinarians in the power of reason made them natural allies of the Enlightenment, a second intellectual current that nourished the rise of deism. Enlightenment thought celebrated the promise of scientific discovery for solving the problems of the world and distrusted traditional sources of religious authority. It emphasized the importance of reason rather than revelation and celebrated a religion nourished more by nature and its glories than by Scripture. Deism's God was a creator but not a redeemer, a deity who fashioned the natural order of the universe but who did not answer prayer. Unhinged as it was from institutional and communal expressions of religious belief, deism failed to secure an enduring place in American religious experience. Within the fraternity of reasonable religion, Unitarianism, the close cousin of deism, would earn a more permanent place in the nation's religious history.

Chronicle of Events

1741

- Count Nicholas Ludwig von Zinzendorf begins an 18-month tour of North America during which period he establishes the Moravian Church in America but is unsuccessful in his efforts, referred to as the "union movement," to unite all German Protestants in Pennsylvania into a single ecclesiastical body. During this period he engages in missionary activities among the American Indians of Pennsylvania.
- *July 8:* Jonathan Edwards preaches the sermon "Sinners in the Hands of an Angry God" in Enfield, Connecticut.
- Gilbert Tennent and other New Side Presbyterians establish the New Brunswick presbytery. Four years later a New Side synod is established in New York. The schism between Old Side and New Side Presbyterians lasts for 17 years.

Henry Muhlenberg was a prominent Lutheran minister in the 18th century. *(Library of Congress, Prints and Photographs Division LC-USZ62-57325)*

1742

- John Philip Boehm opposes Count Nicholas Ludwig von Zinzendorf's attempt to unite the various German Protestant groups in Pennsylvania by publishing a tract against the movement titled *True Letter of Warning addressed to the Reformed Congregations of Pennsylvania.*
- Jonathan Edwards publishes a generally sympathetic discussion of the Great Awakening titled *Some Thoughts Concerning the Present Revival of Religion.*
- Henry Muhlenberg, the father of American Lutheranism, emigrates from Germany to Pennsylvania, where he becomes minister of three Lutheran congregations.
- Connecticut, influenced by opponents of the Great Awakening, enacts a law banning itinerant preaching except when invited by a local minister.

1743

- Charles Chauncy, minister at Boston's First Church, publishes an influential critique of the Great Awakening titled *Seasonable Thoughts on the State of Religion in New England.*
- Christopher Sauer publishes the Germantown Bible, a version of Martin Luther's German translation of the Bible, the first Bible in a European language published in the colonies.
- Massachusetts provides for Quakers to make an affirmation in cases otherwise requiring the swearing of oaths.

1744

- David Brainerd is ordained a Presbyterian minister.
- George Whitefield returns to America.
- Jonathan Edwards discovers that several young men in his Northampton church have acquired books on midwifery and popular medicine and are using what they learned from these books to taunt young women. Edwards's attempts to investigate and censor those involved in what is sometimes called the "bad book case" alienate many members of his congregation.
- Harvard leaders publish a joint statement critical of George Whitefield and other revival preachers.

1745

- Jonathan Dickinson and other New Side Presbyterians (i.e., those generally in support of the Great Awakening) organize the New York synod as an alternative to the Old Side–dominated Philadelphia Presbyterian synod.

- Thomas Clapp, the rector of Yale College, and three Yale tutors publish a joint statement criticizing George Whitefield.
- Samuel Davies and other southern Presbyterian ministers organize the Hanover presbytery in Virginia. Davies will be an important figure in the growth of southern Presbyterianism.
- *August 20:* Francis Asbury, father of American Methodism, is born in Staffordshire, England.

1746

- Jonathan Dickinson and other New Side Presbyterians obtain a charter creating the College of New Jersey (later Princeton University), and Dickinson becomes its first president.
- Jonathan Edwards publishes *A Treatise concerning Religious Affections,* which provides a theological defense of revivalism and of the role of emotions in Christian experience.

1747

- David Brainerd has to withdraw from missionary activities among Native Americans and take up residence at the home of Jonathan Edwards, where, before his death on October 9, he edits his diary. When published posthumously by Edwards, Brainerd's diary will become a classic devotional text among Protestant Christians.
- The Presbyterian minister Samuel Davies arrives in Virginia from Pennsylvania and is greeted with official hostility from Anglican government and religious leaders.
- *September 28:* Thomas Coke, who with Francis Asbury will serve as the first Methodist "bishops" in America, is born in Brecon, South Wales.

1748

- Isaac Backus is ordained a Congregationalist minister in Massachusetts.
- The Presbyterian synod of New York sends Samuel Davies to minister in Virginia.
- Henry Muhlenberg is instrumental in the creation of the first Lutheran ministerium, or synod, and serves as its first president.
- Joseph Conrad Beissel's Ephrata commune of Seventh-Day Baptists prints a Mennonite book titled *Martyr-Spiegel,* or "Martyrs' Mirror," whose pages exceed 1,500, making it the longest book published in America prior to the 19th century.

1749

- Jonathan Edwards publishes *The Life of David Brainerd,* which becomes a classic Christian devotional work.

1750

- Jonathan Edwards is forced to leave his position as minister of the Congregational church in Northampton, Massachusetts, because of personal and theological differences with church members.
- Approximately this year Eleazer Wheelock establishes the Moors Indian Charity School, which will later become Dartmouth College, in Connecticut.

1751

- Jonathan Edwards settles in Stockbridge, Massachusetts, where he serves as minister to the small church there and undertakes missionary activity to American Indians in the area.

1754

- Anglican minister Samuel Johnson becomes president of the newly chartered King's College (present-day Columbia University) in New York.

1756

- Convinced that infant baptism is inconsistent with the teachings of the Bible, Isaac Backus leads his church to reorganize itself as the First Baptist Church of Middleborough.
- Quakers lose control of the Pennsylvania legislature.
- Maryland imposes a scheme of double taxation upon Catholics.

1758

- The first known African-American church, called the African Baptist or Bluestone Church, is established on the William Byrd plantation near the Bluestone River in Mecklenburg, Virginia.
- The New York and Philadelphia synods of Presbyterianism, formed initially out of different responses to the Great Awakening, merge.
- The Philadelphia Yearly Meeting of Quakers determines that members should cease buying and selling slaves.
- *February 16:* Jonathan Edwards becomes president of the College of New Jersey (later Princeton University), but he will die a little more than a month later of fever after being inoculated against smallpox.

1759

- The Presbyterian minister Samuel Davies is appointed president of the College of New Jersey (present-day Princeton University).

1760

- Barbara Ruckle Heck, referred to sometimes as "the mother of American Methodism," immigrates to New York City with her husband, children, and other relatives.
- *February 14:* Richard Allen, the first black ordained in the Methodist Episcopal Church, and founder and first bishop of the African Methodist Episcopal (AME) Church, is born a slave in Philadelphia.

1763

- *December:* The Touro Synagogue, designed by Peter Harrison and home of the Congregation Jeshuat Israel, is dedicated in Newport, Rhode Island. Today it is the only surviving synagogue from the colonial period.

1764

- Rhode Island charters the College of Rhode Island (present-day Brown University), stipulating in the charter that "[i]nto this liberal and catholic institution shall never be admitted any religious tests; but on the contrary, all the members hereof shall forever enjoy full, free, absolute and uninterrupted liberty of conscience."[14]
- George Whitefield visits the colonies again.

1765

- Samson Occom, an American Indian convert to Christianity and graduate of Eleazer Wheelock's Moors Indian Charity School, travels to England to raise money for the school, which is later relocated to New Hampshire and chartered in 1769 as Dartmouth College.

1766

- Barbara Ruckle Heck encourages her cousin Philip Embury to begin preaching and thus participates in the formation of a Methodist fellowship. The Methodist layman Robert Strawbridge also begins preaching the same year.
- Evangelical Dutch Reformed leaders establish Queen's College (present-day Rutgers University) in New Jersey.

1767

- The Warren Baptist Association, the first association of Baptist congregations in New England, is formed.
- *June 25:* The Jesuits are expelled from New Spain.

John Witherspoon was a Presbyterian minister who signed the Declaration of Independence. *(Library of Congress, Prints and Photographs Division LC-USZ62-104656)*

1768

- Presbyterian minister John Witherspoon, the only active minister to sign the Declaration of Independence, arrives with his family in America to become the president of the College of New Jersey (later Princeton University).
- The American Philosophical Society is founded in Philadelphia.
- Canada's first synagogue, Shearith Israel, is established in Montreal.
- *October 30:* A stone chapel is constructed on St. John Street in New York according to a design provided by Barbara Ruckle Heck and opened for use, becoming perhaps the first Methodist church building in America.

1769

- The Spanish Franciscan priest Junípero Serra leads in the establishment of a mission at San Diego.
- At the annual conference of Methodist ministers in England, those in attendance discuss the "pressing call" to bring the message of salvation to America.

- Dartmouth College, an outgrowth of the Moors Indian Charity School founded by Eleazer Wheelock, is chartered.

1770
- George Whitefield makes another visit to the American colonies.
- The Baptist minister Isaac Backus publishes *A Seasonable Plea for Liberty of Conscience Against Some Late Oppressive Proceedings Particularly in the Town of Berwick.*

1771
- At the annual conference of Methodist ministers in England, when John Wesley seeks volunteers to preach in America, Francis Asbury is one of two ministers who volunteer to undertake this mission.
- *October 27:* Methodist minister Francis Asbury arrives in Philadelphia, Pennsylvania. The following year he will make New York a base for his itinerant preaching career.

1773
- Isaac Backus publishes a defense of religious freedom titled *An Appeal to the Public for Religious Liberty.*
- Pope Clement XIV dissolves the Society of Jesus (the Jesuits).
- George Liele, a black slave, is licensed as a Baptist preacher in Georgia.

1774
- Ann Lee and a small group of Shakers immigrate to America.
- The British Parliament adopts the Quebec Act, which recognizes Catholicism as the official religion of Quebec. American colonists are alarmed at this law and refer to it as one of the Intolerable Acts.
- In the face of rising revolutionary sentiments, Quakers at the Philadelphia Yearly Meeting express continued gratitude to the British Crown for the religious liberties they enjoy.
- At the first meeting of the Continental Congress, a proposal to begin the following session with prayer is approved.

1775
- Mennonites in Pennsylvania petition the Pennsylvania assembly about their unwillingness to bear arms.

- *October 12:* Lyman Beecher is born in New Haven, Connecticut.

1776
- The American colonies declare their independence from Britain. Charles Carroll is the only Catholic to sign the Declaration of Independence.
- Catholic priest John Carroll, Benjamin Franklin, Samuel Chase, and Charles Carroll travel to Canada seeking to persuade Canada to remain neutral during the Revolutionary War.
- The Baptist preacher John Leland arrives in Virginia from New England. He will become an important advocate for religious liberty in the state.
- The Continental Congress suggests that states draft constitutions to serve as fundamental political documents.
- *November:* The Continental Congress appoints the first national day of prayer and thanksgiving, designating for this purpose December 18.

1777
- Congregational minister Ezra Stiles is elected president of Yale College.
- Richard Allen is converted through the preaching of Freeborn Garrettson and joins the Methodist Church.

1778
- *May 2:* Future Methodist minister Nathan Bangs is born in Stratford, Connecticut.
- The Loyalist master of black Baptist preacher and slave George Liele is killed in battle during the Revolutionary War, and Liele settles in Savannah, where he establishes a congregation that becomes the First African Baptist Church of Savannah.

1779
- The first conferences of American Methodist ministers are held, one in the North and one in the South.
- Thomas Jefferson composes a Bill for Establishing Religious Liberty. It is not enacted by the Virginia legislature until 1786.

1780
- Lott Cary, an African-American Baptist missionary who will become governor of Liberia, is born a slave around this date on a plantation in Charles City County, Virginia.

Eyewitness Testimony

Let us pray ... for the *out-pouring* of the SPIRIT upon our land. There is room for prayer in this respect. A concern, I am sensible, has been generally awaken'd in the minds of people, in one place or another: And it has, I trust, been of spiritual advantage to many; who, it may be hoped, have been either *savingly converted* to GOD, or *enliven'd* and *quicken'd* in the work of religion, and their soul's everlasting salvation. There are I doubt not, a number in this land, upon whom GOD has graciously *shed* the influences of his blessed SPIRIT; and we ought to be thankful for what of the SPIRIT, we have reason to hope there is among us: But there is yet need of prayer; and the more so, as so many things have arisen among us, which are a dishonour to GOD, and may have a tendency greatly to obstruct the progress of real and substantial religion. Alas! what unchristian heats and animosities are there in many places, to the dividing and breaking in pieces of churches and towns? What a spirit of rash, censorious, uncharitable judging prevails too generally all over the land? What bitterness and wrath and clamour, what evil speaking, reviling and slandering, are become common; and among those too, who would be counted good christians? How alienated are many ministers from each other, and how instrumental of hurting rather than promoting one another's usefulness? What prejudices are there in the minds of too many people against the *standing ministry,* tho' perhaps as faithful a one as any part of the world is favour'd with? And how general is the disposition they discover to flock after every *weak* and *illiterate* EXHORTER, to the contempt of their *pastors,* who have spent, it may be, most of their days, in faithful services for their souls? How heated are the imaginations of a great many, and into what excesses do they betray them?

> *Charles Chauncy, 1742, minister at Boston's First Church, concerning the Great Awakening, in Griffin,* Old Brick, *p. 65.*

The thing was sudden, and though the thoughts of writing an Instrument of Slavery for one of my fellow creatures felt uneasy, yet I remembered I was hired by the year; and that it was my master who [directed] me to do it, and that it was an Elderly man, a member of our society who brought her, so through weakness I gave way, and wrote it, but at the Executing it I was so afflicted in my mind, that I said before my Master and the friend, that I believed Slavekeeping to be a practice inconsistent with the Christian Religion; this in some degree abated my uneasiness, yet as often as I reflected seriously upon it I thought I should have been clearer, if I had desired to be Excused from it, as a thing against my conscience, for such it was.

> *John Woolman, 1742, describing in his journal his reaction to being asked to draw up a bill of sale for a female slave, quoted in Trueblood,* The People Called Quakers, *p. 155.*

Sunday, August 26 [1743, New London, Conn.] I went home at 6 o'clock and Deacon Green's son came to see me. He entertained me with the history of the behaviour of one [James] Davenport, a fanatick preacher there who told his flock in one of his enthusiastic rhapsodies that in order to be saved they ought to burn all their idols. They began this conflagration with a pile of books in the public street, among which were Tillotson's Sermons, Drillincourt on Death, Sherlock and many other excellent authors, and sung psalms and hymns over the pile while it was a burning. They did not stop here, but the women made up a lofty pile of hoop petticoats, silk gowns, short cloaks, cambrick caps, red heeled shoes, fans, neclaces, gloves and other such apparell, and what was merry enough, Davenport's own idol with which he topped the pile, was a pair of old, wore out, plush breaches. But this bone fire was happily prevented by one more moderate than the rest, who found means to perswade them that making such a sacrifice was not necessary for their salvation, and so every one carried of[f] their idols again, which was lucky for Davenport who, had fire been put to the pile, would have been obliged to strutt about bare-arsed, for the devil another pair of breeches had he but these same old plush one which were going to be offered up as an expiatory sacrifice.

> *Dr. Alexander Hamilton, a visiting Edinburgh physician, August 26, 1743, quoted in Williams,* Popular Religion in America, *p. 111.*

When I came *there* [to New Brunswick] which was about *seven Years after* [Theodorus Frelinghuysen], I had the Pleasure of seeing much of the Fruits of his Ministry: divers of his Hearers with whom I had the Opportunity of conversing, appear'd to be converted Persons, by their Soundness in Principle, Christian Experience, and pious Practice: and these Persons declared that the Ministrations of the aforesaid Gentleman, were the Means thereof. This together with a kind *Letter* which he sent me respecting the Necessity of dividing the Word aright, and giving every Man his Portion in due Season, thro' the divine Blessing, excited me to greater Earnestness in ministerial Labours. I [then] began to be very much distressed about my want of Success; for I knew not for *half a Year* or more after I came to *New Brunswick*, that any one was converted by my Labours, altho' several Persons were at Times affected transiently. . . . I was then exceedingly grieved that I had done so little for God, and was very desirous to live one *half Year* more if it was his Will, that I might stand upon the Stage of the World as it were, and plead more faithfully for his Cause, and take more earnest Pains for the *Conversion of Souls.* The secure State of the World appeared to me in a very affecting Light; and one Thing among others pressed me sore; viz. that I had spent much Time in conversing about Trifles, which might have been spent in examining People's States towards God, and persuading them to turn unto him: I therefore prayed to God that he would be pleased to give me one *half Year* more, and I was determined to endeavor to promote his Kingdom with all my Might at all Adventures.

Presbyterian minister Gilbert Tennent, 1744, in Coalter, Gilbert Tennent, Son of Thunder, *pp. 16–17.*

[Revival preachers] thrust themselves into Towns and Parishes, to the Destruction of all Peace and Order, whereby they have to the great impoverishment of the community, taken the People from their Work and Business, to attend their Lectures and Exhortations, always fraught with Enthusiasm, and other pernicious Errors. But, which is worse, and it is the natural effect of these things, the people have been thence ready to despise their own ministers, and their usefulness among them, in too many places, hath been almost destroyed.

"The Testimony of the Presidents, Professors, Tutors, and Hebrew Instructor of Harvard College in Cambridge Against the Reverend Mr. George Whitefield, and His Conduct," 1744, in McGarvie, One Nation Under Law, *p. 34.*

Rev. Sir [George Whitefield],

. . . It has always appeared to us, that you and other Itinerants have laid a Scheme to vilify and subvert our Colleges, and to introduce a Sett of Ministers into our churches, by other Ways and Means of Education. In your Journal . . . you say, As to the Universities, I believe it may be truly said that the Light in them is now become Darkness, even thick Darkness that may be felt. . . .

Upon the best Information, we suppose, that altho' at the first erection of this College, and while it was for some years destitute of a resident Rector and compleat Government, there were sundry Instances of Vice and Irreligion; yet by the good Government of the late Rector, under the Inspection of the venerable Trustees, it was by Degrees brought into a very well regulated State as to Learning, Religion, and Manners. And that as many learned and godly Ministers have been educated here as at any College or private Seminary in the World, of no longer Standing. But this is certain, that soon after the Publication of these Slanders upon the Colleges, this was upon several Accounts in a worse State than it was before. Sundry of the Students ran in Enthusiastic Errors and Disorders, censur'd and reviled their Governours and others; for which some were expell'd, denied their Degrees, or otherwise punished. . . . And we've been inform'd, that the Students were told, that there was no Danger in disobeying their present Governours, because there would in a short Time be a great Change in the civil Government, and so in the Governours of the College.

Thomas Clap, rector of Yale College, along with three Yale tutors, 1745, "Declaration of the Rector and Tutors Against Whitefield," in Documentary History of Yale University: 1701–1745, *pp. 369–370.*

[O]n August the 24, 1741 as I was mowing in the field alone I was thinking of my case; and all my past Life Seemed to be brought fresh to my view And it appeared indeed nothing but a life of Sin. I felt so that I left work and went and sat Down under a Shadey tree; and I was brought to Look Particularly into my duties and strivings How I had tryed to get help by awakening Preaching but found it fail. Had tryed to Mend my Self by my Tears prayers and Promises of doing better but all in vain—my heart was Hard and full of Corruption still. And it Appeared clear to me then that I had tryed Every way that Posibly I Could and if I perished Forever I Could do no more. And the Justice of God Shined so clear Before my eyes in Condemning Such a guilty Rebel that I Could say no more—but fell at his feet. I See that I was in his hands and he had a right To do with me just as he Pleased And I Lay like a Dead Vile Creature before him. I felt a calm in my mind—them tossing And tumults that I felt before seemed to be gone.

And Just in that Critical moment God who caused the light to Shine out of Darkness, Shined into my heart with such A discovery of that glorious Righteousness Which fully Satisfies the Law that I had Broken; and of the Infinite fulness that there Is in Christ to Satisfie the wants of just Such a helpless Creature as I was and these Blessing Were held forth So freely to my Soul—That my Whole Heart was atracted and Drawn away after God and Swallowed up with Admiration in viewing his Divine glories.

Never did his Word appear So before as It did now:—it appeared So glorious and Such Infallible Truth that I could with the greatest Freedom Rest my Eternal all upon what God hath Spoken. Now the way of Salvation appeared so excellent and glorious That I Wondered that I had stood out So long against Such a Blessed Redeemer. Yea I wondered that all the World didn't Come to him.

Baptist minister Isaac Backus, August 16, 1751, The Diary of Isaac Backus, vol. 3, pp. 1,525–1,526.

He [Papounhan] forsook the town and went to the woods in great bitterness of Spirit . . . But at the end of five days it pleased God to appear to him to his Comfort and to give him a sight of his own inward state, and also an acquaintance into the Works of nature—for he apprehended a sense was given him of the virtues, and Natures, of several herbs, Roots, Plants, and trees and the different relation they had one to another, and he was made sensible that Man stood in the nearest relation to God of any Part of the Creation.

Papounhan, a Munsee Delaware Indian, relating a vision then recorded by a Quaker in 1756, in Martin, The Land Looks After Us, p. 52.

They [the residents of Lynch's Creek, Carolina] complained of being eaten up by Itinerant Teachers, Preachers, and Imposters from New England and Pennsylvania—Baptists, New Lights, Presbyterians, Independents, and an hundred other Sects—So that one day you might hear this System of Doctrine—the next day another—next day another, retrograde to both—Thus by the Variety of Taylors who would pretend to know the best fashion in which Christ's Coat is to be worn none will put it on—And among the Various Plans of Religion, they are at a Loss which to adapt, and consequently are without any Religion at all.

Charles Woodmason, 1760s, The Carolina Backcountry on the Eve of the Revolution, p. 13.

Much learning hath been displayed to show the necessity of establishing one church in England in the present form. But these reasonings do not reach the case of this colony.

. . . . .

A general toleration of Religion appears to me the best means of peopling our country, and enabling our people to procure those necessaries among themselves, the purchase of which from abroad has so nearly ruined a colony, enjoying, from nature and time, the means of becoming the most prosperous on the continent.

. . . . .

When I say that the article of religion is deemed a trifle by our people in the general, I assert a known truth. But when we suppose that the poorer sort of European emigrants set as light by it, we are greatly mistaken. The free exercise of religion hath stocked the Northern part of the continent with inhabitants; and although Europe hath in great measure adopted a more moderate policy, yet the profession of Protestantism is extremely inconvenient in many places there. A Calvinist, a Lutheran, or Quaker, who hath felt these inconveniences in Europe, sails not to Virginia, where they are felt perhaps in a (greater degree).

Virgiana politician Patrick Henry, around 1766, in Stokes, Church and State in the United States, vol. 1, pp. 311–312.

I was Born a Heathen and Brought up In Heathenism, till I was between 16 & 17 years of age, at a Place Called Mohegan, in New London, Connecticut, in New England. My Parents Lived a wandering life, for did all the Indians at Mohegan, they Chiefly Depended upon Hunting, Fishing, & Fowling for their Living and had no Connection with the English, excepting to Traffic with them in their small Trifles; and they Strictly maintained and followed their Heathenish Ways, Customs & Religion, though there was Some Preaching among them. Once a Fortnight, in ye Summer Season, a Minister from New London used to come up, and the Indians to attend; not that they regarded the Christian Religion, but they had Blankets given to them every Fall of the Year and for these things they would attend and there was a Sort of School kept, when I was quite young, but I believe there never was one that ever Learnt to read any thing,—and when I was about 10 Years of age there was a man who went about among the Indian Wigwams, and wherever he Could find the Indian Children, would make them read; but the Children Used to take Care to keep out of his way;—and he used to Catch me Some times and make me Say over my Letters; and I believe I learnt Some of them. But this was Soon over too; and all this Time there was not one amongst us, that made a Profession of Christianity.

. . . . .

When I was 16 years of age, we heard a Strange Rumor among the English, that there were Extraordinary Ministers Preaching from place to Place and a Strange

Concern among the White People. This was in the Spring of the Year. But we Saw nothing of these things, till Some Time in the Summer, when Some Ministers began to visit us and Preach the Word of God; and the Common People all Came frequently and exhorted us to the things of God, which it pleased the Lord, as I humbly hope, to Bless and accompany with Divine Influence to the Conviction and Saving Conversion of a Number of us; amongst whom I was one that was Impressed with the things we had heard. These Preachers did not only come to us, but we frequently went to their meetings and Churches. . . . And when I was 17 years of age, I had, as I trust, a Discovery of the way of Salvation through Jesus Christ, and was enabled to put my trust in him alone for Life & Salvation. From this Time the Distress and Burden of my mind was removed, and I found Serenity and Pleasure of Soul, in Serving God.

Native American Christian convert and minister Samson Occom, 1768, "A Short Narrative of My Life," in Mulford, Early American Writings, *pp. 868–869.*

Mr. Wesley says that the first message of the preachers is to the lost sheep of England. Are there none in America? They have strayed from England into the wild woods here and they are running wild after this world. They are drinking their wine in bowls and are jumping and dancing and serving the Devil in the groves and under the green trees. Are these not lost sheep?

Charleston Methodist Thomas Bell, 1768, on the need for Methodist ministers in America, in Hattersley, The Life of John Wesley, *p. 352.*

Here [in Pennsylvania] we mingled like fish at sea, but peaceably. He who would let it be noticed that he was inimical to another because of religion, would be regarded as a fool, although one frankly tells another his mind. A Mennonite preacher is my real neighbor; I do not wish for a better; on the other side stands a large, stone, Catholic church. The present Jesuit father here is a native of Vienna, . . . he confides more in me than in any of the bosom-children. When he encounters a difficulty he comes to me. These men have learned to adjust themselves perfectly to the time. Furthermore, the Lutherans and Reformed have their churches here. . . . On Sundays we meet each other crisscross. That does not signify anything.

Christopher Schultz, a Pennsylvania resident, to Carl Ehrenfried Heintze, 1769, in Schwartz, "A Mixed Multitude," p. 266.

I was frequently under great exercise of mind respecting the dear Americans, and found a willingness to sacrifice everything for their sakes. I was happy enough as to my situation and connexions, and met with the utmost encouragement from the people and from the Preachers, yet I could not be satisfied to continue in Europe. A sense of duty so affected my mind, and my heart was drawn out with such longing desires for the advancement of the Redeemer's kingdom that I was made perfectly willing to forsake my kindred and native land, with all that was the most near and dear to me on earth, that I might spread abrode (abroad) the honours of his glorious Name.

Methodist minister Joseph Pilmore describing why he accepted John Wesley's challenge for Methodist volunteers to preach in the American colonies, 1769, The Journal of Joseph Pilmore, *p. 15.*

On May 15, Pentecost Monday, the day after the founding of the mission [Mission San Fernando Velicata in present-day Baja California], after the two Masses which Father Campa and I celebrated, I had a great consolation. For when the two Masses were over, while I was within the little shelter of my dwelling place, I received notice that pagan Indians were coming and were already near. I praised the Lord and kissed the ground, giving thanks to His divine Majesty that after so many years of longing He had granted me the grace of being among them in their own land. I went forth immediately and found myself in the company of a dozen Indians, all men, all of whom were adults with the exception of two boys, the one about ten years old, the other about sixteen. Then I saw what I could hardly begin to believe when I had read about it or was told about it, namely that they go about entirely naked like Adam in Paradise before the fall. Thus they went about, and thus they presented themselves to us. We treated with them for a long time; and though they saw all of us clothed, they nevertheless showed not the least trace of shame in their manner of nudity. I placed both hands upon the heads of all of them, one after another, in sign of friendship. . . . By means of an interpreter I gave them to understand that a priest was staying there in their midst, the one whom they saw there, and that his name was Father Miguel; that they and the rest of the people of their acquaintance should come to visit him, and that they should spread the word that they had nothing to fear or to suspect, for the father would be a good friend of theirs, Moreover, those soldiers who would remain with the priest would do them much good and inflict no injury. I told them they should not rob the cattle that were grazing in the field. If they should be in want, they should come to the father, and he would always give them what he could. These statements and others, it appears, they understood very well, and all gave signs of approval so that it seemed to me there would be no delay in their being caught in the apostolic and evangelical net.

The Franciscan priest Junípero Serra concerning the founding of the mission San Fernando Velicata, May 1769, in Palóu's Life of Fray Junípero Serra, *pp. 65–66.*

Dear Brother,

Im very much fatigue'd having been to Faneuil Hall to hear, the female Quaker Preacher. 'Twas a very crowded assembly, but perfect order maintain'd. Everything was Novel to me—the approach of a woman into a Desk Dash'd me [so that] I cou'd hardly look up but I soon found She felt none of those perturbations from the Gaze of a Gaping multitude which I pity'd. Shes a Graceful woman & has attain'd a very modest assurance. She spoke clear & Loud Eno' to be heard distinctly into the Entry. Her Language is very Polite & no doubt her mind is Zealously bent on doing good, her Exhortations to seek the Truth & Court that Light which Evidenceth the truth were Lenthy & towards the close workt up to Poesy & produced a tune Not unlike an anthem—her fluency gains the applause She receives for these, nothing like method, & many are her repetitions to my Ear tiresome. I learnt but one thing new which was an Exposition on the Parable of the woman who hid her Leaven in 3 measures of meal till the whole was Leavened this she says presents the Compound of man Soul, Body, and mind in which the spirit of God is hid & shou'd be kept Close, the man being inactive as meal till animated by the spirit as the meal with Leaven. After the Exhortation she rested, rose to Conclude with Prayer which was short & pertinent. She then thanked the Audience for the Decent atendance & reprove'd the Levity she observed in some few faces in a very Polite & kind manner & in the Apostles words Blessed the assembly & dismissed us.

Boston resident Eunice Paine, July 21, 1769, letter to Robert Treat Paine concerning a female Quaker preacher in Boston, in Berkin and Horowitz, Women's Voices, Women's Lives, *pp. 156–157.*

[Simon] said, "Gentlemen, today is my Sabbath, & I do not do business in it; if you will please to call tomorrow, I will wait on you." We observed that the same reasons which prevented his payment of the order on that day would prevent our troubling him the day following [Sun-day]. We apologized for our intruding on his Sabbath, & told him we would wait until Monday. He replied, you are on a journey, & it may be inconvenient to you to wait. He went to call in his neighbor, Dr. Boyd, & took from his Desk a bag, laid it on the table & presented the order to the Dr. The Doctor counted out the money and we gave a recipt. The Jew sat looking on, to see that all was rightly transacted, but said nothing, & thus quieted his conscience against the rebuke of a violation of his Sabbath.

David McClure, a missionary to the Delaware Indians, 1772, concerning a visit to a Jewish merchant on a Saturday, in Sarna, American Judaism, *p. 23.*

My dear fellow traveler into a vast eternity; listen unto me awhile. I am an Indian, known by the name of J—h J—n, a native of this land and of the Mohegan tribe. I am one who am truly sorry for your misfortune, but so it was foreordained by an all-wise God; and so you see it is by woeful experience, but who knows what God has designed by it, perhaps to the good of your immortal soul.

My dear fellow mortal, it is too evident (that there is a God) for us to deny a being of a God, than we say we believe there is a God of allmighty power, who has created all things by the word of his power, and he preserves all things both in heaven and earth; and he over-rules all things by his secret Providence, though we see him not, we do his will, and fulfill his word: Perhaps not designedly, yet he is glorified by us, or will be, either by our eternal salvation, or condemnation. And from this great God's hands no one can deliver; whomsoever he sees fit to save, none can destroy or pluck out of his hands. And we hear likewise, that this great God is the Lord Jesus Christ to pardon, and forgive your soul, and give you his holy Spirit to sanctify, and purify your heart, and make you meet for the inheritance of the saints in light. Pray for true, and genuine conviction, such a conviction as God gives unto his true children; pray for true repentance, that which is unto-life, and faith which purifies the heart; and pray for every grace of a true christian believer in the Lord Jesus Christ: Who knows but God will have mercy upon you, and hear you, and pardon and forgive you at last, for he is a merciful God, delighteth in forgiving iniquities, transgressions and sins, through the merits of his Son Jesus Christ. . . . My spirit mourned within me, when I heard that you were unconcerned about your soul's eternal welfare. But I hope by this time you are of another mind, and things eternal your chiefest concern.

Native American Christian minister Joseph Johnson, March 29, 1772, "Letter from J—h J—n, One of the Mohegan Tribe of Indians, to His Countryman, Moses Paul, Under Sentence of Death, in New-Haven Gaol," in Peyer, The Elders Wrote, *pp. 19–21.*

As neither reason requires, nor religion permits the contrary, every Man living in or out of a state of civil society, has a right peaceably and quietly to worship God according to the dictates of his conscience.—

"Just and true liberty, equal and impartial liberty" in matters spiritual and temporal, is a thing that all Men are clearly entitled to, by the eternal and immutable laws of God and nature, as well as by the law of Nations, & all well grounded municipal laws, which must have their foundation in the former.—

In regard to Religion, mutual toleration in the different professions thereof, is what all good and candid minds in all ages have ever practiced; and both by precept and example inculcated on mankind: And it is now generally agreed among Christians that this spirit of toleration in the fullest extent consistent with the being of civil society "is the chief characteristical mark of the true church" & In so much that Mr. Lock has asserted, and proved beyond the possibility of contradiction on any solid ground, that such toleration ought to be extended to all whose doctrines are not subversive of society. The only Sects which he thinks ought to be, and which by all wise laws are excluded from such toleration, are those who teach Doctrines subversive of the Civil Government under which they live. The Roman Catholics or Papists are excluded by reason of such Doctrines as these "that Princes excommunicated may be deposed, and those they call Heretics may be destroyed without mercy; besides their recognizing the Pope in so absolute a manner, in subversion of Government, by introducing as far as possible into the states, under whose protection they enjoy life, liberty and property, that solecism in politicks, Imperium in imperio leading directly to the worst anarchy and confusion, civil discord, war and blood shed—

The natural liberty of Men by entering into society is abridged or restrained so far only as is necessary for the Great end of Society the best good of the whole.

American Revolutionary figure Samuel Adams, November 20, 1772, in The Writings of Samuel Adams, *vol. 2, pp. 352–353.*

'T was mercy brought me from my *Pagan* land,
Taught my benighted soul to understand

That there's a God, that there's a *Saviour* too:
Once I redemption neither sought nor knew.
Some view our sable race with scornful eye,
"Their colour is a diabolic die."
Remember, *Christians, Negroes,* black as *Cain,*
May be refin'd, and join th' angelic train.

African-American poet Phillis Wheatley, "On Being Brought from Africa to America," 1773, in Gates, The Norton Anthology of African American Literature, *p. 171.*

To my great sorrow, the Society [i.e., the Society of Jesus, or the Jesuits] is abolished; with it must die all that zeal that was founded and raised on it. Labour for our neighbour is a Jesuit's pleasure; destroy the Jesuit, and labour is painful and disagreeable. . . . [W]ith joy I impaired my health and broke my constitution in the care of my flock. It was the Jesuit's call, it was his whole aim and business. The Jesuit is no more; . . . in me, the Jesuit and the Missioner was always combined together; if one falls, the other must of consequence fall with it.

Joseph Mosley, Jesuit priest in Maryland, 1773, after Pope Clement XIV suppressed the Jesuits, quoted in Dolan, The American Catholic Experience, *p. 95.*

I am a Friend to American Liberty; of the final prevalence of which I have not the least doubt, though by what means and in what ways God only knows. But I have perfect Confidence that the future Millions of America

Ezra Stiles was a Congregationalist minister who served as president of Yale College. *(Library of Congress, Prints and Photographs Division LC-USZ62-51840)*

will emancipate themselves from all foreign Oppression. I am a Spectator indeed of Events, but intermeddle not with Politics. We [ministers] have another Department, being called to an Office and Work, which may be successfully pursued (for it has been pursued) under every species of *Civil Tyranny* or *Liberty*. We cannot become the Dupes of Politicians without Alliances, Concessions and Connexions dangerous to evangelical Truth and spiritual Liberty.

Congregational minister and later president of Yale College Ezra Stiles, 1773, in Morgan, The Gentle Puritan, *pp. 262–263.*

Reverend and honored sir,

I have this Day received your obliging kind Epistle, and am greatly satisfied with your Reasons respecting the Negroes, and think highly reasonable what you offer in Vindication of their natural Rights: Those that invade them cannot be insensible that the divine Light is chasing away the thick Darkness which broods over the Land of Africa; and the Chaos which has reign'd so long, is converting into beautiful Order, and [r]eveals more and more clearly, the glorious Dispensation of civil and religious Liberty, which are so inseparably united, that there is little or no Enjoyment of one without the other: Otherwise, perhaps, the Israelites had been less solicitous for their Freedom from Egyptian slavery; I do not say they would have been contented without it, by no means, for in every human Breast, God has implanted a Principle, which we call Love of Freedom; it is impatient of Oppression, and pants for Deliverance; and by the Leave of our modern Egyptians I will assert, that the same Principle lives in us. God grant Deliverance in his own Way and Time, and get him honour upon all those whose Avarice impels them to countenance and help forward the Calamities of their fellow Creatures. This I desire not for their Hurt, but to convince them of the strange Absurdity of their Conduct whose Words and Actions are so diametrically opposite. How well the Cry for Liberty, and the reverse Disposition for the exercise of oppressive Power over others agree,—I humbly think it does not require the Penetration of a Philosopher to determine.—

African-American poet Phyllis Wheatley, letter to Samson Occom, 1774, in Gates, The Norton Anthology of African American Literature, *p. 176.*

CHAPTER SIX

Religion and the New Nation
(1781–1819)

On the eve of America's declaration of independence from Britain, most of the colonies still had established churches. In 1774 nine had specific establishments, and three others had informal variants of ecclesiastical establishments. During the last decades of the 18th century, however, most of these official preferences for particular churches came to an end. Disestablishment did not proceed, though, at the same pace in every colony or state. In particular, the Congregational establishments of New England proved more durable than the Anglican establishments of the southern colonies. Partially, the strength of the Congregational establishments reflected a measure of Puritan success at intertwining the organs of church and state that dated to the earliest days of the New England colonies. More importantly, though, in the revolutionary climate that dominated the second half of the 18th century, Congregationalism was not burdened with the same taint of British connections as Anglicanism (present-day Episcopalianism). American Anglicanism transplanted the Church of England to the New World, and England's church inevitably suffered when the conflict between the colonies and British rule came to dominate colonial attention. It was no surprise, then, that official preferences for the Anglican Church would not survive the revolutionary generation. But the collapse of these preferences did not end the trend toward a greater separation of government and religious institutions. Other state religious establishments crumbled as well, and in 1833 the last surviving establishment—the one planted in Massachusetts more than two centuries earlier—was finally repudiated. In the space of scarcely more than half a century, America had ventured down an uncharted path. Informal connections between government and religion continued to exist, of course. Congressional chaplains, national days of prayer and thanksgiving, and other such examples of civil religion continue to adorn American politics down to the present. But both national and state governments proceeded forward without any formal alliance between civil power and ecclesiastical authority.

Those who insisted that religion would not flourish without government support were abundantly contradicted in the last decades of the 18th century and the first of the 19th. Of course, some religious traditions, those of Jewish and Catholic believers, for example, had not received any government support during the 17th and 18th centuries. Disestablishment, therefore, did not trouble them. If anything, it gradually granted these traditions a measure of religious liberty as government retreated from its former role of enforcing religious orthodoxy. Other traditions, especially those that had resisted the revivalistic enthusiasms of the 18th century, did indeed find themselves often struggling to adapt to existence without official government favors. But a variety of evangelical groups flourished. Emphasizing voluntary rather than government support of religion, groups such as Baptists, Methodists, and Presbyterians prospered in the new environment.

No sooner had "We the people" created a new nation by ratification of the U.S. Constitution than the infant nation experienced a new outburst of revivalism stretching roughly from 1790 to 1820 and referred to as the Second Great Awakening. This period also saw the rapid spread of Christianity among African Americans, both slave and free, especially Baptists and Methodists. Blacks, though, not content to assume the subordinate positions they were often assigned in Protestant churches, responded by establishing their own churches and denominations. Finally, American Indians, some of whom shared the devastation of siding with the British during the Revolutionary War and all of whom endured the displacements occasioned by steady encroachments from white settlers, experienced religious revitalizations of their own during the early years of the new republic.

Church and State in Virginia

Once ratified in 1791, the Constitution's First Amendment prohibited Congress from enacting laws "respecting an establishment of religion or prohibiting the free exercise thereof." This prohibition, however, did not apply to states. Issues of religious liberty and disestablishment at the state and local levels were governed by provisions in state constitutions adopted in the wake of the Declaration of Independence and by other state laws. These various legal provisions did not uniformly repudiate the religious establishments that were common during the colonial period. Gradually, though, official support for religion at the state and local levels collapsed during the late 18th and early 19th centuries. The most famous case of disestablishment occurred in Virginia, just prior to the ratification of the U.S. Constitution. Because the Virginia experience involved three luminaries of early American history—Thomas Jefferson, James Madison, and Patrick Henry—it has always commanded a great deal of attention from historians. Moreover, because Madison, in particular, played a prominent role in the early history of the U.S. Constitution, the events that occurred in Virginia just a few years before the ratification of the Constitution and the Bill of Rights have been seen by some observers as an important source for understanding the meaning of federal constitutional provisions relating to religion. The U.S. Supreme Court, in particular, at least during the middle decades of the 20th century, treated Jefferson as essentially an authoritative interpreter of the First Amendment's religion clauses. The Court was especially enamored of Jefferson's metaphor of the "wall of separation between church and state" that he had penned while he was president but whose idea certainly owed a significant debt to his earlier experiences in revolutionary Virginia.

During most of the colonial period, the Church of England was established by law in Virginia, but the revolutionary generation found this establishment untenable. The fear that England would appoint an American bishop for the Anglican Church was a prominent source of revolutionary dissatisfaction with British rule. Moreover, the growth of evangelical Protestant groups such as Baptists and Presbyterians in Virginia after the Great Awakening also contributed to a climate increasingly hostile to Virginia's Anglican establishment. Soon after Virginia joined the other American colonies in declaring itself independent of British rule, the Virginia legislature first suspended and then abolished state tax support for the Anglican Church. But certain Virginia leaders such as Patrick Henry feared that the absence of state support for religion would deprive the state of an important source for the inculcation of morality, itself viewed as crucial to the success of democracy. Henry and others believed that republican government could not be sustained without a virtuous citizenry. Democracy required that citizens be prepared to labor for the public good and not simply scramble for their own narrow, private interests. Only virtue could produce this kind of self-sacrifice, and leaders such as Henry concluded that virtue itself required the support of religious belief and practice. He thus feared that the end of Virginia's official Anglican establishment would produce a vacuum in which religious impulses—and consequently civic virtue—would suffer decline. To combat this end, he championed legislation in Virginia that would provide support for Christian teachers. This legislation contemplated levying a tax in support of Christian ministers but generally allowing citizens to designate the Christian denomination of their choice to receive their taxes.

Patrick Henry and other supporters of this scheme for supporting Christian ministers found themselves opposed by one of American history's most curious and most significant alliances. In the years after the Great Awakening, Virginia Baptists and Presbyterians had flourished. They did so without official support from Virginia's colonial government, relying instead on voluntary contributions from their members. Presbyterians at least were acquainted with the benefits of official government support, since Presbyterianism was the established church of Scotland. But in America Presbyterians had learned to adapt themselves to voluntary support alone. Baptists, however, never officially supported in colonial America or elsewhere, had a strong tradition of reliance on religious voluntarism rather than official government patronage. They also had a strong memory of the various persecutions and harassments that had ensued from alliances between church and state. Consequently, when Henry and others proposed a new scheme of taxes to support Christian teachers, Baptists immediately opposed the move. Presbyterians were initially favorable to the tax proposal, but they eventually joined Baptists in denouncing the scheme. In their opposition to the bill to support Christian teachers, Baptists and Presbyterians found themselves allied with men such as Thomas Jefferson and James Madison, even though neither of these political leaders shared the religious convictions of the evangelical Protestants. Madison at least seems to have had some sympathy for evangelical believers, though he was not himself one. In a letter to a friend written in 1774, Madison displayed his opposition to official Anglican persecution of religious dissenters.

> That diabolical Hell conceived principle of persecution rages among some and to their eternal Infamy the Clergy can furnish their quota of Imps for such business. This vexes me the most of any thing whatever. There are at this [time?] in the adjacent County not less that 5 or 6 well meaning men in close Gaol for publishing their religious Sentiments which in the main are very orthodox. I have neither patience to hear talk or think any thing relative to this matter, for I have squabbled and scolded abused and ridiculed so long about it, [to so lit]tle purposes that I am without common patience. So I [leave you] to pity me and pray for Liberty of Conscience [to revive among us.].[1]

Jefferson shared Madison's enmity against the Anglican establishment, though not his sympathy for the evangelicals. His religious beliefs were, if anything, even more distant from the orthodox Christianity of either the Baptists or the Presbyterians. He believed that Jesus was a splendid teacher but not God, in later years going so far as to produce an edited version of the New Testament gospels that removed all the miraculous events and retained only Jesus' moral teachings.

In their own way, though, Jefferson, Madison, and Virginia's Protestant dissenters all agreed that the proposal to support Christian teachers with tax revenues offended the principle of religious liberty. As early as 1779 Jefferson drafted proposed legislation, the Bill for Establishing Religious Freedom, that would have prohibited compelled support for religion. The Virginia legislature refused to enact the bill, however. After the Revolutionary War ended in 1783, the issue of tax support for religion returned to the forefront of Virginia's politics. It was the following year that Patrick Henry championed the proposal to provide tax support to Christian teachers. For a time the proposed law seemed to enjoy substantial support, including from Presbyterians in the state. But opposition emerged in 1785, with some 90 petitions being submitted to the Virginia legislature, one of which included a protest against the proposed bill written by James Madison titled "Memorial and Remonstrance." Madison's "Memorial" insisted that religion was an "unalienable right" that must be left to "the conviction and conscience of every man."[2] Although history remembers Madison's petition best, the petitions drawing the most signatures were those circulated among evangelicals such as the Virginia Baptists. These petitions typically began by declaring that the proposed bill for supporting Christian teachers was "contrary to the spirit of the Gospel and the Bill of Rights."[3] Presbyterians in the state eventually joined the opposition against the bill. Ultimately, these protests changed the political tide and resulted in Jefferson's Bill for Establishing Religious Liberty being enacted by the Virginia legislature in 1786. This law denied that government had any role in taxing citizens to support religion. "[T]o compel a man to furnish contributions of money for the propagation of opinions which he disbelieves and abhors," the law insisted, "is sinful and tyrannical; . . . even the forcing him to support this or that teacher of his own religious persuasion, is depriving him of the comfortable liberty of giving his contributions to the particular pastor whose morals he would make his pattern."[4] With the passage of Jefferson's bill, Virginia decisively repudiated the venerable axiom that civil and social stability required financial support of religion by government. Over the years that immediately followed, the nation founded upon the words of the Constitution had to wrestle with similar issues.

The Godless Constitution and American Civil Religion

Of the notable features of the U.S. Constitution, drafted in 1787 and ratified the following year, one of the most significant was its godlessness. America's founding document did not rail against God, of course, or specifically exempt citizens of the new nation from the obligations of piety. It was simply silent about the Almighty, and this fact alone made the Constitution unusual for its day. The revolutionary generation had customarily adorned its formative political documents with references to God. Thomas Jefferson, for example, referred in the Declaration of Independence to "the separate & equal station to which the laws of nature and of nature's God entitle." Following this political declaration, one after another of the original American colonies adopted constitutions to reflect their new identify as states, and these state constitutions invariably referred to God in some way, often in connection with guarantees of religious liberty. The Virginia constitution of 1776, for example, asserted that religion was "the duty which we owe to our Creator," and New Jersey's constitution of the same year spoke comparably of the "inestimable privilege of worshiping Almighty God."[5] Even the Constitution's immediate predecessor, the Articles of Confederation, paid homage to "the Great Governor of the World."[6] But when Americans, acting as We the People in the Constitution's preamble, invented the United States of America, they chose not to clothe their act of political creation in the language of faith. The framers of the Constitution were certainly not ignorant of this language, since they routinely referred to God in other contexts. But in the Constitution itself, they breathed not a syllable of piety. This fact did not go unnoticed by some citizens, who complained bitterly about the absence of any reference to God in the Constitution. For nearly a century afterward, opponents of the Constitution's godlessness would attempt to correct this defect by amending the document to provide some testimony to faith. But they never succeeded in this endeavor.

Even more vigorous than complaints about the Constitution's secularism, however, were objections that the Constitution lacked a Bill of Rights—in particular, an explicit protection of religious liberty. The only reference to religion in the original Constitution was the prohibition in Article VI of any religious test as a qualification for public office. This prohibition itself was remarkable, since religious qualifications for public office were common among the state constitutions of the time. But the federal Constitution explicitly repudiated religious test oaths, as they are referred to. For men such as James Madison, himself a devoted friend of religious liberty, this was all the protection religion needed. Madison initially believed that the structural limitations placed on the federal government in the Constitution made a Bill of Rights in general and a protection of religious freedom in particular unnecessary. He argued that the presence of such provisions in state constitutions had not prevented state governments from trampling on these "parchment barriers." Moreover, he worried that the very enumeration of particular rights in the Constitution would suggest that the federal government had more power than the Constitution intended. But Madison soon found himself in a minority on this issue. Americans wanted the protections of fundamental liberties from federal encroachment in writing. Seven states ratified the Constitution but called at the same time for the Constitution to be amended to include a Bill of Rights. Consequently, after the Constitution was ratified and Congress convened, the newly elected representatives moved quickly to correct the defect identified by their fellow citizens. On September 25, 1789, Congress adopted proposed amendments, including the First Amendment, which barred all federal laws "respecting an establishment of religion or prohibiting the free exercise thereof." The states promptly ratified the amendments that make up the Bill of Rights.

Neither the Constitution's godlessness, however, nor its eventual prohibition against laws "respecting an establishment of religion" or those "prohibiting the free exercise thereof" portended a purely secular political process, though some observers claim it should have. The Almighty may have escaped mention in the text of the Constitution but not in the ordinary politics of the time. George Washington adopted the practice, unvaried by subsequent U.S. presidents, of taking the oath of the presidential office with his hand on a Bible, even though the Constitution makes no reference to this added element of pious solemnity. And Washington was not alone in adorning political practice with piety. On September 26, 1789, the day after Congress adopted the final version of the proposed First Amendment, the House and Senate appointed a joint committee to request that the President

> recommend to the people of the United States a day of thanksgiving and prayer, to be observed by acknowledging with grateful hearts the many signal favors of Almighty God, especially by affording them an opportunity peacefully to establish a constitution of government for their safety and happiness.[7]

President Washington agreed to this request and set aside November 26, 1789, as a day of national thanksgiving. Thereafter, both the House and the Senate moved to appoint chaplains for their respective chambers. These practices have flowed down to the present, though a few presidents, such as Thomas Jefferson, refused to follow Washington's example in declaring national days of thanksgiving and prayer. Jefferson insisted that the Constitution had erected a "wall of separation between church and state."[8] But during the years preceding and immediately following ratification of the Constitution and its First Amendment, Jefferson had few allies on this point. The Constitution had chosen not to speak of God, but this choice did not constrain politicians and citizens during the early republic from adorning the public affairs of the new nation with a vibrant civil religion.

African-American Christianity

One important legacy of the Great Awakening was the strong foothold gained by evangelical Christianity among African Americans. Through the efforts of Baptist and Methodist itinerant preachers, especially, large numbers of African Americans were converted to Christianity during and after the Great Awakening. But the inexorable and corrupting social logic of slavery insinuated itself into Christian communities, frequently causing blacks to be admitted to church fellowship on the condition that they occupy inferior stations. Unpersuaded by the social logic that subordinated them, many black Christians began to form their own communities in the last decades of the 18th century.

Baptist reverence for the relative autonomy of individual congregations made this denomination hospitable to the formation of separate African-American churches. In 1788, for example, former slave Andrew Bryan led in establishing the First African Baptist Church of Savannah, Georgia. Though Andrew Bryan and his brother Sampson were arrested and whipped for holding illegal meetings, they refused to abandon the meetings and were eventually granted permission to conduct services during daylight hours.[9] Some 50 years after Bryan established the church, his nephew Andrew Marshall pastored a congregation that had grown to more than 2,400 members.[10] By that time Savannah also boasted a Second African and a Third African church.

Separate African-American congregations formed in other religious traditions as well. In the latter part of the 1780s, for example, a number of African Americans, including lay preachers Richard Allen and Absalom Jones, worshiped at St. George's Methodist Church in Philadelphia. But segregation made its presence felt even in this racially mixed congregation, as white members of the church insisted that blacks occupy separate and inferior seats assigned to them in the back of the balcony. In 1787 a church official went so far as to interrupt blacks during prayer to insist that they move to their newly assigned seating at the rear of the balcony. This indignity and the general lack of welcome visited on blacks who attended St. George's Church inspired Richard Allen, Absalom Jones, and others to walk out of the church and begin meeting together on their own that year. Allen and Jones soon worked together to establish the Free African Society, a benevolent association for African Americans. Though united in their exodus from St. George's, Allen and Jones eventually followed different spiritual visions and led in the formation of two separate African-American congregations. Absalom Jones, under the auspices of the Free African Society, led one group of blacks who built a church in Philadelphia formally dedicated as the St. Thomas African Episcopal Church on July 17, 1794. There Jones was ordained the first African-American Episcopal deacon the following year and a priest in 1802. Meanwhile, by 1794 Allen had broken away from the Free African Society and led a group that was able to acquire a building formerly used as a blacksmith shop. On June 29 of that year, the group organized the Bethel African Episcopal Church of Philadelphia in this building. Allen served as the church's informal leader until 1799, when he was ordained by Methodist bishop Francis Asbury the first African-American deacon in the Methodist Episcopal Church.

Richard Allen helped to found and served as first bishop of the African Methodist Episcopal Church. *(Library of Congress, Prints and Photographs Division LC-USZ62-15059)*

In the early years after the formation of the Bethel church, Richard Allen tried to maintain ties with St. George's Methodist Church. But that church's attempts to control affairs at Bethel ultimately inspired Allen to contemplate the formation of an association of African-American churches. In 1816 he invited a number of other African-American churches to send delegates to a meeting intended to establish a new denomination. As a result, the African Methodist Episcopal Church, or the AME Church, was formed in April 1816. Richard Allen was ordained first as an elder in the new denomination and then, on April 11, 1816, the first bishop of the AME Church. Other African-American Protestant denominations followed in the wake of the AME, perhaps most significantly the National Baptist Association organized toward the end of the 19th century.

Spiritual Revitalization among American Indians

In the wake of the Revolutionary War, the American states organized themselves first under the Articles of Confederation and still later under the Constitution, ratified in 1789. But the same war that yielded political independence for the American states produced a more bitter legacy for the once vigorous confederacy of Iroquois nations. Most of these had allied themselves with the British during the Revolutionary War and reaped the consequences of this fateful alliance. The defeat of war joined itself with loss of ever more land and the ravages of disease and alcoholism, leaving the Iroquois at a low cultural moment. As the 18th century drew to a close, however, a Seneca shaman named Handsome Lake or Ganeodiyo, the half-brother of Iroquois leader Cornplanter, experienced a series of visions that ultimately prompted a temporary revitalization of Iroquois belief and practice. Partially influenced by Quaker missionaries, Handsome Lake's message emphasized the importance of confessing the sins he claimed had humbled the Iroquois—chiefly alcoholism, witchcraft, and the failure to practice traditional religious ceremonies. Although he traced these sins to European influences, Handsome Lake insisted that his people needed to repent of their participation in these evils and revive their traditional religious practices. A tendency to wield promiscuous accusations of witchcraft, however, ultimately eroded Handsome Lake's immediate influence. Nevertheless, his teachings became the basis for what came to be known as the Handsome Lake Code or Longhouse Religion, which has been passed down among some American Indians to the present.

Farther to the west a comparable revitalization of traditional Indian religious practice occurred in the early years of the 19th century under the leadership of Tenskwatawa, known as the Shawnee Prophet, the brother of Shawnee leader Tecumseh. Prior to 1805 Tenskwatawa had been an alcoholic and a would-be medicine man who failed to gain the respect of his people. He was nicknamed the Rattle or Noisemaker. But in that year he experienced the first of a series of visions in which he saw Shawnee who obtained heaven, on the one hand, and those whose wicked deeds consigned them to a hell-like lodge in which they suffered torment. After this vision he took the name Tenskwatawa, which means *open door*. On the basis of subsequent visions, Tenskwatawa taught that the Shawnee and other American Indians had been made by the Creator of Life but that whites had been created by a great serpent. Indians, he insisted, had to distance themselves from whites, descendants of this primordial evil. Hearing of

Tenskwatawa's claims of religious authority, Indiana's governor, William Henry Harrison, scoffed. "If he really is a prophet," Harrison demanded, "ask of him to cause the sun to stand still—the moon to alter its course—the rivers to cease to flow—or the dead to rise from their graves. If he does these things, you may then believe that he has been sent from God!"[11] Subsequently, in 1806 Tenskwatawa was able to use advance warning of an eclipse to predict the occurrence of a "black sun," and this successful prediction enhanced his religious authority among the Shawnee. Eventually, Tenskwatawa and his brother Tecumseh settled in Prophetstown, Indiana, where Tecumseh tried to use his brother's influence to unite a variety of Indian tribes. Fearful of this effort, Indiana's governor attacked Prophetstown with a military force. In spite of Tenskwatawa's assurance to his followers that the weapons of the white men would not harm them, the inhabitants of Prophetstown were badly defeated, causing a sharp decline in Tenskwatawa's subsequent religious influence.

Tenskwatawa, the Shawnee prophet, led a revitalization of American Indian religion during the early part of the 19th century. *(Library of Congress, Prints and Photographs Division LC-USZ62-23787)*

The Second Great Awakening

By the time of the American Revolution, the spiritual fervor of the Great Awakening had long since subsided. To some observers, at least, America had inaugurated a republic of reason in which religious faith, especially of the evangelical variety, could be expected to suffer steady and irrevocable decline. But within a decade of the new nation's birth, evangelical piety proved itself to be very much alive. Beginning in the late 1790s new murmurs of spiritual awakening accompanied the preaching of Presbyterian minister James McGready in Kentucky. Then in August of 1801, revival arrived in earnest at a camp meeting held at Cane Ridge, near Lexington, Kentucky. An interdenominational group of preachers, including Barton Warren Stone, preached for days to crowds estimated at between 10,000 and 25,000. Preachers occupied various stands scattered around the campground, from which they engaged smaller crowds with sermons that produced multitudes of emotionally charged conversions. Ministers preached against the sinfulness of their listeners but then presented the news of Christ's gracious salvation. Guilt and initial despair gave way to hope and then assurance.

The Cane Ridge Revival exemplified an important difference between the Great Awakening and the Second Great Awakening. The awakening of the 1730s and 1740s occurred against the backdrop of a still dominant Calvinistic theology. Salvation was the gracious gift of a sovereign God to the elect. The elect neither merited nor could do anything to acquire this salvation. Revival, the midwife of salvation, could neither be orchestrated nor predicted—only longed for and awaited. But by the time of the revivals of the Second Great Awakening, Protestant Christianity in America had drifted considerably closer to the Arminian theology that would become increasingly dominant during the 19th century. While still acknowledging the sinfulness of humankind, the implicit theology of the Second Great Awakening insisted that sinners had the capacity to turn in repentance toward God and to receive the gracious gift of salvation he offered through Christ. If Arminianism subtly altered the perspective of revival listeners, it also reshaped the perspective of preachers. Revival, even if it could not quite be orchestrated, could nevertheless be planned for and anticipated. Camp meetings and other forms of revivalism adhered to quite definite forms, including protracted periods of emotional preaching in contexts where listeners were removed from the everyday routines of their lives. Revivals need no longer be waited for—they could be scheduled.

Methodism, especially, flourished in the new spiritual climate. Since the Arminian John Wesley turned down a separate theological avenue from his one-time ally, Anglican and Calvinistic minister George Whitefield, Methodism had emphasized the ability of individuals to turn toward God and live holy lives. In fact, although early camp meetings such as the one held at Cane Ridge joined Presbyterian, Baptist, and Methodist ministers, this form of revivalism soon came to be practiced predominantly by Methodists. Presbyterianism, theologically sympathetic with the older revivalism of Calvinists George Whitefield and Jonathan Edwards, received the revival spirit with some ambivalence. Barton Warren Stone was a case in point. Originally ordained a Presbyterian minister by the Orange presbytery of North Carolina in 1796, Stone soon relocated to Cane Ridge, Kentucky, where he was ordained by the Transylvania presbytery. Stone's revivalism, especially his vigorous participation in the Cane Ridge Revival, ultimately led to his expulsion from the Transylvania presbytery in 1803. He and other like-minded ministers responded by organizing their own Springfield presbytery the following year. But even this move was only a way-station in a journey that eventually led Stone out of Presbyterianism altogether. Within a year of organizing the new presbytery, Stone and his ministerial associates dissolved it, producing in this act "The Last Will and Testament of the Springfield Presbytery," in which they declared that they would be guided henceforth by the Bible alone. Subsequently, the congregations allied with Stone referred to themselves simply as "Christian," and they eventually joined with congregations led by Alexander Campbell to form the Disciples of Christ. Barton Stone's migration away from Presbyterianism marks the beginning of what came to be known as the Restorationist movement within American Protestantism. The Restorationist impulse sought to leap past the various creeds of Christendom to rediscover primitive Christianity, an impulse that would repeatedly resurface in the history of American religion in such various forms as Mormonism and 20th-century fundamentalism.

Chronicle of Events

1780

- By this decade, the black preachers Gowan Pamphlet and Moses organize an independent African Baptist church in Williamsburg, Virginia.
- Richard Allen, formerly a slave, is licensed as a Methodist preacher. He will later lead in establishing the African Methodist Episcopal church.

1781

- Shaker founder Ann Lee and some of her followers begin a 28-month missionary tour through Massachusetts and Connecticut.
- *March 4:* Jewish lay leader Rebecca Gratz is born in Lancaster, Pennsylvania.

1782

- King's Chapel, an Episcopalian church in Boston, invites James Freeman, recently graduated from Harvard, to become its reader. Under his leadership, the church will become a Unitarian congregation.

1783

- A group of American Anglican ministers appoint Samuel Seabury to seek ordination as an Anglican bishop. The Church of England refuses to grant this ordination because Seabury is not in a position to swear the traditional oath of fealty to the British Crown.
- *September 3:* The signing of the Treaty of Paris officially ends the Revolutionary War.

1784

- Samuel Seabury is consecrated bishop of Connecticut by Scottish bishops, referred to as nonjuring bishops because their predecessors had refused to take the oath of allegiance to William and Mary after already having sworn allegiance to King James II.
- At the "Christmas Conference" in Baltimore, Maryland, the Methodist Episcopal Church is organized, and Francis Asbury and Thomas Coke become its first superintendents.
- A liturgy for American Methodists is published, titled the *Sunday Services of the Methodists in North American with Other Occasional Services,* based on the Anglican Book of Common Prayer.
- John Carroll becomes the first Catholic to publish a book in the United States, *Address to the Roman Catholics of the United States of America.* Carroll is also appointed vicar apostolic for America.
- Patrick Henry introduces into the Virginia legislature a proposal to tax citizens for the support of the church of their choice.
- Charles Chauncy, minister of Boston's First Church, publishes a defense of universal salvation titled *The Mystery Hid from Ages and Generations, Made Manifest by the Gospel-Revelation.*

1785

- After revising the Book of Common Prayer to eliminate Trinitarian references, King's Chapel in Boston becomes the first Unitarian congregation in America.
- James Madison composes the "Memorial and Remonstrance," a petition against a proposed bill in Virginia that would have provided tax support for Christian teachers. The "Memorial and Remonstrance" is an important argument for religious liberty and disestablishment in America.
- The first Shaker community is formally "ordered" in New Lebanon, New York.
- *September 1:* Peter Cartwright, future Methodist minister, is born in Amherst County, Virginia.

1786

- The Virginia legislature enacts the Bill for Establishing Religious Liberty, drafted by Thomas Jefferson.

1787

- Richard Allen, a black Methodist minister, begins to meet with other blacks separately after St. George's Methodist Church in Philadelphia refuses to welcome growing numbers of blacks in the church. Together with Absalom Jones, he also founds the Free African Society, a benevolent organization for African Americans.
- At New Lebanon, New York, Shakers establish the first of numerous communal villages.
- *May 14:* The Constitutional Convention begins meeting in Philadelphia. A few weeks after the opening of the convention, Benjamin Franklin suggests that each day's session begin with prayer. The delegates, however, adjourn for the day without voting on this proposal.
- *September 17:* Delegates at the Constitutional Convention sign a final draft of the proposed Constitution. Article six contains a prohibition against religious tests for public office, but the document does not otherwise contain an explicit guarantee of religious liberty or a prohibition against a national church.

Alexander Campbell cofounded the Disciples of Christ with his father. *(Library of Congress, Prints and Photographs Division LC-USZC4-3367)*

- *September 28:* Congress approves the Constitution and sends it to the states for ratification.

1788

- The Constitution is ratified by the necessary nine states. Article six prohibits the imposition of a religious test "as a qualification to any office or public trust under the United States." The lack of any other explicit protection for religious freedom and other civil liberties in the original Constitution will inspire protests and the ultimate ratification of the Bill of Rights in 1791.
- Former slave Andrew Bryan helps to organize the First African Baptist Church of Savannah, Georgia.
- *September 12:* Alexander Campbell, founder of the Disciples of Christ, is born in County Antrim, Ireland.

1789

- The U.S. Constitution takes effect.
- The first general assembly of Presbyterians in the United States is held in Philadelphia.
- The Church of England in America is formally reorganized in Philadelphia as the Protestant Episcopal Church.

- Georgetown University, the oldest Catholic university in America, is founded in Maryland.
- *September 25:* The first Congress proposes the Bill of Rights for ratification by the states as amendments to the U.S. Constitution. When ratified, the First Amendment will bar federal laws "respecting an establishment of religion or prohibiting the free exercise thereof."
- *September 26:* The first Congress appoints a committee to request that President George Washington declare a national day of thanksgiving and prayer.
- *November 6:* John Carroll is appointed the first Roman Catholic bishop in the United States.
- *November 26:* President George Washington accepts the recommendation of Congress and will appoint this the first day of thanksgiving and prayer for the new nation.

1791

- Archibald Alexander is licensed as a Presbyterian minister.
- The Bill of Rights, including the religion clauses of the First Amendment prohibiting abridgements of the free exercise of religion and laws "respecting an establishment of religion," is ratified.
- St. Mary's Seminary and University in Baltimore is established as the first Catholic seminary in the United States.
- *January 1:* The Free African Society begins holding religious services that lead to the formation of the African Episcopal Church of St. Thomas, the first black church in Philadelphia.

1792

- *August 29:* Revivalist Charles Grandison Finney is born in Warren, Connecticut.

1794

- Joseph Priestley, British Unitarian minister and scientist, emigrates to the United States, settling in Pennsylvania.
- *June 29:* Methodist bishop Francis Asbury dedicates the Bethel African Methodist Episcopal Church of Philadelphia, which meets in a converted blacksmith shop purchased by Richard Allen and other African-American Methodists in Philadelphia.
- *July 17:* Absalom Jones and other members of the Free African Society complete construction on the building where St. Thomas African Episcopal Church is dedicated.

1795

- Timothy Dwight becomes president of Yale College.
- Absalom Jones is ordained the first African-American Episcopal deacon.

1796

- The Church of England recognizes and validates Samuel Seabury's previous ordination as an Anglican bishop.
- Presbyterians, Baptists, and Dutch Reformed join to establish the New York Missionary Society with the aim of promoting missions among American Indians.

1797

- Isabella Baumfree, later known as Sojourner Truth, is born a slave in Ulster County, New York.

1798

- Lyman Beecher is licensed to preach as a Congregationalist minister.
- Congregationalists organize the Missionary Society of Connecticut to encourage the establishment of churches on the frontier.

1799

- Richard Allen is ordained the first African-American deacon of the Methodist Episcopal Church.
- Handsome Lake (Ganeodiyo) has the first of a series of religious visions that will eventually make him a Seneca prophet and founder of the Longhouse Religion among Native Americans.

1800

- The first known camp meeting to be held in the United States is conducted in Kentucky.

1801

- Nathan Bangs is licensed as an itinerant Methodist preacher.
- Presbyterian and Congregationalist churches adopt the Plan of Union, by which they agree to participate in joint missionary activities in the western United States.
- *June 1:* Brigham Young, future Mormon leader, is born.
- *August:* Barton Warren Stone and other ministers hold revival services in Cane Ridge, Kentucky, attended by an estimated 10,000 to 25,000 people. This event is frequently thought to mark the beginning of the Second Great Awakening.

1802

- The first Ashkenazic synagogue in North America, Rodeph Shalom, is established in Philadelphia.
- The Massachusetts Baptist Domestic Missionary Society is established.
- *January 1:* Thomas Jefferson suggests in a letter to the Danbury Baptist Association that the U.S. Constitution has erected "a wall of separation" between church and state.
- *April 14:* Horace Bushnell, sometimes called the father of American religious liberalism, is born in Bantam, Connecticut.
- *September 21:* Absalom Jones is ordained an Episcopal priest.

1803

- Presbyterian revivalist Barton Warren Stone is expelled from the Transylvania presbytery. He and other like-minded ministers form the Springfield presbytery.
- In a convention held in Winchester, N.H., Universalists adopt a confession of faith.
- The United States consummates the Louisiana Purchase from France, essentially doubling the size of the territory controlled by the new nation.
- *September 16:* Catholic apologist Orestes Augustus Brownson is born in Stockbridge, Vermont.

1804

- Barton Warren Stone and other organizers of the Springfield presbytery declare it dissolved in "The Last Will and Testament of the Springfield Presbytery." They thus withdraw from the Presbyterian Church and begin to establish new congregations whose members refer to themselves simply as Christians. These congregations subsequently merge with the Disciples of Christ, led by Alexander Campbell.
- The federal act creating the Louisiana Territory includes a protection of religious liberty.
- Henry Ware, Sr. is appointed Hollis Professor of Divinity at Harvard College, and his appointment is taken to represent a decisive victory for liberal Congregationalists.
- While serving as president of the United States, Thomas Jefferson begins preparing a personal version of the New Testament gospels in which he eliminates references to miracles while retaining Jesus' ethical teachings. He will complete the project in 1819.

1805

- Utopian leader George Rapp immigrates with his followers from Germany. They establish the town of

Harmony near Pittsburgh, Pennsylvania, and organize themselves into the Harmony Society.

- Joseph Smith, Jr., founder of the Church of Jesus Christ of Latter-day Saints (the Mormon Church) is born.
- Tenskwatawa, also known as Lalethika or the Shawnee Prophet, experiences the first of a series of visions that will make him a Native American religious leader.
- Construction is completed on the Mother Bethel African Methodist Episcopal Church in Philadelphia, which had originally met in a renovated blacksmith shop in Philadelphia.
- Henry Ware, known for his theological liberalism, becomes professor of divinity at Harvard, prompting theological conservatives to establish Andover Theological Seminary three years later.
- Jedidiah Morse begins publishing a magazine titled the *Panoplist* as a vehicle for combating the spread of liberal theology among Congregationalists.
- Universalist minister Hosea Ballou publishes *A Treatise on the Atonement,* which denies that Christ's death accomplished a substitutionary atonement on behalf of humanity.
- *August 8:* Thomas Paul leads in establishing the First African Baptist Church in Boston.

1806

- Tenskwatawa obtains advance warning of an eclipse and is able to use his knowledge to predict a "black sun," thus increasing his respect among the Shawnee.
- Williams College student Samuel J. Mills and four other fellow students meet for prayer for foreign missions. When rain forces the students to take refuge by the side of a hay stack, the event will subsequently become known as the Haystack Prayer Meeting.
- *January 12:* English evangelist Dorothy Ripley becomes the first woman to speak before the U.S. House of Representatives.
- *December 6:* The African Meeting House, built by black Baptists in Boston, is dedicated. It is the oldest black church still standing.

1807

- John Gloucester helps organize the First African Presbyterian Church in Philadelphia, the first African-American Presbyterian church in the United States.
- *December 18:* Phoebe Worrall Palmer, Holiness lay preacher, is born in New York City.

1808

- William McKendree becomes the first American-born bishop of the Methodist Episcopal Church.
- Andover Seminary is founded by conservative Congregationalists after theological liberals gain control of Harvard College.
- Thomas Paul assists in organizing the Abyssinian Baptist Church in New York, and Josiah Bishop is called to be its minister.

1809

- The Sisters of Charity of St. Joseph, the first Catholic women's order in the United States, is founded by Elizabeth Seton in Maryland.

1810

- The first foreign missions society in the United States, the American Board of Commissioners for Foreign Missions, is established after a number of students at Andover Theological Seminary commit themselves to foreign missionary service.
- *February 4:* Finis Ewing, Samuel King, and Samuel McAdow organize the Cumberland presbytery as an independent presbytery, thus becoming the first Cumberland Presbyterians.

1811

- After Tenskwatawa and his brother Tecumseh move to Prophetstown in Indiana, Tecumseh tries to leverage his brother's spiritual leadership to unite various American Indian tribes against whites. William Henry Harrison, the governor of the Indiana Territory, leads a military force against Prophetstown. Although Tenskwatawa assures his followers that they will be immune to the weapons of the white soldiers, Harrison and his force destroy Prophetstown and kill many of the Indians there.

1812

- Princeton Theological Seminary is founded as a school for Presbyterian ministers.
- Archibald Alexander becomes the first professor of the newly established Princeton Theological Seminary.
- Adoniram Judson is ordained a Congregationalist missionary, but en route to China he rejects the practice of infant baptism, becomes a Baptist, and is subsequently supported by the newly formed Baptist Board of Foreign Missions.

This engraving, originally published in 1814, pictures Christ Church in Philadelphia, Pennsylvania. *(Library of Congress, Prints and Photographs Division LC-USZ62-29187)*

1813

• *June 24:* Henry Ward Beecher is born in Litchfield, Connecticut.

1814

• The New England Tract Society is established.
• *August 23:* James Roosevelt Bayley, future archbishop of Baltimore, is born in New York City.

1815

• Jewish lay leader Rebecca Gratz is instrumental in founding the Philadelphia Orphan Asylum.
• Lott Carey and others organize the Richmond African Baptist Missionary Society.
• Peter Spencer and others found the Union Church of Africans in Wilmington, Delaware.
• The publication of an extract from the *Memoirs of Theophilus Lindsey* includes letters written by New England Unitarians to Lindsey and brings to public light the significant defections from orthodoxy in New England.
• Smohalla, Native American founder of the Dreamer Religion, is born around this time near Walla Walla, Washington.
• Louis William DuBourg is appointed Catholic bishop of Louisiana and the Floridas.

1816

• Richard Allen and others form the African Methodist Episcopal Church, and Allen is ordained the denomination's first bishop.
• The American Bible Society is formed.
• George Bourne, an immigrant from England who became a Presbyterian minister in Virginia in 1814, publishes *The Book and Slavery Irreconcilable;* its condemnation of slavery will be deeply resented in the South.
• The American Colonization Society is founded to repatriate ex-slaves to Africa.

1817

• The Sunday and Adult School Union of Philadelphia is founded (succeeded by the American Sunday School Union, founded in 1824).

1818

• Connecticut abandons its establishment of the Congregationalist church.
• The Presbyterian general assembly condemns slavery and calls for gradual emancipation of all slaves. However, the assembly also strips George Bourne, who published *The Book and Slavery Irreconcilable,* of his status as a Presbyterian minister.
• *June 27:* James Lloyd Breck, Episcopal missionary to the western frontier of the United States, is born in Philadelphia County, Pennsylvania.

1819

• Nathan Bangs and others form the Methodist Missionary Society.
• Jewish lay leader Rebecca Gratz is instrumental in founding the Female Hebrew Benevolent Society in Philadelphia, the first Jewish women's benevolent organization in America.
• In *Trustees of Dartmouth College v. Woodward,* the U.S. Supreme Court declares unconstitutional the attempt by

New Hampshire to seize control of Dartmouth College from evangelical Protestants who control the college.

- Hosea Ballou begins publishing the *Universalist Magazine.*
- *March 29:* Isaac Mayer Wise, "father of Reform Judaism in the United States" and founder of the Union of American Hebrew Congregations and the Hebrew Union College, is born in Bohemia.

- *May 5:* William Ellery Channing preaches an ordination sermon for Jared Sparks at the First Independent Church of Baltimore titled "Unitarian Christianity." The sermon becomes an important early statement of Unitarian beliefs.
- *December 18:* Isaac Thomas Hecker, Catholic priest and founder of the Paulists, is born in New York City.

Eyewitness Testimony

There are but two congregations in this town [Nantucket]. They assemble every Sunday in meeting houses, as simple as the dwelling of the people; and there is but one priest on the whole island. What would a good Portuguese observe?—but one single priest to instruct a whole island, and to direct their consciences! It is even so; each individual knows how to guide his own, and is content to do it, as well as he can. This lonely clergyman is a Presbyterian minister, who has a very large and respectable congregation; the other is composed of Quakers, who you know admit of no particular person, who in consequence of being ordained becomes exclusively entitled to preach, to catechize, and to receive certain salaries for his trouble. Among them, every one may expound the Scriptures, who thinks he is called so to do; beside, as they admit of neither sacrament, baptism, nor any other outward forms whatever, such a man would be useless. Most of these people are continually at sea, and have often the most urgent reasons to worship the parent of nature in the midst of the storms which they encounter. These two sects live in perfect peace and harmony with each other; those ancient times of religious discords are now gone (I hope never to return) when each thought it meritorious, not only to damn the other, which would have been nothing, but to persecute and murder one another, for the glory of that Being, who requires no more of us, than that we should love one another and live! Every one goes to that place of worship which he likes best, and thinks not that his neighbor does wrong by not following him; each busily employed in their temporal affairs, is less vehement about spiritual ones, and fortunately you will find at Nantucket neither idle drones, voluptuous devotees, ranting enthusiasts, nor sour demagogues. I wish I had it in my power to send the most persecuting bigot I could find in to the whale fisheries; in less than three or four years you would find him a much more tractable man, and therefore a better Christian.

J. Hector St. John De Crevecoeur, a French aristocrat turned American farmer, 1782, in Letters from an American Farmer, *pp. 192–194.*

Whereas Absalom Jones and Richard Allen, two men of the African race, who, for their religious life and conversation have obtained a good report among men, these persons, from a love to the people of their complexion whom they beheld with sorrow, because of their

irreligious and uncivilized state, often communed together upon this painful and important subject in order to form some kind of religious society, but there being too few to be found under the like concern, and those who were, differed in their religious sentiments; with these circumstances they labored for some time, till it was proposed, after a serious communication of sentiments, that a society should be formed, without regard to religious tenets, provided, the person lived an orderly and sober life, in order to support one another in sickness, and for the benefit of their widows and fatherless children.

Preamble of the Philadelphia Free African Society, April 12, 1787, in Aptheker, A Documentary History of the Negro People in the United States, *pp. 17–18.*

Wherefore is religious liberty not secured? One honorable gentlemen, who favors adoption, said that he had had his fears on the subject. If I can well recollect, he informed us that he was perfectly satisfied, by the powers of reasoning, (with which he is so happily endowed,) that those fears were not well grounded. There is many a religious man who knows nothing of argumentative reasoning; there are many of our most worthy citizens who cannot go through all the labyrinths of syllogistic, argumentative deductions, when they think that the rights of conscience are invaded. This sacred right ought not to depend on constructive, logical reasoning.

. . . . .

That sacred and lovely thing, religion, ought not to rest on the ingenuity of logical deduction. Holy religion, sir, will be prostituted to the lowest purposes of human policy. What has been more productive of mischief among mankind than religious disputes? Then here, sir, is a foundation for such disputes, when it requires learning and logical deduction to perceive that religious liberty is secure.

Virginia leader Patrick Henry, June 12, 1788, speech to the Virginia ratifying convention concerning the lack of an explicit protection of religious liberty for the proposed constitution of the United States, in Kurland and Lerner, The Founders' Constitution, *vol. 5, p. 88.*

At last we came in sight of the island of Barbadoes, at which the whites on board gave a great shout, and made many signs of joy to us. . . . Many merchants and planters now came on board, though it was in the evening. They put us in separate parcels, and examined us attentively. They also made us jump, and pointed to the land, signifying we were to go there. We thought by this we should be eaten by these ugly men, as they appeared to us; and, when soon after we were all put down under the deck again, there was much dread and trembling among us, and nothing but bitter cries to be heard all the night from these apprehensions, insomuch that at last the white people got some old slaves from the land to pacify us. They told us we were not to be eaten, but to work, and were soon to go on land, where we should see many of our country people. This report eased us much; and sure enough, soon after we were landed, there came to us Africans of all languages. We were conducted immediately to the merchant's yard, where we were all pent up together like so many sheep in a fold, without regard to sex or age. As every object was new to me every thing I saw filled me with surprise. What struck me first, was, that the houses were built with stories, and in every other respect different from those in Africa: but I was still more astonished on seeing people on horseback. I did not know what this could mean; and indeed I thought these people were full of nothing but magical arts. While I was in this astonishment one of my fellow prisoners spoke to a countryman of his about the horses, who said they were the same kind they had in their country. I understood them, though they were from a distant part of Africa, and I thought it odd I had not seen any horses there; but afterwards, when I came to converse with different Africans, I found they had many horses amongst them, and much larger than those I then saw. We were not many days in the merchant's custody before we were sold after their usual manner, which Is this:—On a signal given, (as the beat of a drum) the buyers rush at once into the yard where the slaves are confined, and make choice of that parcel they like best. The noise and clamour with which this is attended, and the eagerness visible in the countenances of the buyers, serve not a little to increase the apprehension of terrified Africans, who may well be supposed to consider them as the ministers of that destruction to which they think themselves devoted. In this manner, without scruple, are relations and friends separated, most of them never to see each other again. I remember in the vessel in which I was brought over, in the men's apartment, there were several brothers, who, in the sale, were sold in different lots; and it was very moving on this occasion to see and hear their cries at parting. O, ye nominal Christians! might not an African ask you—learned you this from your God, who says unto you, Do unto all men as you would men should do unto you? Is it not enough that we Are torn from our country and friends, to toil for your luxury and lust of gain? Must every tender feeling Be likewise sacrificed to your avarice? Are the dearest friends and relations, now rendered more dear by their separation from their kindred, still to be parted from each other, and thus prevented from cheering the gloom of slavery with the small comfort of being together and mingling their sufferings and sorrows? Why are parents to lose their children, brothers their sisters, or husbands their wives? Surely, this is a new refinement in cruelty, which, while it has no advantage to atone for it, thus aggravates distress, and adds fresh horrors even to the wretchedness of slavery.

Olaudah Equiano, an African-born former slave, 1789, The Interesting Narrative of the Life of Olaudah Equiano or Gustavus Vassa, the African, *in* Slave Narratives, *pp. 78–79.*

[I]t would ill become me to conceal the joy I have felt in perceiving the fraternal affection which appears to increase every day among the friends of genuine religion. It affords edifying prospects, indeed, to see Christians of different denominations dwell together in more charity, and conduct themselves, in respect to each other, with a more Christian-like spirit than ever they have done in any former age, or in any other nation.

George Washington, replying to the congratulations conveyed to him by the Episcopal General Convention after his election as president, 1789, in Pointer, Protestant Pluralism and the New York Experience, *p. 117.*

Whereas it is the duty of all nations to acknowledge the providence of Almighty God, to obey His will, to be grateful for His benefits, and humbly to implore His protection and favor; and

Whereas both Houses of Congress have, by their joint committee, requested me "to recommend to the people of the United States a day of public thanksgiving and prayer, to be observed by acknowledging with grateful hearts the many and signal favors of Almighty God, especially by affording them an opportunity peaceably to establish a form of government for their safety and happiness:"

Now, therefore, I do recommend and assign Thursday, the 26th Day of November next, to be devoted by the people of these States to the service of that great and glorious Being who is the beneficent author of all the good that was, that is, or that will be; that we may then all unite in rendering unto Him our sincere and humble thanks for His kind care and protection of the people of this country previous to their becoming a nation; for the signal and manifold mercies and the favorable interpositions of His providence in the course and conclusion of the late war; for the great degree of tranquillity, union, and plenty which we have since enjoyed; for the peaceable and rational manner in which we have been enabled to establish constitutions of government for our safety and happiness, and particularly the national one now lately instituted; for the civil and religious liberty with which we are blessed, and the means we have of acquiring and diffusing useful knowledge; and, in general, for all the great and various favors which He has been pleased to confer upon us.

And also that we may then unite in most humbly offering our prayers and supplications to the great Lord and Ruler of Nations, and beseech Him to pardon our national and other transgressions; to enable us all, whether in public or private stations, to perform our several and relative duties properly and punctually; to render our National Government a blessing to all the people by constantly being a Government of wise, just, and constitutional laws, discreetly and faithfully executed and obeyed; to protect and guide all sovereigns and nations (especially such as have shown kindness to us), and to bless them with good governments, peace, and concord; to promote the knowledge and practice of true religion and virtue, and the increase of science among them and us; and, generally, to grant unto all mankind such a degree of temporal prosperity as He alone knows to be best.

George Washington, Proclamation: A National Thanksgiving, October 3, 1789, in Kurland and Lerner, The Founders' Constitution, *vol. 5, p. 94.*

The situation of religious rights in the American states, though also well known, is too important, too precious a circumstance to be omitted. Almost every sect and form of Christianity is known here—as also the Hebrew church. None are tolerated. All are admitted, aided by mutual charity and concord, and supported and cherished by the laws. In this land of promise for the good men of all denominations, are actually to be found, the independent or Congregational Church from England, the Protestant Episcopal Church (separated by our revolution from the Church of England) the Quaker Church, the English, Scotch, Irish and Dutch Presbyterian or Calvinist Churches, the Roman Catholic Church, the German Lutheran Church, the German Reformed Church, the Baptist and Anabaptist

Churches, the Hugonot or French Protestant Church, the Moravian Church, the Swedish Episcopal Church, the Seceders from the Scotch Church, the Menonist Church, with other Christian sects, and the Hebrew Church. Mere toleration is a doctrine exploded by our general condition; instead of which have been substituted an unqualified admission, and assertion, "that their own modes of worship and of faith equally belong to all the worshippers of God, of whatever church, sect, or denomination."

American political economist Tench Coxe, 1790, Notes Concerning the United States of America, *in Stokes,* Church and State in the United States, *vol. 1, p. 275.*

You desire to know something of my religion. It is the first time I have been questioned upon it. But I cannot take your curiosity amiss, and shall endeavor in a few words to gratify it. Here is my creed. I believe in one God, the creator of the universe. That he governs by his providence. That he ought to be worshiped. That the most acceptable service we render to him is doing good to his other children. That the soul of man is immortal, and will be treated with justice in another life respecting its conduct in this. These I take to be the fundamental points in all sound religion, and I regard them as you do in whatever sect I meet with them.

As to Jesus of Nazareth, my opinion of whom you particularly desire, I think his system of morals and his religion, as he left them to us, the best the world ever saw or is likely to see; but I apprehend it has received various corrupting changes, and I have, with most of the present dissenters in England, some doubts as to his divinity; though it is a question I do not dogmatize upon, having never studied it, and think it needless to busy myself with it now, when I expect soon an opportunity of knowing the truth with less trouble. I see no harm, however, in its being believed, if that belief has the good consequences, as probably it has, of making his doctrines more respected and more observed; especially as I do not perceive that the Supreme takes it amiss, by distinguishing the unbelievers in his government of the world with any peculiar marks of his displeasure.

Benjamin Franklin, March 9, 1790, letter to Congregational minister and Yale president Ezra Stiles, in The Works of Benjamin Franklin, *vol. 12, pp. 185–186.*

Our ancestors, before they ever enjoyed Gospel revelation acknowledged one Supreme Being who dwells above, whom they styled Waun-theet Mon-nit-toow, or the Great, Good Spirit, the author of all things in heaven and on earth, and also believed that there is an evil one, called Mton-toow or Wicked Spirit that loves altogether to do mischief; that he excites person or persons to tell a lie—angry, fight, hate, steal, to commit murder, and to be envious, malicious, and evil-talking; also excites nations to war with one another, to violated their Friendship with the Great, Good Spirit given them to maintain for their mutual good, and their children after them.

Hendrick Aupaumut, a leader among the Mahican Indians, ca. 1790, History of the Muh-he-con-nuk Indians, in Peyer, The Elders Wrote, *p. 28.*

From yon blue wave, to that far distant shore,
Where suns decline, and evening oceans roar,
Their eyes shall view one free elective sway; One
blood, one kindred, reach from sea to sea;
One language spread; one tide of manners run;
One scheme of science, and of morals one;
And, God's own Word the structure, and the base,
One faith extend, one worship, and one praise.

Congregationalist minister and later Yale president, Timothy Dwight, "Greenfield Hill," 1794, in The Major Poems of Timothy Dwight, *p. 526.*

There is in every town or tribe a high priest, usually called by the white people jugglers, or conjurers, besides several juniors or graduates. But the ancient high priest or seer, presides in spiritual affairs, and is a person of consequence; he maintains and exercises great influence in the state; particularly in military affairs, the senate never determine on an expedition against their enemy without his counsel and assistance. These people generally believe that their seer has communion with powerful invisible spirits, who they suppose have a share in the rule and government of human affairs, as well as the elements; that he can predict the result of an expedition, and his influence is so great, that they have been known frequently to stop, and turn back an army, when within a days journey of their enemy, after a march of several hundred miles, and indeed their predictions have surprised many people. They foretell rain or drought, and pretend to bring rain at pleasure, cure diseases, and exercise witchcraft, invoke or expel evil spirits, and even assume the power of directing thunder and lightning. These Indians are by no means idolaters, unless their

puffing the tobacco smoke towards the sun and rejoicing at the appearance of the new moon, may be termed so, so far from idolatry are they, that they have no images amongst them, nor any religious rite or ceremony that I could perceive; but adore the Great Spirit, the giver and taker away of the breath of life, with the most profound and respectful homage. They believe in a future state, where the spirit exists, which they call the world of spirits, where they enjoy different degrees of tranquility or comforts, agreeable to their life spent here: a person who in this life has been an industrious hunter, provided well for his family, an intrepid and active warrior, just, upright, and done all the good he could, will, they say, in the world of spirits, live in a warm, pleasant country, where are expansive, green, flowery savannas and high forests, watered with rivers of pure waters, replenished with deer, and every species of game; a serene, unclouded and peaceful sky; in short, where there is fulness of pleasure, uninterrupted.

American naturalist William Bartram, 1791, describing his perceptions of American Indian religion, in Travels Through North & South Carolina, *pp. 497–498.*

On my way home being much distressed, I alighted from my horse in a lonely wood, and bowed my knees before the Lord; I sensibly felt two spirits, one on each hand. The good spirit set forth to my inmost mind, the beauties of religion; and I seemed almost ready to lay hold on my Saviour. Oh! unbelief! soul damning sin! it kept me from my Jesus. . . . I felt my heart rise sensibly (I do not say with enmity) against my Maker, and immediately I arose from my knees with these words. "I will take my own time, and then I will serve thee. I mounted my horse with a hard unbelieving heart, unwilling to submit to Jesus. Oh! what a good God had I to deal with! I might in justice have been sent to hell.

I had not rode a quarter of a mile, before the Lord met me powerfully with these words, "These three years have I come seeking fruit on this fig tree; and find none." And then the following words were added, "I have come once more to offer you life and salvation, and it is the last time: chuse, or refuse." I was instantly surrounded with a divine power: heaven and hell were disclosed to view, and life and death were set before me. I do believe if I had rejected this call, mercy would have been forever taken from me. Man hath power to chuse, or refuse in religious matters; otherwise God would have no reasonable service from his creatures. I knew the very instant, when I submitted to the Lord; and was willing that Christ should reign over me: I likewise knew the two sins which I parted with last, pride, and unbelief. I threw the reins of the bridle on my horse's neck, and putting my hands together, cried out, Lord, I submit. I was less than nothing in my own sight; and was now, for the first time, reconciled to the justice of God. The enmity of my heart was slain—The plan of salvation was open to me—I saw the beauty in the perfection of the Deity. and felt the power of faith and love that I had ever been a stranger to before.

Methodist minister Freeborn Garrettson, 1791, The Experience and Travels of Mr. Freeborn Garrettson, *referring to his conversion in 1775, in* American Methodist Pioneer, *pp. 44–45.*

The discourse being ended, I immediately retired to the woods alone with my Bible. Here I read and prayed with various feelings, between hope and fear. But the truth I had just heard, "God is love," prevailed. Jesus came to seek and save the lost—"Him that cometh unto me, I will in no wise cast out." I yielded and sunk at his feet a willing subject. I loved him—I adored him—I praised him aloud in the silent night,—in the echoing grove around. I confessed to the Lord my sin and folly in disbelieving his word for so long—and in following so long the devices of men. I now saw that a poor sinner was as much authorized to believe in Jesus at first, as at last—that *now* was the accepted time, and day of salvation.

Barton Warren Stone, a prominent preacher at the Cane Ridge revival and leader in the Christian restorationist movement describing his conversion in 1791, "A Short History of the Life of Barton W. Stone," in Thompson, Voices from Cane Ridge, *p. 41.*

A great queen had among her servants a young minister. Upon a certain occasion she requested him to dust some books that she had hidden in an old chest. Now when the young man reached the bottom of the chest he found a wonderful book which he opened and read. It told that the white men had killed the son of the creator and it said, moreover, that he had promised to return in three days and then again in forty but that he never did. All his followers then began to despair but some said, "He surely will come again some time." When the young preacher read this book he was worried because he had discovered that he had been deceived and

that his Lord was not on earth and had not returned when be promised. So he went to some of the chief preachers and asked them about the matter and they answered that he had better seek the Lord himself and find if he were not on the earth now. So he prepared to find the Lord and the next day when he looked out into the river he saw a beautiful island and marveled that he had never noticed it before. As he continued to look he saw a castle built of gold in the midst of the island and he marveled that he had not seen the castle before. Then he thought that so beautiful a palace on so beautiful an isle must surely be the abode of the son of the Creator. Immediately he went to the wise men and told them what he had seen and they wondered greatly and answered that it must indeed be the house of the Lord. . . . So the young man went boldly over to attend to the business at hand and walking up to the door knocked. A handsome man welcomed him into a room and bade him be of ease. . . . "Listen to me, young man, and you will be rich. Across the ocean there is a great country of which you have never heard. The people there are virtuous, they have no evil habits or appetites but are honest and single-minded. A great reward is yours if you enter into my plans and carry them out. Here are five things. Carry them over to the people across the ocean and never shall you want for wealth, position or power. Take these cards, this money, this fiddle, this whiskey and this blood corruption and give them all to the people across the water. The cards will make them gamble away their goods and idle away their time, the money will make them dishonest and covetous, the fiddle will make them dance with women and their lower natures will command them, the whiskey will excite their minds to evil doing and will turn their minds, and the blood corruption will eat their strength and rot their bones."

The young man thought this a good bargain and promised to do as the man had commanded him. . . . So he looked about and at length found Columbus to whom he told the whole story. So Columbus fitted out some boats and sailed out into the ocean to find the land on the other side. When he had sailed for many days on the water the sailors said that unless Columbus turned about and went home they would behead him but he asked for another day and on that day land was seen and that land was America. Then they turned around and going back reported what they had discovered. Soon a great flock of ships came over the ocean and white men came swarming into the country bringing with them cards, money, fiddles, whisky and blood corruption.

Now the man who had appeared in the gold palace was the devil and when afterward he saw what his words had done he said that he had made a great mistake and even he lamented that his evil had been so enormous.

American Indian religious leader Handsome Lake, 1799, explaining how America came to be discovered, told by his brother Cornplanter, in Parker, Seneca Myths and Folk Tales, *pp. 383–385.*

Believing with you that religion is a matter which lies solely between man and his God, that he owes account to none other for his faith or his worship, that the legislative powers of government reach actions only, and not opinions, I contemplate with sovereign reverence that act of the whole American people which declared that their legislature should "make no law respecting an establishment of religion, or prohibiting the free exercise thereof," thus building a wall of separation between

Thomas Jefferson advocated a "wall of separation between church and state." *(Library of Congress, Prints and Photographs Division LC-D416-9859)*

church and State. Adhering to this expression of the supreme will of the nation in behalf of the rights of conscience, I shall see with sincere satisfaction the progress of those sentiments which tend to restore to man all his natural rights, convinced he has no natural right in opposition to his social duties.

Thomas Jefferson, January 1, 1802, letter to Messrs. Nehemiah Dodge and Others, a Committee of the Danbury Baptist Association, in the State of Connecticut, Thomas Jefferson: Writings, *p. 510.*

Brother!—Our seats were once large, and yours were very small. You have now become a great people, and we have scarcely a place left to spread our blankets. You have got our country, but are not satisfied. You want to force your religion upon us.

Brother!—Continue to listen. You say that you are sent to instruct us how to worship the Great Spirit agreeably to his mind; and if we do not take hold of the religion which you white people teach, we shall be unhappy hereafter. You say that you are right and we are lost. How do we know this to be true? We understand that your religion is written in a book. If it was intended for us as well as for you, why has not the Great Spirit given it to us; and not only to us, but why did he not give to our forefathers the knowledge of that book, with the means of understanding it rightly? We only know what you tell us about it. How shall we know when to believe, being so often deceived by the white people.

Brother!—You say there is but one way to worship and serve the Great Spirit. If there is but one religion, why do you white people differ so much about it? Why not all agree, as you can all read the book?

. . . . .

Brother!—We are told that you have been preaching to white people in this place. These people are our neighbors. We are acquainted with them. We will wait a little while, and see what effect your preaching has upon them. If we find it does them good and makes them honest and less disposed to cheat Indians, we will then consider again what you have said.

Seneca political leader Red Jacket, 1805, speech in response to missionary efforts, in Moquin, Great Documents in American Indian History, *pp. 32–33.*

Father:—it is three years since I first began with that system of religion which I now practice. The white people and some of the Indians were against me; but I had no other intention but to introduce among the Indians, those good principles of religion which the white people profess.

. . . . .

The Great Spirit told me to tell the Indians that he had made them, and made the world—that he had placed them on it to do good, and not evil.

I told all the red skins, that the way they were in was not good, and that they ought to abandon it.

That we ought to consider ourselves as one man; but we ought to live agreeably to our several customs, the red people after their mode, and the white people after theirs; particularly, that they should not drink whiskey; that it was not made for them, but the white people, who alone knew how to use it; and that it is the cause of all the mischief which the Indians suffer; and that they must always follow the directions of the Great Spirit, and we must listen to him, as it was he that made us: determine to listen to nothing that is bad: do not take up the tomahawk, should it be offered by the British, or by the long knives: do not meddle with any thing that does not belong to you, but mind your own business, and cultivate the ground, that your women and children may have enough to live on.

I now inform you, that it is our intention to live in peace with our father and his people forever.

My father, I have informed you what we mean to do, and I call the Great Spirit to witness the truth of my declaration. The religion which I have established for the last three years, has been attended to by the different tribes of Indians in this part of the world. Those Indians were once different people; they are now but one: they are all determined to practice what I have communicated to them, that has come immediately from the Great Spirit through me.

American Indian religious leader Tenkswatawa, August 1808, speech to the governor of Indiana, in Moquin, Great Documents in American Indian History, *pp. 34–35.*

In my sleep I tho't I was traveling and came to a hill that was almost perpendicular. I was much troubled about it, for I had to go to its top. I knew not how to get up. She said she saw the steps which others had gone and tried to put her feet in their steps, but found she could not ascend in this way, because her feet slipped. Having made several unsuccessful attempts to ascend, she became very weary, but although she succeeded in getting near the top, but felt in great danger of falling. While in this distress in doubt whether to try to go forward or return, she saw a bush just above her of which she tho't, if she could get hold it she could get up, and as she reached out her hand to the bush, she saw a little boy standing at the top, who reached out his hand; She grasped his thumb, and at this moment she was on the top and someone told her it was the saviour.

Catharine Brown, a Cherokee convert to Christianity, 1817, in Martin, The Land Looks After Us, *p. 71.*

In Pennsylvania, the Society of Friends were united in opposition to the African trade from their first settlement in the province, and, had they constituted the majority of the population (which their own liberal institutions tended to prevent), it is probable that the European traders would have found the implanting black slavery on the banks of the Delaware impracticable. It must be remembered, however, that the will of the mother country was upon this matter imperative, and that a positive prohibitory statute on the part of Pennsylvania would have been treated in like manner with those of Massachusetts. Her restrictive regulations, however, were numerous, nor could the eager cupidity of the foreign traders ever create a certain market for the enslaved Africans to the north of Maryland. It is a striking fact, and one greatly in favour of religious as well as civil liberty (if in this age of the world either needed the support of argument), that in those provinces where the home authority was insufficient to establish one privileged church this traffic was held in odium from its very commencement. Religion, there ingrafted in the heart, instantly bred scruples as to its legality, humanity, and policy, while in the distant European empires, living under proud hierarchies, and in the neighbouring colonies in which the Church of England had been by law established, the human mind was more slow to acknowledge the crime. It is not to be doubted that the difference of climate between the southern and northern provinces of British America contributed yet more than the differing standard of conscientious scruple among the colonists to produce a more marked reluctance to the trade in the one than the other. Yet we cannot peruse the colonial histories of these states without counting for something the varying influence of religion in those districts where its principles were engrafted in *willing minds,* and those where its forms were established by compulsory edicts.

American reformer Francis ("Fanny") Wright, 1819, Views of Society and Manners in America, *pp. 37–38.*

CHAPTER SEVEN

Reason and Revivalism
(1820–1840)

By the third decade of the 19th century, theological conflict between the conservative and liberal wings of Congregationalism had produced fractures that could not be mended. Unitarianism, which denied the divinity of Jesus, ceased to be simply a subset of Congregationalism and became a new denomination in its own right. Its adherents saw themselves as practicing a rational faith and expected that theirs was the faith of the future. As early as 1801 Thomas Jefferson had confidently predicted in his *Autobiography* that there was not a young man then living who would not die a Unitarian. By the 1820s Unitarian prospects appeared even brighter. Yet

This picture, originally published in 1819, depicts a Methodist camp meeting. *(Library of Congress, Prints and Photographs Division LC-USZ62-2497)*

evangelical Christian piety doggedly refused to surrender the field. The Second Great Awakening refreshed the nation's acquaintance with revival, adding camp meetings to its religious vocabulary and renewed vigor to evangelical denominations such as the Methodists and the Baptists. The 19th century's third decade witnessed the transportation of revivalism from its frontier and rural origins at the beginning of the century to the urban centers of America, where it flourished into the 21st century. The two forces—reason and revivalism—would contend with each other over the coming decades and, contrary to the confident expectations of Jefferson, revivalism would prove to be the more dominant social current.

The Rise of Liberal Religion

Unitarianism debuted in the United States primarily as a liberal subspecies of Congregationalism, which professed to be Christian but denied that Christ was God. It had its origins among Congregationalist ministers who opposed the Great Awakening in the 1730s and 1740s and were sometimes referred to as Old Lights. Their opposition eventually drifted down theological paths that strayed from Calvinistic orthodoxy by questioning the doctrine of the Trinity, according to which Jesus was considered to be one person of the triune God, and the Calvinistic doctrine of divine sovereignty, according to which humanity was deemed utterly incapable of meriting or even choosing salvation. They thus claimed spiritual kinship with two historical figures deemed heretics by orthodox Calvinism: Arius, who claimed in the fourth century that Jesus was a divine emissary rather than God, and Jacob Harmensen Arminius, who rejected strict Calvinism in the early 17th century by insisting that individuals had the power to choose God's gracious offer of salvation through Christ. Unitarianism's roots also were intertwined with other reasonable religions of the 18th century such as deism. Unlike deists, however, Unitarians of the late 18th and early 19th centuries tended to be church members who believed in the authority of the Bible. On the point of Christology and soteriology, however—that is, doctrinal questions involving the nature and work of Christ and the nature of salvation—they concluded that more orthodox Christians had misunderstood the teachings of Scripture.

The first Unitarian congregation in America came into being when King's Chapel in Boston, an Anglican congregation led by lay reader James Freeman, revised the Book of Common Prayer in 1785 to remove all references to the Trinity. When Freeman's anti-Trinitarian views made it impossible for him to obtain ordination as an Anglican minister, his congregation proceeded to ordain him themselves, thus precipitating their severance from the Anglican Church and the birth of a Unitarian congregation. In the main, though, American Unitarianism received most of its early support from the liberal wing of Congregationalism, which increasingly came to reject the doctrines of the Trinity and of divine sovereignty and human depravity, at least as held by more orthodox Congregationalists. By the close of the 19th century's second decade, this rejection made it increasingly unlikely that spiritual fraternity could continue between orthodox Congregationalists and Unitarians. A key moment in the birth of Unitarianism as a separate theological movement rather than a subspecies of Congregationalism occurred in 1819, when Congregationalist minister William Ellery Channing preached an ordination sermon for a young minister at the First Independent Church of Baltimore. Titled *Unitarian Christianity* when later published as a book, Channing's sermon attempted to elaborate the central theological tenets of the movement. This event was soon followed by the formation of the Berry Street Conference, which served as the forerunner of the American Unitarian Association, established in 1825. During the early years of Unitarianism, Boston was its intellectual center, so much so that Unitarians were sometimes said to believe in "the Fatherhood of God, the Brotherhood of Man, and the Neighborhood of Boston."[1]

In spite of his heterodox beliefs, William Channing thought of himself as very much still a member of the Christian household of faith. He believed the Bible was God's inspired word and insisted that Unitarians had simply pierced through Trinitarian distortions that had misled more orthodox Christians. Because his orthodox opponents—and there were many—concluded that Channing and other Unitarians had moved altogether outside the bounds of Christian belief, they waged a vigorous rhetorical battle in sermon and print against Unitarian heresy. Even before the formal split between conservative Congregationalists and Unitarians, minister-geographer Jedidiah Morse had founded the magazine the *Panoplist* in 1805 to combat liberal theological tendencies among Congregationalists. Later, Congregationalist minister Lyman Beecher railed against Unitarianism (and Catholicism, as well) from his pulpit at the Hanover Street Church in Boston. He also established an evangelical magazine, *Spirit of the Pilgrims*, in 1828, which he used as a forum for exposing both the perils and the errors of Unitarianism, and he supported the revivalism that served as the dominant counterforce to the spread of "reasonable" religion during the 19th century.

Another strand of the liberal religious tradition, Universalism, planted its first American congregations by the last quarter of the 18th century, and Universalist conventions began assembling in the 1780s, with first the New England convention of 1785 and the Philadelphia convention of 1790. Rejecting Calvinism's theology of election, under which only a chosen group of the elect would obtain salvation, Universalists believed in the ultimate redemption of all humanity through Jesus Christ. They undertook to produce statements of their core beliefs, of which the most important early example was the Winchester Profession of 1803. The first general convention of Universalists in America took place in 1833. During its second generation, American Universalism had an able champion in Hosea Ballou, the son of a New Hampshire farmer and Baptist minister who was ordained a Universalist minister in 1794. Under Ballou's influence Universalism began to assume the anti-Trinitarian beliefs associated with Unitarians. His most famous work, *A Treatise on the Atonement*, published in 1805, rejected the commonly held orthodox view that Christ by his death on the cross had made an atoning sacrifice for the sins of humanity. Under this view, human sinfulness deserved eternal punishment, but God accepted Christ's death on the cross in substitution for the eternal death owed to sinners, thus allowing him to be reconciled to those who received his gift of salvation through Christ. In contrast, Ballou argued that God, in his great love, did not need to be reconciled with humanity. Humanity, though, needed to be reconciled with God, and Jesus was sent as a messenger to lead humanity back to God.

Unitarian and Universalist congregations spread rapidly during the first few decades of the 19th century, though they remained centered primarily in New England. Among Congregationalism, especially, defection of congregations to Unitarianism became so frequent in the early part of the century that Congregationalism's privileged status as the established church in Massachusetts was in danger of being swallowed up by Unitarian congregations. Years of protest against this establishment by Baptists and other Protestant dissenters had not dislodged it. Nevertheless, in 1833 the prospect that orthodox Congregationalists might have to provide tax support to Unitarian congregations finally joined with continued opposition by Protestant dissenters to dismantle America's last state establishment of religion.

Initially, Unitarians and Universalists differed both in their core beliefs and in the predominant socioeconomic backgrounds of their members. Unitarians focused their theological energies primarily on rebuttals of the idea of human depravity and Trinitarianism. Universalists coalesced around a common abhorrence of the idea that God might punish unbelievers with eternal damnation. Unitarians drew their members mainly from the urban upper classes, Universalists from rural areas less familiar with wealth or social prestige. By the middle decades of the 19th century, a gradual convergence of liberal theological principles led some within the two groups to posit the benefits of a formal alliance. Not until the 20th century, however, did the two religious traditions formally merge.

Revivalism

The revivals of the Great Awakening in the first half of the 18th century were securely fastened to Calvinistic orthodoxy. Both George Whitefield, the awakening's greatest preacher, and Jonathan Edwards, its principal theologian, believed that sinful humanity was powerless to choose salvation on its own. God had to awaken the sinner to receive salvation through faith, and he chose only to awaken the elect. In the 19th century, however, when a new wave of revivalism surged across America, traditional Calvinism was no longer its main current. Presbyterians still nominally attached to this tradition were partners in the early stages of the Second Great Awakening, such as the Cane Ridge Revival. But some of 19th-century revivalism's chief architects eventually drifted away from both Presbyterianism and traditional forms of Calvinistic belief. Barton Warren Stone, a leader in the Cane Ridge Revival, went so far as to join with other ministers to disband a presbytery. Camp meetings, in which some Presbyterians joined in the earliest years of their existence, rapidly became a feature more characteristic of Methodism than of the American heirs of Calvin. Charles Grandison Finney, the leading revivalist of the middle years of the 19th century, migrated from Presbyterianism to Congregationalism.

The century's new forms of revival drifted far closer to Arminianism than did the revivals associated with the Great Awakening. In the previous century Jonathan Edwards preached a kind of theological determinism that emphasized the disabling effects of sin on human capacity to turn toward God. Men and women could only wait patiently to see whether God might awaken them, whether revival might be granted to them. But America of the early 19th century was not in a waiting mood, and it was less conscious of its sinful incapacities than of its potential. The "era of good feelings," as the period from about 1817 to 1823 has been described, was succeeded by the "era of the common man," with the election of Andrew Jackson as president of the United States in 1828. Popular democracy was on the rise, and frontiers lay open to rapid expansion. The mood of the day emphasized possibility rather than peril, self-industry rather than sinful incapacity. Consequently, revivalism in the new century had a good deal more affinity with Arminianism than with Calvinism, more confidence in the power of human activity and choice than pessimism about disabilities associated with inherent sinfulness.

As the theology of Jonathan Edwards anchored the Great Awakening to Calvinism, so the theology of men such as Nathaniel Taylor unfastened 19th-century revivalism from this tradition. Taylor, a professor of divinity at Yale, is the most important representative of what came to be known as the New Haven Theology. Taylor, in particular, rejected Calvin's emphasis on the total depravity of humanity in favor of what he termed "the power to choose." While he and others supplied a new theology of revival, Charles Grandison Finney contributed the revival's science. Finney, who turned away from pursuit of a legal career after his conversion, was licensed as a Presbyterian minister in 1823 and came to national prominence in 1830 when he launched a series of revival services in Rochester, New York, in September that would last until June of the following year. Through Finney's labors 19th-century revivalism found its way to urban America, where successors such as Dwight L. Moody, Billy Sunday, and Billy Graham would regularly return for more than a century to come. As Finney explained in his *Lectures on Revivals of Religion,* there was nothing mysterious about revival. It was simply a matter of making the "right use of constituted means." "There is nothing in religion beyond the ordinary powers of nature," he argued.

> *Religion is the work of man. . . .* It consists entirely in the *right exercise* of the powers of nature. It is just that and nothing else. When mankind become religious, they are not *enabled* to put forth exertions which they were unable before to put forth. They only exert powers which they had before, in a different way, and use them for the glory of God. [A revival] is not a miracle, nor dependent on a miracle, in any sense. It is a purely philosophical result of the right use of constituted means—as much as any other effect produced by the application of means.[2]

For Finney, these means included holding "inquiry meetings" after revival services or inviting those convicted of their need for salvation to come forward and sit on an "anxious bench," where they might be counseled. He did not invite his hearers to a protracted period of spiritual inquiry or a sustained program of preconversion instruction. Instead, he called upon them to receive salvation immediately. Finney's confidence in the ability of his hearers to choose salvation placed him increasingly at odds with the more orthodox Calvinism still dominant in American Presbyterianism, and he eventually became a Congregationalist in 1836. This personal migration mirrored a larger turn of American evangelicalism down a more Arminian path.

It might be tempting to suppose that reason and revivalism are mutually exclusive phenomena, and since the days of the Great Awakening many observers of revival have been quick to conclude this. Critics did not lack examples of religious enthusiasm that seemed naked of thought, ecstasies unperturbed by logic, awakenings divorced from reason. But even then, Jonathan Edwards stood as a powerful counterexample to the common supposition that religious "affections," as he termed them, could not be expected to flourish in the presence of sober thought. To the contrary, Edwards wielded one of America's most copious intellects to marry reason and revivalism. Nineteenth-century revivalism carried forward the tension between reason and revivalism. Sometimes, as in the case of the camp meetings that launched the Second Great Awakening, revival could appear clothed in rustic garb. But as in the case of the earlier awakening, the revivals of the 1800s could as readily flourish in more urbane environments. Charles Finney, for example, whose years as a revival preacher were sandwiched between preparation for a career in law, on one side, and as a professor and later president at Oberlin College, on the other, reproduced something of the Edwardsian marriage between reason and revivalism.

Finney and other urban revivalists who followed him pioneered new models of awakening that replicated important features of the camp meeting style of revival. A crucial feature of the camp meeting was its disruption of normal patterns of church attendance in favor of a concentrated period of soul searching carried out in the presence of fellow spiritual seekers. Ordinary schedules gave way to an intense and collective period of religious preoccupation. Ordinarily, church attendance might involve Sunday services and a weekday lecture or prayer meeting. But the camp meeting replaced occasional gatherings with virtually nonstop revival preaching. This kind of concentrated preoccupation was harder to come by in urban settings, where revival could not absolutely displace the necessity of work or other routines of daily living. But Finney and others launched meeting schedules that extended not simply across days but across weeks and even months. Revival services often lasted hours, during which souls on the brink of conversion could not readily retreat into the mundane routines of life. Moreover, these revival services were often accompanied and sometimes preceded by house-to-house visits and prayer meetings that augmented the monopolylike effect of the revival on everyday schedules. And, as in the case of the camp meeting, the spiritual soul-searching characteristic of revivals had a profoundly corporate dimension. Individual seekers could not help but be aware that their seeking was mirrored by others around them. Urban revivalists relied on inquiry rooms or the anxious bench, which to some extent publicized conversion struggles and made them not simply inner spiritual experiences but collective ones. Protracted meetings in urban settings thus captured both important elements of the camp meeting: its temporal concentration and its group dynamics.

One collateral consequence of revivalism's prominence in 19th-century America was the visibility it gave to the spiritual experiences and contributions of women.[3] So long as religious belief and practice were anchored to institutional churches, women's roles were traditionally subordinated to those of men. Men possessed almost an unbroken monopoly on the organized ministry until well into the 19th century, and this ministry, in turn, exercised a central position in most churches. Revival meetings in the 19th century, however, frequently migrated outside the boundaries of the local church to extracurricular sessions such as the camp meeting and citywide urban revival services. Moreover, revivals gave a prominent place to the testimonies of those, including women, who experienced conversion and were expected to give a public witness to this experience. Women thus found a new place for spiritual expression and leadership not commonly available in ordinary congregations. Revivalism's tendency to value spiritual fervor more than ministerial credentials even paved the way for increased room for women preachers. It is no surprise, then, that the 19th century would produce both a growing movement for the recognition of women's rights and prominent examples of women religious leaders such Ellen Gould Harmon Smith, the founder of the Seventh Day Adventists. Religious enthusiasm—the heartbeat of revivalism—has frequently served to undermine existing social hierarchies, including hierarchies of gender.

Voluntary Societies

Revivalism carried the evangelical Christian influence beyond the borders of specific denominations. It frequently joined evangelical Presbyterians and Congregationalists with Baptists and Methodists who overlooked, to some extent, their doctrinal differences in favor of a common enthusiasm for the salvation of souls and later for the reformation of certain individual and social ills. Moreover, evangelical believers could find spiritual fraternity in their opposition to the currents of religious liberalism, which experienced rapid growth in the early decades of the 19th century. But theological liberalism itself was swept up in the 19th century with utopian fervor as vigorous as that that gripped evangelicals, lending to the period a broad theological consensus over the necessity for and the possibility of human reform. "Not a reading man," Ralph Waldo Emerson wrote to his friend Thomas Carlyle in 1840, "but has a draft of a new community in his waistcoat pocket."[4]

Denominational and regional missionary societies were the first manifestation of the spirit of voluntarism that swept across the early decades of 19th-century America. Rather than navigate the organizational challenges required for collective action at the denominational level, church, ministers, and laity discovered they could move more quickly through separate associations with more focused aspirations. Thus, even before the end of the 18th century, missionary societies sprang into existence. The first significant such organization was the New York Missionary Society, which Presbyterians, Baptists, and Dutch Reformed established in 1796 to carry the Christian gospel to American Indians. Other associations followed quickly, though these tended to concentrate their energies on the planting of churches in frontier areas or in the South. But these domestic aspirations soon proved too narrow to contain the hopes of the era. By 1810 the American Board of Commissioners for Foreign Mission had been created. During the first half of the 19th century, these early voluntary efforts were joined by a flood of new associations intended to support the work of evangelism. Two of the most important were the American Bible Society, formed in 1816, and the American Tract Society, established in 1825. But evangelical Protestants of the period were not content simply to see that Bibles and tracts found their way into the hands of potential readers: they quickly recognized the need for more sustained efforts to improve scriptural literacy. To this end the American Sunday School Union was formed in 1824 to coordinate these efforts.

The voluntary spirit of the early 19th century might to contemporary observers seem predominantly other-worldly in its focus. Nevertheless, the spiritual renewal characteristic of the Second Great Awakening also possessed utopian aspirations rooted in the here and now. Confidence in human capacity to receive the gift of salvation was coupled with confidence that human society might be reformed and sinful and destructive patterns of human conduct restrained. Jonathan Edwards might have been preoccupied in the previous century with the inevitability of human sinfulness; Charles Grandison Finney in the new century was more enamored with the possibility of conversion and the potential for reform. In fact, in the theology of 19th-century revivalism, conversion and social reform were linked. According to theologians such as Samuel Hopkins and Nathaniel Taylor, spiritual regeneration replaced sinful selfishness with "disinterested benevolence." One social evil in particular, alcohol abuse, earned the attention of evangelical reformers, though enthusiasm for temperance manifested itself among theologically liberal sensibilities as well. Reformers gave organizational structure to this enthusiasm by establishing the Society for the Promotion of Temperance in 1826 and a decade later the American Temperance Union. Yet the battle waged by voluntary associations against drink took its place within a larger campaign against a variety of social ills including inhumane treatment of prisoners, illiteracy, and even dueling. Collectively, the vast array of associations came to be known as the Benevolent Empire.

Voluntary associations such as the American Tract Society and the American Temperance Union drew their members from individuals scattered across the larger American society. But the spirit of reform in 19th-century America also expressed itself through the proliferation of smaller utopian societies and communities. These looked to communal living arrangements as a means of remedying on a small scale the ills pervading broader American society. One important such group, the Shakers, dated its history from the last decades of the 18th century, after Mother Ann Lee migrated to America with eight of her followers in 1774. She taught her disciples that sex was the original sin and that they should remain celibate. More controversially, she instructed them that she was the Second Christ and that her presence in the world had inaugurated a millennial kingdom. Shakers, as her followers were called, grew in number slowly during the life of its founder. After her death in 1784, Joseph Meacham assumed leadership of the Shakers, formally known as the United Society of Believers in Christ's Second Coming, and helped to organize the followers of Mother Ann Lee. The first community of Shakers was formally "ordered" in New Lebanon, New York, in 1785. Thereafter, through about 1840 Shaker communities flourished, offering 19th-century Americans an alternative spiritual vision. The Oneida Community, established by John Humphrey

Shakers were one of the many utopian religious communities that flourished in 19th-century America. *(Library of Congress, Prints and Photographs Division LC-USZ62-13659)*

Noyes, was the 19th century's other most famous utopian community. Noyes experienced a revivalistic conversion after graduating from Dartmouth College in 1830. Subsequently, he briefly contemplated a legal career before studying at Andover Theological Seminary and Yale Divinity School. By 1834 he had concluded that Christ had returned to the earth in 70 A.D. and made human perfection possible. Noyes married a few years later but soon began to teach the idea of "complex marriage," which promoted multiple sexual unions among the disciples who soon gathered around him in a community he established in Putney, Vermont. The following decade, after being charged with adultery by his Vermont neighbors, he relocated the community to Oneida, New York, where it continued until the 1880s.

Slavery and Religion

Africans imported to America as slaves brought with them a variety of religious beliefs. At least some of these Africans were Muslims and Christians, though a majority practiced traditional forms of African spirituality. The non-Christian religious traditions most North American slaves inherited from their West African homes did not survive intact the brutality of slavery in the British colonies. Oppressive conditions and the hostility of whites to non-Christian beliefs and practices combined to suppress some of these inherited traditions. But slaves were able to sustain elements of these traditions, such as ceremonies relating to marriage, burial, and magical healing practices. Moreover, they were able to adapt elements of these traditions to the Christianity they encountered in America and adapt Christian beliefs and practices to their inherited traditions and their conditions of servitude. By a process of restructuring, they incubated a living faith that would subsequently take its place within the larger family of American Christianity.

Although practice of African religious traditions among slaves was discouraged as soon as they arrived in America, slaves were not generally the object of sustained efforts at Christian evangelism. White slaveholders frequently feared that the conversion of slaves to Christianity might make it awkward or even illegal to subject them to continued slavery and that exposing slaves to Christian teachings might infect them with egalitarian aspirations inconsistent with slavery. Also, fear of insurrection among slaves discouraged a variety of activities that would have assisted the spread of the Christian gospel among slaves—permitting unsupervised religious gatherings of slaves, for example, or teaching slaves to read and write. Nevertheless, southern clergy generally emphasized the necessity of bringing the Christian gospel to slaves. One preacher, for example, declared that "Whatever men may think or say as to the political, legal, constitutional, social, domestic or personal aspects of slavery, there can be no two opinions among those who profess and call themselves Christians, as to the duty of preaching the Gospel to the slave, and bringing him within the pale of the church."[5] Southern ministers could be sensitive, however, to the possibility that slaves might feign conversion to Christianity as a way of securing their liberty. Thus, for example, Francis le Jau, an Anglican missionary in South Carolina, required slaves to swear an oath before he would baptize them:

> You declare in the presence of God and before this Congregation that you do not ask for the holy baptism out of any design to free yourself from the Duty and Obedience that you owe to your Master while you live, but merely for the good of Your Soul and to partake of the Graces and Blessings promised to the members of the Church of Jesus Christ.[6]

But while southern clergy frequently urged planters to support missionary activity among the slaves, the planters themselves generally resisted this proposal in the early decades of the 19th century. They eventually warmed to this idea in the years after 1840, but before this time such contacts as the slaves had with Christianity occurred without the blessings of the planters. When planters began to recognize the need to expose slaves to the teachings of Christianity, evangelical motives were often coupled with, and even subordinated to practical aims. Slaves introduced to Christian teaching, it was commonly argued, would be less prone to lying, stealing, and insubordination. The agriculturalist Solon Robinson summarized the view that came to predominate in the last years before the Civil War.

> The fact is notorious, that slaves are better treated now than formerly, and that the improvement in their condition is progressing, partly from their masters' becoming more temperate and better men, but mainly from the greatest of all moving causes in human actions—self interest. For masters have discovered in the best of all possible schools—experience—that their true interest is insepa-rably found bound up with the humane treatment, comfort, and happiness of their slaves. And many masters have discovered, too, that their slaves are more temperate, more industrious, more kind to one another, more cheerful, and more faithful and more obedient, under the ameliorating influences of reli-gion, than under all the driving and whipping of all the tyrannical task masters that have existed since the day when the children of Israel were driven to the task of making Egyptian brick without straw.[7]

Planters ultimately came to believe that Christianity, far from inciting rebellion among slaves, actually made them more comfortable with their station in life. Slave-owners would have bristled at Karl Marx's suggestion that religion amounted to a kind of drug for the masses, dulling their sensibility to the hardships of labor. But in the main they embraced the spread of Christianity among the slaves at least partially, if not predominantly, because of its supposed tranquilizing effects.

One important legacy of the Great Awakening in the 18th century and even more significantly the Second Great Awakening of the early 19th century was the spread of Christian belief and practice among African Americans. Baptist and Methodist congregations spread rapidly in the second half of the 18th century, and they were not hesitant to carry the Christian gospel to blacks, both free and slave. Their preaching frequently emphasized the equality of all as sinners in need of God's mercy and, having received it, as brothers and sisters in Christ. Moreover, unlike traditions such as Anglicanism, which viewed conversion as the last step in a lengthy process of study and self-examination, evangelicals emphasized salvation in terms of the immediate turning of the soul to God through Christ. Accordingly, among slaves and poor blacks, as among poor whites, the evangelistic efforts of Bap-tists and Methodists were much more successful than those of traditions emphasizing studious conversion. During the years surrounding the Revolutionary War, at least, many Baptists and Methodists went on record opposing slavery. Although this op-position soon waned among southern adherents to these denominations, it made the Baptists and Methodists initially attractive to slaves. Moreover, these denominations were also enthusiastic about appointing lay black ministers, who were even more ef-fective at introducing the Christian gospel to African-American communities.

As Christianity penetrated slave communities, it joined with older African spiritual traditions to produce a fusion of religious belief and practice that bore the imprint of both African traditions and evangelical Protestant beliefs and practices. The religious enthusiasm characteristic of both 18th- and 19th-century awakenings included forms of emotional expressiveness similar to African forms of spirituality. Ecstatic singing and physical trembling and shaking commonly accompanied revival experiences, and these same physical manifestations of religious practice were also familiar within African traditions. These similarities encouraged the conversion of slaves to evangelical Christianity.

In the North separate congregations of African-American Christians began to spring up in the last decades of the 18th century. The same sometimes occurred in the South, such as in the case of the First African Baptist Church of Savannah, established in 1778 under the leadership of Andrew Bryan. Nevertheless, the religion of southern slaves did not often have the liberty to express itself through separate institutional forms. More commonly, southern law made it illegal for slaves to congregate without a white person present for fear that slave meetings would foment rebellion. Purely autonomous black churches were thus generally unknown in the South, with black congregations typically being at least nominally overseen by whites. In many locations, though, even this kind of superintended black worship was not permitted, and slaves, if they had any contact with Christianity at all, had so as a result of attending the churches of their masters. There, they discovered that southern Christians might be reluctantly willing to welcome slaves into the fraternity of belief, but only so long as the implacable hierarchies of bondage remained undisturbed. Slaves thus could expect to sit in galleries or other segregated seating arrangements. And they were expected to imbibe purported scriptural teachings that supported these hierarchies and segregations. Nevertheless, slaves regularly defied southern law by meeting privately, away from the plantation homes of masters, in "hush harbors." Here, slaves worshiped clandestinely and practiced forms of singing and preaching that included clapping, chanting, and dancing. Lay preachers engaged in a style of extemporaneous preaching intoned rhythmically. Here, also, spirituals were born—songs that meditated on the grievous losses and sufferings visited by slavery upon African Americans and that intertwined heavenly hopes with longing for earthly freedom.

> Steal away, steal away,
> Steal way to Jesus,
> Steal away, steal away home,
> I ain't got long to stay here.
> My Lord calls me,
> He calls me by the thunder,
> The trumpet sounds it in my soul,
> I ain't got long to stay here.[8]

By some accounts, "Steal Away" may have been written by lay preacher Nat Turner, who led a bloody slave uprising in Virginia in the 1830s and who, according to this tradition, used the song to call other slaves to secret meetings. Though evidence supporting these accounts is limited, the more general role of spirituals in sustaining the lives of African-American slaves under brutal conditions and of incubating a longing for freedom is clear.

Chronicle of Events

1820

- William Ellery Channing and others form the Berry Street Conference, a forerunner of the American Unitarian Association.
- Charles Hodge, the 19th century's most prominent Presbyterian theologian, joins the faculty of Princeton Theological Seminary as an instructor of biblical languages and a year later will be appointed professor of Oriental and biblical literature. He will become a leading voice among Old School Presbyterians.
- Fifteen-year-old Joseph Smith, according to his later published recollection, experiences his first vision, in which he is instructed by two "personages" not to join any of the Christian denominations, for they are "all wrong."
- Congress passes the Missouri Compromise, allowing admission of Maine as a free state and Missouri as a slave state, but banning slavery in the Louisiana Territory north of Missouri's southern border.
- John England is appointed bishop of Charleston.
- Catharine Brown, a Cherokee convert to Christianity, helps to establish a school for American Indian women in Alabama.
- The first wave of Irish immigrants arrives in the United States, swelling the ranks of the nation's Catholics.

1821

- Charles Grandison Finney experiences a religious conversion and abandons a legal apprenticeship to begin study for a preaching ministry.
- The African Methodist Episcopal Zion Church is established.
- Episcopalians establish the Domestic and Foreign Missionary Society.
- *July 16:* Mary Baker Eddy, founder of Christian Science, is born.

1822

- John England, the first bishop of South Carolina, establishes the *United States Catholic Miscellany,* the first Catholic newspaper published regularly in America.

1823

- The first Jewish periodical in America, *The Jew,* is established by Solomon H. Jackson.

- Charles Grandison Finney is licensed to preach by the St. Lawrence presbytery.
- Catholic bishop John England of South Carolina introduces a constitution for his diocese that provides for lay participation in the governance of church affairs.

1824

- Philander Chase, Episcopal bishop of Ohio, establishes Kenyon College and Gambier Theological Seminary.
- The American Sunday School Union is founded.
- The Reformed Society of Israelites for Promoting True Principles of Judaism According to Its Purity and Spirit is established in Charleston after Jews led by Isaac Harby unsuccessfully petition the leaders of the Beth Elohim Congregation for changes in the Shabbat service.

1825

- Mordecai Manuel Noah attempts to establish a colony for Jews on an island he has named Ararat in the Niagara River in New York. The venture is ultimately unsuccessful.
- *May 11:* The American Tract Society is founded in New York City to "make Jesus Christ known in His redeeming grace and to promote the interests of vital godliness and sound morality, by the circulation of Religious Tracts, calculated to receive the approbation of all Evangelical Christians."

Philander Chase helped establish Episcopalianism in the western United States. *(Library of Congress, Prints and Photographs Division LC-USZ62-109898)*

- *May 20:* Antoinette Louisa Brown Blackwell, the first woman ordained a minister by a mainline Protestant denomination, is born in Henrietta, New York.
- *July 19:* Liberal members of Congregational churches in New England found the American Unitarian Association.

1826

- John England, the first bishop of South Carolina, becomes the first Catholic to address the U.S. Congress.
- The Society for the Promotion of Temperance is formed in Boston.
- *August 11:* Andrew Jackson Davis, the most prominent spiritualist of the 19th century, is born in Blooming Grove, New York.

1827

- Revival preacher Harriet Livermore becomes the first American woman (and the second woman) to speak before the U.S. House of Representatives.
- *January 24:* Baptist preacher and seminary professor John Albert Broadus is born in Culpeper County, Virginia.
- *September 21:* Joseph Smith, Jr., claims that the angel Moroni hs given him gold plates, part of which are subsequently translated into *The Book of Mormon.*

1828

- Lyman Beecher founds an evangelical magazine called *Spirit of the Pilgrims* to combat the spread of Unitarianism.
- *March:* Lott Cary, a former slave who became a Baptist missionary, is appointed governor of Liberia.
- *September 10:* Congregationalist minister and divinity school professor Nathaniel Taylor delivers a commencement address at Yale College titled "Concio ad Clerum," which is an important articulation of the New Haven Theology. This theological movement has departed from traditional Calvinism in emphasizing the ability of men and women to choose salvation.

1829

- Isaac Leeser is appointed *hazan* of the Mikveh Israel synagogue in Philadelphia. Here he introduces sermons preached in English.
- The Oblate Sisters of Providence, a Catholic religious order established by women of African descent, is formed; the first sisters take their vows.
- The first Provincial Council of Catholic Bishops is held in Baltimore.

Isaac Leeser is sometimes referred to as the father of Conservative Judaism in the United States. *(Library of Congress, Prints and Photographs Division LC-USZ62-97922)*

1830

- Joseph Smith publishes *The Book of Mormon.*
- Bishop Richard Allen of the A.M.E. Church presides over the First National Negro Convention in Philadelphia at the Bethel Church, where African-American leaders discuss political issues including discrimination and poverty.
- Congregationalist minister Elijah Coleman Bridgman arrives in Canton, thus becoming the first American missionary to China.
- *September:* Charles Grandison Finney begins revival services in Rochester, New York, which will last until June of the following year.
- *April 6:* James Augustine Healy, who will become the first black Roman Catholic bishop in America, is born on a plantation near Macon, Georgia.

1831

- Helena Petrovna Blavatsky, cofounder of the Theosophical Society, is born in Ekaterinoslav, Ukraine.

- Joseph Smith relocates the headquarters of the Mormon Church from New York to Kirtland, Ohio.
- William Lloyd Garrison begins publishing the abolitionist newspaper *The Liberator.*
- *August:* Nat Turner, a black lay preacher, leads a group of slaves in a rebellion in Southampton County, Virginia.
- *December 27:* Charles Darwin undertakes his historic voyage aboard the HMS *Beagle.*

1832

- Lyman Beecher becomes the first president and a professor of Lane Theological Seminary in Cincinnati, Ohio.
- The American Baptist Home Mission Society is formed.
- Evangelically oriented Oberlin Collegiate Institute is founded in Ohio. Both women and blacks are permitted as students.
- Charles Grandison Finney becomes minister of a church that meets at the Chatham Street Theater in New York City. This congregation subsequently builds the Broadway Tabernacle to serve as the center of Finney's preaching ministry.
- Brigham Young embraces Mormonism. After Joseph Smith's murder the following decade, Young will become the new leader of the Mormons.
- Christian believers associated with Barton Stone (Stoneites) and Alexander Campbell (Campbellites) informally unite in Lexington, Kentucky. They will subsequently come to be known as Disciples of Christ.

1833

- The last state religious establishment ends when the Congregational church ceases to be the established church of Massachusetts.
- Quaker minister Lucretia Mott establishes the Female Anti-Slavery Society in Philadelphia.
- The General Convention of Universalists in the United States is founded.
- The sermon preached by John Keble in England titled "On National Apostasy" is thought to mark the beginning of the Oxford Movement, or Tractarianism. This reform movement within the Church of England, which stresses the importance of liturgical worship, will have a significant influence on Episcopal churches in the United States.
- Parliament abolishes slavery in the British Empire.
- An anti-Catholic Boston mob destroys an Ursuline convent.

1834

- Hartford Seminary is established by conservative Congregationalists in East Windsor, Connecticut, to combat the theologically liberal influence of Yale.
- After the trustees of the Lane Theological Seminary in Cincinnati, Ohio, attempt to suppress an antislavery student society, many students (thereafter known as the Lane rebels) withdraw from the seminary and enroll in the newly founded Oberlin Collegiate Institute.
- In Ohio black Baptists form the Providence Baptist Association.
- *July:* St. Philip's African Episcopal Church in New York is destroyed by a mob.

1835

- Lyman Beecher is charged with heresy and tried by a Presbyterian ecclesiastical court but is acquitted of the charges. The same year he publishes *A Plea for the West,* in which he warns Protestants against allowing Catholics to overrun the west.
- Charles Grandison Finney accepts a position as professor of theology at Oberlin Collegiate Institute in Ohio on the condition that he be permitted to return each winter to preach at the Broadway Tabernacle in New York City. The same year he publishes *Lectures on Revivals of Religion.*
- Charlotte Elliot composes the evangelical hymn "Just as I Am, Without One Plea."
- German theologian David Strauss publishes *Leben Jesu* ("The Life of Jesus"), which argues that the miracles recorded in the New Testament gospels are mythical rather than true historical accounts of events.
- Samuel F. B. Morse publishes *Imminent Dangers to the Free Institutions of the United States Through Foreign Immigration,* which raises alarm concerning the dangers of "popery."
- Phoebe Worrall Palmer, future Holiness preacher, begins holding a "Tuesday Meeting for the Promotion of Holiness" at the home of her sister, Sarah Worrall Lankford, in New York City.
- Brigham Young is appointed one of the 12 apostles who assist Joseph Smith in governing the Mormon Church.
- *December 13:* Phillips Brooks, noted Episcopal preacher and bishop and author of the lyrics to "Oh Little Town of Bethlehem," is born in Boston, Massachusetts.

1836

- Frederick Henry Hedge, a Unitarian minister, establishes the Transcendental Club in Boston and four years later persuades the club to begin publication of *The Dial,* the main periodical of the Transcendentalist movement.

- Mormons build and consecrate a temple in Kirtland, Ohio.
- African-American revivalist Jarena Lee publishes her *Life and Religious Experience.* In this book she argues that women are entitled to preach the gospel.
- The American Temperance Union is formed as an outgrowth of the Society for the Promotion of Temperance.
- Mary Lyon establishes Mount Holyoke Female Seminary.
- Angelina Grimké publishes *An Appeal to the Christian Women of the South,* urging an end to slavery.
- Marcus and Narcissa Whitman establish a mission to the Cayuse Indians sponsored by the American Board of Commissioners for Foreign Missions at Waiilatpu on the Walla Walla River in Oregon.
- Union Theological Seminary is established in New York by New School Presbyterians.
- The publication of *Awful Disclosures of the Hotel Dieu Nunnery,* which contains lurid accounts of infanticide and other supposed acts of barbarism among Catholic priests and nuns, stimulates anti-Catholic feeling in the United States.

1837

- The Presbyterian general assembly votes to end its cooperative arrangement with Congregationalists, called the Plan of Union, adopted in 1801. The assembly also expels three synods in New York and one in Ohio. These actions culminate theological differences among Old School and New School Presbyterians.
- Charles Grandison Finney, though originally ordained as a Presbyterian minister, becomes a Congregationalist after the Arminian tendencies of his revival preaching place him at odds with Calvinistic theology. He ends his association with the Broadway Tabernacle in New York City and becomes minister of the First Church in Oberlin.
- Theodore Dwight Weld, converted under the revival preaching of Charles Grandison Finney, publishes *The Bible against Slavery.*
- Antislavery Lutherans form the Franckean synod.
- Phoebe Worrall Palmer, future Holiness preacher, experiences a spiritual awakening after the death of three of her children. She will subsequently characterize this experience as one of having received "entire sanctification."
- *February 5:* Revivalist Dwight L. Moody is born in Northfield, Massachusetts.
- *June 13:* Mormon missionaries set off to proselytize in England.

1838

- Rebecca Gratz persuades the Female Hebrew Benevolent Society to begin a Hebrew Sunday school, the first Jewish Sunday school in America.
- Many Mormons settle in Missouri near present-day Kansas City. After friction and violence erupts between the Mormons and their neighbors, Missouri governor Lilburn Boggs threatens Mormons with extermination if they do not leave the state.
- Lutheran minister Samuel S. Schmucker issues his *Fraternal Appeal,* urging American Protestants to join in an Apostolic Protestant Church.

Rebecca Gratz was a prominent leader in Philadelphia's Jewish community. *(Library of Congress, Prints and Photographs Division LC-USZ62-109117)*

- Sarah Grimké publishes a biblically based defense of public roles for women in *Letters on the Equality of the Sexes, and the Condition of Women.*
- Frederick Douglass escapes from slavery to Massachusetts.
- Phineas Parkhurst Quimby begins to study Mesmerism, an event sometimes characterized as the inauguration of the New Thought movement, of which Christian Science and the Unity School of Christianity are tributaries.
- After a fire destroys the building of Beth Elohim in Charleston, South Carolina, in 1838, reform-minded members of the congregation successfully lead a drive to have an organ installed in the new building.
- In Illinois black Baptists form the Wood River Baptist Association.
- *July 15:* Ralph Waldo Emerson delivers a controversial address at Harvard Divinity School often understood to mark the public beginning of Transcendentalism in the United States.
- *December 31:* Phineas Franklin Bresee, founder of the Church of the Nazarene, is born in Franklin, New York.

1839

- Joseph Smith and approximately 15,000 Mormons relocate to Commerce, Illinois, which they rename Nauvoo.

1840

- Russian Orthodox missionary Ivan Veniaminov is ordained bishop of Alaska.
- Abraham Rice, the first ordained rabbi in America, arrives in Baltimore from Bavaria.
- A controversy begins in Charleston that will over the next several years result in a split between Reform and Orthodox Jews.
- Ralph Waldo Emerson and others join in establishing *The Dial* as a journal for the expression of Transcendentalist thought.
- Roman Catholic bishop John Hughes petitions for Catholic parochial schools to receive a portion of New York public education funds.
- *January 3:* Joseph de Veuster, known as Father Damien, the "leper priest of Molokai," is born in Tremeloo, Belgium.

Eyewitness Testimony

I am about to leave you and expect to see your faces no more. I long to preach to the poor Africans the way of life and salvation. I don't know what may befall me, whether I may find a grave in the ocean, or among the savage men, or more savage wild beasts on the coast of Africa; nor am I anxious what may become of me. I feel it my duty to go; and I very much fear, that many of those who preach the gospel in this country, will blush when the Saviour calls them to give an account of their labors in His cause and tell them, "I commanded you to go into all the world, and preach the gospel to every creature;" and . . . the Saviour may ask, where have you been? what have you been doing? have you endeavored to the utmost of your ability to fulfill the commands I gave you? or have you sought your own gratification, and your own ease, regardless of My commands?

> *Lott Cary, 1821, farewell address to the First Baptist Church of Richmond, Virginia, delivered before he left for missionary work in Africa, in Taylor,* Biography of Elder Lott Cary, Late Missionary of Africa, *pp. 24–25.*

The bill for establishing religious freedom, the principles of which had, to a certain degree, been enacted before, I had drawn in all the latitude of reason and right. It still met with opposition; but, with some mutilations in the preamble, it was finally passed; and a singular proposition proved that its protection of opinion was meant to be universal. Where the preamble declares, that coercion is a departure from the plan of the holy author of our religion, an amendment was proposed, by inserting the word "Jesus Christ," so that it should read, "a departure from the plan of Jesus Christ, the holy author of our religion;" the insertion was rejected by a great majority, in proof that they meant to comprehend, within the mantle of its protection, the Jew and the Gentile, the Christian and Mahometan, the Hindoo, and Infidel of every denomination.

> *Thomas Jefferson, 1821, describing the enactment of the Bill for Establishing Religious Freedom by the Virginia legislature, in* Autobiography, *in Kurland and Lerner,* The Founders' Constitution, *vol. 5, p. 85.*

The Church of Christ at Little Flock holding Believers Baptism by immersion eternal election effectual calling and the final perseverance of the saints through grace and the judgement to come Send greeting to any other church of the same faith and order,

Beloved Brethern

Whereas our very dear Sister Elizabeth Smith have applied to us for a letter of dismission in consequence of her being about to remove from our State and County we recommend her as a worthy member in full fellowship with us and when received by you will be dismissed from our immediate care we hope dear Brethern that you will prove a blessing to one another and may God in his goodness bless you all.

Farewell

By Order of the Church

> *Paul French, clerk of the Baptist church in Little Flock, Harrison County, Indiana, October 1821, providing a letter of good standing to a departing church member, in* Sweet, Religion on the American Frontier, *vol. 1, p. 244.*

Ship Thames, at Sea.

Nov. 20, 1822.—Here begins the history of things known only to those who have bid the American shores a long adieu. We were employed in arranging our births, clothes, &c. all day; and as the weather was calm, we were enabled to go on without much difficulty.

21. The weather became stormy, and the sea-sickness commenced.

22. It blew very hard in the day, and in the night increased to a gale; sea-sickness increased with it. I was myself very sick.

23. Saturday morning at daybreak shipped a sea. The water rushed into the cabin. I saw it with very little fear; and felt inclined to say, The Lord reigneth, let us all rejoice. I was so weak that I was almost unable to help myself. At 10 o'clock I went on deck: the scene that presented itself was, to me, the most sublime I ever witnessed. How, thought I, can "those who go down to the sea in ships" deny the existence of God. The day was spent in self-examination. This, if ever, is the time to try my motives in leaving my native land. I found myself at times unwilling to perish so near my friends; but soon became composed, and resigned to whatever should be the will of my Heavenly Father. I believed that my motives were pure: and a calm and heavenly peace soon took possession of my breast. Oh that it were always with me as it is this day!

24. Sabbath. The weather still squally, and our family still in bad health. We had no publick service to-day. My soul longed for the courts of the Lord; but my heart was still rejoicing in the strength of my God.

25. The ocean has become much smoother than it has been for some time. Our family are recovering very fast; nothing particular has occurred to-day.

26. The weather is delightful, and we feel much better. The ladies wanted a pudding for dinner. Two or three volunteered their services, and a pudding was made. I, for my part, felt no inclination either to make or eat it. I stayed with Mrs. S. In the midst of their business the man on the mast called out, A sail ho! We were all elate for a few minutes. If we had seen a friend who had been absent for a long time we could not have hailed him with more delight. We bore for the ship, and soon discovered her to be the Penn of Philadelphia. Preparations were made for speaking her. The sea was too rough to permit us to send letters. She came near enough to hail us, but we could only say All's well after being at sea a week.

December 1. Sabbath. My soul longed again for the house of the Lord; I endeavoured to find him present with me; and soon indeed found that he was near to all that call on him. I enjoyed the day although we were prevented from having worship until afternoon—owing to the roughness of the weather and the unsettled state of the ship.

Betsey Stockton, 1822, from her journal of her voyage to the Hawaiian Islands as part of a missionary company sponsored by the American Board of Commissioners of Foreign Missions, in African-American Religion: A Documentary History Project, Available online at URL: http://www.amherst.edu/~aardoc/Betsey_Stockton_Journal.html. *Accessed on May 18, 2005.*

Act righteously, act justly, towards all men, whether he be thy brother, or whether he be a stranger unto thee. Restrain every propensity to acts vicious and abandoned. Our happiness depends on our virtue; our virtue depends on the conformity of our hearts and conduct to the rules of right prescribed to us by our beneficent creator whose attributes are perfect holiness, inflexible justice. The virtuous man stands in a relation to God which is peculiarly delightful—his divine perfections are all engaged in his defence; he feels powerful in God's power—wise in his wisdom; good in his goodness. Worship him in holiness of spirit. Approach this house of prayer erected to his service in lowliness of mind. Observe a serious, devout, and respectful demeanor whilst performing your solemn duties; bear in your minds that all your present and future happiness depends on his merciful, kindness. . . . As members of a nation distinguished for its religious customs and ceremonies, it is incumbent on us, so to conduct ourselves, as to manifest obedience to the laws of the country which God has been pleased to allot to us, under the shadow of whose government we enjoy comfort and security.

Jacob Mordecai, September 15, 1822, dedicating the Beth Shalome synagogue in Richmond, Virginia, in Marcus, The Jew in the American World, *p. 144.*

I must inform you, that we rejoice to hear that some people are found yet in your City, and particularly among your Society, who meditate upon the Condition of the present Generation, with all the existing political as well as religious Societies and undoubtedly see how every thing is Shaked in its base by the present periode, how every Kingdom and State tremble and totter, even every Religious Society, Sect or party have no longer a Solid hold upon their old Systems or forms, after which they modelled themselves and also how deep Moral coruptness had universally Crept into all ranks, that the most of People have become licentious and unconscionable and nither regard Civil order, nor mind to exercise true Christian Religion (allthough she produced at all times the best of Man) but Yield to the propensities of their lusts, which outran the Limits of Necessaries long ago, And are not yet nor never will be Satiated—else there were not so many Complaints of hard times, and Scarcity of Money &c among all classes of people. Of all those evils & calamities Harmonie knows nothing; Eighteen years ago she laid the foundation and plan for a New periode, after the Original Pattern of the primitive church described in the 2 & 4 Chapter of the Acts and since that time we lived, although unnoticed, covered with ignominy and contempt, yet happy and in peace, for, our temporary as well as Spiritual Union became every year more perfect, and how our Community stands proof, firm and unmoveable upon its Rock of truth, the World and hell have but very few means remaining untried to overthrow Harmonie, and yet she Stands, and will also well maintain her Ground, for the strength of faith which penetrates into the invisible Realm of Spirits will even reach him whom all Power is given in Heaven and upon earth, he will for certain be Sufficiently interested to promote the preparations of his approaching Kingdom wherever he finds people for it; and with that belief Harmonie is prepossessed in a high degree.

Frederick Rapp, adopted son of George Rapp, the founder of the Harmony Society, December 19, 1822, letter to Samual Worester, in Alexander, American Personal Religious Accounts, 1600–1980, *pp. 145–146.*

MY DEAR SIR,—We think ourselves possessed, or at least we boast that we are so, of liberty of conscience on all subjects and of the right of free inquiry and pri-

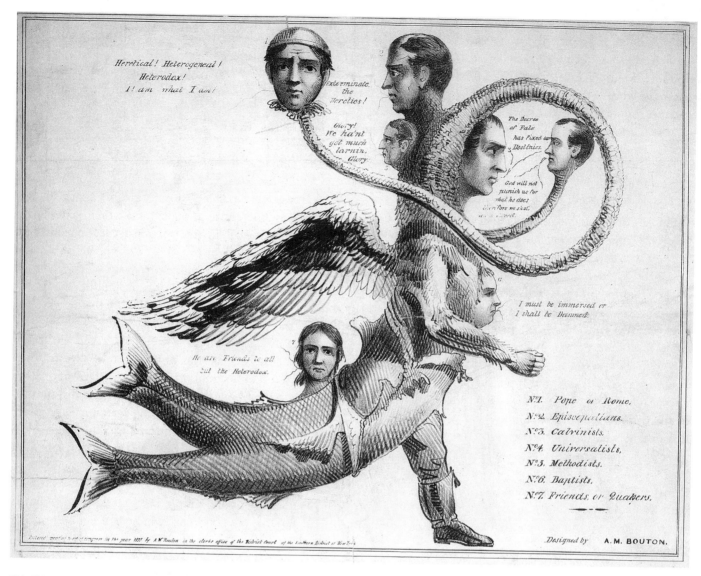

This lithograph, originally published in 1835, satirizes the major religious groups of the 19th century. *(Library of Congress, Prints and Photographs Division LC-USZ62-91361)*

vate judgment in all cases, and yet how far are we from these exalted privileges in fact. There exists, I believe, throughout the whole Christian world, a law which makes it blasphemy to deny, or to doubt the divine inspiration of all the books of the Old and New Testaments, from Genesis to Revelations. In most countries of Europe it is punished by fire at the stake, or the rack, or the wheel. In England itself, it is punished by boring through the tongue with a red-hot poker. In America it is not much better; even in our Massachusetts, which, I believe, upon the whole, is as temperate and moderate in religious zeal as most of the States, a law was made in the latter end of the last century, repealing the cruel punishments of the former laws, but substituting fine and imprisonment upon all those blasphemies upon any book of the Old

Testament or New. Now, what free inquiry, when a writer must surely encounter the risk of fine or imprisonment for adducing any arguments for investigation into the divine authority of those books? Who would run the risk of translating Volney's *Recherches Nouvelles?* Who would run the risk of translating Dapin's? But I cannot enlarge upon this subject, though I have it much at heart. I think such laws a great embarrassment, great obstructions to the improvement of the human mind. Books that cannot bear examination, certainly ought not to be established as divine inspiration by penal laws. It is true, few persons appear desirous to put such laws in execution, and it is also true that some few persons are hardy enough to venture to depart from them; but as long as they continue in force as laws, the human mind must make an awkward and clumsy progress in its investigations. I wish they were repealed. The substance and essence of Christianity, as I understand it, is eternal and unchangeable, and will bear examination forever; but it has been mixed with extraneous ingredients, which, I think, will not bear examination, and they ought to be separated. Adieu.

John Adams, January 23, 1825, letter to Thomas Jefferson, concerning laws prohibiting blasphemy, in The Writings of Thomas Jefferson, *vol. 7, pp. 396–397.*

Having travelled over a considerable portion of these United States, and having, in the course of my travels, taken the most accurate observations of things as they exist—the result of my observations has warranted the full and unshaken conviction, that we, (coloured people of these United States,) are the most degraded, wretched, and abject set of beings that ever lived since the world began; and I pray God that none like us ever may live again until time shall be no more. They tell us of the Israelites in Egypt, the Helots in Sparta, and of the Roman Slaves, which last were made up from almost every nation under heaven, whose sufferings under those ancient and heathen nations, were, in comparison with ours, under this enlightened and Christian nation, no more than a cypher—or, in other words, those heathen nations of antiquity, had but little more among them than the name and form of slavery; while wretchedness and endless miseries were reserved, apparently in a phial, to be poured out upon our fathers, ourselves and our children, by *Christian* Americans!

African-American protest writer David Walker, 1829, arguing for forcible resistance against slavery, Appeal in Four Articles; Together with a Preamble, to the Coloured Citizens of the World, *in Gates,* The Norton Anthology of African American Literature, *pp. 178–179.*

Before I came to the Christian country, my religion was the religion of Mohammed, the Apostle of God—may God have mercy upon him and give him peace. I walked to the mosque before daybreak, washed my face and head and hands and feet. I prayed at noon, prayed in the afternoon, prayed at sunset, prayed in the evening. I gave alms every year, gold, silver, seeds, cattle, sheep, goats, rice, wheat, and barley. I gave tithes of all the above-named things. I went every year to the holy war against the infidels. I went on pilgrimage to Makkah, as all did who were able. My father had six sons and five daughters, and my mother had three sons and one daughter. When

I left my country I was thirty-seven years old; I have been in the country of the Christians twenty-four years. Written A.D. 1831.

Omar Ibn Seid, a West African Muslim brought to America as a slave, 1831, in Eck, A New Religious America, *p. 243.*

Camp-Meeting Rules

1. The people will be notefied of the commencement of Publick Worship from time by the sound of the trumpet; when all persons within the space formed by the tents, are requested to take their seats in the congregation and form to the order [of] Meeting.
2. The seats, and the grove of timber on the right hand of the stand are for the use, & retirement of the females: and the seats & grove of timber on the left hand are for the use & retirement of the men.
3. The trumpet will sound in the morning at 5 as a signal to rise & have prayer in the tents.
4. At the close of worship in the evening, the trumpet will sound as a signal of rest: when all are requested to go to their beds & be quiet; so as not to disturb others. And all persons not having tents to sleep in are required to leave the encampment till morning.
5. The hours for eating will be as follows: vis, breakfast at 7, dinner at 12 and supper at 5
6. All persons commiting any act, or making any disturbance, in, or about this meting, such as are prohibited by the state laws of Ohio, will be delt with according to law.

Rules adopted September 2, 1831, for a Methodist camp meeting in Granville Circuit, Ohio Conference, in Sweet, Religion on the American Frontier, *vol. 4, pp. 720–721.*

A number of us usually attended St. George's Church in Fourth street; and when the colored people began to get numerous in attending the church, they moved us from the seats we usually sat on, and placed us around the wall, and on Sabbath morning we went to church and the sexton stood at the door, and told us to go in the gallery. He told us to go, and we would see where to sit. We expected to take the seats over the ones we formerly occupied below, not knowing any better. We took those seats. Meeting had begun, and they were nearly done singing, and just as we got to the seats, the elder said, "let us pray." We had not been long upon our knees before I heard considerable scuffling and low talking. I raised my head up and saw one of the trustees, H—M—, having hold of the Rev. Absalom Jones, pulling him up off of his knees, and saying, "You must get up—you must not kneel here." Mr. Jones replied, "wait until prayer is over." Mr. H—M—said "no, you must get up now, or I will call for aid and I force you away." Mr. Jones said, "wait until prayer is over, and I will get up and trouble you no more." With that he beckoned to one of the other trustees, Mr. L—S—to come to his assistance. He came, and went to William White to pull him up. By this time prayer was over, and we all went out of the church in a body, and they were no more plagued with us in the church. This raised a great excitement and inquiry among the citizens, in so much that I believe they were ashamed of their conduct. But my dear Lord was with us, and we were filled with fresh vigor to get a house erected to worship God in. Seeing our forlorn and distressed situation, many of the hearts of our citizens were moved to urge us forward; notwithstanding we had subscribed largely towards finishing St. George's Church, in building the gallery and laying new floors, and just as the house was made comfortable, we were turned out from enjoying the comforts of worshiping therein. We then hired a store room, and held worship by ourselves.

Richard Allen, founder and first bishop of the African Methodist Episcopal Church, 1833, The Life Experiences and Gospel Labors of the Rt. Rev. Richard Allen, *pp. 13–14.*

Having a desire to place a few things before my fellow creatures who are travelling with me to the grave, and to God who is the maker and preserver both of the white man and the Indian, whose abilities are the same, and who are to be judged by one God, who will show no favor to outward appearances, but will judge righteousness. Now I ask if degradation has not been heaped long enough upon the Indians? And if so, can there not be a compromise; is it right to hold and promote prejudices? If not, why not put them all away?

. . . . .

But, reader, I acknowledge that this is a confused world, and I am not seeking for office; but merely placing before you the black inconsistency that you place before me—which is ten times blacker than any skin that you will find in the Universe. And now let me exhort you to do away that principle, as it appears ten times worse in the sight of God and candid men, than skins of color—more disgraceful than all the skins that Jehovah ever made. If black or red skins, or any other skin of color is disgraceful to God, it appears that he has disgraced himself a

great deal—for he has made fifteen colored people to one white, and placed them here upon this earth.

. . . . .

Do not get tired, ye noble-hearted—only think how many poor Indians want their wounds done up daily; the Lord will reward you, and pray you stop not till this tree of distinction shall be leveled to the earth, and the mantle of prejudice torn from every American heart—then shall peace pervade the Union.

William Apes, a Native American Methodist minister, 1833, An Indian's Looking-Glass for the White Man, *in Peyer,* The Elders Wrote, *pp. 44–50.*

Probably at the time of the adoption of the constitution, and of the amendment to it, now under consideration, the general, if not the universal, sentiment in America was, that Christianity ought to receive encouragement from the state, so far as was not incompatible with the private rights of conscience, and the freedom of religious worship. An attempt to level all religions, and to make it a matter of state policy to hold all in utter indifference, would have created universal disapprobation, if not universal indignation.

. . . . .

The real object of the amendment was, not to countenance, much less to advance Mahometanism, or Judaism, or infidelity, by prostrating Christianity; but to exclude all rivalry among Christian sects, and to prevent any national ecclesiastical establishment, which should give to an hierarchy the exclusive patronage of the national government. It thus cut off the means of religious persecution, (the vice and pest of former ages,) and of the subversion of the rights of conscience in matters of religion, which had been trampled upon almost from the days of the Apostles to the present age. The history of the parent country had afforded the most solemn warnings and melancholy instructions on this head; and even New England, the land of the persecuted puritans, as well as other colonies, where the Church of England had maintained its superiority, would furnish out a chapter, as full of the darkest bigotry and intolerance, as any, which could be found to disgrace the pages of foreign annals. Apostasy, heresy, and nonconformity had been standard crimes for public appeals, to kindle the flames of persecution, and apologize for the most atrocious triumphs over innocence and virtue.

Joseph Story, associate justice of the U.S. Supreme Court, 1833, Commentaries on the Constitution, *in Kurland and Lerner,* The Founders' Constitution, *vol. 5, p. 109.*

Agreeably to appointment the church met at the school house near bro. Samuel Goodrich's 3. o'clock P.M. Rev. N. C. Clark presided as moderator.

The subjects under consideration by the session, in the morning were brought before the church.

Rev. N. C. Clark & bro. Pomroy Goodrich were appointed a committee to consult with the church & Christians in this country & vicinity respecting the form of church government to be adopted, in this region of country; & to request a general conference of the churches & Christians for consultation on this subject, that, if possible there may be unison.

Resolved, That a church meeting for prayer & conversation be held on the last Friday of each month at the place & hour previously designated.

Resolved, That our next communion, by the leave of providence, be on the first Sabbath in October next.

Brother Isaac Clark was appointed as committee to see that the sabbath schools books were repaired & numbered & registered.

Resolved, That the minister, as soon as practicable, visit every family in the settlement, & that each of the brethren in turn when called upon, accompany him; to ascertain the state of religious feeling, & to awake attention on the subject.—Especially to explain the object & plan of sabbath schools, & distribution of tracts, & to distribute tracts according to the manner of monthly distribution.

Resolved, That a contribution for the purpose of defraying the expenses of the church, be taken at the monthly church meeting.

Resolved, That there be a weekly prayer meeting in the neighbourhood of bro. Strong. Brothers Blodget, S. Goodrich, Strong & I. Clark pledged themselves to maintain it.

Resolved, That there be a weekly prayer meeting in the neighbourhood of bro. Pomroy Goodrich.

Records of the Congregational church at Du Page, Cook County, Illinois, August 29, 1833, Sweet, Religion on the American Frontier—1783–1850, *vol. 3, pp. 121–122.*

There is an innumerable multitude of sects in the United States. All differ in the worship one must render to the Creator, but all agree on the duties of men toward one another. Each sect therefore adores God in its manner, but all sects preach the same morality in the name of God. If it serves man very much as an individual that his religion be true, this is not so for society. Society has nothing to fear nor to hope from another life; what is most important to it is not so much that all citizens profess the true religion but that they profess religion. Besides, all the sects in the United States are within the great Christian unity, and the morality of Christianity is everywhere the same.

It is permissible to think that a certain number of Americans follow their habits more than their convictions in the worship they render to God. In the United States, moreover, the sovereign is religious, and consequently hypocrisy ought to be common; America is, however, still the place in the world where the Christian religion has most preserved genuine powers over souls; and nothing shows better how useful and natural to man it is in our day, since the country in which it exercises the greatest empire is at the same time the most enlightened and the most free. . . .

Religion, which, among Americans, never mixes directly in the government of society, should therefore be considered as the first of their political institutions; for if it does not give them the taste for freedom, it singularly facilitates their use of it.

It is also from this point of view that the inhabitants of the United States themselves consider religious beliefs. I do not know if all Americans have faith in their religion—for who can read to the bottom of hearts?—but I am sure that they believe it necessary to the maintenance of republican institutions. This opinion does not belong only to one class of citizens or to one party, but of the entire nation; one finds it in all ranks.

Alexis de Tocqueville, 1835, Democracy in America, *pp. 278–280.*

The churches must take right ground on the subject of slavery. . . . It is a great national sin. . . . The fact is, that slavery is, pre-eminently, the *sin of the church.* It is the very fact that ministers and professors of religion of different denominations hold slaves, which sanctifies the whole abomination, in the eyes of ungodly men. Who does not know that on the subject of temperance, every drunkard in the land, will skulk behind some rum-selling deacon, or wine-drinking minister? . . . Let the churches of all denominations . . . close their doors against all who have anything to do with the death-dealing abomination, and the cause of temperance is triumphant. A few years would annihilate the traffic. Just so with slavery.

It is the church that mainly supports this sin. Her united testimony upon the subject would settle the question. Let Christians of all denominations . . . write on the head and front of this great abomination, SIN! and in three years, a public sentiment would be formed that would carry all before it. . . .

Revival preacher Charles Grandison Finney, 1835, Lectures on Revivals of Religion, *in Crowe,* A Documentary History of American Thought and Society, *pp. 112–113.*

I do not know that it has ever been questioned and especially by those who have had the best opportunities to learn by *experience and observation,* that the Indian possesses as perfect a physical constitution as the whites, or any other race of men—especially in the matter of hardy body, swift foot—sharp and true eye, accompanied by a hand that scarcely ever drew the bow-string amiss or raised the tomahawk in vain.

I believe, that it is not denied that he is susceptible of *hatred*—and equally of friendship—that he even can love and pity, and feel gratitude—that he is prone to adoration of the Great Spirit—that he possesses an imagination, by which he pictures fields of the blessed in a purer and more glorious world than this; that he possesses the faculty of memory and judgement, and such a combination of faculties as enabled him to invent and imitate; that he is susceptible of ambition, emulation, pride, vanity; that he is sensitive to honor and disgrace; and necessarily has the *elements* of a *moral sense* or conscience. All these are granted as entering into his *native spiritual constitution.*

Maris B. Pierce, a Seneca sachem, 1838, "Address on the Present Condition and Prospects of the Aboriginal Inhabitants of North America," in Peyer, The Elders Wrote, *p. 59.*

My mind at times was greatly excited, the cry and tumult were so great and incessant. The Presbyterians were most decided against the Baptists and Methodists, and used all the powers of both reason and sophistry to prove their errors, or, at least, to make the people think they were in error. On the other hand, the Baptists and Methodists in their turn were equally zealous in endeavoring to establish their own tenets and disprove all others.

In the midst of this war of words and tumult of opinions, I often said to myself: what is to be done? Who of all these parties are right; or, are they all wrong together? If any one of them be right, which is it, and how shall I know it? While I was laboring under the extreme difficulties caused by the contests of these parties of religionists, I was one day reading the Epistle of James, first chapter and fifth verse, which reads: "If any of you lack wisdom, let him ask of God, that giveth to all men liberally, and upbraideth not; and it shall be given him."

. . . . .

At length I came to the conclusion that I must either remain in darkness and confusion, or else I must do as

James directs, that is, ask of God. . . . So, in accordance with this, my determination to ask of God, I retired to the woods to make the attempt. It was on the morning of a beautiful, clear day, early in the spring of eighteen hundred and twenty. It was the first time in my life that I had made such an attempt, for amidst all my anxieties I had never as yet made the attempt to pray vocally.

After I had retired to the place where I had previously designed to go, having looked around me, and finding myself alone, I kneeled down and began to offer up the desires of my heart to God. I had scarcely done so, when immediately I was seized upon by some power which entirely overcame me, and had such an astonishing influence over me as to bind my tongue so that I could not speak. Thick darkness gathered around me, and it seemed to me for a time as if I were doomed to sudden destruction. But, exerting all my powers to call upon God to deliver me out of the power of this enemy which had seized upon me, and at the very moment when I was ready to sink into despair and abandon myself to destruction . . . I saw a pillar of light exactly over my head, above the brightness of the sun, which descended gradually until it fell upon me.

It no sooner appeared than I found myself delivered from the enemy which held me bound. When the light rested upon me I saw two personages, whose brightness and glory defy all description, standing above me in the air. One of them spoke unto me, calling me by name, and said, pointing to the other—"THIS IS MY BELOVED SON. HEAR HIM!"

My object in going to inquire of the Lord was to know which of all the sects was right, that I might know which to join. No sooner, therefore, did I get possession of myself, so as to be able to speak, than I asked the personages who stood above me in the light, which of all the sects was right—and which I should join. I was answered that I must join none of them, for they were all wrong, and the personage who addressed me said that all their creeds were an abomination in His sight; that those professors were all corrupt. . . . He again forbade me to join with any of them: and many other things did he say unto me, which I cannot write at this time. When I came to myself again, I found myself lying on my back, looking up into heaven. When the light had departed, I had no strength; but soon recovering in some degree, I went home.

Mormon founder Joseph Smith, 1838, in Gaustad, A Documentary History of Religion in America to the Civil War, *pp. 350–352.*

The intuition of the moral sentiment is an insight of the perfection of the laws of the soul. These laws execute themselves. They are out of time, out of space, and not subject to circumstance. Thus in the soul of man there is a justice whose retributions are instant and entire. He who does a good deed is instantly ennobled. He who does a mean deed is by the action itself contracted. He who puts off impurity, thereby puts on purity. If a man is at heart just, then in so far is he God; the safety of God, the immortality of God, the majesty of God do enter into that man with justice.

    . . . . .

The perception of this law of laws awakens in the mind a sentiment which we call the religious sentiment, and which makes our highest happiness.

    . . . . .

This sentiment lies at the foundation of society, and successively creates all forms of worship. . . . And the unique impression of Jesus upon mankind, whose name is not so much written as ploughed into the history of this world, is proof of the subtle virtue of this infusion.

Meantime, whilst the doors of the temple stand open, night and day, before every man, and the oracles of this truth cease never, it is guarded by one stern condition; this, namely; it is an intuition. It cannot be received at second hand. Truly speaking, it is not instruction, but provocation, that I can receive from another soul. What he announces, I must find true in me, or reject; and on his word, or as his second, be he who he may, I can accept nothing. On the contrary, the absence of this primary faith is the presence of degradation. As is the flood, so is the ebb. Let this faith depart, and the very words it spake and the things it made become false and hurtful. . . . The doctrine of inspiration is lost; the base doctrine of the majority of voices usurps the place of the doctrine of the soul. Miracles, prophecy, merely; they are not in the belief, nor in the aspiration of society; but, when suggested, seem ridiculous.

    . . . . .

Jesus Christ belonged to the true race of prophets. He saw with open eye the mystery of the soul. Drawn by its severe harmony, ravished with its beauty, he lived in it, and had his being there. Alone in all history he estimated the greatness of man. One man was true to what is in you and me. . . . He spoke of miracles; for he felt that man's life was a miracle, and all that man doth, and he knew that this daily miracle shines as the character ascends. But the word Miracle, as pronounced by Christian churches, gives a false impression; it is

Monster. It is not one with the blowing clover and the falling rain.

New England poet and philosopher Ralph Waldo Emerson, 1838, "Divinity School Address," in Crowe, A Documentary History of American Thought and Society, *pp. 125–126.*

Tired of new creeds and new parties in religion, and of the numerous abortive efforts to reform the reformation; convinced from the Holy Scriptures, from observation and experience, that the union of the disciples of Christ is essential to the conversion of the world, and that the correction and improvement of no creed, or partisan establishment in Christendom, could ever become the basis of such a union, communion, and co-operation, as would restore peace to a church militant against itself, or triumph to the common salvation; a few individuals, about the commencement of the present century, began to reflect upon the ways and means to restore primitive Christianity.

This led to a careful, most conscientious, and prayerful examination of the grounds and reasons of the present state of things in all the Protestant sects. On examination of the history of all the platforms and constitutions of all these sects, it appeared evident as mathematical demonstration itself, that neither the Augsburg articles of faith and opinion, nor the Westminister, nor the Wesleyan, nor those of any state creed or dissenting establishment, could ever improve the condition of things, restore union to the church, peace to the world, or success to the gospel of Christ.

As the Bible was said and constantly affirmed to be the religion of Protestants, it was for some time a mysterious problem why the Bible alone, confessed and acknowledged, should work no happier results than the strifes, divisions, and retaliatory excommunications of rival Protestant sects. It appeared, however, in this case, after a more intimate acquaintance with the details of the inner temple of sectarian Christianity, as in many similar cases, that it is not the acknowledgment of a good rule, but the walking by it, that secures the happiness of society. The Bible in the lips, and the creed in the head and in the heart, will not save the church from strife, emulation, and schism. There is no moral, ecclesiastical, or political good, by simply acknowledging it in word. It must be obeyed.

Alexander Campbell, Disciples of Christ founder, 1839, in The Christian System in Reference to the Union of Christians, and a Restoration of Primitive Christianity, as Plead in the Current Reformation, *pp. ix–x.*

CHAPTER EIGHT

Expansion and Fractures
(1841–1860)

In the generation leading up to the Civil War, the nation spread westward even as tensions between the North and the South escalated toward conflict. Denominational bodies hurried to bring religious influences to the frontier as Americans spilled across the Mississippi, lapping up new land and opportunities provided by western expansion. Evangelical Protestant groups such as the Methodists and the Baptists grew rapidly during this period, but other religious groups prospered as well. Catholics continued their long tradition of missionary activity in the West and Southwest. An influential Jewish community sprang up in Cincinnati, Ohio, and would become the center of what would soon become the dominant expression of Jewish faith in America: Reform Judaism. This period also saw the birth of one of America's most influential indigenous religious traditions, the Mormons. Led initially by Joseph Smith and after his murder by Brigham Young, Mormons migrated in stages westward, ultimately settling in Utah. But whatever optimism this national expansion westward might have produced was clouded by the growing American conflict over slavery. By the middle decade of the 19th century, this conflict accelerated toward war, and religious believers and institutions were swept up in a moral and political dispute that ultimately ignited the Civil War. Denominational fractures split churches along sectional lines, producing rifts such as that between Northern and Southern Baptists, that remained long after war had ended.

Religion and the West

In the first half of the 19th century, territory encompassed in or controlled by the United States grew radically. First the Louisiana Purchase, accomplished in a treaty with France in 1803, nearly doubled the size of the territory controlled by the nation. Subsequently, the United States acquired the Pacific Southwest from Mexico as a consequence of the U.S.-Mexican War and the Pacific Northwest by a treaty with Great Britain. By mid-century the nation spread from the Atlantic to the Pacific Ocean, from Canada to Mexico. Americans rushed westward, and religious influences—sometimes preceding but generally following this expansion—reached westward as well. Missionaries found their way to California and even to the Hawaiian Islands and Alaska.

The territory gained during this period had in some cases been the object of French and Spanish Catholic influence prior to its acquisition by the United States. Beginning in the 1820s, for example, Pierre-Jean de Smet joined a missionary expedition to the United States, was ordained a Jesuit priest, and ultimately became an important emissary between the United States and American Indians in the West. He is credited with founding St. Joseph's Mission among the Potowatomi at Council Bluffs, Iowa, and St. Mary's Mission among the Salish tribe in Montana. Known as Black Robe by the American Indians among whom he ministered, de Smet traveled more than 180,000 miles in his long missionary career, mainly among the tribes of the Pacific Northwest. In the years leading up to the Civil War and the decade following, the federal government relied extensively on de Smet in its dealings with American Indians.

Though federal authorities welcomed the assistance of de Smet, Protestant leaders were frequently alarmed at Catholic missionary activity in the West. Congregationalist minister Lyman Beecher from his outpost in Cincinnati, Ohio, where he had assumed the presidency of Lane Theological Seminary in 1832, warned his readers in *A Plea for the West* (1835) of the growing threat of Catholic presence in the West. He characterized the competing presence of Protestants and Catholics in the West as a "conflict which is to decide the destiny of the West . . . a conflict of institutions for the education of her sons, for purposes of superstition, or evangelical light; of despotism, or liberty."[1] Beecher was certainly not alone in his distress at the spread of Catholicism in the United States. Samuel F. B. Morse published the tract *Imminent Dangers to the Free Institutions of the United States Through Foreign Immigration* (1835), which warned in arguments similar to those of Beecher, of the dangers of "popery." Toward the end of the following decade, the steady flow of Catholic immigrants into the country prompted the formation of the Know-Nothing Party in 1849, which was animated by a fierce anti-Catholic spirit. Prejudice against Catholics in the United States found nourishment in the cartoons of Thomas Nast and in lurid accounts of supposed Catholic barbarities in works such as *Awful Disclosures of the Hotel Dieu Nunnery*, published in 1836. But anti-Catholic zeal proved insufficient to stifle the growth of Catholicism in the United States. By the middle of the 19th century, Catholics had become the largest single denomination of Christians in the country, a position they have not since surrendered. Moreover, Catholic apologists such as Orestes Brownson countered the charges leveled by anti-Catholic polemicists by insisting that Catholicism posed no danger to democracy. To the contrary, Brownson argued in *Catholicity Necessary to Sustain Popular Liberty* (1845), liberty needed some source of authority free from popular control, and Catholic tradition and teaching provided just such a source of authority.

Even without the incitement of anti-Catholic fears, Protestants were unwilling to leave the frontier to be overwhelmed by moral laxity and spiritual indifference. In the second decade of the 19th century, mission societies organized in the Northeast launched exploratory expeditions to the newly acquired Louisiana Territory and received discouraging reports about the general absence of spiritual influences in the territory. Such elements of Catholicism as survived in the territory, of course, did not impress them. They hurried to plant churches, colleges, and schools in an exuberance of institution-building that was characteristic of 19th-century Christianity. Among the Protestant denominations, evangelicals such as Methodists and Baptists tended to devote the most copious resources to this activity. Methodist circuit-riding preachers were not hindered by the lack of travel amenities on the frontier, and Baptist farmer-preachers helped extend the reach of evangelical preaching and teaching even as they helped settle the land. Congregationalists and Presbyterians also joined forces through the Plan of Union, adopted in 1801, specifically intended to pool the resources necessary to plant churches and launch missionary activities in the West.

Liturgical denominations such as the Episcopalians turned their attentions westward as well. For example, Philander Chase, who served first as bishop of Ohio and later bishop of Illinois, established Kenyon College and Gambier Theological Seminary in 1824. Chase had to war against the more settled inclinations of eastern Episcopalians, who doubted whether any supplement to New York's General Theological Seminary was necessary. But through a program of energetic fund-raising in England, Chase succeeded in raising the money necessary to bring Anglican education to the frontier. After relocating to Illinois in the next decade, Chase was able to repeat the process with somewhat less success and establish Jubilee College in 1839. Chase brought low-church Anglicanism to the western frontier; Episcopal missionary James Lloyd Breck, on the other hand, demonstrated that high-church Anglicans were also drawn to the west. Breck settled with associates at Nashotah Lakes, Wisconsin, in the early 1840s and established a mission and a semimonastic order there centered around the Nashotah House Seminary. The following decade he relocated to Minnesota, where he undertook missionary ventures among the American Indians there.

Expectation and Disappointment

For most of the 19th century a majority of Protestants shared a common theological perspective about the nature of the end of times that inspired the general spirit of reform and institution building characteristic of the century. The shared view is referred to as postmillennialism. According to postmillennialists, Jesus was expected to return at the end of a thousand-year period of spiritual and moral improvement that would preface the establishment of his kingdom on Earth. A minority view, premmillennialism, located the return of Christ before the establishment of his millennial kingdom. Postmillennialists, to characterize matters most generally, believed that the world would get better and better before the coming of Christ. Premillennialists, on the other hand, thought matters would get worse and worse before his coming. While the nation stumbled toward catastrophe in the two decades preceding the Civil War, at least some Americans became convinced that history itself would soon run its course. One man in particular galvanized attention by predicting that Christ would return to Earth and establish his kingdom before the 19th century reached its midway mark. William Miller experienced a conversion at a camp meeting in the early decades of the century. Subsequently, he turned his attention to Bible study and in particular to an investigation of scriptural teachings concerning the return of Christ. In 1836 he published an influential tract whose title announced an astonishing prediction: *Evidences from Scripture and History of the Second Coming of Christ about the Year A.D. 1843, and of His Personal Reign of 1000 Years.* Miller highlighted attention on chapter eight of the Old Testament book of Daniel, which referred to an interval of 2,300 days preceding the inauguration of the Messiah's millennial kingdom. He concluded that the reference to days should be understood as actually meaning years and that Daniel's prophesy itself should be dated at 457 B.C. Consequently, he argued, Christ would return to Earth in

1843. His disciples, known as Millerites, were impressed with his calculations and urged him to even greater specificity of prediction. Miller subsequently announced that Christ's return would occur sometime between March 21, 1843, and March 21, 1844. When Christ did not appear during this interval, Miller turned again to Scripture to recalculate. This time he announced that Jesus would return to Earth on October 22, 1844. The passage of this date also without any messianic appearance produced a falling away among Miller's disciples, known to history as the Great Disappointment. Many of Miller's followers returned to the denominations among which they had previously made their homes, but some abandoned evangelical religion altogether.

Though the influence of Miller himself waned drastically after 1844, one of his disciples, Ellen Gould Harmon, who had experienced conversion at a Methodist camp meeting in 1841, insisted that Miller had not been completely wrong after all. That year she fell into a trance and experienced the first of many visions that confirmed her faith. Christ, she declared, had indeed inaugurated his millennial kingdom on the date predicted by Miller, though the cleansing of the temple Jesus was expected to accomplish at the beginning of his reign had occurred in heaven rather than on Earth. As Miller himself retired from public view, Ellen Gould Harmon White, now married to another Millerite, James S. White, began an itinerant preaching ministry of her own. James White served as editor and publisher for his wife's teachings and continued visions. In 1860 the churches they loosely superintended were named Seventh-Day Adventists. Three years later White and her husband organized the churches as a separate denomination. Led by her teaching, the denomination embraced Sabbatarian worship—that is, worship on Saturday, the Jewish Sabbath—and a concentration on health-related issues such as reliance on water treatments and natural remedies rather than physicians and the avoidance of tobacco and alcohol.

Joseph Smith and the First Generation of Mormons

The middle decades of the 19th century saw expansive growth among one of the century's most controversial religious groups, the Mormons, founded by Joseph Smith, Jr. In 1830 the Church of Jesus Christ of Latter-day Saints, as it was soon called, arose out of visions Smith reported to have received and golden tablets he claimed to have discovered and translated as a result of these visions. Smith had arrived with his family in the area of Palmyra, New York, in 1816. There, in what historians refer to as part of the "burned over district" of western New York for its frequent revivals and episodes of religious enthusiasm, the teenaged Smith found himself baffled by the various competing theological claims of different religious groups. By his account, he prayed to discover which group to join and received by way of answer a vision of two beings—the Father and the Son—who told him not to join any church, for none of them possessed the truth. Later, in 1823, Smith claimed to have received a new vision of an angel named Moroni who instructed him where to find certain golden plates buried nearby. These were reportedly inscribed with an ancient language and buried together with two stones that he called the Urim and the Thummim, which were intended to assist in the translation of the plates. Still later Smith claimed to have recovered the plates and translated them. He published the resulting work as the *Book of Mormon* in 1830 and in the same year

Joseph Smith published *The Book of Mormon* in 1830 and subsequently founded the Church of Jesus Christ of Latter-day Saints. *(Library of Congress, Prints and Photographs Division LC-USZ62-90309)*

founded the Church of Jesus Christ, later renamed the Church of Jesus Christ of Latter-day Saints.

Smith soon relocated his church to Kirtland, Ohio, where in 1836 construction was completed on a Mormon temple. While in Kirtland Smith also opened a bank whose subsequent failure provoked enough local animosity to force Smith and his followers to relocate to Far West, Missouri. Here also, however, tensions with neighbors quickly blossomed, and in 1838 the governor of Missouri threatened the Mormons with extinction if they did not leave the state. Smith was arrested for treason and jailed for five months before he was permitted to leave the state with the rest of the Mormons. Toward the end of 1839, Smith relocated his followers once again to a community he named Nauvoo, in Illinois on the Mississippi River. Once settled, the group engaged in missionary activities successful enough to prompt Smith to declare himself a candidate for the presidency of the United States in 1844. Smith, now mayor of Nauvoo as well as leader of the Mormons, soon found himself the object of criticism by a group that had broken away from his church and begun publishing a newspaper to expose Smith's alleged errors. When Smith summarily closed the paper, he was arrested and confined to jail in Carthage, Illinois. There, on June 27, 1844, a mob attacked the jail and killed Smith and his brother Hyrum.

After Smith's death Brigham Young assumed leadership of the Mormons and led them in one further migration to the Great Salt Lake Valley in Utah, where he arrived in 1847. Here the Mormons rapidly grew in numbers and also generated new controversy when in 1852 Brigham Young publicly announced the church's commitment to the practice of plural marriage, or polygamy. During the course of Joseph Smith's lifetime, Mormonism had drifted ever further away from the evangelical Protestantism from which it at least nominally sprang. The idea that the Bible might be supplemented by additional revelations to Smith drove a significant wedge between Mormonism and more orthodox Protestant denominations. Additional revelations purportedly received by Smith included pronouncements that God was material rather than spiritual and mandated that Mormons receive baptism for their dead ancestors. These doctrinal innovations created a significant gulf between Mormons and orthodox Christians, but Young's endorsement of plural marriages made this gulf all but impassable. Joseph Smith had reportedly received a vision in 1841 authorizing the practice of plural marriage, but he had limited knowledge of this vision—and practice consistent with the knowledge—to a core of Mormon leaders. Young's public announcement concerning plural marriages aroused new opposition to the Mormons and inspired political efforts to prohibit polygamy. It also inspired Joseph Smith's wife, Emma Hale Smith, and his son Joseph Smith III to break away from the main body of Mormons and eventually establish the Reorganized Church of Jesus Christ of Latter Day Saints in 1860 at Amboy, Illinois. The formation of this splinter church did little to abate the growth of the main Mormon Church, but the political consequences of Brigham Young's announcement about polygamy were far more serious. This announcement followed Congress's recognition of Utah as a U.S. territory in 1850 and the appointment of Brigham Young as territorial governor. Mormon commitment to the practice of plural marriage collided with an increasing federal dedication to oppose this practice. The Republican Party, organized in 1856, declared itself implacably opposed to both slavery and polygamy. The following year newly elected president James Buchanan aligned himself fully with those who feared that Mormons, though clamoring for statehood, were busy erecting a theocracy around Brigham Young that was hostile to federal law. Accordingly, he removed Young from his territorial post as governor and sent federal troops to Utah to defend federal law. Afterward he explained in an address to Congress the reasoning behind this step.

> The people of Utah almost exclusively belong to this [Mormon] church, and, believing with a fanatical spirit that he [Young] is Governor of the Territory by divine appointment, they obey his commands as if these were direct revelations from heaven. If, therefore, he chooses that his government shall come into collision with the government of the United States, the members of the Mormon church will yield implicit obedience to his will. Unfortunately, existing facts leave but little doubt that such is his determination. Without entering upon a minute history of occurrences, it is sufficient to say that all the officers of the United States, judicial and executive, with the single exception of two Indian agents, have found it necessary for their own safety to withdraw from the Territory, and there no longer remained any government in Utah but the despotism of Brigham Young. This being the condition of affairs in the Territory, I could not mistake the path of duty. As chief executive magistrate, I was bound to restore the supremacy of the constitution and laws within its limits. In order to effect this purpose, I appointed a new governor and other federal officers for Utah, and sent with them a military force for their protection, and to aid as a posse comitatus in case of need in the execution of the laws.[2]

A bloodless war followed in which federal authorities reasserted control of Utah. The matter did not end here, however, as Congress soon took steps to make the practice of polygamy illegal.

The Houses That Slavery Divided

In the decades leading up to the Civil War, the issue of slavery increasingly polarized both the politics and the religious life of the nation. Southern Anglicanism had long since made its peace with slavery. Younger denominations such as the Baptists and the Methodists had initially opposed the traffic in human souls, but by the 1830s their southern representatives also came to support slavery as a divinely sanctioned institution. Proslavery Christians routinely identified blacks as the descendants of Ham in the Old Testament book of Genesis, burdened by the curse of perpetual enslavement Noah pronounced upon Ham's son Canaan.[3] And they happily noted that Old Testament patriarchs practiced forms of indentured servanthood equivalent to slavery. They also observed that the New Testament contains no specific proscription against slavery and, in fact, generally encouraged slaves to practice obedience toward their masters rather than to clamor for freedom. Christians who defended slavery were especially quick to point to the New Testament book of Philemon, in which the apostle Paul urged a converted slave to return to his Christian master. In their minds, though slavery might be subject to abuses, it was not itself an abuse of human relations so long as slaves were treated humanely. Slave masters might be guilty of sin individually to the extent they treated their slaves harshly, but the institution of slavery was not sinful in itself in the view of proslavery advocates. In fact, they calculated the spiritual benefits of slavery as outweighing any of its negative features, since slaves—even if deprived of liberty in their transport to the New World—had gained exposure to the good tidings of the Christian gospel and to the uplifting benefits of civilization.

Abolitionists, however, were appalled by these rationalizations of a corrupt institution. They denied the connection between slaves and the descendants of Ham and contrasted the cruelties visited upon slaves in the South with the more benign Old Testament models of indentured servanthood. More fundamentally, however, they insisted that broad scriptural principles relating to justice and love were more appropriately looked to for guidance concerning the morality of slavery than past practices or the absence of specific scriptural prohibitions against slavery. Sometimes abolitionists displayed impatience with literal proslavery readings of Scripture, and southerners hurried to characterize slavery's opponents as opponents of Christian orthodoxy. In fact, some abolitionists, such as William Lloyd Garrison, whose paper, the *Liberator,* launched issue after issue of attacks on the institution of slavery beginning in 1831, were no particular friends of orthodox Christianity. But the growing protest against slavery could not be contained within the bounds of any particular theological persuasion: it leaped across doctrinal lines. Unitarian minister William Ellery Channing condemned slavery, and fellow Unitarian Julia Ward Howe gave the Union its anthem in "The Battle Hymn of the Republic." But theological liberals possessed no monopoly on abolitionist spirit. Northern evangelical heirs of the First and Second Great Awakening such as the Methodists and the Baptists were increasingly resolute in their condemnations of slaveholding.

The broad consensus eventually shared by northern Christians against slavery and in favor of some immediate deconstruction of the institution of slavery did not make its appearance until the decades immediately preceding the Civil War. In the early decades of the 19th century, northern Christians tended to be moderately antislavery in their outlook. They were inclined to view slaveholding as wrong in God's eyes but were tolerant of gradual schemes for abolishing the institution of slavery. Thus, for example, many northern believers initially supported the aims of the American Colonization Society, established in 1816 with the aim of repatriating slaves to Africa. Through the society's efforts a significant number of free blacks were assisted in migrating to Africa, where they established the nation of Liberia. But the society made no equivalent effort to encourage the emancipation of slaves and thus lost the support of influential African-American leaders, who could rightly question the merits of a program more interested in removing blacks from America than in toppling the institution of slavery. Support for the American Colonization Society reflected early 19th-century support by many northern Christians of a gradual elimination of slavery in the United States. But the evangelical piety inherited from the Second Great Awakening eventually helped kindle a more vigorous abolitionism among northern Christians. Evangelicals, at least in the North, came to view slavery as an individual sin and increasingly emancipation as the only response consistent with true repentance concerning this sin. Moreover, as some evangelicals embraced perfectionism, which maintained the possibility for believers to live sinlessly, the pressure against tolerating the evil of slavery escalated.

African Americans added the voice of bitter experience to the chorus of antislavery condemnation. Frederick Douglass, escaped from slavery himself, asked: "Just God and holy! is that church which lends / Strength to the spoiler thine?"[4] And Presbyterian minister Henry Highland Garnet, an ex-slave ordained a Presbyterian minister in 1842, specifically urged rebellion when he called on southern slaves to rise up against their bondage in a speech the following year to the National Negro Convention in Buffalo, New York.

The sectional divides among Americans over the issue of slavery gradually threatened the denominational unity of major Christian groups. Catholics, Episcopalians, and Lutherans split along sectional lines over the issue of slavery but quickly recombined after the war. Episcopalians in the South, for example, organized themselves during the years of the Civil War as the Protestant Episcopal Church in the Confederate States of America and declined to attend the general convention in 1862. By the end of war, though, they had reunited with the main body of American Anglicans. Congregationalism was generally confined to the northern states and so did not find its peace much troubled by internal dissension over the issue of slavery. But Baptists, Methodists, and Presbyterians claimed significant members in both the North and the South, and these evangelical denominations suffered the most severe and enduring divisions. For a time they wrestled to secure ecclesiastical unity in the face of increasingly bitter disputes over the issue of slavery, typically by muzzling one side or the other in the fierce debate. Methodist authorities, for example, turned aside protests against slavery at the general convention in 1840. By 1843, however, the abolitionist-minded Wesleyan Methodist Connexion was formed in New York, and the following year the general conference adopted antislavery positions that resulted in an outright split along sectional lines and the creation of the Methodist Episcopal Church, South in 1845. The same year saw the birth of the Southern Baptist Convention. Presbyterians, recently divided along theological lines between Old School and New School, resisted further fractures over slavery for a time. But New School Presbyterians split over slavery in 1857, and after the Civil War began Old School Presbyterians followed suit.

Jewish Life

From the beginning of the 19th century to the start of the Civil War, the Jewish population in America grew from roughly 1,600 to 150,000.[5] The latter years of this period saw the beginning of demarcations between two main branches of Jewish faith in America: Orthodoxy and Reformed. Orthodoxy represented the strand of Jewish experience that remained committed to the observance of Mosaic law and to the traditional practices of Jewish religion. Orthodoxy also maintained a vigilant hope for the restoration of Israel to its historic homeland in Palestine. Reform Judaism, on the other hand, substituted concern for the broad moral principles of Jewish teaching for strict observance of Jewish law. Moreover, during the 19th century Reform Jews generally disavowed any hope of a restoration of the traditional Jewish homeland, concerning themselves rather with finding their place in America.

Philadelphia served as an important center for traditional Jewish practice in the 19th century, and it was the home of two important Jewish leaders, Isaac Leeser and Rebecca Gratz. Both belonged to the city's most influential Jewish congregation, Mikveh Israel. Congregation Mikveh Israel invited Leeser to become its *hazzan* (reader) in 1829, and for more than two decades in this office Leeser labored to make Jewish traditions available to his English-speaking congregants. His prolific pen produced translations of the prayers and traditions of both Sephardic and Ashkenazic Judaism. Leeser also began publication in 1843 of a monthly newspaper called the *Occident and American Jewish Advocate*. Two years later he published an English translation of the Torah. Philadelphia's other leading Jewish religious leader during the middle decades of the 19th century was Rebecca Gratz. Gratz gained prominence through her tireless devotion to and organization of a variety of Jewish benevolent and educational activities. As early as 1801 she participated in the founding of the Female Association for the Relief of Women and Children in Reduced Circumstances and subsequently served as the organization's secretary. In the next decade she helped establish the Philadelphia Orphan Asylum in 1815 and again assumed the role of secretary for the organization. Perhaps most significantly, she played a major role in founding the Female Hebrew Benevolent Society (FHBS) in 1819 and devoted some 40 years of her life to work as the organization's secretary. One of the most important activities of the FHBS was the founding of a Hebrew Sunday school in 1838 along the lines of the Sunday schools adopted by Christian churches in the early part of the century.

The 19th century also saw the rise of what became the most prominent expression of Jewish belief in the United States, Reform Judaism. The position of preeminence can be traced to the decades immediately following the Civil War. Reform Judaism, originating in Germany during the earlier part of the 19th century, adopted beliefs and practices untethered from strict adherence to Jewish law and from aspirations of a return to the Jews' historic homeland in Palestine. Reform Jews emphasized general principles of morality rather than careful observation of Jewish law and, especially in America during the 19th century, saw the United States as a sufficient homeland. In the 20th century many Reform Jews became staunch Zionists, supporting the creation of a Jewish homeland in Palestine, but in the 19th century Reform Jews distinguished themselves from more Orthodox Jews by their lack of enthusiasm for the creation of such a homeland.

The growth and eventual dominance of Reform Judaism in America can be traced to the efforts of Isaac Mayer Wise, often described as the father of Reform Judaism in the United States. A rabbi from Bohemia, Wise arrived with his family in the United States in 1846 and settled in Albany, New York, where he served as rabbi of Congregation Beth-El until his Reform sympathies clashed with some of his more orthodox congregants in 1850. He eventually relocated to Cincinnati, Ohio, where he became rabbi for Congregation B'nai Yeshrun, a position he held for the remainder of his life. In Cincinnati Wise cast himself into the work of bringing order and organization to the many Jewish congregations in America, apparently believing he could transcend the divisions already hardening between Orthodox and Reform Jews. He proved unable to surmount these divisions, however, and his organizational labors, which were prolific, served less to strengthen Jewish belief and practice in America generally than to make Reform Judaism the dominant expression of Jewish faith. His accomplishments included publishing a reformed prayer book, *Minhag America*, in 1857, as well as helping to found the Union of American Hebrew Congregations in 1873 and in 1875 the Hebrew Union College in Cincinnati. When the Central Conference of American Rabbis was established in 1883, he assumed its presidency, an office he held until his death. At the time when Wise led in establishing the Hebrew Union College, he enjoyed the support of more conservative Jews such as Sabato Morais, rabbi of the Mikveh Israel congregation in Philadelphia, one of the oldest Jewish congregations in the United States. But a fateful event in the summer of 1883 disrupted the spirit of cordial cooperation that had given birth to Hebrew Union College. At a banquet (known as the "trefa banquet") celebrating the ordination of the college's first graduates, nonkosher shellfish were served, and Wise's perceived lack of sympathy for more conservative dietary scruples sparked a rift between Wise and Morais. Subsequently, the success of Wise's institution building inspired more conservative Jews, led by Sabato Morais and H. Pereira Mendes, to established the Jewish Theological Seminary in New York in 1885. The birth of this institution cemented the division, reaching into the present, between Orthodox and Reform Jews. This division would be reinforced in the 20th century by the emergence of a further major Jewish tradition, Conservative Judaism, which would occupy a middle theological territory between Orthodox and Reform Jews.

The Union Revival of 1858

The revivals ignited by the Second Great Awakening toward the beginning of the 19th century continued episodically throughout the decades that followed. Revivalism in the 19th century initially flowered in the rural settings most famously characterized by the Cane Ridge Revival. Nevertheless, the spirit of revivalism gradually came to plant itself in America's urban life, especially through the preaching of Charles Grandison Finney and Dwight L. Moody. Revivals flourished in spite of criticism leveled at their emphasis on sudden and dramatic conversion as the quintessential entrance into the Christian community. Congregationalist minister Horace Bushnell, for example, who presided over Hartford's North Church for a quarter of a century beginning in 1834, questioned the effectiveness of revival experience in spiritual life. In his 1847 book, *Christian Nurture*, he insisted that instead of the abruptness of revivalistic conversion, churches should aspire to cocoon children in a steady environment of Christian learning so that they would essentially grow up within the church and never perceive themselves to exist outside it. Bushnell's gradual vision of Christian nurture, however, did not offer a satisfactory account of Christian spirituality to many Americans. Urban and industrial growth during the century spawned new forms of dislocation, and revivalistic conversion transmitted to the spiritual realm the kind of abrupt changes increasingly experienced by ordinary Americans.

The looming prospect of war between the North and the South did not dam up the revival currents that flowed across the 19th century. In 1857 one of the century's most significant revivals began in New York and Boston. Although the preaching of ministers such as George Whitefield helped to ignite both the Great Awakening and the Second Great Awakening, what came to be known as the Union or Businessmen's Revival leaned more heavily on the activity of lay believers. Revival was sparked as lay men and women scheduled lunchtime prayer meetings, often with different occupational groups joining in prayer together. Charles Grandison Finney is often credited with having introduced revival to 19th-century urban America, but the Union Revival demonstrated that this introduction was not a passing moment in the history of the nation's religious life. Under the influences of revivalists such as Dwight L. Moody, Aimee Semple McPherson, Billy Sunday, and Billy Graham, cities have remained at the center of America's revival experience. But the Union Revival also revealed that spiritual renewal might proceed even in the absence of charismatic preachers, as ordinary men and women sought a vital religious faith.

Chronicle of Events

1841

- Unitarian minister Theodore Parker preaches an influential sermon titled "The Transient and Permanent in Christianity."
- Joseph Smith claims to have received a vision authorizing the practice of plural marriages (polygamy), shares this vision with other Mormon leaders, and convinces them to join him in this practice.
- Ellen Gould Harmon White, who will become a prominent Adventist leader, experiences conversion at a Methodist camp meeting.

1842

- Former slave Henry Highland Garnet is ordained a minister by the Troy presbytery of New York.
- The American Oriental Society is founded.
- The University of Notre Dame is founded by Reverend Edward Sorin, a priest of the Congregation of the Holy Cross.
- In New Orleans Henriette Delille founds the Sisters of the Holy Family, a Catholic order for black nuns.

1843

- African-American minister Henry Highland Garnet delivers a speech titled "Call to Rebellion" at the National Negro Convention in Buffalo, New York, urging southern slaves to revolt against their masters.
- The Jewish fraternal organization B'nai B'rith (Sons of the Covenant) is founded.
- Former slave Isabella van Wagener takes the name Sojourner Truth and begins an itinerant preaching career for the A.M.E. Church.
- Isaac Lesser begins publication of the *Occident and American Jewish Advocate*.
- Methodist minister and abolitionist Orange Scott and others form the Wesleyan Methodist Connexion.
- Abolitionist Baptists form the Free Mission Society.
- *March 21:* This is the first date proclaimed by William Miller as the date when the Second Coming of Christ will occur. Miller subsequently revises this date to October 22, 1844.
- *July 12:* Joseph Smith, Mormon leaders subsequently announce, receives a revelation concerning plural marriage. Initially he reveals the revelation about plural marriage only to a few trusted Mormon leaders. He and these leaders begin to practice polygamy.

1844

- African-American Alexander Crummell is ordained an Episcopalian priest.
- Mormon leader Joseph Smith declares himself a candidate for president of the United States.
- Anti-Catholic riots occur in Philadelphia.
- Unitarian minister Orestes Brownson converts to Catholicism.
- The Transcendentalist periodical *The Dial* publishes a translation by Elizabeth Palmer Peabody of parts of the *Lotus Sutra*, an important early step in exposing Americans to Buddhism.
- *January 15:* The University of Notre Dame, founded in 1842, is officially chartered by the state of Indiana.
- *June 25:* Joseph Smith and his brother Hyrum are arrested after being accused of instigating a riot when Mormons in Nauvoo smash the presses of a newspaper critical of the Mormons. On June 27, while in jail in Carthage, Illinois, Joseph and his brother will be killed by a mob. Brigham Young subsequently becomes leader of the Mormons.
- *October 22:* The Great Disappointment occurs when William Miller's revised prediction that Christ will return to Earth on this date fails to happen.

1845

- Isaac Leeser publishes an English version of the Torah.
- Holiness preacher Phoebe Worrall Palmer publishes her first book, *The Way of Holiness*.
- Methodist minister Peter Cartwright runs for Congress against Abraham Lincoln. Lincoln wins the election.
- Former slave Frederick Douglass publishes *Narrative of the Life of Frederick Douglass*.
- *May:* Southern Methodists form the Methodist Episcopal Church, South, after northern Methodists attempt to curtail the authority of Bishop James O. Andrew, who owns slaves.
- *May 8:* Baptists in the South split from those in the North over the issue of slavery and form the Southern Baptist Convention.
- *October 8:* Brigham Young announces the planned exodus of Mormons from Nauvoo.

1846

- Isaac Mayer Wise, Reform Judaism rabbi, immigrates to the United States with his family and soon settles in Albany, New York, where he serves as rabbi of the Congregation Beth-El.

- After the U.S.-Mexican War the United States obtains significant new territory in the Pacific Southwest that was formerly controlled by Mexico.
- The American Missionary Association is established. After the Civil War the association will sponsor evangelism and educational efforts among the freed slaves.
- *February 4:* Mormon settlers leave Nauvoo, Illinois, to begin the settlement of the West.

1847

- Henry Ward Beecher becomes the minister of the Plymouth Church in Brooklyn, New York, where he will serve for 40 years.
- Andrew Jackson Davis, called the Seer of Poughkeepsie, publishes *The Principles of Nature, Her Divine Revelations, and a Voice to Mankind,* an important 19th-century work on spiritualism.
- Carl Ferdinand Wilhelm Walther is instrumental in organizing the German Evangelical Lutheran Synod of Missouri, Ohio, and Other States, later known simply as the Missouri Synod of the Lutheran Church.
- Horace Bushnell publishes *Christian Nurture,* which advocates a vigorous program of Christian education in contrast with revivalism's influence on conversion.
- The first wave of Mormon settlers arrives in Utah.

Henry Ward Beecher championed the cause of theological liberalism in late 19th-century America. *(Library of Congress, Prints and Photographs Division LC-USZ62-102767)*

- *November 29:* Marcus and Narcissa Whitman, missionaries to the Cayuse Indians in Oregon, are massacred along with other members of their mission outpost.

1848

- John Humphrey Noyes, after being charged with adultery in Vermont the previous year as a result of his practice of complex marriage, relocates his disciples to New York, where he founds the Oneida Community.
- The Daughters of Zion, a women's auxiliary group within the A.M.E. Church, petitions the general conference of the church to recognize female preachers. This petition, along with one made is 1852, is denied.
- Elizabeth Cady Stanton and Lucretia Mott organize the Women's Rights Convention.

1849

- James S. White begins editing and publishing *Present Truth* as a vehicle for spreading the visions and teachings of his wife, Ellen Gould Harmon White. The following year he begins publishing *Review and Herald.*
- A secret society called the Order of the Star Spangled Banner is formed in New York. Its opposition to immigration and the spread of Catholicism in the United States will characterize the rise of the Know-Nothing Party during the early years of the next decade.

1850

- Isaac Mayer Wise's congregation in Albany, New York, attempts to dismiss him because of his Reform Judaism views, but he refuses to accept the dismissal. During new year services physical conflict erupts in the synagogue, and Wise is arrested for inciting a mob. He and his supporters within the congregation subsequently establish the Anshe Emeth congregation.
- John Joseph Hughes becomes the first archbishop of New York.
- Utah is organized as a U.S. territory, and Brigham Young subsequently becomes territorial governor.
- Jean-Baptiste Lamy is appointed vicar apostolic of New Mexico.
- Catholics in the United States become the largest Christian denomination.
- *July 15:* Francesca Xavier Cabrini, Catholic nun and missionary, is born in Italy.

1851

- The Boston Young Men's Christian Association (YMCA) is established, the first branch of the YMCA in the United States. The same year a branch of the YMCA is established in Montreal.

- The Jewish Anshe Emeth congregation in Albany, New York, becomes the first to seat men and women together.

- Charles Grandison Finney assumes the position of president of Oberlin Collegiate Institute (later Oberlin College) in Ohio, a position he will hold until 1865.

- After Congregationalist minister Horace Bushnell asserts that the Trinity is just the form in which God manifests himself to humanity rather than an intrinsic aspect of God's identity, ministers of the Hartford North Consociation consider trying him for heresy. Rather than submit to such a possibility, Bushnell leads his church, Hartford's North Church, in withdrawing from the Consociation.

1852

- American Indian religious leader Quanah Parker is born around this year.

- Harriet Beecher Stowe publishes *Uncle Tom's Cabin*.

- The Mormon Church publicly advocates the practice of polygamy. Mormon leader Parley Parker Pratt has previously defended the practice in a book titled *"Mormonism! Plurality of Wives!" An especial chapter, for the especial edification of certain inquisitive news editors.*

- Congregationalists formally repudiate the Plan of Union adopted with Presbyterians in 1801 and rejected by Presbyterians in 1837.

- Beth Hamidrash, the first east European Orthodox synagogue, is established in New York by immigrants from Lithuania and Poland.

- The General Convention of Universalists founds Tufts College in Massachusetts.

- *May 9:* The First Plenary Council of Baltimore for U.S. Catholics begins.

1853

- James Roosevelt Bayley becomes the first bishop of Newark, New Jersey.

- Isaac Leeser publishes the first complete translation of the Jewish Bible into English.

- The first Chinese temple in America opens in San Francisco.

- *September 15:* Antoinette Louisa Brown Blackwell is ordained a minister by the Congregationalist church in South Butler, New York, thus becoming the first woman ordained a minister in a mainline Protestant church.

1854

- The Young Men's Hebrew Association (YMHA) is established in Baltimore, Maryland.

- James Augustine Healy is ordained in Paris, France, becoming the first African-American Catholic priest. He will subsequently be ordained the first African-American bishop in 1875.

- Isaac Mayer Wise arrives in Cincinnati, Ohio, where he becomes rabbi of Congregation B'nai Yeshrun and where he begins to publish the *Israelite* (later renamed *American Israelite*).

1855

- David Einhorn, a leading figure of Reform Judaism, immigrates to the United States and becomes rabbi of the Har Sinai congregation in Baltimore, Maryland.

- A conference of rabbis in Cleveland fails to produce unity among Reform and Orthodox Jews.

- Mormon leader Parley Parker Pratt publishes an account of Mormon theology titled *Key to the Science of Theology.*

- Rebecca Gratz leads in establishing the Jewish Foster Home in Philadelphia, the first Jewish orphanage in the United States.

1856

- Wovoka, also known as Jack Wilson, the founder of the Ghost Dance religion, is born around this date.

- The newly formed Republican Party makes the eradication of "the twin relics of barbarism"—slavery and polygamy—central to its platform.

- The first American branch of the Young Women's Christian Association (YMCA) is organized in New York.

1857

- Isaac Mayer Wise publishes a prayer book for Reform Judaism called *Minhag America.*

- Mass prayer meetings beginning in New York City spread to other urban centers, sparking a two-year-long period of revival among many American Christians. The event is variously referred to as the Union Revival or the Businessmen's Revival.

- President James Buchanan removes Brigham Young from his position as territorial governor of Utah and dispatches federal troops to Utah.

- New School Presbyterians divide over the issue of slavery.

- *March 6:* The U.S. Supreme Court holds in *Dred Scott v. Sandford* that African Americans cannot be citizens of the United States and that the Missouri Compromise is unconstitutional.

1858

- Isaac Thomas Hecker establishes the Missionary Priests of St. Paul the Apostle (the Paulists), the first male religious order to originate within the United States, and becomes the order's first superior.
- George Duffield, Jr., publishes the evangelical Christian hymn "Stand Up, Stand Up for Jesus."
- Dwight L. Moody begins a Sunday school mission for disadvantaged children in Chicago.

1859

- Charles Darwin publishes *The Origin of Species.*
- The Board of Delegates of American Israelites is formed. It is the first national organization of Jewish congregations.

- Phoebe Palmer publishes *Promise of the Father,* which defends the role of women preachers.

1860

- The Reorganized Church of Jesus Christ of Latter Day Saints is established in Amboy, Illinois, by Mormons disaffected with Brigham Young and his advocacy of polygamy. Joseph Smith III serves as its first president.
- Rabbi Morris Jacob Raphall delivers a prayer at the opening of a session of the U.S. House of Representatives, the first Jewish clergyman to do so.
- Anna B. Warner writes the lyrics to "Jesus Loves Me, This I Know."
- The churches associated with the teachings of Ellen Gould Harmon White come to be known as Seventh-Day Adventists.
- *December 20:* In a state convention convened by its legislature, South Carolina declares its relationship to the United States to be dissolved.

Eyewitness Testimony

Many tenets, that pass current in our theology, seem to be the refuse of idol temples; the offscourings of Jewish and heathen cities, rather than the sands of virgin gold, which the stream of Christianity has worn off from the rock of ages, and brought in its bosom for us. It is wood, hay, and stubble, wherewith men have built on the corner stone Christ laid. What wonder the fabric is in peril when tried by fire? The stream of Christianity, as men receive it, has caught a stain from every soil it has filtered through, so that now it is not the pure water from the well of Life, which is offered to our lips, but streams troubled and polluted by man with mire and dirt. If Paul and Jesus could read our books of theological doctrines, would they accept as their teaching, what men have vented in their name? Never till the letters of Paul had faded out of his memory; never till the words of Jesus had been torn out from the Book of Life. It is their notions about Christianity men have taught as the only living word of God. They have piled their own rubbish against the temple of Truth where Piety comes up to worship; what wonder the pile seems unshapely and like to fall? But these theological doctrines are fleeting as the leaves on the trees.

Unitarian minister Theodore Parker, 1841, ordination sermon, in Three Prophets of Religious Liberalism: Channing, Emerson, Parker, *p. 123.*

With all deference, I beg leave to introduce some of the religious views and ceremonies of the Shakers.

From the conversation of the elders, I learned that they considered it doing God service, to sever the sacred ties of husband and wife, parent and child—the relationship existing between them being contrary to their religious views—views which they believe were revealed from heaven to "Mother Ann Lee," the founder of their sect, and through whom they profess to have frequent revelations from the spiritual world. These communications, they say, are often written on gold leaves, and sent down from heaven to instruct the poor, simple Shakers in some new duty. They are copied, and perused, and preserved with great care. I one day heard quite a number of them read from a book, in which they were recorded, and the names of several of the brethren and sisters to whom they were given by the angels, were told me. One written on a gold leaf, was (as I was told) presented to Proctor Sampson by an angel, so late as the summer of 1841. These "revelations" are written partly in English, and partly in some unintelligible jargon, or unknown tongue, having a spiritual meaning, which cannot be understood only by those who possess the spirit in an eminent degree. They consist principally of songs, which they sing at their devotional meetings, and which are accompanied with dancing, and many unbecoming gestures and noises.

Often in the midst of a religious march, all stop, and with all their might set to stamping with both feet. And it is no uncommon thing for many of the worshipping assembly to crow like a parcel of young chanticleers, while others imitate the barking of dogs; and many of the young women set to whirling round and round—while the old men shake and clap their hands; the whole making a scene of noise and confusion, which can be better imagined than described. The elders seriously told me that these things were the outward manifestations of the spirit of God.

Anonymous author writing as C.B., 1841, "A Second Visit to the Shakers," in Lowell Offering; A Repository of Original Articles, Written Exclusively by Females Actively Employed in the Mills. . . . First Volume, *in* Bode, American Life in the 1840s, *pp. 194–195.*

Brethren, arise, arise! Strike for your lives and liberties. Now is the day and the hour. Let every slave throughout the land do this, and the days of slavery are numbered. You cannot be more oppressed than you have been—you cannot suffer greater cruelties than you have already. *Rather die freemen than live to be slaves.* . . . Awake, awake; millions of voices are calling you! Your dead fathers speak to you from their graves. Heaven, as with a voice of thunder, calls on you to arise from the dust.

Presbyterian minister Henry Highland Garnet, August 1843, "An Address to the Slaves of the United States of America," delivered at the National Negro Convention in Buffalo, N.Y., in Gates, Norton Anthology of African American Literature, *p. 285.*

B'nai B'rith has taken upon itself the mission of uniting Israelites in the work of promoting their highest interests and those of humanity; of developing and elevating the mental and moral character of the people of our faith; of inculcating the purest principles of philanthropy, honor and patriotism; of supporting science and art; alleviating the wants of the poor and needy; visiting and attending the sick; coming to the rescue of victims of persecution; providing for, protecting and assisting the widow and orphan on the broadest principles of humanity.

Preamble to the constitution of B'nai B'rith, 1843, in Schappes, A Documentary History of the Jews in the United States, 1654–1875, *pp. 216–217.*

I find, since reading over the foregoing Narrative, that I have, in several instances, spoken in such a tone and manner, respecting religion, as may possibly lead those unacquainted with my religious views to suppose me an opponent of all religion. To remove the liability of such misapprehension, I deem it proper to append the following brief explanation. What I have said respecting and against religion, I mean strictly to apply to the *slaveholding religion* of this land, and with no possible reference to Christianity proper; for, between the Christianity of this land, and the Christianity of Christ, I recognize the widest possible difference—so wide, that to receive the one as good, pure, and holy, is of necessity to reject the other as bad, corrupt, and wicked. To be the friend of the one, is of necessity to be the enemy of the other. I love the pure, peaceable, and impartial Christianity of Christ: I therefore hate the corrupt, slaveholding, women-whipping, cradle-plundering, partial and hypocritical Christianity of this land. Indeed, I can see no reason, but the most deceitful one, for calling the religion of this land Christianity. I look upon it as the climax of all misnomers, the boldest of all frauds, and the grossest of all libels. Never was there a clearer case of "stealing the livery of the court of heaven to serve the devil in." I am filled with unutterable loathing when I contemplate the religious pomp and show, together with the horrible inconsistencies, which every where surround me. We have men-stealers for ministers, women-whippers for missionaries, and cradle-plunderers for church members. The man who wields the blood-clotted cowskin during the week fills the pulpit on Sunday, and claims to be a minister of the meek and lowly Jesus. The man who robs me of my earnings at the end of each week meets me as a class-leader on Sunday morning, to show me the way of life, and the path of salvation. He who sells my sister, for purposes of prostitution, stands forth as the pious advocate of purity. He who proclaims it a religious duty to read the Bible denies me the right of learning to read the name of the God who made me. He who is the religious advocate of marriage robs whole millions of its sacred influence, and leaves them to the ravages of wholesale pollution. The warm defender of the sacredness of the family relation is the same that scatters whole families,—sundering husbands and wives, parents and children, sisters and brothers,—leaving the hut vacant, and the hearth desolate. We see the thief preaching against theft, and the adulterer against adultery. We have men sold to build churches, women sold to support the gospel, and babes sold to purchase Bibles for the *poor heathen! all for the glory of God and the good of souls!* The slave auctioneer's bell and the church-going bell chime in with each other, and the bitter cries of the heart-broken slave are drowned in the religious shouts of his pious master. Revivals of religion and revivals in the slave-trade go hand in hand together. The slave prison and the church stand near each other. The clanking of fetters and the rattling of chains in the prison, and the pious psalm and solemn prayer in the church, may be heard at the same time. The dealers in the bodies and souls of men erect their stand in the presence of the pulpit, and they mutually help each other. The dealer gives his blood-stained gold to support the pulpit, and the pulpit, in return, covers his infernal business with the garb of Christianity. Here we have religion and robbery the allies of each other—devils dressed in angels' robes, and hell presenting the semblance of paradise.

. . . . .

Such is, very briefly, my view of the religion of this land; and to avoid any misunderstanding, growing out of the use of general terms, I mean, by the religion of this land, that which is revealed in the words, deeds, and actions, of those bodies, north and south, calling themselves Christian churches, and yet in union with slaveholders. It is against religion, as presented by these bodies, that I have felt it my duty to testify.

African-American leader Frederick Douglass, 1845, Narrative of the Life of Frederick Douglass, *in Gates,* The Norton Anthology of African American Literature, *pp. 365–367.*

Farewell to thee, brother! We meet but to part,
And sorrow is struggling with joy in each heart;
There is grief—but there's hope, all its anguish to quell;
The Master goes with thee—Farewell! oh, farewell!

Farewell! Thou art leaving the home of thy youth,
The friends of thy God, and the temples of truth,
For the land where is heard no sweet Sabbath bell;
Yet the Master goes with thee—Farewell! oh, farewell!

Farewell! for thou treadest the path that He trod;
His God is thy Father, His Father thy God;

And if ever with doubtings thy bosom shall swell,
Remember He's with thee—Farewell! oh, farewell!

Farewell! and God speed thee, glad tidings to bear,
To the desolate isles in their night of despair;
On the sea, on the shore, all the promises tell,
His wings shall enfold thee. Farewell! oh, farewell!

Farewell! but in spirit we often shall meet
(Though the ocean divide us) at one mercy-seat;
And above, ne'er to part, but for ever to dwell
With the Master in glory—Till then, oh! farewell!

George W. Bethune, 1848, "The Departing Missionary," in Bode, American Life in the 1840s, *p. 205.*

The history of mankind is a history of repeated injuries and usurpations on the part of man toward woman, having in direct object the establishment of an absolute tyranny over her. To prove this, let facts be submitted to a candid world.

· · · · ·

He allows her in Church, as well as State, but a subordinate position, claiming Apostolic authority for her exclusion from the ministry, and, with some exceptions, from any public participation in the affairs of the Church.

· · · · ·

He has usurped the prerogative of Jehovah himself, claiming it as his right to assign for her a sphere of action, when that belongs to her conscience and to her God.

Declaration of Sentiments, 1848, written by women's rights activist Elizabeth Cady Stanton, and adopted at the Seneca Falls Conference, in Langley and Fox, Women's Rights in the United States, *pp. 83–84.*

I now began to think seriously of breaking up housekeeping, and forsaking all to preach the everlasting Gospel. I felt a strong desire to return to the place of my nativity, at Cape May, after an absence of about fourteen years. To this place, where the heaviest cross was to be met with, the Lord sent me, as Saul of Tarsus was sent to Jerusalem, to preach the same gospel which he had neglected and despised before his conversion. I went by water, and on my passage was much distressed by sea sickness, so much so that I expected to have died, but such was not the will of the Lord respecting me. After I had disembarked, I proceeded on as opportunities offered toward where my mother lived. When within ten miles of that place, I appointed an evening meeting. There were a goodly number came out to hear. The Lord was pleased to give me light and liberty among the people. After meeting, there came an elderly lady to me and said, she believed the Lord had sent me among them: she then appointed me another meeting there two weeks from that night. The next day I hastened forward to the place of my mother, who was happy to see me, and the happiness was mutual between us. With her I left my poor sickly boy while I departed to do my Master's will. In this neighborhood I had an uncle, who was a Methodist and who gladly threw open his door for meetings to be held there. At the first meeting which I held at my uncle's house, there was, with others who had come from curiosity to hear the woman preacher, an old man, who was a Deist, and who said he did not believe the colored people had any souls—he was sure they had none. He took a seat very near where I was standing, and boldly tried to look me out of countenance. But as I labored on in the best manner I was able, looking to God all the while, though it seemed to me I had but little liberty, yet there went an arrow from the bent bow of the gospel, and fastened in his till then obdurate heart. After I had done speaking, he went out, and called the people around him, said that my preaching might seem a small thing, yet he believed I had the worth of souls at heart. This language was different from what it was a little time before, as he now seemed to admit that colored people had souls, as it was to these I was chiefly speaking; and unless they had souls, whose good I had in view, his remark must have been without meaning. He now came into the house, and in the most friendly manner shook hands with me, saying, he hoped God had spared him to some good purpose. This man was a great slave holder, and had been very cruel; thinking nothing of knocking down a slave with a fence stake, or whatever might come to hand. From this time it was said of him that he became greatly altered in his ways for the better. At that time he was about seventy years old, his head as white as snow; but whether be became a converted man or not, I never heard.

Jarena Lee, a minister in the African Methodist Episcopal church, 1849, The Life and Religious Experience of Jarena Lee, *in Andrews,* Sisters of the Spirit, *pp. 46–47.*

I trust that some may be as near and dear to Buddha, or Christ, or Swedenborg, who are without the pale of their churches. It is necessary not to be Christian to appreciate the beauty and significance of the life of Christ. I know that some will have hard thoughts of me, when they hear their Christ named beside my Buddha, yet I am sure that I am willing they should love their Christ more than my

Buddha, for the love is the main thing, and I like him too.

. . . . .

The New Testament is an invaluable book, though I confess to having been slightly prejudiced against it in my very early days by the church and the Sabbath school, so that it seemed, before I read it, to be the yellowest book in the catalogue. Yet I early escaped from their meshes. It was hard to get the commentaries out of one's head and taste its true flavor.—I think that Pilgrim's Progress is the best sermon which has been preached from this text; almost all other sermons that I have heard, or heard of, have been but poor imitations of this.—It would be a poor story to be prejudiced against the Life of Christ because the book has been edited by Christians. In fact, I love this book rarely, though it is a sort of castle in the air to me, which I am permitted to dream. Having come to it so recently and freshly, it has the greater charm, so that I cannot find any to talk with about it. I never read a novel, they have so little real life and thought in them. The reading which I love best is the scriptures of the several nations, though it happens that I am better acquainted with those of the Hindoos, the Chinese, and the Persians, than of the Hebrews, which I have come to last. Give me one of these Bibles and you have silenced me for a while. When I recover the use of my tongue, I am wont to worry my neighbors with the new sentences; but commonly they cannot see that there is any wit in them. Such has been my experience with the New Testament. I have not yet got to the crucifixion, I have read it over so many times. I should love dearly to read it aloud to my friends, some of whom are seriously inclined; it is so good, and I am sure that they have never heard it, it fits their case exactly, and we should enjoy it so much together,—but I instinctively despair of getting their ears. They soon show, by signs not to be mistaken, that it is inexpressibly wearisome to them. I do not mean to imply that I am any better than my neighbors; for, alas! I know that I am only as good, though I love better books than they.

It is remarkable that, notwithstanding the universal favor with which the New Testament is outwardly received, and even the bigotry with which it is defended, there is no hospitality shown to, there is no appreciation of, the order of truth with which it deals. I know of no book that has so few readers. There is none so truly strange, and heretical, and unpopular. To Christians, no less than Greeks and Jews, it is foolishness and a stumbling-block.

Henry D. Thoreau, 1849, A Week on the Concord and Merrimack Rivers, *in* Henry David Thoreau, *pp. 55, 58–59.*

Day after day for about two weeks, I found myself more deeply convicted of personal guilt before God. . . . Burning with a recollection of the wrongs man had done me—mourning for the injuries my brethren were still enduring, and deeply convicted of the guilt of my own sin against God . . . one evening in the third week of the struggle, while alone in my chamber, and after solemn reflection for several hours, I concluded that I could never be happy or useful in that state of mind, and resolved that I would try to become reconciled to God.

African-American Congregationalist and Presbyterian minister James W. C. Pennington, 1849, from The Fugitive Blacksmith, *in Thomas,* James W. C. Pennington, *p. 46.*

The mode generally adopted for the introduction of Christianity among the Indians. This mode has not, I think, been one that would induce them to speedily relinquish their habits of life. I am aware that I here tread on delicate ground. There is zeal enough among the missionaries who labor among them to move the world, if there was any *system* of operation. There is piety enough to enkindle and fan to a blaze the fine devotional feelings of the Indians, if there was one uniform course taken by all those who go to teach them.

The *doctrines* which have been preached in this civilized country may be necessary for the purpose of stimulating various denominations to zealous labor, but in our country they have had a tendency to retard the progress of the gospel. The strenuous efforts that have been made to introduce doctrinal views, and forms of worship, have perplexed and prejudiced the mind of the Indian against Christianity.

It is true that every man who has been among the Indians as a missionary to them has not been as judicious as he should have been. The idea that *anything* will do for the Indian, has been a mistaken one.

. . . . .

When they preach love to God and to all men, and act otherwise toward ministers of differing denominations, it creates doubts in the mind of the watchful Indian as to the truth of the word he hears. Let the men advocating the sacred cause of God go on together, let them labor side by side for the good of the Indian, and he will soon see that they intend his good. The Indian is not wilfully blind to his own interests.

American Indian Methodist missionary George Copway, 1851, "The American Indians," in Peyer, The Elders Wrote, *pp. 79–80.*

One of the most unique and interesting speeches of the convention was made by Sojourner Truth, an emancipated slave. It is impossible to transfer it to paper, or convey any adequate idea of the effect it produced upon the audience. Those only can appreciate it who saw her powerful form, her whole-souled, earnest gesture, and listened to her strong and truthful tones. She came forward to the platform and addressing the President said with great simplicity: "May I say a few words?" Receiving an affirmative answer, she proceeded:

I want to say a few words about this matter. I am a woman's rights. I have as much muscle as any man, and can do as much work as any man. I have plowed and reaped and husked and chopped and mowed, and can any man do more than that? I have heard much about the sexes being equal. I can carry as much as any man, and can eat as much too, if I can get it. I am as strong as any man that is now. As for intellect, all I can say is, if a woman have a pint, and a man a quart—why can't she have her little pint full? You need not be afraid to give us our rights for fear we will take too much,—for we can't take more than our pint'll hold. The poor men seem to be all in confusion, and don't know what to do. Why children, if you have woman's rights, give it to her and you will feel better. You will have your own rights, and they won't be so much trouble. I can't read, but I can hear. I have heard the bible and have learned that Eve caused man to sin. Well, if woman upset the world, do give her a chance to set it right side up again. The Lady has spoken about Jesus, how he never spurned woman from him, and she was right. When Lazarus died, Mary and Martha came to him with faith and love and besought him to raise their brother. And Jesus wept and Lazarus came forth. And how came Jesus into the world? Through God who created him and the woman who bore him. Man, where was your part? But the women are coming up blessed be God and a few of the men are coming up with them. But man is in a tight place, the poor slave is on him, woman is coming on him, he is surely between a hawk and a buzzard.

Marcus Robinson, 1851, recounting the speech of Sojourner Truth to the Women's Rights Convention in Akron, Ohio, in Gates, The Norton Anthology of African American Literature, *p. 198.*

In calm and cool and silence, once again
I find my old accustomed place among

My brethren, where, perchance, no human tongue
Shall utter words; where never hymn is sung,
Nor deep-toned organ blown, nor censer swung,
Nor dim light falling through the pictured pane!
There, syllabled by silence, let me hear
The still small voice which reached the prophet's ear;
Read in my heart a still diviner law
Than Israel's leader on his tables saw!
There let me strive with each besetting sin,
Recall my wandering fancies, and restrain
The sore disquiet of a restless brain;
And, as the path of duty is made plain,
May grace be given that I may walk therein,
Not like the hireling, for his selfish gain,
With backward glances and reluctant tread,
Making a merit of his coward dread,
But, cheerful, in the light around me thrown,
Walking as one to pleasant service led;
Doing God's will as if it were my own,
Yet trusting not in mine, but in His strength alone!

Poet and Quaker John Greenleaf Whittier, 1853, "First-Day Thoughts," in West, The Quaker Reader, *p. 300.*

There are persons, I believe, in our community, opposed to the policy of the law in question [prohibiting anyone from teaching African Americans to read or write]. They profess to believe that universal intellectual culture is necessary to religious instruction and education, and that such culture is suitable to a state of slavery; and there can be no misapprehension as to your opinions on this subject, judging from the indiscreet freedom with which you spoke of your regard for the colored race in general. Such opinions in the present state of our society I regard as manifestly mischievous. It is not true that our slaves cannot be taught religious and moral duty, without being able to read the Bible and use the pen. Intellectual and religious instruction often go hand in hand, but the latter may well exist without the former.

. . . . .

[T]he slave population of the South are peculiarly susceptible of good religious influences. Their mere residence among a Christian people has wrought a great and happy change in their condition: they have been raised from the night of heathenism to the light of Christianity, and thousands of them have been brought to a saving knowledge of the Gospel.

Of the one hundred millions of the Negro race, there cannot be found another so large a body as the three millions of slaves in the United States, at once so intelligent, so inclined to the Gospel, and so blessed by the elevating influence of civilization and Christianity. Occasional instances of cruelty and oppression, it is true, may sometimes occur, and probably will ever continue to take place under any system of laws: but this is not confined to wrongs committed upon the negro; wrongs are committed and cruelly practiced in a like degree by the lawless white man upon his own color; and while the negroes of our town and State are known to be surrounded by most of the substantial comforts of life, and invited both by precept and example to participate in proper, moral and religious duties, it argues, it seems to me, a sickly sensibility towards them to say their persons, and feelings, and interests are not sufficiently respected by our laws, which, in effect, tend to nullify the act of our Legislature passed for the security and protection of their masters.

. . . . .

There might have been no occasion for such enactments in Virginia, or elsewhere, on the subject of negro education, but as a matter of self-defense against the schemes of Northern incendiaries, and the outcry against holding our slaves in bondage.

. . . . .

For these reasons, as an example to all others in like cases disposed to offend, and in vindication of the policy and justness of our laws, which every individual should be taught to respect, the judgment of the Court is, in addition to the proper fine and costs, that you be imprisoned for the period of one month in the jail of this city.

From the sentence of the court in the trial of Mrs. Margaret Douglass for teaching black children to read in Norfolk, Virginia, 1853, in Blaustein and Zangrando, Civil Rights and African Americans, *pp. 134–138.*

We usually spent our Sabbaths at the opening, on which days our master would gather all his slaves about him, and read and expound the Scriptures. He sought to inculcate in our minds feelings of kindness towards each other, of dependence upon God—setting forth the rewards promised unto those who lead an upright and prayerful life. Seated in the doorway of his house, surrounded by his man-servants and his maid-servants, who looked earnestly into the good man's face, he spoke of the loving kindness of the Creator, and of the life that is to come. Often did the voice of prayer ascend from his lips to heaven, the only sound that broke the solitude of the place.

Solomon Northrup, a free black captured and sold into slavery in the South, 1853, in Boles, Masters & Slaves in the House of the Lord, *pp. 115–116.*

[Y]ou have excommunicated me, on the charge of "disobeying both the laws of God and men," "in absconding from the service of my master, and refusing to return voluntarily."

I admit that I left my master (so called), and refused to return; but I deny that in this I disobeyed either the law of God, or any real law of men.

Look at my case, I was stolen and made a slave as soon as I was born. No man had any right to steal me. That mansteer who stole me trampled on my dearest rights. He committed an outrage on the law of God; therefore his manstealing gave him no right, in me, and laid me under no obligation to be his slave. God made me a *man*—not a *slave;* and gave me the same right to myself that he gave the man who stole me to himself. The great wrongs he has done me, in stealing me and making me a slave, in compelling me to work for him many years without wages, and in holding me as merchandise,—these wrongs could never put me under obligation to stay with him, or to return voluntarily, when once escaped.

You charge me that, in escaping, I disobeyed God's law. No, indeed! That law which God wrote on the table of my heart, inspiring the love of freedom, and impelling me to seek it at every hazard, I obeyed; and, by the good hand of my God upon me, I walked out of the house of bondage.

. . . . .

You charge me with disobeying the *laws of men*. I utterly deny that those things which outrage all right are laws. To be real laws, they must be founded in equity.

You have thrust me out of your church fellowship. So be it. You can do no more. You cannot exclude me from heaven; you cannot hinder my daily fellowship with God.

You have used your liberty of speech freely in exhorting and rebuking me. You are aware, that I too am now where I may think for myself, and can use great freedom of speech, too, if I please. I shall therefore be only returning the favor of your exhortation if I exhort you to study carefully the golden rule, which reads, "All things whatsoever ye would that men should do to you, do ye even so to them; for this is the law and the prophets." Would you like to be *stolen*, and then *sold?* And then worked without wages? and forbidden to read the Bible? and be torn from your wife and children? and then, if you were able to make yourself free, and should, as Paul said, *"use it rather,"* would you think it quite right to be cast out of the church for this? If it were done, so wickedly, would you be afraid

God would indorse it? Suppose you were to put your soul in my soul's stead; how would you read the law of love?

Fugitive slave Anthony Burns, responding to his excommunication by the Baptist church at Union, Fauquier County, Virginia, 1855, in Stevens, Anthony Burns, *pp. 280–283.*

Somewhere between 1800 and 1801, in the upper part of Kentucky, at a memorable place called "Cane Ridge," there was appointed a sacramental meeting by some of the Presbyterian ministers, at which meeting, seemingly unexpected by ministers or people, the mighty power of God was displayed in a very extraordinary manner; many were moved to tears, and bitter and loud crying for mercy. The meeting was protracted for weeks. Ministers of almost all denominations flocked in from far and near. The meeting was kept up by night and day. Thousands heard of the mighty work, and came on foot, on horse back, in carriages and wagons. It was supposed That there were in attendance at times during the meeting from twelve to twenty-five thousand people. Hundreds fell prostrate under the mighty power of God, as men slain in battle. Stands were erected in the woods from which preachers of different churches proclaimed repentance toward God and faith in Our Lord Jesus Christ, and it was supposed, by eye and ear witnesses, that between one and two thousand souls were happily and powerfully converted to God during the meeting. It was not unusual for one, two, three, and four to seven preachers to be addressing the listening thousands at the sate Time from the different stands erected for the purpose. The heavenly fire spread in almost every direction. It was said, by truthful witnesses, that at times more than one thousand persons broke into loud shouting all at once, and that the shouts could be heard for miles around.

Methodist preacher Peter Cartwright, 1856, describing the Cane Ridge revival, in Autobiography of Peter Cartwright, the Backwoods Preacher, *pp. 30–31.*

If the red slayer think he slays,
Or if the slain think he is slain,
They know not well the subtle ways
I keep, and pass, and turn again.

Far or forgot to me is near;
Shadow and sunlight are the same;
The vanished gods to me appear;
And one to me are shame and fame.

Peter Cartwright, pictured here with his wife, forged a reputation as a backwoods Methodist preacher. *(Library of Congress, Prints and Photographs Division LC-USZ62-095736)*

They reckon ill who leave me out;
When me they fly, I am the wings;
I am the doubter and the doubt,
And I am the hymn the Brahmin sings.

The strong gods pine for my abode,
And pine in vain the sacred Seven;
But thou, meek lover of the good!
Find me, and turn thy back on heaven.

Ralph Waldo Emerson, 1857, "Brahma," in Tweed and Prothero, Asian Religions in America, *p. 93.*

I do not pretend that I have found the Catholic population perfect . . . yet I have found that population superior to what I expected, more intellectual, more cultivated, more moral, more active, living, and energetic. Undoubtedly, our Catholic population, made up in great part of the humbler classes of the Catholic populations of the Old World, for three hundred years subjected to the bigotry, intolerance, persecutions, and oppressions of Protestant or quasi-Protestant governments, have traits of character, habits, and manners, which the outside non-Catholic American finds unattractive, and even repulsive. . . . This is certainly to be deplored, but can easily be explained without prejudice to the church, by adverting to the condition to which these individuals were reduced before coming here; to their disappointments and discouragements in a strange land; . . . and to our great lack of schools, churches, and priests. . . . Yet there is a respectable Catholic-American literature springing up among us, and Catholics have their representatives among the first scholars and scientific men in the land. In metaphysics, in moral and intellectual philosophy, they take already the lead; in natural history and the physical sciences, they are not far behind; and let once the barrier between them and the non-Catholic public be broken down, and they will soon take the first position in general and polite literature.

Catholic apologist Orestes Brownson, 1857, The Convert, *in Crowe,* A Documentary History of American Thought and Society, *p. 299.*

CHAPTER NINE

War and Reconstruction
(1861–1880)

The Civil War made enemies of fellow citizens and of fellow believers. The rhetoric of conflict, whether uttered by the North or the South, frequently clothed itself in the vocabulary of faith, as ministers rushed to lend support to battle, sometimes with words and sometimes even with weapons, secure in the confidence that a righteous God would vindicate their cause. When the Union proved ultimately victorious, new theologies of both victory and defeat arose to explain the results of war. Bitterness colored more than a few of these theologies, as some northern voices heaped blame upon the South for subjecting the country to the wounds of war, and southern counterparts chastised the North for tyranny. But other, less polarized theologies also bloomed in the years after the Civil War. The North, while triumphant on the field of battle, nevertheless suffered significant losses, and some

An African-American camp meeting in the late 19th century is represented in this drawing. *(Library of Congress, Prints and Photographs Division LC-USZ62-063867)*

of its theologians saw these losses as evidence of God's chastening, correcting a nation that had forgotten the great Governor of the Universe. The South, too, could sometimes accept this reading of history and see in the war less a judgment upon slavery than a providential restoration of national purpose.

The end of slavery created new opportunities for the growth of African-American religion, which had flourished before the war even in the face of prominent social obstacles. Independent black churches had existed since the late 18th century, and denominations such as the African American Methodist Episcopal Church and the African Methodist Episcopal Zion Church date from early in the 19th century. Emancipation, though, facilitated the growth of African-American churches, especially Methodist and Baptist ones. Predominantly white churches and denominations engaged in missionary activity among the freed men and women, but these did not prompt the rise of integrated churches. Autonomous black churches and denominations flourished in the decades after the war and became central features of African-American community life.

The years immediately after the Civil War saw revivalism harnessed to organizational planning by evangelist Dwight L. Moody, who became the most well-known preacher in the second half of the 19th century. By some accounts the revivals spawned by the Second Great Awakening never totally subsided during the 19th century but flowed across the decades in an unbroken tide that washed into the next century: Cane Ridge, Charles Finney, the urban revivals of 1857 and 1858, revival among the Confederate troops, and Dwight L. Moody. The 18th century, punctuated by the Great Awakening, was followed by the 19th century, in which revivalism took up a kind of semipermanent residence in the household of American faith. Moody's evangelistic preaching thus crowned a century-long tradition of revivalism. But it also partially modified this tradition to introduce tools of organization and management for the planning and execution of revivals that fitted a religious phenomenon originally more at home in the field for life in the great cities of the nation. Like his predecessor Charles Grandison Finney, Moody believed that revivals were not simply random occurrences to be sought after but never counted upon. They were instead, he believed, the predictable results of meticulous planning and organization.

While Moody reinvigorated evangelical America, other religious currents followed different paths. Unitarianism, estranged from the orthodox Christian doctrines of the Trinity and the divinity of Jesus, still counted among its number many

Dwight L. Moody abandoned a career as a shoe salesman to become the most famous revivalist of the late 19th century. *(Library of Congress, Prints and Photographs Division LC-USZ62-122752)*

believers who thought of themselves as Christians. When these, led by Henry Whitney Bellows, organized themselves as the National Conference of Unitarian Churches in 1865, more liberal Unitarian congregations quickly followed by forming the Free Religious Association in 1867. Another established religious tradition, Methodism, gave birth during the middle decades of the 19th century to a subsidiary movement in the form of the Holiness revival, which emphasized the possibility of Christians obtaining perfection in the present life. This religious movement ultimately drifted down a spiritual pathway different from that pursued by mainstream Methodists. Toward the end of the century, the Holiness movement itself spawned Pentecostalism, which was born of the same spiritual hunger for a "second blessing," but which pursued forms of ecstatic worship even less conventional than that common among other Holiness groups. During the central decades of the 19th century, Judaism in America also experienced something of the kinds of divisions long prevalent among Christian denominations. Reform Judaism, introduced in the United States from its original birthplace in Germany, gradually distinguished itself from what came to be known as Orthodox Judaism and in the decades after the Civil War became the dominant expression of Jewish faith in America.

Workers quarry granite in 1872 for the Mormon temple. *(National Archives NWDNS-57-HS-146)*

But reformulations among existing religious traditions were also accompanied by the birth during this period of one of America's indigenous religious faiths, Christian Science, and the maturing of another, the Mormon Church. For a nation that had seen a surfeit of suffering and horror during the Civil War, Christian Science arrived with the hopeful message that sickness and death were ultimately inconsistent with reality. Mary Baker Eddy, influenced by ideas associated with mesmeric healing, authored a new religious tradition by melding these ideas to a strain of Christianity. Another indigenous American religious specimen, the Mormon Church, found itself besieged during this period by a federal government implacably hostile to the Mormon practice of plural marriage. After the death of Joseph Smith, Mormons led by Brigham Young, the church's second president, migrated to Utah. There Young announced publicly on behalf of the church a commitment to the practice of plural, or polygamous, marriage. This announcement ultimately precipitated federal opposition so fierce and so effective that Mormons in the last decade of the 19th century repudiated the practice entirely. Thereafter polygamy would endure only among splinter sects of the main Mormon body.

Theologies of War and Reconstruction

Religious voices were prominent among those who encouraged and sustained the Civil War, both in the North and in the South. Ministers, especially, used their pulpits to uphold the respective causes and to petition the Almighty for his expected vindication. They also provided support and assistance to the war's combatants, organizing relief efforts and serving as military chaplains. Initially, both North and South produced theologies of triumph, confident that a just God would assure them victory in the field of battle, and armed their respective combatants with the vocabularies of holy war. Thus, Julia Ward Howe penned "The Battle Hymn of the Republic" shortly after the war's beginning, confident that God's truth "was marching on" and leaving no doubt that truth marched under a northern banner.

> In the beauty of the lilies Christ was born across the sea,
> With a glory in His bosom that transfigures you and me:
> As He died to make men holy, let us die to make men free,
> While God is marching on.[1]

Similarly, after the fall of Richmond in 1865, Episcopal priest and future bishop Phillips Brooks was effusive in a prayer of thankfulness for victory, for "the triumph of right over wrong."[2] The South also wrapped fury at Northern meddlesomeness in the uniform of faith. God was no friend of tyrants, and the federal government had demonstrated itself to be tyrannical in its repudiation of southern liberties. Thus, Episcopalian bishop Leonidas Polk of Louisiana wrote to a friend in the summer of 1861, "it is for constitutional liberty, which seems to have fled to us for refuge, for our hearth-stones, and our altars that we strike."[3]

Victory, though, whether of particular engagements or of the war itself in the case of the Union, could not disguise the awful toll the conflict had exacted from both the North and the South. A contemplation of the death and suffering sown by battle produced other, less triumphalist theologies. For example, one of the nation's great lay theologians, President Abraham Lincoln, declined to find even in the prospect of victory a straightforward sign of divine approval for the cause of the Union. A month before a bullet fired by John Wilkes Booth ended his life, Lincoln took the oath of office for his second term as president. He chose the moment to engage the nation in a meditation upon the Almighty's purposes. In his second inaugural address, Lincoln hesitated to read victory as a matter of answered prayer and suggested instead that both North and South had besieged heaven with prayer, yet neither could point to a straightforward vindication of these prayers.

> Both read the same Bible and pray to the same God, and each invokes His aid against the other. It may seem strange that any men should dare to ask a just God's assistance in wringing their bread from the sweat of other men's faces, but let us judge not, that we be not judged. The prayers of both could not be answered. That of neither has been answered fully. The Almighty has His own purposes.[4]

The president declined to declare these purposes or to predict that they included a prompt victory on the field of battle. War, he suggested, might continue "until all the wealth piled by the bondsman's two hundred and fifty years of unrequited toil shall be sunk, and until every drop of blood drawn with the lash shall be paid by another drawn with the sword." Even so, this result would only confirm that "the judgments of the Lord are true and righteous altogether." The nation should devote itself less to the task of divining the Almighty's purposes in allowing the conflict than in striving "to finish the work we are in":

> to bind up the nation's wounds, to care for him who shall have borne the battle and for his widow and his orphan, to do all which may achieve and cherish a just and lasting peace among ourselves and with all nations.[5]

When the North ultimately proved victorious, there were theologians of both the Union and the now defeated Confederacy who saw the war as divine retribution on a nation that had lost its way, forgetting the God who had formed it. For some the fundamental liberties announced by the Declaration of Independence had been distorted by the institution of slavery, and only the bloody conflict could awaken America from its slumbering disregard for the rights secured by nature and nature's God. Even southerners could accept that war and defeat had accorded with the providence of God, and some, at least, were anxious to imagine the future toward which God's providential purposes were inclined. Atticus Haygood, a Methodist minister who became president of Emory College, exemplified those in the South who refused to pine for an antebellum southern world and advocated instead the erection of a "new South." In particular, Haygood insisted that African Americans should be made full partners in American life and provided the education necessary to sustain this partnership.

But the sting of defeat ultimately nourished contrary ambitions that came to flourish in the South in the form of a religion of the lost cause. Nostalgia for the past became the devotion of the present, dislocating the work of Reconstruction and reconciliation and entrenching the spiritual sectionalism that had produced denominational schisms in the years leading up to the Civil War. Though American Anglicans promptly reunited after the war, the three other major Protestant denominations—Methodists, Baptists, and Presbyterians—failed to secure reconciliation. Not until the 20th century would northern and southern Methodists and Presbyterians reunite. Baptists never repaired the schism occasioned by slavery and war. Even into the 21st century, Southern Baptists remain a distinct denominational structure separate from Baptists in the North.

New Freedom and Divisions

The end of slavery inaugurated a period of rapid expansion for African-American Christianity. Northern denominations, especially Congregationalists, spearheaded efforts to evangelize the freed men and women, the most important of which were those launched under the auspices of the American Missionary Association (AMA), established in 1846. After the end of the Civil War, the AMA was especially successful in establishing educational institutions in the South intended both to secure the political participation of the freed men and women and their evangelization. Fiske University and Tougaloo University are among the institutions founded by the AMA. But missionary efforts by the AMA and other northern enterprises supplemented previously existing traditions of African-American Christianity among the slaves. Emancipation allowed the worship practiced in "hush harbors" to find more public expressions, and it gave a more prominent voice to black spiritual leaders who had covertly helped to sustain faith among the slaves during the antebellum years. The growing importance of evangelical Christianity among the African-American community during the last decades of the 19th century and the first of the 20th made black ministers extraordinarily influential during this period.

The spread of Christianity among the African Americans, however, did not result in the widespread integration of churches in either the North or the South. One of the "scars of race" manifested in the decades after the Civil War was the racial segregation of Protestant churches.[6] Separation along racial lines had partially preceded the war, reaching back into the late 18th century, when African Americans subjected to second-class spiritual citizenship in white churches abandoned those churches and formed their own denominations. In the antebellum South this kind of exodus was not generally possible. Some nominally separate African-American congregations existed in the South before the war, such as the Baptist congregations in Savannah. More commonly, though, Christian slaves were expected to worship under the same roof as their masters, though they were inevitably allocated segregated seating. After the war the continuation of racist practices such as discrimination and segregation inspired blacks to form their own congregations rather than acquiesce in the kinds of subordination whites still thought appropriate for their black fellow believers. To practices existing within the churches were added those in the broader society. Apart from a brief experience of political empowerment during Reconstruction, African Americans found themselves largely excluded from the main institutions of American life, especially in the South, where Jim Crow segregation attempted to reinstitute the social hierarchies implicit in slavery. Separate black churches, accordingly, became a central feature of African-American communal life.

In the 20th century Dr. Martin Luther King, Jr., would announce that 11 o'clock on Sunday morning—the traditional hour for many Christian worship

Artist Thomas Nast chastises white churches that practiced segregation in this engraving originally published in *Harper's Weekly* in 1875. *(Library of Congress, Prints and Photographs Division LC-USZ61-1422)*

services—was the most segregated hour in America. The roots of that segregation, which reaches even into the 21st century, can be found especially in the decades immediately after the Civil War. The white Methodist preacher David Sullins described the movement of increasing segregation among congregations.

> My negro membership was large and a somewhat puzzling factor in our work. Our custom before the war was to have our colored people sit on the rear seats below or in the gallery, and to give them an afternoon service about twice a month. But now they were free and beginning to assert their independence. I told them of the organization of their people in Philadelphia, Pa., the Zion Methodists; and believing they would do better in that church than in ours, I called their leaders together and explained it to them, and advised them to go into that organization. A letter to this effect soon brought a representative of

that church to see me. We got the colored folks together, and after a little talk they agreed to go in a body to that church. So I took the church register and transferred them. The work was done, and all were pleased.[7]

What Sullins saw in his own congregation was duplicated across the South. Some African-American Methodists abandoned white churches in favor of the black Methodist denominations organized in the early years of the century. Others formed new denominations. In 1870, for example, most of the African Americans remaining in the Methodist Episcopal Church, South, retired from that denomination to form the Colored Methodist Episcopal Church.

After the Civil War church attendance among blacks increased dramatically. Among African-American churches Baptist and Methodist congregations grew and spread most rapidly: by 1916, 90 percent of blacks who attended church attended Baptist or Methodist congregations.[8] Black Baptist churches flourished most of all. Methodism maintained a strong presence among African Americans dating back to the formation of the African Methodist Episcopal Church and the African Methodist Episcopal Zion Church, established in 1816 and 1821,

Though Baptist and Methodist denominations attracted most African Americans after the Civil War, a smaller number of blacks joined the Catholic Church, such as the nuns of the Sisters of the Holy Family in New Orleans. *(Library of Congress, Prints and Photographs Division LC-USZ62-053509)*

respectively. But the congregational structure of Baptist church government, according to which each church is essentially autonomous, made Baptist churches easier to establish. By the end of the 19th century, Baptist churches claimed the largest number of African-American Christians, and in 1895 the National Baptist Convention was formed out of preexisting regional associations of black Baptist churches. In addition to the growth of African-American Methodist and Baptist churches, the second half of the 19th century saw many blacks attracted to the Holiness revival, which began as a subspecies of Methodism but eventually developed into new forms of religious experience, including Pentecostalism. Holiness groups in general and Pentecostal groups in particular practiced forms of enthusiastic or ecstatic worship compatible with older traditions of African-American spirituality.

The Holiness Movement

Methodism has a long history of association with the idea of *entire sanctification*—the belief that Christian perfection is possible in the present life and is not, as Protestant denominations have more commonly insisted, a lifelong process of increasing holiness not completed until after the death of a believer. Toward the middle of the 19th century, as mainstream Methodism moved further away from this ideal, a reemphasis on the possibility of Christian perfectionism inspired the birth of the Holiness movement as a subspecies of American Wesleyanism. Central to Holiness theology was the idea of the "second blessing." For Holiness believers conversion consisted of the sinner's experience of God's forgiveness for past sins. But it remained for those converted to experience also the second blessing, a spiritual turning point that freed the sinner from the shackles of sinful inclinations and made possible entire sanctification. Claiming to be faithful to scriptural teaching and the theology of John Wesley, Holiness groups began to take shape in the years leading up to the Civil War. After the war these groups experienced significant growth. Camp meetings, dating from early in the century and especially prominent among Methodists, became a vehicle for the spread of Holiness theology, prompting the formation of the National Camp Meeting Association for the Promotion of Holiness in 1867.

As mainstream Methodism became a domesticated faith for middle-class Americans, Holiness groups offered a less sedate alternative. As is commonly the case with religious traditions operating outside the mainstream, the Holiness movement was more amenable to leadership by women and minorities. Phoebe Worrall Palmer, for example, was an influential lay preacher drawn to the movement after her own experience of entire sanctification in 1837. Following this experience Palmer became a prominent revival preacher in the United States, Canada, and Great Britain and conducted regular meetings called the Tuesday Meeting for the Promotion of Holiness for nearly 40 years. She was a writer as well as a preacher, publishing *The Way of Holiness*, her first book, in 1845 and editing *Guide to Holiness* from 1862 to 1874.

Although the Holiness movement sprang out of Methodism, the theological parent and its offspring found themselves increasingly unable to remain within the same denominational household as the 19th century moved to its close. Mutual recriminations between the two strained relations, and independent-minded Holiness preachers did not hesitate to gather nondenominational congregations with no organizational ties to Methodism. Holiness groups also shared a distinctive regard for faith healing and drifted theologically toward premillennialist views, according to which the physical return of Christ to the Earth was seen as imminent. These emphases pushed Holiness believers ever further from mainline Methodism. Moreover, toward the beginning of the 20th century the Holiness movement gave birth to a variant of religious experience even more removed from middle-class Methodism. As the Holiness movement matured into the 20th century, Pentecostalism, one of its tributaries, insisted that the experience of the second blessing included being "baptized in the Spirit" and receiving supernatural gifts of the Spirit such as glossolalia, the ability to speak in a heavenly language or an unknown tongue. Speaking in tongues thus became one of the signature features of the ecstatic worship common in Pentecostal services. In the 20th century this kind of ecstatic worship escaped the bounds of Pentecostalism and energized the nondenominational charismatic movement, which emphasized the possession and practice of spiritual gifts such as speaking in tongues.

Urban Revivalism and the Sunday School Movement

At the beginning of the 19th century, the characteristic expression of revival was the camp meeting, none more famous than the Cane Ridge Revival meetings of 1801 in Kentucky. But as the center of American life moved in the 19th century from rural to urban settings, the center of revival migrated as well. Charles Grandison Finney was a leading figure in the introduction of revival to urban America before the Civil War, but it was Dwight L. Moody whose name became most closely associated with urban revivalism. After he left work as a shoe salesman to devote himself full time to Christian mission work in the slums of Chicago in 1858, war briefly interrupted Moody's career as an evangelist. In 1866, though, he began working with the YMCA and in 1870 met and formed an association with singer Ira Sankey. Three years later the two traveled to England, where they held revival meetings that became internationally prominent. After two years they returned to the United States and traveled for a decade, launching revival meetings in the great urban centers of America's North and Midwest. Moody's message was anything but a jeremiad of fire and brimstone, and in spite of his talents as a businessman and organizer his sermons were warm-hearted calls for men and women to receive God's gracious gift of salvation. Like Charles Grandison Finney earlier in the century, Moody was theologically quite distant from Calvinistic voices of the Great Awakening such as George Whitefield and Jonathan Edwards. These men had labored to cause their listeners to see their stark peril and their absolute dependency for salvation on God's sovereign grace. Finney and Moody, on the other hand, preached an Arminian message that emphasized the ability of their listeners to turn at once toward God and to receive salvation in Christ. One of Moody's chief contributions to revivalism in America, however, was to apply his business and organizational skills to the preparation of urban revival meetings. His meetings were preceded by an elaborate structure of advance committees that oversaw planning for the various aspects of the revival sessions. Moody was more than just a revival preacher and organizer. He understood that revival experiences often subside in the wake of revival meetings, and he therefore took steps in the late 1870s and early 1880s to fashion educational institutions devoted to cultivating Christian devotion and practice armed with biblical teaching. In addition, he established the influential Northfield Conferences, at which students gathered during the summer to engage in Bible study and Christian fellowship. One important outgrowth of these meetings was the Student Volunteer Movement for Foreign Missions, established in 1888, whose motto was "the evangelization of the world in this generation."

Dwight L. Moody also used his considerable influence after the Civil War to encourage the revitalization of the Sunday school movement, turning to wealthy Chicago businessman B. F. Jacobs for leadership. Dating from the 1820s, the American Sunday School Union represented one of the ecumenical impulses of prewar America inherited from the Second Great Awakening. After the war, however, Sunday school increasingly became an instrument not only for Christian education but for evangelism. B. F. Jacobs's most important contribution to the Sunday school movement was to lobby successfully for the adoption of uniform lesson plans created for separate age groups in 1872. Under his leadership the Sunday school movement became an interdenominational collaboration that enlisted and trained volunteer teachers who met regularly together in county and state rallies to maintain their enthusiasm and share teaching strategies. The use of common lesson plans facilitated this collaboration. The impetus of this new vision of Sunday school was not simply to communicate biblical teaching but to spread an evangelistic message comparable to the one Moody had made internationally prominent in his revival services.

New Religious Currents

While evangelical Protestantism was nourished by revivalism and a reinvigorated Sunday school movement, other nontraditional faiths took root in the American soil during the decades following the Civil War. Unitarianism, though estranged from orthodox Christianity, nevertheless still considered itself within the household of the Christian church. Relatively conservative Unitarians, led by Henry Whitney Bellows, formed the National Conference of Unitarian Churches in 1865, and Bellows served as the organization's president for its first decade. The conference did not fully realize Bellow's dream of establishing a "Liberal Christian Church of America," and, because its constitution acknowledged the "Lordship of Christ," it alienated Unitarians who had more vigorously repudiated any tie to Christianity. These quickly organized themselves into the Free Religious Association, established in 1867. Yet a more decisive movement away from any kind of religious identity was the Society for Ethical Culture, established by Felix Adler in the spring of 1876. Adler proposed a series of Sunday lectures that would be devoid of any religious content—substituting a focus on morality rather than faith—but retain some of the echoes of more traditional services such as readings and music.

The decades after the Civil War also gave birth to one of America's indigenous religious traditions, Christian Science. Its founder, Mary Baker Eddy, arrived at midlife beset by physical ailments, having experienced widowhood and then an unhappy second marriage. In 1862 she met Phineas Parkhurst Quimby,

Mary Baker Eddy founded Christian Science.
(Library of Congress, Prints and Photographs Division LC-USZ62-100584)

a psychic healer who had since before the Civil War undertaken a successful career as a psychic healer. After receiving healing herself at Quimby's hand, Eddy became his student and an energetic advocate of his theories about healing. In 1866, though, Quimby died, and Eddy experienced a fall on ice that left her seriously injured. A few days later, while reading an account of a New Testament healing, Eddy experienced healing herself. The next decade she published the first edition of *Science and Health* in 1875, expanded in 1883 as *Science and Health: With Key to the Scriptures.* In 1879 she established the Church of Christ, Scientist.

During the period when Christian Science was being born, another of America's indigenous religious traditions, Mormonism, entered its second generation. Not even the Civil War distracted the nation from alarm at the Mormon practice of polygamy, formally announced by the church in 1852 and promptly denounced by the infant Republican Party in 1856. Preoccupation with the great conflict against the South did not prevent Congress from taking the first steps to achieve its ambition of defeating polygamous practice in 1862, when it passed the Morrill Act, which made bigamy a crime in U.S. territories, including Utah. The following decade George Reynolds, secretary to Mormon leader Brigham Young, agreed to serve as a test case for a Mormon challenge against the constitutionality of the Morrill Act. He was arrested, convicted of polygamy, but appealed his conviction, ultimately to the Supreme Court. He argued that the antipolygamy law abridged the free exercise of religion of Mormons, as protected by the First Amendment of the U.S. Constitution. Mormons who expected the Constitution's free exercise clause to shield them from unfriendly federal legislation were destined to be disappointed, however. In *Reynolds v. United States* (1878) the Supreme Court rejected Reynold's appeal and affirmed the constitutionality of the federal antipolygamy law. The Court was unwilling to grant Mormons a religiously based exemption to the federal law. Construing the First Amendment's free exercise clause to require such an exemption, the Court reasoned, would allow every man to become "a law unto himself." As a result of the *Reynolds* decision, Mormons who felt religiously obligated to continue the practice of plural marriage had the option of either going to jail or going into hiding. Congress soon passed new legislation to strengthen the campaign against polygamy. The Edmunds Act of 1882 and the Edmunds-Tucker Act of 1887 made it easier to prosecute Mormons who engaged in the practice of plural marriage, denied the right to vote to polygamists, and provided for the seizure of property of the Mormon Church. The implacability of U.S. law to polygamy eventually caused the fourth president of the church,

Wilford Woodruff, to announce in 1890 that after prayer, God had revealed to him that Mormons should discontinue their practice of plural marriages. This announcement subsequently cleared the way for the admission of Utah into the Union as a state in 1896 and for Mormons to enter the mainstream of American life in the 20th century.

Chronicle of Events

1861

- The Civil War begins.
- After the Presbyterian general assembly pledges loyalty to the federal government, southern commissioners withdraw, and the Presbyterian Church in the Confederate States of America is subsequently organized in Augusta, Georgia.
- Julia Ward Howe publishes "Battle Hymn of the Republic."
- Sarah R. Doremus leads in establishing the Women's Union Missionary Society.

1862

- Following a change in federal law inspired by Jewish protests, non-Christian ministers are allowed to serve as chaplains in the Union army.
- General Ulysses S. Grant expels Jews from the territory he controls, blaming them for engaging in smuggling operations and cotton speculation. President Abraham Lincoln reverses this order.
- Congress passes the Morrill Act, which makes polygamy in U.S. territories, including Utah, illegal.
- Mary Baker Eddy is healed by and begins to study with Phineas Parkhurst Quimby, who believes that sicknesses are mental illusions.
- *November 19:* Revival preacher Billy Sunday is born in Story County, Iowa.

1863

- Unitarian minister Edward Everett Hale publishes "The Man without a Country" in *Atlantic Monthly.*
- Ellen Gould Harmon White and her husband, James S. White, organize the churches that have gathered around her teachings as the Seventh-Day Adventist denomination. On June 5 of this year she has a visionary experience that forms the basis for subsequent prohibitions against eating meat, drinking alcohol, and using tobacco; avoiding physicians and medical drugs; and maintaining a proper diet.
- Representatives from various Protestant denominations establish the National Reform Association for the purpose of seeking an amendment to the U.S. Constitution that will explicitly acknowledge Jesus Christ.
- *January 1:* The Emancipation Proclamation, issued by President Abraham Lincoln, takes effect.

- *December:* American Indian religious leader Black Elk is born on the Little Powder River in what is today the state of Wyoming.

1864

- The Methodist Church Extension Society is founded.
- The National Reform Association proposes an amendment to the preamble of the constitution of the United States, that would recognize Jesus Christ as "Ruler among the nations" and "constitute a Christian government." The proposed amendment never passes Congress.
- The first Greek Orthodox Church in the United States is established in New Orleans, Louisiana.
- Dwight L. Moody dedicates the Illinois Street Church, which grew out of his Sunday School Mission in Chicago.

Unitarian minister Edward Everett Hale was a writer as well as a preacher and is famous for his short story, "The Man without a Country." *(Library of Congress, Prints and Photographs Division LC-USZ62-99518)*

- *April 22:* The motto "In God We Trust" first appears on U.S. coins.

1865

- Henry Whitney Bellows and other theologically conservative Unitarians found the National Conference of Unitarian and Other Christian Churches, whose constitution recognizes "the Lordship of Christ."
- Henry Highland Garnet becomes the first African-American minister to address Congress.
- William and Catherine Mumford Booth found the Christian Mission (later the Salvation Army) in London.
- *April 9:* Robert E. Lee surrenders to Ulysses S. Grant at Appomattox Courthouse in Virginia.
- *April 14:* John Wilkes Booth shoots President Abraham Lincoln at Washington's Ford's Theater on Good Friday.
- *April 15:* Lincoln dies.

1866

- The first conference for Reform rabbis in the United States is held in Philadelphia.
- The Universalist General Convention is organized.
- Ellen Gould Harmon White establishes a sanatarium in Battle Creek, Michigan, called the Western Health Reform Institute.
- Dwight L. Moody becomes president of the Chicago YMCA.
- The Methodist Episcopal Church (North) establishes the Freedmen's Aid Society.
- The African Union Church and the First Colored Methodist Protestant Church unite to form the African Union First Colored Methodist Protestant Church of America.
- *February:* Mary Baker Eddy, founder of Christian Science, experiences physical healing while reading an account of one of Jesus' healings in the New Testament.
- *August 20:* President Andrew Jackson proclaims the "close of the Rebellion."
- *October 7:* The Second Plenary Council of Baltimore for U.S. Catholics begins.

1867

- Isaac Leeser leads in establishing Maimonides College in Philadelphia, the first rabbinical school in America.
- Mary Prout, a former slave, establishes the Order of St. Luke, which becomes one of the most influential benevolent societies for African-American women.

- James Freeman Clarke is appointed a lecturer on non-Christian religions at Harvard.
- Theologically liberal Unitarians, dismayed at the formation of the more conservative National Association of Unitarian Churches in 1865, establish the Free Religious Association.
- The National Camp Meeting Association for the Promotion of Holiness is formed.

1868

- The Fourteenth Amendment to the U.S. Constitution is ratified. Among its key provisions are the equal protection clause and the due process clause. The due process clause will be construed in the 20th century to protect certain fundamental rights from state and local interference. This protection will be applied to make the First Amendment's free exercise and establishment clauses applicable to state and local governments.
- Catholic priest and missionary Pierre Jean de Smet visits the camp of Sioux leader Sitting Bull and helps persuade the Sioux to accept a peace treaty with the U.S. government.

1869

- Fanny Jackson Coppin becomes principal of the Institute for Colored Youth in Philadelphia.
- Old School and New School general assemblies of Presbyterianism in America are reconciled after 30 years of division.
- The Women's Board of Missions is organized.
- *December:* The First Vatican Council begins, lasting until September 1870, during which the Catholic Church officially adopts the doctrine of papal infallibility.

1870

- Revivalist Dwight L. Moody and singer Ira David Sankey meet at an international YMCA conference held in Indianapolis, Indiana, and form an association that will eventually make them partners in revival work.
- Hiram R. Revels, ordained a minister in the A.M.E. Church, becomes the first African American elected to the U.S. Senate.
- Most of the remaining African-American members of the Methodist Episcopal Church, South, leave to form the Colored Methodist Episcopal Church (today the Christian Methodist Episcopal Church).
- Paiute prophet Wodziwob teaches an early version of the Ghost Dance around this date, suggesting to the

Paiute that carrying out the dance will revive the dead, destroy whites, and inaugurate an earthly paradise.

- Around this date Charles Taze Russell begins a home Bible study that will eventually lead to the organization of the group now known as Jehovah's Witnesses.

1871

- Charles Hodge publishes the first volume of his influential three-volume work *Systematic Theology.*
- Charles Darwin publishes *The Descent of Man.*
- James Freeman Clarke publishes *Ten Great Religions,* which eventually goes through 21 editions.

1872

- James Roosevelt Bayley becomes archbishop of Baltimore.
- The American Sunday School Union adopts a plan of uniform lessons.

1873

- Father Damien, a Catholic priest, begins working among the lepers on the island of Molokai in Hawaii, from which labor he will eventually contract leprosy himself.
- Dwight L. Moody accompanied by Ira Sankey begins a two-year revival tour of the British Isles that will make him one of the world's best-known revival preachers.
- Ira Sankey publishes his first hymn book, titled *Sacred Songs and Solos,* in England.
- The Union of American Hebrew Congregations is established in Cincinnati, Ohio, for the purpose of joining all Jewish congregations in the United States, but it soon becomes the center of Reform Judaism congregations.
- Bethiah Ogle and other women march on the saloons of Washington Court House, Ohio, eventually causing the saloons to surrender their liquor supplies and cease further sales. This march inspires others like it elsewhere and helps to ignite the women's temperance movement.

1874

- In a high-profile ecclesiastical trial, Henry Ward Beecher is exonerated of charges of having had an affair with Elizabeth Tilton, though a civil trial the following year arising out of the same allegations results in a hung jury.
- George Reynolds, secretary to Brigham Young, agrees to serve as a test case for Mormons who wish to chal-

lenge the constitutionality of the Morrill Act, passed by Congress in 1862, which made polygamy illegal in the U.S. territories. He is convicted of polygamy and appeals.

- The Women's Christian Temperance Union is organized in Cincinnati, Ohio, and Frances Willard is elected corresponding secretary of the organization. She later serves as the organization's president beginning in 1879 until her death in 1898. Under Willard's leadership (characterized by the motto Do Everything) the Union supports a variety of progressive causes, including women's suffrage.
- The Judiciary Committee of the U.S. House of Representatives votes against passage of the "Christian amendment" proposed by the National Reform Association in 1864.
- Charles Hodge publishes *What Is Darwinism?* in which he argues that Darwin's theory of natural selection is not consistent with biblical teaching.

1875

- Mary Baker Eddy publishes *Science and Health.* In 1883 she will append *A Key to the Scriptures* to the original book, and the new text, *Science and Health: With Key to the Scriptures,* becomes the central religious book of Christian Science.
- Representative James G. Blaine offers the proposed Blaine Amendment to the U.S. Constitution in the House of Representatives. The amendment, aimed at restricting government support of Catholic parochial schools, would prohibit public funds or assets from being given to or controlled by any religious denomination. The amendment passes in the House on August 4, 1876, but fails to receive the necessary two-thirds majority vote in the Senate to be submitted for ratification to the states. Subsequently, however, the substance of the Blaine amendment will be incorporated into a number of state constitutions.
- Isaac Mayer Wise helps to found the Hebrew Union College in Cincinnati, Ohio, and serves as its president for the remainder of his life. The college promotes Reform Judaism.
- Dwight L. Moody and Ira Sankey return from a successful revival tour in England and launch a series of revival campaigns in the northern and midwestern United States.
- Henry Steel Olcott and Helena Petrovna Blavatsky found the Theosophical Society, with Olcott as president.

A room from Mary Baker Eddy's home in Boston, Massachusetts, is pictured here. *(Library of Congress, Prints and Photographs Division LC-USZ62-073247)*

- In England the Keswick Convention begins a series of annual meetings focused on the "higher" Christian life. Earlier during this year the Brighton Conventions for the Promotion of Holiness convenes and helps initiate the Higher Life Movement. These meetings emphasize the baptism of the Spirit as empowering believers to engage in Christian service, and they subsequently influence the rise of Pentecostalism and still later the charismatic movement in the United States.
- Holiness preacher and author Hannah Whitall Smith publishes the Christian devotional classic *The Christian's Secret of a Happy Life.*
- James Augustine Healy is consecrated bishop of Portland, Maine, becoming the first African-American bishop of the Catholic Church in the United States.
- Jean-Baptiste Lamy is consecrated archbishop of Sante Fe.

1876
- James Cardinal Gibbons publishes *The Faith of Our Fathers,* an influential apologetic for Catholicism.
- Felix Adler establishes the Society for Ethical Culture in New York.
- *June:* Following the destruction of the Illinois Street Church, founded by Dwight L. Moody, in the Chicago fire of 1871, the Chicago Avenue Church, with seats for 10,000 people, is built and dedicated. In 1908 the church will be renamed the Moody Church.

1877
- Helena Petrovna Blavatsky, cofounder of the Theosophical Society with Henry Steel Olcott, publishes her first major work, *Isis Unveiled.*

Ira D. Sankey traveled with Dwight L. Moody, supplying music for Moody's revival campaigns. *(Library of Congress, Prints and Photographs Division LC-USZ62-108534)*

1878

- *May 5:* The U.S. Supreme Court in *Reynolds v. United States* determines that the protection of religious free exercise in the U.S. Constitution's First Amendment does not exempt Mormons from the prohibition against polygamy in a federal law.

1879

- Mary Baker Eddy founds the Church of Christ, Scientist.
- Helena Petrovna Blavatsky and Henry Steel Olcott, the cofounders of the Theosophical Society, after having relocated to India, begin publishing the *Theosophist.*
- Dwight L. Moody founds the Northfield Seminary for Girls in his hometown of Northfield, Massachusetts.

1880

- Francesca Xavier Cabrini founds the Missionaries of the Sacred Heart.
- Dwight L. Moody founds the Northfield Conferences, annual evangelical religious meetings for students.
- The Salvation Army begins work in the United States.
- Methodist minister and president of Emory College, Atticus Greene Haygood delivers a commencement address titled "The New South" in which he urges southerners to cease lamenting the Old South.
- A total of 150 black Baptist ministers meet in Montgomery, Alabama, and form the Baptist Mission Convention, one of the predecessors of the National Baptist Convention, organized in 1895.

Eyewitness Testimony

Dear Beauregard:

... The grand news here is that he is dead—"our Savonarola," dead, appropriately, in the city of Savonarola. You ask who I mean by *he.* I mean, of course, the man who has been the heart and soul of the religionists who have stirred up our fanatics not only in this commonwealth but as far west as Ohio and Illinois. I mean, of course, the one who is not far from being Satan himself in his rank unbelief, his smooth and slippery and hypocritical invocation of Scripture, and the energy and determination he has thrown into the cause of wrecking our peaceful land. I mean no other than the Reverend (?) Theodore Parker.

. . . . .

You are, I know, of a philosophical turn of mind and must wonder how this murderous creature came to occupy one of our pulpits. On that point a little recent religious history is relevant. To begin with, the antislavery agitation began—I say it to my shame—in this city on the Fourth of July 1829, in the Park Street Church. William Lloyd Garrison, who had hitherto been crusading against Sabbath-breaking and alcoholism, announced that he had been converted to a new cause—abolition. Five years later 124 ministers of the Gospel, chiefly Congregationalists from this part of the world, issued a manifesto addressed to the public, in which they made the discovery that slavery was "a great and crying national sin" and that every man, in every part of the country, had a personal duty to secure its extinction by what they called "Immediate Emancipation." Thereafter, a network of ministers was formed which kept up the attack. They were always a small portion of the ministry. They did not have the countenance of the main church bodies, Methodist, Baptists, Presbyterian, Episcopalian, Roman Catholic. But they were insistent, persistent, and very noisy; and as you know, they insulted you and your fellow owners of human property to the point where you justifiably were angry and almost maddened.

. . . . .

Parker called his God "A Father and Mother Person," a kind of hybrid hermaphrodite blessed with hebetude, a spectator not an actor in the world, a being of moral insensibility. He believed Christ to be no more divine than Daniel Webster and the Church to be no more sacred than a tavern. The Music Hall or Faneuil Hall were equally good auditoriums for his religious discourses. He could have been prosecuted for fraud, calling himself a minister of the Gospel and his church a Christian church.

. . . . .

A wise Frenchman, who visited our country and this city almost thirty years ago, noted at the time the religious peace that reigned and ventured the observation that if a religion were to be successful it should not meddle with partisan politics and practical reform. Would that Mr. Parker had meditated on that advice of Alexis de Tocqueville! I should not have to spend this afternoon in these melancholy reflections that fill my mind with news of his none too timely demise.

George Frothingham, May 30, 1860, in Noonan, The Lustre of Our Country, *pp. 119–129.*

My period had come for Prayer—
No other Art—would do—
My Tactics missed a rudiment—
Creator—Was it you?

God grows above—so those who pray
Horizons—must ascend—
And so I stepped upon the North
To see this Curious Friend—

His House was not—no sign had He—
By Chimney—nor by Door
Could I infer his Residence—
Vast Prairies of Air

Unbroken by a Settler—
Were all that I could see—
Infinitude—Had'st Thou no Face
That I might look on Thee?

The Silence condescended—
Creation stopped—for Me—
But awed beyond my errand—
I worshipped—did not "pray"—

Emily Dickinson, ca. 1862, in The Complete Poems of Emily Dickinson, *pp. 274–275.*

We are gathered to celebrate the emancipation, yea, rather, the *Redemption* of the enslaved people of the District of Columbia, the exact number of whom we have no means of ascertaining, because, since the benevolent intention of Congress became manifest, many have been removed by their owners beyond the reach of this beneficent act.

Our pleasing task then, is to welcome to the Churches, the homestead, and circles of free colored Americans, those who remain to enjoy *the boon of holy Freedom.*

Brethren, sisters, friends, we say welcome to our Churches, welcome to our homesteads, welcome to our social circles.

Enter the great family of Holy Freedom; not to *lounge in sinful indolence,* not to *degrade yourselves by vice,* nor to *corrupt society by licentiousness,* neither to *offend the laws by crime,* but to the *enjoyment of a well regulated liberty,* the offspring of generous laws; of law as just as generous, as righteous as just—a liberty to be *perpetuated* by equitable law, and sanctioned by the divine; for law is never equitable, righteous, just, until it harmonizes with the will of Him, who is "*King* of kings, and *Lord* of lords," and who commanded Israel to *have but one law for the home-born* and the *stranger.*

We repeat ourselves, welcome then *ye ransomed ones;* welcome *not* to indolence, to vice, licentiousness, and crime, but to a well-regulated liberty, sanctioned by the Divine, maintained by the Human law.

Welcome to habits of industry and thrift—to duties of religion and piety—to obligations of law, order, government—of government divine, of government human: these two, though not one, are inseparable. The man who refuses to obey divine law, will never obey human laws. *The divine first,* the *human next.* The latter is the consequence of the former, and follows it as light does the rising sun.

We invite you to our Churches, because we desire you to be religious; to be more than religious; we urge you *to be godly.* We entreat you to never be content until you are emancipated from sin, from sin without, and from sin within you. But this kind of freedom is attained only through the faith of Jesus, love for Jesus, obedience to Jesus. As certain as the American Congress has *ransomed* you, so certain, yea, more certainly has Jesus redeemed you from the guilt and power of sin by his own precious blood.

As you are now free in body, so now seek to be free in soul and spirit, from sin and Satan. The *noblest freeman is he whom Christ makes free.*

Daniel Alexander Payne, 1862, African Methodist Episcopal Church bishop, "Welcome to the Ransomed; or Duties of the Coloured Inhabitants of the District of Columbia," *after President Abraham Lincoln signed into law on April 16, 1862, a bill passed by Congress abolishing slavery in the District of Columbia, in Sernett,* African American Religious History, *pp. 233–234.*

The will of God prevails. In great contests each party claims to act in accordance with the will of God. Both

Juliann Jane Tillman was a preacher for the African Methodist Episcopal Church in the mid-19th century. *(Library of Congress, Prints and Photographs Division LC-USZ62-54596)*

may be, and one *must* be, wrong. God cannot be *for,* and *against* the same thing at the same time. In the present civil war it is quite possible that God's purpose is something different from the purpose of either party—and yet the human instrumentalities, working just as they do, are of the best adaptation to effect His purpose. I am almost ready to say this is probably true—that God wills this contest, and wills that it shall not end yet. By his mere quiet power, on the minds of the now contestants, He could have either *saved* or *destroyed* the Union without a human contest. Yet the contest began. And, having begun He could give the final victory to either side any day. Yet the contest proceeds.

Abraham Lincoln, September, 1862, in Abraham Lincoln: Speeches and Writings, 1859–1865, *vol. 2, p. 359.*

I. The Jews, as a class, violating every regulation of trade established by the Treasury Department, and also Department orders, are hereby expelled from the Department.

II. Within twenty-four hours from the receipt of this order by Post Commanders, they will see that all of this class of people are furnished passes and are required to leave, and any one returning after such notification, will be arrested and held in confinement until an opportunity occurs of sending them out as prisoners unless furnished with permits from these Head Quarters. III. No permits will be given these people to visit Head Quarters for the purpose of making personal application for trade permits.

Major General U.S. Grant, December 17, 1862, in Marcus,
The Jew in the American World, *pp. 199–200.*

On one occasion, when our house was filled with company, several eminent clergymen being our guests, notice was brought up to me that Sojourner Truth was below, and requested an interview. Knowing nothing of her but her singular name, I went down, prepared to make the interview short, as the pressure of many other engagements demanded.

When I went into the room, a tall, spare form arose to meet me. She was evidently a full-blooded African, and though now aged and worn with many hardships, still gave the impression of a physical development which in early youth must have been as fine a specimen of the torrid zone as Cumberworth's celebrated statuette of the Negro Woman at the Fountain. Indeed, she so strongly reminded me of that figure, that, when I recall the events of her life, as she narrated them to me, I imagine her as a living, breathing impersonation of that work of art.

I do not recollect ever to have been conversant with any one who had more of that silent and subtle power which we call personal presence than this woman. In the modern Spiritualistic phraseology, she would be described as having a strong sphere. Her tall form, as she rose up before me, is still vivid to my mind. She was dressed in some stout, grayish stuff, neat and clean, though dusty from travel. On her head, she wore a bright Madras handkerchief, arranged as a turban, after the manner of her race. She seemed perfectly self-possessed and at her ease,—in fact, there was almost an unconscious superiority, not unmixed with a solemn twinkle of humor, in the odd, composed manner in which she looked down on me. Her whole air had at times a gloomy sort of drollery which impressed one strangely.

"So this is you," she said.

"Yes," I answered.

"Well, honey, de Lord bless ye! I jes' thought I'd like to come an' have a look at ye. You's heerd o' me, I reckon?" she added.

"Yes, I think I have. You go about lecturing, do you not?"

"Yes, honey, that's what I do. The Lord has made me a sign unto this nation, an' I go round a'testifyin', an' showin' on 'em their sins agin my people."

So saying, she took a seat, and, stooping over and crossing her arms on her knees, she looked down on the floor, and appeared to fall into a sort of reverie. Her great gloomy eyes and her dark face seemed to work with some undercurrent of feeling; she sighed deeply, and occasionally broke out,—

"O Lord! O Lord! Oh, the tears, an' the groans, an' the moans! O Lord!" . . .

By this time I thought her manner so original that it might be worth while to call down my friends; and she seemed perfectly well pleased with the idea. An audience was what she wanted,—it mattered not whether high or low, learned or ignorant. She had things to say, and was ready to say them at all times, and to any one.

I called down Dr. Beecher, Professor Allen, and two or three other clergymen, who, together with my husband and family, made a roomful. No princess could have received a drawing-room with more composed dignity than Sojourner her audience. She stood among them, calm and erect, as one of her own native palm-trees waving alone in the desert. I presented one after another to her, and at last said,—

"Sojourner, this is Dr. Beecher. He is a very celebrated preacher."

"Is he?" she said, offering her hand in a condescending manner, and looking down on his white head. "Ye dear lamb, I'm glad to see ye! De Lord bless ye! I loves preachers. I'm a kind o' preacher myself."

"You are?" said Dr. Beecher. "Do you preach from the Bible?"

"No, honey, can't preach from de Bible,—can't read a letter."

"Why, Sojourner, what do you preach from, then?"

Her answer was given with a solemn power of voice, peculiar to herself, that hushed every one in the room.

"When I preaches, I has jest one text to preach from, an' I always preaches from this one.

My text is, 'WHEN I FOUND JESUS.'"

Harriet Beecher Stowe, author of Uncle Tom's Cabin,
April 1863, "Sojourner Truth, The Libyan Sibyl" Atlantic
Monthly, Available online at URL: http://etext.
lib.virginia.edu/etcbin/toccer-reldem?id=StoSojo.
sgm&images=images/mod eng&data=/texts/
english/modeng/parsed&tag=public&part=all.
Accessed on May 18, 2005.

Dear Sir:

I take the liberty of addressing you these lines, with the prayerful hope that you may spare one moment from the multitudinous and important affairs which engage your attention, to listen to my simple appeal.

I am a colored woman; having a slight admixture of negro blood in my veins; and have been for several years a teacher in the public schools of Ohio. Since the providence of God has opened in the South, so vast a field for earnest and selfabnegating missionary labor, I have felt a strong conviction of duty, an irresistible desire to engage in teaching the freed people; to aid to the extent of what ability God has given me, in bringing these poor outcasts from the pale of humanity, into the family of man.

Possessing no wealth and having nothing to give but my life to the work, I therefore make this application to you. Can I become a teacher under the auspices of the American Missionary Association? I should be very glad and happy if it might be so, for my warmest and deepest feelings are enlisted in the cause.

"This is the way, walk ye on it," speaks a voice within my heart, and I know that no thought of suffering and privation, nor even death, should deter me from making every effort possible for the moral and intellectual salvation of these ignorant and degraded people; children of a benificent Father, and heirs of the kingdom of Heaven. And I feel moreover how much greater my own spiritual advancement will be, for while laboring for them, while living a life of daily toil, self sacrifice and denial, I can dwell nearer to God and my Savior and become constantly, by divine aid, richer in faith, richer in love, richer in all the graces of the Holy Spirit.

. . . . .

I shall be very grateful if you will send me word in reply to this. I know that the efforts of a single individual seem small and insignificant, but to me this is of the most vital importance.

Hoping that you will kindly bestow upon me a moment's attention.

Sara G. Stanley, January 19, 1864, letter to George Whipple of the American Missionary Association, in Lawson, The Three Sarahs, *pp. 78–79.*

I made a brief address and wound up as requested, by singing the "Battle Hymn," Col. Powell singing bass. When we came to the chorus the audience rose. O, how they sang! I happened to strike exactly the right key and the band helped us. I kept time for them with my hand and the mighty audience sang in exact time. Some shouted out loud at the last verse, and above all the uproar Mr. Lincoln's voice was heard: "Sing it again!"

Charles Cardwell McCabe, chaplain in the Union Army and later bishop of the Methodist Episcopal Church, February 1864, describing to his wife the singing of the "Battle Hymn of the Republic" at a meeting of the U.S. Christian Commission at the hall of the House of Representatives at which President Abraham Lincoln was present, in Bristol, The Life of Chaplain McCabe: Bishop of the Methodist Episcopal Church, *p. 199.*

All places of public worship in Norfolk and Portsmouth are hereby placed under the control of the provost marshals of Norfolk and Portsmouth respectively, who shall see the pulpits properly filled by displacing, when necessary, the present incumbents, and substituting men of known loyalty and the same sectarian denomination, either military or civil, subject to the approval of the commanding general. They shall see that all churches are open free to all officers and soldiers, white or colored, at the usual hour of worship, and at other times, if desired; and they shall see that no insult or indignity be offered to them, either by word, look, or gesture on the part of the congregation. The necessary expenses will be levied as far as possible, in accordance with the previous usages or regulations of each congregation respectively.

General Order No. 3, February 11, 1864, Norfolk, Virginia, in Fleming, Documentary History of Reconstruction, *vol. 2, p. 223.*

On the occasion corresponding to this four years ago, all thoughts were anxiously directed to an impending civil-war. All dreaded it—all sought to avert it. While the inaugural address was being delivered from this place, devoted altogether to *saving* the Union without war, urgent agents were in the city seeking to *destroy* it without war—seeking to dissolve the Union, and divide effects, by negotiation. Both parties deprecated war; but one of them would *make* war rather than let the nation survive; and the other would *accept* war rather than let it perish. And the war came.

. . . . .

Neither party expected for the war, the magnitude, or the duration, which it has already attained. Neither anticipated that the *cause* of the conflict might cease with, or even before, the conflict itself should cease. Each looked for an easier triumph, and a result less fundamental and astounding. Both read the same Bible, and pray to the same God, and each invokes His aid against the other. It may seem strange that any men should dare to ask a just God's assistance in wringing their bread from the sweat of other men's faces; but let us judge not that we be not judged. The prayers of both could not be answered; that of neither has been answered fully. The Almighty has His own purposes. "Woe unto the world because of offences! for it must needs be that offences come; but woe to that man by whom the offence cometh!" If we shall suppose that American Slavery is one of those offenses which, in the providence of God, must needs come, but which, having continued through His appointed time, He now wills to remove, and that He gives to both North and South, this terrible war, as the woe due to those by whom the offence came, shall we discern therein any departure from those divine attributes which the believers in a Living God always ascribe to Him? Fondly do we hope—fervently do we pray—that this mighty scourge of war may speedily pass away. Yet, if God wills that it continue, until all the wealth piled by the bond-man's two hundred and fifty years of unrequited toil shall be sunk, and until every drop of blood drawn with the lash, shall be paid by another drawn with the sword, as was said three thousand years ago, so still it must be said "the judgments of the Lord, are true and righteous altogether."

Abraham Lincoln, March 4, 1865, from his Second Inaugural Address, in Abraham Lincoln: Speeches and Writings, 1859–1865, *vol. 2, pp. 686–687.*

Do not say that it [slavery] is dead. It is not, while its essential spirit lives. While one man counts another man his born inferior for the color of his skin, while both in North and South prejudices aud practices, which the law cannot touch, but which God hates, keep alive in our people's hearts the spirit of the old iniquity, it is not dead. . . . We must grow like our President in his truth, his independence, his religion, and his wide humanity. Then the character by which he died shall be in us, and by it we shall live. Then Peace shall come that knows no War, and Law that knows no Treason, and full of his spirit, a grateful land shall gather round his grave, and in the daily psalm of prosperous and righteous living, thank God forever for his Life and Death.

Episcopal minister and later bishop Phillips Brooks, April 23, 1865, in The Life and Death of Abraham Lincoln, *p. 22.*

The first and most obvious consequence of the dreadful civil war just ended, has been the final and universal overthrow of slavery within the limits of the United States. This is one of the most momentous events in the history of the world. That it was the design of God to bring about this event cannot be doubted. . . . Almost all foreigners, and a large class of our own people predicted the success of the South. . . . But God has ordered it otherwise. . . . The inevitable difficulties and sufferings consequent on such an abrupt change in the institutions and social organization of a great people, must be submitted to, as comprehended in the design of God in these events.

Presbyterian theologian Charles Hodge, July 1865, "President Lincoln," Biblical Repertory and Princeton Review, *in Noll,* America's God, *pp. 433–434.*

The Protestant Episcopal Church of the United States has established a form of prayer to be used for "the President of the United States and all in civil authority." During the continuance of the late wicked and groundless rebellion the prayer was changed for one for the President of the Confederate States, and so altered, was used in Protestant Churches of the Diocese of Alabama.

Since the "lapse" of the Confederate government, and the restoration of the authority of the United States over the late rebellious States, the prayer for the President has been altogether omitted in the Episcopal Churches of Alabama.

This omission was commended by the Rt. Rev. Richard Wilmer, Bishop of Alabama, in a letter to the clergy and laity, dated June 20, 1865.

. . . . .

The advice of the bishop to omit this prayer, and its omission by the clergy, is not only a violation of the canons of the church, but shows a factious and disloyal spirit, and is a marked insult to every loyal citizen within the department. Such men are unsafe public teachers, and not to be trusted in places of power and influence over public opinion.

It is, therefore, ordered, pursuant to the directions of Major-General Thomas, commanding the military division of Tennessee, that said Richard Wilmer, bishop of the Protestant Episcopal Church of the Diocese of Alabama, and the Protestant Episcopal clergy of said diocese be, and they are hereby suspended from their functions, and forbidden to preach, or perform divine service; and that their places of worship be closed until such time as said bishop and clergy show a sincere return to their allegiance to the government of the United States, and give evidence of a loyal and patriotic spirit by offering to resume the use of the prayer for the President of the

United States and all in civil authority, and by taking the amnesty oath prescribed by the President.

This prohibition shall continue in each individual case until special application is made through the military channels to these headquarters for permission to preach and perform divine service, and until such application is approved at these or superior headquarters.

District commanders are required to see that this order is carried into effect.

Major-General Chas. R. Woods, September 20, 1865, Mobile, Alabama, General Order No. 38, in Fleming, Documentary History of Reconstruction, *vol. 2, pp. 223–226.*

There came one of those awful, snowy, windy nights, such as blew across the Western plains occasionally, with the thermometer twenty degrees below zero. Not many were out to church that night. I tried hard to preach a little, the best I could. I tried to rally the people to the altar, the few that were there, and went back to the stove, and tried to get somebody to the Lord. I did not find anyone. I turned toward the altar; in some way it seemed to me that this was my time, and I threw myself down across the altar and began to pray for myself. I had come to the point where I seemingly could not go on. My religion did not meet my needs. It seemed as though I could not continue to preach with this awful question of doubt on me, and I prayed and cried to the Lord. . . . . [I]n my ignorance, the Lord helped me, drew me and impelled me, and, as I cried to Him that night, He seemed to open heaven on me, and gave me, as I believe, the baptism with the Holy Ghost, though I did not know either what I needed, or what I prayed for.

Phineas F. Bresee, late 1860s, Church of the Nazarene founder, describing his experience of being baptized with the Holy Ghost, in Brickley, Man of the Morning, *pp. 74–75.*

I shall never, never forget how, yesterday, the clouds dispersed from my mind—the light that never was on sea or shore shown into my dark heart, & Jesus, man's Saviour, was revealed to me as I had not before seen Him *for myself*. So now, to use dear Mother's favorite illustration, "I am like air to sunshine";—that is, I am continually helped to yield my being as the medium through which Christ's strength & righteousness may shine. This is all that I do, or can do, or, thanks be to God!—am *wished* to do. The hand of *faith* grasps the spotless robe of my Redeemer—the eye of faith rests on His matchless face—the heart of faith murmurs "Not as I will, but as *thou wilt* O, Saviour."

Women's Temperance leader Frances E. Willard, April 17, 1866, in Writing Out My Heart, *pp. 227–228.*

They were a gaily dressed crowd of worshippers, and the female portion of it seemed to have come out *en masses* in fresh apparel, and dazzled the eye with their exhibition of shade and color in the multitudinous and variegated hues of their garments. Fifth avenue, from Tenth street to Central Park, from ten o'clock in the morning till late in the afternoon, was one long procession of men and women, whose attire and bearing betokened refinement, wealth and prosperity, and nearly all these were worshippers of some denomination or another, as the crowds that poured in and out of the various religious edifices along the line of the avenue amply testified.

New York Herald, *April 14, 1873, quoted in "The Easter Parade: Piety, Fashion, and Display," in Hackett,* Religion and American Culture, *p. 244.*

And all the way my Savior leads me,
Oh the fullness of His love!
Perfect rest in me is promised
In my Father's house above;
When my spirit, clothed, immortal
Wings its flight to realms of day,
This my song through endless ages—
Jesus led me all the way.

Fanny J. Crosby, 1874, "All the Way My Savior Leads Me," in Jackson, Fanny Crosby's Story of Ninety-Four Years, *p. 100.*

The maturity of Christian experience cannot be reached in a moment, but is the result of the work of God's Holy Spirit, who, by His energizing and transforming power, causes us to grow up into Christ in all things. . . . But the sanctification the Scriptures urge, as a present experience upon all believers, does not consist in maturity of growth, but in purity of heart; and this may be as complete in the early as in our later experiences.

. . . . .

All that we claim, then, in this life of sanctification is that by a step of faith we put ourselves into the hands of the Lord, for Him to work in us all the good pleasure of His will, and then, by a continuous exercise of faith, keep ourselves there. This is our part in the matter. And when we do it, and while we do it, we are, in the Scripture sense, truly pleasing to God, although it may require years of training and discipline to mature us into a vessel that shall be in all respects to His honor, and fitted to every good work.

Holiness preacher Hannah Whitall Smith, 1875, The Christian's Secret of a Happy Life, *pp. 33–34.*

A higher and more practical Christianity, demonstrating justice and meeting the needs of mortals in sickness and in health, stands at the door of this age, knocking for admission. Will you open or close the door upon this angel visitant, who cometh in the quiet of meekness, as he came of old to the patriarch at noonday?

. . . . .

(Slavery abolished)

Legally to abolish unpaid servitude in the United States was hard; but the abolition of mental slavery is a more difficult task. The despotic tendencies, inherent in mortal mind and always germinating in new forms of tyranny, must be rooted out through the action of the divine Mind.

Men and women of all climes and races are still in bondage to material sense, ignorant how to obtain their freedom. The rights of man were vindicated in a single section and on the lowest plane of human life, when African slavery was abolished in our land. That was only prophetic of further steps towards the banishment of a world-wide slavery, found on higher planes of existence and under more subtle and depraving forms.

(Liberty's crusade)

The voice of God in behalf of the African slave was still echoing in our land, when the voice of the herald of this new crusade sounded the keynote of universal freedom, asking a fuller acknowledgment of the rights of man as a Son of God, demanding that the fetters of sin, sickness, and death be stricken from the human mind and that its freedom be won, not through human warfare, not with bayonet and blood, but through Christ's divine Science.

(Cramping systems)

God has built a higher platform of human rights, and He has built it on diviner claims. These claims are not made through code or creed, but in demonstration of "on earth peace, good-will toward men." Human codes, scholastic theology, material medicine and hygiene, fetter faith and spiritual understanding. Divine Science rends asunder these fetters, and man's birthright of sole allegiance to his Maker asserts itself.

I saw before me the sick, wearing out years of servitude to an unreal master in the belief that the body governed them, rather than Mind.

(House of bondage)

The lame, the deaf, the dumb, the blind, the sick, the sensual, the sinner, I wished to save from the slavery of their own beliefs and from the educational systems of the Pharaohs, who to-day, as of yore, hold the children of Israel in bondage. I saw before me the awful conflict, the Red Sea and the wilderness; but I pressed on through faith in God, trusting Truth, the strong deliverer, to guide me into the land of Christian Science, where fetters fall and the rights of man are fully known and acknowledged.

Mary Baker Eddy, 1875, Science and Health with Key to the Scriptures, *pp. 224–227.*

As I went in and shut the door after me, it seemed as if I met the Lord Jesus Christ *face to face.* It did not occur to me then, nor did it for sometime afterward, that it was wholly a *mental* state. On the contrary, it seemed to me that I met him face to face, and saw him as I would see any other man. He said nothing, but looked at me in such a manner as to break me right down at his feet. I have always since regarded this as a most remarkable state of mind; for it seemed to me a reality that he stood before me, and that I fell down at his feet and poured out my soul to him. I wept aloud like a child, and made such confessions as I could with my choked utterance. It seemed to me as if I bathed his feet with my tears; and yet I had no distinct impression that I *touched* him, that I recollect. I must have continued in this state for a good while; but my mind was too much absorbed with the interview to recollect scarcely anything that I said.

But I know as soon as my mind became calm enough to break off from the interview, I returned to the front office and found that the fire that I had just made of large wood was nearly burned out. But as I returned and was about to take a seat by the fire, I received *a mighty baptism of the Holy Ghost.* Without expecting it, without ever having the thought in my mind that there was any such thing for me, without any recollection that I had ever heard the thing mentioned by any person in the world, at a moment entirely unsuspected by me, the Holy Spirit descended upon me in a manner that seemed *to go through me,* body and soul. I could feel the impression, *like a wave of electricity,* going through and through me. Indeed it seemed to come in *waves* and *waves of liquid love;*—for I could not express it in any other way. And yet it did not seem like water, but rather as *the breath of God.* I can recollect distinctly that it seemed to *fan* me, like immense wings; and it seemed to me, as these waves passed over me, that they literally *moved my hair like a passing breeze.*

No words can express the wonderful love that was shed abroad in my heart. It seemed to me that I should burst. I wept aloud with joy and love; and I do not know but I should say, I literally *bellowed out* the unutterable gushings of my heart. These waves came over me, and over me, and over me one after the other, until I recollect I cried out, "I shall *die* if these waves continue to pass over me." I said to the Lord, "Lord, I cannot *bear* any more." yet I had no fear of death.

Revival preacher Charles Grandison Finney, 1876, in Memoirs, *pp. 23–24.*

The exercises of our meetings are to be simple and devoid of all ceremony and formalism. They are to consist of a *lecture* mainly, and, as a pleasing and grateful auxiliary, of music to elevate the heart and give rest to the feelings. The object of the lectures shall be twofold: First, to illustrate the history of human aspirations, its monitions and its examples; to trace the origin of many of those errors of the past whose poisonous tendrils still cling to the life of the present, but also to exhibit its pure and bright examples and so *to enrich the little sphere of our earthly existence by showing the grander connections in which it everywhere stands with the large life of the race.*

Felix Adler, May 15, 1876, on the founding of the Ethical Culture Society, in Friess, Felix Adler and Ethical Culture, *p. 48.*

Can a man excuse his practices to the contrary because of his religious belief? To permit this would be to make the professed doctrines of religious belief superior to the law of the land, and in effect to permit every citizen to become a law unto himself. Government could exist only in name under such circumstances.

Chief Justice Waite for the U.S. Supreme Court in Reynolds v. United States, 98 U.S. 145, 166–67 (1878), *concluding that Mormons were not exempted from the prohibitions against polygamy in a federal law by virtue of their religiously inspired belief in the practice of polygamy.*

CHAPTER TEN

Immigrants, Industry, and the Social Gospel
(1881–1899)

The long sweep of revivalism across the 19th century had a tendency to treat religious experience primarily as a matter of the individual heart and evil as the expression of individual sin. Revivalism could and did inspire concrete action in the realm of society, but this action generally proceeded from a spiritual diagnosis focused on the individual. As the industrial revolution during the last half of the 19th century remade American society, however, many religious observers began to doubt whether this individual focus was well equipped to deal with contemporary conditions. Waves of immigration washed against America's cities during the 19th century, flooding the nation with social problems associated with increased urbanization. New concentrations of wealth and power, the offspring of industrialization, unbalanced the fabric of laws inherited from a simpler age. The effects of urbanization and industrialization, of course, could be felt at the individual level and could surely be traced in some sense to the actions of individuals, both the powerful and the powerless. But something larger was at work, something not amenable to an individual religious conversion or remedied by the inculcation of individual virtue. What if evil were systemic, locating itself in public or private institutions or in law or bureaucracies? What if sins were social as well as individual, and the remedy to social problems—and these increasingly seemed many and intractable—lay in a reordering of society itself, not simply in the reordering of individual hearts and lives? Had religious principles anything to say to these new conditions?

For the leaders of what came to be known as the Social Gospel movement, it was apparent that society's ills could not be traced simply to individual sin, nor could they be remedied merely by individual religious conversions, no matter how numerously multiplied. Revivals would not cure the unsanitary conditions in urban tenements or resolve disputes between laborers and their industrial employers. Individual philanthropy could not eradicate deeper inequities in the distribution of the nation's wealth. Systems and sources of power and aggregations of wealth had to be confronted, and for the architects of the Social Gospel movement Christian principles were on hand to support this confrontation. They were, in fact, generally

214

optimistic about the potential of these principles to remold society. Many progressive believers of the late 19th century found themselves in sympathy with the views of social Darwinism, according to which society was continually evolving upward just as biological organisms were. For these believers the problems of city and industry were not cause for despair but opportunities for positive change.

But the prospect of change did not excite equal enthusiasm from all religious believers at the end of the 19th century. The changes experienced by American Indians, for example, had more to do with suffering and loss than improved circumstances. Some of the Native American religious traditions that developed during this period shared a belief that the present world would eventually be replaced by one in which Native Americans were no longer hemmed in on reservations and besieged by the loss of traditional ways of life. In the future world contemplated by Smohalla, a shaman in the Pacific Northwest, and by followers of the Ghost Dance, for example, American Indians would be resurrected to a land no longer peopled by whites. Other religious traditions, including Judaism and Catholicism, experienced internal disagreement about the desirability of religious change. Orthodox Jews, often immigrants from eastern European nations, resisted the willingness of Reform Jews, drawn especially from Germany, to modify elements of Jewish tradition. More conservative Catholics viewed with alarm the accommodations made by more progressive Catholics—whom they labeled "Americanizers"—to worldly American values such as secularization and materialism. During the closing decades of the 19th century, Americanizers such as Archbishop John Ireland viewed American traditions such as the separation between government and official religious dogma as a healthy environment for the prospering of Catholicism in the United States. Conservative Catholic voices, however, had an ally in the pope, who went so far as to declare "Americanism" a heresy. Nevertheless, the spirit of assimilation to American culture embraced by Archbishop Ireland and others would, in the next century, come to dominate Catholic thought in the United States and would eventually pave the way for the election of a Catholic president, John F. Kennedy, in the last half of the 20th century.

Responding to the Economies of Modernity

As industrialization and urbanization accelerated in America during the last two decades of the 19th century, some Protestant clergy began to insist on the application of Christian principles to the new economic environment. Friends of labor and the poor, outspoken ministers such as Josiah Strong, Washington Gladden, and Walter Rauschenbusch, argued that Christians had a responsibility to secure social justice within American society. This engagement between Christian theology and social conditions was not new in and of itself. The cultural landscape inherited by the Social Gospel movement, as it came to be called, had only recently witnessed a catastrophic national struggle in which theologically inspired abolitionists had an important voice. Even earlier in the 19th century, the expansive network of voluntary societies sometimes referred to as the Benevolent Empire had harnessed confidence in the possibility of human reform to combat a variety of social ills, including alcoholism, prisoner abuse, and illiteracy. The Social Gospel movement, then, did not invent Christian social activism, but the forms of activism previously characteristic of Christian encounters with society had tended to focus on the importance of individual acts of benevolence or the aggregation of such acts through the work of voluntary societies. The Social Gospel movement was not indifferent to the importance of such acts, but it also emphasized that Christian principles had something to say about the laws and policies necessary to sustain a just society. The movement was not interested only in the private sphere of individual virtuous conduct but in the public sphere of just laws and just arrangements between, say, laborers and the industries in which they labored. This focus on the application of the Christian gospel to the nation's public life was a significant contribution of the Social Gospel movement and one that would inspire a variety of civil engagements by Christians during the 20th century, the most important of which was the Civil Rights movement.

The leaders of the Social Gospel movement generally arrived at socially activist convictions through concrete encounters with late 19th-century poverty and workers' conditions. Congregationalist minister Washington Gladden, sometimes called the father of the Social Gospel, gained first-hand experience with the problems of labor in modern industrial society while serving as minister of a Congregational church in Columbus, Ohio, beginning in 1882 until his retirement in 1914. Though denying the label of socialist, Gladden declared that Christian principles dictated that the wealth created by the industrial revolution not be accumulated into the hands of a few industrialists but be shared broadly by all those workers whose labor generated that wealth. He was not satisfied with being simply a theorist of social change but aspired to be an active architect of it as well, even serving as an alderman for the city of Columbus, Ohio, from 1900 to 1902. Overall, he proved to be an ally of the rights of labor and an enemy of pietistic forms of Christianity that saw in the gospel only a cure for individual sinfulness rather than an agenda for the transformation of earthly society into the kingdom of Christ.

Walter Rauschenbusch, another early proponent of the Social Gospel and its most prominent theologian, arrived at similar conclusions through years he spent as pastor of the Second German Baptist Church in the part of New York City's West Side known as Hell's Kitchen. Within several years of undertaking this ministry in 1886, he helped organize a social service group called the Brotherhood of the Kingdom. Although he eventually joined the faculty of Rochester Seminary toward the end of the following decade, he used his new academic post as a perch from which to provide theological support for the Social Gospel movement, publishing works such as *Christianity and the Social Crisis* (1907) and *Christianizing the Social Order* (1913). Like Gladden, Rauschenbusch was a progressive Protestant impatient with forms of Christianity that did not see the necessity of bringing the principles of Christ to bear upon the social ills of the day, not just in the form of individual acts of charity but through concrete efforts to achieve social justice.

The last of a triumvirate of important leaders in the Social Gospel movement, Josiah Strong, demonstrated that the progressive Protestantism of the period could easily drift toward anti-Catholicism and nativism. As early as 1885 in his first book, *Our Country: Its Possible Future and Its Present Crisis*, Strong argued that Catholic immigration (along with Mormonism, intemperance, socialism, wealth, and urbanization) was one of the chief ills of modern American society. Later critics have chastised Strong for racism on the basis of his confidence in this book as well as *The New Era: or the Coming Kingdom* (1893) that the Anglo-Saxon race was poised to become a saving force in the entire world and the exemplar of civilization. But at the time, Josiah Strong numbered himself and was numbered by many of his contemporaries as a voice of progressivism. Strong also illustrated the ease with which adherents of the Social Gospel became advocates of the ecumenical movement in the early 20th century, since the impetus to accomplish large-scale social change naturally inspired a desire to find allies across denominational lines. He thus participated actively in the affairs of the Federal Council of Churches after its creation in 1908, especially its Commission on the Church and Social Service.

The Social Gospel movement was generally animated by a spirit of optimism consistent with social Darwinianism, the view derived from Charles Darwin's account of biological evolution that suggested that society, also, is in the process of upward evolution. World War I ultimately corroded this optimistic view of social potential, but in the last years of the 19th century and the first of the 20th, progressive Christians especially approached the work of social reform confident that significant cures to the ills of society lay close at hand. The most popular expression of this progressive Christian optimism took the form of a work of fiction published by Congregationalist minister Charles Sheldon in 1897, *In His Steps*. Pastor of a church in Topeka, Kansas, Sheldon was dedicated to the work of social reform, leading his church in a variety of ministries to the poor of Topeka, including African Americans in a nearby black ghetto called Tennesseetown. Beginning in the early 1890s, Sheldon wrote stories that he read on Sunday evenings to his congregation centered around a fictional town where Christians asked themselves, "What would Jesus do?" The characters in the stories responded to this question by engaging in the kind of social service activities in which Sheldon encouraged his church members to participate. Ultimately, *In His Steps*, derived from these stories, sold millions of copies and became not only a popular manifesto of the Social Gospel movement but one of the best-selling books of the 20th century. Its influence continues into the 21st century among Christians who still ask the same question (and sometimes sport jewelry bearing the letters WWJD for "what would Jesus do?").

The Temperance Movement

One important tributary of the Social Gospel movement among progressive Christians was a renewed dedication to the cause of temperance. Today, lingering remnants of the temperance movement find expression chiefly among conservative strands of Christianity. But the great temperance crusade of the late 19th and early 20th centuries that ultimately produced the Prohibition era owed as much to progressive Protestantism as to theological conservativism. Germinated in the same theological soil as the Social Gospel movement, the progressive incarnation of the temperance movement was concerned less with individual vice than with the social and corporate dimensions of drinking. Progressive believers opposed what they saw as the predatory practices of the liquor industry, its corruption of the political process, and its shadowy connections to the criminal underworld. As a poem from this period illustrated, the cause of temperance had to focus on laws that protected distillers from the deadly consequences of their product:

> I know that the Bible says, "Thou shalt not kill,"
> But the court says I may with the juice of the still,
> I know that no drunkard shall Paradise gain,
> And as I make drunkards no doubt I'd be slain
> *Did not Legislators step in to my aid,*
> *And by their enactment take the guilt of my trade.*[1]

The temperance movement had briefly enjoyed significant success in the antebellum period, an adopted child of the Benevolent Empire of volunteer reform efforts during this period. After the Civil War Protestant women reinvigorated the movement in the 1870s, beginning in 1873 with a series of local marches protesting saloons in which women laid siege to drinking establishments armed with Bibles and hymnals.[2] These protests prefaced the creation of the Women's Christian Temperance Union in 1874. The union initially confined its reform efforts to the cause of temperance, but with the election of Frances Willard as the organization's second president in 1879, it added a variety of social reforms to its activist agenda. The cause of temperance often found allies among advocates of women's rights, since 19th-century saloons were largely patronized by men and women were often the invisible victims of alcoholic men. Arguments supporting women's right to vote, for example, often assumed that recognizing this right would secure new allies for social reform. Willard, at least, epitomized the progressive strand of the temperance movement. After reading Edward Bellamy's utopian novel *Looking Backward* (1888), Willard became a socialist and thereafter added to her repertoire of social causes the transfer of ownership of railroads, utilities, and factories to the public, thereafter being happy to announce that "in every Christian there is a socialist; and in every socialist a Christian."[3]

Frances Willard's Do Everything motto, representing her commitment to a variety of progressive and even radical causes, ultimately hampered her ability to forge a sufficient alliance with conservative opponents of drink to effect sweeping social change. Conservative Protestants often shared her devotion to the temperance movement but viewed many of her other causes with alarm. The organization that would pursue the cause of temperance relentlessly and with the most singleness of purpose was the Anti-Saloon League, established in Oberlin, Ohio, in 1893 and then given national scope at a convention held in Washington, D.C., in 1895. Chiefly through its efforts, the Eighteenth Amendment to the U.S. Constitution was eventually ratified in January 1919, prohibiting the manufacture, sale, or transportation of intoxicating liquors.

The Ghost Dance and Peyoteism

The 19th century produced widespread millennial expectations among Protestant Christians. The most well known of these occurred toward the middle of the century, when William Miller predicted that Christ would shortly return to the Earth. Predictions of an earthly paradise soon to appear were not confined to Christians, however. Among American Indians similar expectations flourished in the second half of the 19th century. In the Pacific Northwest, for example, Smohalla, a shaman of the Sahaptian-speaking branch of the Wanapum tribe, taught that in a future millennial period American Indians would be resurrected and replanted in a land cleansed of whites. In the interim, he proclaimed, Native Americans should resist the encroachments of white civilization, such as the practice of farming.

The Ghost Dance movement also nurtured millennial expectations. Beginning in 1870 a prophet of the Northern Paiute named Wodziwob taught his followers that the practice of a Ghost Dance would help to usher in an age of paradise in which whites would be destroyed and dead Indians revived. Nearly 20 years later Wovoka, also known as Jack Wilson, taught an even more influential version of the Ghost Dance. Toward the end of the 1880s he experienced a vision in which he received a revelation that a messiah would shortly appear, that dead American

This photograph shows Arapaho participating in the Ghost Dance in 1900. *(National Archives NWDNS-111-SC-87767)*

Indians would soon return to life, and that whites would shortly vanish. He instructed his followers to conduct a series of ritual dances over four or five nights to inaugurate this earthly paradise, and the ritual became known as the Ghost Dance. In 1889 Wovoka's credibility as a prophet and speculation that he himself might be the messiah increased after his followers came to believe that he had been able to produce rain in an area of Nevada afflicted with drought.

Although Wovoka apparently counseled his followers to live at peace among themselves and with whites, some of the American Indians who adopted the Ghost Dance—the Sioux, in particular—embraced it as a charter for conflict with whites. Coupled with belief in the efficacy of the "ghost shirt," a supposedly invulnerable spiritual armor granted by Wovoka to his followers and with the readiness of federal authorities to see the Ghost Dance as a shield for rebellion among American Indians, the Ghost Dance partially contributed to the massacre at Wounded Knee on the Pine Ridge Indian Reservation in South Dakota on December 29, 1890, in which U.S. troops killed more than 200 Sioux men, women, and children. The massacre effectively spelled the end of the Ghost Dance movement, though Wovoka eventually resumed teaching the Ghost Dance around 1905, and this teaching sparked a brief period of revival for the movement.

The Ghost Dance, to the extent that it was construed as promising the triumph of American Indians over whites, was irrevocably discredited by the massacre at Wounded Knee. Subsequent developments within American Indian religion tended to take the form of beliefs or practices that accommodated American Indian life to white culture while also seeking to preserve traditional aspects of Native American religion. One prominent form of American Indian religious practice during this period was peyoteism. Peyote is a small variety of spineless cactus whose top may be harvested and dried in the form of a small button. It is hallucinogenic and has been used by a variety of American Indian groups in connection with sacred ceremonies.

During the second half of the 19th century, circumstances of American Indian life combined to spread religious ideas and practices among tribes. Overlapping reservations, the cessation of warfare between tribes and the development of intertribal councils, better roads, and the spread of English as a common language resource

Quanah Parker helped to establish peyoteism among American Indians during the late 19th century. *(Library of Congress, Prints and Photographs Division LC-USZ62-98166)*

among tribes helped to create a cultural climate in which religious traditions originating in one tribe might find a broader audience of adherents.[4] Peyoteism is a case in point. Its modern expression is sometimes traced to the Carrizo tribe, on the Texas-Mexico border, an area where peyote grew. The Carrizo are thought to have taught the peyote ceremony to the Lipan Apache, who in turn communicated it more broadly to the Kiowa, the Kiowa-Apache, and the Comanche.[5] As peyoteism spread among different tribal groups, it tended to organize around one of two broad ritual systems: the Comanche Half Moon ritual and the Wilson Big Moon ritual, partially distinguished by the incorporation of some Christian elements in the Wilson Big Moon ritual. During the last part of the 19th century, Comanche leader Quanah Parker was an important advocate of peyoteism among American Indians, in particular the Half Moon ritual. In 1916 American Indian practitioners of peyoteism joined to establish the Native American Church.

The East Arrives in the West

As America was poised to enter the 20th century, Protestants and Catholics held so dominant a position in the cultural landscape that the U.S. Supreme Court was willing in the case of *Holy Trinity Church v. U.S.*, decided in 1892, to declare that America was "a Christian nation." The very next year, however, the World's Parliament of Religions convened in conjunction with the Chicago Columbian Exposition, and this assembly boasted speakers who publicly announced the arrival of the great religious traditions of the East in America. The Parliament, as was to be expected, did not neglect to showcase speakers from the Christian and Jewish traditions already well settled in America: James Cardinal Gibbons spoke on behalf of Catholicism and Isaac Mayer Wise for Judaism, for example. But the religious diversity that would increasingly characterize American religious life during the 20th century was also represented. Muslims, Hindus, Zoroastrians, Buddhists, Confucians, Jains, Shintos, and Taoists took their place at the parliament alongside Christians and Jews. Delivering the parliament's opening address, Presbyterian minister John Henry Barrows greeted the assembled delegates effusively: "Welcome, most welcome, O wise men of the East and of the West!"[6]

For those alert to developments in American religion, the 1893 parliament only tendered greater visibility to Eastern influences already well under way.[7] As early as 1888 Philangi Dasa (Herman C. Vetterling) had begun publication of *The Buddhist Ray*, the first English-language Buddhist magazine in the United States. And even before this a curiously American amalgamation of the occult and Eastern religion had taken root in the United States with the founding of the Theosophical Society in the 1870s. Established by Helena Petrovna Blavatsky (called H. P. B. by her close friends) and lawyer and journalist Henry Steel Olcott, the Theosophical Society grew out of the shared interest of Blavatsky and Olcott in spiritualism and their curiosity about Eastern religious principles and practices. Blavatsky was the chief architect and spokesperson for the society's religious ideas; Olcott its organizing force. In 1878 both Blavatsky and Olcott left the United States for India, and, once there, both studied and helped reinvigorate the Hindu and Buddhist traditions they encountered, ultimately becoming Buddhists themselves. Four years later they relocated the world headquarters of the Theosophical Society to Adyar, India, near Madras. Though Blavatsky had died by the time of the World's Parliament of Religions, Annie Besant, a British representative of Theosophy, was on hand to speak at the parliament.

Henry S. Olcott founded the Theosophical Society together with Helena Blavatsky. *(Library of Congress, Prints and Photographs Division LC-USZ62-105248)*

The parliament inaugurated a period of increased exposure of Eastern religious traditions in America. After the conclusion of its proceedings, Hindu religious leader Swami Vivekanada remained in the United States for three years to lecture on Hindu religious teaching and practice. The year after the parliament concluded he established the New York Vedanta Society, and by 1906 the San Francisco Vedanta Society had built the first Hindu temple in America. While Hinduism began to take root in American soil, Buddhism also began to establish a public presence in the United States. In 1893 in the city that had hosted the World's Parliament of Religions, Jewish businessman C. T. Strauss became the first U.S. citizen formally to convert to Buddhism in America, participating in a ceremony conducted by Anagarika Dharmapala of Ceylon. Even more influential as an evangelist of Buddhism in America was Paul Carus, who published *The Gospel of Buddha According to Old Records* in 1894. But Carus's own influence was significantly augmented when in 1897 Daisetz Teitaro Suzuki arrived in the United States from Japan and began work with Carus on the *Open Court* magazine, a leading periodical devoted to Eastern religious thought in the late 19th and early 20th centuries. Suzuki became the most influential spokesman for Zen Buddhism in America. He helped Carus translate the *Tao te ching* into English and in 1907 published his own English introduction to Eastern religious thought, *Outlines of Mahayana Buddhism.* Two years later Suzuki returned to Japan, but after World War II he settled again in the United States, teaching at Columbia University, where he had a significant influence on psychoanalyst Erich Fromm, composer John Cage, and poet Allen Ginsberg.

Catholics and "Americanism"

Catholic Christianity arrived early in the New World but during the 17th century saw its influence eclipsed by European Protestantism. American explorations during the 16th century were dominated by Catholics, and efforts to colonize the New World during the 17th century included the prominent case of Maryland, founded by Lord Baltimore. But Protestant arrivals soon overwhelmed the Catholic presence in America, dominating especially the colonial, revolutionary, and early national periods of American history. Strong surges of Catholic immigration washed across the shores of the United States in the 19th century, however. Famine and economic depression in Ireland beginning in the 1820s tempted some 2 million Irish-Catholic immigrants to find their way to America. In subsequent decades German, Polish, and Italian Catholics joined them. By the end of the Civil War Catholics in America numbered approximately 3.5 million, forming the largest single Christian body in the United States. In spite of their rapidly increasing numbers—and certainly *because of* fears among some Protestants relating to this increase—19th-century Catholics in America had good reason to feel unwelcome. Sensationally lurid accounts of supposed misdeeds by Catholics, such as *Awful Disclosures of the Hotel Dieu Nunnery,* published in 1836, which described accounts of infanticide and other alleged acts of barbarism among Catholic priests and nuns, found a wide readership. Anti-Catholic feeling ran high enough in the 1850s to prompt the organization of a political party, the Order of United Americans, commonly known as the Know Nothing Party for the secrecy with which its members clothed its doings. Fiercely anti-immigrant and anti-Catholic, the Know Nothing Party accumulated a string of electoral victories in the middle of the 1850s but then quickly dissolved. But the anti-Catholic animus that gave birth to the Know Nothing Party survived the party itself. Toward the end of the 19th century it would be reincarnated in the American Protective Association, an anti-Catholic organization founded in Iowa in 1887 by Henry F. Bowers, and in the early 20th century by the reemergence of the Ku Klux Klan.

Catholic immigrants in the 19th century had not only to contend with nativist hostility, but with assimilation to American culture, especially a steady pressure to assimilate to the dominant Protestant culture. This culture impinged on Catholic identity from any number of directions, but nowhere more insistently and—to Catholic minds—with more peril than in the public schools. As the various established churches were repudiated in the last decades of the 18th century and the first of the 19th, a more general Protestant culture assumed the place of these former establishments. This culture dominated the public schools and was widely acceptable to Protestant parents and their children, but most decidedly unacceptable to their Catholic neighbors. Threatened by the influence of this culture in the public schools, Catholics established parochial schools of their own and labored to finance them. The choice to abandon the public schools posed financial hardship to Catholics, since the public schools were generally financed with tax revenues, and Catholics who chose not to send their children to public school continued to pay taxes toward schools from which they derived no personal benefit.

If American Catholics stood united against the encroachment of assimilation to the dominant Protestant culture, they nevertheless divided over the issue of whether assimilation to American culture, more broadly conceived, represented a threat to Catholic identity. By the last decade of the 19th century, a sharp division had emerged between Catholics who generally supported assimilation to American values and those who saw this assimilation as not only a repudiation of their previous national loyalties but as antagonistic to Catholic faith and practice itself.

Cardinal James Gibbons supported progressive trends in American Catholicism in the late 19th and early 20th centuries. *(Library of Congress, Prints and Photographs Division LC-USZ62-068593)*

On the side of assimilation was Archbishop John Ireland of St. Paul, Minnesota, who urged Catholics to find a home within the institutions and cultural values of American society. Anxious to see Catholic immigrants surmount language barriers that would otherwise confine them to cultural enclaves patterned after their various nations of origin, Ireland cast his support behind a Wisconsin law that would have mandated that instruction in all public and private schools be conducted in English. He also devised a program to lease parochial school property in one Minnesota city to the public schools so long as he retained the right to oversee the education offered in these facilities. Finally, Ireland appreciated the American pattern of church-state separation, finding it not a threat to Catholic faith and worth being replicated in other nations. Ireland had an influential ally in James Gibbons, the archbishop of Baltimore elevated to the rank of cardinal in 1887 by Pope Leo XIII. Gibbons and Ireland, joined by other progressive Catholics, were able to secure the establishment of the Catholic University of America that same year, and in subsequent years the university became a prominent institutional voice in support of engagement by Catholics with American culture. Gibbons also played an important role in persuading the pope not to condemn the Knights of Labor in America.

The most prominent adversary of Archbishop Ireland's enthusiasm for the assimilation of Catholic immigrants in America was Archbishop Michael Corrigan of New York, who feared that Americanizers, as he called leaders such as Ireland, were surrendering authentic Catholic values for the corrupt American values of secularization and materialism. But Americanists such as Archbishop Ireland had to contend not only with the opposition of other American Catholic leaders, such as Archbishop Corrigan, but of the pope as well. In 1895 Pope Leo XIII issued the encyclical letter *Longingqua Oceani*, which announced that the pattern of church-state relations in America, characterized by a significant measure of separation, was not an appropriate model for European nations. Even more damaging to the cause of Americanism was the pope's declaration in his encyclical letter *Testem benevolentiae*, published in 1899, that Americanism was a heresy. Leaders such as John Ireland denied, of course, that the views condemned by Pope Leo XIII were, in fact, the views they advanced. Nevertheless, the cumulative weight of these late 19th-century papal announcements was to strengthen the hands of more conservative American Catholics during this period.

Chronicle of Events

1881

- Francis Edward Clark, a Congregationalist minister, establishes the first Christian Endeavor society, an organization for youth.
- Following the assassination of Alexander II in Russia, pogroms and legislation against Jews begin to prompt significant Jewish immigrations to the United States from Russia and eastern Europe.
- Charles Taze Russell organizes the Watch Tower Bible and Tract Society as an unincorporated association. He subsequently incorporates the organization in 1884. The group will eventually become known as the Jehovah's Witnesses.
- Atticus Haygood, Methodist minister, president of Emory College, and advocate of a "new South," publishes *Our Brother in Black*. Haygood insists that African Americans should be equal partners in the nation's life and urges that they be provided educational opportunities conducive to this partnership.

1882

- Congress enacts the Edmunds Act, which strips Mormons of various citizenship rights.
- Congress passes the Chinese Exclusion Act, which will suspend immigration from China for 10 years. This moratorium on Chinese immigration will be extended again in 1892 and then made permanent in 1904. This policy of exclusion will ultimately be repealed in 1943.
- Father Michael McGiveny founds the Knights of Columbus.
- The Salvation Army begins work in Canada.
- Helena Petrovna Blavatsky and Henry Steel Olcott relocate the world headquarters of the Theosophical Society to Adyar, India, near Madras.

1883

- Future revivalist Billy Sunday plays the first of five seasons with the Chicago White Stockings baseball team.
- The Niagara Bible Conference meets for the first time and becomes an important precursor of the fundamentalist movement within Protestantism.
- *July 11:* At a banquet (sometimes referred to as the trefa banquet—*trefa* meaning "nonkosher") to celebrate the first graduating class from Hebrew Union College, the presence of shellfish (which are nonkosher) on the

menu exacerbates existing tensions between more traditional Jewish religious leaders and those of Reform Judaism. These tensions will ultimately led Orthodox Jews, led by Sabato Morais and H. Pereira Mendes, to establish the Jewish Theological Seminary in New York in 1887.

1884

- Charles Taze Russell incorporates the Watch Tower Bible and Tract Society (later known as the Jehovah's Witnesses).
- J. W. MacMurray visits the Wanapum dreamer-prophet Smohalla and records some of his teachings.
- The Protestant magazine *Christian Oracle* (later renamed *Christian Century*) is established.
- New York minister Samuel D. Burchard calls the Democrats the party of Rum, Romanism, and Rebellion. In spite of this charge Democratic presidential candidate Grover Cleveland wins the election.
- *November 9:* The Third Plenary Council of Baltimore for U.S. Catholics begins.

1885

- Congregationalist minister Josiah Strong publishes the book *Our Country: Its Possible Future and Its Present Crisis*, which warns of the dangers of Romanism—that is, Catholicism.
- *November:* The Pittsburgh Platform is adopted as a statement of theological principles for Reform Judaism.

1886

- Orthodox Jewish lay leaders establish Etz Chaim Yeshiva in New York.
- The Student Volunteer Movement, an organization devoted to encouraging foreign missions, grows out of Dwight L. Moody's Northfield Conference for this year. The movement's motto is "the evangelization of the world in this generation."
- Walter Rauschenbusch graduates from Rochester Seminary and becomes the minister of the Second German Baptist Church in the Hell's Kitchen area of New York's West Side. His experiences in this pastorate make him a leading theologian of the Social Gospel movement.
- *August 20:* Theologian Paul Tillich is born in Starzeddel, East Prussia.

1887

- Cyrus Adler receives the first Ph.D. awarded in Semitics in the United States from Johns Hopkins University.

- Henry Pereira Mendes and Sabato Morais are instrumental in founding the Jewish Theological Seminary in New York City, intended as an Orthodox counterpart to Reform Judaism's Hebrew Union College in Cincinnati, Ohio.
- Dwight L. Moody establishes a Bible training school called the Chicago Evangelization Society, renamed the Moody Bible Institute after his death.
- The American Protective Association, an anti-Catholic organization, is founded in Iowa.
- Catholic bishops in the United States found the Catholic University of America in Washington, D.C. The university will actually open to students in 1889.
- Southern Anglicans establish the Bishop Payne Divinity School to train black Episcopalian priests.
- Congress passes the Edmunds-Tucker Act, which unincorporates the Mormon Church and provides for the seizure of certain church property.
- *February 20:* James Cardinal Gibbons signs a letter to Giovanni Cardinal Simeoni, prefect of the Congregation de Propaganda Fide, the branch of Catholic ecclesiastical government with authority over the Catholic Church in America, urging the church not to condemn the Knights of Labor.

1888

- Cyrus Adler helps establish the Jewish Publication Society.
- *The Buddhist Ray,* edited by Philangi Dasa (Herman C. Vetterling), begins publication, the first English-language Buddhist magazine in the United States.
- Wovoka, also known as Jack Wilson, experiences the first of a series of religious visions and subsequently founds the Ghost Dance religion.
- Helena Petrovna Blavatsky, cofounder of the Theosophical Society with Henry Steel Olcott, publishes her second major work, *The Secret Doctrine,* after having relocated to London.

1889

- Francesca Xavier Cabrini, founder of the Missionaries of the Sacred Heart, arrives in New York.
- Charles Sherlock Fillmore begins publishing *Modern Thought,* a religious magazine associated with the beginning of the Unity School of Christianity, founded by Charles and his wife, Myrtle Fillmore.
- The Central Conference of American Rabbis is founded and comes to serve as the rabbinical arm of Reform Judaism.

Catholic missionary Frances Xavier Cabrini was the first American citizen canonized as a saint. *((Library of Congress, Prints and Photographs Division LC-USZ62-103568)*

1890

- Wilford Woodruff, president of the Church of Jesus Christ of Latter-day Saints, leads the Mormon Church to renounce polygamy.
- Jacob Riis publishes *How the Other Half Lives,* which describes the bleak conditions of urban life, including the marginal impact of organized religion on the lives of those inhabiting American cities.
- *February 3:* The U.S. Supreme Court in *Davis v. Beason* unanimously upholds the constitutionality of a federal law (the Edmunds Act) that denies the right to vote to those who advocate or practice polygamy or who belong to an organization that advocates or practices polygamy.
- *October 9:* Aimee Semple McPherson, founder of the Four Square Gospel Church, is born in Ontario, Canada.
- *December 29:* More than 200 Sioux are killed by U.S. soldiers at Wounded Knee on the Pine Ridge Indian Reservation in South Dakota.

1891

- Katharine Drexel, later declared a saint by the Catholic Church, establishes the Sisters of the Blessed Sacrament for Indians and Colored People.

- Charles Randolf Uncles becomes the first black ordained a Catholic priest in America.
- The Rosary and Altar Society for Catholic women is founded.
- Billy Sunday gives up his career as a baseball player to work full time as assistant secretary of the Chicago YMCA. He subsequently becomes a revival preacher.

1892

- Walter Rauschenbusch helps organize a nondenominational group called the Brotherhood of the Kingdom, which devotes its energies to practical social service to immigrants and poor laborers.
- *June 21:* Theologian Reinhold Niebuhr is born.

1893

- Charles Augustus Briggs, on the faculty of Union Theological Seminary in New York City, is suspended as a minister by the general assembly of the Presbyterian Church in the United States of America after expressing support for higher critical theories concerning the Bible.
- The National Council of Jewish Women is organized in Chicago.
- Hindu religious leader Swami Vivekanada will remain in America for three years after attending the World's Parliament of Religions, undertaking a lecture tour that will continue until mid-1895.
- The Anti-Saloon League is established. Two years later it will be organized at the national level at a convention in Washington, D.C.
- The Foreign Missions Conference of North America is established.
- In Chicago C. T. Strauss becomes the first U.S. citizen formally to convert to Buddhism in America.
- *September:* The World's Parliament of Religions is held in conjunction with the Chicago Columbian Exposition.
- *September 14:* Pope Leo XIII appoints Archbishop Francesco Satolli the first apostolic delegate to the United States.

1894

- Quaker leader Rufus M. Jones begins publishing *The American Friend.*
- Swami Vivekananda establishes the New York Vedanta Society.
- Paul Carus publishes *The Gospel of Buddha According to Old Records.*

- Ibrahim George Kheiralla immigrates to the United States and introduces the Baha'i Faith to America.
- *September 3:* Theologian H. Richard Niebuhr is born in Wright City, Missouri.

1895

- Phineas Franklin Bresee helps to establish the First Church of the Nazarene in Los Angeles.
- The National Baptist Convention of the United States of America is formed out of existing conventions of African-American Baptists.
- The African Methodist Episcopal Zion Church becomes the first black denomination to grant official recognition to female preachers when it ordains Julia Foote.
- Elizabeth Cady Stanton and others produce *The Women's Bible.*

1896

- William Jennings Bryan runs for president of the United States for the first time. He will later serve as prosecuting attorney in the "Scopes monkey trial" in Tennessee.
- Following the repudiation of plural marriages by Mormons in 1890, Utah enters the Union as a state.
- William S. Crowdy founds the Church of God and Saints of Christ and declares that blacks are descendants of the "lost tribes of Israel."
- *January:* Billy Sunday holds a series of revival services in Garner, Iowa, launching his career as an evangelistic preacher.
- *May 18:* In *Plessy v. Ferguson* the U.S. Supreme Court upholds the constitutionality of racial segregation. The case is generally understood to adopt the "separate but equal" test, approving racial segregation as long as benefits and facilities segregated by race are equal.

1897

- The first advanced Talmudical school is established in New York, the Rabbi Isaac Elchanan Theological Seminary.
- Daisetz Teitaro Suzuki arrives in the United States from Japan and begins work with Paul Carus on the *Open Court* magazine. He will be a leading figure in popularizing Zen Buddhism in America.
- Charles H. Mason founds the Church of God in Christ, at first a Holiness denomination. Later, after attending the Azusa Street Revival which will begin in 1906, Mason will lead the denomination to become Pentecostal.

- Congregationalist minister Charles Monroe Sheldon publishes *In His Steps,* a novel that explores the consequences when its characters ask themselves, "What would Jesus do?"
- Theodor Herzl, a Hungarian Jew, publishes *The Jewish State,* which contributes to the rise of Zionism.
- The *Jewish Daily Forward* is launched as a Yiddish-language daily newspaper in New York.
- Baptist minister Walter Rauschenbusch joins the faculty of Rochester Seminary and uses his academic influence to further the Social Gospel movement.
- *October 7:* Elijah Mohammed, Nation of Islam leader, is born in Sandersville, Georgia.
- *November 8:* Dorothy Day, cofounder of the Catholic Worker Movement, is born in Brooklyn, New York.

1898

- The Orthodox Jewish Congregational Union of America is established to counter developments in Reform Judaism, including the Reform-minded Union of American Hebrew Congregations.
- The Federation of American Zionists is founded in New York.
- Josiah Strong, a leader in the Social Gospel movement, organizes the American League for Social Service.

1899

- Pope Leo XIII issues his encyclical *Testem Benevolentiae,* which condemns Americanism as a heresy.
- The first full-time Buddhist missionaries arrive in the United States.

Eyewitness Testimony

The traditions of our people are handed down from father to son. The chief is considered to be the most learned, and the leader of the tribe. The doctor, however, is thought to have more inspiration. He is supposed to be in communion with spirits; and we call him "doctor," as you white people call your medicine-man; and the word is not taken from the English language, as may be supposed, but purely Indian. We do not call him a medicine-man, because he does not dose us, as your doctors do, and therefore we call him "doctor." He cures the sick by the laying on of hands, and prayers and incantations and heavenly songs. He infuses new life into the patient, and performs most wonderful feats of skill in his practice. It is one of the most solemn ceremonies of our tribe. He clothes himself in the skins of young, innocent animals, such as the fawn; and decorates himself with the plumage of harmless birds, such as the dove and hummingbird and little birds of the forest—no such things as hawks' feathers, eagles', or birds of prey. His clothing is emblematic of innocence. If he cannot cure the sick person, he tells him that the spirits of his relations hover around and await his departure. Then they pray and sing around his deathbed, and wait for the spirit to take its flight; and then, after the spirit leaves the body, they make merry, because he is beyond care, and they suppose in heaven. They believe there is only joy in that place; that sorrow is before and not after death; that when the soul departs, it goes to peace and happiness, and leaves all its misery behind.

American Indian lecturer and teacher Sarah Winnemucca, 1882, "The Pah-utes," in Peyer, The Elders Wrote, *pp. 110–111.*

Once the world was all water and God lived alone. He was lonesome, he had no place to put his foot, so he scratched the sand up from the bottom and made the land, and he made the rocks, and he made trees, and he made a man; and the man had wings and could go anywhere. The man was lonesome, and God made a woman. They ate fish from the water, and God made the deer and other animals, and he sent the man to hunt and told the woman to cook the meat and to dress the skins. Many more men and women grew up, and they lived on the banks of the great river whose waters were full of salmon. The mountains contained much game and there were buffalo on the plains. There were so many people that the stronger ones sometimes oppressed the weak and drove them from the best fisheries, which they claimed as their own. They fought and nearly all were killed, and their bones are to be seen in the hills yet. God was very angry at this and he took away their wings and commanded that the lands and fisheries should be common to all who lived upon them; that they were never to be marked off or divided, but that the people should enjoy the fruits that God planted in the land, and the animals that lived upon it, and the fishes in the water. God said he was the father and the earth was the mother of mankind; that nature was the law; that the animals, and fish, and plants obeyed nature, and that man only was sinful. This is the old law.

. . . . .

Those who cut up the lands or sign papers for lands will be defrauded of their rights and will be punished by God's anger.

. . . . .

You ask me to plough the ground! Shall I take a knife and tear my mother's bosom? Then when I die she will not take me to her bosom to rest.

You ask me to dig for stone! Shall I dig under her skin for her bones! Then when I die I can not enter her body to be born again.

You ask me to cut grass and make hay and sell it, and be rich like white men! But how dare I cut off my mother's hair?

It is a bad law, and my people can not obey it. I want my people to stay with me here. All the dead men will come to life again. Their spirits will come to their bodies again. We must wait here in the homes of our fathers and be ready to meet them in the bosom of our mother.

Wanapum Shaman Smohalla, 1884, in Moquin, Great Documents in American Indian History, *pp. 26–27.*

We think we can claim to be acquainted with the laws, institutions, and spirit of the Catholic Church, and with the laws, institutions, and spirit of our country; and we emphatically declare that there is no antagonism between them. A Catholic finds himself at home in the United States; for the influence of his Church has constantly been exercised in behalf of individual rights and popular liberties. And the right-minded American nowhere finds himself more at home than in the Catholic Church, for nowhere else can he breathe more freely that atmosphere of Divine truth, which alone can make us free.

American Catholic bishops at the Third Plenary Council of Baltimore, 1884, in Gillis, Roman Catholicism in America, *p. 64.*

It is not necessary to argue to those for whom I write that the two great needs of mankind, that all men may be lifted up into the light of the highest Christian civilization, are, first, a pure, spiritual Christianity, and, second, civil liberty. Without controversy, these are the forces which, in the past, have contributed most to the elevation of the human race, and they must continue to be, in the future, the most efficient ministers to its progress. It follows, then, that the Anglo-Saxon, as the great representative of these two ideas, the depositary of these two greatest blessings, sustains peculiar relations to the world's future, is divinely commissioned to be, in a peculiar sense, his brother's keeper. Add to this the fact of his rapidly increasing strength in modern times, and we have well nigh a demonstration of his destiny.

. . . . .

There can be no reasonable doubt that North America is to be the great home of the Anglo-Saxon, the principal seat of his power, the center of his life and influence. Not only does it constitute seven-elevenths of his possessions, but here his empire is unsevered, while the remaining four-elevenths are fragmentary and scattered over the earth.

. . . . .

What is the significance of such facts? These tendencies infold the future; they are the mighty alphabet with which God writes his prophecies. May we not, by a careful laying together of the letters, spell out something of his meaning? It seems to me that God, with infinite wisdom and skill, is training the Anglo-Saxon race for an hour sure to come in the world's future. Heretofore there has always been in the history of the world a comparatively unoccupied land westward, into which the crowded countries of the East have poured their surplus populations. But the widening waves of migration, which millenniums ago rolled east and west from the valley of the Euphrates, meet to-day on our Pacific coast. There are no more new worlds. The unoccupied arable lands of the earth are limited, and will soon be taken. The time is coming when the pressure of population on the means of subsistence will be felt here as it is now felt in Europe and Asia. Then will the world enter upon a new stage of its history—*the final competition of races, for which the Anglo-Saxon is being schooled.* Long before the thousand millions are here, the mighty *centrifugal* tendency, inherent in this stock and strengthened in the United States, will assert itself. Then this race of unequaled energy, with all the majesty of numbers and the might of wealth behind it—the representative, let us

hope, of the largest liberty, the purest Christianity, the highest civilization—having developed peculiarly aggressive traits calculated to impress its institutions upon mankind, will spread itself over the earth. If I read not amiss, this powerful race will move down upon Mexico, down upon Central and South America, out upon the islands of the sea, over upon Africa and beyond. And can any one doubt that the result of this competition of races will be the "survival of the fittest"?

. . . . .

Every civilization has its destructive and preservative elements. The Anglo-Saxon race would speedily decay but for the salt of Christianity. Bring savages into contact with our civilization, and its destructive forces become operative at once, while years are necessary to render effective the saving influences of Christian instruction. Moreover, the pioneer wave of our civilization carries with it more scum than salt. Where there is one missionary, there are hundreds of miners or traders or adventurers ready to debauch the native.

. . . . .

Thus, while on this continent God is training the Anglo-Saxon race for its mission, a complemental work has been in progress in the great world beyond. God has two hands. Not only is he preparing in our civilization the die with which to stamp the nations, but, by what Southey called the "timing of Providence," he is preparing mankind to receive our impress.

Social Gospel leader Josiah Strong, 1885, arguing for the historic role of Anglo-Saxon civilization, including Christianity, in Our Country, *pp. 201–216.*

I was on a solitary walk, absorbed with my thoughts about the meaning and purpose of my life, wondering whether I should ever get myself organized and brought under the control and direction of some constructive central purpose of life, when I felt the walls between the visible and the invisible suddenly grow thin, and I was conscious of a definite mission of life opening out before me. I saw stretch before me an unfolding of labor in the realm of mystical religion, almost as clearly as Francis heard himself called at St. Damiens to "repair the Church." I remember kneeling down alone in a beautiful forest glade and dedicating myself then and there in the quiet and silence, but in the presence of an invading Life, to the work of interpreting the deeper nature of the soul and its relation with God.

Quaker theologian Rufus Matthew Jones, 1887, in Vining, Friend of Life, *p. 51.*

That there exists among us, as in the other countries of the world, grave and threatening social evils, public injustices, which call for strong resistance and legal remedy, is a fact which no one dares to deny, and the truth of which has been already acknowledged by the Congress and the President of the United States. Without entering into the sad details of these wrongs,—which does not seem necessary here,—it may suffice to mention only that monopolies on the part of both individuals and of corporations, have already called forth not only the complaints of our working classes but also the opposition of our public men and legislators; that the efforts of these monopolists, not always without success, to control legislation to their own profit, cause serious apprehension among the disinterested friends of liberty; that the heartless avarice which, through greed of gain, pitilessly grinds not only the men, but particularly the women and children in various employments, make it clear to all who love humanity and justice that it is not only the right of the laboring classes to protect themselves, but the duty of the whole people to aid them in finding a remedy against the danger with which both civilization and the social order are menaced by avarice, oppression and corruption.

James Cardinal Gibbons, February 20, 1887, letter to Giovanni Cardinal Simeoni, prefect of the Congregation de Propaganda Fide, the branch of Catholic ecclesiastical government with authority over the Catholic Church in America, urging the church not to condemn the Knights of Labor, in Browne, The Catholic Church and the Knights of Labor, *p. 368.*

My grandfather, Moses Menahem Zieve, came to this country in the early 1880s from Lithuania where he had been a shochet, a ritual slaughterer. He left behind, to follow him some six years later, his wife and four children: three boys and one girl, my mother.

After living in America for six years, he decided against pursuing his profession of shechitah. His visits to slaughtering establishments in New York, Chicago, and Los Angeles led him to the conclusion that his American coreligionists—he considered them "goyim," non-Jews by comparison with what he had known in Europe—would not or could not appreciate his meticulousness nor accept his high standards. He settled in Minneapolis and, for a livelihood, turned to peddling.

Grandfather's "territory" was the area out of Northfield, Minnesota, forty miles south of Minneapolis. When he set out on his trips he carried with him on his wagon, in addition to his goods for sale, his own utensils for pre-

paring meals in accordance with the requirements of kashruth, ritual purity [the dietary laws]. Many weekends he could not return to Minneapolis and spent the Sabbath in the home of a friendly farmer in Northfield. He would arrive at the farmer's house on Friday—or possibly Thursday night—in time to slaughter a chicken, do his Sabbath cooking, and make his personal preparations for the Sabbath. In the farmer's home, from sundown on Friday until dark on Saturday evening, he observed the Sabbath in the traditional manner. At twilight on Saturday a child in the family would go outside to watch for three stars and then come in to advise him: "You can smoke now, Moses."

The German immigrants who settled the area around Northfield worshipped together in a community church. For lack of funds, they had no regular preacher. On Sunday mornings, then, in this community church, my grandfather occupied the pulpit and preached to this German-speaking congregation. His language? A carefully selected non-Hebraic Yiddish. His subjects? The Torah portions of the week. And in serving this Christian community over many months, he won their gratitude—and an affectionate but reverent title. They called him "Holy Moses."

Beryl B. Gordon, ca. 1890, in Marcus, The Jew in the American World, *pp. 341–342.*

Where God builds a church the devil builds next door a saloon, is an old saying that has lost its point in New York. Either the devil was on the ground first, or he has been doing a good deal more in the way of building. I tried once to find out how the account stood, and counted to 111 Protestant churches, chapels and places of worship of every kind below Fourteenth Street, 4,065 saloons. The worst half of the tenement population lives down there, and it has to this day the worst half of the saloons. Uptown the account stands a little better, but there are easily ten saloons to every church to-day. I am afraid, too, that the congregations are larger by a good deal; certainly the attendance is steadier and the contributions more liberal the week round, Sunday included.

Social reformer Jacob Riis, 1890, How the Other Half Lives, *quoted in Butler, et al.,* Religion in American Life: A Short History, *p. 341.*

You belong, sir, to a sect—I believe my sect . . . which has enjoyed, and partly failed to utilize, an exceptional advantage in the islands of Hawaii. The first missionaries came; they found the land already self-purged of its old and bloody faith; they were embraced, almost on their arrival, with enthusiasm. . . . In the course of their evangelical calling, they—or too many of them—grew rich. It may be news to you that the houses of missionaries are a cause of mocking on the streets of Honolulu. . . . [W]hen leprosy descended and took root in the Eight Islands, a *quid pro quo* was to be looked for. To that prosperous mission, and to you, as one of its adornments, God had sent at last an opportunity. I know I am touching here upon a nerve acutely sensitive. I know that others of your colleagues look back on the inertia of your Church, and the intrusive and decisive heroism of Damien, with something almost to be called remorse. . . . But, sir, when we have failed, and another has succeeded; when we have stood by, and another has stepped in; when we sit and grow bulky in our charming mansions, and a plain, uncouth peasant steps into the battle, under the eyes of God, and succors the afflicted, and consoles the dying, and is himself af-

flicted in his turn, and dies upon the field of honor—the battle cannot be retrieved as your unhappy irritation has suggested. It is a lost battle, and lost for ever.

Open letter of Robert Louis Stevenson to the Reverend Charles McEwen Hyde, a Presbyterian minister, responding to Hyde's criticisms of Father Damien, the Leper Priest of Molokai, February 25, 1890, in Stewart, Leper Priest of Molokai, *p. 381.*

You say, "If the United States army would kill a thousand or so of the dancing Indians there would be no more trouble." I judge by the above language you are a "Christian," and are disposed to do all in your power to advance the cause of Christ. You are doubtless a worshiper of the white man's Saviour, but are unwilling that the Indians should have a "Messiah" of their own. The Indians have never taken kindly to the Christian religion as preached and practiced by the whites. Do you know why this is

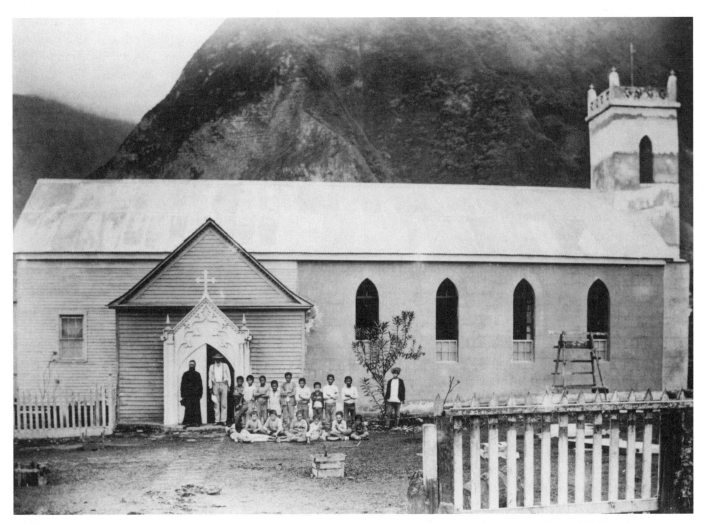

Father Damien, "the Leper Priest of Molokai," pictured here with members of his mission on the island of Molokai in Hawaii, was eloquently defended by Robert Louis Stevenson. *(Library of Congress, Prints and Photographs Division LC-USZ62-103862)*

the case? Because the Good Father of all has given us a better religion—a religion that is all good and no bad, a religion that is adapted to our wants. You say if we are good, obey the Ten Commandments and never sin any more, we may be permitted eventually to sit upon a white rock and sing praises to God forevermore, and look down upon our heathen fathers, mothers, brothers and sisters who are howling in hell.

It won't do. The code of morals as practiced by the white race will not compare with the morals of the Indians. We pay no lawyers or preachers, but we have not one-tenth part of the crime that you do. If our Messiah does come we shall not try to force you into our belief. We will never burn innocent women at the stake or pull men to pieces with horses because they refuse to join in our ghost dances. . . . You are anxious to get hold of our Messiah, so you can put him in irons. This you may do—in fact, you may crucify him as you did that other one, but you cannot convert the Indians to the Christian religion until you contaminate them with the blood of the white man. The white man's heaven is repulsive to the Indian nature, and if the white man's hell suits you, why, you keep it. I think there will be white rogues enough to fill it.

Masse Hadjo, a Sioux, defending the Ghost Dance religion, December 5, 1890, "An Indian on the Messiah Craze," Chicago Tribune, available online at URL: http://www. digitalhistory.uh.edu/native_voices/voices_display. cfm?id=81. Accessed on May 16, 2005.

When you get home you must make a dance to continue five days. Dance four successive nights, and the last night keep up the dance until the morning of the fifth day, when all must bathe in the river and then disperse to their homes. You must all do in the same way.

I, Jack Wilson, love you all, and my heart is full of gladness for the gifts you have brought me. When you get home I shall give you a good cloud [rain?] which will make you feel good. I give you a good spirit and give you all good paint. I want you to come again in three months, some from each tribe there [the Indian territory].

There will be a good deal of snow this year and some rain. In the fall there will be such a rain as I have never given you before.

Grandfather [a universal title of reverence among Indians and here meaning the messiah] says, when your friends die you must not cry. You must not hurt anybody or do harm to anyone. You must not fight. Do right always. It will give you satisfaction in life.

. . . . .

Do not tell the white people about this. Jesus is now upon the earth. He appears like a cloud. The dead are still alive again. I do not know when they will be here; maybe this fall or in the spring. When the time comes there will be no more sickness and everyone will be young again.

Do not refuse to work for the whites and do not make any trouble with them until you leave them. When the earth shakes [at the coming of the new world] do not be afraid. It will not hurt you.

I want you to dance every six weeks. Make a feast at the dance and have food that everybody may eat. Then bathe in the water. That is all. You will receive good words again from me some time. Do not tell lies.

Wovoka (Jack Wilson), 1891, "The Messiah Letter (free rendering)," in Mooney, The Ghost-Dance Religion and the Sioux Outbreak of 1890, p. 23.

Have mercy upon me. Give me knowledge that I may not say or do evil things. To you, O God, I am trying to pray. Do thou, O Son of God, help me, too. This [peyote] religion, let me know. Help me, O medicine grandfather, help me.

Prayer of an unknown Winnebago after consuming eight peyote buttons, 1893, in Gaustad and Schmidt, The Religious History of America, pp. 13–14.

MR. PRESIDENT AND FRIENDS,—If my heart did not overflow with cordial welcome at this hour, which promises to be a great moment in history, it would be because I had lost the spirit of mankind and had been forsaken by the Spirit of God. The whitest snow on the sacred mount of Japan, the clearest water springing from the sacred fountains of India are not more pure and bright than the joy of my heart and of many hearts here that this day has dawned in the annals of time, and that, from the farthest isles of Asia; from India, mother of religions; from Europe, the great teacher of civilization; from the shores on which breaks the "long wash of Australasian seas"; that from the neighboring lands and from all part of this republic, which we love to contemplate as the land of earth's brightest future, you have come here at our invitation in the expectation that the world's first Parliament of Religion must prove an event of race-wide and perpetual significance.

. . . . .

Welcome, most welcome, O wise men of the East and of the West! May the star which has led you hither be like that luminary which guided the sages of old, and may this meeting by the inland sea of a new continent be blessed of heaven to the redemption of men from error and from sin and despair. I wish you to understand that this great undertaking, which has aimed to house under one friendly roof in brotherly council the representatives of God's aspiring and believing children everywhere, has been conceived and carried on through strenuous and patient toil, with an unfaltering heart, with a devout faith in God, and with most signal and special evidences of his divine guidance and favor.

Presbyterian minister John Henry Barrows, 1893, opening address for the World's Parliament of Religions, quoted in Tweed and Prothero, Asian Religions in America, *pp. 127–128.*

I am an American of the Americans. I carried with me for years the same errors that thousands of Americans carry with them to-day. Those errors have grown into history, false history has influenced your opinion of Islam. It influenced my opinion of Islam and when I began, ten years ago, to study the Oriental religions, I threw Islam aside as altogether too corrupt for consideration. But when I came to go beneath the surface, to know what Islam really is, to know who and what the prophet of Arabia was, I changed my belief very materially, and I am proud to say I am now a Mussulman.

American convert to Islam Mohammed Russell Alexander Webb, 1893, speech before the World's Parliament of Religions, in Eck, A New Religious America, *p. 234.*

The Secret Doctrine then establishes three fundamental propositions:

I. An Omnipresent, Eternal, Boundless and Immutable PRINCIPLE, on which all speculation is impossible, since it transcends the power of human conception and could only be dwarfed by any human expression or similitude. It is beyond the range and reach of thought—in the words of *Mândûkya,* "unthinkable and unspeakable."

. . . . .

II. The Eternity of the Universe *in toto* as a boundless plane; periodically "the playground of numberless Universes incessantly manifesting and disappearing," called the "Manifesting Stars," and the "Sparks of Eternity."

. . . . .

This second assertion of the Secret Doctrine is the absolute universality of that law of periodicity, of flux and reflux, ebb and flow, which physical science has observed and recorded in all departments of nature. An alternation such as that of Day and Night, Life and Death, Sleeping and Waking, is a fact so common, so perfectly universal and without exception, that it is easy to comprehend that in it we see one of the absolutely fundamental Laws of the Universe.

Moreover, the Secret Doctrine teaches:

III. The fundamental identity of all Souls with the Universal Over-Soul, the latter being itself an aspect of the Unknown Root; and the obligatory pilgrimage for every Soul—a spark of the former—through the Cycle of Incarnation, or Necessity, in accordance with Cyclic and Karmic Law, during the whole term. In other words, no purely spiritual Buddhi (Divine Soul) can have an independent conscious existence before the spark which issued from the pure Essence of the Universal Sixth principle—or the OVER-SOUL—has (a) passed through every elemental form of the phenomenal world of that Manvantara, and (b) acquired individuality, first by natural impulse, and then by self-induced and self-devised efforts, checked by its Karma, thus ascending through all the degrees of intelligence, from the lowest to the highest Manas, from mineral and plant, up to the holiest archangel (Dhyâni-Buddha). The pivotal doctrine of the Esoteric Philosophy admits no privileges or special gifts in man, save those won by his own Ego through personal effort and merit throughout a long series of metempsychoses and reincarnations. This is why the Hindûs say that the Universe is Brahman and Brahmâ, for Brahman is in every atom of the universe, the six Principles in Nature being all the outcome—the variously differentiated aspects—of the Seventh and One, the only Reality in the Universe whether cosmic or micro-cosmic; and also why the permutations, psychic, spiritual and physical, on the plane of manifestation and form, of the Sixth (Brahmâ the vehicle of Brahman) are viewed by metaphysical antiphrasis as illusive and mâyâvic. For although the root of every atom individually and of every form collectively, is that Seventh Principle or the One Reality, still, in its manifested phenomenal and temporary appearance, it is no better than an evanescent illusion of our senses.

Theosophist founder H. P. Blavatsky, 1893, The Secret Doctrine, *vol. 1, pp. 42–46.*

The first moral cause of permanence of which the American republic has the advantage is the principle of toleration in religion—a principle which, though not recently enunciated . . . has been very recently put in practice, not, by any means, in all parts of the civilized world, but in a few favored regions, and notably in the United States. On one of the tablets of the Water-gate at Chicago was written this sentence: "Toleration in religion the best fruit of the last four centuries." This statement is no exaggeration but the literal truth. Toleration in religion is absolutely the best fruit of all the struggles, labors, and sorrows of the civilized nations during the last four centuries.

Harvard University president Charles William Eliot, 1894, "Why the Republic may Endure," in Hart, American History Told by Contemporaries, *vol. 4, p. 658.*

Everybody wants me to come over to India. They think we shall be able to do more if I come over. They are mistaken, my friend. Here is a grand field. What have I to do with this "ism" or that "ism"? I am the servant of the Lord, and where on earth is there a better field than here for propagating all high ideas?

Swami Vivekanada, Hindu religious leader, October 1894, letter to a disciple in India while in America on a lecture tour, in Jackson, Vedanta for the West, *p. 28.*

Boston, Massachusetts, December 27, 1894. Twenty six years ago my uncle left for the far West. For the last 22 years we had not heard from him and all our efforts to learn his whereabouts were in vain. Discouraged, we gave up all hopes, thinking our uncle had died. Upon the advice of a good Franciscan we prayed fervently to St. Anthony. A short time after and in the most unexpected manner I found a book, which enabled me to correspond with one of the Fathers in whose parish my uncle was. You may imagine our happiness at once more being in communication with one, loved so dearly. Thanks to St. Anthony for his intercession.

Letter from "C.A." published in St. Anthony's Messenger, *a Catholic magazine, reprinted in McDannell,* Religions of the United States in Practice, *vol. 1, pp. 341–342.*

When I look at the religious question as it really puts itself to concrete men, and when I think of all the possibilities which both practically and theoretically it involves, then this command that we shall put a stopper on our heart, instincts and courage, and *wait*—acting of course meanwhile more or less as if religion were *not* true—till doomsday, or till such time as our intellect and senses working together may have raked in evidence enough— this command, I say, seems to me the queerest idol every manufactured in the philosophic cave.

American philosopher William James, 1897, "The Will to Believe," in William James: Writings, 1878–1899, *pp. 477–478.*

It is simply justice to state that the Methodist Episcopal Church, South, at the beginning of the late war, had over two hundred thousand members of color within her pales, having churches of their own, and ministers sent to them regularly from the conferences. Often one pastor served both the white and the colored members, preaching to the whites in the forenoon and to the colored in the afternoon. Of this two hundred thousand, the great majority informally dissolved their relationship with the Methodist Episcopal Church, South, and went into other branches of Methodism, the African Methodist Episcopal Church receiving the largest share of them. However, there still remained about forty thousand who adhered to the Methodist Episcopal Church, South, and who could not be induced to disband their church relation and enter others which came upon the ground immediately after the emancipation. For some years after the war the reduced number of members of color who still remained adherents of the Methodist Episcopal Church, South, was looked after and cared for as was the case during the years of slavery. As the General Conference of the Methodist Episcopal Church, South, which met in New Orleans, May, 1866, had authorized the bishops to organize conferences of colored ministers, so, four years after, the same body held its quadrennial session in Memphis, Tenn.; and upon the petition of some of the leading colored ministers, the General Conference of the Mother Church delegated their bishops, with other distinguished ministers and laymen, to organize the colored members into a separate and distinct body, which was satisfactorily consummated in December of the same year (1810).

The organization of this branch of our common Methodism seemed necessary for several reasons.

Among them we may note the following: As a result, the war had changed the ancient relation of master and servant. The former, though divested of his slaves, yet carried with him all the notions, feelings and elements in his religious and social life that characterized his former years. On the other hand, the emancipated slave had but little in common with the former master. In fact, he had nothing but his religion, poverty and ignorance. With social elements so distinct and dissimilar, the best results of a common church relation could not be expected. Harmony, friendship and peaceful co-operation between the two peoples in the propagation of a divine and vital Christianity, were among the essential elements of a successful evangelization of the people of color. Social religious equality, as well as any other kind of social equality, was utterly impracticable and undesirable, and coveted by neither class of persons composing a churchship.

With this state of things steadily in view, we had but one horn of the dilemma left us, and that was a free, friendly and authorized separation from the mother body. Although we are become two bands, yet it is, and was understood that this does not, in any sense, release the Methodist Episcopal Church, South, from those duties and obligations that Providence seems to have imposed upon her, in aiding the American African in his Christian development.

Lucius Henry Holsey, bishop of the Methodist Episcopal Church, South, 1898, Autobiography, Sermons, Addresses, and Essays of Bishop L. H. Holsey, D. D., *pp. 214–216, available online at URL: http://docsouth.unc. edu/holsey/holsey.html. Accessed on January 15, 2006.*

The white people made war on the Lakotas to keep them from practicing their religion. Now the white people wish to make us cause the spirits of our dead to be ashamed. They wish us to be a stingy people and send our spirits to the spirit world as if they had been conquered and robbed by the enemy. They wish us to send our spirits on the spirit trail with nothing so that when they come to the spirit world, they will be like beggars. . . . Tell this to the agent and maybe he will not cause us to make our spirits ashamed.

American Indian religious leader Short Bull, 1898, on a prohibition imposed by authorities preventing burial bundles in which a lock of hair of a deceased was saved in a ritual bundle for a year, quoted in "The Lakota Ghost Dance: An Ethnohistorical Account," in Religion and American Culture, *p. 327.*

My Dear Sir,

I desire to send a letter to thank you for your kindness shown to my assistant Mr. Nishijima and to inform you of our public lectures on Buddhism which were opened at last Sunday. I knew your name at home through your excellent writing tinted with candidness.

. . . . .

Though weak handed, we are now carrying on our work trusting to the protection of the merciful Buddha.

. . . . .

After my lecture some questions were raised by the audience which Mr. Nishijima and I explained away. The first meeting was pretty satisfactory. This is the first attempt at the propagation of the new light of the truth in the New World, though our doctrine has been brought here in books by the endeavours of such learned scholars as you. I find much difficulty in conveying the oriental faith to occidental people. So we require your valuable aid.

I can not close my letter without expressing our indebtedness to you for your noble effort to cause the Christian people to understand Buddhism.

Buddhist missionary to America Shuye Sonoda, 1899, letter to Paul Carus, reprinted in Tweed and Prothero, Asian Religions in America, *pp. 80–82.*

CHAPTER ELEVEN

Modernity and Its Critics
(1900–1920)

In the final decades of the 19th and the first of the 20th centuries, two intellectual developments posed new challenges for orthodox Christian belief. The first was the emergence and gradual acceptance in scientific circles of Darwinism. The second was the importation from Germany of critical theories about the composition of biblical texts, theories that questioned traditional views concerning the authorship and inspiration of the Bible. Both developments created new fissures among Christian congregations and forged new alliances among denominations who in spite of other doctrinal differences shared common perspectives on the challenges of modernity.

Mainstream Christian denominations quickly adjusted to the new scientific environment as well as to the currents of modern biblical scholarship. This adjustment prompted these denominations to drift gradually away from tenets of orthodoxy prominent among most 19th-century Christian denominations. Jesus's divinity and resurrection from the dead, for example, seemed less compelling anchors for contemporary theological reflection than his role as a moral exemplar. The Bible was seen less as an authoritative guide than a record of human religious experience, bound by its particular cultural and historical contexts but suggestive under proper interpretation of enduring spiritual issues. Theologians such as Shailer Mathews, dean of the University of Chicago Divinity School, complained that conservatives were disconnected from the issues facing modern believers, issues, in fact, facing the modern world:

> The world needs new control of nature and society and is told that the Bible is verbally inerrant.
> It needs a means of composing class strife, and is told to believe in the substitutionary atonement.
> It needs a spirit of love and justice and is told that love without orthodoxy will not save from hell.
> It needs international peace and sees the champions of peace incapable of fellowship even at the table of their Lord.
> It needs to find God in the processes of nature and is told that he who believes in evolution cannot believe in God.

It needs faith in the divine presence in human affairs and is told it must accept the virgin birth of Jesus Christ.

It needs hope for a better world order and is told to await the speedy return of Jesus Christ from heaven to destroy sinners, cleanse the world by fire, and establish an ideal society composed of those whose bodies have been raised from the sea and earth.[1]

If Mathews's references to conservative orthodoxy were tinged with exasperation for their lack of engagement with the modern world, conservative Christians tended to view the enthusiasm of Mathews and other liberal theologians for such engagement with alarm. Opponents of the Social Gospel movement had already questioned whether theological liberals had exchanged social activism for fidelity to orthodox doctrine. But liberal repudiation of such tenets as the resurrection of Jesus caused some conservatives to question whether modernist Christians were Christians at all. During the first decades of the 20th century, theological conflict between conservatives and liberals reached a new pitch of intensity, one that would eventually sunder mainstream denominations such as the Presbyterians and the Baptists. Those conservatives who mounted a vigorous assault on theological liberalism came to be known as fundamentalists. They generally failed to prevent the mainline Protestant churches from drifting toward liberalism and subsequently withdrew from these churches to form denominations and organizations consistent with their orthodox vision.

While some American believers wrestled self-consciously with modernity, others attempted to retrace their theological steps to an earlier, more primitive period, seeking guidance more from the early New Testament church than from creeds or traditions, no matter how venerable. The primitivist impulse had been prominent during the 19th century and had given rise to the Restorationist movement within Protestant Christianity, which, under the guidance of figures such as Alexander Campbell and Barton Stone, sought to restore primitive patterns of worship and practice consistent with examples they derived from the New Testament church. A new expression of the primitivist impulse appeared toward the beginning of the 20th century in the form of the Pentecostal movement. Generally growing out of the Holiness tradition, Pentecostalism sought to restore forms of spiritual power and life thought to be neglected by other Christian traditions. Believing supernatural spiritual gifts such as prophecy, healing, and speaking in tongues to be authentic marks of Christian experience, Pentecostalism elaborated theology and, even more important, practice that gave a central place to spiritual gifts.

The Influence of Darwinism and Critical Theories of Biblical Interpretation

The publication by Charles Darwin in 1871 of *The Origin of Species* set off a longstanding argument with conservative Christians that still reverberates into the 21st century. Some progressive Protestants, such as Congregationalist minister Henry Ward Beecher and his protégé, Lyman Abbott, embraced evolution as not only a scientifically accurate account of human origins but as a metaphor for God's dealings with the cosmos. Shailer Mathews, the influential dean of the Chicago Divinity School beginning in 1908, argued that evolution was "the history of an ever more complete revelation of how the infinite Person produces finite personalities."[2] Other

Congregationalist minister and magazine editor Lyman Abbott articulated an optimistic view of human progress. *(Library of Congress, Prints and Photographs Division LC-USZ62-125670)*

Christians, though, saw evolutionary theory as an assault on biblical truth designed to unhinge humanity from dependence on a creator.

The prominence of evolutionary theory in the last part of the 19th century threatened traditional Christian views of nature and of God's superintendence over it. A corollary development threatened orthodox views about history and God's governance of it. Imported mainly from Germany, scholarship questioning the unitary authorship of the books of the Pentateuch and Isaiah attracted significant interest in the latter decades of the 19th century. In contrast with "lower criticism" of biblical books, aimed at ascertaining the most accurate text of a particular passage, "higher criticism," or "historical criticism," focused on the historical and cultural circumstances surrounding the composition of the books of the Bible. New critical views relating to the Old Testament insisted that the first five books of the Bible, traditionally attributed to Moses, had actually been written by multiple authors across many centuries. Other scholars suggested that some prophetic books in the Old Testament had been composed after the events prophesied, thus casting doubt on the miraculousness of prophecy itself. And critical treatment of scriptural texts did not confine itself to the Old Testament books. German theologian David Strauss published *Leben Jesu* (The Life of Jesus) in 1835, which suggested that miracles recorded in the New Testament gospels were mythical, the product of the early church's attempt to wrestle with the meaning of Jesus' life rather than historical accounts of that life. These views emphasized the human authorship of Scripture within specific historical and cultural contexts, in contrast to the focus on the divine inspiration of Scripture characteristic of traditional Christian thought. Some supporters of historical-critical scholarship, as it is sometimes referred to, found room in their understandings of the Bible to embrace both the conclusions of this scholarship and continued confidence that the Bible was divinely inspired. But the conclusions of this scholarship also supported more skeptical assessments about the Bible. Darwin, for example, concluded that the Old Testament "was no more to be trusted than the sacred books of the Hindoos."[3] Moreover, more conservative believers aware of the emerging findings of historical critical scholarship found them inconsistent with their understandings of the inspiration of Scripture.

Influenced by these developments in modern thought, theological liberals became disaffected from a focus on the supernatural. Scripture was not so much to be studied for evidence of God's miraculous power but for the moral precepts and principles to be found there. Even such pillars of Christian orthodoxy as the bodily resurrection of Jesus from the dead seemed to the liberals a misguided distraction from the enduring moral significance of Jesus' life. Just as the books of the Bible had themselves—as liberals saw it—been authored out of specific historical and cultural circumstances, the most important work of theology was not to preserve and defend the orthodoxies of the past but to adapt theological truth to the specific circumstances of the present.

In the first skirmishes between theological conservatives and liberals over the application of historical-critical methods to the Bible, conservatives were able to push back some of the encroachments of modernity on the mainline churches. An important early case involved Presbyterian minister and Union Theological Seminary professor Charles Augustus Briggs. With the publication of his book *Whither? A Theological Question for the Times* (1889), Briggs revealed that his theological sympathies lay with the liberals. Two years later he was installed in the Edward Robinson Chair of Biblical Theology at his seminary and used the occasion to deliver a lecture clearly supportive of modern critical claims about the authorship of the Bible and clearly dismissive of conservative suggestions that Scripture was inerrant. This lecture precipitated his being tried for heresy by the New York presbytery of the Presbyterian Church of the United States. The general assembly of that denomination eventually suspended Briggs from the Presbyterian ministry in May 1893. Thereafter Briggs became an Episcopalian and was ordained a priest in 1899.

The Fundamentalist Controversy

Many Protestant leaders of the late 19th century embraced Darwinism and the findings about the Bible suggested by historical-critical scholarship. Consequently, they modified their theology in ways that made it more compatible with these new developments. For more conservative believers, however, the incompatibility between traditional Christian teaching and the conclusions of Darwinism and higher criticism was sufficient reason in and of itself to reject these modern developments. Whether acceptance of these conclusions was necessarily inconsistent with historic

Christian orthodoxy, believers sympathetic to modernity seemed to their conservative counterparts to have abandoned crucial tenets of the faith. The fundamentalist controversy produced a distinct brand of Protestant evangelicals often referred to as fundamentalists. Evangelicals, the heirs of 19th-century revivalism, shared a common belief in salvation through Jesus Christ and in a form of Christian spirituality that emphasized the believer's personal relationship to God through Christ. Fundamentalists differed from evangelicals in the militancy of their opposition to tenets of theological liberalism, secularism, and other religious traditions, including Catholicism, which they perceived as having abandoned historic Christian orthodoxy.

In the early years of the 20th century, conservatives attempted to articulate these fundamental aspects of orthodoxy: a belief in the inerrancy of the Bible, the deity of Jesus, his virgin birth, his substitutionary atonement, and his bodily resurrection from the dead. Biblical inerrancy was understood to mean that God had inspired the work of the Bible authors without necessarily dictating the books they authored and that he had preserved these authors from inserting any errors into their original manuscripts. In the early decades of the 20th century, theological conservatives still held significant power within denominations such as the Presbyterian Church, U.S.A. The general assembly of this denomination announced its adherence to five core theological principles in 1910 and reaffirmed its commitment to these principles in 1916 and 1923: biblical inerrancy, the virgin birth, substitutionary atonement, the bodily resurrection of Christ, and the historicity of miracles. This summary of key principles was intended to stand against the drift in mainline churches toward theological liberalism, often characterized by a willingness to admit the presence of errors in the Bible and to doubt that miracles recorded in the Bible, including a literal, bodily resurrection of Jesus from the dead, had actually occurred. But conservative Presbyterians were not alone in challenging the creeping influence of modernism on theology. Two wealthy California businessmen, Milton and Lyman Stewart, financed the publication and distribution of a series of articles by prominent conservative scholars and ministers titled *The Fundamentals* and published in 12 volumes between 1910 and 1915. Edited initially by Amzi Dixon, a well-known evangelical minister, 3 million copies of *The Fundamentals* were distributed free of charge to "every pastor, evangelist, missionary, theological professor, theological student, Sunday school superintendent, Y.M.C.A. and Y.W.C.A. secretary in the English speaking world."[4] Lyman Stewart explained the issues at stake in a letter to his brother:

> Of course there are a great many "wolves in sheep's clothing" among such a multitude, but there are also among them the "salt of the earth." These are the men from whom the present generation of the Anglo-Saxon people, as well as the large portion of the heathen world, are, in a large measure, to receive their spiritual instruction, and hence the great importance of getting them, as far as possible into line for true service. The spiritual warfare of the present generation requires it; the safety of foreign missionary work demands it. It is a work that will count for both time and eternity. . . . The best and most loyal Bible teachers in the world are supposed to be enlisted in the preparation of this "Testimony," and . . . these articles will doubtless be the masterpiece of the writers.[5]

The theological liberalism against which fundamentalists railed was not without its own resources. Harry Emerson Fosdick, a minister at First Presbyterian

Church of New York City and member of the faculty of Union Theological Seminary, preached an important sermon in 1922 to his congregation titled "Shall the Fundamentalists Win?"[6] In the sermon he admitted that modernity had inspired some Christians to question theological principles dear to conservatives but denied that this questioning disqualified these believers from being considered Christians. The sin of fundamentalism, Fosdick insisted, was the sin of intolerance, and he concluded his sermon with the hope that this sin would not take root in his own congregation.

> Never in this church have I caught one accent of intolerance. God keep us always so and ever increasing areas of the Christian fellowship; intellectually hospitable, open-minded, liberty-loving, fair, tolerant, not with the tolerance of indifference, as though we did not care about the faith, but because always our major emphasis is upon the weightier matters of the law.[7]

The ideas expressed in the sermon gained a wide currency when Fosdick's friend, John D. Rockefeller, Jr., paid to have copies of the sermon distributed to every ordained minister in America.

The career of conservative Presbyterian theologian J. Gresham Machen paralleled the larger currents of the time. Machen was ordained a minister in the Presbyterian Church, U.S.A., and joined the regular faculty of that denomination's flagship educational institution, Princeton Theological Seminary, in 1914. In the years that followed he battled against the drift within his denomination toward liberalism, publishing an influential critique of theological modernism titled *Christianity and Liberalism* in 1923, which argued that liberal Christianity was no longer even recognizably Christian but rather "an un-Christian and sub-Christian form of the religious life."[8] Although his denomination had reiterated support for core tenets of conservative orthodoxy as late as that year, the tide quickly changed, and Machen felt increasingly at odds with his denomination. He left Princeton in 1929 to help establish a new home for conservative Presbyterian theology, Westminister Theological Seminary. When reports surfaced of theological liberalism on the field of Presbyterian foreign missions, Machen responded by helping to found the Independent Board for Presbyterian Foreign Missions in 1933, intended to secure greater orthodoxy among the missionaries it supported. This act precipitated confrontation with the general assembly of the Presbyterian Church, U.S.A., which ordered Machen the next year to abandon his connection with the independent board. When Machen declined to do so, the general assembly expelled him from the ordained ministry in 1935, prompting Machen and others to organize the Presbyterian Church in America, later renamed the Orthodox Presbyterian Church, the next year.

Many theological conservatives of this period adhered to a system of belief referred to as dispensationalist premillennialism, derived from the teaching of John Nelson Darby, a leader among the Plymouth Brethren in England during the first half of the 19th century. Dwight L. Moody helped popularize this view of end times through an annual Northfield Prophecy Conference held beginning in 1880.[9] Dispensationalists believed that history—according to the Bible—was divided into different periods, or dispensations. God dealt with humanity differently in these various periods. Dispensationalists believed that the period in which they were living was the church age but that this age was drawing to a close and would shortly be followed by the physical return from heaven of Jesus Christ. This return would itself be followed by the thousand-year reign of Christ on the Earth (premillennialism being the theological belief that Christ will return *prior to* a literal thousand-year reign on earth). Prior to the growing influence of premillennialist views, most American Protestants of the early 19th century had been postmillennialists. They believed that Christ would physically return to the Earth *after* a period when his kingdom was established on Earth. This view tended to march hand in hand with a spirit of optimism about the progress of the church and the gospel in the world, since this progress was viewed as a sign that Christ's earthly kingdom was being established. Premillennialists tended to take a more negative view concerning the influence of righteousness in the world. In their minds the world was becoming a steadily darker place, and only the return of Christ himself would cure this creeping darkness. Dispensationalist premillennialism tended to align itself with fundamentalism, because it viewed contemporary history as poised on the brink of a climactic conclusion in which Christ would return to the Earth and do battle with the Anti-Christ before establishing his millennial kingdom. Fundamentalists tended to see the issues of their day in terms of a great warfare between the worldly forces of light and darkness. The congeniality of premillennialism to fundamentalism also owed something to fundamentalists' suspicion of the optimistic spiritual temper of theological liberals generally and the Social Gospel movement in particular, a temper more aligned with postmillennialism.[10]

Dispensationalism benefited enormously from the publication of the Scofield Reference Bible by Oxford University Press in 1909. This study Bible, with elaborate notes by C. I. Scofield, defended the orthodoxies of fundamentalism generally as well as the tenets of dispensationalist premillennialism in particular. C. I. Scofield was associated with Dwight L. Moody, the 19th century's most famous revivalist, and served as a Congregationalist minister until his theological conservativism prompted him to migrate to Presbyterianism around the time of the publication of the Scofield Reference Bible. Premillennialism, already well rooted in America prior to the publication of this Bible, would flourish even more after the brutalities of World War I, waged among the nations of the "civilized" world, humbled 19th-century optimism about the gradual spread of righteousness in the world.

The Rise of Pentecostalism

The Holiness movement that took firm root in America during the second half of the 19th century emphasized the possibility of a "second blessing." Derived from aspects of the theology of John Wesley, the theology of the second blessing posited that the Christian life should involve two separate and formative experiences. The first of these was conversion, in which a sinner received forgiveness from past sins. The second experience involved an episode of sanctification, in which a Christian gained freedom from the continued presence of a sinful nature. This second experience introduced the believer to the possibility of "entire sanctification," as a result of which true Christian perfection was attainable in the present. During the middle years of the 19th century, revivalist Charles Grandison Finney, then on the faculty of Oberlin College, and the Oberlin perfectionists, as they are called, taught that a spiritual experience subsequent to conversion could equip a believer to be fully consecrated to Christ.[11] For a time Holiness believers tended to find their home within Methodism. In the second half of the 19th century, however, Holiness believers increasingly abandoned or were driven out of mainstream Method-

The Holiness movement took root in the second half of the 19th century and frequently sponsored missions in urban areas in the next century. *(Library of Congress, Prints and Photographs Division LC-USF33-006592-M2)*

ist congregations and gradually joined denominations that shared a belief in the possibility of Christian perfection. In the final years of the 19th century, one of the more prominent Holiness denominations, the Church of the Nazarene, took form when Phineas Bresee withdrew from the Methodist ministry and helped establish the First Church of the Nazarene in Los Angeles in 1895. Subsequently, in 1914, churches associated with Bresee joined together in a denominational structure to form the Pentecostal Church of the Nazarene (subsequently renamed Church of the Nazarene). Finally, Holiness theology in America was influenced during the last decades of the 19th century by the Keswick movement in England, beginning with a series of annual conferences in 1875, which focused attention on the "higher" Christian life. Hannah Whitall Smith, an American Holiness author and preacher associated with the Higher Life movement, penned one of its most enduring texts, *The Christian's Secret of a Happy Life* (1875).

Among some Holiness groups the experience of the second blessing or entire sanctification became associated with the idea of being "baptized in the Spirit." The baptism of the Spirit among these groups included access to supernatural spiritual gifts such as healing, prophecy, and speaking in tongues (referred to in the New Testament as glossolalia). Toward the beginning of the 20th century, those groups emphasizing the baptism of the Spirit and the possession of spiritual gifts such as glossolalia gave birth to Pentecostalism. Pentecostals take their name from events described in the New Testament book of Acts on the day of Pentecost shortly after the resurrection and ascension of Jesus. According to this account, the disciples of Jesus were assembled together in an upper room and were suddenly "filled with the Spirit" and began speaking in other languages.[12] By finding in this scriptural episode a model for contemporary Christian experience, Pentecostals demonstrated a primitivist and restorationist spirit not wholly dissimilar from that that inspired the birth of the restorationist-minded Disciples of Christ in the first half of the 19th century.[13]

A formative episode in the rise of Pentecostalism in America was the Azusa Street Revival of 1906, led by African-American preacher William Joseph Seymour, sometimes referred to as "the father of modern Pentecostalism." Seymour had been influenced by Charles Fox Parham, a faith healer who preached for a time in Houston, Texas, in 1905 and taught that speaking in tongues was the evidence of a Christian having been baptized in the Spirit. Parham had presided over Bethel Gospel School in Topeka, Kansas, several years earlier, where he and his students had studied the book of Acts in the New Testament and then held a service to pray for the baptism of the Spirit toward the start of the new year in 1901.[14] First Agnes Ozman and then Parham and others meeting with him experienced the baptism of the Spirit and began to speak in tongues. Parham introduced one of Pentecostalism's defining theological axioms: that speaking in tongues always accompanies the baptism of the Spirit.[15] Seymour had briefly attended classes taught by Parham at a Bible school in Houston, though he had to listen to Parham's lessons through a half-opened door so as not to offend southern sensibilities about racial segregation.[16] Beginning in 1906, after having received the gift of tongues himself, Seymour was invited to become the minister of a small African-American church in Los Angeles. There he presided over a Pentecostal revival in which thousands of attendees of his services would eventually experience Spirit baptism and speak in tongues. For three years, seven days a week and more than 12 hours each day,

As this photograph shows, some Pentecostal churches believe in handling poisonous snakes as evidence of faith. *(National Archives NWDNS-245-MS-2621L)*

Pentecostalism in America had its roots in the Holiness movement. *(National Archives NWDNS-83-G-41337)*

the revival meetings continued. Beginning first in a small house, meetings quickly moved to a storage building at 312 Azusa Street, where the attention they soon attracted was not altogether complimentary. A reporter for the *Los Angeles Times* claimed that the "night is made hideous . . . by the howlings of the worshippers" and offered a terse summation: "The devotees of the weird doctrine practice the most fanatical rites, preach the wildest theories and work themselves into a state of mad excitement."[17] Another headline from the period announced that "Whites and Blacks Mix in a Religious Frenzy."[18] African Americans made up a large portion of those who participated in the revival, but the experience crossed racial lines to include Caucasians, Latinos, Orientals, and other racial and ethnic groups as well. The multiracial aspect of the Azusa Street Revival characterized many of the

Pentecostal congregations to which it gave birth. Not infrequently, visitors already attached to Holiness churches or denominations returned home to guide these spiritual bodies into the Pentecostal fold.

Two important denominational tributaries flowed from the revival sparked in Los Angeles. The first of these claims as its spiritual father Charles H. Mason, a black preacher who was tending a congregation of the Church of God in Christ in Memphis, Tennessee, at the time of the Azusa Street Revival. Mason had co-founded this Holiness denomination in 1897 with Charles Price Jones in Jackson, Mississippi. Mason traveled to the Azusa Street Revival himself, received the gift of tongues, and then returned to Memphis, where he directed the Church of God in Christ down the path of Pentecostalism beginning in 1907. The second main denominational outgrowth of the Azusa Street Revival took shape in 1914, when delegates from a number of Pentecostal congregations assembled in Hot Springs, Arkansas. There they laid the foundation for what would become the largest Pentecostal denomination, the Assemblies of God, a mainly white and Hispanic variant of Pentecostalism, whose late 20th century exemplars included such controversial figures as Jim Bakker and Jimmy Swaggart.

Revivalism and the Successors of Finney and Moody

Beginning with the Great Awakening of the early 18th century and followed by recurring revival movements throughout the 19th century, revivalism has been a relatively constant aspect of American religious experience. During the Great Awakening the most prominent revival preachers—men such as George Whitefield and Jonathan Edwards—were Calvinists who emphasized the inability of sinful humanity to receive spiritual awakening apart from the sovereign grace of God. With the advent of the Second Great Awakening, beginning around the turn of the 18th century, revivalism assumed a more Arminian aspect, emphasizing that men and women, even though sinful, had the capacity to turn toward God if they only would. Revival under this theological view was not something mysterious that had to be waited upon but rather an experience that could be orchestrated and planned. During the 19th century evangelists, Dwight L. Moody especially, pioneered the art of orchestrating revivals by elaborate advance planning.

The 20th century also witnessed the continuation of the tradition of mass urban revivals. In the first two decades of the century, the most prominent revivalist was Billy Sunday, an ex-baseball player whose dynamic preaching gathered thousands of listeners into tents where they were encouraged to "hit the sawdust trail." Beginning in 1883 Sunday played successively for teams including the Chicago White Stockings and the Philadelphia Phillies. In 1885, however, he was converted at a mission in Chicago and in 1891 retired from baseball to become assistant secretary of the Chicago YMCA. Later, after working for a time with revivalist J. Wilbur Chapman, Sunday began a career of his own as a revival preacher in 1896. For the next 20 years he won fame as "the Baseball evangelist," bringing the gospel message to towns and cities in the Midwest and preaching as well in New York City. After World War I he tried to win the Republican presidential nomination in 1920 but was not successful. Neither, according to the song "Chicago," made famous by Frank Sinatra, was he successful in shutting Chicago down. But he became the archetype for later evangelists such as Billy Graham.

Billy Sunday gave up his career as a professional baseball player to become a revival preacher. *(Library of Congress, Prints and Photographs Division LC-USZ62-108493)*

Like Protestantism generally, Pentecostalism proved fertile ground for the germination of new churches and denominations, especially centered around particular charismatic personalities such as Maria Beulah Woodworth-Etter and Aimee Semple McPherson. Toward the beginning of the 1880s, Woodworth-Etter began an itinerant preaching ministry that made her one of the most well-known evangelists of the late 19th and early 20th centuries. Her evangelistic services included elements of ecstatic worship that were foretastes of Pentecostalism. She was known, for example, to stand still for long periods during these services with her hands raised, experiencing what she characterized as "the power" and leading some critics to dub her "voodoo priestess." It

Aimee Semple McPherson founded the Church of the Foursquare Gospel, a Pentecostal denomination. *(Library of Congress, Prints and Photographs Division LC-USZ62-92329)*

was no surprise, then, when she became a Pentecostal in the latter part of her evangelistic career.

Aimee Semple McPherson was a faith healer who had briefly served as a missionary to China before her husband died suddenly in 1910. McPherson eventually became an itinerant preacher in 1915 and by 1919 had returned to the city that had given birth to the Azusa Street Revival and begun to preach at Victoria Hall in downtown Los Angeles. Within two years she was able to begin construction of the 5,300-seat Angelus Temple, near Echo Park in Los Angeles, which opened in 1923. Her dynamic preaching and reputation as a faith healer attracted large crowds, and by 1927 McPherson had organized the Church of the Foursquare Gospel, which became yet another tributary of Pentecostalism in America. Scandal and intrigue clouded the subsequent years of her life, but the Church of the Foursquare Gospel survives into the 21st century.

Chronicle of Events

1900

- The Friends General Conference is formed.
- The International Congress of Free Christians and Other Religious Liberals (later renamed the International Association for Religious Freedom) is organized.
- The National Women's Convention is established as an auxiliary to the National Baptist Convention, an association of African-American Baptist churches.
- A Young Men's Buddhist Association is established in Hawaii.

1901

- The American Federation of Catholic Societies is organized.

1902

- Jewish scholar Solomon Schechter immigrates to New York from England and assumes the presidency of the Jewish Theological Seminary.
- The Missionary Education Movement is established.
- Harvard psychologist William James presents the Gifford Lecture Series at the University of Edinburgh. The lectures are subsequently published as *The Varieties of Religious Experience*.
- The Union of Orthodox Rabbis (Agudath ha-Rabbanim) is founded as a means of strengthening the authority of Orthodox Rabbis trained in Europe and to resist Americanization.
- *April 18:* Menachem Mendel Schneerson, rebbe of the Lubavitcher Hasidim, is born in Nikolayev, Ukraine.

1904

- American Indian religious leader Black Elk converts to Catholicism and subsequently changes his name to Nicholas Black Elk after Saint Nicholas.
- The U.S. government bans the American Indian practice of the Sun Dance.
- The North American Shinto Church is established.
- *May:* Martha Gallison Moore Avery converts to Catholicism and begins a career as a Catholic lay preacher.

1905

- William J. Seymour hears the preaching of Charles Parham in Houston, Texas. Parham teaches that speaking in tongues is a necessary sign of believers who receive the baptism of the Holy Spirit.

1906

- Black evangelist William J. Seymour begins leading a series of revival meetings that result in the Azusa Street Revival in Los Angeles, California, a precursor to the Pentecostal and charismatic movements.
- Jewish leaders establish the American Jewish Committee "to prevent infringement of the civil and religious rights of Jews, and to alleviate the consequences of persecution."
- The Watch Tower Bible and Tract Society, led by Charles Taze Russell, begins publication of a series of Bible studies written by Russell and eventually titled *Studies in Scripture*.
- Joseph Franklin Rutherford, who will become the leader of the Watch Tower Bible and Tract Society after Charles Taze Russell's death in 1916, joins the society.
- The first Hindu temple in America is built by the San Francisco Vedanta Society.
- The Central Conference of American Rabbis publishes a pamphlet titled *The Bible Should Not Be Read in Public Schools*.
- Oscar Straus is appointed secretary of labor and commerce, becoming the first Jewish American to hold a cabinet position.
- Catholic priest John Ryan publishes his dissertation, titled *A Living Wage: Its Ethical and Economic Aspects*.

1907

- Walter Rauschenbusch publishes *Christianity and the Social Crisis*, an important book in the Social Gospel movement.
- Russian Orthodox bishop Tikhon Bellavin convenes the first council of Orthodox Churches in America.
- The National Primitive Baptist Convention is organized from black Primitive Baptist churches.
- The American Mohammedan Society is organized in New York City.
- Daisetz Teitaro Suzuki publishes an introduction to Eastern religious thought titled *Outlines of Mahayana Buddhism*.
- *January 11:* Abraham Joshua Heschel, a prominent Jewish theologian, is born in Warsaw, Poland.

1908

- Adam Clayton Powell, Sr., becomes pastor of the Abyssinian Baptist Church in New York City, where he preaches for almost 30 years and becomes one of the most prominent ministers of his generation.

- John Haynes Holmes, a founding member of the NAACP and the ACLU, helps to establish the Unitarian Fellowship for Social Justice.
- *The Melting Pot,* a play by Jewish writer Israel Zangwill, opens.
- The Federal Council of Churches in Christ, an ecumenical organization, is formed.
- *June 29:* Pius X, in the document *Sapienti Consilio,* removes the Catholic Church in the United States from the jurisdiction of the Congregatio de Propaganda Fide, thus ending the missionary status of American Catholicism.

1909

- Louis Ginzberg publishes the first of seven volumes of *Legends of the Jews,* a multivolume work he will not complete until 1938.
- Cyrus Ingerson Scofield publishes the Scofield Reference Bible, which popularizes dispensational premillennialist theology.
- Rabbi Judah Leon Magnes leads in the formation of the New York Kehillah (community), an attempt to unite the Jewish community in New York around various social and educational projects. He directs the organization until its dissolution in 1922.

1910

- Milton and Lyman Stewart, wealthy California businessmen, persuade Amzi Clarence Dixon to serve as initial editor of *The Fundamentals,* a collection of theologically conservative essays published in 12 volumes between 1910 and 1915, which give rise to the description of certain conservative evangelical beliefs as "fundamentalism."
- Future Pentecostal preacher Aimee Semple McPherson and her husband, Robert Semple, travel to China as missionaries, but Robert dies of malaria soon afterward. McPherson returns to the United States with her daughter, born in Hong Kong a month after her husband's death.
- The World Missionary Conference held in Edinburgh marks the beginning of the modern international ecumenical movement.

1911

- American Catholic bishops establish the Maryknoll Catholic Foreign Mission Society of America.

- Conservative Baptists dismayed at the theological liberalism of the University of Chicago Divinity School found the Northern Baptist Theological Seminary.
- *March 13:* L. Ron Hubbard, science fiction author and founder of Scientology, is born.

1912

- A study group of which Henrietta Szold is a member becomes the nucleus of a Zionist women's organization initially called Daughters of Zion but later renamed Hadassah, and Szold serves as the organization's first president.
- Walter Rauschenbusch publishes *Christianizing the Social Order,* an important articulation of the Social Gospel.
- *December 24:* Lottie (Charlotte Diggs) Moon, Baptist missionary to China, dies in a Japanese harbor while en route to the United States as a result of giving her own food away to destitute Chinese.

1913

- Timothy Drew ("Noble Drew Ali") founds the Moorish Holy Temple of Science in Newark, New Jersey.
- The Anti-Defamation League of the B'nai B'rith is founded to combat anti-Semitism.
- The United Synagogue of America, an organization of Conservative Jewish congregations, is established in association with the Jewish Theological Seminary, a move reflecting growing tensions between Conservative and Orthodox congregations.

1914

- At a conference with delegates from various Pentecostal churches in Hot Springs, Arkansas, the Assemblies of God denomination is born.
- Phineas Franklin Bresee is elected general superintendent of the newly united Pentecostal Church of the Nazarene (renamed Church of the Nazarene four years later).
- Baptist minister Russell Herman Conwell publishes *Acres of Diamonds,* a best-selling inspirational book that advocates a gospel of success.
- The Buddhist Mission of North America is established.
- Mizrachi, a Zionist organization established in 1902, holds its first national convention, with the motto "The Land of Israel for the people of Israel according to the Torah of Israel."

This photograph of the celestial room in the Mormon Temple in Salt Lake City, Utah, was taken in 1912. *(Library of Congress, Prints and Photographs Division LC-USZ62-071558)*

- J. Gresham Machen, an influential opponent of theological liberalism, joins the faculty of Princeton Theological Seminary.
- *January 31:* Thomas Merton, a Trappist monk and religious writer, is born in Prades, France.
- *February 10:* The Church Peace Union is established.

1915
- Aimee Semple McPherson begins an itinerant preaching career.
- The National Baptist Convention of America is formed after a schism occurs in the National Baptist Convention, and it becomes the largest black denomination in the United States.

- *August 16:* After the conviction of Leo Frank, a Jewish plant superintendent for the National Pencil Company in Atlanta, for the murder of 14-year-old Mary Phagan and the commutation of his death sentence by Georgia governor John Slaton to life in prison, a mob storms the prison in Milledgeville, abducts Frank, and lynches him.
- *November 21:* The first Sikh *gurdwara,* or temple, in America is dedicated in Stockton, California.

1916
- The American Jewish Congress is created.
- Louis Brandeis becomes the first Jewish justice appointed to serve on the U.S. Supreme Court.

This Church is behind The UNITED WAR WORK CAMPAIGN For the Boys Over There

A church conveys its support for war efforts in this World War I poster. *(National Archives NWDNS-4-P-258)*

- After the death of Charles Taze Russell this year, Joseph Franklin Rutherford assumes leadership of the Watch Tower Bible and Tract Society (later known as Jehovah's Witnesses).

1917

- The United States enters World War I.
- Martha Gallison Moore Avery and David Goldstein establish the Catholic Truth Guild, a street preaching project to make the Catholic Church "better known and loved."
- The National Catholic War Council is established to recruit and train military chaplains. After World War I is over, the council is renamed the National Catholic Welfare Conference.
- The American Friends Service Committee is formed.
- The National Jewish Welfare Board is founded.
- Thomas Wyatt Turner, a biology professor at Howard University, leads in establishing the Federated Colored Catholics.
- *December 12:* Father Edward Joseph Flanagan establishes his boys' home in Omaha, Nebraska.

1918

- The Native American Church, whose members practice sacramental use of peyote, is founded in Oklahoma.
- Joseph Franklin Rutherford and other leaders of the Watch Tower Bible and Tract Society are arrested and convicted of violating the Espionage Act of 1917 for alleged obstruction of the draft. After serving nine months in jail, they are released on bail. Their sentences are later overturned on appeal, and the government does not retry them.
- American archbishops create the National Catholic War Council.
- The American Jewish Congress is founded.
- President Woodrow Wilson expresses approval of the Balfour Declaration announced by Great Britain in 1917, which supports the creation of a Jewish homeland in Palestine.
- *November 7:* Revivalist Billy Graham is born on a farm near Charlotte, North Carolina.

1919

- The first Islamic mosque in the United States is built in Highland Park, Michigan.
- The National Catholic Welfare Council (later Conference) is established as a successor to the National Catholic War Council.
- Baptist and premillennialist William B. Riley founds the World's Christian Fundamentals Association to combat theological modernism.
- Reverend Major Jealous Divine (Father Divine) purchases a house in the village of Sayville in Suffolk County, Long Island, where he establishes a religious community eventually known as the Peace Mission Movement.
- *January 18:* The Versailles Peace Treaty ends World War I.
- *January 19:* With the support of many religious groups, the Eighteenth Amendment to the U.S. Constitution, which prohibits use or sale of alcoholic beverages, is ratified. The amendment will subsequently be repealed in 1933.

1920

- Revivalist Billy Sunday is a candidate for the Republican nomination for president of the United States.
- A mosque is built in Ross, North Dakota, one of the first of its kind in the United States.
- Curtis Lee Laws, a Baptist who is editor of the *Watchman-Examiner,* coins the term *fundamentalists* to refer to conservative Protestants who aggressively defend the fundamentals of Christian orthodoxy against liberal attacks.

The Jewish Welfare Board announced its support for the United War Work Campaign during World War I. *(National Archives NWDNS-4-P-47)*

- *January 6:* Sun Myung Moon, the founder of the Unification Church, is born in Kwangju Sangsa Ri, North Korea.

- *August 18:* The Nineteenth Amendment to the U.S. Constitution, guaranteeing women the right to vote, is ratified.

Eyewitness Testimony

On 25th May [1880], H. P. B. [Helena Petrovna Blavatsky] and I "took *pānsil*" from the venerable Bulatgama, at the temple of the Ramanya Nikāya, whose name at the moment escapes me, and were formally acknowledged as Buddhists. A great arch of greenery, bearing the words: "Welcome to the members of the Theosophical Society," had been erected within the compound of the Vihāra. We had previously declared ourselves Buddhists long before, in America, both privately and publicly, so that this was but a formal confirmation of our previous confessions. H. P. B. knelt before the huge statue of the Buddha, and I kept her company. We had a good deal of trouble in catching the Pāli words that we were to repeat after the old monk, and I don't know how we should have got on if a friend had not taken his place just behind us and whispered them *seriatim*. A great crowd was present and made the responses just after us, a dead silence being preserved while we were struggling through the unfamiliar sentences. When we had finished the last of the *Sīlas*, and offered flowers in the customary way, there came a mighty shout to make one's nerves tingle, and the people could not settle themselves down to silence for some minutes, to hear the brief discourse which, at the Chief Priest's request, I delivered. I believe that attempts have been made by some of my leading colleagues of Europe and America to suppress this incident as much as possible, and cover up the fact that H. P. B. was as completely accepted a Buddhist as any Sinhalese in the Island. This mystification is both dishonest and useless, for, not only did several thousand persons, including many *bhikkus*, see and hear her taking the *pānsil*, but she herself boldly proclaimed it in all quarters. But to be a regular Buddhist is one thing, and to be a debased modern Buddhist sectarian quite another. Speaking for her as well as for myself, I can say that if Buddhism contained a single dogma that we were compelled to accept, we would not have taken the *pānsil* nor remained Buddhists ten minutes. Our Buddhism was that of the Master-Adept Gautama Buddha, which was identically the Wisdom Religion of the Aryan Upanishads, and the soul of all the ancient world-faiths. Our Buddhism was, in a word, a philosophy, not a creed.

Theosophist founder Henry Steel Olcott, 1900, Old Diary Leaves, *in Tweed and Prothero,* Asian Religions in America, *p. 143.*

The railroad train, with its splendid long cars, was a great novelty, and diverted me for a little while; but it was not

An altar in a joss house in Chinatown, New York, is pictured in this 1911 photograph. *(Library of Congress, Prints and Photographs Division LC-USZ62-072478)*

long ere I again succumbed to a feeling of despondency, which not even the fertile and charming Mohawk Valley, with its many beautiful towns, could dissipate. I had a small Pentateuch with two *Targumim* and *Rashi* in my valise. I took it out, hoping thereby to regain my equilibrium. On the same seat with me sat an inquisitive Yankee, who regarded me curiously, and finally asked what sort of a book that was. I told him. . . . When a little later he learned that I had arrived in the country but recently, he said: "Ah, now I know who you are; you are a Jewish bishop." I explained to him that the Jews had no hierarchy, but he drew a New Haven newspaper out of his pocket, and showed me black on white that a Jewish bishop, Wess or Wiss, who had lately arrived from Jerusalem had dedicated the synagogue in New Haven. I remonstrated in vain. He continued to call me bishop, bought lemonade, ice-cream, and everything else that could be procured at the railroad stations, and treated me in quite a princely manner. It is more than likely that he understood but half of what I said, for my English was decidedly Germanic. We arrived at Syracuse at a late hour. My friendly fellow-passenger accompanied me to a hotel, spoke to the proprietor in my behalf, and then took his leave. Upon looking over the newspaper on the following morning, I found to my astonishment the following notice: "N. Traveled yesterday from Albany to this city in company with the Jewish Bishop Wess or Wiss (the pronunciation of the name is uncertain), who has lately arrived from Jerusalem." . . . I had thus an experience similar to that of Lord Byron. I awoke one morning, and found myself famous. I had no time to be vexed at the untruths, for I had scarcely read the notice when a Yankee approached me, and asked whether I was the Jewish bishop. "I am no bishop." "But a rabbi," said he. Upon my affirming this, he continued: "We here in America have never seen a rabbi, although we have been told that there are several in New York, and the rabbi is certainly also a bishop." Thus I became also a bishop for this individual.

Reform rabbi Isaac M. Wise, 1901, recalling a trip in 1846, the year he arrived in the United States from Bohemia, in Reminiscences, *pp. 34–35.*

The Christian religion is the exponent of the highest civilization, the highest moral and social condition of the race to-day. Where it has been accepted, and its faith and doctrines incorporated into the life and character of any people, it has in a very potential manner affected the moral, intellectual and social condition of such people.

. . . . .

No people or race is excluded from its all-embracing provisions, nor from its divinely uplifting power when it is embraced. It should produce in the race in America, or in Africa, worthy examples of its power to save and elevate in proportion to individual or race conformity to its spirit and precepts. . . The large number of the race in America who are Baptists is a living evidence of the readiness with which the race has accepted the Gospel and conformed to its doctrines and ordinances as did the eunuch of the race in the apostolic period of planting and training of Christian churches. A larger percentage of the race in America are members of evangelical Churches than of any other race in the land; and a large number of them are members of Baptist churches than of all other evangelical bodies.

. . . . .

These should be a power as a missionary force for the evangelization of the world. They should, by their numerical strength, give to the race a distinctive character in active and effective missionary work among Christian evangelizing workers. . . . This large number of Christian workers of the race owe it to Christ, who has called them into His service, to the world in which they live, the field in which Christ instructs them work, and to Africa in particular, "The rock from which they have been hewn," the original home of the race, whose benighted millions still grope in darkest heathenism, outraged and neglected, to individually measure up to the fullest possibility of resources and effort in the work of human redemption. A great work remains to be done for the race in this and other lands, and every Baptist should therefore be intensely a missionary Baptist.

R. D. Baptist, 1903, "How the Material Growth of Baptists Should and Will Affect the Race in America and Africa," in L. G. Jordan, Up the Ladder in Foreign Missions, *pp. 160–162.*

It was out in the country, far from home, far from my foster home, on a dark Sunday night. The road wandered from our rambling log-house up the stony bed of a creek, past wheat and corn, until we could hear dimly across the fields a rhythmic cadence of song,—soft, thrilling, powerful, that swelled and died sorrowfully in our ears. I was a country school-teacher then, fresh from the East, and had never seen a Southern Negro revival. To be sure, we in Berkshire were not perhaps as stiff and formal as they in Suffolk of olden time; yet we were very quiet and subdued, and I know not what would have happened those clear Sabbath mornings had some one punctuated the sermon with a wild scream, or interrupted the long prayer with a loud Amen! And so most striking to me, as I approached the village and the little plain church perched aloft, was the air of intense excitement that possessed that mass of black folk. A sort of suppressed terror hung in the air and seemed to seize us,—a pythian madness, a demoniac possession, that lent terrible reality to song and word. The black and massive form of the preacher swayed and quivered as the words crowded to his lips and flew at us in singular eloquence. The people moaned and fluttered, and then the gaunt-cheeked brown woman beside me suddenly leaped straight into the air and shrieked like a lost soul, while round about came wail and groan and outcry, and a scene of human passion such as I had never conceived before.

Those who have not thus witnessed the frenzy of a Negro revival in the untouched backwoods of the South can but dimly realize the religious feeling of the slave; as described, such scenes appear grotesque and funny, but as seen they are awful. Three things characterized this religion of the slave,—the Preacher, the Music, and the

Frenzy. The Preacher is the most unique personality developed by the Negro on American soil. A leader, a politician, an orator, a "boss," an intriguer, an idealist,—all these he is, and ever, too, the centre of a group of men, now twenty, now a thousand in number. The combination of a certain adroitness with deep-seated earnestness, of tact with consummate ability, gave him his preeminence, and helps him maintain it. The type, of course, varies according to time and place, from the West Indies in the sixteenth century to New England in the nineteenth, and from the Mississippi bottoms to cities like New Orleans or New York.

The Music of Negro religion is that plaintive rhythmic melody, with its touching minor cadences, which, despite caricature and defilement, still remains the most original and beautiful expression of human life and longing yet born on American soil. Sprung from the African forests, where its counterpart can still be heard, it was adapted, changed, and intensified by the tragic soul-life of the slave, until, under the stress of law and whip, it became the one true expression of a people's sorrow, despair, and hope.

Finally the Frenzy of "Shouting," when the Spirit of the Lord passed by, and, seizing the devotee, made him mad with supernatural joy, was the last essential of Negro religion and the one more devoutly believed in than all the rest. It varied in expression from the silent rapt countenance or the low murmur and moan to the mad abandon of physical fervor,—the stamping, shrieking, and shouting, the rushing to and fro and wild waving of arms, the weeping and laughing, the vision and the trance. All this is nothing new in the world, but old as religion, as Delphi and Endor. And so firm a hold did it have on the Negro, that many generations firmly believed that without this visible manifestation of the God there could be no true communion with the Invisible.

African-American intellectual W. E. B. DuBois, 1903, The Souls of Black Folk, *in* W. E. B. DuBois: Writings, *pp. 493–495.*

Israel in America has particularly distinguished itself in [the] holy work of altar-building. The Talmud speaks of certain commandments which Israel received in joy, and at all times joyfully fulfilled. Considering the comparatively short period since this country of ours was opened to civilization, the number of places of worship erected under these skies by both Jew and Christian proves altar building to be an especial and favorite duty of the American people, received in joy from the very beginning, and to this day joyfully continued.

. . . . .

The first settlers in this country were mostly men who had left their native land for conscience' sake, despairing of the Old World as given over to the powers of darkness, despotism and unbelief. And I can quite realize how they must have gloried in the idea of being chosen instruments of Providence who were to restore the spiritual equilibrium of the world by the conquest of new spheres of religious influence and their dedication to the worship of Almighty God.

As a Jew coming from the East of Europe, where my people are trodden down, where seats of Jewish learning and Jewish piety are daily destroyed, I am greatly animated by the same feelings and am comforted to see the New World compensating us for our many losses in the Old.

Solomon Schechter, a Romanian-born rabbi who served as president of the Jewish Theological Seminary of America, 1904, "Altar Building in America," in Seminary Addresses and Other Papers, *pp. 82–83.*

God has given me a mean fight, a dirty and dangerous fight; for it is a war on the hidden things of darkness. . . . If the liquor men could bring back saloons into Kansas then a great blow would be struck against prohibition in all the states. This would discourage the people all over. Their great word was, "you can't," "prohibition will not prohibit." I do not belong to the "can't" family. When I was born my father wrote my name Carry A. Moore, then later it was Nation, which is more still. C. A. N. are the initials of my name, the C. (see) A. Nation! And all together Carry A. Nation! This is no accident but Providence. This does not mean that I will carry a nation, but that the roused heart and conscience will, as I am the roused heart and conscience of the people. There are just two crowds, God's crowd and the Devil's crowd. One gains the battle by can, and the other loses it by can't.

Temperance leader Carry A. Nation, 1904, The Use and Need of the Life of Carry A. Nation, *quoted in* American Spiritualities: A Reader, *pp. 320–321.*

In everything that I have been able to read about the religious life of the Negro, it has seemed to me that writers have been too much disposed to treat of it as something fixed and unchanging. They have not sufficiently emphasized the fact that the Negro people, in respect to their religious life, have been, almost since they landed in America, in a process of change and growth.

The Negro came to America with the pagan idea of his African ancestors; he acquired under slavery a number of Christian ideas, and at the present time he is slowly learning what those ideas mean in practical life. He is learning, not merely what Christians believe, but what they must do to be Christians.

. . . . .

Slavery, with all its disadvantages, gave the Negro race, by way of recompense, one great consolation, namely, the Christian religion and the hope and belief in a future life. The slave, to whom on this side of the grave the door of hope seemed closed, learned from Christianity to lift his face from earth to heaven, and that made his burden lighter. In the end, the hope and aspiration of the race in slavery fixed themselves on the vision of the resurrection, with its "long white robes and golden slippers."

This hope and this aspiration, which are the theme of so many of the old Negro hymns, found expression in the one institution that slavery permitted to the Negro people—the Negro Church. It was natural and inevitable that the Negro Church, coming into existence as it did under slavery, should permit the religious life of the Negro to express itself in ways almost wholly detached from morality. There was little in slavery to encourage the sense of personal responsibility.

. . . . .

It has been said that the trouble with the Negro Church is that it is too emotional. It seems to me that what the Negro Church needs is a more definite connection with the social and moral life of the Negro people. Could this connection be effected in a large degree, it would give to the movement for the upbuilding of the race the force and inspiration of a religious motive. It would give to the Negro religion more of that missionary spirit, the spirit of service, that it needs to purge it of some of the worst elements that still cling to it.

. . . . .

A large element of the Negro Church must be recalled from its apocalyptic vision back to the earth; the members of the Negro race must be taught that mere religious emotion that is guided by no definite idea and is devoted to no purpose is vain.

. . . . .

In this great modern world, where every individual has so many interests and life is so complicated there is a tendency to let religion and life drift apart. I meet men every day who, honest and upright though they be, have lost in their daily lives this connection with religion, and are striving vainly to regain it. There is no one great dominating motive in their lives which enters into every task and gives it significance and zest.

. . . . .

Slowly but surely, and in ever larger numbers, the members of my race are learning that lesson; they are realizing that God has assigned to their race a man's part in the task of civilization; they are learning to understand their duty, and to face uncomplainingly and with confidence the destiny that awaits them.

African-American leader Booker T. Washington, July 1905, "The Religious Life of the Negro," North American Review, *reprinted at URL:* http://etext.lib. virginia.edu/etcbin/toccer-reldem?id=WasReli. sgm&images=images/mo deng&data=/texts/ english/modeng/parsed&tag=public&part=all. *Accessed on May 18, 2005.*

We who wear the name Christian only have climbed a hundred rugged steps and today, standing on God's balcony, we look down the past, and yonder is Jesus moving in that mightiest drama of all time. The cross is still stained with his blood, the tomb of Arimathaea lies broken, and the ascension from the Mount of Olives is as fresh as though it were the action of yesterday. Yonder are the apostles telling the story of Jesus and the resurrection from the dead. Yonder is Paul preaching in Ephesus, Philippi, Athens and Corinth.

Yonder is Luther nailing the ninety-five theses to the door of the castle church in Wittenberg, and Calvin, a refugee from persecution, writing his *Institutes.* Yonder are the Wesleys calling all believers in Jesus to the life of personal holiness, and the Campbells pleading for a united church by the return to the New Testament in name, in ordinances and in life. What a host of saints! Some were called "Nazarenes," others "Christians," still others "Roman Catholics," others "Reformers" and some "Disciples," but whatever be their names all these are our brethren. If they were authors, we have their books in our libraries and we quote their sayings; if they were artists, we have their paintings in our homes and admire their achievements; and whatever may have been their contribution to Christ, we hold them as our brothers. Some of them thought differently from what we think but they all loved our Lord and sought to reproduce him in their lives. Say what you will, they live because Christ lived in them.

Peter Ainslie, a Disciples of Christ minister and ecumenical leader, 1910, address at the general convention of the Disciples of Christ, in Peter Ainslie: Ambassador of Good Will, *p. 62.*

The days are evil and forces mighty
Against the Christ now stand array'd
And He is calling for manly workers,
The strong of heart and unafraid.
Ye men of purpose, arise and serve Him,
The manly man of Galilee,
That you may hasten the day of promise,
The golden day that is to be.
The noise of battle, the clash of armies,
The din of strife, will not be long;
For men are waking to high endeavor
And soon shall swell the victor's song.
Then let our banner, the cross of Jesus,
Be lifted high till all shall see
And hail as Saviour and King all-glorious
The blessed Christ of Galilee.

"Men Are Wanted," 1910, in Manly Songs for Christian Men, *in Fox,* Jesus in America: Personal Savior, Cultural Hero, National Obsession, *p. 304.*

Their ways [i.e., that of the Chinese] are not as our ways and their gods are not as our God, and never will be. They bring with them a degraded civilization and debased religion of their own ages older, and to their minds, far superior to ours. We look to the future with hope for improvement and strive to uplift our people; they look to the past, believing that perfection was attained by their ancestors centuries before our civilization began and before Jesus brought us the divine message from the Father. They profane this Christian land by erecting here among us their pagan shrines, set up their idols and practice their shocking heathen religious ceremonies.

Proceedings of the Asiatic Exclusion League, *July 16, 1911, quoted in Eck,* A New Religious America: How a "Christian Country" Has Become the World's Most Religiously Diverse Nation, *p. 51.*

When I first went to Oberlin I boarded in what was known as the Ladies' Hall, and altho the food was good, yet, I think, that for lack of variety I began to run down in health. About this time I was invited to spend a few weeks in the family of Professor H. E. Peck, which ended in my staying a few years, until the independence of the Republic of Hayti was recognized, under President Lin-

coln, and Professor Peck was sent as the first U.S. Minister to that interesting country; then the family was broken up, and I was invited by Professor and Mrs. Charles H. Churchill to spend the remainder of my time, about six months, in their family. The influence upon my life in these two Christian homes, where I was regarded as an honored member of the family circle, was a potent factor in forming the character which was to stand the test of the new and strange conditions of my life in Philadelphia. I had been so long in Oberlin that I had forgotten about my color, but I was sharply reminded of it when, in a storm of rain, a Philadelphia street car conductor forbid my entering a car that did not have on it "for colored people," so I had to wait in the storm until one came in which colored people could ride. This was my first unpleasant experience in Philadelphia. Visiting Oberlin not long after my work began in Philadelphia, President Finney asked me how I was growing in grace; I told him that I was growing as fast as the American people would let me. When told of some of the conditions which were meeting me, he seemed to think it unspeakable.

. . . . .

I never rose to recite in my classes at Oberlin but I felt that I had the honor of the whole African race upon my shoulders. I felt that, should I fail, it would be ascribed to the fact that I was colored. At one time, when I had quite a signal triumph in Greek, the Professor of Greek concluded to visit the class in mathematics and see how we were getting along. I was particularly anxious to show him that I was as safe in mathematics as in Greek.

African-American educator Fanny Jackson Coppin, 1913, Reminiscences of School Life and Hints on Teaching, *pp. 13–14, 15.*

I say that you ought to get rich, and it is your duty to get rich. How many of my pious brethren say to me, "Do you, a Christian minister, spend your time going up and down the country advising young people to get rich, to get money?" "Yes, of course I do." They say, "Isn't that awful! Why don't you preach the gospel instead of preaching about man's making money?" "Because to make money honestly is to preach the gospel." That is the reason. The men who get rich may be the most honest men you find in the community.

Baptist minister Russell Conwell, 1915, Acres of Diamonds, *p. 18.*

As a nation we are facing the danger of the domination of the material over the spiritual; we are commercially drunk. Take a bushel of nickels and walk down the street of the average town and you can lead that grasping bunch so close to hell they can smell the brimstone and sulphur. . . . We have got a wonderful country; wonderful. The American advances in industry, but I am mighty sorry to say we have not had a corresponding advance in the morality and decency of the country.

Andrew Carnegie can build libraries on every street; you can build high schools in every block; you can build a university in every town, but you cannot save the people or the country without religion.

If this country has the sins of Babylon, she will go to hell like Babylon. Education will not save you; nothing will save you but the gospel of Jesus Christ.

Revival preacher Billy Sunday, 1915, in Crowe, A Documentary History of American Thought and Society, *pp. 293–294.*

The American Indian must have restored to him moral standards that he can trust. A weak and hypocritical Christianity will make the red man of today what his ancestors never were—an atheist.

It has been difficult for some to realize what the disruption of an ancient faith can mean to the moral nature of a man. The old way is abandoned; its precepts and superstitions are cast to the scrap heap. Yet no wrath of the spirits comes as punishment. The new way is more or less not understood. Perhaps the convert may find that the magic and the taboos of the new religion have far less potency than he imagined, for no horrible calamity befalls him when he violates the laws of his new-found religion. The convert may then become morally worse than before. All restraint has been eliminated and every sea seems safe to sail, for there are no monsters there, as superstition said. He moral anchor is torn from its moorings and he is free and adrift. Thousands of Indians who have not understood Christianity, who have been unable to distinguish between the ethics of Christ and the immorality of some individual who was presumably a Christian, have become moral wrecks, just as thousands of others who have seen the light have gone their way rejoicing, singing:

God's in his heaven,
All's right with the world!

Children in this photograph pose in front of an adobe church in New Mexico in 1908. *(National Archives NWDNS-95-G-75383)*

The red man as he is today, more than even he himself realizes, needs to know God. The basis of all his ancient faith was God. To him God was the beginning and the end of all human experience. Though he could not comprehend the Deity, he could revere him as the Great Mystery, whose all-seeing eye looked upon his every act.

Civilization through its churches and mission agencies must restore the Indian to a knowledge of his Maker. Civilization through its schools and social institutions must give back to the red man great ideals over which he may map his life and by which he may rebuild his character.

Arthur C. Parker a Seneca Indian who played an active role in the Society of American Indians, 1916, "The Social Elements of the Indian Problem," in Peyer, The Elders Wrote, *pp. 176–177.*

Sixteen millions of Catholics live their lives on our land with undisturbed belief in the perfect harmony existing between their religion and their duties as American citizens. It never occurs to their minds to question the truth of a belief which all their experience confirms. Love of religion and love of country burn together in their hearts.

They love their Church as the divine spiritual society set up by Jesus Christ, through which they are brought into closer communion with God, learn His revealed truth and His holy law, receive the help they need to lead Christian lives, and are inspired with the hope of eternal happiness. They love their country with the spontaneous and ardent love of all patriots, because it is their country, and the source to them of untold blessings. They prefer its form of government before any other. They admire its institutions and the spirit of its laws. They accept the Constitution without reserve, with no desire, as Catholics, to see it changed in any feature. They can, with a clear conscience, swear to uphold it.

James Cardinal Gibbons, 1916, in A Retrospective of Fifty Years, *p. 210.*

Being licensed to preach, I was frequently called upon to preach and exhort, especially on Sunday afternoons, not only to my people, but the white people also would come out in large numbers to hear me. At first I was very much embarrassed to preach before such large crowds, because I realized fully that I was without education and had but little opportunity of learning anything. But God helped me wonderfully and blessed my work.

From the time I was licensed to exhort up to 1865 I held meetings for our people. We had glorious times, and many converts would rise and "tell of Jesus and his love." These meetings made our country famous for Methodism during the war. At some places we had stormy times. The old days of the beginning of the Wesleyan Movement in England, in Ireland, and in Wales had their reflex in these. Many times my life was in great danger, and the white people were constantly being reviled and reprimanded because they had encouraged me in preaching. The persecutors went so far as to burn down the church houses in which I had preached to my people. But I had gone too far in the work to be stopped by such methods. Too many people, both white and colored, believed in me to be sidetracked by any such methods; for at this time not only Methodists, but Christian people of all denominations, upheld me and sought to give encouragement. One good old Presbyterian brother said to me after I had preached in his church: "Brother Lane, keep on preaching the gospel, and we will keep on building church houses until the trumpet blows. Let them burn down. We will build, and you shall preach."

Isaac Lane, bishop of the Colored Methodist Church in America, 1916, Autobiography of Bishop Isaac Lane, LL.D, with a Short History of the C.M.E. Church in America and of Methodism, *pp. 54–55, available online at URL:* http://docsouth.unc.edu/lane/lane.html. *Accessed on January 15, 2006.*

Billy Sunday is going to make it just as rough on the dusky crap-shooter and other negro sinners in Atlanta as he is on the white people. Plans are being perfected right now so that Billy can get a good fair shot at the devil in the souls of the Auburn avenue and Decatur street crowds and all the rest of the colored race in Atlanta. The great evangelist will give his personal attention to this work in periodical sermons in the big Billy Sunday tabernacle, the first sermon of Mr. Sunday to negroes to be preached in the tabernacle Monday night, November 19. Dates of other Sunday sermons to negroes will be announced when the full details of the plans are completed.

In the meantime the same sort of a campaign will be organized among the negroes as is already progressing among the white people of the city.

There will be sectional meetings all over the city for the negroes; that is, meetings in different sections of the city, mostly in negro churches, when members of Billy Sunday's staff will be present to address the negroes and assist in the work which negro workers will carry on.

"Rody," the chorus leader, will be on hand from time to time to find out how just is the reputation of the southern negro for singing, and Bob Matthews and Ashley Brewster, pianists at the Sunday tabernacle, will go, too, whenever they can be spared from the work at the tabernacle. Other workers of Billy Sunday's staff will also take a hand in the work among the negroes. Neighborhood prayer meetings and other campaign work will be taken up.

Organization work among negroes is already under way, under the direction of a committee of negro ministers.

Atlanta Constitution, November 7, 1917, report of revival services to be held by evangelist Billy Sunday for African-American audiences, in African-American Religion: A Documentary History Project, *available online at URL:* http://www.amherst.edu/~aardoc/Atlanta_1.htm. *Accessed on May 18, 2005.*

When I went among the Osage people, some of the leaders of the peyote religion were anxious for me to attend their meetings . . . and I accepted the invitation. . . . At about 6 o'clock in the evening the people entered their "meeting house" and sat in a circle around a fire kindled over some symbolic figures marked in the center of a shallow excavation in the middle of the room. The peyote was passed around, some of it in pellets of the consistency of dough, and some prepared in liquid form. The drum was ceremoniously circulated and accompanied by singing. From all that I had heard of the intoxicating effects of the peyote I expected to see the people get gloriously drunk and behave as drunken people do. While I sat waiting to see fighting and some excitement the singing went on and on and I noticed that all gazed at the fire or beyond, at a little mound on top of which lay a single peyote. I said to the man sitting next to me, "What do you expect to see?" He said, "We expect to see the face of Jesus and the face of our dead relatives. We are worshiping God and Jesus, the same God that the white people worship." All night long the singing went on and I sat watching the worshipers. It was about 5 o'clock in the morning when suddenly the singing ceased, the drum and the ceremonial staff were put away, and the leader, beginning at the right of the door, asked each person: "What did you see?" Some replied, "I saw nothing." Others said, "I saw the face of Jesus and it made me happy." Some answered, "I saw the faces of my relatives, and they made me glad." . . . I noticed that there were only a few who had been able to see faces, the greater number of the men and women saw nothing. It was explained to me by the leader that these revelations come quickly to those whose thoughts and deeds are pure. To those who are irreverent, they come slowly, although they may come in time.

Native American scholar Francis La Flesche, 1918, testimony before Congress, in Martin, The Land Looks After Us, *pp. 111–112.*

After praying thus earnestly—storming heaven, as it were, with my pleadings for the Holy Spirit, a quietness seemed to steal over me, the holy presence of the Lord to envelop me. The Voice of the Lord spoke tenderly:

"Now, child, cease your strivings and your begging; just begin to praise Me, and in simple, childlike faith, receive ye the Holy Ghost."

Oh, it was not hard to praise Him. He had become so near and so inexpressibly dear to my heart. Hallelujah! Without effort on my part I began to say:

"Glory to Jesus! Glory to Jesus!! GLORY TO JESUS!!!" Each time I said "Glory to Jesus!" it seemed to

In this photograph American Indian Slow Bull prays to "the Great Mystery." *(Library of Congress, Prints and Photographs Division LC-USZ62-048425)*

come from a deeper place in my being than the last, and in a deeper voice, until great waves of "Glory to Jesus" were rolling from my toes up; such adoration and praise I had never known possible.

All at once my hands and arms began to shake, gently at first, then violently, until my whole body was shaking under the power of the Holy Spirit.

. . . . .

Almost without my notice my body slipped gently to the floor, and I was lying stretched out under the power of God, but felt as though caught up and floating upon the billowy clouds of glory.

. . . . .

My lungs began to fill and heave under the power as the Comforter came in. The cords of my throat began to twitch—my chin began to quiver, and then to shake violently, but Oh, so sweetly! My tongue began to move up and down and sideways in my mouth. Unintelligible sounds as of stammering lips and another tongue, spoken of in Isaiah 28:11, began to issue from my lips.

. . . . .

I shouted and sang and laughed and talked in tongues until it seemed that I was too full to hold another bit of blessing lest I should burst with the glory. The Word of God was true. . . . The Comforter had come, lifting my soul in ecstatic praises to Jesus in a language I had never learned.

Revival preacher Aimee Semple McPherson, 1919, in This Is That: Personal Experiences, Sermons, and Writings, *pp. 48–50.*

CHAPTER TWELVE

Under the Shadows of World Wars
(1921–1950)

The second quarter of the 20th century began with a highly publicized struggle between the forces of fundamentalism and modernism. This was a struggle inherited from the first two decades of the century, when fundamentalists took liberals to task for repudiating what they believed to be the essential orthodoxies of the Christian faith such as the authority and inerrancy of Scripture. At the beginning of the century, theological conservatives still dominated most Protestant denominations and were able to police orthodoxy by launching heresy investigations and trials against theological liberals in seminaries and pulpits. But by the 20th century's second quarter the balance of power had shifted to the liberals, leaving fundamentalists to withdraw from mainline denominations to establish more conservative churches, denominations, and organizations of their own. These ecclesiastical struggles did not automatically resolve the even more controversial struggles over the content of education and activities in the public schools. These schools, which were the primary home of the nation's future since they were the primary home of its children, became the focus for intense conflict that remains alive even into the 21st century.

The most significant early conflict in the long-standing struggles concerning religion in the public schools occurred in Tennessee, when a high school biology teacher was prosecuted and ultimately convicted of teaching evolution in violation of a state law. The Scopes, or monkey, trial, as it was called, ended as a technical victory for fundamentalism. Nevertheless, fundamentalism emerged from the trial as an object of ridicule for many American elites. Moreover, in the decades that followed the forces that had successfully barred the teaching of evolution in Tennessee's public schools found themselves increasingly embattled as the Supreme Court in later decades methodically struck down efforts by religious believers to make public schools active partners in the inculcation of faith.

Theological liberals, though, did not emerge from the 20th century's second quarter unscathed. World War I and still later World War II did much to tarnish the generally optimistic temper of theological liberalism about human potential for good. Germany, having exported to America in the 19th century critical views about Scripture that had nurtured liberalism, now exported forms of theological

A 1920 poster advertized the Interchurch World Movement, an ecumenical organization. *(Library of Congress, Prints and Photographs Division LC-USZ62-09185)*

reflection known as neo-orthodoxy. Theologians such as Karl Barth suggested that liberals had wrongly constructed "anthropocentric" rather than "Christocentric" theologies—man-centered rather than Christ-centered. And American scholars such as Reinhold Niebuhr insisted that liberals had underestimated the reality of human sin and the necessity of power in political affairs.

Catholicism in America did not escape its own conflicts between conservative and liberal theological forces. These had climaxed partially in the Americanism controversy of the late 19th century, when the pope's condemnation of Americanism as a heresy dealt a blow to progressive elements within American Catholicism. But progressive Catholic thought, however chastened by this episode, nevertheless made important institutional advances during the second quarter of the 20th

Religion has followed Americans even as they followed work, as illustrated by this photograph of a religious service in 1942 in an agricultural workers' camp. *(Library of Congress, Prints and Photographs Division LC-USF34-83350)*

century. The National Catholic Welfare Conference, established after World War I, exhibited much of the same kind of social conscience as the Social Gospel movement had animated within American Protestantism. And particular Catholic leaders such as priest and theologian John Ryan and social reformer Dorothy Day played increasingly active roles on the national scene as advocates of progressive social reform.

Against the backdrop of these larger theological currents, smaller communities of faith wrestled to find their own place within the American religious landscape. Jehovah's Witnesses learned to use the First Amendment's protections of free speech and freedom of religion as a shield against burdensome local laws. American Jews, divided theologically among Reform, Conservative, and Orthodox Judaism, came to share a common zeal for the creation of a Jewish homeland in Palestine, a goal they were able to see accomplished in 1948. And black Americans, though largely gathered into their own Baptist, Methodist, and Pentecostal denominations, also followed other religious impulses, leading to the birth of the Nation of Islam and urban religious communities such as Daddy Grace's House of Prayer and Father Divine's Peace Mission movement.

Old and New Responses to Theological Liberalism

By the third decade of the 20th century, the theological debates between liberalism and fundamentalism had erupted into public acrimony. Presbyterian minister

Harry Emerson Fosdick sounded the alarm for liberals when he asked from his pulpit at New York's First Presbyterian Church in 1922, "Shall the Fundamentalists Win?" J. Gresham Machen, a more conservative Presbyterian, suggested in *Christianity and Liberalism* (1923) that liberals did not even deserve to be called Christian any longer, since they had turned their backs on the beliefs that had historically defined Christianity. The controversy reached the level of spectacle when national attention was focused on the fate of a young high school biology teacher named John T. Scopes who was brought to trial in Dayton, Tennessee, in the summer of 1925 for teaching evolution in his classes. The Tennessee law at issue, enacted in February 1925, made it unlawful "for any teacher in any of the Universities, Normals and all other public schools of the State which are supported in whole or in part by the public school funds of the State, to teach any theory that denies the story of the Divine Creation of man as taught in the Bible, and to teach instead that man has descended from a lower order of animals."[1] The law had earned vociferous praise from evangelist Billy Sunday, who proclaimed at a revival in Memphis in February 1925 "a star of glory to the Tennessee legislature, or that part of it involved, for its action against that God forsaken gang of evolutionary cutthroats."[2] Widely publicized in the media, the trial pitted three-time presidential candidate William Jennings Bryan, serving as prosecutor, against legendary lawyer Clarence Darrow, representing the defendant, Scopes. At one point in the trial, Darrow called Bryan himself as a witness and used the occasion to challenge Bryan's biblical literalism. The exchanges between the two lawyers were spirited.

> Q—[Darrow] Do you know anything about how many people there were in Egypt 3,500 years ago, or how many people there were in China 5,000 years ago?
> A—[Bryan] No.
> Q—Have you ever tried to find out?
> A—No, sir. You are the first man I ever heard of who has been in interested in it. (Laughter.)
> Q—Mr. Bryan, am I the first man you ever heard of who has been interested in the age of human societies and primitive man?
> A—You are the first man I ever heard speak of the number of people at those different periods.
> Q—Where have you lived all your life?

William Jennings Bryan conducted this Presbyterian Bible class for tourists in Miami, Florida, in 1921. *(Library of Congress, Prints and Photographs Division LC-USZ62-126497)*

A—Not near you. (Laughter and applause.)

Q—Nor near anybody of learning?

A—Oh, don't assume you know it all. . . .

Q—Mr. Bryan, do you believe that the first woman was Eve?

A—Yes.

Q—Do you believe she was literally made out of Adams's rib?

A—I do.

Q—Did you ever discover where Cain got his wife?

"A—No, sir; I leave the agnostics to hunt for her.[3]

Ultimately, Scopes was found guilty and fined $100, but coverage of the case by national journalists such as H. L. Mencken portrayed the religious and cultural forces aligned against Scopes as bigoted and ludicrous. Thus, while fundamentalism won a local victory, it also acquired new critics.

If the Scopes trial discredited fundamentalism in the eyes of many Americans, it nevertheless did not usher in a new ascendency for theological liberalism among American churches. In the years leading up to World War II, the optimistic temper of liberalism seemed increasingly dated to some observers. New currents of theological reflection imported from Europe questioned modernism's confidence in human ability to solve the crises of the day. Neo-orthodoxy, represented especially by the work of German theologian Karl Barth, attempted to restore a high view of Scripture inherited from the Reformation. Another German theologian, Paul Tillich, lost his academic post after the Nazis came to power and immigrated to America, where he joined the faculty of Union Theological Seminary in the 1930s and became an American citizen in 1940. He brought with him an enthusiasm for marrying theological reflection with existentialist philosophy to confront the anxieties of modernity. Tillich's association with Union Theological Seminary was engineered by Reinhold Niebuhr, who had himself been deeply influenced by neo-orthodox theology. A keen sense of the reality of sin led to Niebuhr's estrangement from the liberal Christianity of earlier in the century and inspired him to champion the wise use of power to cure society's ills rather than simply trust in more optimistic views of human nature. His book *Moral Man and Immoral Society* (1932) was especially critical of those who imagined that the benevolent impulses of individuals were a sufficient foundation on which to erect public policy. Reinhold Niebuhr's brother, theologian H. Richard Niebuhr, also drew heavily on neo-orthodox thought in his own work. In *The Meaning of*

This sign on a tree along a highway in Greene County, Georgia, photographed in 1939 illustrates the enduring presence of religious messages communicated to 20th-century drivers. *(Library of Congress, Prints and Photographs Division LC-USF34-51274)*

Revelation (1941), for example, he criticized theological liberals for making individual faith a subjective matter rather than the response to divine revelation.

Fundamentalist Protestants busied themselves with institution building in the years after the Scopes trial. Having largely retired from the mainline denominations, now generally controlled by those with more liberal theological tendencies, fundamentalists erected new denominations, mission boards, Bible institutes, and seminaries. These believers would resurface on the national scene in the 1970s. Other conservative Protestants attempted to craft a theological identity less hostile to the culture in which they found themselves. They tended to characterize themselves as evangelicals, even though they generally shared a theological orthodoxy in common with fundamentalism. They also framed institutions in which to house their spiritual vision, among which the National Association of Evangelicals, organized in 1942, was a prominent example. The fundamentalist firebrand Carl McIntire, who had established the American Council of Christian Churches in 1941 as a rallying point for fundamentalist churches against the older Federal Council of Churches, attended the meetings out of which the new association of evangelicals was born. He attempted to secure support at these meetings for his organization and for his generally polemical stance against mainstream Protestant churches and their theological liberalism. But it was precisely this antagonistic spirit against modernity that evangelicals wished to suppress in favor of a more positively orientated gospel witness. Evangelicals, to be

Church members leave services in New Hampshire (1941). *(National Archives NWDNS-83-G-41243)*

sure, differed from the mainstream denominations across a whole front of theological issues and could generally be described accurately as fundamentalists with respect to their theological views. But they wished to move beyond their debates with modernism to focus instead on bearing witness to the gospel of Christ to their generation.

Catholic Responses to Modernity

By the latter part of the 19th century, American Catholic leaders had encountered and befriended the modern labor movement. After the archbishop of Quebec persuaded the Vatican to issue a ruling forbidding Catholic membership in the Knights of Labor in 1884, American bishops John Ireland and John Keane prepared a defense of such membership that Cardinal James Gibbons signed and presented to the Vatican in 1887. When the Vatican retreated from its condemnation of the Knights of Labor, the church earned the reputation in America of being a friend to organized labor.[4] Subsequently, although Pope Leo XIII's encyclical *Rerum Novarum*, published in 1891, condemned socialism, it also affirmed the church's broader commitment to social reform and its unwillingness to declare blind fealty to capitalism.

In the decades that followed, progressive American Catholics turned their attention to the social issues given birth by the industrial revolution. One of the most important Catholic voices during this period was that of John Ryan, a Catholic priest, academic, and social reformer. Ryan's dissertation, *A Living Wage: Its Ethical and Economic Aspects*, published in 1906, established the pattern of his future intellectual and social commitments. After joining the faculty of Catholic University in 1915, Ryan used his academic post to advance a variety of progressive causes, such as progressive taxation and a minimum wage. Beginning in 1919 he served as director of the Social Action Department of the National Catholic Welfare Conference, a position he held for more than 25 years. He was also the author of an outline of social reform adopted and published by the National Catholic Welfare Conference in 1920, titled *The Bishops' Program of Social Reconstruction*. Ryan's social progressivism made him a natural ally of President Franklin D. Roosevelt's New Deal policies during the 1930s, an alliance noticed and denounced by popular radio personality Father Charles Coughlin, a fierce critic of Roosevelt who dubbed Ryan "Right Reverend New Dealer."

Father Ryan, though, was not alone in believing that the Catholic Church had a responsibility to engage the problems of modern American society. Anxious to show their solidarity with the American war effort during World War I, American Catholic bishops established the National Catholic War Council in 1918. This patriotic gesture did not protect Catholic believers from a lingering strand of anti-Catholicism in American society, represented both by the popularity of the KKK during the 1920s and at least partially responsible for Al Smith's unsuccessful candidacy for president of the United States in 1928. But it helped create an organizational structure for social engagement that would evolve into the National Catholic Welfare Council (later "Conference"), established in 1921. Ryan's commitment to social reform was also shared by Dorothy Day, a socialist who was converted to Catholicism in 1927. Five years later Day met Peter Maurin, and together the two began publication in 1932 of a periodical they named the *Catholic Worker*, which itself prompted the creation of the Catholic Worker movement.

The Growth of the Jehovah's Witnesses

During the 19th century one of America's indigenous religious traditions, the Mormons, experienced significant government hostility. Though Mormons sought protection for their practice of plural marriage from the U.S. Supreme Court, they found no ally there and ultimately had to abandon the practice. In the 20th century another of America's indigenous religious groups, the Jehovah's Witnesses, also found itself the object of government hostility. But when this group sought constitutional protection from a variety of legal burdens inflicted upon it, it proved far more successful in wielding the First Amendment's guarantees of religious liberty and freedom of speech to defend itself.

Dating from the 19th century, the Jehovah's Witnesses began as a Bible study taught by Charles Taze Russell in the early 1870s, incorporated the next decade as the Watch Tower Bible and Tract Society. Sharing millennial expectations similar to other 19th-century Adventist groups, Russell taught that Jesus had spiritually re-

Dorothy Day, together with Peter Maurin, cofounded the Catholic Worker movement. *(Library of Congress, Prints and Photographs Division LC-USZ62-111099)*

turned to the Earth in 1874 and that his millennial kingdom would begin in 1914. Beginning in 1906 Russell wrote a series of Bible studies advancing this and other interpretations of the Bible as *Studies in Scripture.* Although he died in 1916, the Watch Tower Bible and Tract Society found an able successor to Russell in Joseph Franklin Rutherford, a member of the society and one of its legal advisers, who gained control of the organization after Russell's death. Rutherford led the society to practice conscientious objection to military service during World War I, and this stance eventually caused him to be arrested and convicted for opposing the draft. Although this conviction was later overturned, Rutherford and other members of the society spent nine months in prison before they were released. This encounter with the American legal system would not be the last for the group. After the war Rutherford encouraged efforts by members of the society to engage in house-to-house and street corner evangelism, often using phonographs to play records of

Rutherford's sermons, including sermons that provided scathing condemnations of other religious traditions, especially Catholicism. This evangelism frequently resulted in members of the society being arrested or fined for preaching without licenses or breaching the peace. Members of the society defended themselves from these prosecutions by appealing to the protection of religious free exercise and freedom of speech in the First Amendment of the U.S. Constitution, and in a series of important cases decided in the 1920s, 1930s, and 1940s the Supreme Court frequently vindicated the rights of the society, known after 1931 as the Jehovah's Witnesses. One of these decisions, *Cantwell v. Connecticut* (1940), provided the opportunity for the Supreme Court to announce for the first time that the protections of religious free exercise and freedom of speech in the First Amendment protected individuals not only from federal laws but laws passed by state and local governments as well.

A more severe legal trial for the Jehovah's Witnesses began in the 1940s, after various state and local governments began passing legislation requiring schoolchildren to recite the Pledge of Allegiance. The Jehovah's Witnesses believed saluting the American flag to be an act of idolatry and steadfastly refused to engage in this recitation.[5] Schools responded by expelling the children of Jehovah's Witnesses who failed to recite the pledge. Parents of such children were subjected to fines or imprisonments. A case called *Minersville v. Gobitis*, in which parents threatened with these punishments attempted to secure the protection of the First Amendment, reached the Supreme Court and was decided against the Jehovah's Witnesses in 1940. A majority of the Court reasoned that even sincerely held religious beliefs did not entitle the Jehovah's Witnesses to an exemption from the legal requirement of reciting the pledge. But three years later, in *West Virginia State Board of Education*

While many Americans, such as the sailors pictured here worshipping at the Naval Training Center chapel in San Diego in 1942, saw no conflict between their patriotism and their faith, others, such as the Jehovah's Witnesses, viewed patriotism as a kind of idolatry. *(National Archives file no. 181-05-006)*

In this photograph a street evangelist spreads the gospel outside a warehouse conducting tobacco sales in Durham, North Carolina. *(Library of Congress, Prints and Photographs Division LC-USF33-030740-M5)*

v. Barnette, the Supreme Court reversed its earlier decision. This time a new majority of the Court ruled that the First Amendment prohibited government from requiring citizens either to pledge allegiance to the flag or to adopt other statements of political orthodoxy inconsistent with their beliefs. Writing for the Court, Associate Justice Robert Jackson declared the core principle vindicated by the decision:

> If there is any fixed star in our constitutional constellation, it is that no official, high or petty, can prescribe what shall be orthodox in politics, nationalism, religion, or other matters of opinion or force citizens to confess by word or act their faith therein. If there are any circumstances which permit an exception, they do not now occur to us. We think the action of the local authorities in compelling the flag salute and pledge transcends constitutional limitations on their power and invades the sphere of intellect and spirit which it is the purpose of the First Amendment to our Constitution to reserve from all official control.[6]

Today this decision as well as the other First Amendment decisions vindicating rights of the Jehovah's Witnesses are considered to be cornerstones of the modern principle of freedom of religion and speech.

Zionism in America

The Reform Jews who played a predominant role in American Jewish life during the last half of the 19th century were generally not Zionists: they did not embrace the idea of a Jewish homeland as a core feature of Jewish belief. If anything, America, with its manifold opportunities, seemed to 19th-century Reform Jews a kind of homeland itself. It was no surprise, then, that the Pittsburgh Platform of 1885, a late 19th-century statement of Reform Judaism's theological principles, was staunchly anti-Zionist: "We consider ourselves no longer a nation but a religious community and therefore expect neither a return to Palestine nor a sacrificial worship under the administration of the sons of Aaron nor the restoration of any of the laws concerning the Jewish state."[7] Reform Jews, anxious to forge a place for themselves in American society, worried that talk of a Jewish homeland would stigmatize American Jews as disloyal and thus frustrate the process of assimilation. During the early decades of the 20th century, most Reform Jews continued to express disinterest or even opposition to the cause of Zionism, though this position changed rapidly after the Nazis came to power in Germany in 1933 and began the systematic persecution of Jews.

If Reform Judaism in America came late to the Zionist movement, other American Jews supported the Zionist cause much earlier. In the latter decades of the 19th century and the first of the 20th, new waves of Jewish immigrants from eastern Europe and Russia came bearing more recent memories of the virulent anti-Semitism that had regularly erupted in these areas of the world. And these immigrants, generally Orthodox Jews, were not so enamored as Reform Jews with the prospect of assimilation to American values. Thus, they were not so ready to proclaim America as Zion, a proclamation some Reform Jews were prepared to announce. American Jews could also witness the growing international Zionist movement, fueled especially by the publication of Theodor Herzl's pamphlet *The Jewish State* (1896) and the first meeting the year after its publication of the World Zionist Congress.

That same year in Baltimore, Maryland, the Zionist Association of Baltimore added to its membership a woman who would greatly advance the cause of Zionism in America. Henrietta Szold became a member of the executive council of the Federation of American Zionists in 1897. Three years later she moved to New York, where she became the first female student at the Jewish Theological Seminary and joined a small group of Zionist women named the Hadassah Study Circle. In 1912 this group became Daughters of Zion, later renamed simply Hadassah, and Szold was elected to serve as its first president, a position she held until 1926.

Critics among Reform Jews continued to denounce the Zionist movement, none perhaps more forcefully than Rabbi Isaac Mayer Wise, the father of Reform Judaism in America. In a speech delivered in the summer of 1897 to the Central Conference of American Rabbis, he protested the "prostitution of Israel's holy cause to a madman's dance of unsound politicians" who had "compromised in the eyes of the public the whole of American Judaism as the phantastic dupes of a thoughtless Utopia."[8] In the early decades of the 20th century, as Orthodox and Conservative Jews grew more enthusiastic about the prospect of a Jewish homeland, Reform Jews, with few exceptions, remained suspicious of the enterprise. Notable exceptions existed, however, such as Reform rabbis Stephen S. Wise and Abba Hillel Silver. For four decades beginning in 1907, Wise was the rabbi of an independent Jewish congregation in New York City called the Free Synagogue. He worked closely with Louis Brandeis, associate justice of the U.S. Supreme Court, to advance the cause of Zionism. In the years after Hitler came to power, Wise sounded a growing alarm against Nazism, though later observers have sometimes criticized him for not being even more vehement after he discovered in 1942 the German plan to exterminate Jews. His more radical contemporary, Rabbi Abba Hillel Silver, was less patient about the urgency of creating a Jewish homeland after the Nazis seized power in Germany during the early

1930s and prodded American and British authorities to increase Jewish immigration to Palestine and subsequently to recognize Israel as a nation in 1948.

Beginnings of Islam in America

The first Muslims arrived in America as slaves captured from West Africa, estimated by one account to have represented 10 percent of the slaves brought to America.[9] The conditions of slavery, however, eventually dissolved the connections between Muslim slaves and their Islamic heritage. Thereafter, the public presence of Islam in America lay dormant until the end of the 19th century, when after being appointed consul general by President Glover Cleveland for Manila in the Philippines in 1887, Alexander Russell Webb, later known as Muhammad Alexander Russell Webb, converted to Islam. When he returned to the United States in 1893, he began publishing *Moslem World,* a periodical that propagated Islam, and he spoke on behalf of Islam at the World's Parliament of Religions in Chicago that year. There he explained the misperceptions about Islam that had originally caused him to dismiss it as a spiritual possibility.

> Those errors have grown into history; false history has influenced your opinion of Islam. It influenced my opinion of Islam and when I began, ten years ago, to study the Oriental religions, I threw Islam aside as altogether too corrupt

After the death of Wallace Fard, Elijah Muhammad assumed leadership of the Nation of Islam. *(Library of Congress, Prints and Photographs Division LC-USZ62-116389)*

for consideration. But when I came to go beneath the surface, to know what Islam really is, to know who and what the prophet of Arabia was, I changed my belief very materially, and I am proud to say I am now a Mussulman.[10]

Although Webb helped to introduce Islamic thought to the United States, a significant Muslim presence in the United States did not begin until about the first quarter of the 20th century. Around that period immigrants from Syria and Lebanon began to arrive in the United States in significant numbers, many of them to be employed in the factories springing up across the nation, some of them to work as peddlers. By the end of this period, Muslim immigrants established the Federation of Islamic Associations.

In the second quarter of the 20th century, the birth of the Nation of Islam added a more indigenous form of Muslim faith to that introduced to America primarily by Muslim immigrants. In the summer of 1930, Wallace Fard, an itinerant salesman, established the Lost-Found Nation of Islam in a rented hall in Detroit, Michigan. Fard taught that the original humans had been blacks but that a mad scientist named Yacub had created a devilish white race. In Fard's cosmology whites would rule the earth for six millennia, but blacks would ultimately be restored to their rightful place after an apocalypse. Robert Poole, an automobile factory worker, met Fard the following year, soon became Fard's chief lieutenant, and changed his name to Elijah Muhammad. After Fard disappeared mysteriously in 1934, Muhammad relocated to Chicago in 1936, establishing what became the headquarters of the Nation of Islam, teaching that Fard had been an incarnation of Allah and that Muhammad was his prophet. Muhammad was imprisoned for four years from 1942 to 1946 for his refusal to submit to the draft during World War II, but after his release the Nation of Islam spread rapidly. The year of Muhammad's release from prison saw another young African-American man, Malcolm Little, imprisoned for grand larceny and breaking and entering. While in prison Little was converted to the Nation of Islam and began corresponding with Muhammad. When released on parole in 1952, Little changed

Black Muslim women listen to Elijah Muhammad's annual Savior's Day message in Chicago in 1974. *(National Archives NWDNS-412-DA-13793)*

his name to Malcolm X and rapidly came to occupy a position among the Black Muslims (as they are also known) second only to that of Elijah Muhammad. By 1954 Muhammad had appointed Malcolm X to lead Temple No. 7 in Harlem, New York, and in 1962 he designated Malcolm X his national representative.

The Nation of Islam may have sprung from an even earlier expression of black Islamic faith founded by Timothy Drew, later known as Noble Drew Ali. Ali founded the Moorish Holy Temple of Science in Newark, New Jersey, in 1913. He taught his followers that blacks had originally been Muslims before being forcibly converted to Christianity and that their ancestral home was the Middle East rather than Africa. In the mid-1920s Ali relocated his group to Chicago, Illinois, and in 1927 he published a collection of his teachings, *Holy Koran of the Moorish Holy Temple of Science.* He died in 1929, apparently of a beating, and the Moorish Holy Temple of Science suffered decline, though it continued to number some followers even into the 21st century.

Father Divine and Sweet Daddy Grace

The growth of the Nation of Islam represented a religious counterpoint to the forms of Protestant Christianity dominant among African Americans during the first half of the 20th century. Methodist, Pentecostal, and, most of all, Baptist congregations formed the spiritual homes of most blacks during this period. But African-American faith sometimes ran down tributaries somewhat removed from these broader currents. The Peace Mission movement and the United House of Prayer for All People were two alternative strands of black spirituality during the middle decades of the 20th century. The founder of the first, Father Divine, claimed to be God. The leader of the second, Charles Emmanuel Grace, offered disciples a Pentecostal-style religious experience suffused with the promise of material opulence.

Major J. Divine, also known as Father Divine to his followers, was born George Baker, Jr., and exposed early in life to the Unity School of Christianity, which taught

George Baker announced to his followers that he was, in fact, God. *(Library of Congress, Prints and Photographs Division LC-USF34-56457)*

that believers could attain divinity themselves by properly channeling the spirit of God present within them. Later he participated in the Azusa Street Revival and still later joined a Baptist church in Baltimore, Maryland. Around 1907 Baker came into contact with Samuel Morris, who claimed to be Father God, and Baker soon began to claim that he was the son of God. By 1912 Baker was claiming that he alone was the authentic expression of the divine presence on Earth. Two years later, when he settled for a time in Georgia, local authorities responded to this claim by first attempting to have him committed as insane and then, when this failed, charging him with vagrancy. Baker left Georgia for New York and soon established a religious community in Brooklyn, where he assumed the name Reverend Major Jealous Divine, shortened by his followers to Father Divine. In 1919 the community relocated to the village of Sayville in Suffolk County, Long Island, where Father Divine and his wife became the first black homeowners. Over the next decade he encouraged his followers to practice thrift and abstinence from tobacco, alcohol, and drugs. By 1931 he was serving meals for as many as a thousand people on weekends, causing local authorities to arrest him for disturbing the peace. He was convicted and sentenced to time in jail and a fine, but an appeals court overturned his conviction due to misconduct by the trial judge. Divine, however, relocated once again, this time to Harlem, where his community became known as the Peace Mission movement and emphasized the provision of necessary social services for nominal charges.

Father Divine's contemporary, Charles Manuel Grace, made less extravagant spiritual claims about his identity but established a religious community that provided a similar measure of social support for his followers. Grace appears to have established the first House of Prayer in the 1920s, and by 1927 he had incorporated the United House of Prayer for All People on the Rock of the Apostolic Faith in Washington, D.C. Other centers soon sprang up in other cities, practicing a Pen-

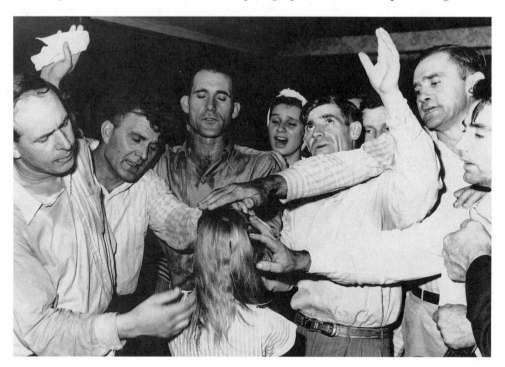

In this 1946 photograph members of a Pentecostal Church of God congregation in Lejunior, Kentucky, participate in a healing service. *(National Archives NWDNS-245-MS-3623L)*

tecostal form of worship, including experiences of healing. Daddy Grace, as his followers referred to him, was not reluctant to emphasize his role as a mediator between his people and God. "Grace has given God a vacation," he quipped, "and since God is on His vacation, don't worry Him. . . . If you sin against God, Grace can save you, but if you sin against Grace, God cannot save you."[11] He collected significant donations from followers and supporters, funneling some of these into social services such as free cafeterias for urban poor but also using them to construct an extravagant lifestyle for himself.

Chronicle of Events

1921
• Conservative Baptists organize the National Federation of the Fundamentalists of the Northern Baptists.

1922
• Rabbi Mordecai M. Kaplan establishes the Society for the Advancement of Judaism, thus founding Reconstructionist Judaism.
• Henry Sloan Coffin and other theological liberals produce the Auburn Affirmation, a response to the fundamentalist movement.
• Arnold Josiah Ford, an African-American Jewish leader, leaves the black Jewish group known as the Moorish Zionist Temple, Inc., and establishes the synagogue Beth B'nai Abraham.
• Stephen S. Wise founds the Jewish Institute of Religion, a rabbinical seminary in New York.
• Aimee Semple McPherson is the first woman to preach a sermon over the radio.
• *March 18:* Judith Kaplan, daughter of Mordecai M. Kaplan, participates in the first bat mitzvah conducted in the United States.
• *May 21:* Liberal Protestant minister Harry Emerson Fosdick preaches a sermon titled "Shall the Fundamentalists Win?" which John D. Rockefeller, Jr., distributes to every minister in America.

1923
• Theologically conservative Presbyterian seminary professor J. Gresham Machen publishes *Christianity and Liberalism*, which argues that theological liberalism should not be considered a species of Christianity.
• Construction is completed on the Angelus Temple, a 5,300-seat auditorium at the edge of Echo Park in Los Angeles that will become the center of Aimee Semple McPherson's preaching ministry.

1924
• The Federation of Colored Catholics is organized by Howard University professor Thomas W. Turner.

1925
• American rabbi Judah Leon Magnes becomes the first chancellor of Hebrew University in Jerusalem, a post he occupies until 1935.

Migrant workers from the Southwest did not leave their faith behind after they arrived in Tranquility, California. *(Library of Congress, Prints and Photographs Division LC-USF34-018780-E)*

• Bruce Barton publishes *The Man Nobody Knows*, which describes Jesus as a shrewd businessman.
• *June 1:* In *Pierce v. Society of Sisters*, the U.S. Supreme Court rules that a state cannot require that all school-aged children attend public rather than private schools.
• *June 10:* The United Church of Canada is founded by the merger of the Methodist Church, Canada, the Congregational Union of Canada, most of the Presbyterian Church in Canada, and the General Council of Union Churches.
• *July 10:* The Scopes "monkey" trial, begins in Dayton, Tennessee, with William Jennings Bryan as prosecuting attorney and Clarence Darrow as defense attorney. It concludes with John Scopes convicted on July 21 for teaching evolution in school and fined $100.

1926
• Revivalist Bob Jones founds Bob Jones College in St. Andrews, Florida. The college later relocates to Cleveland, Tennessee, and then to Greenville, South Carolina.
• A meeting of Jewish religious leaders in New York City results in the formation of the Synagogue Council of America.
• Pentecostal preacher Aimee Semple McPherson becomes the center of controversy when she disappears

in the spring while swimming at a beach in Venice, California, and then reappears in the summer, claiming to have been kidnaped and to have escaped. Rumors circulate suggesting that she had an affair with an employee at her church. A prosecuting attorney charges her with obstructing justice and falsifying police records but eventually drops the charges.

1927

- Dorothy Day, later cofounder of the Catholic Worker Movement, is converted to Catholicism.
- Timothy Drew (Noble Drew Ali) publishes the *Holy Koran of the Moorish Holy Temple of Science*, a collection of his teachings.
- Sweet Daddy Grace (Charles Manuel Grace) incorporates the United House of Prayer for All People on the Rock of the Apostolic Faith in Washington, D.C.
- Aimee Semple McPherson founds the Church of the Foursquare Gospel.
- The National Conference of Christians and Jews is established.
- W. Y. Evans-Wentz publishes the *Tibetan Book of the Dead.*

1928

- Catholic politician Alfred E. Smith wins the Democratic nomination for president of the United States but is defeated by Republican candidate Herbert Hoover.
- The National Conference of Christians and Jews (now known as the National Conference for Community and Justice) is founded to combat religious prejudice.

1929

- Robert Dick Wilson, J. Gresham Machen, Oswald T. Allis, and Cornelius Van Til withdraw from the faculty of Princeton Theological Seminary because of its liberal theology and found Westminster Theological Seminary in Philadelphia.
- *January 15:* Martin Luther King, Jr., is born in Atlanta, Georgia.

1930

- Poet John G. Neihardt interviews American Indian religious leader Black Elk. This meeting leads to Neihardt's publication of *Black Elk Speaks* in 1932. This book will be reprinted in the 1960s and will contribute to a renewed interest in Native American religion.
- CBS begins broadcasting Father Charles Edward Coughlin's radio program *The Golden Hour of the Little Flower*, which will eventually attract an estimated audience of 40 million listeners.
- Catholic priest and later bishop Fulton John Sheen begins a radio broadcast called *The Catholic Hour*.
- Wallace Fard founds the Lost-Found Nation of Islam.

1931

- The Watch Tower Bible and Tract Society is renamed the Jehovah's Witnesses.
- The Buddhist Society of America is incorporated in New York City by Shigetsu Sasaki (also known as Sokei-an).
- Meher Baba, born Merwan Shehariarji Irani, visits the United States from India and develops a following in America.
- *May 25:* In *United States v. Macintosh*, the U.S. Supreme Court finds that the constitutional rights of Douglas Clyde Macintosh, a Baptist theologian on the faculty of Yale University, had not been violated by the refusal of immigration officials to award him U.S. citizenship when he declined to indicate on his application an unreserved willingness to bear arms in defense of the United States. As a result, Macintosh remains a Canadian citizen.

1932

- John G. Neihardt publishes *Black Elk Speaks.*
- Dorothy Day and Peter Maurin begin publication of the *Catholic Worker*, which leads to the formation of the Catholic Worker movement.
- Reinhold Niebuhr publishes *Moral Man and Immoral Society.*
- The I Am movement is founded by Guy Ballard.
- Dwight Goddard publishes *The Buddhist Bible.*
- The Hocking Commission (named for its chair, William Ernest Hocking, a professor of philosophy at Harvard University), established by the Laymen's Foreign Missions Inquiry with the financial support of John D. Rockefeller, Jr., produces an influential study of Protestant missions, summarized in a work titled *Re-Thinking Missions*, calling for greater respect for non-Christian religious traditions and better qualified missionaries. Although the report wins the praise of Pearl S. Buck, Pulitzer prize–winning author of *The Good Earth* and wife of a Presbyterian missionary in China, it is condemned by conservative Protestants.

1933

- The National Fraternal Council of Negro Churches in established.
- After German theologian Paul Tillich is ousted from the faculty of the University of Frankfurt, he obtains

An Orthodox rabbi taught children at Jersey Homesteads in New Jersey in 1936. *(Library of Congress, Prints and Photographs Division LC-USF33-011049-M4)*

a teaching position with Union Theological Seminary in New York through the help of American theologian Reinhold Niebuhr.
- *August 11:* Jerry Falwell is born in Lynchburg, Virginia.

1934
- Mordecai Kaplan publishes *Judaism as a Civilization: Toward a Reconstruction of American-Jewish Life.*
- Construction of the "Mother Mosque of America" is completed in Cedar Rapids, Iowa.
- Wallace Fard, founder of the Nation of Islam, disappears. Subsequently, Elijah Muhammad will take charge of the Nation of Islam, making the Nation of Islam temple in Chicago the new national headquarters of the group.
- *November 11:* Controversial Catholic priest and radio personality Charles Edward Coughlin founds the National Union for Social Justice (Union Party).

1935
- Universalists adopt the Washington Statement of Faith.

- The Arab American Banner Society is founded in Boston.
- William Griffith Wilson (Bill W.) and Dr. Robert Holbrook Smith (Dr. Bob) found Alcoholics Anonymous in New York City.
- Victor Houteff founds Mount Carmel Center near Waco, Texas, as an off-shoot of the Seventh-Day Adventist Church. In 1942 he will break with the Seventh-Day Adventists and rename his group the Davidian Seventh-Day Adventist Association, of which the Branch Davidians will subsequently become a splinter group.

1936
- J. Gresham Machen and other conservative Presbyterians establish the Presbyterian Church in America, later renamed the Orthodox Presbyterian Church.
- Elijah Muhammad settles in Chicago, Illinois, where the Temple of Islam No. 2 becomes the national headquarters of the Nation of Islam after the disappearance of Wallace Fard in 1934. Muhammad announces that Fard had been an incarnation of Allah and that he himself is Allah's messenger.

1937

- Reform Jews adopt the Columbus Platform, which emphasizes the goal of establishing a Jewish homeland in Palestine.
- Charles Edward Fuller begins airing the *Old Fashioned Revival Hour.*
- The Friends World Committee for Consultation is formed.

1938

- Father Charles Coughlin begins denouncing Jews on his radio station and through a newspaper he publishes called *Social Justice.*
- Thomas Merton is converted to Catholicism and receives his first Communion. He will become one of the 20th century's most influential Catholic writers.

1939

- William Griffith Wilson and Dr. Robert Holbrook Smith, the founders of Alcoholics Anonymous, publish *Alcoholics Anonymous,* the group's basic handbook, referred to as the Big Book.
- *May 10:* The Methodist Episcopal Church, the Methodist Protestant Church, and the Methodist Episcopal Church, South, reunite.

1940

- Joseph I. Schneerson, the sixth Lubavitcher rebbe, arrives in the United States and settles in Crown Heights, Brooklyn.
- German-born theologian Paul Tillich, who immigrated to the United States after the Nazis came to power in the early 1930s, becomes a U.S. citizen.
- *May 30:* In *Cantwell v. Connecticut,* the U.S. Supreme Court holds that the First Amendment prevents states from prohibiting Jehovah's Witnesses from engaging in proselytizing that includes comments critical of Catholics. The case also establishes the principle that the protections of religious free exercise and freedom of speech guaranteed by the First Amendment apply to the actions of state and local governments in addition to those of the federal government.
- *June 3:* In *Minersville School District v. Gobitis,* the U.S. Supreme Court holds that Jehovah's Witness children can be forced to say the Pledge of Allegiance, even though they believe that reciting the pledge is an act of idolatry. The Court denies that the First Amendment shields the Jehovah's Witnesses from this compulsion. The decision will be overturned by a new majority of the Court in 1943.

A teacher led a Sunday school class in a Norwegian Lutheran Church near Irwin, Iowa, in 1941. *(National Archives NWDNS-83-G-41864)*

1941

- Thomas Merton becomes a postulate in the Trappist order.
- Fundamentalist minister Carl McIntire establishes the American Council of Christian Churches as a conservative alternative to the Federal Council of Churches, which had been established as an ecumenical organization of mainstream Protestant churches in 1908.
- Young Life, an evangelical youth organization begun by Dallas Theological Seminary student Jim Rayburn in Gainesville, Texas, is officially incorporated.
- *October 8:* Jesse Jackson is born Jesse Louis Burns in Greenville, South Carolina.

1942

- Under pressure from Roman Catholic authorities after publicly speaking favorably of Adolf Hitler and Nazism and portraying communist Jews as America's greatest threat, Father Charles Edward Coughlin abandons his radio broadcasts and other public appearances.
- Wycliffe Bible Translators is founded, an outgrowth of a linguistics training school established in 1932 by William Cameron Townsend, a Guatemalan missionary.
- Stephen Wise learns of German plans to exterminate European Jews and reveals that 2 millions Jews have already been killed.
- The National Association of Evangelicals is organized.
- Anti-Zionist Reform Jews who oppose the creation of a Jewish homeland in Palestine found the American Council for Judaism.
- President Franklin D. Roosevelt issues Executive Order 9066, which authorizes the forced relocation of Japanese Americans to internment camps.

1943

- Orthodox rabbis march on Washington to pressure the rescue of European Jews from the Holocaust. President Roosevelt refuses to speak to the rabbis.
- *June 14:* In *West Virginia v. Barnette*, the U.S. Supreme Court reverses its decision in *Minersville School District v. Gobitis* and holds that the Constitution's First Amendment prohibits states from requiring the children of Jehovah's Witnesses to say the Pledge of Allegiance.

Those of Japanese ancestry forced to relocate to an internment camp held a religious service on their first night at the Colorado River Indian reservation in 1942. *(National Archives NWDNS-210-G-C37)*

Buddhists of Japanese ancestry forced to relocate to camps during World War II met in churches such as this one at the Gila River Relocation Center in Rivers, Arizona. *(National Archives NWDNS-210-G-D647)*

1944

- The Canadian Council of Churches is formed.
- The Buddhist Mission of North America is renamed the Buddhist Churches of America.
- *January 31:* In *Prince v. Massachusetts,* the U.S. Supreme Court holds that the First Amendment's protection of religious free exercise does not prevent a state from punishing a Jehovah's Witness who allowed a nine-year-old girl to engage in nighttime proselytizing activities in violation of a state child labor law.

1945

- Sponsored by the American Jewish Committee, *Commentary* magazine begins publication.
- Adam Clayton Powell, Jr., pastor of the Abyssinian Baptist Church in Harlem, is elected to the U.S. House of Representatives. He will subsequently serve 11 successive terms.
- A number of evangelical Christian youth organizations consolidate to form Youth for Christ with Torrey Johnson its first president and Billy Graham its first field representative.

1946

- Malcolm X (Malcolm Little) is imprisoned for grand larceny and breaking and entering. While in prison he is converted to the Nation of Islam.

After the beginning of the Pentecostal movement with the Azusa Street Revival, Pentecostal churches, such as the one pictured here from Alameda County, California, in the 1940s, rapidly spread across the country. *(National Archives NWDNS-83-G-41565)*

- Paramhansa Yogananda publishes *Autobiography of a Yogi.*
- *July 7:* Pope Pius XII declares Francesca Xavier Cabrini, Catholic nun and missionary, a saint; she becomes the first American citizen canonized.

1947

- The first of what will become many thousands of reported healings occurs in services conducted by charismatic preacher Kathryn Kuhlman.
- Quakers in the United States and Great Britain are awarded the Nobel Peace Prize.
- *February 10:* In *Everson v. Board of Education* the U.S. Supreme Court holds that the Constitution's establishment clause does not prevent states from paying the costs of transporting students to private parochial schools. The Court announces, however, that the First Amendment's prohibition of laws "respecting an establishment of religion" applies to the actions of state and local governments as well as to those of the federal government.

1948

- The first assembly of the World Council of Churches occurs in Amsterdam.
- The General Assembly of the United Nations adopts the Universal Declaration of Human Rights, which includes a guarantee of religious freedom.
- Brandeis University is established as a Jewish-sponsored nonsectarian institution.
- Catholic writer Thomas Merton publishes his autobiographical account, *The Seven Storey Mountain.*

- *May 14:* Israel is established as an independent nation and is diplomatically recognized by the United States.

1949

- Billy Graham gains national prominence after a revival campaign in Los Angeles is extended from three weeks to eight.
- Thomas Merton is ordained a Trappist monk.
- Paul Blanshard publishes *American Freedom and Catholic Power*, which argues that Catholics are a danger to American democracy.
- The first registered and dedicated Muslim cemetery in America is opened in Cedar Rapids, Iowa.

1950

- The National Council of the Churches of Christ in the United States of America is established.
- Billy Graham begins airing his *Hour of Decision* radio program.
- L. Ron Hubbard, founder of Scientology, publishes *Dianetics: The Modern Science of Mental Health.*
- After settling in the Crown Heights area of Brooklyn, New York, Menachem Mendel Schneerson becomes the seventh Lubavitch rebbe.
- Conservative Judaism, in contrast to Orthodox Judaism, approves using electricity and driving on the Sabbath.

Eyewitness Testimony

For the last ten years our nation has been under conviction of sin. We had long been living a double life, but without realizing it. Our business methods and the principles of our religion and our democracy have always been at strife, but not until our sin had matured and brought forth wholesale death did we understand our own obliquity.

. . . . .

Sin is the greatest preacher of repentance. Give it time, and it will cool our lust in shame. When God wants to halt a proud man who is going wrong, he lets him go the full length and find out the latter end for himself. That is what he has done with our nation in its headlong ride on the road of covetousness. Mammonism stands convicted by its own works. It was time for us to turn.

We are turning.

. . . . .

The . . . sense of a great change comes over any one who watches the life of this nation with an eye for the stirring of God in the souls of men. There is a new shame and anger for oppression and meanness; a new love and pity for the young and frail whose slender shoulders bear our common weight; a new faith in human brotherhood; a new hope of a better day that is even now in sight. . . . We are passing through a moral adolescence. When the spirit of manhood comes over a boy, his tastes change. The old doings of his gang lose interest. A new sense of duty, a new openness to ideal calls, a new capacity of self-sacrifice surprise those who used to know him. So in our conventions and clubs, our chambers of commerce and our legislatures, there is a new note, a stiffening of will, an impatience for cowardice, an enthusiastic turning toward real democracy. The old leaders are stumbling off the stage bewildered.

. . . . .

Were you ever converted to God? Do you remember the change in your attitude to all the world? Is not this new life which is running through our people the same great change on a national scale? This is religious energy, rising from the depth of that infinite spiritual life in which we all live and move and have our being. This is God.

Social Gospel leader Walter Rauschenbusch, 1921,
Christianizing the Social Order, pp. 1–6.

Christianity means to me:

A new spirit of love service and sacrifice in humanity.

A new and ever developing life in art, literature, music, philosophy, government, industry, worship.

A relief from the heavy burden of remorse for past errors, blunders, and sins.

An ever growing aspiration for the future and an ever increasing power toward achievement.

Faith in ourselves and in our fellow men; in our infinite possibilities because in our infinite inheritance.

Faith in the great enterprise in which God's loyal children are engaged, that of making a new world out of this old world, a faith which failure does not discourage nor death destroy.

Faith in a Leader who both sets our task and shares it with us; the longer we follow him and work with him, the more worthy to be loved, trusted, and followed does he seem to us to be.

Faith in a companionable God whom we cannot understand, still less define, but with whom we can be acquainted, as a little child is acquainted with his mysterious mother.

Faith in our present possession of a deathless life of the spirit, which we share with the Father of our spirits and our divinely appreciated leader.

Congregationalist minister Lyman Abbott, 1922,
What Christianity Means to Me: A Spiritual
Autobiography, pp. 184–186.

[T]he world is beginning to realize the source of Notre Dame's brand of sportsmanship. The teamwork of a Notre Dame eleven is not inspired by the philosophy of Nietzsche, it has none of the earmarks of Schopenhauer or Kant; it is neither bloodless pessimism, nor festering selfishness; it is neither cynical nor brutal; it is a red-blooded play of men full of life, full of hope, full of charity, of men who learn at the foot of the altar what it means to love one another, of men who believe that clean play can be offered as a prayer in honor of the Queen of Heaven. Notre Dame football is a new crusade: it kills prejudice and it stimulates faith.

John O'Hara, Notre Dame University's prefect of religion,
1924, after Notre Dame wins the national football
championship, in Dolan, The American Catholic
Experience, *p. 391.*

Dayton, Tennessee, July 13—There is a Unitarian clergyman here from New York, trying desperately to horn into the trial and execution of the infidel Scopes. He will fail. If Darrow ventured to put him on the stand the whole audience, led by the jury, would leap out of the courthouse windows, and take to the hills. Darrow himself, indeed, is as much as they can bear. The whisper that he is an atheist has been stilled by the bucolic make-up and by the public report that he has the gift of prophecy and can reconcile Genesis and evolution. Even so, there is ample space about him when he navigates the streets. The other day a newspaper woman was warned by her landlady to keep out of the courtroom when he was on his legs. All the local sorcerers predict that a bolt from heaven will fetch him in the end. The night he arrived there was a violent storm, the town water turned brown, and horned cattle in the lowlands were afloat for hours. A woman back in the mountains gave birth to a child with hair four inches long, curiously bobbed in scallops.

The Book of Revelation has all the authority, in these theological uplands, of military orders in time of war. The people turn to it for light upon all their problems, spiritual and secular. If a text were found in it denouncing the Anti-Evolution law, then the Anti-Evolution law would become infamous overnight. But so far the exegetes who roar and snuffle in the town have found no such text. Instead they have found only blazing ratifications and reinforcements of Genesis. Darwin is the devil with seven tails and nine horns. Scopes, though he is disguised by flannel pantaloons and a Beta Theta Pi haircut, is the harlot of Babylon. Darrow is Beelzebub in person.

. . . . .

I have hitherto hinted an Episcopalian down here in the coca-cola belt is regarded as an atheist. It sounds like one of the lies that journalists tell, but it is really an understatement of the facts. Even a Methodist, by Rhea county standards, is one a bit debauched by pride of intellect. It is the four Methodists on the jury who are expected to hold out for giving Scopes Christian burial after he is hanged. They all made it plain, when they were examined, that they were free-thinking and independent men, and not to be run amuck by the superstitions of the lowly. One actually confessed that he seldom read the Bible, though he hastened to add that he was familiar with its principles. The fellow had on a boiled shirt and a polka dot necktie. He sits somewhat apart. When Darrow withers to a cinder under the celestial blowpipe, this dubious Wesleyan, too, will lose a few hairs.

. . . . .

When we got to Dayton [after attending a Church of God service outside the town], after 11 o'clock—an immensely late hour in these parts—the whole town was still gathered on the courthouse lawn, hanging upon the disputes of theologians.

. . . . .

Such is human existence among the fundamentalists, where children are brought up on Genesis and sin is unknown. . . . I have done my best to show you what the great heritage of mankind comes to in regions where the Bible is the beginning and end of wisdom, and the mountebank Bryan, parading the streets in his seersucker coat, is pointed out to sucklings as the greatest man since Abraham.

H. L. Mencken, 1925, in a Baltimore Evening Sun *article reporting on the Scopes trial in Tennessee, in* The Impossible Mencken: A Selection of His Best Newspaper Stories, *pp. 576–582.*

When I first went to India I was trying to hold a very long line—a line that stretched clear from Genesis to Revelation, on to Western Civilization and to the Western Christian Church. I found myself bobbing up and down that line fighting behind Moses and David and Jesus and Paul and Western Civilization and the Christian Church. I was worried. There was no well-defined issue. I found the battle almost invariably being pitched at one of these three places: the Old Testament, or Western Civilization, or the Christian Church. I had the ill-defined but instinctive feeling that the heart of the matter was being left out. Then I saw that I could, and should, shorten my line, that I could take my stand at Christ and before that non-Christian world refuse to know anything save Jesus Christ and him crucified. The sheer storm and stress of things had driven me to a place that I could hold. Then I saw that there is where I should have been all the time. I saw that the gospel lies in the person of Jesus, that he himself is the Good News, that my one task was to live and to present him. My task was simplified.

. . . . .

Jesus is forcing modification everywhere. He stands unmodified. In all this battle and struggle of things—and Jesus hasn't won this place in the soul of India without his Calvarys of misunderstanding and abuse, and there are more to come—nevertheless, in this clash of ideas and ideals we have not been called upon to modify a single thing about him. We are called upon, with deep insistence, to modify our civilization, our church, ourselves—everything, except him. A Hindu principal of a college said to me, "Your trouble is with the Christian Church." Even so, but that is remediable. We can remedy our church, our civilization, ourselves. But suppose he had been able to say, "Your trouble is with your Christ"— that would be irremediable; it would be fatal. "Smite the shepherd, and the sheep will be scattered abroad." Smite Jesus with legitimate moral or spiritual criticism, and we are worse than scattered abroad. We are done for. But I say the literal truth when I say that men are not asking for modification there; the demand is for interpretation and imitation.

Methodist missionary E. Stanley Jones, 1925, in The Christ of the Indian Road, *pp. 11–12, 219.*

I was reared in the Roman Catholic faith, but never thoroughly espoused it, though I loved going to mass, especially to the Cathedral; the quiet solemnity of the services, the soft coloring, the sublime music, all appealing to my mystic temperament.

An unsatisfied craving for something, I knew not what, pursued me. I sought a solution in many ways. First, I took up philanthropic work, then the study of the different sciences.

I observed greed, selfishness, and deceit everywhere and in every sphere of life; it seem to me one could not succeed in the feverish life of the world without pulling another down. Everything was unreal, artificial, my own life no less so than that of others. Sometimes the emptyness of my life appalled me; at such times I turned to religion but found no comfort. Those who profess to live the most pious lives were, upon the whole, the most egotistical and selfish of people; they were incessantly wrangling over creeds. The prevalent idea of God as given by the early protestant teachers, and still held as a cornerstone of orthodox theology, confused rather than gave peace. I studied and searched deeply, but everywhere the same old platitudes met me; then my soul cried out, "Can I ever find answers to my longings?" Thus my mind rocked back and forth.

. . . . .

At last I left the silence which had meant so much to me during the last three years and came from my retreat, I sought kindred spirits, whom I found in the Theosophical Society.

Through connection with this fraternity, I came to know a Buddhist from Ceylon. I told him of my long search for truth, and explained that I had not yet found what I was seeking. He then told me of the Buddha and his long search for truth. He spoke no ill of anyone, and had sympathy for everything that lived. I became interested, and commenced the study of Buddha's scriptures. In these I came to know the meaning of Christ and that many Christs had lived before Jesus, even before time was, and would live when time had ceased to be. That Truth

(as Buddha had termed what the Christians call God) was above all in reality; that there was a divine law of cause and effect which balanced good and evil and that this law can be reasoned out, also pointing the way to reach this understanding, and that moreover there was nothing preventing any mortal from attaining the same goal, but that the Self, which through ignorance had caused the world often to err, had brought suffering even to the innocent.

. . . . .

The study of Buddhist scriptures satisfied my craving for Truth and led me to embrace that religion and venerate that concept of my relation to things about me.

Buddhist convert Marie De S. Canavarro, 1925, in Insight into the Far East, *pp. 13–15.*

Dear Sir:

In your open letter to me in the April *Atlantic Monthly* you "impute" to American Catholics views which, if held by them, would leave open to question the loyalty and devotion to this country and its Constitution of more than twenty million American Catholic citizens. . . . These convictions are held neither by me nor by any other American Catholic, as far as I know.

. . . . .

[Y]ou imply that there is conflict between religious loyalty to the Catholic faith and patriotic loyalty to the United States. Everything that has actually happened to me during my long public career leads me to know that no such thing as that is true. . . . I have never known any conflict between my official duties and my religious belief. No such conflict could exist. . . .

Under our system of government the electorate entrusts to its officers of every faith the solemn duty of action according to the dictates of conscience. I may fairly refer once more to my own record to support these truths. No man, cleric or lay, has every directly or indirectly attempted to exercise Church influence on my administration of office I have ever held, nor asked me to show special favor to Catholics or exercise discrimination against non-Catholics.

. . . . .

I summarize my creed as an American Catholic. I believe in the worship of God according to the faith and practice of the Roman Catholic Church. I recognize no power in the institutions of my Church to interfere with the operations of the Constitution of the United States or the enforcement of the law of the land. I believe in absolute freedom of conscience for all men and in equality of all churches, all sects, and all beliefs before the law as a matter of right and not as a matter of favor. I believe in the absolute separation of Church and State and in the strict enforcement of the provisions of the Constitution that Congress shall make no law respecting an establishment of religion or prohibiting the free exercise thereof.

. . . . .

In this spirit I join with fellow Americans of all creeds in a fervent prayer that never again in this land will any public servant be challenged because of the faith in which he has tried to walk humbly with his God.

Presidential candidate Alfred E. Smith, May 1927, open letter to Charles C. Marshall published in Atlantic Monthly, *in Wilson and Drakeman,* Church and State in American History, *pp. 183–185.*

There is a discouraging pettiness about human nature which makes me hate myself each time I make an analysis of my inner motives and springs of action. Here I am prodding and criticizing people continually because they have made too many compromises with the necessities of life and adjusted the Christian ideal until it has completely lost its original meaning. Yet I make my own compromises all the time.

It is Christian to trust people, and my trust is carefully qualified by mistrust and caution.

It is Christian to love, and to trust in the potency of love rather than in physical coercion. Logically that means non-resistance. Yet I believe that a minimum of coercion is necessary in all social tasks, or in most of them.

It is Christian to forgive rather than to punish; yet I do little by way of experimenting in the redemptive power of forgiveness.

I am not really a Christian. . . . I am too cautious to be a Christian. I can justify my caution, but so can the other fellow who is more cautious than I am.

The whole Christian adventure is frustrated continually not so much by malice as by cowardice and reasonableness.

. . . . .

A reasonable person adjusts his moral goal somewhere between Christ and Aristotle, between an ethic of love and an ethic of moderation. I hope there is more of Christ than of Aristotle in my position. But I would not be too sure of it.

Theologian Reinhold Niebuhr, 1928, from Leaves from the Notebook of a Tamed Cynic, *pp. 166–167.*

It was overwhelmingly proved that the more open-minded, honest, just, and generous we were in dealing with the non-Christian faiths, the higher Christ loomed in His absolute uniqueness, sufficiency, supremacy, and universality. More than ever before, we saw Him as One other than all the rest—other than the saints and sages of ancient Hinduism, other than Buddha, Confucius, and Mohammed, other than Moses and St. Paul—"strong among the weak, erect among the fallen, believing among the faithless, clean among the defiled, living among the dead." In all the many months of fresh study of the values of the non-Christian systems across the world, or the comprehensive or luminous sharing of knowledge, spiritual insight, and personal experience at Jerusalem, nothing was discovered or took place which would tend in the least to invalidate the claim and belief that in Christ we have the Central Figure of the Ages and the Eternities, the Fountain Head of Spiritual Life, the Unfailing Source of Creative Energy, the World's Redeemer, the Desire of All Nations.

Ecumenical leader John Mott, 1931, The Present-Day Summons to the World Mission of Christianity, *quoted in* John R. Mott: World Citizen, *p. 269.*

My friend, I am going to tell you the story of my life, as you wish; and if it were only the story of my life I think I would not tell it; for what is one man that he should make much of his winters, even when they bend him like a heavy snow? So many other men have lived and shall live that story, to be grass upon the hills.

It is the story of all life that is holy and is good to tell, and of us two-leggeds sharing in it with the four-leggeds and the wings of the air and all green things; for these are children of one mother and their father is one Spirit.

This, then, is not the tale of a great hunter or of a great warrior, or of a great traveler, although I have made much meat in my time and fought for my people both as boy and man, and have gone far and seen strange lands and men. So also have many others done, and better than I. These things I shall remember by the way, and often they may seem to be the very tale itself, as when I was living them in happiness and sorrow. But now that I can see it all as from a lonely hilltop, I know it was the story of a mighty vision given to a man too weak to use it; of a holy tree that should have flourished in a people's heart with flowers and singing birds, and now is withered; and of a people's dream that died in bloody snow.

But if the vision was true and mighty, as I know, it is true and mighty yet; for such things are of the spirit, and it is in the darkness of their eyes that men get lost.

Ogala Lakota Sioux holyman Black Elk, 1932, in Black Elk Speaks: Being the Life Story of a Holy Man of the Oglala Sioux, as Told through *John G. Neihardt (Flaming Rainbow), pp. 1–2.*

The steel doors closed. Locked. Here, too, was Brown America. . . . The State Penitentiary at Kilby, Alabama, in the year of our Lord, 1932.

Our Lord . . . Pilate . . . and the thieves on the cross.

. . . . .

Daily, I watch the guards washing their hands.

The world remembers for a long time a certain washing of hands. The world remembers for a long time a certain humble One born in a manger—straw, manure, and the feet of animals—standing before Power washing its hands. No proven crime. Farce of a trial. Lies. Laughter. Mob. Hundreds of years later Brown America sang: *My Lord! What a morning when the stars began to fall!*

For eight brown boys in Alabama the stars have fallen. In the death house, I heard no song at all. Only a silence more ominous than song. All of Brown America locked up there. And no song.

Even as ye do unto the least of these, ye do it unto Me.

White guard.
The door that leads to DEATH.
Electric chair.
No song.

African-American poet Langston Hughes, June 1932, "In the Death House with the Scottsboro Boys," in Colbert, Eyewitness to America, *pp. 373–375.*

Judaism is the soul of which Israel [the Jewish people] is the body. Living in all parts of the world, Israel has been held together by the ties of a common history, and above all, by the heritage of faith. Though we recognize in the group-loyalty of Jews who have become estranged from our religious tradition, a bond which still unites them with us, we maintain that it is by its religion and for its religion that the Jewish people has lived. The non-Jew who accepts our faith is welcomed as a full member of the Jewish community.

In all lands where our people live, they assume and seek to share loyally the full duties and responsibilities of citizenship and to create seats of Jewish knowledge and religion. In the rehabilitation of Palestine, the land hallowed by memories and hopes, we behold the promise of renewed life for many of our brethren. We affirm the obligation of all Jewry to aid in its upbuilding as a Jewish

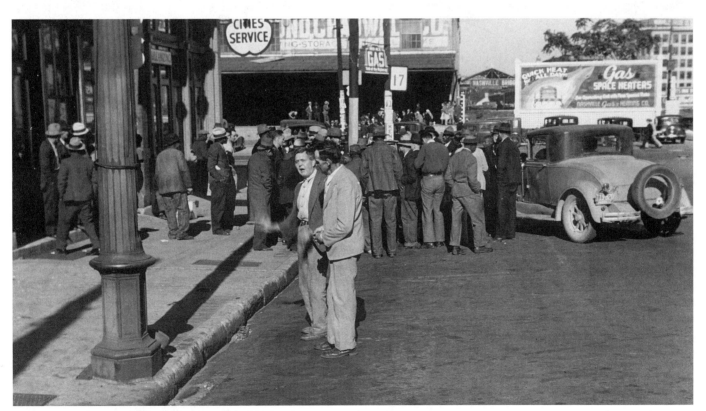

A religious gathering took place on the streets of Nashville, Tennessee, in 1935. *(Library of Congress, Prints and Photographs Division LC-USF33-006144-M1)*

Church members attended services in a black church in a mining town in West Virginia in 1946. *(National Archives NWDNS-245-MS-1297L)*

homeland by endeavoring to make it not only a haven of refuge for the oppressed but also a center of Jewish culture and spiritual life.

Throughout the ages it has been Israel's mission to witness to the Divine in the face of every form of paganism and materialism. We regard it as our historic task to cooperate with all men in the establishment of the kingdom of God, of universal brotherhood, justice, truth and peace on earth. This is our Messianic goal.

From the Columbus Platform, May 27, 1937, a statement of principles adopted by Reform Jews supportive of Zionism, in Marcus, The Jew in the American World, *p. 437.*

My fellow Americans: Last night when I spoke with you about the fall of Rome, I knew at that moment that troops of the United States and our Allies were crossing the Channel in another and greater operation. It has come to pass to success thus far.

And so in this poignant hour, I ask you to join with me in prayer:

Almighty God: Our sons, pride of our nation, this day have set upon a mighty endeavor, a struggle to preserve our Republic, our religion, and our civilization and to set free a suffering humanity.

President Franklin Delano Roosevelt, June 6, 1944, radio broadcast to the nation on D-Day, the date of the Normandy invasion, in The Lustre of Our Country: The American Experience of Religious Freedom, *p. 213.*

So the problem of all spiritual life, no matter whether you are a Christian, a Buddhist or a Hindu, simply amounts to this: How can I kill the ego? And the answer given by every one of these religions is the same: Surrender yourself. Give yourself up to God, completely and wholeheartedly. Love God with all your heart, all your soul and all your mind. Become absorbed, and forget yourself in the consciousness of God. The ego is the only obstacle to God-consciousness.

. . . . .

It sounds so simple: to love God, to surrender ourselves to Him, to kill this ego. But it is the hardest thing one can possibly do. It involves great spiritual disciplines; and the practice of these disciplines with the utmost patience and perseverance. The mind is always straining to go outward, toward everything that seems pleasant in the external world. And the ego reasserts itself perpetually. However we may try to banish it, it keeps reappearing, as it were, in different disguises. So we have to keep on trying.

Swami Prabhavananda, founder of the Vedanta Society of Southern California, 1946, "Self Surrender," in Isherwood, Vedanta for the Western World, *pp. 419–420.*

The science of *Kriya Yoga* . . . became widely known in modern India through the instrumentality of Lahiri Mahasaya, my guru's guru. The Sanscrit root of *kriya* is *kri*, to do, to act and react; the same root is found in the word *karma*, the natural principle of cause and effect. *Kriya Yoga* is thus "union (*yoga*) with the Infinite through a certain action or rite (*kriya*)." A yogi who faithfully practices the technique is gradually freed from karma or the lawful chain of cause-effect equilibriums.

. . . . .

Kriya Yoga is a simple, psychophysiological method by which human blood is decarbonated and recharged with oxygen. The atoms of this extra oxygen are transmuted into life current to rejuvenate the brain and spinal centers. By stopping the accumulation of venous blood, the yogi is able to lessen or prevent the decay of tissues. The advanced yogi transmutes his cells into energy. Elijah, Jesus, Kabir, and other prophets were past master in the use of *Kriya* or a similar technique, by which they caused their bodies to materialize and dematerialize at will.

Indian guru Paramahansa Yogananda, 1946, Autobiography of a Yogi, *p. 275.*

The night before landing in Liverpool I awoke in my berth with a strange sense of trouble and sadness. As I lay wondering what it meant, I felt myself invaded by a Presence and held by Everlasting Arms. It was the most extraordinary experience I had ever had. But I had no intimation that anything was happening to Lowell [his only child, a boy of eleven]. When we landed in Liverpool a cable informed me that he was desperately ill, and a second cable, in answer to one from me, brought the dreadful news that he was gone.

Quaker scholar Rufus Jones, 1947, The Luminous Trail, *describing the death of an only child in 1903, quoted in* Trueblood, The People Called Quakers, *p. 218.*

The "establishment of religion" clause of the First Amendment means at least this: neither a state nor the Federal Government can set up a church. Neither can pass laws which aid one religion, aid all religions, or prefer one religion over another. Neither can force nor influence a person to go to or to remain away from church against his will or force him to profess a belief or disbelief in any religion. No person can be punished for entertaining or professing religious beliefs or disbeliefs, for church attendance or non-attendance. No tax in any amount, large or small, can be levied to support any religious activities or institutions, whatever they may be called, or whatever form they may adopt to teach or practice religion. Neither a state nor the Federal Government can, openly or secretly, participate in the affairs of any religious organizations or groups, and vice versa.

Associate Justice Hugo Black, U.S. Supreme Court, 1947, for the majority of the Court in Everson v. Board of Education, *330 U.S. 1, 16.*

I hear You saying to me:

"I will give you what you desire. I will lead you into solitude. I will lead you by the way that you cannot possibly understand, because I want it to be the quickest way.

"Therefore all the things around you will be armed against you, to deny you, to hurt you, to give you pain, and therefore to reduce you to solitude.

"Because of their enmity, you will soon be left alone. They will cast you out and forsake you and reject you and you will be alone.

"Everything that touches you will burn you, and you will draw your hand away in pain, until you have withdrawn yourself from all things. Then you will be all alone.

"Everything that can be desired will sear you, and brand you with a cautery, and you will fly from it in pain, to be alone. Every created joy will only come to you as pain, and you will die to all joy and be left alone. All the good things that other people love and desire and seek will come to you, but only as murderers to cut you off from the world and its occupations.

"You will be praised, and it will be like burning at the stake. You will be loved, and it will murder your heart and drive you into the desert.

"You will have gifts, and they will break you with their burden. You will have pleasures of prayer, and they will sicken you and you will fly from them.

"And when you have been praised a little and loved a little I will take away all your gifts and all your love and all your praise and you will be utterly forgotten and abandoned and you will be nothing, a dead thing, a rejection. And in that day you shall begin to possess the solitude you have so long desired. And your solitude will bear immense fruit in the souls of men you will never see on earth.

"Do not ask when it will be or where it will be or how it will be: On a mountain or in a prison, in a desert or in a concentration camp or in a hospital or at Gethsemani. It does not matter. So do not ask me, because I am not going to tell you. You will not know until you are in it.

"But you shall taste the true solitude of my anguish and my poverty and I shall lead you into the high places of my joy and you shall die in Me and find all things in My mercy which has created you for this end.

. . . . .

"That you may become the brother of God and learn to know the Christ of the burnt men."

Trappist monk Thomas Merton, 1948, concluding his autobiographical account, The Seven Storey Mountain, *pp. 472–473.*

Dear Fellow Worker in Christ: Unless the seed fall into the ground and die, itself remaineth alone. But if it die it bringeth forth much fruit. So I don't expect any success in anything we are trying to do, either in getting out a paper, running houses of hospitality or farming groups, or retreat houses on the land. I expect that everything we do will be attended with human conflicts, and the suffering that goes with it, and that this suffering will water the seed to make it grow in the future. I expect that all our natural love for each other which is so warming and so encouraging and so much a reward of this kind of work and living, will be killed, put to death painfully by gossip, intrigue, suspicion, distrust, etc., and that this painful dying to self and the longing for the love of others will be rewarded by a tremendous increase of supernatural love amongst us all. I expect the most dangerous of sins cropping up amongst us, whether of sensuality or pride it does not matter, but that the struggle will go on to such an extent that God will not let it hinder the work but that the work will go on, because that work is our suffering and our sanctification.

Dorothy Day, cofounder of the Catholic Worker movement, "Letter on Hospices" in The Catholic Worker, *January 1948. Available online at URL:* http://www.catholicworker. org/dorothyday/daytext.cfm?TextID=183. dorothydaydaytext.cfm?TextID=183&SearchTerm= philosophy. *Accessed on November 11, 2006.*

There are no substitutes in Jewish life for religion. Neither philanthropy nor culture nor nationalism is adequate for the stress and challenge of our lives. All these interests can and must find their rightful place within the general pattern of Judaism. But the pattern must be of Judaism, the Judaism of the priest, the prophet, the saint, the mystic and the rabbi; the Judaism which speaks of God and the worship of God, and the commandments of God and the quest for God.

Abba Hillel Silver, November 1948, address before the 1948 biennial assembly of the Union of American Hebrew Congregations in Boston, in Raider, et al., Abba Hillel Silver and American Zionism, *p. 6.*

O God, I have tasted Thy goodness, and it has both satisfied me and made me thirsty for more. I am painfully conscious of my need of further grace. I am ashamed of my lack of desire. O God, the Triune God, I want to want Thee; I long to be filled with longing; I thirst to be made more thirsty still. Show me Thy glory, I pray Thee, so that I may know Thee indeed. Begin in mercy a new work of love within me. Say to my soul, "Rise up, my love, my fair one, and come away." Then give me grace to rise and follow Thee up from this misty lowland where I have wandered so long. In Jesus' Name, Amen.

A. W. Tozer, a minister of the Christian and Missionary Alliance, 1948, The Pursuit of God, *in Lundin and Noll,* Voices from the Heart, *p. 300.*

CHAPTER THIRTEEN

Equality and Explorations
(1951–1979)

During the second half of the 20th century, the diversity characteristic of American religion since the colonial period had become increasingly prominent. New waves of immigration, prompted especially by changes to immigration law in 1965, imported the world's religions to America, making the appearance of Muslim mosques and Buddhist temples scarcely more remarkable in urban—and even suburban—centers of the United States than the presence of Methodist or Episcopalian churches. Even as some observers were predicting that secularism was crowding religious faith out of contemporary American life and some theologians mediated on the "death of God," these new arrivals added to a bustling religious scene in which faith was anything but in decline.

This energetic religious landscape did not mean that every variety of faith flourished. Mainline Protestant denominations continued a long decline in numbers that had been in process throughout most of the 20th century. Other groups, though—evangelical Protestants and Mormons in particular—experienced significant growth. Southern Baptists, Assemblies of God, and Pentecostal churches flourished. And less denominationally anchored "electric churches" led by television personalities such as Pat Robertson and Jim and Tammy Bakker created an environment in which faith often expressed itself in forms other than traditional religious community. Moreover, the charismatic movement, born out of the Pentecostalism of the early 20th century, swept into Protestant and Catholic churches, renovating worship and adding guitars and drums to the standard repertoire of church instruments. At the same time the century's most prominent revivalist, Billy Graham, launched a preaching career that made him the most recognized minister in America by the end of the 20th century.

Though evangelical Christian groups experienced the most significant growth during this period, mainline Protestants and Catholics did experience significant changes, even if their membership numbers did not swell alongside those of evangelicals. The mid-20th century marked the rise of the ecumenical movement as mainline denominations attempted to bridge the doctrinal differences that had historically divided them from one another through a variety of cooperative ventures. The ecumenical impulse gave birth not only to organizations such as the World Council of Churches and the National Council of Churches but to actual denominational

Jehovah's Witnesses sang at a convention in Chicago in 1973. *(National Archives NWDNS-412-DA-13789)*

mergers. For Catholics, the 1960s produced revisions of practice as a consequence of the ecumenical council called Vatican II, which was convened in that decade.

If revivalists such as Billy Graham emphasized the personal nature of religious faith, religion after the mid-point of the 20th century also could be found grappling with the social issues of America, none more prominent in this period than civil rights. The Civil Rights movement of the 1960s was partially inspired by the NAACP's landmark victory in *Brown v. Board of Education* (1954), in which the Supreme Court held that segregation in public schools violated the Constitution's equal protection clause. The movement found its most effective leader when Martin Luther King, Jr., recently installed as the pastor of the Dexter Avenue Baptist Church in Montgomery, Alabama, was elected president of the Montgomery Improvement Association, organized to boycott racially segregated buses in Montgomery. Beginning in Montgomery, King's nonviolent protests, anchored firmly in his religious faith, helped remake the face of American society.

A good deal of the history of the Civil Rights movement played out in public schools, where racial desegregation required by *Brown v. Board of Education* was at first frustrated and then gradually accomplished. But battles over the integration of schools were not the only significant conflict public education endured during this period. Two important Supreme Court decisions during the 1960s that prohibited government-sponsored prayer and Bible reading in schools had the effect of untangling the close relationship between religion and the public schools common since the previous century. These decisions made public schools more hospitable to the diversity of faiths that found residence there in the latter years of the 20th century, but they also contributed to a growing sense among conservative Christians that they could no longer avoid political engagement if they wished to preserve America as a "Christian nation." The school prayer decisions, when combined with the decision in *Roe v. Wade* (1973), striking down most of the nation's antiabortion laws, had the effect of energizing a new wave of conservative Christian involvement in politics that would bear fruit in the last two decades of the 20th century.

Religion and the Civil Rights Movement

In 1954 the U.S. Supreme Court, in *Brown v. Board of Education,* finally repudiated the legal doctrine of "separate but equal," which had provided constitutional shelter for racial segregation in America since the 19th century. This decision, resulting from legal strategy engineered by Thurgood Marshall and the National Association for the Advancement of Colored People (NAACP), served to ignite a broad movement to secure basic civil rights for African Americans. Among the many actors within this movement, none would play a more important or prominent role than black Christians, most notably Martin Luther King, Jr.

King came to national prominence as pastor of the Dexter Avenue Baptist Church in Montgomery, Alabama, after being elected president of the Montgomery Improvement Association when he was 26 years old. This association was organized in 1955 to oversee a boycott of the Montgomery bus system to protest Rosa Parks's arrest for refusing to surrender her bus seat to a white person. The ultimate success of the Montgomery boycott prompted King to establish the Southern Christian Leadership Conference in 1957, an organization of black Christian leaders devoted to the cause of securing civil rights for African Americans. In 1960 he joined his father as copastor of the Ebenezer Baptist Church in Atlanta, Georgia, though his continued work in the Civil Rights movement engaged far more of his time than this ecclesiastical post. This work reached its climax in 1963, when King helped organize civil rights demonstrations in Birmingham, Alabama. Arrested during the course of these demonstrations, King wrote his famous "Letter from a Birmingham Jail," addressed to white ministers who had opposed the demonstrations. That same year after his release from jail, King participated in the March on Washington and delivered from the steps of the Lincoln Memorial on August 28 his most famous speech, "I Have a Dream." "I have a dream," he proclaimed,

> that one day on the red hills of Georgia the sons of former slaves and the sons of former slaveowners will be able to sit down together at a table of brotherhood.

I have a dream that one day even the state of Mississippi, a desert state, sweltering with the heat of injustice and oppression, will be transformed into an oasis of freedom and justice.

I have a dream that my four children will one day live in a nation where they will not be judged by the color of their skin but by the content of their character. I have a dream today!

I have a dream that one day . . . right there in Alabama, little black boys and black girls will be able to join hands with little white boys and white girls and walk together as sisters and brothers.[1]

Though awarded the Nobel Peace Prize in 1964, King did not live to see his dream achieved. In 1968 while in Memphis, he was assassinated by James Earl Ray on April 4.

Martin Luther King, Jr., was awarded the Nobel Peace Prize in 1964 for his leadership in the Civil Rights movement. *(Library of Congress, Prints and Photographs Division LC-USZ62-122990)*

In this photograph a family signs the church registry at Chicago's Church of the Messiah after an infant baptism (1973). *(National Archives NWDNS-412-DA-13782)*

Martin Luther King, Jr.'s, leadership in the Civil Rights movement was firmly attached to his religious convictions, and these had been nurtured by reading modern theologians such as Reinhold Niebuhr and Paul Tillich and studying the example of the independence movement in India led by Mohandas Gandhi.[2] Though the Civil Rights movement had, of course, its secular activists who championed equality without reference to any religious underpinnings, King, like an Old Testament prophet, moored his nonviolent demands for equal rights in his faith that God was just and required justice. As he pressed forward against the racial discrimination that had entwined itself around the roots of American public life, he found allies who shared his religiously oriented opposition to segregation. Presbyterian minister Eugene Carson Blake, for example, one of the century's most prominent ecumenical leaders, stood on the podium in Washington, D.C., when King delivered his "I Have a Dream" speech. Blake's fierce opposition to racial discrimination saw him arrested for trying to integrate an amusement park in Baltimore, Maryland. Likewise, Jewish scholar Abraham Joshua Heschel joined King in civil rights protests conducted in Selma, Alabama, in 1965. The Selma protests also attracted the energies of a young black Baptist named Jesse Jackson, who had recently dropped out of the Chicago Theological Seminary, where he was studying to become a minister, to undertake work for the Southern Christian Leadership Conference. By the last decades of the 20th century, Jackson had clearly proven himself to be King's most visible successor as a civil rights leader.

Martin Luther King's nonviolent protests against racial discrimination also inspired religiously rooted opposition as well as support. Nation of Islam leader Malcolm X was himself deeply involved in civil rights activities during the late 1950s and early 1960s. But he saw nothing to praise in King's nonviolent approach to protest. Islam, he suggested, counseled more vigorous opposition to those who would deny blacks their civil rights.

There is nothing in our book, the Koran, that teaches us to suffer peacefully. Our religion teaches us to be intelligent. Be peaceful, be courteous, obey the law, respect everyone; but if someone puts his hand on you, send him to the cemetery. That's a good religion. In fact, that's that old-time religion. That's the one that Ma and Pa used to talk about: an eye for an eye, and a tooth for a tooth, and a head for a head, and a life for a life. That's a good religion. And nobody resents that kind of religion being taught but a wolf, who intends to make you his meal.[3]

Malcolm X was an important leader within the Nation of Islam until disagreements with Elijah Mohammad caused him to withdraw from the organization shortly before he was assassinated. *(Library of Congress, Prints and Photographs Division LC-USZ62-115058)*

Although Malcolm X attended the March on Washington in the summer of 1964, he called the event a "farce" and expressed little enthusiasm for the idea of participating in a demonstration in which whites played such a prominent part.

If Malcolm X represented religiously rooted impatience with King's nonviolent protests, Baptist minister Jerry Falwell expressed views common among fundamentalists when he suggested that ministers had no business pouring their energies into political protests. In a sermon delivered in 1965, he argued that Scripture provided no authorization for a general war against social wrongs. "We are not told to wage war against bootleggers, liquor stores, gamblers, murderers, prostitutes, racketeers, prejudiced persons or institutions, or any other existing evil as such." The role of preachers was one of "transformation" rather than "reformation." "The gospel," he declared, "does not clean up the outside but rather regenerates the inside."[4] At the time Falwell's resistance to the idea of religiously inspired social reform reflected a common position staked out by fundamentalists, who during much of the 20th century had treated the world as an alien place and had directed their attention toward creating relatively insular communities and institutions. But toward the end of the 1970s, Falwell himself underwent a transformation about the value of Christian participation in social reform. The fruit of this transformation was the Moral Majority, a conservative political action group organized by Falwell and sometimes credited with helping to elect Ronald Reagan president of the United States. As might be expected, Jerry Falwell's late 20th-century conversion to the cause of social reform tended to express itself through advocacy of politically conservative causes, such as opposition to abortion.

The movement for racial equality in America was accompanied by a corollary struggle for gender equality. Sparked especially by Betty Friedan's 1963 book *The Feminine Mystique*, the feminist movement warred against traditions that subordinated women in society, including in the nation's churches and synagogues. In the mainline churches especially, barriers to the ordination of women as ministers crumbled during the 1960s and 1970s, and in 1972 Sally Priesand was ordained a rabbi in the comparatively liberal Reform branch of American Judaism. Catholics and more conservative Protestants, however, resisted these developments in their churches and resisted, as well, some key aims of the feminist movement, such as ratification of the proposed Equal Rights Amendment to the U.S. Constitution. This amendment ultimately failed to be ratified by a sufficient number of states, and religious conservatives played a prominent role in the defeat of the proposed amendment.

The Ecumenical Movement

Though the ecumenical movement is generally thought of as a creature of the 20th century, it did not introduce the idea of ecclesiastical harmony. During the first half of the 19th century, the Second Great Awakening produced a general willingness on the part of evangelical Christians to work together in service of a variety of social reforms, creating a network of voluntary associations referred to as the Benevolent Empire. The modern international ecumenical movement had its origins in the early 20th century, when more than a thousand church leaders from around the world met in Edinburgh, Scotland, for the World Mission Conference, an event largely inspired by the vision of John R. Mott, whose long career as an ecumenical leader ultimately led to his receiving the Nobel Peace Prize in 1946 and being named the first honorary president of the World Council of Churches. Though not attended by Roman Catholic or Orthodox delegates, the conference nevertheless embraced a vast array of Christian denominations brought together to achieve "the evangelization of the world in this generation." Even before this event, mainline Protestant churches in the United States had joined cooperatively together to form the Federal Council of Churches in 1908. This spirit of cooperation owed much to the general temper of the Social Gospel movement, which saw the work of social reform as sufficiently important to justify ecumenical harmony. The impulse toward ecumenical cooperation was not peculiar to the liberal Protestants who inhabited the mainline denominations: evangelical Protestants also saw the benefit of collective action and formed the National Association of Evangelicals in 1942. But ecumenism became a defining characteristic of mainstream Protestants during the middle decades of the 20th century. The international expression of this impulse created the World Council of Churches in 1948, soon followed by the formation of the National Council of Churches in 1950.

These interfaith cooperative ventures, however, did not exhaust the sum of ecumenical energy during the 20th century. Even more aggressive plans to heal the fractures long characteristic of Protestantism came to prominence in the middle decades of the century. As early as 1931 Congregationalists had united with the Christian Church to form the Congregational Christian Churches. Unitarians and Universalists agreed to merge in 1961. Moreover, some of the splinters occasioned by the Civil War were finally healed when, for example, northern and southern Methodists reunited in 1939 and Presbyterians in 1983. But the most far-reaching plan for ecclesiastical merger took the form of the Consultation on Church Union, which began meeting in 1960. Nine denominations began a long attempt to find a basis for ecclesiastical union: the African Methodist Episcopal Church, African Methodist Episcopal Zion Church, Christian Church-Disciples of Christ, Christian Methodist Episcopal Church, Episcopal Church, International Council of Community Churches, Presbyterian Church (USA), United Church of Christ, and United Methodist Church. In spite of strenuous efforts to find a pathway to unity, however, by the late 1980s the participating denominations had reduced their sights to working toward a "covenant communion" that would allow for some shared practices and traditions but generally leave each denomination to conducts its own internal affairs. By the beginning of the 21st century, the consultation continued to press forward without a clear sign that unity among the several participant denominations would be shortly forthcoming.

Religion and Public Schools

The First Amendment of the Constitution prohibits Congress from making laws "respecting an establishment of religion or abridging the free exercise thereof." By its terms the amendment did not originally apply to the actions of state or local governments that threatened religious liberty or amounted to a religious establishment. After the Civil War, however, the nation adopted the Fourteenth Amendment to the Constitution, which bars state and local governments from depriving individuals of "life, liberty, or property" without "due process of law." The Supreme Court eventually construed this provision to protect certain fundamental rights, including the rights safeguarded by the First Amendment. During the 1940s, accordingly, the Court ruled that states could neither abridge religious free exercise nor pass laws "respecting an establishment of religion." Since public schools are regulated primarily by state and local laws, this ruling placed the Court at the center of controversies relating to religion and education, one of the 20th century's most volatile issues. Two subjects, especially, dominated the Court's attention: the constitutionality of various religious practices, such as prayer and Bible readings in the public schools, and the constitutionality of government aid to private religious schools.

In its earliest encounters with these subjects, the Court adopted Thomas Jefferson's reference to a "wall of separation between church and state" as a guiding metaphor for interpreting the meaning of the First Amendment's establishment clause.[5] Applying this metaphor, the Court invalidated most forms of direct aid to religious institutions such as parochial schools, finding that this aid amounted to a breach in the so-called wall of separation. At the time when the Court began to strike down this aid in the 1960s and 1970s, these decisions impacted Catholics most, since the majority of private religious schools were Catholic. Protestants, accordingly, did not generally object to the Court's early school aid cases. More controversial, however, were decisions of the Court declaring unconstitutional official prayers in public schools. In *Engel v. Vitale* (1962) the Court struck down daily recitations of a prayer composed by New York school authorities for public schools in that state, and in *Abington v. Schempp* (1963), the Court added daily recitations of the Lord's Prayer and daily Bible readings to the list of activities prohibited by the establishment clause. In subsequent cases the Court demonstrated an almost implacable hostility to state-sponsored forms of public religiosity and religious teaching in public schools. Thus, the Court struck down laws requiring the posting of the Ten Commandments in public schools in *Stone v. Graham* (1980) and providing for a moment of silence for prayer in *Wallace v. Jaffree* (1985). In *Jaffree*, although a majority of the justices indicated that they might approve moment-of-silence laws in some circumstances, they concluded that the Alabama statute at issue had been passed with the impermissible purpose of returning prayer to school. Moreover, in *Lee v. Weisman* (1992) the Court held unconstitutional prayers offered by a Jewish rabbi at a middle school graduation ceremony. And subsequently, in *Santa Fe Independent School District v. Doe* (2000), the Court invalidated a school district's policy of allowing students to vote on whether to have an "invocation" at football games and on who would deliver the invocation. Earlier, in *Edwards v. Aguillard* (1987), the Court had struck down a Louisiana statute that required schools to balance the teaching of evolution with the teaching of creation science—a view of the world's origins that emphasizes the role of a divine Creator.

The Prominence of Pluralism

America has never been religiously homogeneous. It has had its dominant religious traditions, to be sure. The various forms of Protestant Christianity have enjoyed the greatest number of adherents throughout the nation's history. Even this label, though, suggests a monolithic reality that has not ever existed, since Protestantism has flowered in multitudinous forms on American soil. But alongside the many varieties of Protestantism, other faiths have flourished as well, from the numerous American Indian religious traditions that existed on the continent even before the first European explorers arrived, to Jewish and Catholic traditions that stretch back to the country's colonial period, to the Islam and Eastern religious traditions imported in significant numbers beginning in the 20th century.

Immigrants in the 19th century vastly increased the measure of America's religious diversity. Catholic arrivals, especially, made it less plausible to refer to the United States as a Protestant nation, but these were supplemented by immigrants who practiced other faiths as well. Restrictive immigration policies adopted toward the end of the 19th century, however, stifled this fertile source of pluralism. But in 1965 important changes to immigration law revived the migration of other religious faiths to American soil, including Islam, Buddhism, Hinduism, Confucianism, and other world religions. Moreover, alongside the increasing presence in America of representatives of the world's main religious traditions, new religious movements became prominent as well, often imported from other areas of the world. In 1965, for example, A. C. Bhaktivedanta Swami Prabhupāda (born Abhay Charan De) immigrated to the United States and the following year founded the International Society for Krishna Consciousness (ISKCON). ISKCON popularized a form of Hinduism characterized by devotion to the Hindu god Vishnu and his incarnation Krishna. Also during the 1960s, the United States received the first missionaries dispatched by the Holy Spirit Association for the Unification of World Christianity, commonly referred to as the Unification Church, established by Sun Myung Moon in Seoul, Korea, in 1954. Moon taught that the human race had been corrupted by the sexual seduction of Eve by Satan in the Garden of Eden. Christ had brought spiritual redemption to the world, but physical redemption awaited a new messiah, which Moon claimed to be, who would find a perfect wife and produce sinless children. The Unification Church earned a controversial reputation in the United States, frequently being labeled a cult and accused of brainwashing young followers. Moon himself spent significant time in America and even spent time in prison after being convicted of tax evasion in the early 1980s.

Evangelical Influence

Since the Great Awakening in the early 18th century, Protestant evangelicalism has been a major component of the American religious experience. During the second half of the 20th century, it continued to hold a prominent place in American life. Evangelical faith continued its long familiar alliance with revivalism, most prominently exemplified by the career of Billy Graham. Before the century ended he had preached to an estimated 200 million people. Evangelicalism also assumed new forms such as the "electric" church, that is, the proliferation of radio and television programming that acted as surrogates for or supplements to more traditional forms of communal religious experience. Finally, one important tributary of evangelical Christian faith, Pentecostalism, surged into the mainstream of American religious experience by way of the charismatic movement. In 1976 born-again evangelical Jimmy Carter was elected president of the United States, prompting *Newsweek* magazine to announce "the year of the evangelical."

Although Billy Graham was ordained a Southern Baptist minister on the eve of World War II, like many prominent American revivalists he came to articulate a religious message unmoored from any particular denominational theology. Soon after the end of World War II, he began a career as an evangelist, preaching initially in meetings sponsored by Youth for Christ and subsequently as an independent revivalist. In 1949 he came to national prominence after his revival campaign in Los Angeles was extended from three to eight weeks. Graham followed this success with activity via a wide range of communications media, including a radio program

Jimmy Carter and Rosalynn Carter sang with Martin Luther King, Sr., Coretta Scott King, Andrew Young, and others during a visit to Atlanta's Ebenezer Baptist Church in 1979. *(Jimmy Carter Library NLC 08963.19)*

established in 1950 called the *Hour of Decision,* a religious film company—World Wide Pictures—which released its first feature film, *Mr. Texas,* in 1951, and an evangelical magazine founded in 1955 called *Christianity Today.* Over the coming decades Graham carried his evangelistic crusades to one after another major U.S. city and to every continent but Antarctica. His influence reached even into the White House, as Truman and successive American presidents invited him to visit regularly. Although steeped in conservative evangelical faith, Graham generally managed to escape the shrill tone that sometimes characterized other conservative preachers of the 20th century's second half.

Billy Graham brought his revival message to audiences measured in the hundreds of millions through more than a half century of crusades. Even as he did, however, other preachers discovered the power of radio and television programming to reach immeasurably more viewers than could be assembled in any single physical venue. Evangelicals were not alone in appreciating the uses of communications technology. Father Charles Coughlin's radio program, *The Golden Hour of the Little Flower,* was broadcast by CBS beginning in 1930. The same year Bishop Fulton Sheen launched a radio program called the *Catholic Hour,* and Sheen earned national recognition over the following years as a leading 20th-century apologist for Catholicism. With the advent of television Sheen hosted a program called *Life Is Worth Living* from 1951 to 1957, and still later, *The Bishop Sheen Program* from 1961 to 1968. It was evangelicals, however, who dominated radio and even more so television programming.[6] In the first half of the 20th century, revivalists such as Aimee Semple McPherson, who established the city's third radio station in 1924 at her Angelus Temple in Los Angeles, were quick to recognize radio's potential for spreading the gospel message.[7] The following decade evangelist Charles Fuller popularized the *Old Fashioned Revival Hour*, the most widely listened to radio program of all time. But the second half of the 20th century was increasingly dominated by television programming. Pat Robertson's *700 Club* and Jerry Falwell's *Old Time Gospel Hour* reached millions of viewers and by the end of the century provided these men with influence that they attempted to turn to political purposes, Falwell by founding the Moral Majority and Robertson by establishing the Christian Coali-

Billy Graham, the most famous evangelist of the 20th century who was also a confidant of presidents, including Richard Nixon, is pictured here. *(National Archives NLNP-WHPO-MPF-C3587(04))*

This photograph shows members of the Church of God in Christ in North Las Vegas participating in a baptism ceremony in 1972. *(National Archives NWDNS-412-DA-6503)*

tion and seeking unsuccessfully to obtain the Republican nomination for president of the United States.

One early 20th century fruit of evangelical religion was the Pentecostal movement, which emphasized the contemporary relevance of miraculous spiritual gifts such as speaking in tongues and healing. This influential movement then settled into a fairly narrow segment of Protestant Christian experience. Beginning in the 1960s, however, the Pentecostal impulse escaped into the broader current of American Christianity through what came to be known as the charismatic movement. Prominent Episcopalian minister Dennis J. Bennett shocked many members of his congregation when he announced in April 1960 his own charismatic experience of being "baptized in the Spirit" and speaking in tongues. His subsequent book, *Nine O'Clock in the Morning,* became an important testament of the charismatic movement.[8] Though the movement's roots lay securely in the Protestant evangelical tradition, it reached even into the experience of American Catholics. Professors at Duquesne University in Pittsburgh launched a series of prayer meetings that sparked charismatic experiences. Notre Dame hosted an annual series of conferences in the 1970s called the National Conference on Charismatic Renewal in the Catholic Church.

American Catholicism and Vatican II

After Angelo Giuseppe Roncalli became Pope John XXIII in 1958, one of his first important acts was to summon a general council of the Catholic Church, known as the Second Vatican Council or Vatican II, the first session of which began in October 1962. Pope John XXIII did not live to see the end result of the council, and another pope, Paul VI, presided over the council's conclusion. Vatican II's greatest impact on American religious life resulted from the renovations in Catholic liturgy it inspired. Prior to the council the celebration of Mass was an essentially solitary ritual performed by a priest speaking in Latin with his back turned to parishioners. After Vatican II Mass in America was generally conducted in English—except in parishes that balked at the council's reforms—in ways that made parishioners more active spectators. Church services increasingly included greater lay participation and often even collaboration in the planning of worship.

Vatican II also inaugurated new attitudes about the relationship between Catholics and other Christians as well as between Catholics and Jews and other non-Christian religious traditions. One consequence of the ecumenical temper that flourished in the second half of the 20th century was the more cordial spirit that came to exist between American Protestants and Catholics. By 1960 a Catholic candidate, John F. Kennedy, was elected president of the United States. Along the way he had to assure voters that he would not be a tool for the implementation of Vatican policy on American soil. Vatican II also resulted in a revision of earlier Catholic doctrine dealing with the appropriate relationship between church and state. The fears that John F. Kennedy tried to allay about the influence of the Vatican on American government were he to be elected president could reasonably be traced at least partially to the Vatican's own stance toward church-state relations. Catholic doctrine prior to the 1960s had generally taken the stance that the best form of government was one in which the Catholic Church was established by law as a nation's religion. Catholics, however, recognized that in the United States and elsewhere they were not always in the majority. Consequently, they admitted that forms of church-state separation such as were exhibited in the United States might be appropriate where Catholics lacked the political power to secure a first place for Catholicism. Thus, prior to the council Catholic teaching had generally treated religious pluralism and religious liberty as regrettable facts necessarily endured in countries where Catholics were not a majority, but not otherwise appreciated. An American Jesuit, John Courtney Murray, contested this view, however, arguing that religious liberty was valuable in and of itself, even in circumstances under which Catholics might have the political strength to make theirs the official established faith. In the years before Vatican II, Murray endured the disapproval of authorities in Rome, but after the start of the council in 1962, Cardinal Francis Spellman persuaded Murray to serve as an expert on church-state relations for the U.S. delegation to the council. In this capacity Murray eventually was able to influence the content of the council's final statement concerning religious liberty, *Dignitatis humanae personae*. Vatican II also brought about changes in Catholic teachings about Jews. Partially as a result of work by Jewish theologian Abraham Heschel behind the scenes, the council eventually produced a statement concerning non-Christian religions, known as *Nostra Aetate*, that prodded the church to begin eliminating anti-Semitic references in liturgical and educational materials.

Such revisions in church practice as grew out of Vatican II did not extend to wholesale reconsideration of Catholic doctrine. Revisions concerning the church's understanding of religious liberty were significant, but in other areas Catholic doctrine remained unchanged. One of the most controversial issues of the 1960s involved birth control. Pope John XXIII appointed a commission to study the issue

President Richard Nixon met Pope Paul VI at the Vatican in 1970. *(National Archives NLNP-WHPO-MPF-C4584(14))*

of birth control, but his successor, Pope Paul VI, issued an encyclical in 1968 called *Humanae Vitae* that reaffirmed the prohibition against the use of artificial forms of birth control. Surveys of American Catholic opinion in the following decade demonstrated that nearly 90 percent of the Catholic laity rejected this teaching.[9]

In spite of Vatican II's attempt to revitalize faith and practice—some conservative Catholics disgruntled by new innovations would say *because of* this attempt—the late 1960s witnessed the beginning of a decline in the numbers of priests and members of religious orders. From 1966 to 1969 more than 3,000 priests left the ministry, and from 1966 to the beginning of the 1980s the number of women in Catholic religious orders in the United States declined by some 30 percent.[10] The church's continued requirement of celibacy for priests and members of religious orders accounted for some of the departures. But whatever the reasons for the decline, it created an urgent need for greater lay participation in Catholic affairs, a participation fully within the spirit of Vatican II itself. In fact, the increasingly prominent role of the laity in the Catholic Church would be a major feature of American Catholic experience in the last decades of the 20th century.

Chronicle of Events

1951

- Catholic bishop Fulton John Sheen begins hosting the television program *Life Is Worth Living* and will subsequently host *The Bishop Sheen Program.*
- William F. Buckley, a Catholic and a conservative commentator, publishes *God and Man at Yale.*
- Campus Crusade for Christ is founded by William R. (Bill) Bright on the campus of the University of California, Los Angeles (UCLA).
- Canadian law is amended to remove restrictions on certain Native American religious practices.
- Paul Tillich publishes the first of three volumes of his *Systematic Theology.*

1952

- L. Ron Hubbard founds the Hubbard Association of Scientologists International; two years later the Church of Scientology is formed in Los Angeles, California.
- The Federation of Islamic Organizations is organized.
- An Islamic center is built in Washington, D.C.
- Malcolm Little is paroled, and upon his release from prison he changes his name to Malcolm X and becomes a minister for the Nation of Islam.
- Methodist minister Norman Vincent Peale publishes *The Power of Positive Thinking.*
- The Federation of Islamic Associations of America is established.
- *April 28:* In *Zorach v. Clauson* the U.S. Supreme Court holds that a program that releases public school children from school to attend religious classes does not violate the establishment clause of the First Amendment.

1954

- Martin Luther King, Jr., becomes pastor of the Dexter Avenue Baptist Church in Montgomery, Alabama.
- Congress adds the phrase *under God* to the Pledge of Allegiance.
- Sun Myung Moon founds the Holy Spirit Association for the Unification of World Christianity (the Unification Church) in South Korea.

1955

- Louis Abdul Farrakhan joins the Nation of Islam.
- *Christianity Today* begins publication.
- Will Herberg publishes his influential study of American religion, *Protestant-Catholic-Jew.*

- The Committee on Jewish Law and Standards of the Rabbinical Assembly approves the calling of women to the Torah (aliyot).
- The congregation initially known as Community Unity changes its name to Peoples Temple Full Gospel Church. Jim Jones will subsequently lead a number of the church's members to commit mass suicide in Guyana on November 18, 1978.
- *December 1:* Rosa Parks is arrested after refusing to surrender her seat on a Montgomery, Alabama, bus to a white man.
- *December 5:* African-American clergy in Montgomery form the Montgomery Improvement Association and elect Martin Luther King, Jr., the pastor of Dexter Avenue Baptist Church, its president.

1956

- Jerry Falwell founds the Thomas Road Baptist Church in Lynchburg, Virginia, and begins broadcasting a radio program called *The Old-Time Gospel Hour.*

1957

- An estimated 2 million people attend Billy Graham's 16-week evangelistic crusade in Madison Square Garden in New York City.
- Martin Luther King, Jr., organizes the Southern Christian Leadership Conference and serves as its first president.
- Buddhist teacher Daisetz Teitaro Suzuki joins the faculty of Columbia University, where he influences such figures as psychoanalyst Erich Fromm, poet Allen Ginsberg, and composer John Cage.
- *June 25:* The Congregational Christian Church and the Evangelical and Reformed Church merge, creating the United Church of Christ.

1958

- Jack Kerouac publishes *Dharma Bums.*
- *October 28:* Angelo Giuseppe Roncalli is elected Pope John XXIII.

1959

- Young Oon Kim becomes the first missionary of the Unification Church to the United States and settles in Eugene, Oregon.
- Maharishi Mahesh Yogi introduces Transcendental Meditation to America.
- The Presbyterian Church (USA) and the United Presbyterian Church of North America unite to form the

United Presbyterian Church (USA), the largest Presbyterian denomination in the United States.

- Alan Watts publishes *Beat Zen, Square Zen, and Zen,* which chastises those who had toyed with Zen Buddhism rather than struggling to absorb its teachings.

1960

- Martin Luther King, Jr., leaves the Dexter Avenue Baptist Church in Montgomery, Alabama, and joins his father as copastor of the Ebenezer Baptist Church in Atlanta, Georgia.
- John F. Kennedy is elected the first Catholic president of the United States.
- The Christian Broadcasting Network, established and operated by Pat Robertson, is founded and will begin broadcasting in 1961.
- Reform Judaism establishes the Religious Action Center in Washington, D.C., to advocate the cause of social justice and religious liberty.
- *December 8, 1960:* Madalyn Murray (later O'Hair) files suit in Baltimore to force the end of required Bible readings and recitations of the Lord's Prayer in public schools.

1961

- *Black Elk Speaks,* originally published by John G. Neihardt in 1932, is re-released in paperback and helps to renew interest in American Indian religion.
- Malcolm X begins publishing the newspaper, *Muhammad Speaks.*
- Unitarians and Universalists in the United States merge to form the Unitarian-Universalist Association.
- Shunryu Suzuki-roshi establishes the San Francisco Zen Center.
- *June 19:* In *Torcaso v. Watkins* the U.S. Supreme Court holds that a Maryland constitutional provision requiring public officials—including notaries public—to declare their belief in the existence of God is an unconstitutional violation of religious freedom.

1962

- *Time* magazine designates Pope John XXIII Man of the Year.
- The Consultation of Church Union is established to investigate a possible ecumenical union among American Methodist, Episcopal, United Presbyterian, United Church of Christ, and other denominations.
- *June 25:* In *Engel v. Vitale* the U.S. Supreme Court holds unconstitutional the practice of having New York pub-

lic school children begin the day by reciting a prayer composed by the state board of education.

- *October 11:* The first session of the Second Vatican Council (Vatican II) begins. The Council will end in 1965.

1963

- Martin Luther King, Jr., leads civil rights demonstrations in Birmingham, Alabama, where he is arrested and writes "Letter from a Birmingham Jail."
- The Evangelical Friends Alliance (later Evangelical Friends International) is formed.
- Betty Friedan publishes *The Feminine Mystique,* which launches the modern feminist movement.
- The Muslim Students' Association of the United States and Canada is founded.
- Witness Lee, the brother of Local Church movement founder Watchman Nee, immigrates to the United States and settles in Anaheim, California, where the movement is launched in America.
- *June 17:* In *Abington Township v. Schempp* the U.S. Supreme Court declares unconstitutional the practice of having public school children listen to Bible readings and recite prayers at the beginning of the school day.
- *June 17:* In *Sherbert v. Verner* the U.S. Supreme Court rules that religious believers who are burdened by legal requirements are generally entitled to an exemption from those requirements unless government has compelling justification for denying the exemption.
- *August 28:* Martin Luther King, Jr., participates in the March on Washington and delivers his "I Have a Dream" speech.

Members of the Church of the Saviour participate in the March on Washington on August 28, 1963. *(National Archives NWDNS-306-SSM-4C(48)13)*

- *September 15:* A bomb explodes in the basement of the Sixteenth Street Baptist Church in Birmingham, Alabama, killing four black children.

1964
- Malcolm X leaves the Nation of Islam following conflicts with Elijah Muhammad and organizes Muslim Mosque, Inc. He makes a pilgrimage to Mecca and on his return to the United States changes his name to el-Hajj Malik el-Shabazz.
- Congress passes the 1964 Civil Rights Act, which includes among its provisions prohibitions against certain forms of religious discrimination.
- Martin Luther King, Jr., receives the Nobel Peace Prize.
- Robert Thurman is the first American to be ordained a Tibetan Buddhist monk.
- The Catholic Traditionalist Movement is founded in response to Vatican II.
- The San Francisco Council on Religion and Homosexuality is organized.

1965
- Pope Paul VI visits the United Nations in New York.
- Chuck Smith becomes the minister of Calvary Chapel in Costa Mesa, California, and under his leadership the church grows exponentially and ultimately becomes the parent church for numerous new congregations modeled after it.
- *February 21:* Malcolm X is assassinated by three Black Muslims while speaking to an audience in Harlem, New York City.
- *July 4:* President Lyndon Baines Johnson signs the 1965 Immigration and Naturalization act into law; the act's easing of previous immigration restrictions increases the flow of immigrants and their various religious traditions into the United States.
- *October 28:* Pope Paul VI promulgates *Nostra Aetate,* a statement concerning the relation between the Catholic Church and non-Christian religions, which includes a condemnation of anti-Semitism.

1966
- A. C. Bhaktivedanta Swami Prabhupāda (born Abhay Charan De) at 70 founds the International Society for Krishna Consciousness after arriving in the United States the previous year.
- The American Bible Society publishes a paraphrase of the New Testament called *Good News for Modern Man.*

- The cover of *Time* magazine asks "Is God Dead?"
- Anton Szandor Lavey founds the Church of Satan.

1968
- The Beatles visit India and study meditation there, and *Life* magazine announces 1968 the Year of the Guru.
- Reverend Troy Perry founds the Universal Fellowship of Metropolitan Community Churches in Los Angeles, a denomination for gay ministers and church members.
- The Islamic Circle of North America is established.
- David Brandt Berg (also known as Moses David or Mo) founds the Children of God (the Family).
- The lay Catholic organization Catholics United for Faith is established in St. Paul, Minnesota, to oppose the spread of pluralism within the Catholic Church.
- The encyclical *Humanae Vitae,* issued by Pope Paul VI, prohibits Catholics from using birth control. A number of Catholic leaders publish a dissent to this encyclical in the *New York Times.*
- *April 4:* Martin Luther King, Jr., is assassinated by James Earl Ray in Memphis, Tennessee.
- *May:* Catholic priests Daniel and Philip Berrigan, along with other Catholic activists, seize draft records of a Maryland draft board and burn them publicly.
- *November 12:* In *Epperson v. Arkansas* the U.S. Supreme Court holds that a state law prohibiting the teaching of evolution violates the first amendment's establishment clause.

1969
- The popular Catholic writer Thomas Merton dies from accidental electrocution while attending a conference in Thailand.
- The Krishnamurti Foundation of America is established.
- Sister M. Martin de Porres Grey leads in organizing the National Black Sisters' Conference.
- The Roman Catholic Church in America appoints its first Hispanic bishop, Patricio F. Flores.
- Union Theological Seminary professor James H. Cone publishes *Black Theology and Black Power.*
- Anton Szandor Lavey publishes *The Satanic Bible.*
- *May 4:* Civil rights leader James Forman interrupts Communion at Riverside Church in New York City to present *The Black Manifesto.* The manifesto demands reparations of $500 million from white churches and synagogues for their role in supporting slavery.

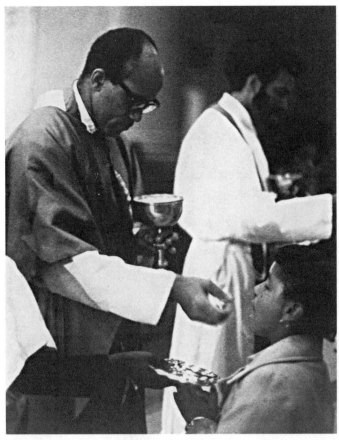

The priest in this photograph administers mass in Holy Angel Catholic Church on Chicago's south side. *(National Archives NWDNS-412-DA-13784)*

1970

- The organization Jews for Jesus originates in San Francisco.
- Hal Lindsey publishes *The Late, Great Planet Earth,* a best-selling novel which popularizes premillennialist theology, depicting the world as on the verge of the end times in which the forces of the Antichrist will war against the forces of God.

1971

- Jesse Jackson founds Operation PUSH (People United to Serve Humanity).
- The Bawa Muhaiyaddeen Fellowship is founded in Philadelphia.
- The Jesus People movement begins about this time.
- George Harrison's song "My Sweet Lord," which includes the lyrics "Hare Krishna, Hare Rama," becomes popular.
- Teenaged guru Maharaj Ji (Prem Pal Singh Rawat) introduces the Divine Light Mission (subsequently named Elan Vital) to the United States.

- *June:* The cover of *Time* magazine headlines the Jesus Revolution.
- *June 28:* In *Lemon v. Kurtzman* the U.S. Supreme Court declares that the First Amendment's establishment clause bars government from enacting laws that do not have a secular purpose and a secular effect or that amount to an excessive entanglement between government and religion.

1972

- In *Wisconsin v. Yoder* the U.S. Supreme Court holds that the free exercise clause of the First Amendment prevents a state from forcing Amish children to attend school after the eighth grade.
- Sally J. Priesand is ordained by Hebrew Union College the first woman rabbi.
- John Africa (born Vincent Leaphart) founds the American Christian Movement for Life, later known simply as MOVE, in Philadelphia.
- The Council of Muslim Communities in Canada is founded.

1973

- The Presbyterian Church in America (PCA) is formed as a more theologically conservative alternative to mainline Presbyterian denominations in the North and South.
- The U.S. Supreme Court's decision in *Roe v. Wade* recognizes the right to an abortion and is opposed by many Catholics. Although many conservative Protestants do not initially oppose the decision, subsequently opposition to abortion will galvanize many evangelical

This photograph shows worshippers gathered at Holy Angel Catholic Church on Chicago's South Side (1973). *(National Archive NWDNS-412-DA-13787)*

During the fuel crisis of 1973–74, abandoned gasoline stations sometimes became religious meeting places, as illustrated by this station in Potlatch, Washington. *(National Archives NWDNS-412-DA-13061)*

and fundamentalist Christians and prompt them to become more involved in political activity.

- Rousas John Rushdoony publishes *Institutes of Biblical Religion*, a key text for Christian Reconstructionists, who advocate the application of Biblical law to the entire range of social activities.

1974

- Robert Pirsig publishes *Zen and the Art of Motorcycle Maintenance.*
- Ted Patrick establishes the Citizens' Freedom Foundation (later named the Cult Awareness Network) to promote the idea of deprogramming the members of cults.

1975

- Sociologist Peter L. Berger, Lutheran pastor Richard J. Neuhaus, and other theologians adopt the Hartford Affirmation, which seeks a "renewal of Christian witness and mission."
- Nation of Islam leader Elijah Muhammad dies and is succeeded by his son, Wallace D. Muhammad. Wallace Muhammad steers the Nation of Islam toward a more mainstream version of Sunni Islam and in 1985 disbands what is left of the organization he inherited from his father. Prior to this, however, in the late 1970s Louis Farrakhan reinvigorates a separate version of the Nation of Islam organization more consistent with Elijah Muhammad's teaching.

- Elizabeth Bayley Seton becomes the first native-born American to be canonized by the Roman Catholic Church as a saint.
- Willow Creek Community Church, a forerunner to today's megachurches, is established outside of Chicago by Reverend Bill Hybels.

1976

- After a Gallup poll announces that half of American Protestants claim to be born again or to have made or accepted Jesus as their personal savior, *Newsweek* declares this to be the Year of the Evangelical.
- Jimmy Carter, a self-proclaimed evangelical Christian, is elected president of the United States.
- The Episcopal Church approves the ordination of women as priests.

- Many Roman Catholic women organize the Women's Ordination Conference and protest the Roman Catholic Church's refusal to ordain women as priests, a position that will be confirmed the following year when the Vatican releases its *Declaration on the Question of the Admission of Women to the Ministerial Priesthood.*

1977

- James Dobson establishes Focus on the Family, a conservative Christian organization.

A Nation of Islam audience listened to Elijah Muhammad's annual Savior's Day message in Chicago in 1974. *(National Archives NWDNS-412-DA-13792)*

1978

- The Congress of National Black Churches is organized.
- Spencer Woolley Kimball, president of the Church of Jesus Christ of Latter-day Saints, announces a new revelation that ends the Mormon Church's refusal to admit blacks to the Mormon priesthood and to temple ordinances.
- Congress enacts the American Indian Religious Freedom Act.
- *November 18:* Jim Jones, founder of the People's Temple, after relocating to Guyana the previous year, persuades 913 members of the temple to commit mass suicide.

1979

- Jerry Falwell forms the Moral Majority to influence the presidential election scheduled for the following year.
- Concerned Women of America, a conservative religious organization, is founded by Beverly LaHaye.
- Pope John Paul II becomes the first Catholic pontiff to visit America's capital.
- The Messianic Jewish Alliance of America, whose members believe that Jesus of Nazareth is the messiah, is founded.
- A majority of the faculty of Jewish Theological Seminary in New York City vote against ordaining women.
- The general convention of the Episcopal Church passes a resolution opposing openly gay priests.

Eyewitness Testimony

Ultimate concern is the abstract translation of the great commandment: "The Lord, our God, the Lord is one; and you shall love the Lord your God with all your heart, and with all your soul and with all your mind, and with all your strength." The religious concern is ultimate; it excludes all other concerns from ultimate significance; it makes them preliminary. The ultimate concern is unconditional, independent of any conditions of character, desire, or circumstance. The unconditional concern is total: no part of ourselves or of our world is excluded from it; there is no "place" to flee from it. The total concern is infinite: no moment of relaxation and rest is possible in the face of a religious concern which is ultimate, unconditional, total, and infinite.

The word "concern" points to the "existential" character of religious experience. We cannot speak adequately of the "object of religion" without simultaneously removing its character as an object. That which is ultimate gives itself only to the attitude of ultimate concern. It is the correlate of an unconditional concern but not a "highest thing" called "the absolute" or "the unconditioned," about which we could argue in detached objectivity. It is the object of total surrender, demanding also the surrender of our subjectivity while we look at it. It is a matter of infinite passion and interest (Kierkegaard), making us its object whenever we try to make it our object.

Theologian Paul Tillich, 1951, Systematic Theology, *vol. 1, pp. 11–12.*

I walked out to the hill just now. It is exalting, delicious. To stand embraced by the shadows of a friendly tree with the wind tugging at your coattail and the heavens hailing your heart, to gaze and glory and give oneself again to God, what more could a man ask? Oh the fullness, pleasure, sheer excitement of knowing God on earth. I care not if I never raise my voice again for Him, if only I may love Him, please Him. Mayhap in mercy, He shall give me a host of children that I may lead them through the vast star fields to explore His delicacies whose fingers' ends set them to burning. But if not, if only I may see Him, smell His garments and smile into my Lover's eyes; ah, then, not stars, nor children, shall matter, only Himself.

Jim Elliot, January 16, 1951, subsequently killed while serving as a missionary for Wycliffe Bible Translators in Ecuador, The Journals of Jim Elliot, *p. 309.*

Personally, I believe that prayer is a sending out of vibrations from one person to another and to God. All of the universe is in vibration. There are vibrations in the molecules of a table. The air is filled with vibrations. The reaction between human beings is also in vibration. When you send out a prayer for another person, you employ the force inherent in a spiritual universe. You transport from yourself to the other person a sense of love, helpfulness, support—a sympathetic, powerful understanding—and in this process you awaken vibrations in the universe through which God brings to pass the good objectives prayed for. Experiment with this principle and you will know its amazing results.

For example, I have a habit, which I often use, of praying for people as I pass them. I remember being on a train traveling through West Virginia when I had a curious thought. I saw a man standing on a station platform, then the train moved on and he passed from sight. It occurred to me that I was seeing him for the first and last time. His life and mine touched lightly for just a fraction of an instant. He went his way and I went mine. I wondered how his life would turn out.

Then I prayed for that man, sending out an affirmative prayer that his life would be filled with blessings. Then I began praying for other people I saw as the train passed.

Methodist and Reformed Minister Norman Vincent Peale, 1952, The Power of Positive Thinking, *pp. 53–54.*

When I declare, "I believe in God, the Father Almighty," I affirm the theistic faith and strike at the fundamental falla-

Norman Vincent Peale popularized the "gospel of success" through his best-selling book, *The Power of Positive Thinking.* (Library of Congress, Prints and Photographs Division LC-USZ62-126496)

cy of communism, which is atheism. I thereby reaffirm the basic conviction upon which this republic rests, namely, that all men are created by the Eternal and in His image, beings of infinite worth, members of one family, brothers. We are endowed by the Creator with certain inalienable rights. The State does not confer them; it merely confirms them. They belong to man because he is a son of God. When I say, "I believe in God," I am also saying that moral law is written into the nature of things. There are moral absolutes. Marxism, by definition, rules out moral absolutes. Because I believe the will of God is revealed in the Gospel of Christ, I hold that all historically conditioned political, economic, social, and ecclesiastical systems must be judged by the Gospel, not identified with it. This is to say I reject communism, first, because of its atheism.

. . . . .

I believe the churches have done and are doing far more to destroy the Communist threat to faith and to freedom than all the investigating committees put together. . . . This Committee might well have the co-operation of millions of citizens who belong to the churches if it would cease practices that many of us believe to be un-American and would turn itself to the real task and the real threat. But those citizens will never co-operate in practices that jeopardize the rights of free men won after a thousand years' struggle for political and religious freedom. They will co-operate effectively with agencies everywhere that honestly seek to build the free society, where free men may worship God according to the dictates of conscience, and serve their fellow men in accordance with Christ's law of love.

Methodist bishop G. Bromley Oxnam, 1953, testimony before the House Un-American Activities Committee, I Protest, *pp. 35–40.*

The little Saint Teresa bum was the first genuine Dharma Bum I'd met, and the second was the number one Dharma Bum of them all and in fact it was he, Japhy Ryder, who coined the phrase. Japhy Ryder was a kid from eastern Oregon brought up in a log cabin deep in the woods with his father and mother and sister, from the beginning a woods boy, an axman, farmer, interested in animals and Indian lore so that when he finally got to college by hook or crook he was already well equipped for his early studies in anthropology and later in Indian myth and in the actual texts of Indian mythology. Finally he learned Chinese and Japanese and became an Oriental scholar and discovered the greatest Dharma Bums of them all, the Zen Lunatics of China and Japan. At the same time, being a Northwest boy with idealistic tendencies, he got interested in oldfash-

ioned I.W.W. anarchism and learned to play the guitar and sing old worker songs to go with his Indian songs and general folksong interests. I first saw him walking down the street in San Francisco the following week (after hitchhiking the rest of the way from Santa Barbara in one long zipping ride given me, as though anybody'll believe this, by a beautiful darling young blonde in a snow-white strapless bathing suit and barefooted with a gold bracelet on her ankle, driving a next-year's cinnamon-red Lincoln Mercury, who wanted benzedrine so she could drive all the way to the City and when I said I had some in my duffel bag yelled "Crazy!")—I saw Japhy loping along in that curious long stride of the mountainclimber, with a small knapsack on his back filled with books and toothbrushes and whatnot which was his small "goin-to-the-city" knapsack as apart from his big full rucksack complete with sleeping bag, poncho, and cookpots.

Beat-era author Jack Kerouac, 1958, The Dharma Bums, *pp. 9–10.*

[B]ecause I am a Catholic, and no Catholic has ever been elected President, the real issues in this campaign have been obscured—perhaps deliberately in some quarters less responsible than this. So it is apparently necessary for me to state once again—not what kind of church I believe in, for that should be important only to me, but what kind of America I believe in.

I believe in an America where the separation of church and state is absolute—where no Catholic prelate would tell the President (should he be a Catholic) how to act and no Protestant minister would tell his parishioners for whom to vote—where no church or church school is granted any public funds or political preference—and where no man is denied public office merely because his religion differs from the President who might appoint him or the people who might elect him.

I believe in an America that is officially neither Catholic, Protestant nor Jewish—where no public official either requests or accepts instructions on public policy from the Pope, the National Council of Churches or any other ecclesiastical source—where no religious body seeks to impose its will directly or indirectly upon the general populace or the public acts of its officials—and where religious liberty is so indivisible that an act against one church is treated as an act against all.

. . . . .

Finally, I believe in an America where religious intolerance will someday end—where all men and all churches are treated as equal—where every man has the same right to attend or not to attend the church of his choice—where there is no Catholic vote, no anti-Catholic vote, no bloc voting of any kind—and where Catholics, Protestants and Jews, both the lay and the pastoral level, will refrain from those attitudes of disdain and division which have so often marred their works in the past, and promote instead the American ideal of brotherhood.

. . . . .

I ask you tonight to follow in that tradition, to judge me on the basis of fourteen years in the Congress—on my declared stands against an ambassador to the Vatican, against unconstitutional aid to parochial schools, and against any boycott of the public schools (which I attended myself)—instead of judging me on the basis of these pamphlets and publications we have all seen that carefully select quotations out of context from the statements of Catholic Church leaders, usually in other countries, frequently in other centuries, and rarely relevant to any situation here—and always omitting, of course, that statement of the American bishops in 1948 which strongly endorsed church-state separation.

. . . . .

I do not speak for my church on public matters—and the church does not speak for me.

Whatever issue may come before me as President, if I should be elected—on birth control, divorce, censorship, gambling, or any other subject—I will make my decision in accordance with these views, in accordance with what my conscience tells me to be in the national interest, and without regard to outside religious pressure or dictate. And no power or threat of punishment could cause me to decide otherwise.

But if the time should ever come—and I do not concede any conflict to be remotely possible—when my office would require me to either violate my conscience, or violate the national interest, then I would resign the office, and I hope any other conscientious public servant would do likewise.

. . . . .

[I]f . . . I should win this election, I shall devote every effort of mind and spirit to fulfilling the oath of the Presidency—practically identical, I might add, with the oath I have taken for fourteen years in the Congress. For, without reservation, I can, and I quote, "solemnly swear that I will faithfully execute the office of President of the

This photograph shows a Catholic priest celebrating mass. *(National Archives NWDNS-412-DA-15948)*

United States and will to the best of my ability preserve, protect and defend the Constitution, so help me God."

Presidential candidate and Catholic John F. Kennedy, September 12, 1960, speech to the Greater Houston Ministerial Association, in Wilson and Drakeman, Church and State in American History, *pp. 188–191.*

I certainly don't think that the death required that "ye be born again," is the death of reason. If what the Church teaches is not true, then the security and emotional release and sense of purpose it gives you are of no value and you are right to reject it. One of the effects of modern liberal Protestantism has been gradually to turn religion into poetry and therapy, to make truth vaguer and vaguer and more and more relative, to banish intellectual distinctions, to depend on feeling instead of thought, and gradually to come to believe that God has no power, that he cannot communicate with us, cannot reveal himself to us, indeed has not done so, and that religion is our own sweet invention. This seems to be about where you find yourself now.

Of course, I am a Catholic and I believe the opposite of all this. I believe what the Church teaches—that God has given us reason to use and that it can lead us toward a knowledge of him, through analogy; that he has revealed himself in history and continues to do so through the Church, and that he is present (not just symbolically) in the Eucharist on our altars. To believe all this I don't take any leap into the absurd. I find it reasonable to believe, even though these beliefs are beyond reason.

Fiction writer Flannery O'Connor, June 16, 1962, letter to poet Alfred Corn, in The Habit of Being: Letters, *p. 479.*

Once upon a time, many years ago, on a sunny afternoon in the garden of a Cuernavaca villa, I ate seven of the so-called sacred mushrooms which had been given to me by a scientist from the University of Mexico. During the next five hours, I was whirled through an experience which could be described in many extravagant metaphors but which was, above all and without question, the deepest religious experience of my life.

. . . . .

I have repeated this biochemical and (to me) sacramental ritual several hundred times, and almost every time I have been awed by religious revelations as shattering as the first experience. During this period I have been lucky enough to collaborate in this work with several hundred scientists and scholars who joined in our various research projects. In our centers at Harvard, in Mexico, and at Millbrook we have arranged transcendent experiences for several thousand persons from all walks of life,

including more than 200 full-time religious professionals, about half of whom profess the Christian or Jewish faiths and about half of whom belong to Eastern religions.

. . . . .

At this point it is conservative to state that over 75 percent of these subjects report intense mystico-religious responses, and considerably more than 50 percent claim that they have had the deepest spiritual experience of their life.

Psychologist Timothy Leary, 1963, The Politics of Ecstasy, *pp. 13–14.*

MY DEAR FELLOW CLERGYMEN,

While confined here in the Birmingham city jail, I came across your recent statement calling our present activities "unwise and untimely." Seldom, if ever, do I pause to answer criticism of my work and ideas. If I sought to answer all the criticisms that cross my desk, my secretaries would be engaged in little else in the course of the day, and I would have no time for constructive work. But since I feel that you are men of genuine goodwill and your criticisms are sincerely set forth, I would like to answer your statement in what I hope will be patient and reasonable terms.

. . . . .

But despite . . . notable exceptions I must honestly reiterate that I have been disappointed with the church. I do not say that as one of the negative critics who can always find something wrong with the church. I say it as a minister of the gospel, who loves the church; who was nurtured in its bosom; who has been sustained by its spiritual blessings and who will remain true to it as long as the cord of life shall lengthen.

. . . . .

I have traveled the length and breadth of Alabama, Mississippi and all the other southern states. On sweltering summer days and crisp autumn mornings I have looked at her beautiful churches with their lofty spires pointing heavenward. I have beheld the impressive outlay of her massive religious education buildings. Over and over again I have found myself asking: "What kind of people worship here? Who is their God? Where were their voices when the lips of Governor Barnett dripped with words of interposition and nullification? Where were they when Governor Wallace gave the clarion call for defiance and hatred? Where were their voices of support when tired, bruised and weary Negro men and women decided to rise from the dark dungeons of complacency to the bright hills of creative protest?"

Yes, these questions are still in my mind. In deep disappointment, I have wept over the laxity of the church.

In this photograph a woman and two girls read a religious tract. (National Archives NWDNS-412-DA-14912)

But be assured that my tears have been tears of love. There can be no deep disappointment where there is not deep love. Yes, I love the church; I love her sacred walls. How could I do otherwise? I am in the rather unique position of being the son, the grandson and the great-grandson of preachers. Yes, I see the church as the body of Christ. But, oh! How we have blemished and scarred that body through social neglect and fear of being nonconformists.

. . . . .

I hope this letter finds you strong in the faith. I also hope that circumstances will soon make it possible for me to meet each of you, not as an integrationist or a civil rights leader, but as a fellow clergyman and a Christian brother. Let us all hope that the dark clouds of racial prejudice will soon pass away and the deep fog of misunderstanding will be lifted from our fear-drenched communities and in some not too distant tomorrow the radiant stars of love and brotherhood will shine over our great nation with all their scintillating beauty.

Civil rights leader Martin Luther King, Jr., April 16, 1963, "Letter from a Birmingham Jail," I Have a Dream, pp. 84–100.

Never have I witnessed such sincere hospitality and the overwhelming spirit of true brotherhood as is practiced by people of all colors and races here in this Ancient Holy Land, the home of Abraham, Muhammad, and all the other prophets of the Holy Scriptures. For the past week, I have been utterly speechless and spellbound by the graciousness I see displayed around me by people *of all colors.*

I have been blessed to visit the Holy City of Mecca. I have made my seven circuits around the Ka'ba, led by a young *Mutawaf* named Muhammad. I drank water from the well of Zem Zem. I ran seven times back and forth between the hills of Mt. Al-Safa and Al-Marwah. I have prayed in the ancient city of Mina, and I have prayed on Mt. Arafat.

There were tens of thousands of pilgrims, from all over the world. They were of all colors, from blue-eyed blonds to black-skinned Africans. But we were all participating in the same ritual, displaying a spirit of unity and brotherhood that my experience in America had led me to believe never could exist between the white and the non-white.

America needs to understand Islam, because this is the one religion that erases from its society the race problem. Throughout my travels in the Muslim world, I have met, talked to, even eaten with people who in America would have been considered "white"—but the "white" attitude was removed from their minds by the religion of Islam. I have never before seen *sincere* and *true* brotherhood practiced by all colors together, irrespective of their color.

. . . . .

We were *truly* all the same (brothers)—because their belief in one God had removed the "white" from their *minds,* the "white" from their *behavior,* and the "white" from their *attitude.*

I could see from this, that perhaps if white Americans could accept the Oneness of God, then perhaps, too, they could accept *in reality* the Oneness of Man—and cease to measure, and hinder, and harm others in terms of their "differences" in color.

A letter from civil rights leader El-Hajj Malik El-Shabazz (Malcolm X), at the conclusion of his pilgrimage to Mecca, to his assistants and others, 1964, The Autobiography of Malcolm X, pp. 339–340.

[I]n the figure of Jesus we saw Immanuel, that is, God, that is, Love. It was a figure who, appearing so inauspiciously among us, broke up our secularist and our religious categories, and beckoned us and judged us and damned us and saved us, and exhibited to us a kind of life that participates in the indestructible.

. . . . .

It was a figure we could neither own nor manage.

. . . . .

And we experienced his announcement as death deal-ing again, because it knocked over all the little pickets and wickets that we had tapped carefully into place to guaran-tee the safety of our religion. He saw our masses and rosa-ries and prayer meetings and study groups and devotions, and he said yes, yes, yes, you are quite right to think that goodness demands rigor and vigilance and observance, but your new moons and sabbaths and bullocks and altars and vestments and Gospel teams and taboos and Bible studies are trumpery, and they nauseate me because you have elevated *them*, and I alone am the Host. Your incense is foetid, and your annotated Bibles are rubbish paper. Your meetings are a bore and your myopic exegesis is suffocat-ing. Return, return, and think again what I have asked of you: to follow justice, and love mercy, and do your job of work, and love one another, and give me the worship of your heart—your *heart*—and be merry and thankful and lowly and not pompous and gaunt and sere.

But we experienced the announcement as life-giving because it was an announcement, appearing in a dirty barn, and heard among the dry provincial hills and then in the forum of Rome and in the halls of royal princes and in the kitchens and streets of Paris and Calcutta and Harlem and Darien, that Joy and not Havoc is the last word. It an-nounced to us what we could not hope. It saw limitation and contingency and disparity and irrevocability and mutability and decay and death, and it said yes, yes, yes, you are quite right: terror and horror and despair are the only eventually realistic responses . . . *if* this is all there is to it. But it is not.

Protestant and later Catholic writer Thomas Howard, 1967,
Christ the Tiger, *pp. 154–158.*

The transcendental vibration established by the chanting of HARE KRSNA, HARE KRSNA, KRSNA KRSNA, HARE HARE/HARE RĀMA, HARE RĀMA, RĀMA RĀMA, HARE HARE is the sublime method of reviving our transcendental consciousness. As living spiritual souls, we are all originally KRSNA conscious entities, but due to our association with matter from time immemorial, our con-sciousness is now adulterated by the material atmosphere. The material atmosphere, in which we are now living, is called *māyā,* or illusion. *Māyā* means that which is not. And what is this illusion? The illusion is that we are all trying to be lords of material nature, while actually we are under the grip of her stringent laws. When a servant artificially tries to imitate the all-powerful master, it is called illusion. We are trying to exploit the resources of material nature, but actually we are becoming more and more entangled in her complexities. Therefore, although we are engaged in a hard struggle to conquer nature, we are ever more dependent on her. This illusory struggle against material nature can be stopped at once by revival of our KRSNA consciousness.

A. C. Bhaktivedanta Swami Prabhupāda, founder of the International Society for Krishna Consciousness, 1970, in Ellwood, Religious and Spiritual Groups in Modern America, *p. 244.*

What we were doing in San Francisco in the 1950s must, of course, be seen in the context of America's military involve-ments in Japan, Korea, and then Vietnam, for these exploits were bound to bring the cultures of those areas back home. My own interest in this cultural encounter was peculiar, in the sense that I was not simply a fact-seeker, like a historian or journalist, nor a missionary trying to convert Westerners to Buddhism—though I have been taken for that. No one, however, has ever accused me of being a scholarly Orien-talist. I am more often considered a popularizer of Zen, Vedanta, and Taoism, who often twists the facts to suit his own views. One reason for this impression is that my style of writing does not lend itself to the tortuous course of inter-minable qualifications, reservations, and drawing of fine dis-tinctions. . . . Another is that I am not interested in studying, say, Buddhism in terms of what most Buddhists think about it—that is, as an anthropological phenomenon. I am inter-ested in the work of those who are, and have been, its most creative exponents, and, above all, in the actual nature of the inner experiences which they describe. . . . It is therefore also said—perhaps with truth—that my easy and free-floating at-titude to Zen was largely responsible for the notorious "Zen boom" which flourished among artists and "pseudointel-lectuals" in the late 1950s, and led on to the frivolous "beat Zen" of Kerouac's *Dharma Bums,* or Franz Kline's black and white abstractions, and of John Cage's silent concerts.

British-born popularizer of Eastern religion in America, Alan Watts, 1972, In My Own Way, *pp. 301–303.*

New confidence in Christ provided me with a rational an-swer to a number of important questions. I had of course long believed in God, and I had recognized the force of the cumulative evidence for theism, but now I had a new approach. With Christ as my center of certitude, I was driven inevitably to God because Christ believed in Him! The logic was sharp and clear: either God is, or Christ was wrong. I found that such reasoning could be made clear to "average" people who made no claims to intel-lectual competence.

What emerged was a new theological approach. I discovered that when I spoke of God, people were polite but unimpressed, partly because so much of the sharp-ness of meaning had been eroded by talk of God as an impersonal Force. It was obvious that no thoughtful person would be greatly interested in a Power so abstract as the law of gravity. At least one kind of agnosticism can be maintained with integrity, but it is something about which no one ever becomes excited. . . . If God is, but is not a Person, ours is a desert universe indeed.

The new strategy, which influenced my ministry, was to move, not from God to Christ, but from Christ to God. Thereby we start in our epistemological pilgrimage at the point of most reasonable assurance. If Christ is trustworthy, it follows that God really and objectively *is*, for Christ prayed to Him in a completely personal way.

. . . . .

When I found that thoughtful people would listen to a Christ-centered approach, I realized where the power of the Christian faith resides. While many churches are declining in strength, the churches which exhibit both Christ-centeredness and rationality are marked by evident vitality. A natural consequence of this fruitful combination is devotion to justice and a real concern for persons. Once a ministry accepts unapologetically the conviction of the Christlikeness of God, we have a firm launching pad from which we can operate with confidence and make a consequent difference in the world.

Quaker scholar Elton Trueblood, 1974, While It Is Day: An Autobiography, *pp. 102–103.*

America is experiencing a spiritual rebirth as people discover that a materialistic existence, an ego-dominated life, is unsatisfying. We are looking for meaning in our life, pleasure in our bodies, and honest communication rather than image, money, or power. This decline in chasing after symbols and objects is eroding the moral of capitalism.

. . . . .

The consciousness movement is bringing Eastern philosophies to the West, modifying the aggressive, masculine, control philosophies of Western industrialism. Our traditional, competitive outlook effectively industrialized the West, but it does not work in the atomic age when sharing and distribution are bigger problems than production. For this era a new value system is needed. We are importing Zen, yoga, and Buddhism and combining them with our emphsis on technology, achievement, and control over nature, in a new synthesis of East and West.

The growth movement must also grow. It must eliminate its internal contradictions of authoritarianism, sexism, economic barriers, spiritual escapism. The men got kicked out by women as political leaders in the 1960's, so they came back as gods. The movement is heavily dominated by male gurus who use spiritual evolution to justify authoritarianism.

. . . . .

At the moment, therefore, the consciousness movement is not addressing itself to problems of economic inequality, political torture, war and peace. Until it does, it will be incomplete. No spiritual movement can claim to deal with the suffering of humanity if it neglects physical oppression.

Social activist Jerry Rubin, 1974, Growing (Up) at Thirty-Seven, *pp. 200–201.*

On June 3, 1972 I was ordained rabbi by Hebrew Union College-Jewish Institute of Religion in Cincinnati, Ohio. As I sat in the historic Plum Street Temple, waiting to accept the ancient rite of *s'micha* (ordination), I couldn't help but reflect on the implications of what was about to happen. For thousands of years women in Judaism had been second-class citizens. They were not permitted to own property. They could not serve as witnesses. They did not have the right to initiate divorce proceedings. They were not counted in the *minyan* [quorum]. Even in Reform Judaism, they were not permitted to participate fully in the life of the synagogue. With my ordination all that was going to change; one more barrier was about to be broken.

. . . . .

It is still too soon to assess the impact of my ordination, but I would hope that it would at least mark a transition in our congregations, that sole involvement on the part of women in the synagogue kitchen and the classroom should move toward complete and full participation on the pulpit and in the boardroom as well.

When I accepted ordination on June 3, 1972, I affirmed my belief in Judaism and publicly committed myself to the survival of Jewish tradition. I did so knowing that Judaism had traditionally discriminated against women; that it had not always been sensitive to the problems of total equality. I know that there has been a tremendous flexibility in our tradition—it enabled our survival. Therefore, I chose to work for change through constructive criticism. The principles and ideals for which our ancestors have lived and died are much too important to be cast aside. Instead we must accept the responsibilities of the covenant upon ourselves, learn as much as possible of our heritage, and make the necessary changes which will grant women total equality within the Jewish community.

Rabbi Sally Priesand, the first woman ordained a rabbi in America, 1975, Judaism and the New Woman, *pp. xiii, xvi.*

[D]oubts about my motives continued to nag at me. Was I seeking a safe port in the storm, a temporary hiding place? . . . Despite the arrow to my heart and my awakening on the Maine coast to the incredible realization about Jesus Christ, was I somehow looking to religion as a last-gasp effort to save myself as everything else in my world was crashing down on me?

. . . . .

No, I knew that the time had come for me: I could not sidestep the central question [C. S.] Lewis (or God) had placed squarely before me. Was I to accept without reservation Jesus Christ as Lord of my life? It was like a gate before me. There was no way to walk around it. I would step through, or I would remain outside.

. . . . .

And as something pressed that question home, less and less was I troubled by the curious phrase "accept Jesus Christ." It had sounded at first both pious and mystical, language of the zealot, maybe blackmagic stuff. But "to accept" means no more than "to believe." Did I believe what Jesus said? If I did, if I took it on faith or reason or both, then I accepted. Not mystical or weird at all, and with no in-between ground left. Either I would believe or I would not—and believe it all or none of it.

. . . . .

And so early that Friday morning, while I sat alone staring at the sea I love, words I had not been certain I could understand or say fell naturally from my lips: "Lord Jesus, I believe You. I accept You. Please come into my life. I commit it to You."

Charles W. Colson, a prominent participant in the Watergate scandal and subsequent founder of the Prison Fellowship organization, 1976, Born Again, *pp. 129–130.*

The higher Christian churches—where, if anywhere, I belong—come at God with an unwarranted air of professionalism, with authority and pomp, as though they knew what they were doing, as though people in themselves were an appropriate set of creatures to have dealings with God. I often think of the set pieces of liturgy as certain words which people have successfully addressed to God without their getting killed. In the high churches they saunter through the liturgy like Mohawks along a strand of scaffolding who have long since forgotten their danger. If God were to blast such a service to bits, the congregation would be, I believe, genuinely shocked. But in the low churches you expect it any minute. This is the beginning of wisdom.

Writer Annie Dillard, 1977, Holy the Firm, *p. 59.*

I *chose* to believe in the Father, Son, and Holy Ghost—in Christ, my lord and my God. Christianity has the ring, the

feel, of unique truth. Of *essential* truth. By it, life is made full instead of empty, meaningful instead of meaningless. Cosmos becomes beautiful at the *Centre,* instead of chillingly ugly beneath the lovely pathos of spring. But the emptiness, the meaninglessness, and the ugliness can only be seen, I think, when one has glimpsed the fullness, the meaning, and the beauty. It is when heaven and hell have *both* been glimpsed that going back is impossible. But to go on seemed impossible, also. A glimpse is not a vision. A choice was necessary: and there is no certainty. One can only choose a side. So I—I now choose my side: I choose beauty; I choose what I love. But choosing to believe *is* believing. It's all I can do: choose. I confess my doubts and ask my Lord Christ to enter my life. I do not *know* God is, I do but say: Be it unto me according to Thy will. I do not affirm that I am without doubt, I do but ask for help, having chosen, to overcome it. I do but say: Lord, I believe—help Thou mine unbelief.

Sheldon Vanauken, educator and writer, describing his conversion to Christianity, 1977, in A Severe Mercy, *p. 99.*

I returned to the Mediterranean coast and began thinking of putting an end to it all by committing suicide. I really began to think about that. I was sitting up on my balcony one night, on the thirteenth floor—just sitting there. . . . I was brooding and downcast, at the end of my rope. I looked up at the moon saw certain shadows . . . and the shadows became a man in the moon, and I saw a profile of myself (a profile used on posters for the Black Panther Party—something I had seen a thousand times). I was already upset and this scared me. I started trembling. It was a shaking that came from deep inside, and it had a threat about it that this mood was getting worse, that I could possibly disintegrate on the scene and fall apart. As I stared at this image, it changed, and I saw my former heroes paraded before my eyes. Here were Fidel Castro, Mao Tse-tung, Karl Marx, Frederick Engels, passing in review—each one appearing for a moment of time, and then dropping out of sight, like fallen heroes. Finally, at the end of the procession, in dazzling, shimmering light, the image of Jesus Christ appeared. That was the last straw.

I just crumbled and started crying. I fell to my knees, grabbing hold of the banister, and in the midst of this shaking and crying the Lord's Prayer and the 23rd Psalm came into my mind.

Eldridge Cleaver, who initially became prominent as a leader in the Black Panthers, describing a Christian conversion experience, 1978, in Mandelker and Powers, Pilgrim Souls, *pp. 139–140.*

CHAPTER FOURTEEN

Religion and Politics Redux
(1980–Present)

Conservative Christians at the end of the century reentered American politics after a long period of absence. They joined liberal believers—already active in a variety of social and political causes—but frequently on the opposite side of contested issues such as abortion, nuclear disarmament, and gay rights. Of course, the appearance of religious rhetoric in politics was nothing new. During the Civil Rights movement, for example, leaders such as Martin Luther King, Jr., regularly clothed their advocacy of equal rights in the language of religious faith. Earlier in the century religiously inspired temperance advocates had helped rouse the nation to embrace Prohibition. And in the 19th century abolitionists often appealed to religious justifications for ending slavery. But at the end of the 20th century, the arrival of conservative religious believers on the national political scene prompted some prominent observers to wonder whether religious voices were appropriately raised in the public square. Equally prominent conservative believers, such as Lutheran pastor and later Catholic priest Richard John Neuhaus, decried the *Naked Public Square,* as a book published by Neuhaus in 1984 characterized the matter, arguing that public discourse was already too secular.[1] Whatever the force of these arguments, conservative religious views occupied a significant place in contemporary politics as the 20th century ended and the 21st began.

The increased prominence of religious voices in a public square—not nearly so naked of religion as Neuhaus claimed—made it perhaps inevitable that scandals regarding religious leaders would achieve equal prominence at the end of the 20th century. Television personality Jim Bakker, who, along with his wife, Tammy Faye Bakker, presided over a multimillion dollar religious empire, was convicted of fraud and sentenced to prison. Popular television evangelist Jimmy Swaggart was defrocked after his transactions with prostitutes came to light. And American Catholicism was battered in the last decade of the century with news that some of its priests—with the complicity of superiors such as Boston's Cardinal Bernard Law—had engaged in sexual abuse of children.

The intersection between religion and the law took less scandalous forms during the late 20th century. Not infrequently, religious believers found themselves at odds with secular laws. Mormons in the 19th century, for example, clashed with federal laws prohibiting polygamy and argued unsuccessfully that the First

Amendment's protection of religious free exercise entitled them to exemptions from these laws. Jehovah's Witnesses in the 20th century ran afoul of laws requiring the recitation of the Pledge of Allegiance in public schools, since they believed that saying the pledge amounted to idolatry. The Jehovah's Witnesses, however, were ultimately more successful than the Mormons in obtaining relief from these kinds of laws. But it was not until the second half of the 20th century that the U.S. Supreme Court finally addressed squarely the issue of whether religious believers were constitutionally protected from laws that inadvertently burdened their beliefs or practices. Its resolution of this issue seemed not sufficiently protective of religious liberty to many American observers and prompted Congress to make attempts of its own to secure equal religious liberty for citizens. At the same time, the Supreme Court revisited the wall of separation between church and state and approved at least some instances of government support of religious symbols or practices as well as some forms of government aid to religious institutions.

Tension between particular religious traditions and the broader currents of American society have been a recurring element of religious experience in the United States. The events of September 11, 2001, when Islamic terrorists attacked the World Trade Center in New York and the Pentagon in Washington, D.C., focused particular attention on Islam in America. Muslims in the United States experienced indiscriminate suspicion and endured acts of violence in some cases

In this photograph an army chaplain from Fort Stewart, Georgia, reads Scripture (1980). *(National Archives NWDNS-111-SC-680030)*

after 9/11. Consequently, American Islamic leaders and scholars rushed to defend themselves and their faith as compatible with democratic life and as implacably opposed to terrorist strategies. American Muslims also claimed their right to religious free exercise and to respect as fellow citizens.

Whose Morality? Which Majority?

Religious involvement in politics has been a recurring feature of American political life. Christian abolitionists warred against slavery, evangelists of the Social Gospel confronted the consequences of industrialism, and African-American ministers protested against Jim Crow segregation. For much of the 20th century, the religious voices heard most often in the public square tended to be liberal and progressive. After the fundamentalism controversy of the early 20th century, conservative believers frequently adopted a stance of separation toward the broader society, treating political activity in particular as inevitably compromising and as a distraction from more weighty religious duties such as evangelism. Accordingly, they tended to retreat into the security of their own churches, educational institutions, and missionary societies. Two legal developments during the 1960s and 1970s caused religious conservatives to reevaluate their separatism, however. First, the school prayer cases decided in the 1960s, which ruled unconstitutional officially sanctioned prayers and Bible reading in public schools, alarmed conservative Christians. A decade later in *Roe v. Wade* (1973), the Supreme Court announced that the Constitution protected a woman's right to an abortion and invalidated most legal restrictions on abortions. These decisions eventually generated significant opposition among religious conservatives and inspired many of them to become politically engaged.

Baptist minister Jerry Falwell proved successful at mobilizing conservative Christian dissatisfaction with these developments through the Moral Majority, which he founded in 1979. Pastor of the Thomas Road Baptist Church in Lynchburg, Virginia, which he had established in the 1950s and which had grown to 22,000 members by the beginning of the 21st century, Falwell gained a national following from viewers of his popular television program, the *Old-Time Gospel Hour.* Toward the end of the 1970s, he was able to translate this popularity into the basis for organizing the Moral Majority, a political action group devoted to conservative causes such as opposition to abortion and support of missile defense. The very name of the organization rankled religious progressives, who fiercely insisted then, as now, that conservatives had no monopoly on either religious or moral values. But Falwell's organization, whether or not appropriately named, succeeded in inspiring a new engagement with political action among conservative Christians and is sometimes credited with helping to elect Ronald Reagan president of the United States in 1980. Before that decade was over, however, the Moral Majority had ceased operations and the political power of the Christian right, as it was frequently characterized, was widely questioned.

In 1986, however, the year that the Moral Majority ceased operations, television personality Pat Robertson published *America's Date With Destiny* (1986), which complained about America's drift away from the Christian values he saw as animating its founding. Robertson earned national prominence during the 1970s and 1980s as the founder of the Christian Broadcast Network and the host of a popular Christian talk show, *The 700 Club.* Like Falwell, Robertson used his popularity as a television personality as a platform for his political aspirations, though unlike

Falwell, Robertson aspired to political office rather than simply political influence. In 1988 he attempted to capture the Republican nomination for president of the United States. When this attempt failed, he established a new political action group in 1989 named the Christian Coalition, an organization that remains active into the 21st century. Equally prominent groups, led by conservative evangelicals such as James Dobson and Beverly LaHaye, founders of Focus on the Family and Concerned Women of America, respectively, also worked actively to advance conservative Christian values. As America entered the 21st century conservative Christians remained important players in the nation's politics, though the measure of their actual influence continued to be debated.

Some conservative believers turned aside from political activism in favor of more direct forms of protest, including civil disobedience and in some cases even violence. Controversy over abortion inspired many of these protests. The election of Ronald Reagan as president in 1980 created expectations that the Supreme Court's decision in *Roe v. Wade* (1973) might be reversed by new presidential appointments to the Court. By the second half of that decade, it was less clear that this result would be forthcoming, and impatience with continued abortions inspired some prolife advocates to stage protests designed to curtail the activities of abortion clinics. Religious believers—predominantly conservative Catholics at first and later conservative Protestants—contributed significantly to these protests.[2] Evangelical activist Randall Terry organized the most famous of the antiabortion protest groups, Operation Rescue, in 1987. The group insisted its tactics were nonviolent and legitimate forms of civil disobedience, but it staged massive demonstrations around abortion clinics designed to frustrate attempts by women seeking abortions to enter the clinics and by police to secure access to the clinics for these women. Across the nation demonstrations such as those orchestrated by Operation Rescue resulted in more than 11,000 arrests for blockading clinics in 1988 and more than 12,000 the next year.[3] These two years marked the height of the abortion clinic protests. By the early 1990s, though, jail sentences, fines, and civil liability had largely curtailed the ability of Operation Rescue and other groups to stage large-scale antiabortion demonstrations. More violent opponents of abortion, however, moved beyond protest to murder. On March 10, 1993, antiabortion activist Michael Griffin shot and killed abortion doctor David Gunn in front of an abortion clinic in Pensacola, Florida. The following year on July 29, 1994, Paul Hall killed John Britton, the doctor who had replaced David Gunn.

Toward the close of the 20th century and the beginning of the 21st, a new issue came to dominate conservative religious engagement with politics. Spurred by state court decisions in some jurisdictions that suggested that gay couples had the same right to marry as heterosexuals, many social conservatives, including those animated by religious beliefs, announced their opposition to gay marriage. Conservatives feared that states opposed to gay marriages would nevertheless be forced to recognize such marriages when couples married in states allowing gay marriages moved to other states. Accordingly, Pat Robertson's Christian Coalition and other conservative religious groups supported the passage by Congress in 1996 of the Defense of Marriage Act, a federal law that gave states the right to refuse recognition of same-sex marriages performed in other states. The act also defined marriage for purposes of federal law as including only heterosexual couples. Early in the 21st century a similar coalition of religious and traditionalist groups continued to press for an amendment to the U.S. Constitution to limit marriage to heterosexual couples.

The political controversy over gay marriage also paralleled ecclesiastical debates over the ordination of openly gay ministers. Both controversies found religious believers often divided over the morality of gay sexual activity, with conservative believers typically concluding that gay sex was sinful. With this premise they easily concluded that ordination should be denied openly gay ministers and the sanction of marriage denied to gay couples. Gay believers contested this view and as early as 1968 established the United Fellowship of Metropolitan Community Churches as a separate denomination for gay Christians. Other mainline Protestant denominations wrestled with the ordination issue, none perhaps more traumatically than American Episcopalians. In 1979 the General Convention of the Episcopal Church in the United States passed a resolution declaring it "inappropriate" to ordain either practicing homosexuals or anyone engaged in heterosexual relations outside of marriage. A little more than a decade later, however, in 1990, Walter Righter, an assistant bishop of Newark, New Jersey, ordained Barry Stopfel an openly gay deacon, and Newark's bishop, John Spong, ordained Stopfel a priest the next year. Spong had already ordained Robert Williams, another openly gay man, a priest in 1989, which led to his censure by the Episcopal House of Bishops the following year. After Righter's ordination of Stopfel as a deacon, conservative Episcopalians attempted to try the assistant bishop for heresy, but the case was dismissed in 1996 for lack of specific Episcopal doctrine prohibiting ordination of gays. In June 2003 New Hampshire elected Vicky Gene Robinson the first openly lesbian bishop in the Anglican Church. The House of Bishops subsequently confirmed the election later that summer, setting in motion a possible fracture with conservative Episcopalian congregations.

Although conservative Christians arrived late to the world of 20th-century politics, liberal believers during this period continued their long-standing practice of addressing political questions from the standpoint of progressive ideas about life and faith. In the last two decades two important such questions involved the appropriateness of nuclear armament and of American support for governments—especially in Central America—viewed by liberals as corrupt. While President Ronald Reagan championed the continued development of nuclear arms and a missile defense system known as Star Wars, liberal Christians, including many Catholics and mainline Protestants, insisted that nuclear armament was un-Christian and immoral. They pressed unsuccessfully for American endorsement of the 1978 Strategic Arms Limitation Treaty (known as SALT II). They also opposed Reagan's support of the anticommunist contra guerrillas in Nicaragua against the Soviet-backed Sandinista government and his support of the government of El Salvador, where thousands of citizens had been tortured and killed. When refugees from regions such as El Salvador, formally supported by the U.S. government, began to arrive on American soil, liberal believers were appalled that these refugees were generally denied political asylum. Many of these believers subsequently became involved in the Sanctuary movement, which attempted to harbor the refugees in violation of American law. Presbyterian minister John Fife explained the views that led his congregation to participate in the movement:

> We believe that justice and mercy require that people of conscience actually assert our God-given right to aid anyone fleeing from persecution and murder.

. . . . .

> [My congregation] declared sanctuary because they determined after Bible study, prayer and agonizing reflection that they could not remain faithful to the God of the Exodus and prophets and do anything less. It was for us a question of faith.[4]

Fife and other members of the Sanctuary movement were arrested in 1985 for transporting illegal aliens, and most of those arrested were subsequently found guilty in a highly publicized trial. But the judge in the case eventually entered suspended sentences for the defendants instead of sending them to prison, chiefly as a result of widespread appeals for clemency toward them.

During the last decades of the 20th century African-American religious leaders continued to press for civil rights in the public sphere. None was more prominent during this period than Jesse Jackson, a black minister who had worked with Martin Luther King, Jr., during the 1960s and had subsequently become the foremost civil rights leader of the late 20th century. Jackson ran twice for the Democratic nomination for president of the United States, first in 1984 and then again in 1988, each time making a significant showing even though ultimately losing the nomination. Nation of Islam leader Louis Farrakhan campaigned for Jackson after the latter announced his candidacy for president in 1983, but Farrakhan stirred controversy by his anti-Semitic remarks, including a reference to Judaism as a "gutter religion."

Jesse Jackson was the most prominent civil rights leader of the late 20th century. *(National Archive NWDNS-412-DA-13800)*

Farrakhan had assumed an important place of leadership in the Nation of Islam after Malcolm X left the organization in 1963. When Elijah Muhammad, founder of the Black Muslims, died in 1975, and his son attempted first to steer the Nation of Islam toward more traditional Islamic belief and practice and then disbanded the organization altogether, Farrakhan reestablished the Black Muslims in keeping with Elijah Muhammad's teaching. Farrakhan earned a less controversial prominence by orchestrating the Million Man March in Washington, D.C., for black men in 1995. By the end of the century he had moved somewhat closer to traditional Islam and had become less prone to the kind of racist remarks that had sometimes characterized his earlier career.

By the beginning of the 21st century, social commentators on the religious right regularly complained that America had lost its way and that only a return to God would avert disaster. Jerry Falwell, for example, interpreted the terrorist attacks of September 11, 2001, as a judgment from God for America's sins—sins he laid at the door of the political and cultural left:

> The abortionists have got to bear some burden for this because God will not be mocked. And when we destroy 40 million little innocent babies, we make God mad. I really believe that the pagans and the abortionists, and the feminists, and the gays and lesbians who are actively trying to make that an alternative lifestyle, the ACLU, People for the American Way—all of them who have tried to secularize America—I point the finger in their faces and say: "You helped this happen."[5]

Observers from the middle and left of the political spectrum variously proclaimed that religious conservatives—the Christian right—were either a threat to democracy or a spent political force with no real power. One prominent scholar suggested that these mutual recriminations amounted to a cultural war between Christian fundamentalists, Orthodox Jews, and conservative Catholics on one hand and their progressive counterparts on the other hand.[6] The truth of this appraisal remains uncertain. It is clear, though, that religious believers of the early 21st century showed no inclination to retire from their engagement in American public affairs, whether on the right, the left, or the middle of the political spectrum.

The Scandals of Faith

The last two decades of the 20th century did not invent the idea of religious scandal. Religious leaders accused of misdeeds were nothing new on the American scene. Henry Ward Beecher, one of the most famous preachers of the 19th century, endured accusations, never conclusively proved, that he had committed adultery with the wife of a friend. And American literature, in works such as Nathaniel Hawthorne's *The Scarlet Letter* and Sinclair Lewis's *Elmer Gantry*, has a long history of fascination with religious leaders and their misdeeds. But toward the end of the 20th century, as religious leaders increasingly turned to the instruments of mass media to publicize and propagate their ministries, they discovered the same media could devour them. Sometimes, media attention showered little more than mockery on prominent religious personalities, such as when Oklahoma television evangelist Oral Roberts announced in 1987 that God would "call him home" unless his supporters tendered $8 million in contributions to support fellowships at the Oral Roberts University medical school. The following year Baptist minister

Jerry Falwell learned from the U.S. Supreme Court that the First Amendment prevented him from successfully suing *Hustler* magazine for damages to his reputation occasioned by a lurid sexual parody of Falwell published by the magazine.[7] But sometimes media attention could deal out more than mockery and actually topple particular religious ministries. Two prominent television personalities, Jim Bakker and Jimmy Swaggart, suffered spectacular downfalls during this period when their private misdeeds became public.

Jim and Tammy Fay Bakker, members of the Assemblies of God denomination, were associated early in their careers with Pat Robertson's Christian Broadcasting Network (CBN) in the late 1960s. In 1972, though, they left CBN and later that decade began to work for the PTL (Praise the Lord) television ministry, of which they soon assumed control. Broadcasting on-the-air prayer sessions and conversations between Jim, Tammy, and other guests, PTL programming proved extraordinarily successful at gaining audiences and just as successful at coaxing viewers to contribute to the ministry. By the early 1980s the Bakkers were managing not only PTL but an evangelical theme park in South Carolina called Heritage USA, for which they solicited "partnership" contributions that purportedly guaranteed donors an annual right to lodging at the park. Allegations of financial improprieties soon began to surface, however, and it was eventually discovered that the Bakkers had diverted partnership contributions to fund their television ministry and to purchase a lavish lifestyle for themselves. Coupled with the financial scandal was news that Tammy Faye Bakker had received treatment at the Betty Ford Center for drug addiction and that Jim Bakker had had an affair with 19-year-old church secretary Jessica Hahn. In late 1988 Jim Bakker was indicted for mail and wire fraud and ultimately convicted and sentenced to 45 years in prison, of which he served six.[8]

The same year that saw Bakker indicted for fraud witnessed the fall of another popular Assemblies of God personality, evangelist Jimmy Swaggart. From a 270-acre complex in Louisiana, which included a Bible college along with television and radio studios, Swaggart broadcast television programs seen around the world by millions of viewers. He had been harshly critical of the Bakkers, rejecting the glossiness of their television programming and theme park in favor of his own more traditional evangelistic preaching ministry. But Swaggart's popularity suffered precipitous decline after a photograph of him leaving a hotel with a prostitute surfaced. The photograph, ironically, had been taken by another former Assemblies of God minister who had been defrocked for a similar sexual scandal. Temporarily defrocked himself by his denomination, Swaggart eventually resumed his career as a televangelist, but with significantly less prominence.[9]

The Bakkers and Swaggart may have flirted with scandal by deliberately courting public prominence, but their televised lives were quite removed from the less public careers of the Catholic priests whose acts of sexual abuse became news in the late 1990s. The resulting crisis eventually toppled one of America's most prominent Catholic leaders, Cardinal Bernard Law, archbishop of Boston since 1984. Widely publicized occurrences of sexual abuse by priests of children came to light in the mid-1980s and early 1990s, and the Dallas diocese gained national attention when it was forced to pay more than $31 million to victims of former priest Rudolf Kos in 1998. The following year, though, a former Massachusetts priest, John Geoghan, was indicted on child rape charges. This case ultimately implicated the supervisory role of Cardinal Bernard Law. In January 1999 Geoghan was convicted of indecent assault and battery of a 10-year-old boy and sentenced to 10 years in prison. The same year former priest Paul Shanley was arrested and charged with child rape, and it was subsequently discovered that Cardinal Law had repeatedly transferred Shanley from parish to parish in the face of allegations that he had engaged in acts of sexual abuse. Shanley was ultimately convicted of child rape and sentenced to prison in 2005, and Law was forced to resign as archbishop and retire to Rome at the end of 2002.

Equal Religious Freedom and Walls of Separation

By the last decades of the 20th century, religious pluralism had to be reckoned as a prominent feature of American life, and this very prominence inspired new attempts to understand the nature of religious freedom and the appropriate relationship between government and religion. The U.S. Supreme Court, accordingly, wrestled repeatedly during the waning years of the century with the meaning of the Constitution's First Amendment, which prohibits laws abridging religious free exercise or respecting an establishment of religion. Two issues predominated. First, the Court had to resolve the issue of whether religious believers were entitled to exemptions from the requirements of laws that burdened their religious beliefs or practices. Second, the Court turned its attention to the so-called wall of separation between church and state, especially the relationship between this wall and access by religious groups to public facilities and benefits.

On one front the last decade of the 20th century saw the Supreme Court revise its approach to religious liberty claims. It remained committed to the principle that the Constitution prevented government from targeting minority religious groups for burdensome treatment *because of* their particular religious beliefs or practices. Thus, in the 1980s Santerians, a syncretistic religious tradition imported to the United States from the Caribbean combining elements of African religious tradition with Catholicism, began practicing animal sacrifice in the Florida city of Hialeah. The city responded by passing ordinances prohibiting animal sacrifice, and when prosecuted for violating these ordinances the Santerians invoked the protections of the free exercise clause in response. When the case eventually arrived at the U.S. Supreme Court, the Court held that the local ordinances violated the First Amendment because they singled out a particular religion for burdensome treatment precisely because of its religious practices.[10]

But laws intended to persecute a religious minority in America are rare. More commonly, governments pass laws that unintentionally make it more difficult for religious minorities to carry out the requirements of their faiths. In some cases governments may possess sufficiently weighty interests to justify overriding religious conscience. For example, the government interest in preserving life would certainly allow laws against homicide to be applied or punish religiously inspired human sacrifice. And laws regulating firearms and explosives would probably take precedence over the asserted beliefs of a religious group to stockpile these items. Precisely such a conflict between federal authorities and the Branch Davidians near Waco, Texas, occurred in 1993. In February of that year agents of the Federal Bureau of Alcohol, Tobacco and Firearms attempted to arrest David Koresh, the leader of the Branch Davidians, for illegal possession of firearms and explosives. The ensuing gun battle left both a number of federal agents and Davidians dead or wounded and resulted in a standoff between the Branch Davidians and the F.B.I. When negotiations failed to resolve the issue, the F.B.I. eventually attempted to penetrate the compound occupied by the Davidians under cover of a tear gas attack. While this attack was ongoing, fires erupted in the compound causing the death of David Koresh and some 80 of his followers, including at least 17 children. Though a subsequent investigation and civil trial exonerated the federal government for these deaths, many observers maintained that federal agents had acted, at the very least, imprudently in their dealings with the Branch Davidians.

In many cases of conflict between law and religious conscience, though, the government interests might not be so compelling. In these circumstances, when majority or popular religious faiths collide with legal requirements, lawmakers generally take care to exempt these faiths from those requirements. Thus, for example, when the nation embraced Prohibition in the early 20th century, Congress made sure to exempt the sacramental use of wine from laws banning the sale or use of alcohol, thus preserving a central Christian rite from legal disturbance. But lawmakers may be unaware of or not sufficiently attentive to the burdens imposed by laws on minority religious practices. Were minority religious groups entitled to protection under the First Amendment from the kinds of burdens that majority religious groups typically obtained through the political process?

Beginning in the 1960s the Court had declared that the free exercise clause of the First Amendment prevented government at all levels from incidentally burdening religious belief or practice without overwhelmingly persuasive justification for doing so.[11] Thus, in *Wisconsin v. Yoder* (1972) the Court held that a state law requiring compulsory attendance at school after the eighth grade lacked sufficient justification to be enforced against Amish parents, who had religious convictions against educating their children after the eighth grade. But in a controversial case decided in 1990, the Court announced that ordinarily, unintentional burdens on religious belief or practice would not be protected by the First Amendment. In *Employment Division v. Smith* (1990) a narrow majority of the Court rejected claims brought by members of the Native American church that a state's drug control law should not be applied to prevent them from engaging in religiously motivated use of peyote. The Court's opinion was widely denounced, and Congress quickly responded to this decision by passing the Religious Freedom Restoration Act of 1993, which was more protective of religious liberty. The act reinstated the requirement that religious believers be exempted from laws burdening their faith or practice unless overwhelmingly persuasive reasons existed for not granting an exemption. Nevertheless, the Court in its turn ruled subsequently that Congress lacked the power to adopt this law, at least as it applied to state and local governments.[12] Thus, at the beginning of the 21st century, federal, state, and local governments had a good deal of power to enact and enforce laws even when these laws conflicted with the sincerely held religious beliefs of individuals.

Although the Court was vigilant in preventing state-sponsored endorsements of religious practice or religious teaching in the public schools after the middle of the 20th century, it became increasingly committed to protecting religious speakers from discrimination in the final two decades of that century. Public officials have sometimes argued that religious individuals or groups cannot be permitted to use public facilities for gatherings because this use would amount to a violation of the separation between church and state. But in a series of cases decided in the 1980s and 1990s, the Supreme Court ruled that the establishment clause was generally not offended when religious speakers were allowed the same rights to meet on pub-

New York's historic Trinity Church stands on lower Broadway at the foot of Wall Street, as shown in this photo from May 1973. *(National Archives NWDNS-412-DA-7433)*

lic property as other citizens. The Court held additionally that the right to freedom of speech generally meant that religious speakers had to be treated the same as nonreligious speakers, even if this meant giving them access to particular public facilities or benefits. Thus, in *Widmar v. Vincent* (1981) the Court held that a Christian student organization could not be prevented from meeting in a room at a university when other student organizations enjoyed this privilege. Congress subsequently enacted the Equal Access Act in 1984, which adopted a similar principle for public secondary schools. Under this act religious clubs cannot be prevented from having comparable access to school facilities as that enjoyed by other non–course-related student clubs. The Court has since recognized a similar principle for public elementary schools: when a variety of community groups are given access to elementary school classrooms after school hours, religious groups are entitled to comparable access.[13]

During this same period the Court also revisited the "height" of the wall of separation between church and state. During the third quarter of the 20th century, the Court had been fairly vigorous in policing this so-called wall of separation. It had rebuffed numerous attempts by governments to sponsor religious activities such as prayer and Bible reading in the public schools, and it had also prohibited most forms of government aid to religious institutions such as parochial schools. Toward the end of the 20th century, however, the Court became more tolerant of government support of religious symbols, at least in some contexts, and more willing to permit government aid that had the result of benefiting religious institutions. Though it remained vigilant concerning government sponsorship of religious activities in public schools, holding unconstitutional practices that allowed prayers at graduation ceremonies and football games, it was more tolerant of government support for religious symbols and activities in other public contexts.[14] Thus, the Court approved prayers offered before a state legislature in *March v. Chambers* (1983) and the display of a nativity scene on public property along with other holiday symbols in *Lynch v. Donnelly* (1984). As to government aid that benefits religious institutions, the Court followed a pattern in the 1980s and 1990s of allowing a greater variety of such aid to stand, especially when the choices of private individuals were responsible for the receipt by a religious institution of public aid. Most significantly, in *Zelman v. Simmons-Harris* (2002) the Court upheld a voucher program that provided vouchers for private school tuition to low-income families. Although many of the families used these vouchers to pay for tuition at private religious schools, the Court held that this fact did not make the program an unconstitutional establishment of religion.

Islam in America

Muslims arrived in America long before the 21st century. Scholars have pondered whether these first arrivals may have appeared around 1492, both the year that Columbus "discovered" America and the year that Spanish monarchs drove the last Muslims from their stronghold in Grenada. In any event, when African slaves were forcibly transported to America beginning in the 16th century, at least some of these were adherents of Islam. But it remained until the 19th and especially the 20th centuries for significant numbers of Muslim immigrants to reach America's shores. During approximately the last quarter of the 20th century, as a result of more liberal U.S. immigrations policies, the number of Muslim immigrants to the United States swelled. These joined many African Americans who were members of the Nation of Islam or practiced other forms of Islam. In all, the number of adherents of Islam in the United States grew from roughly half a million to 6 million during the last three decades of the 20th century.[15]

Muslims in the United States believe themselves to share a measure of spiritual fraternity with Jews and Christians, since these traditions, along with Islam, are for Muslims "people of the book." The sacred book of Islam is the Qur'an (Koran), believed by Muslims to be the revelation of God to Muhammad. Jewish and

Christian sacred books are also, according to Islam, divine revelations but had been sufficiently distorted by Jews and Christians to prompt God to make a further, final revelation to Muhammad. Included in this revelation are the five pillars of Islam, a word that itself means "submission." Submission to God for Muslims begins with the first pillar, the affirmation or *shahadah:* "There is no God but God, and Muhammad is God's messenger.[16] The second pillar is prayer, to be offered five times a day toward Mecca. The third is almsgiving, or payment of the alms tax (*zakat*). The fourth pillar is fasting during the month of Ramadan, and the fifth is the obligation of making a pilgrimage to Mecca once in one's life.

On September 11, 2001, terrorists hijacked passenger jets and crashed them into each of the Twin Towers of the World Trade Center in New York and the Pentagon in Washington, D.C. A fourth hijacked plane crashed in Pennsylvania, killing all aboard after passengers attempted to retake control of the plan from the hijackers. In all, the attacks resulted in the deaths of nearly 3,000 people. An Islamic terrorist group called Al Qaeda, led by Osama bin Laden, a Saudi Arabian national, ultimately claimed responsibility for these attacks. In the wake of these acts of terrorism, American Muslims suffered from indiscriminate suspicions widely directed against all Muslims or even individuals, such as Sikhs, thought to look like Muslims. Reports of violence against mosques and those who dressed in a "Middle Eastern" fashion were common in the days after September 11. Most Muslims in the United States vehemently repudiated terrorism and sought to remind other Americans that the followers of Islam in the United States continued to be neighbors and fellow-citizens and that they, in fact, were numbered among the victims of the September 11 attacks. They also insisted that terrorism was flatly inconsistent with the teachings and values of Islam.

Before 9/11 and the public dialogue about Islam it inspired, many Americans may have been unaware of the significant number of Muslims who have made their homes in the United States. Today there are as many adherents of Islam in America as there are Jews and more Muslims than many specific Christian denominations. There are, for example, more Muslims in America than there are Episcopalians. In fact, there are more Hindus and Buddhists in American today than there are Episcopalians. Those who imagine the United States to be a Judeao-Christian nation have generally failed to recognize the significant demographic changes of the last 40 years. But as the 21st century unfolds, it is becoming ever more difficult to ignore the diversity of American religious belief and practice.

Chronicle of Events

1980

- Two churches in Tucson, Arizona, provide sanctuary for the surviving members of a group of Salvadorans who had been abandoned in the Arizona desert by a professional smuggler. In the course of the decade, the Sanctuary movement will involve many believers in the cause of providing sanctuary to Central American refugees in the face of U.S. immigration policies hostile to the claims of these refugees.
- Kateri Tekakwitha, a Native American convert to Catholicism who died at the age of 24 as a result of severe ascetic practices, is beatified by Pope John Paul II.
- Marjorie Matthews becomes the first female bishop for the United Methodists.
- *November 17:* In *Stone v. Graham* the U.S. Supreme Court holds that it is unconstitutional for a school to post copies of the Ten Commandments in classrooms.

1981

- Vernon Howell, who subsequently changes his name to David Koresh in 1990, joins the Branch Davidians near Waco, Texas. He will assume control of the group in 1988.
- The Islamic Society of North America is formed.
- *December 8:* In *Widmar v. Vincent* the U.S. Supreme Court holds that a public university violated the free speech rights of a Christian student organization when it refused to let the organization hold meetings in university facilities under terms comparable to those enjoyed by other student groups.

1982

- Sun Myung Moon, founder and leader of the Unification Church, is found guilty in federal court of income tax evasion.

1983

- The American Islamic College is established in Chicago.
- Jesse Jackson announces his candidacy for the Democratic nomination for president of the United States.
- President Ronald Reagan declares this the "year of the Bible."
- The union of northern and southern branches of mainline Presbyterianism, the United Presbyterian Church (northern) and the Presbyterian Church in the United States (southern), produces the Presbyterian Church in the United States of America.
- Conservative Catholic Michael Novak publishes a defense of nuclear armament titled *Moral Clarity in the Nuclear Age.*
- *July 5:* In *March v. Chambers,* the U.S. Supreme Court holds that prayers offered at the beginning of state legislative sessions do not violate the First Amendment's establishment clause.

1984

- Congress passes the Equal Access Act, which requires that public schools grant religious student organizations the same rights as other noncurricular student organizations.
- Jesse Jackson is the first black candidate to run for president of the United States and receives 3½ million votes in the Democratic primary.
- The United States establishes official diplomatic relations with the Vatican.
- Lutheran minister and later Catholic priest Richard John Neuhaus publishes *The Naked Public Square: Religion and Democracy in America,* which champions the necessity of religious participation in the political process.
- *March 5:* In *Lynch v. Donnelly* the U.S. Supreme Court rules that the inclusion of a nativity scene in a public holiday display does not violate the First Amendment's establishment clause.

1985

- Presbyterian minister John Fife and other leaders and participants in the Sanctuary movement are arrested for transporting illegal aliens. In a subsequent trial most of the defendants will be found guilty, but the judge, besieged by letters supporting their activities, grants them suspended sentences rather than time in prison.
- *June 4:* In *Wallace v. Jaffree* the U.S. Supreme Court rules that an Alabama statute providing for a moment of silence at the beginning of the school day in public schools violates the establishment clause of the First Amendment because it is an attempt to restore prayer to public schools.

1986

- Jewish writer and activist Elie Wiesel is awarded the Nobel Peace Prize.
- The Moral Majority ceases operations.

1987

- Jesse Jackson announces his candidacy for the Democratic nomination for U.S. president.
- Pat Robertson declares his candidacy for the Republican nomination for president.
- The American Buddhist Congress is founded.
- Randall Terry, a Christian minister, organizes Operation Rescue, a group devoted to disrupting the business and protesting the practices of abortion clinics.
- Televangelist Oral Roberts of Oklahoma announces that God will "call him home" unless supporters contribute $8 million to Oral Roberts University.
- *June 19:* In *Edwards v. Aguillard* the U.S. Supreme Court holds that a state law requiring the balanced treatment of evolution and creation science violates the establishment clause of the First Amendment.

1988

- The Evangelical Lutheran Church in America is organized.
- Jim Bakker is indicted for mail and wire fraud. He is ultimately convicted.
- Assembly of God minister Jimmy Swaggart is temporarily defrocked after news of his relations with a prostitute surfaces.
- *February 24:* In *Hustler Magazine v. Falwell* the U.S. Supreme Court holds that Jerry Falwell, a prominent Baptist minister, cannot recover damages from *Hustler* magazine for a sexual parody it published concerning him.

1989

- Pat Robertson founds the Christian Coalition.
- The North American Conference on Religion and Ecology is founded.
- Episcopal bishop John Spong ordains Robert Williams, an openly gay man, a priest.

1990

- Congress passes the Native American Graves Protection and Repatriation Act.
- Warith Deen Mohammed is the first Muslim to open the U.S. Senate with prayer.
- The Promise Keepers, a conservative Christian men's organization, is founded by Bill McCartney and Dave Wardell.
- Assistant Episcopal bishop of Newark, Walter Righter, ordains Barry Stopfel, an openly gay man, deacon. Bishop John Spong ordains Stopfel a priest the next year.

- *April 17:* In *Employment Division v. Smith* the U.S. Supreme Court holds that Native Americans who practice sacramental use of peyote are not entitled to an exemption from a state controlled-substance law that makes possession and use of peyote a crime.

1991

- The first Promise Keepers conference is held at the University of Colorado at Boulder.
- Catholic George Weigel publishes *Just War and the Gulf War*, which argues that the Gulf War satisfies the requirements of being a just war under Catholic teaching.
- Russian Orthodox patriarch Aleksy II visits the United States.
- *June 25:* Muslim iman Siraj Wahaj, an African American from Brooklyn, New York, offers a prayer before the U.S. House of Representatives, the first Muslim to do so.

1992

- *June 24:* In *Lee v. Weisman* the U.S. Supreme Court holds that it is unconstitutional for a public school to invite a rabbi to deliver prayers at a middle school graduation ceremony.
- *August:* Federal agents raid the Idaho home of Randy Weaver, a Christian survivalist influenced by the white supremacist group Christian Identity. A federal agent along with Weaver's 13-year-old son and his wife are killed before Weaver surrenders after an 11-day standoff.

1993

- The Islamic Assembly of North America is established.
- In the centennial year celebrating the original World's Parliament of Religions in Chicago in 1893, a second World's Parliament of Religions is held.
- Congress passes the Religious Freedom Restoration Act, which protects religious believers from the effects of laws burdening their beliefs or practise in the absence of overwhelmingly persuasive government justification for such burdens.
- The Evangelical Environmental Network is established, representing a new enthusiasm for environmental causes among evangelical Christians. The same year the National Religious Partnership for the Environment is founded.
- The first Islamic chaplain is commissioned in the U.S. Army.

- Religiously inspired antiabortion activist Michael Griffin of Pensacola shoots and kills abortion doctor David Gunn.
- *February 28:* The Bureau of Alcohol, Tobacco and Firearms along with the FBI and other federal agents stage a raid on the Branch Davidian compound at Waco, Texas.
- *April 19:* An FBI assault on the Branch Davidian compound in Waco, Texas, leads to a fire that kills more than 70 people, including Davidian leader David Koresh.
- *June 11:* In *Church of Lukumi Babalu Aye v. Hialeah* the U.S. Supreme Court holds that local ordinances targeted to prohibit animal sacrifice by Santerians violated the free exercise clause of the First Amendment.

1994

- The Council on American Islamic Relations is organized.
- *July 29:* Religiously inspired antiabortion activist Paul Hill shoots and kills abortion doctor John Britton. He also kills James Barrett and wounds Barrett's wife, June. The couple were members of a Pensacola Unitarian church who were accompanying Britton from the airport to his abortion clinic.

1995

- Nation of Islam leader Louis Farrakhan organizes the Million Man March, which attracts hundreds of thousands of African-American men to the National Mall in Washington, D.C.
- Deepak Chopra establishes the Chopra Center for Well Being in La Jolla, California.
- The Southern Baptist Convention apologizes to African Americans for defending slavery in the antebellum South and for condoning racism.

1996

- With the support of the Christian Coalition and other conservative Christian groups, Congress passes the Defense of Marriage Act, which defines marriage as "a union between one man and one woman." The act is partially a response to religious opposition to gay marriages.
- *May:* Heresy proceedings against Assistant Bishop Walter Righter of New Jersey for having ordained an openly gay deacon (who was subsequently ordained a priest by Bishop John Spong) are dismissed because of a lack of Episcopal doctrine specifically prohibiting gay ordinations.

1997

- In *City of Boerne v. Flores* the U.S. Supreme Court holds that Congress lacks the power to pass the Religious Freedom Restoration Act, which protects religious believers from the unintentionally burdensome effect of certain state and local laws.
- *March:* A total of 38 members of the Heaven's Gate UFO cult in California commit mass suicide in anticipation of the arrival of the comet Hale-Bopp. Members of the group, established by Marshall Applewhite and Bonnie Lu Nettles, believed that a flying saucer concealed behind the comet would transplant them to the kingdom of heaven but that group members had to escape their mortal bodies to board the flying saucer.
- *October:* Promise Keepers sponsors a rally in Washington, D.C., called Stand in the Gap. The rally marks the high point of the group's public prominence.

1998

- Promise Keepers suffers severe financial difficulties, ending a period of rapid expansion.

1999

- The Reverend Jimmy Creech performs a lesbian marriage in North Carolina, is subsequently tried by the United Methodist Church, and is stripped of his ministerial credentials.

2001

- Justice Roy Moore, chief justice of the Alabama supreme court, oversees the installation of a granite display of the Ten Commandments in the rotunda of the Alabama Judicial Building. He is ultimately ordered by federal courts to remove the display, and when he refuses to do so, is removed from his judicial office.
- Bishop Wilton Gregory is the first African American to be elected president of the U.S. Conference of Catholic Bishops.
- The Reorganized Church of Jesus Christ of Latter Day Saints is renamed the Community of Christ.
- *September 11:* Terrorists later linked to Islamic militant Osama bin Laden crash two airliners into the World Trade Center, one into the Pentagon, and one into a field in Pennsylvania. The United States subsequently launches war against the Taliban in Afghanistan.

2002

- The Boston archdiocese of the Roman Catholic Church is caught up in controversy after allegations that the church had not dealt appropriately with priests accused of having sexually abused children and teenagers. Cardinal Bernard Law, archbishop of the Boston archdiocese, resigns on December 13 after allegations that he had not taken strong enough action to resolve the issues relating to sexual abuse.

2003

- The Episcopal Church approves the ordination of Rev. V. Gene Robinson, an openly gay priest, as bishop of New Hampshire.
- *September 3:* Antiabortion activist Paul Hill is executed by lethal injection for murdering abortion doctor John Britton and James Barrett.

2004

- *The Passion of the Christ,* a film directed by Mel Gibson about Jesus' final days, grosses $89.3 million in its first three days in theaters.

2005

- The U.S. Supreme Court holds that older Ten Commandment monuments on public property do not generally offend the First Amendment's establishment clause, but that newer monuments placed in courthouses are unconstitutional because they are intended to advance religion.

2006

- Religious believers take an active part in political debates concerning immigration reform and a proposed constitutional amendment banning same-sex marriage.
- *February:* Muslims around the world protest the publication of Danish cartoons in September 2005 that include representations of Muhammad.
- *February 8:* Eighty-six evangelical leaders urge Congress to enact legislation to reduce global warning.
- *February 29:* In *Gonzales v. O Centro Espirita,* the Supreme Court holds that under the Religious Freedom Restoration Act, the federal government had not demonstrated a compelling reason for preventing the members of a church known as Uniao Do Vegtal or the Union of the Plants from using a hallucinogenic tea as a means of connecting with God.

- *March 10:* Catholic Charities of Boston abandons arranging adoptions after failing to obtain an exemption from a state law prohibiting discrimination against gays in adoption.
- *June 18:* Katherine Jefferts Schori, bishop of Nevada, is elected as presiding bishop of the Episcopal Church in the United States.
- *September 27:* President George W. Bush signs into law a bill that awards the congressional medal of honor to the Dalai Lama, the leader of Tibetan Buddhism, over the protests of Chinese leaders.
- *November:* Ted Haggard, president of the National Association of Evangelicals, is forced to resign from this post, and fired from his position as pastor of the New Life Church in Colorado Springs, Colorado, after news surfaces of his alleged sexual liaisons with a male prostitute.
- *November:* Congressional elections produce a new Congress that will include, for the first time, a Muslim, two Buddhists, and the highest ranking Mormon in congressional history (Senator Harry Reid, the incoming Democratic majority leader).
- *December 1:* The Supreme Court agrees to hear a case concerning whether private citizens should be allowed to bring a case charging that President George W. Bush's "faith-based initiative" violates the First Amendment's prohibition against laws "respecting" an establishment of religion.
- *December 6:* The Rabbinical Assembly of Conservative Judaism votes to allow ordination of gay rabbis and the celebration of same-sex commitment ceremonies.
- *December 11:* A gathering of Holocaust deniers in Iran prompts protests around the globe.

The Dalai Lama converses with monks before a prayer session in northern India. (*JITENDRA PRAKASH/Reuters/Landov*)

Eyewitness Testimony

Our nation is now faced with serious challenges and choices which may require sacrifice, even from those assembled here in this great hall. But it's important that we keep our perspective and realize what is truly valuable. It is not a sacrifice to give up waste. It's not a sacrifice to submit to God's will. It's not a sacrifice to care for others or to struggle for peace or to tell the truth.

President Jimmy Carter, January 1980, speech to the National Association of Religious Broadcasters, in Hutcheson, God in the Whitehouse, *p. 144.*

The Divine Potter can change the circumstances of the human clay, maybe adding a little suffering here and there. If we refuse to be molded into the original shape meant for us, namely, holiness and perfect imitation of Christ, He molds us into useful pitchers from which He can pour out His Divine Grace. God does not make anything with the purpose of destroying it. There is no waste in life. Childhood is not a waste. It has relationship to the rest of life.

That portion of us which is tried and tested, which is subjected to many trials, is not a waste. The tears, the agonies, the frustrations, the toils are not loss. All of these, which seem to militate against life, are worked into new forms. Life may be marred into a broken thing, but God can make it into a thing of beauty. So if I were asked if I had my life to live over again, would I love the priesthood as I have, the answer is "No, I would try to love Christ more." The only sorrow in my life, or any life, is not to have loved Him enough.

Catholic bishop Fulton Sheen, 1980, Treasure in Clay, *p. 35.*

There is a singing group in this Catholic church today, a singing group which calls itself "Wildflowers." The lead is a tall, square-jawed teen-aged boy, buoyant and glad to be here. He carries a guitar; he plucks out a little bluesy riff and hits some chords. With him are the rest of the Wildflowers. There is an old woman, wonderfully determined; she has long orange hair and is dressed country-and-western style. A long embroidered strap around her neck slings a big western guitar low over her pelvis. Beside her stands a frail, withdrawn fourteen-year-old boy, and a large Chinese man in his twenties who seems to want to enjoy himself but is not quite sure how to. He looks around wildly as he sings, and shuffles his feet. There is also a very tall teen-aged girl, presumably the lead singer's

In this photograph a guitarist plays at a Catholic folk mass. *(National Archives NWDNS-412-DA-15937)*

girl friend; she is delicate of feature, half serene and half petrified, a wispy soprano. They straggle out in front of the altar and teach us a brand new hymn.

It all seems a pity at first, for I have overcome a fiercely anti-Catholic upbringing in order to attend Mass simply and solely to escape Protestant guitars. Why am I here? Who gave these nice Catholics guitars? Why are they not mumbling in Latin and performing superstitious rituals? What is the Pope thinking of?

Writer Annie Dillard, 1982, Teaching a Stone to Talk, *pp. 17–18.*

Nor is it only the joy of God and the comfort of God that come at unforeseen times. God's coming is always unforeseen, I think, and the reason, if I had to guess, is that if he gave us anything much in the way of advance warning, more often than not we would have made ourselves scarce long before he got there.

. . . . .

[F]or the first time in my life that year in New York, I started going to church regularly, and what was farcical about it was not that I went but my reason for going, which was simply that on the same block where I lived there happened to be a church with a preacher I had heard of and that I had nothing all that much better to do with my lonely Sundays. The preacher was a man named George Buttrick, and Sunday after Sunday I went, and sermon after sermon I heard. . . . And then there came one particular sermon with one particular phrase in it that does not even appear in a transcript of his words that somebody sent me more than twenty-five years later so I can only assume that he must have dreamed it up at the last minute and ad-libbed it—and on just such foolish, tenuous, holy threads as that, I suppose, hang the destinies of us all. Jesus Christ refused the crown that Satan offered him in the wilderness, Buttrick said, but he is king nonetheless because again and again he is crowned in the heart of people who believe in him. And that inward coronation takes place, Buttrick said, "among confusion, and tears, and great laughter."

It was the phrase *great laughter* that did it, did whatever it was that I believe must have been hiddenly in the doing all the years of my journey up till then. It was not so much that a door opened as that I suddenly found that a door had been open all along which I had only just then stumbled upon.

American writer Frederick Buechner, 1982, The Sacred Journey, *pp. 105–109.*

Those of you in the National Association of Evangelicals are known for your spiritual and humanitarian work. And I would be especially remiss if I didn't discharge right now one personal debt of gratitude. Thank you for your prayers. Nancy and I have felt their presence many times in many ways. And believe me, for us they've made all the difference.

The other day in the East Room of the White House at a meeting there, someone asked me whether I was aware of all the people out there who were praying for the President. And I had to say, "Yes, I am. I've felt it. I believe in intercessionary prayer." But I couldn't help but say to that questioner after he'd asked the question that—or at least say to them that if sometimes when he was praying he got a busy signal, it was just me in there ahead of him. I think I understand how Abraham Lincoln felt when he said, "I have been driven many times

to my knees by the overwhelming conviction that I had nowhere else to go."

I'll tell you there are a great many God-fearing, dedicated, noble men and women in public life, present company included. And, yes, we need your help to keep us ever mindful of the ideas and the principles that brought us into the public arena in the first place. The basis of those ideals and principles is a commitment to freedom and personal liberty that, itself, is grounded in the much deeper realization that freedom prospers only where the blessings of God are avidly sought and humbly accepted.

President Ronald Reagan, 1983,
"National Association of Evangelicals; Remarks at the
Annual Convention in Orlando, Florida," in Harvey and Goff,
The Columbia Documentary History of Religion
in America since 1945, *p. 68.*

The churches are disappointing, even for most believers. If Christ brings us new life, it is all the more remarkable that the church, the very bearer of this good news, should be among the most dispirited institutions of the age. The alternatives to the institutional churches are even more grossly disappointing, from TV evangelists with their blown-dry hairdos to California cults led by prosperous gurus ignored in India but embraced in La Jolla.

Novelist Walker Percy, 1983, Lost in the Cosmos,
pp. 179–180.

Forty years ago, a young man awoke and he found himself an orphan in an orphaned world. What have I learned in the last 41 years? Small things. I learned the perils of language and those of science. I learned that in extreme situations when human lives and dignity are at stake, neutrality is a sin. It helps the killers, not the victims. I learned the meaning of solitude, Mr. President. We were alone, desperately alone.

Today is April 19, and April 19, 1943, the Warsaw Ghetto rose in arms against the onslaught of the Nazis. There were so few and so young and so helpless. And nobody came to their help. And they had to fight what was then the mightiest legion in Europe. Every underground received help except the Jewish underground. And yet they managed to fight and resist and push back those Nazis and their accomplices for six weeks. And yet the leaders of the free world, Mr. President, knew everything and did so little, or nothing, or at least nothing specifically to save Jewish children from death. . . . One million Jewish children perished. If I spent my entire life reciting their names, I would die before finishing the task.

. . . . .

I have learned that the Holocaust was a unique and uniquely Jewish event, albeit with universal implication. Not all victims were Jews. But all Jews were victims. I have learned the danger of indifference, the crime of indifference. For the opposite of love, I have learned, is not hate, but indifference. Jews were killed by the enemy but betrayed by their so-called allies, who found political reasons to justify their indifference of passivity.

But I have also learned that suffering confers no privileges. It all depends what one does with it. And this is why survivors, of whom you spoke, Mr. President, have tried to teach their contemporaries how to build on ruins, how to invent hope in a world that offers none, how to proclaim faith to a generation that has seen it shamed and mutilated. And I believe, we believe, that memory is the answer, perhaps the only answer.

Writer and Holocaust survivor Elie Wiesel, April 19, 1985, statement to President Ronald Reagan on receiving the Congressional Gold Medal of Achievement, in Marcus, The Jew in the American World, *pp. 604–605.*

Abortion was not a national issue until the Supreme Court, in *Roe v. Wade,* set national standards for state laws. Abortion did *not* become an issue because Fundamentalists wanted to *strengthen* prohibitions against abortion, but because liberals wanted to abolish them. Equal rights for women did *not* become an issue because Fundamentalists wanted to *limit* women's rights, but because the proposed Equal Rights Amendment raised fears, both rational and irrational, that all traditional distinctions between men's and women's roles would be overturned. (That these fears were not so irrational is evidenced by the litigation against a military draft for men only.) Pornography in the 1980s did *not* become an issue because Fundamentalists wanted to *ban* D. H. Lawrence, James Joyce, or even Henry Miller, but because in the 1960s and 1970s under-the-table pornography moved to the top of the newsstands. Prayer in the schools did *not* become an issue because Fundamentalists wanted to *introduce* new prayers or sectarian prayers but because the Supreme Court ruled against all prayers. Freedom for religious schools became an issue *not* because of any legal effort to expand their scope, but because the Internal Revenue Service and various state authorities tried to impose restrictions on them that private schools had not faced before.

Conservative commentator Nathan Glazer, 1987, "Fundamentalism: A Defensive Offensive," in Hutcheson, God in the Whitehouse, *pp. 159–160.*

Vatican II has become, for many Catholics, a center of controversy. Some voices from the extreme right and the extreme left frankly reject the council. Reactionaries of the traditionalist variety censure it for having yielded to Protestant and modernist tendencies. Radicals of the far left, conversely, complain that the council, while making some progress, failed to do away with the church's absolutistic claims and its antiquated class structures. The vast majority of Catholics, expressing satisfaction with the results of the council, are still divided because they interpret it in contrary ways.

Catholic theologian and, subsequently, cardinal Avery Dulles, 1988, "The Reshaping of Catholicism: Current Challenges in the Theology of the Church," *in Gillis,* Roman Catholicism in America, *p. 95.*

Contemporary American politics faces few greater dilemmas than deciding how to deal with the resurgence of religious belief. On the one hand, American ideology cherishes religion, as it does all matters of private conscience, which is why we justly celebrate a strong tradition against state interference with private religious choice. At the same time, many political leaders, commentators, scholars, and voters are coming to view any religious element in public moral discourse as a tool of the radical right for reshaping American society. But the effort to banish religion for politics' sake has led us astray: In our sensible zeal to keep religion from dominating our politics, we have created a political and legal culture that presses the religiously faithful to be other than themselves, to act publicly, and sometimes privately as well, as though their faith does not matter to them.

. . . . .

Yet religion matters to people, and matters a lot. Surveys indicate that Americans are far more likely to believe in God and to attend worship services regularly than any other people in the Western world. True, nobody prays on prime-time television unless religion is a part of the plot, but strong majorities of citizens tell pollsters that their religious beliefs are of great importance to them in their daily lives. Even though some popular histories wrongly assert the contrary, the best evidence of this is that this deep religiosity has always been a facet of the American character and that it has grown consistently through the nation's history. And today, to the frustration of many opinion leaders in both the legal and political cultures, religion, as a moral force and perhaps a political one too, is surging. Unfortunately, in our public life, we prefer to pretend that it is not.

Legal scholar Stephen Carter, 1993, The Culture of Disbelief, *pp. 3–4.*

Fear is not a bad place to start a spiritual journey. If you know what makes you afraid, you can see more clearly that the way out is through the fear. For me, this has meant acknowledging that the strong emotions dredged up by the few Christian worship services—usually weddings or funeral—I attended during the twenty-year period when I would have described my religion as "nothing," were trying to tell me something. It has meant coming to terms with my fundamentalist Methodist ancestors, no longer ignoring them but respecting their power.

. . . . .

At its Latin root, the word religion is linked to the words ligature and ligament, words having both negative and positive connotations, offering both bondage and freedom of movement. For me, religion is the ligament that connects me to my grandmothers, who representing so clearly the negative and positive aspects of the Christian tradition, made it impossible for me either to reject or accept the religion wholesale. They made it unlikely that I would settle for either the easy answers of fundamentalism or the overintellectualized banalities of a conventionally liberal faith. Instead, the more deeply I've reclaimed what was good in their faith, the more they have set me free to find my own way.

Step by step, as I made my way back to church, I began to find that many of the things modern people assume are irrelevant—the liturgical year, the liturgy of the hours, the Incarnation as an everyday reality—are in fact essential to my identity and my survival. I'm not denying the past, or trying to bring it back, but am seeking in my inheritance what theologian Letty Russell terms "a usable past." Perhaps I am also redefining frontier not as a place you exploit and abandon but as a place where you build on the past for the future. When we journey here, we discover it is no less old than new. T. S. Eliot wrote, "The end of our exploring / Will be to arrive where we started / And know the place for the first time." Against

all odds, I rediscovered the religion I was born to, and found in it a home.

Kathleen Norris, poet, 1993, Dakota: A Spiritual Geography, *reprinted in Mandelker & Powers, eds.,* Pilgrim Souls: A Collection of Spiritual Biographies, *pp. 144–146.*

The world is in agony. The agony is so pervasive and urgent that we are compelled to name its manifestations so that the depth of this pain may be made clear. Peace eludes us—the planet is being destroyed—neighbors live in fear—women and men are estranged from each other—children die!

This is abhorrent.

We condemn the abuses of Earth's ecosystems. We condemn the poverty that stifles life's potential; the hunger that weakens the human body, the economic disparities that threaten so many families with ruin. We condemn the social disarray of the nations; the disregard for justice which pushes citizens to the margin; the anarchy overtaking our communities; and the insane death of children from violence. In particular we condemn aggression and hatred in the name of religion. But this agony need not be. It need not be because the basis for an ethic already exists. This ethic offers the possibility of a better individual and global order, and leads individuals away from despair and societies away from chaos.

We are women and men who have embraced the precepts and practices of the world's religions: We affirm that a common set of core values is found in the teachings of the religions, and that these form the basis of a global ethic. We affirm that this truth is already known, but yet to be lived in heart and action. We affirm that there is an irrevocable, unconditional norm for all areas of life, for families and communities, for races, nations, and religions. There already exist ancient guidelines for human behavior which are found in the teachings of the religions of the world and which are the condition for a sustainable world order.

We declare:

We are interdependent. Each of us depends on the well-being of the whole, and so we have respect for the community of living beings, for people, animals, and plants, and for the preservation of Earth, the air, water and soil. We take individual responsibility for all we do. All our decisions, actions, and failures to act have consequences.

We must treat others as we wish others to treat us. We make a commitment to respect life and dignity, individuality and diversity, so that every person is treated humanely, without exception. We must have patience and acceptance. We must be able to forgive, learning from the past but never allowing ourselves to be enslaved by memories of hate. Opening our hearts to one another, we must sink our narrow differences for the cause of the world community, practicing a culture of solidarity and relatedness. We consider humankind our family. We must strive to be kind and generous. We must not live for ourselves alone, but should also serve others, never forgetting the children, the aged, the poor, the suffering, the disabled, the refugees, and the lonely. No person should ever be considered or treated as a second-class citizen, or be exploited in any way whatsoever. There should be equal partnership between men and women. We must not commit any kind of sexual immorality. We must put behind us all forms of domination or abuse. We commit ourselves to a culture of non-violence, respect, justice, and peace. We shall not oppress, injure, torture, or kill other human beings, forsaking violence as a means of settling differences. We must strive for a just social and economic order, in which everyone has an equal chance to reach full potential as a human being. We must speak and act truthfully and with compassion, dealing fairly with all, and avoiding prejudice and hatred. We must not steal. We must move beyond the dominance of greed for power, prestige, money, and consumption to make a just and peaceful world. Earth cannot be changed for the better unless the consciousness of individuals is changed first. We pledge to increase our awareness by disciplining our minds, by meditation, by prayer, or by positive thinking. Without risk and a readiness to sacrifice there can be no fundamental change in our situation. Therefore we commit ourselves to this global ethic, to understanding one another, and to socially beneficial, peace-fostering, and nature-friendly ways of life. We invite all people, whether religious or not, to do the same.

"Toward a Global Ethic," 1993, statement discussed and adopted by many of the leaders of the 1993 World Parliament of Religions in Chicago, available online at URL: http://www.cpwr.org/resource/ethic.pdf. *Accessed on July 22, 2005.*

The house of Judaism in North America has not been satisfactorily built—it does not have a spiritual dimension for many Jews. Too many Jews are like me: our Jewishness has been an inchoate mixture of nostalgia, family feeling, group identification, a smattering of Hebrew, concern for Israel, and so forth. Yet we feel we are Jews, very strongly, and sense that somehow none of the current denominations really speak to our needs.

. . . . .

The dialogue with Tibetans has heightened my awareness of the precious value and fragility of all of our world's ancient spiritual traditions.

. . . . .

I worry too about my own people. I am grateful we have an Israel and that some remnants of the great Talmudic and Hasidic traditions have survived the Holocaust and propagate themselves in America. Perhaps it is true that the only Judaism to survive in the long run will be among these separationists, these preservationists. Or perhaps in the future there will only be two types of Jews: totally assimilated and Israelis. I am hoping for a third alternative. I am hoping Judaism will survive and renew itself, because it has something vital to offer the world.

Poet Rodger Kamenetz, 1994, The Jew in the Lotus, *pp. 282, 287–288.*

Nearly three decades ago I wrote a book, *The Secular City,* in which I tried to work out a theology for the "postreligious" age that many sociologists had confidently assured us was coming. Since then, however, religion—or at least some religions—seems to have gained a new lease on life. Today it is secularity, not spirituality, that may be headed for extinction.

. . . . .

[I]t had become obvious that instead of the "death of God" some theologians pronounced not many years ago, or the waning of religion that sociologists had extrapolated, something quite different has taken place. Perhaps I was too young and impressionable when the scholars made those sobering projections. In any case I had swallowed them all too easily and had tried to think about what their theological consequences might be. But it had now become clear that the predictions themselves had been wrong. The prognosticators had written that the technological pace and urban bustle of the twentieth century would increasingly shove religion to the margin where, deprived of roots, it would shrivel. They allowed that faith might well survive as a valued heirloom, perhaps in ethnic or family customs, but insisted that religion's days as shaper of culture and history were over.

This did not happen. Instead, before the academic forecasters could even begin to draw their pensions, a religious renaissance of sorts is under way all over the globe. Religions that some theologians thought had been stunted by western materialism or suffocated by totalitarian repression have gained a whole new vigor.

Harvard Divinity School professor Harvey Cox, 1994, Fire from Heaven, *pp. xv–xvi.*

On one of the Knicks' road trips, I picked up a copy of William James' *The Varieties of Religious Experience,* a book filled with firsthand accounts by Quakers, Shakers, and other Christian mystics. I couldn't put it down. Reading their stories, it was clear that mystical experience didn't have to be a big production. It didn't require hallucinogenic drugs or a major Pentecostal-style catharsis. It could be as uneventful as a moment of reflection.

When I finished the book, I put it down, said a prayer and, all of a sudden, experienced a quiet feeling of inner peace. Nothing special—and yet there it was. This was the experience I had longed for as a teenager. It wasn't the big, crashing moment of transcendence that I expected, but it came close enough to give me an idea of what I had been missing. It also gave me a deeper understanding of my Pentecostal roots and helped lift the curtain of guilt that had shrouded me most of my life. I no longer felt compelled to run from my past or cling to it out of fear. I could take from it what worked for me and let the rest go. I could also explore other traditions more fully without feeling as if I was committing a major sacrilege against God and family.

Professional basketball coach Phil Jackson, 1995, Sacred Hoops, *p. 46.*

You came not at the call of Louis Farrakhan, but you have gathered here at the call of God. For it is only the call of Almighty God, no matter through whom that call came, that could generate this kind of outpouring. God called us here to this place. At this time. For a very specific reason.

. . . . .

So, we stand here today at this historic moment. We are standing in the place of those who couldn't make it here today. We are standing on the blood of our ancestors. We are standing on the blood of those who died in the middle passage, who died in the fields and swamps of America, who died hanging from trees in the South, who died in the cells of their jailers, who died on the highways and who died in the fratricidal conflict that rages within our community. We are standing on the sacrifice of the lives of those heroes, our great men and women that we today may accept the responsibility that life imposes upon each traveler who comes this way.

We must accept the responsibility that God has put upon us, not only to be good husbands and fathers and builders of our community, but God is now calling upon the despised and rejected to become the cornerstone and the builders of a new world.

Nation of Islam leader Louis Farrakhan, 1995, "Minister Farrakhan Challenges Black Men" (Transcript from Remarks at the Million Man March), in Harvey and Goff, The Columbia Documentary History of Religion in America since 1945, *p. 303.*

"Those who lose their life for my sake will find it," Jesus says. There is no day without many losses. If we are attentive to our inner life, we quickly realize how many times things are not happening in the way we hoped, people aren't saying what we expected, the day is not evolving as we wanted, et cetera, et cetera. All these little "losses" can make us bitter people who complain that life is not fair to us. But if we live these losses for the sake of Jesus—that is, in communion with his redemptive death—then our losses can gradually free us from our self-centeredness and open our hearts to the new life that comes from God. The real question is: "Do I live my losses for my sake or for Jesus' sake?" That choice for death or life.

Henri J. M. Nouwen, Catholic priest, educator, and writer, August 9, 1996, in Sabbatical Journey: The Diary of His Final Year, *p. 211.*

And there was Watergate, which some people thought rubbed off on my reputation.

. . . . .

The Watergate break-in, an undeniable personal and national tragedy, should never have happened in the first place. And it should have been laid to rest long before now. If the Lord were as unforgiving to us sinful and disobedient humans as were are to each other, even the best among us wouldn't stand a chance at the Great Judgment. It may not be in the Bible, but there is God's own truth in Alexander Pope's proverb, "To err is human, to forgive divine."

The whole library of literature that has been written detailing the Watergate break-in and the subsequent cover-up has not explained for me what came over President Richard Nixon at that time. I deliberately chose the words *came over* because I cannot accept in my heart that his conduct and conversation during that crisis sprang from the deep wells of his character. The evidence on the tapes and the testimony of many associates leave no doubt that he was culpable. I did not absolve him—but neither did I judge him.

Evangelist Billy Graham, 1997, Just as I Am, *p. 456.*

I hadn't gone shopping for a new religion. After twenty-five years as a writer in America, I wanted something to soften my cynicism. I was searching for new terms by which to see. . . . I could not have drawn up a list of demands, but I had a fair idea of what I was after. . . . There would be no priests, no separation between nature and things sacred. There would be no war with the flesh, if I could help it. Sex would be natural, not the seat of a curse upon the species. Finally, I'd want a ritual component, a daily routine to sharpen the senses and discipline my mind. Above all, I wanted clarity and freedom. I did not want to trade away reason simply to be saddled with a dogma. The more I leaned about Islam, the more it appeared to conform to what I was after.

American writer Michael Wolfe, 1998, The Hadj: An American Pilgrimage to Mecca, *quoted in Smith,* Islam in America, *p. ix.*

There's never a time that I sit in a fast and testimony meeting . . . that I don't think about how grateful I am for a young boy who wanted to know which church to join. It's this time of the year that the pageant in Palmyra is going on, the Hill Cumorah. . . . I'm grateful for him and the many struggles he had in his short life, and what he accomplished. Surely the Prophet Joseph Smith was a prophet of God. And I'm grateful for President Hinckley, and the message he leaves and the kind of life he lives. You can't go wrong if you follow the prophet. I'm grateful for my wife and our children and grandchildren for their commitment to serve the Lord, and their desire to do so. I know that Jesus is the Christ, the Son of God, that he is the only person whereby we can receive exaltation in our lives, that this is his church,

that the Bible and the Book of Mormon are true. [The Book of Mormon] is a powerful book and can be a great solace to us, which solves our problems, answers our questions, and is a guidance to us throughout our lives. The scriptures are a great blessing to us, but they are only a blessing when we search and ponder and pray about them. Again I testify that this is the Lord's work, and that Jesus is the Christ, and that we have a prophet. And I leave these things with you in the name of Jesus Christ. Amen.

Testimony of an unnamed retired Mormon, an adult Sunday school teacher, at a Mormon fast and testimony meeting, August 1, 1999, in McDannell, Religions of the United States in Practice, *vol. 2, pp. 70–71.*

All Christians are under obligation to seek to make the will of Christ supreme in our own lives and in human society. Means and methods used for the improvement of society and the establishment of righteousness among men can be truly and permanently helpful only when they are rooted in the regeneration of the individual by the saving grace of God in Jesus Christ. In the spirit of Christ, Christians should oppose racism, every form of greed, selfishness, and vice, and all forms of sexual immorality, including adultery, homosexuality, and pornography. We should work to provide for the orphaned, the needy, the abused, the aged, the helpless, and the sick. We should speak on behalf of the unborn and contend for the sanctity of all human life from conception to natural death. Every Christian should seek to bring industry, government, and society as a whole under the sway of the principles of righteousness, truth, and brotherly love. In order to promote these ends Christians should be ready to work with all men of good will in any good cause, always being careful to act in the spirit of love without compromising their loyalty to Christ and His truth.

Excerpt from The Baptist Faith and Message, *an updated version adopted by the Southern Baptist Convention, June 14, 2000, in Brasher,* Encyclopedia of Fundamentalism, *p. 51.*

I stand before you today as an advocate of anti-hate crimes legislation. Hate crimes are a challenge to all religious believers. While religion preaches that we are all God's children, hate crimes are evidence of a pernicious belief that those who are different, be it in race, creed, ethnicity, or sexual orientation not only cannot claim

God's grace, but may actually be subjected to physical harm. This is a belief that no religion can accept, and it is particularly anathma to Sikhs, with their traditions of tolerance and mutual understanding. . . . America is a nation of diversity, and it is strong to the extent that we respect each other's beliefs, customs, and achievements. Passage of anti-hate crime legislation will put the practitioners of hate on notice that they cannot do violence to those whom they may not like and expect to get away with it.

Dr. Rajwant Singh, president of the Sikh Council on Religion and Education, September 2000, at a rally in support of anti–hate crime legislation pending before Congress, in Eck, A New Religious America, *p. 75.*

Asian and Pacific Catholic Americans and immigrants migrated with the experience and sensibilities of the great religions and spiritual traditions of the world together with Christianity: Judaism, Islam, Hinduism, Buddhism, Taoism, Confucianism, Zoroastrianism, Jainism, Sikhism and Shintoism. In its best expressions, the important values of harmonious relationship with one another, with society, and with nature; the realization of a cosmic design that gives meaning to an apparently chaotic world; the belief in salvation from the senseless suffering in this world; the necessity of silence and contemplation, detachment from the world, simplicity, frugal living, consonance with neighbors and all of creation, respect for life; nonviolence; the spirit of hard work—all these shape the cultures of the peoples of Asia and the Pacific Islands. Their experience of the great religions and spiritual traditions teach them how to live with, and have the deepest respect for these traditions.

. . . . .

Despite the fact that many Christian immigrants from Asia have suffered persecution in their homelands, we are mindful that their religiosity has roots in their Asian spiritual traditions. Their experience demonstrates the values of these religions and spiritual traditions, and how these values await their fulfillment in the revelation of Jesus Christ.

National Conference of Catholic Bishops, July 2001, "Asian and Pacific Presence: Harmony in Faith," in Obo, The Columbia Documentary History of the Asian American Experience, *p. 562.*

We are here in the middle hour of our grief. So many have suffered so great a loss, and today we express our nation's sorrow. We come before God to pray for the missing and the dead, and for those who love them.

On Tuesday, our country was attacked with deliberate and massive cruelty. We have seen the images of fire and ashes, and bent steel.

Now come the names, the list of casualties we are only beginning to read. They are the names of men and women who began their day at a desk or in an airport, busy with life. They are the names of people who faced death, and in their last moments called home to say, be brave, and I love you.

They are the names of passengers who defied their murderers, and prevented the murder of others on the ground. They are the names of men and women who wore the uniform of the United States, and died at their posts.

They are the names of rescuers, the ones whom death found running up the stairs and into the fires to help others. We will read all these names. We will linger over them, and learn their stories, and many Americans will weep.

To the children and parents and spouses and families and friends of the lost, we offer the deepest sympathy of the nation. And I assure you, you are not alone.

. . . . .

God's signs are not always the ones we look for. We learn in tragedy that his purposes are not always our own. Yet the prayers of private suffering, whether in our homes or in this great cathedral, are known and heard, and understood.

There are prayers that help us last through the day, or endure the night. There are prayers of friends and strangers, that give us strength for the journey. And there are prayers that yield our will to a will greater than our own.

This world He created is of moral design. Grief and tragedy and hatred are only for a time. Goodness, remembrance, and love have no end. And the Lord of life holds all who die, and all who mourn.

It is said that adversity introduces us to ourselves. This is true of a nation as well. In this trial, we have been reminded, and the world has seen, that our fellow Americans are generous and kind, resourceful and brave. We see our national character in rescuers working past exhaustion; in long lines of blood donors; in thousands of citizens who have asked to work and serve in any way possible.

And we have seen our national character in eloquent acts of sacrifice. Inside the World Trade Center, one man who could have saved himself stayed until the end at the side of his quadriplegic friend. A beloved priest died giving the last rites to a firefighter. Two office workers, finding a disabled stranger, carried her down sixty-eight floors to safety. A group of men drove through the night from Dallas to Washington to bring skin grafts for burn victims.

In these acts, and in many others, Americans showed a deep commitment to one another, and an abiding love for our country. Today, we feel what Franklin Roosevelt called the warm courage of national unity. This is a unity of every faith, and every background.

It has joined together political parties in both houses of Congress. It is evident in services of prayer and candlelight vigils, and American flags, which are displayed in pride, and wave in defiance.

Our unity is a kinship of grief, and a steadfast resolve to prevail against our enemies. And this unity against terror is now extending across the world.

America is a nation full of good fortune, with so much to be grateful for. But we are not spared from suffering. In every generation, the world has produced enemies of human freedom. They have attacked America, because we are freedom's home and defender. And the commitment of our fathers is now the calling of our time.

On this national day of prayer and remembrance, we ask almighty God to watch over our nation, and grant us patience and resolve in all that is to come. We pray that He will comfort and console those who now walk in sorrow. We thank Him for each life we now must mourn, and the promise of a life to come.

As we have been assured, neither death nor life, nor angels nor principalities nor powers, nor things present nor things to come, nor height nor depth, can separate us from God's love. May He bless the souls of the departed. May He comfort our own. And may He always guide our country.

God bless America.

President George W. Bush, September 14, 2001, remarks at the Washington National Cathedral on the occasion of a National Day of Prayer and Remembrance of the attacks of September 11, 2001, available online at URL: http://www. whitehouse.gov/news/releases/2001/09/20010914-2.html. Accessed on November 15, 2006.

We, the undersigned Muslims, wish to state clearly that those who commit acts of terror, murder and cruelty in the name of Islam are not only destroying innocent lives, but are also betraying the values of the faith they claim to represent. No injustice done to Muslims can ever justify the massacre of innocent people, and no act of terror will ever serve the cause of Islam. We repudiate and dissociate ourselves from any Muslim group or individual who commits such brutal and un-Islamic acts. We refuse to allow our faith to be held hostage by the criminal actions of a tiny minority acting outside the teachings of both the Quran and the Prophet Muhammad, peace be upon him.

As it states in the Quran: "Oh you who believe, stand up firmly for justice, as witnesses to God, even if it be against yourselves, or your parents, or your kin, and whether it be against rich or poor; for God can best protect both. Do not follow any passion, lest you not be just. And if you distort or decline to do justice, verily God is well-acquainted with all that you do." (Quran 4:135)

Muhammad Nur Abdullah, president of the Islamic Society of North America, and other members of the society, May 22, 2004, available online at URL: http://islam. about.com/gi/dynamic/offsite.htm?site=http:// www.phillyburbs.com/pb%2Ddyn/news/ 1%2D09092003%2D155967.html. Accessed on January 22, 2006.

The religious and political Right gets the public meaning of religion mostly wrong—preferring to focus only on sexual and cultural issues while ignoring the weightier matters of justice. And the secular Left doesn't seem to get the meaning and promise of faith for politics at all—mistakenly dismissing spirituality as irrelevant to social change. I actually happen to be conservative on issues of personal responsibility, the sacredness of human life, the reality of evil in our world, and the critical importance of individual character, parenting, and strong "family values." But the popular presentations of religion in our time (especially in the media) almost completely ignore the biblical vision of social justice and, even worse, dismiss such concerns as merely "left wing."

It is indeed time to take back our faith.

Take back our faith from whom? To be honest, the confusion comes from many sources. From religious right-wingers who claim to know God's political views on every issue, then ignore the subjects that God seems to care the most about. From pedophile priests and cover-up bishops who destroy lives and shame the church.

From television preachers whose extravagant lifestyles and crass fund-raising tactics embarrass more Christians than they know. From liberal secularists who want to banish faith from public life and deny spiritual values to the soul of politics. And even from liberal theologians whose cultural conformity and creedal modernity serve to erode the foundations of historic biblical faith. From New Age philosophers who want to make Jesus into a nonthreatening spiritual guru. And from politicians who love to say how religious they are but utterly fail to apply the values of faith to their public leadership and political policies.

Christian political activist Jim Wallis, founder of Sojourners *magazine, 2005,* God's Politics, *pp. 3–4.*

Appendix A
Documents

1. Bartolome de Las Casas, *Brief Account of the Devastation of the Indies*, 1542
2. The Fundamental Orders of Connecticut, 1639
3. Maryland Act Concerning Religion, 1649
4. Massachusetts law banishing Quakers, 1658
5. Pennsylvania Charter of Privileges, 1701
6. Delaware Charter, 1701
7. Benjamin Franklin, letter to the London *Packet*, 1772
8. Virginia Declaration of Rights, 1776
9. The Declaration of Independence, 1776
10. Thomas Jefferson, bill for establishing Religious Freedom, 1779
11. James Madison, Memorial and Remonstrance, 1785
12. Article VI of the U.S. Constitution, 1787; ratified 1788
13. Thomas Jefferson, *Notes on the State of Virginia*, 1787
14. The Federalist 51 (Publius [James Madison]), February 6, 1788
15. George Washington, letter to the General Committee of the United Baptist Churches in Virginia, 1789
16. Debates in the House of Representatives concerning the proposed amendments to the Constitution, August 15, 1789
17. Amendment I, U.S. Constitution, 1791
18. Plan of Union adopted by Congregationalists and Presbyterians, 1801
19. James Madison, Detached Memoranda, ca. 1817
20. Amendment XIV, sec. 1, U.S. Constitution, 1868
21. The Blaine Amendment, 1875
22. Preamble to the Constitution of the Jewish Theological Seminary, 1886
23. Charter of the Kehillah (Jewish Community) of New York City, April 5, 1914
24. Amendment XVIII, U.S. Constitution, 1919
25. Amendment XXI, U.S. Constitution, 1933
26. Student Non-Violent Coordinating Committee (SNCC) Statement of Purpose, 1960
27. Opinion of Justice Hugo Black for the U.S. Supreme Court in *Engel v. Vitale*, 1963
28. Civil Rights Act, 1964
29. Declaration on the relation of the Church to Non-Christian Religions, *Nostra Aetate*, proclaimed by Pope Paul VI, October 28, 1965
30. *Black Manifesto*, 1969
31. *The Williamsburg Charter*, 1988

1. Bartolome de Las Casas, *Brief Account of the Devastation of the Indies* (1542)

The Indies were discovered in the year one thousand four hundred and ninety-two. In the following year a great many Spaniards went there with the intention of settling the land. Thus, forty-nine years have passed since the first settlers penetrated the land, the first so claimed being the large and most happy isle called Hispaniola, which is six hundred leagues in circumference. Around it in all directions are many other islands, some very big, others very small, and all of them were, as we saw with our own eyes, densely populated with native peoples called Indians. This large island was perhaps the most densely populated place in the world. There must be close to two hundred leagues of land on this island, and the seacoast has been explored for more than ten thousand leagues, and each day more of it is being explored. And all the land so far discovered is a beehive of people; it is as though God had crowded into these lands the great majority of mankind.

And of all the infinite universe of humanity, these people are the most guileless, the most devoid of wickedness and duplicity, the most obedient and faithful to their native masters and to the Spanish Christians whom they serve. They are by nature the most humble, patient, and peaceable, holding no grudges, free from embroilments, neither excitable nor quarrelsome. These people are the most devoid of rancors, hatreds, or desire for vengeance of any people in the world. And because they are so weak and complaisant, they are less able to endure heavy labor and soon die of no matter what malady. The sons of nobles among us, brought up in the enjoyments of life's refinements, are no more delicate than are these Indians, even those among them who are of the lowest rank of laborers. They are also poor people, for they not only possess little but have no desire to possess worldly goods. For this reason they are not arrogant, embittered, or greedy. Their repasts are such that the food of the holy fathers in the desert can scarcely be more parsimonious, scanty, and poor. As to their dress, they are generally naked, with only their pudenda covered somewhat. And when they cover their shoulders it is with a square cloth no more than two varas in size. They have no beds, but sleep on a kind of matting or else in a kind of suspended net called bamacas. They are very clean in their persons, with alert, intelligent minds, docile and open to doctrine, very apt to receive our holy Catholic faith, to be endowed with virtuous customs, and to behave in a godly fashion. And

once they begin to hear the tidings of the Faith, they are so insistent on knowing more and on taking the sacraments of the Church and on observing the divine cult that, truly, the missionaries who are here need to be endowed by God with great patience in order to cope with such eagerness. Some of the secular Spaniards who have been here for many years say that the goodness of the Indians is undeniable and that if this gifted people could be brought to know the one true God they would be the most fortunate people in the world.

Yet into this sheepfold, into this land of meek outcasts there came some Spaniards who immediately behaved like ravening wild beasts, wolves, tigers, or lions that had been starved for many days. And Spaniards have behaved in no other way during the past forty years, down to the present time, for they are still acting like ravening beasts, killing, terrorizing, afflicting, torturing, and destroying the native peoples, doing all this with the strangest and most varied new methods of cruelty, never seen or heard of before, and to such a degree that this Island of Hispaniola once so populous (having a population that I estimated to be more than three million), has now a population of barely two hundred persons.

The island of Cuba is nearly as long as the distance between Valladolid and Rome; it is now almost completely depopulated. San Juan [Puerto Rico] and Jamaica are two of the largest, most productive and attractive islands; both are now deserted and devastated. On the northern side of Cuba and Hispaniola the neighboring Lucayos comprising more than sixty islands including those called Gigantes, beside numerous other islands, some small some large. The least felicitous of them were more fertile and beautiful than the gardens of the King of Seville. They have the healthiest lands in the world, where lived more than five hundred thousand souls; they are now deserted, inhabited by not a single living creature. All the people were slain or died after being taken into captivity and brought to the Island of Hispaniola to be sold as slaves. When the Spaniards saw that some of these had escaped, they sent a ship to find them, and it voyaged for three years among the islands searching for those who had escaped being slaughtered, for a good Christian had helped them escape, taking pity on them and had won them over to Christ; of these there were eleven persons and these I saw.

More than thirty other islands in the vicinity of San Juan are for the most part and for the same reason depopulated, and the land laid waste. On these islands I estimate there are 2,100 leagues of land that have been ruined and depopulated, empty of people.

As for the vast mainland, which is ten times larger than all Spain, even including Aragon and Portugal, containing more land than the distance between Seville and Jerusalem, or more than two thousand leagues, we are sure that our Spaniards, with their cruel and abominable acts, have devastated the land and exterminated the rational people who fully inhabited it. We can estimate very surely and truthfully that in the forty years that have passed, with the infernal actions of the Christians, there have been unjustly slain more than twelve million men, women, and children. In truth, I believe without trying to deceive myself that the number of the slain is more like fifteen million.

The common ways mainly employed by the Spaniards who call themselves Christian and who have gone there to extirpate those pitiful nations and wipe them off the earth is by unjustly waging cruel and bloody wars. Then, when they have slain all those who fought for their lives or to escape the tortures they would have to endure, that is to say, when they have slain all the native rulers and young men (since the Spaniards usually spare only the women and children, who are subjected to the hardest and bitterest servitude ever suffered by man or beast), they enslave any survivors. With these infernal methods of tyranny they debase and weaken countless numbers of those pitiful Indian nations.

Their reason for killing and destroying such an infinite number of souls is that the Christians have an ultimate aim, which is to acquire gold, and to swell themselves with riches in a very brief time and thus rise to a high estate disproportionate to their merits. It should be kept in mind that their insatiable greed and ambition, the greatest ever seen in the world, is the cause of their villainies. And also, those lands are so rich and felicitous, the native peoples so meek and patient, so easy to subject, that our Spaniards have no more consideration for them than beasts. And I say this from my own knowledge of the acts I witnessed. But I should not say "than beasts" for, thanks be to God, they have treated beasts with some respect; I should say instead like excrement on the public squares. And thus they have deprived the Indians of their lives and souls, for the millions I mentioned have died without the Faith and without the benefit of the sacraments. This is a well known and proven fact which even the tyrant Governors, themselves killers, know and admit. And never have the Indians in all the Indies committed any act against the Spanish Christians, until those Christians have first and many times committed countless cruel aggressions against them or against neighboring nations. For in the beginning the Indians regarded the Spaniards as angels from Heaven. Only after the Spaniards had used violence against them, killing, robbing, torturing, did the Indians ever rise up against them. . . .

On the Island Hispaniola was where the Spaniards first landed, as I have said. Here those Christians perpetrated their first ravages and oppressions against the native peoples. This was the first land in the New World to be destroyed and depopulated by the Christians, and here they began their subjection of the women and children, taking them away from the Indians to use them and ill use them, eating the food they provided with their sweat and toil. The Spaniards did not content themselves with what the Indians gave them of their own free will, according to their ability, which was always too little to satisfy enormous appetites, for a Christian eats and consumes in one day an amount of food that would suffice to feed three houses inhabited by ten Indians for one month. And they committed other acts of force and violence and oppression which made the Indians realize that these men had not come from Heaven. And some of the Indians concealed their foods while others concealed their wives and children and still others fled to the mountains to avoid the terrible transactions of the Christians.

And the Christians attacked them with buffets and beatings, until finally they laid hands on the nobles of the villages. Then they behaved with such temerity and shamelessness that the most powerful ruler of the islands had to see his own wife raped by a Christian officer.

From that time onward the Indians began to seek ways to throw the Christians out of their lands. They took up arms, but their weapons were very weak and of little service in offense and still less in defense. (Because of this, the wars of the Indians against each other are little more than games played by children.) And the Christians, with their horses and swords and pikes began to carry out massacres and strange cruelties against them. They attacked the towns and spared neither the children nor the aged nor pregnant women nor women in childbed, not only stabbing them and dismembering them but cutting them to pieces as if dealing with sheep in the slaughter house. They laid bets as to who, with one stroke of the sword, could split a man in two or could cut off his head or spill out his entrails with a single stroke of the pike. They took infants from their mothers' breasts, snatching them by the legs and pitching them headfirst against the crags or snatched them by the arms and threw them into the rivers, roaring with laughter and saying as the babies fell into the water, "Boil there, you offspring of the devil!" Other infants they put to the sword along with their mothers and anyone else who happened to be nearby. They made some low wide gallows on which the hanged victim's feet almost touched the ground, stringing up their victims in lots of thirteen, in memory of Our Redeemer and His twelve Apostles, then set burning wood at their feet and thus burned them alive. To others they attached straw or wrapped their whole bodies in straw and set them afire. With still others, all those they wanted to capture alive, they cut off their hands and hung them round the victim's neck, saying, "Go now, carry the message," meaning, Take the news to the Indians who have fled to the mountains. They usually dealt with the chieftains and nobles in the following way: they made a grid of rods which they placed on forked sticks, then lashed the victims to the grid and lighted a smoldring fire underneath, so that little by little, as those captives screamed in despair and torment, their souls would leave them. . . .

After the wars and the killings had ended, when usually there survived only some boys, some women, and children, these survivors were distributed among the Christians to be slaves. The repartimiento or distribution was made according to the rank and importance of the Christian to whom the Indians were allocated, one of them being given thirty, another forty, still another, one or two hundred, and besides the rank of the Christian there was also to be considered in what favor he stood with the tyrant they called Governor. The pretext was that these allocated Indians were to be instructed in the articles of the Christian Faith. As if those Christians who were as a rule foolish and cruel and greedy and vicious could be caretakers of souls! And the care they took was to send the men to the mines to dig for gold, which is intolerable labor, and to send the women into the fields of the big ranches to hoe and till the land, work suitable for strong men. Nor to either the men or the women did they give any food except herbs and legumes, things of little substance. The milk in the breasts of the women with infants dried up and thus in a short while the infants perished. And since men and women were separated, there could be no marital relations. And the men died in the mines and the women died on the ranches from the same causes, exhaustion and hunger. And thus was depopulated that island which had been densely populated.

Source: Available online at URL: http://www.uctp. org/Devastation. html. Accessed on January 16, 2006.

2. The Fundamental Orders of Connecticut (1639)

January 14, 1639

For as much as it hath pleased Almighty God by the wise disposition of his divine providence so to order and dispose of things that we the Inhabitants and Residents of Windsor, Hartford and Wethersfield are now cohabiting and dwelling in and upon the River of Connecticut and the lands thereunto adjoining; and well knowing where a people are gathered together the word of God requires that to maintain the peace and union of such a people there should be an orderly and decent Government established according to God, to order and dispose of the affairs of the people at all seasons as occasion shall require; do therefore associate and conjoin ourselves to be as one Public State or Commonwealth; and do for ourselves and our successors and such as shall be adjoined to us at any time hereafter, enter into Combination and Confederation together, to maintain and preserve the liberty and purity of the Gospel of our Lord Jesus which we now profess, as also, the discipline of the Churches, which according to the truth of the said Gospel is now practiced amongst us; as also in our civil affairs to be guided and governed according to such Laws, Rules, Orders and Decrees as shall be made, ordered, and decreed as follows:

1. It is Ordered, sentenced, and decreed, that there shall be yearly two General Assemblies or Courts, the one the second Thursday in April, the other the second Thursday in September following; the first shall be called the Court of Election, wherein shall be yearly chosen from time to time, so many Magistrates and other public Officers as shall be found requisite: Whereof one to be chosen Governor for the year ensuing and until another be chosen, and no other Magistrate to be chosen for more than one year: provided always there be six chosen besides the Governor, which being chosen and sworn according to an Oath recorded for that purpose, shall have the power to administer justice according to the Laws here established, and for want thereof, according to the Rule of the Word of God; which choice shall be made by all that are admitted freemen and have taken the Oath of Fidelity, and do cohabit within this Jurisdiction having been admitted Inhabitants by the major part of the Town wherein they live or the major part of such as shall be then present. . . .

January 1639 the 11 Orders above said are voted.

Source: Available online at URL: http://www. constitution.org/bcp/fo_1639.htm. Accessed on January 16, 2006.

3. Maryland Act Concerning Religion (1649)

Forasmuch as in a well governed and Christian Commonwealth matters concerning Religion and the honor of God ought in the first place to be taken into serious consideration and endeavored to be settled. Be it therefore ordered and enacted by the Right Noble Cecil Lord Baron of Baltimore absolute Lord and Proprietary of this Province with the advise and consent of this General Assembly. That whatsoever person or persons within this Province and the Islands thereunto belonging shall from henceforth blaspheme God, that is Curse him, or deny our Savior Jesus Christ to bee the son of God, or shall deny the holy Trinity the father son and holy Ghost, or the Godhead of any of the said Three persons of the Trinity or the Unity of the Godhead, or shall use or utter any reproachful Speeches, words or language concerning the said Holy Trinity, or any of the said three persons thereof, shall be punished with death and confiscation or forfeiture of all his or her lands and goods to the Lord Proprietary and his heirs, And bee it also Enacted by the Authority and with the advise and assent aforesaid. That whatsoever person or persons shall from henceforth use or utter any reproachful words or Speeches concerning the blessed Virgin Mary the Mother of our Savior or the holy Apostles or Evangelists or any of them shall in such case for the first offence forfeit to the said Lord Proprietary and his heirs Lords and Proprietaries of this Province the sum of five pound Sterling or the value thereof to be Levied on the goods and chattels of every such person so offending, but in case such Offender or Offenders, shall not then have goods and chattels sufficient for the satisfying of such forfeiture, or that the same bee not otherwise speedily satisfied that then such Offender or Offenders shall be publically whipped and bee imprisoned during the pleasure of the Lord Proprietary or the Lieut. or chief Governor of this Province for the time being. And that every such Offender or Offenders for every second offence shall forfeit ten pound serling or the value thereof to bee Levied as aforesaid, or in case such Offender or Offenders shall not then have goods and chattels within this Province sufficient for that purpose then to bee publically and severely whipped and imprisoned as before is expressed. And that every person or persons before mentioned offending herein the third time, shall for such third Offence forfeit all his lands and Goods and bee for ever banished and expelled out of this Province. And be it also further Enacted by the same authority advise and assent

that whatsoever person or persons shall from henceforth upon any occasion of Offence or otherwise in a reproachful manner or Way declare call or denominate any person or persons whatsoever inhabiting residing trafficking trading or commercing within this Province or within any the Ports, Harbors, Creeks or Havens to the same belonging an heretic, Schismatic, Idolater, puritan, Independent, Presbyterian popish priest, Jesuit, Jesuited papist, Lutheran, Calvinist, Anabaptist, Brownist, Antinomian, Barrowist, Roundhead, Separatist, or any other name or term in a reproachful manner relating to matter of Religion shall for every such Offence forfeit and loose the some or ten shillings sterling or the value thereof to bee Levied on the goods and chattels of every such Offender and Offenders, the one half thereof to be forfeited and paid unto the person and persons of whom such reproachful words are or shall be spoken or uttered, and the other half thereof to the Lord Proprietary and his heirs Lords and Proprietaries of this Province, But if such person or persons who shall at any time utter or speake any such reproachful words or Language shall not have Goods or Chattels sufficient and overt within this Province to bee taken to satisfy the penalty aforesaid or that the same bee not otherwise speedily satisfied, that then the person or persons so offending shall be publically whipped, and shall suffer imprisonment. without bails or maineprise until he, she or they respectively shall satisf the party so offended or grieved by such reproachful Language by asking him or her respectively forgiveness publically for such his Offence before the Magistrate or chief Officer or Officers of the Town or place where such Offence shall be given. And be it further likewise Enacted by the Authority and consent aforesaid That every person and persons within this Province that shall at any time hereafter profane the Sabbath or Lords day called Sunday by frequent swearing, drunkenness or by any uncivil or disorderly recreation, or by working on that day when absolute necessity doth not require it shall for every such first offence forfeit 2s 6d sterling or the value thereof, and for the second offence 5s sterling or the value thereof, and for the third offence and so for every time he shall offend in like manner afterwards 10s sterling or the value thereof. And in case such offender and offenders shall not have sufficient goods or Chattels within this Province to satisfy any of the said Penalties respectively hereby imposed for profaning the Sabbath or Lords day called Sunday as aforesaid, That in Every such case the party so offending shall for the first and second offence in that kind be imprisoned till he or she shall publically in open Court before the chief Commander Judge or Magistrate, of that County Town or precinct where such offence shall be committed acknowledge the Scandal and offence he hath in that respect given against God and the good and civil Government. of this Province And for the third offence and for every time after shall also bee publically whipped. And whereas the enforcing of the conscience in matters of Religion hath frequently fallen out to be of dangerous Consequence in those commonwealths where it hath been practiced, And for the more quiet and peaceable government. of this Province, and the better to preserve mutual Love and amity amongst the Inhabitants thereof. Be it Therefore also by the Lo: Proprietary with the advise and consent of this Assembly Ordained & enacted (except as in ths present Act is before Declared and sett forth) that no person or persons whatsoever within this Province, or the Islands, Ports, Harbors, Creeks, or havens hereunto belonging professing to believe in Jesus Christ, shall from henceforth bee any ways troubled, Molested or discountenanced for or in respect of his or her religion nor in the free exercise thereof within this Province or the Islands hereunto belonging nor any way compelled to the belief or exercise of any other Religion against his or her consent, so as they be not unfaithful to the Lord Proprietary, or molest or conspire against the civil Government. established or to bee established in this Province under him or his heirs. And that all & every person and persons that shall presume Contrary to this Act and the true intent and meaning thereof directly or indirectly either in person or estate willfully to wrong disturb trouble or molest any person whatsoever within this Province professing to believe in Jesus Christ for or in respect of his or her religion or the free exercise thereof within this Province other than is provided for in this Act that such person or persons so offending, shall be compelled to pay treble damages to the party so wronged or molested, and for every such offence shall also forfeit 20s sterling in money or the value thereof, half thereof for the use of the Lo: Proprietary, and his heirs Lords and Proprietaries of this Province, and the other half for the use of the party so wronged or molested as aforesaid, Or if the party so offending as aforesaid shall refuse or bee unable to recompense the party so wronged, or to satisfy such fine or forfeiture, then such Offender shall be severely punished by public whipping & imprisonment. during the pleasure of the Lord Proprietary, or his Lieutenant or chief Governor of this Province for the time being without bails or maineprise. And be it further also Enacted by the authority and consent aforesaid That the Sheriff or other Officer or Officers from time to time

to bee appointed & authoized for that purpose, of the County Town or precinct where every particular offence in this present Act contained shall happen at any time to bee committed and whereupon there is hereby a forfeiture fine or penalty imposed shall from time to time distrain and seize the goods and estate of every such person so offending as aforesaid against this present Act or any pt thereof, and sell the same or any part thereof for the full satisfaction of such forfeiture, fine, or penalty as aforesaid, Restoring unto the party so offending the Remainder or overplus of the said goods or estate after such satisfaction so made as aforesaid.

Source: The Founders' Constitution, *vol. 5, pp. 49–50.*

4. An Act made at a General Court, held at Boston, the 20th of October, 1658

Whereas there is a pernicious sect (commonly called Quakers), lately risen, who by word and writing have published and maintained many dangerous and horrid tenets, and do take upon them to change and alter the received laudable customs of our nation, in giving civil respect to equals, or reverence to superiors, whose actions tend to undermine the civil government, and also to destroy the order of the churches, by denying all established forms of worship, and by withdrawing from orderly church-fellowship, allowed and approved by all orthodox professors of the Truth, and instead thereof, and in opposition thereunto, frequently meeting themselves, insinuating themselves into the minds of the simple, or such as are least affected to the order and government of church and commonwealth, hereby divers of our inhabitants have been infected, notwithstanding all former laws, made upon the experience of their arrogant and bold obtrusions, to disseminate their principles among us, prohibiting their coming in this jurisdiction, they have not been deterred from their impetuous attempts to undermine our peace, and hazard our ruin.

For prevention thereof, this court doth order and enact, that every person, or persons, of the cursed sect of the Quakers, who is not all inhabitant of, but is found within this jurisdiction, shall be apprehended without warrant, where no magistrate is at hand, by any constable, commissioner, or select man, and conveyed from constable to constable, to the next magistrate, who shall commit the said person to close prison, there to remain, without bail, unto the next court of assistants, where they shall have a legal trial: and being convicted to be of the sect of the Quakers, shall be sentenced to be banished upon pain of death: and that every inhabitant of this jurisdiction, being convicted to be of the aforesaid sect, either by taking up, publishing, or defending the horrid opinions of the Quakers, or the stirring up mutiny, sedition, or rebellion against the government, or by taking up their absurd and destructive practices, viz. Denying civil respect to equals and superiors, and withdrawing from our church assemblies, and instead thereof frequent meetings of their own, in opposition to our church order; or by adhering to, or approving of any known Quaker, and the tenets and practices of the Quakers, that are opposite to the orthodox received opinions of the godly, and endeavouring to disaffect others to civil government, and church orders, or condemning the practice and proceedings of this court against the Quakers, manifesting thereby their complying with those, whose design is to overthrow the order established in church and state, every such person, upon conviction before the said court of assistants, in manner as aforesaid, shall be committed to close prison for one month, and then, unless they choose voluntarily to depart this jurisdiction, shall give bond for their good behaviour, and appear at the next court, where continuing obstinate, and refusing to retract and reform the aforesaid opinions, they shall be sentenced to banishment upon pain of death; and any one magistrate, upon information given him of any such person, shall cause him to be apprehended, and shall commit any such person to prison, according to his discretion, until he come to trial, as aforesaid.

Source: The History of the Rise, Increase, and Progress, of the Christian People Called Quakers, *vol. 1, pp. 222–223.*

5. Pennsylvania Charter of Privileges (1701)

Because no People can be truly happy, though under the greatest Enjoyment of Civil Liberties, if abridged of the Freedom of their Consciences, as to their Religious Profession and Worship: And Almighty God being the only Lord of Conscience, Father of Lights and Spirits; and the Author as well as Object of all divine Knowledge, Faith and Worship, who only doth enlighten the Minds, and persuade and convince the Understandings of People, I [William Penn] do hereby grant and declare, That no Person or Persons, inhabiting in this province of Territories, who shall confess and acknowledge *One* almighty God, the Creator, Upholder and Ruler of the World; and

profess him or themselves obliged to live quietly under the Civil Government, shall be in any Case molested or prejudiced, in his or their Person or Estate, because of his or their conscientious Persuasion or Practice, nor be compelled to frequent or maintain any religious Worship, Place or Ministry, contrary to his or their Mind, or to do or suffer any other Act or Thing, contrary to their religious Persuasion.

And that all Persons who also profess to believe in *Jesus Christ*, the Savior of the world, shall be capable (notwithstanding their other Persuasions and Practices in Point of Conscience and Religion) to serve this Government in any Capacity, both legislatively and executively, he or they solemnly promising, when lawfully required, Allegiance to the King as Sovereign, and Fidelity to the Proprietary and Governor, and taking the Attests as now established by the Law. . . .

Source: William Penn, Pennsylvania Charter of Privileges, *October 28, 1701, in Commager,* Documents of American History, *pp. 40–41.*

6. Delaware Charter, 1701

Because no People can be truly happy, though under the greatest Enjoyment of Civil Liberties, if abridged of the Freedom of their Consciences, as to their Religious Profession and Worship: And Almighty God being the only Lord of Conscience, Father of Lights and Spirits; and the Author as well as Object of all divine Knowledge, Faith and Worship, who only doth enlighten the Minds, and persuade and convince the Understandings of People, I do hereby grant and declare, That no Person or Persons, inhabiting in this Province or Territories, who shall confess and acknowledge One almighty God, the Creator, Upholder and Ruler of the World; and professes him or themselves obliged to live quietly under the Civil Government, shall be in any Case molested or prejudiced, in his or their Person or Estate, because of his or their conscientious Persuasion or Practice, nor be compelled to frequent or maintain any religious Worship, Place or Ministry, contrary to his or their Mind, or to do or suffer any other Act or Thing, contrary to their religious Persuasion.

And that all Persons who also profess to believe in Jesus Christ, the Saviour of the World, shall be capable (notwithstanding their other Persuasions and Practices in Point of Conscience and Religion) to serve this Government in any Capacity, both legislatively and executively, he or they solemnly promising, when lawfully required, Allegiance to the King as Sovereign, and Fidelity to the

Proprietary and Governor, and taking the Attests as now established by the Law made at Newcastle, in the Year One Thousand and Seven Hundred, entitled, An Act directing the Attests of several Officers and Ministers, as now amended and confirmed this present Assembly. . . .

But, because the Happiness of Mankind depends so much upon the Enjoying of Liberty of their Consciences, as aforesaid, I do hereby solemnly declare, promise and grant, for me, my Heirs and Assigns, That the First Article of this Charter relating to Liberty of Conscience, and every Part and Clause therein, according to the true Intent and Meaning thereof, shall be kept and remain, without any Alteration, inviolably for ever.

Source: Available online at URL: http://www.yale. edu/lawweb/avalon/states/de01.htm. Accessed on January 16, 2006.

7. Benjamin Franklin, Letter to the London *Packet* (June 3, 1772)

I Understand from the public papers, that in the debates on the bill for relieving the Dissenters in the point of subscription to the Church Articles, sundry reflections were thrown out against that people, importing, "that they themselves are of a persecuting intolerant spirit, for that when they had here the superiority they persecuted the church, and still persecute it in America, where they compel its members to pay taxes for maintaining the Presbyterian or independent worship, and at the same time refuse them a toleration in the full exercise of their religion by the administrations of a bishop."

If we look back into history for the character of present sects in Christianity, we shall find few that have not in their turns been persecutors, and complainers of persecution. The primitive Christians thought persecution extremely wrong in the Pagans, but practised it on one another. The first Protestants of the Church of England, blamed persecution in the Roman church, but practised it against the Puritans: these found it wrong in the Bishops, but fell into the same practice themselves both here and in New England. To account for this we should remember, that the doctrine of toleration was not then known, or had not prevailed in the world. Persecution was therefore not so much the fault of the sect as of the times. It was not in those days deemed wrong in itself. The general opinion was only, that those who are in error ought not to persecute the truth: But the possessors of truth were in the right to persecute error, in order to destroy it. Thus every sect believing itself possessed of all truth, and that every

tenet differing from theirs was error, conceived that when the power was in their hands, persecution was a duty required of them by that God whom they supposed to be offended with heresy. By degrees more moderate and more modest sentiments have taken place in the Christian world; and among Protestants particularly all disclaim persecution, none vindicate it, and few practise it. We should then cease to reproach each other with what was done by our ancestors, but judge of the present character of sects or churches by their present conduct only.

Now to determine on the justice of this charge against the present dissenters, particularly those in America, let us consider the following facts. They went from England to establish a new country for themselves, at their own expence, where they might enjoy the free exercise of religion in their own way. When they had purchased the territory of the natives, they granted the lands out in townships, requiring for it neither purchase-money nor quit-rent, but this condition only to be complied with, that the freeholders should for ever support a gospel minister (meaning probably one of the then governing sects) and a free-school within the township. Thus, what is commonly called Presbyterianism became the established religion of that country. All went on well in this way while the same religious opinions were general, the support of minister and school being raised by a proportionate tax on the lands. But in process of time, some becoming Quakers, some Baptists, and, of late years some returning to the Church of England (through the laudable endeavours and a proper application of their funds by the society for propagating the gospel) objections were made to the payment of a tax appropriated to the support of a church they disapproved and had forsaken. The civil magistrates, however, continued for a time to collect and apply the tax according to the original laws which remained in force; and they did it the more freely, as thinking it just and equitable that the holders of lands should pay what was contracted to be paid when they were granted, as the only consideration for the grant, and what had been considered by all subsequent purchasers as a perpetual incumbrance on the estate, bought therefore at a proportionably cheaper rate; a payment which it was thought no honest man ought to avoid under the pretense of his having changed his religious persuasion. And this I suppose is one of the best grounds of demanding tithes of dissenters now in England. But the practice being clamored against by the Episcopalians as persecution, the legislature of the Province of the Massachusets-Bay, near thirty years since, passed an act for their relief, requiring indeed the tax to be paid as usual, but directing that the several sums levied from members of the Church of England, should be paid over to the Minister of that Church, with whom such members usually attended divine worship, which Minister had power given him to receive and on occasion to recover the same by law.

It seems that legislature considered the end of the tax was, to secure and improve the morals of the people, and promote their happiness, by supporting among them the public worship of God and the preaching of the gospel; that where particular people fancied a particular mode, that mode might probably therefore be of most use to those people; and that if the good was done, it was not so material in what mode or by whom it was done. The consideration that their brethren the dissenters in England were still compelled to pay tithes to the clergy of the Church, had not weight enough with the legislature to prevent this moderate act, which still continues in full force, and I hope no uncharitable conduct of the church toward the dissenters will ever provoke them to repeal it.

With regard to a bishop, I know not upon what ground the dissenters, either here or in America, are charged with refusing the benefit of such an officer to the church in that country. Here they seem to have naturally no concern in the affair. There they have no power to prevent it, if government should think fit to send one. They would probably dislike, indeed, to see an order of men established among them, from whose persecutions their fathers fled into that wilderness, and whose future domination they may possibly fear, not knowing that their natures are changed. But the non-appointment of bishops for America seems to arise from another quarter. The same wisdom of government, probably, that prevents the sitting of convocations, and forbids, by noli prosequi's, the persecution of Dissenters for non-subscription, avoids establishing bishops where the minds of people are not yet prepared to receive them cordially, lest the public peace should be endangered.

And now let us see how this persecution-account stands between the parties.

In New-England, where the legislative bodies are almost to a man Dissenters from the Church of England,

1. There is no test to prevent Churchmen holding offices.
2. The sons of Churchmen have the full benefit of the Universities.
3. The taxes for support of public worship, when paid by Churchmen, are given to the Episcopal minister.

In Old England,

1. Dissenters are excluded from all offices of profit and honour.
2. The benefits of education in the Universities are appropriated to the sons of Churchmen.
3. The clergy of the Dissenters receive none of the tythes paid by their people, who must be at the additional charge of maintaining their own separate worship.

But it is said, the Dissenters of America oppose the introduction of a Bishop. In fact, it is not alone the Dissenters there that give the opposition (if not encouraging must be termed opposing) but the laity in general dislike the project, and some even of the clergy. The inhabitants of Virginia are almost all Episcopalians. The Church is fully established there, and the Council and General Assembly are perhaps to a man its members, yet when lately at a meeting of the clergy, a resolution was taken to apply for a Bishop, against which several however protested; the assembly of the province at their next meeting, expressed their disapprobation of the thing in the strongest manner, by unanimously ordering the thanks of the house to the protesters: for many of the American laity of the church think it some advantage, whether their own young men come to England for ordination, and improve themselves at the same time by conversation with the learned here, or the congregations are supplied by Englishmen, who have had the benefit of education in English universities, and are ordained before they come abroad. They do not therefore see the necessity of a Bishop merely for ordination, and confirmation is among them deemed a ceremony of no very great importance, since few seek it in England where Bishops are in plenty. These sentiments prevail with many churchmen there, not to promote a design, which they think must sooner or later saddle them with great expences to support it. As to the Dissenters, their minds might probably be more conciliated to the measure, if the Bishops here should, in their wisdom and goodness, think fit to set their sacred character in a more friendly light, by dropping their opposition to the Dissenters application for relief in subscription, and declaring their willingness that Dissenters should be capable of offices, enjoy the benefit of education in the universities, and the privilege of appropriating their tythes to the support of their own clergy. In all these points of toleration, they appear far behind the present Dissenters of New-England, and it may seem to some a step below the dignity of Bishops, to follow the example of such inferiors.

I do not, however, despair of their doing it some time or other, since nothing of the kind is too hard for true christian humility. I am, Sir, your's, &c.

A New-England-Man.

Source: The Founders' Constitution, *vol. 5, pp. 58–60.*

8. The Virginia Declaration of Rights (June 12, 1776)

I. That all men are by nature equally free and independent, and have certain inherent rights, of which, when they enter into a state of society, they cannot, by any compact, deprive or divest their posterity; namely, the enjoyment of life and liberty, with the means of acquiring and possessing property, and pursuing and obtaining happiness and safety.

II. That all power is vested in, and consequently derived from, the people; that magistrates are their trustees and servants, and at all times amenable to them. . . .

XVI. That religion, or the duty which we owe to our Creator and the manner of discharging it, can be directed by reason and conviction, not by force or violence; and therefore, all men are equally entitled to the free exercise of religion, according to the dictates of conscience; and that it is the mutual duty of all to practice Christian forbearance, love, and charity towards each other.

Source: Available online at URL: http://www.yale. edu/lawweb/avalon/virginia.htm. Accessed on January 16, 2006.

9. From The Declaration of Independence (July 4, 1776)

The unanimous Declaration of the thirteen united States of America,

When in the Course of human events, it becomes necessary for one people to dissolve the political bands which have connected them with another, and to assume among the powers of the earth, the separate and equal station to which the Laws of Nature and of Nature's God entitle them, a decent respect to the opinions of mankind requires that they should declare the causes which impel them to the separation.

We hold these truths to be self-evident, that all men are created equal, that they are endowed by their Creator with certain unalienable Rights, that among these are Life, Liberty and the pursuit of Happiness.—That to secure these rights, Governments are instituted among

Men, deriving their just powers from the consent of the governed,—That whenever any Form of Government becomes destructive of these ends, it is the Right of the People to alter or to abolish it, and to institute new Government, laying its foundation on such principles and organizing its powers in such form, as to them shall seem most likely to effect their Safety and Happiness. Prudence, indeed, will dictate that Governments long established should not be changed for light and transient causes; and accordingly all experience hath shewn, that mankind are more disposed to suffer, while evils are sufferable, than to right themselves by abolishing the forms to which they are accustomed. . . .

We, therefore, the Representatives of the United States of America, in General Congress, Assembled, appealing to the Supreme Judge of the world for the rectitude of our intentions, do, in the Name, and by the Authority of the good People of these Colonies, solemnly publish and declare, That these United Colonies are, and of Right ouht to be Free and Independent States; that they are Absolved from all Allegiance to the British Crown, and that all political connection between them and the State of Great Britain, is and ought to be totally dissolved; and that as Free and Independent States, they have full Power to levy War, conclude Peace, contract Alliances, establish Commerce, and to do all other Acts and Things which Independent States may of right do. And for the support of this Declaration, with a firm reliance on the protection of divine Providence, we mutually pledge to each other our Lives, our Fortunes and our sacred Honor.

Available online at URL: http://www.law.indiana. edu/uslawdocs/declaration.html. Accessed on January 16, 2006.

10. A Bill for Establishing Religious Freedom, by Thomas Jefferson (1779; enacted by the Virginia assembly in 1786)

SECTION I. Well aware that the opinions and belief of men depend not on their own will, but follow involuntarily the evidence proposed to their minds; that Almighty God hath created the mind free, and manifested his supreme will that free it shall remain by making it altogether insusceptible of restraint; that all attempts to influence it by temporal punishments, or burthens, or by civil incapacitations, tend only to beget habits of hypocrisy and meanness, and are a departure from the plan of the holy author of our religion, who being lord both of body and mind, yet chose not to propagate it by coercions on either, as was in his Almighty power to do, but to exalt it by its influence on reason alone; that the impious presumption of legislators and rulers, civil as well as ecclesiastical, who, being themselves but fallible and uninspired men, have assumed dominion over the faith of others, setting up their own opinions and modes of thinking as the only true and infallible, and as such endeavoring to impose them on others, hath established and maintained false religions over the greatest part of the world and through all time: That to compel a man to furnish contributions of money for the propagation of opinions which he disbelieves and abhors, is sinful and tyrannical; that even the forcing him to support this or that teacher of his own religious persuasion, is depriving him of the comfortable liberty of giving his contributions to the particular pastor whose morals he would make his pattern, and whose powers he feels most persuasive to righteousness; and is withdrawing from the ministry those temporary rewards, which proceeding from an approbation of their personal conduct, are an additional incitement to earnest and unremitting labours for the instruction of mankind; that our civil rights have no dependence on our religious opinions, any more than our opinions in physics or geometry; that therefore the proscribing any citizen as unworthy the public confidence by laying upon him an incapacity of being called to ofices of trust and emolument, unless he profess or renounce this or that religious opinion, is depriving him injuriously of those privileges and advantages to which, in common with his fellow citizens, he has a natural right; that it tends also to corrupt the principles of that very religion it is meant to encourage, by bribing, with a monopoly of worldly honours and emoluments, those who will externally profess and conform to it; that though indeed these are criminals who do not withstand such temptation, yet neither are those innocent who lay the bait in their way; that the opinions of men are not the object of civil government, nor under its jurisdiction; that to suffer the civil magistrate to intrude his powers into the field of opinion and to restrain the profession or propagation of principles on supposition of their ill tendency is a dangerous fallacy, which at once destroys all religious liberty, because he being of course judge of that tendency will make his opinions the rule of judgment, and approve or condemn the sentiments of others only as they shall square with or differ from his own; that it is time enough for the rightful purposes of civil government for its officers to interfere when principles break out into overt acts against peace and good order; and finally, that truth is great and will prevail if left to herself; that she is the proper and sufficient antagonist to error, and has nothing to fear from the conflict unless by human interposition disarmed of her natural weapons, free argument and debate; errors ceasing to be dangerous when it is permitted freely to contradict them.

SECTION II. We the General Assembly of Virginia do enact that no man shall be compelled to frequent or support any religious worship, place, or ministry whatsoever, nor shall be enforced, restrained, molested, or burthened in his body or goods, nor shall otherwise suffer, on account of his religious opinions or belief; but that all men shall be free to profess, and by argument to maintain, their opinions in matters of religion, and that the same shall in no wise diminish, enlarge, or affect their civil capacities.

SECTION III. And though we well know that this Assembly, elected by the people for the ordinary purposes of legislation only, have no power to restrain the acts of succeeding Assemblies, constituted with powers equal to our own, and that therefore to declare this act irrevocable would be of no effect in law; yet we are free to declare, and do declare, that the rights hereby asserted are of the natural rights of mankind, and that if any act shall be hereafter passed to repeal the present or to narrow its operation, such act will be an infringement of natural right.

Source: Julian P. Boyd, ed., The Papers of Thomas Jefferson *(Princeton, N.J.: Princeton University Press, 1950), vol. 2, pp. 345–347.*

11. Memorial and Remonstrance, by James Madison (June 20, 1785)

To the Honorable the General Assembly of the Commonwealth of Virginia

A Memorial and Remonstrance

We the subscribers, citizens of the said Commonwealth, having taken into serious consideration, a Bill printed by order of the last Session of General Assembly, entitled "A Bill establishing a provision for Teachers of the Christian Religion," and conceiving that the same if finally armed with the sanctions of a law, will be a dangerous abuse of power, are bound as faithful members of a free State to remonstrate against it, and to declare the reasons by which we are determined. We remonstrate against the said Bill,

1. Because we hold it for a fundamental and undeniable truth, "that religion or the duty which we owe to our Creator and the manner of discharging it, can be directed only by reason and conviction, not by force or violence." The Religion then of every man must be left to the conviction and conscience of every man; and it is the right of every man to exercise it as these may dictate. This right is in its nature an unalienable right. It is unalienable, because the opinions of men, depending only on the evidence contemplated by their own minds cannot follow the dictates of other men: It is unalienable also, because what is here a right towards men, is a duty towards the Creator. It is the duty of every man to render to the Creator such homage and such only as he believes to be acceptable to him. This duty is precedent, both in order of time and in degree of obligation, to the claims of Civil Society. Before any man can be considerd as a member of Civil Society, he must be considered as a subject of the Governour of the Universe: And if a member of Civil Society, do it with a saving of his allegiance to the Universal Sovereign. We maintain therefore that in matters of Religion, no man's right is abridged by the institution of Civil Society and that Religion is wholly exempt from its cognizance. True it is, that no other rule exists, by which any question which may divide a Society, can be ultimately determined, but the will of the majority; but it is also true that the majority may trespass on the rights of the minority.

2. Because Religion be exempt from the authority of the Society at large, still less can it be subject to that of the Legislative Body. The latter are but the creatures and viceregents of the former. Their jurisdiction is both derivative and limited: it is limited with regard to the co-ordinate departments, more necessarily is it limited with regard to the constituents. The preservation of a free Government requires not merely, that the metes and bounds which separate each department of power be invariably maintained; but more especially that neither of them be suffered to overleap the great Barrier which defends the rights of the people. The Rulers who are guilty of such an encroachment, exceed the commission from which they derive their authority, and are Tyrants. The People who submit to it are governed by laws made neither by themselves nor by an authority derived from them, and are slaves.

3. Because it is proper to take alarm at the first experiment on our liberties. We hold this prudent jealousy to be the first duty of Citizens, and one of the noblest characteristics of the late Revolution. The free men of America did not wait till usurped power had strengthened itself by exercise, and entangled the question in precedents. They saw all the consequences in the principle, and they avoided the consequences by denying the principle. We revere this lesson too much soon to forget it. Who does not see that the same authority which can establish Christianity, in exclusion of all other Religions, may establish with the same ease any particular sect of Christians, in exclusion of all other Sects? that the same authority which can force a citizen to contribute three pence only of his property for the support of any one establishment, may force him to conform to any other establishment in all cases whatsoever?

4. Because the Bill violates the equality which ought to be the basis of every law, and which is more indispensable, in proportion as the validity or expediency of any law is more liable to be impeached. If "all men are by nature equally free and independent," all men are to be considered as entering into Society on equal conditions; as relinquishing no more, and therefore retaining no less, one than another, of their natural rights. Above all are they to be considered as retaining an "equal title to the free exercise of Religion according to the dictates of Conscience." Whilst we assert for ourselves a freedom to embrace, to profess and to observe the Religion which we believe to be of divine origin, we cannot deny an equal freedom to those whose minds have not yet yielded to the evidence which has convinced us. If this freedom be abused, it is an offence against God, not against man: To God, therefore, not to man, must an account of it be rendered. As the Bill violates equality by subjecting some to peculiar burdens, so it violates the same principle, by granting to others peculiar exemptions. Are the Quakers and Menonists the only sects who think a compulsive support of their Religions unnecessary and unwarrantable? can their piety alone be entrusted with the care of public worship? Ought their Religions to be endowed above all others with extraordinary privileges by which proselytes may be enticed from all others? We think too favorably of the justice and good sense of these denominations to believe that they either covet pre-eminences over their fellow citizens or that they will be seduced by them from the common opposition to the measure.

5. Because the Bill implies either that the Civil Magistrate is a competent Judge of Religious Truth; or that he may employ Religion as an engine of Civil policy. The first is an arrogant pretension falsified by the contradictory opinions of Rulers in all ages, and throughout the world: the second an unhallowed perversion of the means of salvation.

6. Because the establishment proposed by the Bill is not requisite for the support of the Christian Religion. To say that it is, is a contradiction to the Christian Religion itself, for every page of it disavows a dependence on the powers of this world: it is a contradiction to fact; for it is known that this Religion both existed and flourished, not only without the support of human laws, but in spite of every opposition from them, and not only during the period of miraculous aid, but long after it had been left to its own evidence and the ordinary care of Providence. Nay, it is a contradiction in terms; for a Religion not invented by human policy, must have pre-existed and been supported, before it was established by human policy. It is moreover to weaken in those who profess this Religion a pious confidence in its innate excellence and the patronage of its Author; and to foster in those who still reject it, a suspicion that its friends are too conscious of its fallacies to trust it to its own merits.

7. Because experience witnesses that ecclesiastical establishments, instead of maintaining the purity and efficacy of Religion, have had a contrary operation. During almost fifteen centuries has the legal establishment of Christianity been on trial. What have been its fruits? More or less in all places, pride and indolence in the Clergy, ignorance and servility in the laity, in both, superstition, bigotry and persecution. Enquire of the Teachers of Christianity for the ages in which it appeared in its greatest luster; those of every sect, point to the ages prior to its incorporation with Civil policy. Propose a restoration of this primitive State in which its Teachers depended on the voluntary rewards of their flocks, many of them predict its downfall. On which Side ought their testimony to have greatest weight, when for or when against their interest?

8. Because the establishment in question is not necessary for the support of Civil Government. If it be urged as necessary for the support of Civil Government only as it is a means of supporting Religion, and it be not necessary for the latter purpose, it cannot be necessary for the former. If Religion be not within the cognizance of Civil Government how can its legal establishment be necessary to Civil Government? What influence in fact have ecclesiastical establishments had on Civil Society? In some instances they have been seen to erect a spiritual tyranny on the ruins of the Civil authority; in many instances they have been seen upholding the thrones of political tyranny: in no instance have they been seen the guardians of the liberties of the people. Rulers who wished to subvert the public liberty, may have found an established Clergy convenient auxiliaries. A just Government instituted to

secure & perpetuate it needs them not. Such a Government will be best supported by protecting every Citizen in the enjoyment of his Religion with the same equal hand which protects his person and his property; by neither invading the equal rights of any Sect, nor suffering any Sect to invade those of another.

9. Because the proposed establishment is a departure from the generous policy, which, offering an Asylum to the persecuted and oppressed of every Nation and Religion, promised a luster to our country, and an accession to the number of its citizens. What a melancholy mark is the Bill of sudden degeneracy? Instead of holding forth an Asylum to the persecuted, it is itself a signal of persecution. It degrades from the equal rank of Citizens all those whose opinions in Religion do not bend to those of the Legislative authority. Distant as it may be in its present form from the Inquisition, it differs from it only in degree. The one is the first step, the other the last in the career of intolerance. The magnanimous sufferer under this cruel scourge in foreign Regions, must view the Bill as a Beacon on our Coast, warning him to seek some other haven, where liberty and philanthropy in their due extent, may offer a more certain response from his Troubles.

10. Because it will have a like tendency to banish our Citizens. The allurements presented by other situations are every day thinning their number. To super-add a fresh motive to emigration by revoking the liberty which they now enjoy, would be the same species of folly which has dishonored and depopulated flourishing kingdoms.

11. Because it will destroy that moderation and harmony which the forbearance of our laws to intermeddle with Religion has produced among its several sects. Torrents of blood have been spilt in the old world, by vain attempts of the secular arm, to extinguish Religious discord, by proscribing all difference in Religious opinion. Time has at length revealed the true remedy. Every relaxation of narrow and rigorous policy, wherever it has been tried, has been found to assuage the disease. The American Theater has exhibited proofs that equal and complete liberty, if it does not wholly eradicate it, sufficiently destroys its malignant influence on the health and prosperity of the State. If with the salutary effects of this system under our own eyes, we begin to contract the bounds of Religious freedom, we know no name that will too severely reproach our folly. At least let warning be taken at the first fruits of the threatened innovation. The very appearance of the Bill has transformed "that Christian forbearance, love and charity," which of late mutually prevailed, into animosities and jealousies, which

may not soon be appeased. What mischiefs may not be dreaded, should this enemy to the public quiet be armed with the force of a law?

12. Because the policy of the Bill is adverse to the diffusion of the light of Christianity. The first wish of those who enjoy this precious gift ought to be that it may be imparted to the whole race of mankind. Compare the number of those who have as yet received it with the number still remaining under the dominion of false Religions; and how small is the former! Does the policy of the Bill tend to lessen the disproportion? No; it at once discourages those who are strangers to the light of revelation from coming into the Region of it; and countenances by example the nations who continue in darkness, in shutting out those who might convey it to them. Instead of Leveling as far as possible, every obstacle to the victorious progress of Truth, the Bill with an ignoble and unchristian timidity would circumscribe it with a wall of defense against the encroachments of error.

13. Because attempts to enforce by legal sanctions, acts obnoxious to so great a proportion of Citizens, tend to enervate the laws in general, and to slacken the bands of Society. If it be difficult to execute any law which is not generally deemed necessary or salutary, what must be the case, where it is deemed invalid and dangerous? And what may be the effect of so striking an example of impotency in the Government, on its general authority?

14. Because a measure of such singular magnitude and delicacy ought not to be imposed, without the clearest evidence that it is called for by a majority of citizens, and no satisfactory method is yet proposed by which the voice of the majority in this case may be determined, or its influence secured. The people of the respective counties are indeed requested to signify their opinion respecting the adoption of the Bill to the next Session of Assembly. But the representation must be made equal, before the voice either of the representatives or of the Counties will be that of the people. Our hope is that neither of the former will, after due consideration, espouse the dangerous principle of the Bill. Should the event disappoint us, it will still leave us in full confidence, that a fair appeal to the latter will reverse the sentence against our liberties.

15. Because finally, "the equal right of every citizen to the free exercise of his Religion according to the dictates of conscience" is held by the same tenure with all our other rights. If we recur to its origin, it is equally the gift of nature; if we weigh its importance, it cannot be less dear to us; if we consult the "Declaration of those rights which pertain to the good people of Virginia, as the basis and foundation of Government," it is enumerated with equal solemnity, or rather studied emphasis. Either then, we must say, that the Will of the Legislature is the only measure of their authority; and that in the plenitude of this authority, they may sweep away all our fundamental rights; or, that they are bound to leave this particular right untouched and sacred: Either we must say, that they may control the freedom of the press, may abolish the Trial by Jury, may swallow up the Executive and Judiciary Powers of the State; nay that they may despoil us of our very right of suffrage, and erect themselves into an independent and hereditary Assembly or, we must say, that they have no authority to enact into the law the Bill under consideration. We the Subscribers say, that the General Assembly of this Commonwealth have no such authority: And that no effort may be omitted on our part against so dangerous an usurpation, we oppose to it, this remonstrance; earnestly praying, as we are in duty bound, that the Supreme Lawgiver of the Universe, by illuminating those to whom it is addressed, may on the one hand, turn their Councils from every act which would affront his holy prerogative, or violate the trust committed to them: and on the other, guide them into every measure which may be worthy of his [blessing, may re]dound to their own praise, and may establish more firmly the liberties, the prosperity and the happiness of the Commonweath.

Source: Madison Writings, *pp. 29–36.*

12. Article VI, Clause 3, of the U.S. Constitution (1787; ratified 1788)

The Senators and Representatives before mentioned, and the Members of the several State Legislatures, and all executive and judicial Officers, both of the United States and of the several States, shall be bound by Oath or Affirmation, to support this Constitution; but no religious Test shall ever be required as a Qualification to any Office or public Trust under the United States.

Source: Available online at URL: http://www.law.cornell.edu/constitution/constitution.articlevi.html. Accessed on January 16, 2006.

13. Thomas Jefferson, from *Notes on the State of Virginia* (1787)

The error seems not sufficiently eradicated, that the operations of the mind, as well as the acts of the body, are subject to the coercion of the laws. But our rulers can have authority over such natural rights only as we have submitted to them. The rights of conscience we never submitted, we could not submit. We are answerable for them to our God. The legitimate powers of government extend to such acts only as are injurious to others. But it does me no injury for my neighbour to say there are twenty gods, or no god. It neither picks my pocket nor breaks my leg. If it be said, his testimony in a court of justice cannot be relied on, reject it then, and be the stigma on him. Constraint may make him worse by making him a hypocrite, but it will never make him a truer man. It may fix him obstinately in his errors, but will not cure them. Reason and free enquiry are the only effectual agents against error. Give a loose to them, they will support the true religion, by bringing every false one to their tribunal, to the test of their investigation. They are the natural enemies of error, and of error only. Had not the Roman government permitted free enquiry, Christianity could never have been introduced. Had not free enquiry been indulged, at the aera of the reformation, the corruptions of Christianity could not have been purged away. If it be restrained now, the present corruptions will be protected, and new ones encouraged. Was the government to prescribe to us our medicine and diet, our bodies would be in such keeping as our souls are now. Thus in France the emetic was once forbidden as a medicine, and the potatoe as an article of food. Government is just as infallible too when it fixes systems in physics. Galileo was sent to the inquisition for affirming that the earth was a sphere: the government had declared it to be as flat as a trencher, and Galileo was obliged to abjure his error. This error however at length prevailed, the earth became a globe, and Descartes declared it was whirled round its axis by a vortex. Th government in which he lived was wise enough to see that this was no question of civil jurisdiction, or we should all have been involved by authority in vortices. In fact, the vortices have been exploded, and the Newtonian principle of gravitation is now more firmly established, on the basis of reason, than it would be were the government to step in, and to make it an article of necessary faith. Reason and experiment have been indulged, and error has fled before them. It is error alone which needs the support of government. Truth can stand by itself. Subject opinion to coercion: whom will you make your inquisitors? Fallible men; men governed by bad passions, by private as well as public reasons. And why subject it to coercion? To produce uniformity. But is uniformity of opinion desireable? No more than of face and stature. Introduce the bed of Procrustes then, and as there is danger that the large men may beat the small, make us all of a size, by

lopping the former and stretching the latter. Difference of opinion is advantageous in religion. The several sects perform the office of a Censor morum over each other. Is uniformity attainable? Millions of innocent men, women, and children, since the introduction of Christianity, have been burnt, tortured, fined, imprisoned; yet we have not advanced one inch towards uniformity. What has been the effect of coercion? To make one half the world fools, and the other half hypocrites. To support roguery and error all over the earth. Let us reflect that it is inhabited by a thousand millions of people. That these profess probably a thousand different systems of religion. That ours is but one of that thousand. That if there be but one right, and ours that one, we should wish to see the 999 wandering sects gathered into the fold of truth. But against such a majority we cannot effect this by force. Reason and persuasion are the only practicable instruments. To make way for these, free enquiry must be indulged; and how can we wish others to indulge it while we refuse it ourselves But every state, says an inquisitor, has established some religion. No two, say I, have established the same. Is this a proof of the infallibility of establishments? Our sister states of Pennsylvania and New York, however, have long subsisted without any establishment at all. The experiment was new and doubtful when they made it. It has answered beyond conception. They flourish infinitely. Religion is well supported; of various kinds, indeed, but all good enough; all sufficient to preserve peace and order: or if a sect arises, whose tenets would subvert morals, good sense has fair play, and reasons and laughs it out of doors, without suffering the state to be troubled with it. They do not hang more malefactors than we do. They are not more disturbed with religious dissensions. On the contrary, their harmony is unparalleled, and can be ascribed to nothing but their unbounded tolerance, because there is no other circumstance in which they differ from every nation on earth. They have made the happy discovery, that the way to silence religious disputes, is to take no notice of them. Let us too give this experiment fair play, and get rid, while we may, of those tyrannical laws. It is true, we are as yet secured against them by the spirit of the times. I doubt whether the people of this country would suffer an execution for heresy, or a three years imprisonment for not comprehending the mysteries of the Trinity. But is the spirit of the people an infallible, a permanent reliance? Is it government? Is this the kind of protection we receive in return for the rights we give up? Besides, the spirit of the times may alter, will alter. Our rulers will become corrupt, our people careless. A single zealot may commence persecutor, and better men be his victims. It can never be too often repeated, that the time for fixing every essential right on a legal basis is while our rulers are honest, and ourselves united. From the conclusion of this war we shall be going down hill. It will not then be necessary to resort every moment to the people for support. They will be forgotten, therefore, and their rights disregarded. They will forget themselves, but in the sole faculty of making money, and will never think of uniting to effect a due respect for their rights. The shackles, therefore, which shall not be knocked off at the conclusion of this war, will remain on us long, will be made heavier and heavier, till our rights shall revive or expire in a convulsion.

Source: Thomas Jefferson: Writings, *pp. 285–287.*

14. The Federalist 51 (Publius (James Madison), February 6, 1788)

It is of great importance in a republic, not only to guard the society against the oppression of its rulers; but to guard one part of the society against the injustice of the other part. Different interests necessarily exist in different classes of citizens. If a majority be united by a common interest, the rights of the minority will be insecure. There are but two methods of providing against this evil: The one by creating a will in the community independent of the majority, that is, of the society itself; The other, by comprehending in the society so many separate descriptions of citizens, as will render an unjust combination of a majority of the whole, very improbable, if not impracticable. The first method prevails in all governments possessing an hereditary or self appointed authority. This at best is but a precarious security; because a power independent of the society may as well espouse the unjust views of the major, as the rightful interests, of the minor party, and may possibly be turned against both parties. The second method will be exemplified in the federal republic of the United States. Whilst all authority in it will be derived from and dependent on the society, the society itself will be broken into so many parts, interests and classes of citizens, that the rights of individuals or of the minority, will be in little danger from interested combinations of the majority. In a free government, the security for civil rights must be the same as that for religious rights. It consists in the one case in the multiplicity of interests, and in the other, in the multiplicity of sects. The degree of security in both cases will depend on the number of interests and sects; and this may be presumed to depend on the extent of country and number of people comprehended under the same government. This view of the subject must particularly recommend a proper federal system to all the sincere and considerate friends of republican government: Since it shows that in exact proportion as the territory of the union may be formed into more circumscribed confederacies or States, oppressive combinations of a majority will be facilitated, the best security under the republican form, for the rights of every class of citizens, will be diminished; and consequently, the stability and independence of some member of the government, the only other security, must be proportionately increased. Justice is the end of government. It is the end of civil society. It ever has been, and ever will be pursued, until it be obtained, or until liberty be lost in the pursuit. In a society under the forms of which the stronger faction can readily unite and oppress the weaker, anarchy may as truly be said to reign as in a state of nature where the weaker individual is not secured against the violence of the stronger: And as in the latter state even the stronger individuals are prompted by the uncertainty of their condition, to submit to a government which may protect the weak as well as themselves: So in the former state, will the more powerful factions or parties be gradually induced by a like motive, to wish for a government which will protect all parties, the weaker as well as the more powerful. It can be little doubted, that if the state of Rhode Island was separated from the confederacy, and left to itself, the insecurity of rights under the popular form of government within such narrow limits, would be displayed by such reiterated oppressions of factious majorities, that some power altogether independent of the people would soon be called for by the voice of the very factions whose misrule had proved the necessity of it. In the extended republic of the United States, and among the great variety of interests, parties, and sects which it embraces, a coalition of a majority of the whole society could seldom take place on any other principles than those of justice and the general good; and there being thus less danger to a minor from the will of a major party, there must be less pretext also, to provide for the security of the former, by introducing into the government a will not dependent on the latter; or in other words, a will independent of the society itself. It is no less certain than it is important, notwithstanding the contrary opinions which have been entertained, that the larger the society, provided it lie within a practical sphere, the more duly capable it will be of self government. And happily for the republican cause, the practicable sphere may be carried to a very great extent, by a judicious modification and mixture of the federal principle.

Source: The Federalist, 351–353.

15. George Washington, Letter to the United Baptist Churches in Virginia (1789)

If I could have entertained the slightest apprehension that the Constitution framed in the Convention, where I had the honor to preside, might possibly endanger the religious rights of any ecclesiastical society, certainly I would never have placed my signature to it; and if I could now conceive that the general government might ever be so administered as to render the liberty of conscience insecure, I beg you will be persuaded that no one would be more zealous than myself to establish effectual barriers against the horrors of spiritual tyranny, and every species of religious persecution. For you, doubtless, remember that I have often expressed my sentiment, that every man, conducting himself as a good citizen, and being accountable to God alone for his religious opinions, ought to be protected in worshiping the Deity according to the dictates of his own conscience.

While I recollect with satisfaction that the religious society of which you are members, have been, throughout America, uniformly, and almost unanimously, the firm friends to civil liberty, and the persevering promoters of our glorious revolution; I cannot hesitate to believe that they will be the faithful supporters of a free, yet efficient general government. Under this pleasing expectation I rejoice to assure them that they may rely on my best wishes and endeavors to advance their prosperity.

In the mean time be assured, Gentlemen, that I entertain a proper sense of your fervent supplications to God for my temporal and eternal happiness.

Source: Available online at URL: http://www.founding.com/library/lbody.cfm?id=198&parent=60. Accessed on January 19, 2006.

16. Debates in the House of Representatives Concerning the Proposed Amendments to the Constitution (August 1789)

[15 Aug.]

The House again went into a Committee of the whole on the proposed amendments to the constitution, Mr. Boudinot in the chair.

The fourth proposition being under consideration, as follows:

Article 1. Section 9. Between paragraphs two and three insert "no religion shall be established by law, nor shall the equal rights of conscience be infringed."

Mr. Sylvester had some doubts of the propriety of the mode of expression used in this paragraph. He apprehended that it was liable to a construction different from what had been made by the committee. He feared it might be thought to have a tendency to abolish religion altogether.

Mr. Vining suggested the propriety of transposing the two members of the sentence.

Mr. Gerry said it would read better if it was, that no religious doctrine shall be established by law.

Mr. Sherman thought the amendment altogether unnecessary, inasmuch as Congress had no authority whatever delegated to them by the constitution to make religious establishments; he would, therefore, move to have it struck out.

Mr. Carroll—As the rights of conscience are, in their nature, of peculiar delicacy, and will little bear the gentlest touch of governmental hand; and as many sects have concurred in opinion that they are not well secured under the present constitution, he said he was much in favor of adopting the words. He thought it would tend more towards conciliating the minds of the people to the Government than almost any other amendment he had heard proposed. He would not contend with gentlemen about the phraseology, his object was to secure the substance in such a manner as to satisfy the wishes of the honest part of the community.

Mr. Madison said, he apprehended the meaning of the words to be, that congress should not establish a religion, and enforce the legal observation of it by law, nor compel men to worship God in any manner contrary to their conscience. Whether the words are necessary or not, he did not mean to say, but they had been required by some of the State Conventions, who seemed to entertain an opinion that under the clause of the constitution, which gave power to Congress to make all laws necessary and proper to carry into execution the constitution, and the laws made under it, enabled them to make laws of such a nature as might infringe the rights of conscience, and establish a national religion; to prevent these effects he presumed the amendment was intended, and he thought it as well expressed as the nature of the language would admit.

Mr. Huntington said that he feared, with the gentleman first up on this subject, that the words might be taken in such latitude as to be extremely hurtful to the cause of religion. He understood the amendment to mean what had been expressed by the gentleman from Virginia; but others might find it convenient to put another construction upon it. The ministers of their congregations to the Eastward were maintained by the contributions of those who belonged to their society; the expense of building meeting-houses was contributed in the same manner. These things were regulated by bylaws. If an action was brought before a Federal Court on any of these cases, the person who had neglected to perform his engagements could not be compelled to do it; for a support of ministers, or building of places of worship might be construed into a religious establishment.

By the charter of Rhode Island, no religion could be established by law; he could give a history of the effects of such a regulation; indeed the people were now enjoying the blessed fruits of it. He hoped, therefore, the amendment would be made in such a way as to secure the rights of conscience, and a free exercise of the rights of religion, but not to patronize those who professed no religion at all.

Mr. Madison thought, if the word national was inserted before religion, it would satisfy the minds of honorable gentlemen. He believed that the people feared one sect might obtain a pre-eminence, or two combine together, and establish a religion to which they would compel others to conform. He thought if the word national was introduced, it would point the amendment directly to the object it was intended to prevent.

Mr. Livermore was not satisfied with that amendment; but he did not wish them to dwell long on the subject. He thought it would be better if it was altered, and made to read in this manner, that Congress shall make no laws touching religion, or infringing the rights of conscience.

Mr. Gerry did not like the term national, proposed by the gentleman from Virginia, and he hoped it would not be adopted by the House. It brought to his mind some observations that had taken place in the conventions at the time they were considering the present constitution. It had been insisted upon by those who were called antifederalists, that this form of Government consolidated the Union; the honorable gentleman's motion shows that he considers it in the same light. Those who were called antifederalists at that time complained that they had injustice done them by the title, because they were in favor of a Federal Government, and the others were in favor of a national one; the federalists were for ratifying the constitution as it stood, and the others not until amendments were made. Their names then ought not to have been distinguished by federalists and antifederalists, but rats and antirats.

Mr. Madison withdrew his motion, but observed that the words "no national religion shall be established by law," did not imply that the Government was a national one; the question was then taken on Mr. Livermore's motion, and passed in the affirmative, thirty-one for, and twenty against it.

[17 Aug]

The committee then proceeded to the fifth proposition:

Article 1, section 10, between the first and second paragraph, insert "no State shall infringe the equal rights of conscience, nor the freedom of speech or of the press, nor of the right of trial by jury in criminal cases."

Mr. Tucker—This is offered, I presume, as an amendment to the Constitution of the United States, but it goes only to the alteration of the constitutions of particular States. It will be much better, I apprehend, to leave the State Governments to themselves, and not to interfere with them more than we already do; and that is thought by many to be rather too much. I therefore move, sir, to strike out these words.

Mr. Madison conceived this to be the most valuable amendment in the whole list. If there was any reason to restrain the Government of the United States from infringing upon these essential rights, it was equally necessary that they should be secured against the State Governments. He thought that if they provided against the one, it was as necessary to provide against the other, and was satisfied that it would be equally grateful to the people.

Mr. Livermore had no great objection to the sentiment, but he thought it not well expressed. He wished to make it an affirmative proposition; "the equal rights of conscience, the freedom of speech or of the press, and the right of trial by jury in criminal cases, shall not be infringed by any State."

This transposition being agreed to, and Mr. Tucker's motion being rejected, the clause was adopted.

[20 Aug]

On motion of Mr. Ames, the fourth amendment was altered so as to read "Congress shall make no law establishing religion, or to prevent the free exercise thereof, or to infringe the rights of conscience." This being adopted. . . .

The Founders' Constitution, *vol. 5, pp. 92–94.*

17. Amendment I, U.S. Constitution (1791)

Congress shall make no law respecting an establishment of religion, or prohibiting the free exercise thereof; or abridging the freedom of speech, or of the press; or the right of the people peaceably to assemble, and to petition the Government for a redress of grievances.

Source: Available online at URL: http://www.law. cornell.edu/constitution/constitution.billofrights. html. Accessed on January 19, 2005.

18. Plan of Union adopted by Congregationalists and Presbyterians, 1801

Regulations adopted by the General Assembly of the Presbyterian Church in America, and by the General Association of the State of Connecticut, with a view to prevent alienation, and to promote union and harmony in those new settlements which are composed of inhabitants from these bodies.

1. It is strictly enjoined on all their missionaries to the new settlements, to endeavor, by all proper means, to promote mutual forbearance, and a spirit of accommodation, between those inhabitants of the new settlements who hold the Presbyterian, and those who hold the Congregational, form of Church government.

2. If, in the new settlements, any church of the Congregational order shall settle a minister of the Presbyterian order, that church may, if they choose, still conduct their discipline according to Congregational principles, settling their difficulties among themselves, or by a council mutually agreed upon for that purpose. But, if any difficulty shall exist, between the minister and the church, or any member of if, it shall be referred to the Presbytery to which the minister shall belong, provided both parties agree to it; if not, to a council consisting of an equal number of Presbyterians and Congregationalists, agreed upon by both parties.

3. If a Presbyterian church shall settle a minister of Congregational principles, that church may still conduct their discipline according to Presbyterian principles, excepting that if a difficulty arise between him and his church, or any member of it, the cause shall be tried by the Association to which the said minister shall belong, provided both parties agree to it; otherwise by a council, one half Congregationalists and the other Presbyterians, mutually agreed upon by the parties.

4. If any congregation consist partly of those who hold the Congregational form of discipline, and partly of those who hold the Presbyterian form, we recommend to both parties, that this be no obstruction to their uniting in one church and settling a minister; and that, in this case, the church choose a standing committee, from the communicants of said church, whose business it shall be to call to account every member of the church who shall conduct himself inconsistently with the laws of Christianity, and to give judgment on such conduct. That if the person condemned by their judgment be a Presbyterian, he shall have liberty to appeal to the Presbytery; if he be a Congregationalist, he shall have liberty to appeal to the body of the male communicants of the church. In the former case, the determination of the Presbytery shall be final, unless the church shall consent to a further appeal to the Synod, or to the General Assembly; and, in the latter case, if the party condemned shall wish for a trial by a mutual council, the cause shall be referred to such a council. And provided the standing committee of any church shall depute one of themselves to attend the Presbytery, he may have the same right to sit and act in the Presbytery as a ruling elder of the Presbyterian church.

Source: Williston Walker, The Creeds and Platforms of Congregationalism *(Boston: Pilgrim Press, 1960), pp. 530–531.*

19. James Madison, Detached Memoranda (ca. 1817)

The danger of silent accumulations & encroachments by Ecclesiastical Bodies have not sufficiently engaged attention in the U.S. They have the noble merit of first unshackling the conscience from persecuting laws, and of establishing among religious Sects a legal equality. If some of the States have not embraced this just and this truly Xn principle in its proper latitude, all of them present examples by which the most enlightened States of the old world may be instructed; and there is one State at least, Virginia, where religious liberty is placed on its true foundation and is defined in its full latitude. The general principle is contained in her declaration of rights, prefixed to her Constitution: but it is unfolded and defined, in its precise extent, in the act of the Legislature, usually named the Religious Bill, which passed into a law in the year 1786. Here the separation between the authority of human laws, and the natural rights of Man excepted from the grant on which all political authority is founded, is traced as distinctly as words can admit, and the limits to this authority established with as much solemnity as the forms of legislation can express. The law has the further advantage of having been the result of a formal appeal to the sense of the Community and a deliberate sanction of a vast majority, comprising every sect of Christians in the State. This act is a true standard of Religious liberty: its principle the great barrier against usurpations on the rights of conscience. As long as it is respected & no longer, these will be safe. Every provision for them short of this principle, will be found to leave crevices at least through which bigotry may introduce persecution; a monster, that feeding & thriving on its own venom, gradually swells to a size and strength overwhelming all laws divine & human.

Ye States of America, which retain in your Constitutions or Codes, any aberration from the sacred principle of religious liberty, by giving to Caesar what belongs to God, or joining together what God has put asunder, hasten to revise & purify your systems, and make the example of your Country as pure & complete, in what relates to the freedom of the mind and its allegiance to its maker, as in what belongs to the legitimate objects of political & civil institutions.

Strongly guarded as is the separation between Religion & Govt in the Constitution of the United States the danger of encroachment by Ecclesiastical Bodies, may be illustrated by precedents already furnished in their short history. (See the cases in which negatives were put by J. M. on two bills passed by Congress and his signature withheld from another. See also attempt in Kentucky for example, where it was proposed to exempt Houses of Worship from taxes.)

The most notable attempt was that in Virginia to establish a General assessment for the support of all Christian sects. This was proposed in the year [ ] by P. H. and supported by all his eloquence, aided by the remaining prejudices of the Sect which before the Revolution had been established by law. The progress of the measure was arrested by urging that the respect due to the people required in so extraordinary a case an appeal to their deliberate will. The bill was accordingly printed & published with that view. At the instance of Col: George Nicholas, Col: George Mason & others, the memorial & remonstrance against it was drawn up, (which see) and printed

Copies of it circulated thro' the State, to be signed by the people at large. It met with the approbation of the Baptists, the Presbyterians, the Quakers, and the few Roman Catholics, universally; of the Methodists in part; and even of not a few of the Sect formerly established by law. When the Legislature assembled, the number of Copies & signatures prescribed displayed such an overwhelming opposition of the people, that the proposed plan of a genl assessmt was crushed under it; and advantage taken of the crisis to carry thro' the Legisl: the Bill above referred to, establishing religious liberty. In the course of the opposition to the bill in the House of Delegates, which was warm & strenuous from some of the minority, an experiment was made on the reverence entertained for the name & sanctity of the Saviour, by proposing to insert the words "Jesus Christ" after the words "our lord" in the preamble, the object of which, would have been, to imply a restriction of the liberty defined in the Bill, to those professing his religion only. The amendment was discussed, and rejected by a vote of agst [ ] (See letter of J. M. to Mr Jefferson dated [ ]) The opponents of the amendment having turned the feeling as well as judgment of the House agst it, by successfully contending that the better proof of reverence for that holy name wd be no to profane it by making it a topic of legisl. discussion, & particularly by making his religion the means of abridging the natural and equal rights of all men, in defiance of his own declaration that his Kingdom was not of this world. This view of the subject was much enforced by the circumstance that it was espoused by some members who were particularly distinguished by their reputed piety and Christian zeal.

But besides the danger of a direct mixture of Religion & civil Government, there is an evil which ought to be guarded agst in the indefinite accumulation of property from the capacity of holding it in perpetuity by ecclesiastical corporations. The power of all corporations, ought to be limited in this respect. The growing wealth acquired by them never fails to be a source of abuses. A warning on this subject is emphatically given in the example of the various Charitable establishments in G. B. the management of which has been lately scrutinized. The excessive wealth of ecclesiastical Corporations and the misuse of it in many Countries of Europe has long been a topic of complaint. In some of them the Church has amassed half perhaps the property of the nation. When the reformation took place, an event promoted if not caused, by that disordered state of things, how enormous were the treasures of religious societies, and how gross the corruptions engendered by them; so enormous & so gross as to produce in the Cabinets & Councils of the Protestant states a disregard, of all the pleas of the interested party drawn from the sanctions of the law, and the sacredness of property held in religious trust. The history of England during the period of the reformation offers a sufficient illustration for the present purpose.

Are the U.S. duly awake to the tendency of the precedents they are establishing, in the multiplied incorporations of Religious Congregations with the faculty of acquiring & holding property real as well as personal? Do not many of these acts give this faculty, without limit either as to time or as to amount? And must not bodies, perpetual in their existence, and which may be always gaining without ever losing, speedily gain more than is useful, and in time more than is safe? Are there not already examples in the U. S. of ecclesiastical wealth equally beyond its object and the foresight of those who laid the foundation of it? In the U.S. there is a double motive for fixing limits in this case, because wealth may increase not only from additional gifts, but from exorbitant advances in the value of the primitive one. In grants of vacant lands, and of lands in the vicinity of growing towns & Cities the increase of value is often such as if foreseen, would essentially controul the liberality confirming them. The people of the U.S. owe their Independence & their liberty, to the wisdom of descrying in the minute tax of 3 pence on tea, the magnitude of the evil comprized in the precedent. Let them exert the same wisdom, in watching agst every evil lurking under plausible disguises, and growing up from small beginnings. Obsta principiis. . . .

Is the appointment of Chaplains to the two Houses of Congress consistent with the Constitution, and with the pure principle of religious freedom?

In strictness the answer on both points must be in the negative. The Constitution of the U.S. forbids everything like an establishment of a national religion. The law appointing Chaplains establishes a religious worship for the national representatives, to be performed by Ministers of religion, elected by a majority of them; and these are to be paid out of the national taxes. Does not this involve the principle of a national establishment, applicable to a provision for a religious worship for the Constituent as well as of the representative Body, approved by the majority, and conducted by Ministers of religion paid by the entire nation.

The establishment of the chaplainship to Congs is a palpable violation of equal rights, as well as of Constitutional principles: The tenets of the chaplains elected [by the majority] shut the door of worship agst the members whose creeds & consciences forbid a participation in that of the majority. To say nothing of other sects, this is the case with that of Roman Catholics & Quakers who have always had members in one or both of the Legislative branches. Could a Catholic clergyman ever hope to be appointed a Chaplain? To say that his religious principles are obnoxious or that his sect is small, is to lift the evil at once and exhibit in its naked deformity the doctrine that religious truth is to be tested by numbers. or that the major sects have a right to govern the minor.

If Religion consist in voluntary acts of individuals, singly, or voluntarily associated, and it be proper that public functionaries, as well as their Constituents shd discharge their religious duties, let them like their Constituents, do so at their own expence. How small a contribution from each member of Congs wd suffice for the purpose? How just wd it be in its principle? How noble in its exemplary sacrifice to the genius of the Constitution; and the divine right of conscience? Why should the expence of a religious worship be allowed for the Legislature, be paid by the public, more than that for the Ex. or Judiciary branch of the Govt.

Were the establishment to be tried by its fruits, are not the daily devotions conducted by these legal Ecclesiastics, already degenerating into a scanty attendance, and a tiresome formality? "Rather than let this step beyond the landmarks of power have the effect of a legitimate precedent, it will be better to apply to it the legal aphorism de minimis non curat lex: or to class it cum "maculis quas aut incuria fudit, aut humana parum cavit natura."

Better also to disarm in the same way, the precedent of Chaplainships for the army and navy, than erect them into a political authority in matters of religion. The object of this establishment is seducing; the motive to it is laudable. But is it not safer to adhere to a right principle, and trust to its consequences, than confide in the reasoning however specious in favor of a wrong one. Look thro' the armies & navies of the world, and say whether in the appointment of their ministers of religion, the spiritual interest of the flocks or the temporal interest of the Shepherds, be most in view: whether here, as elsewhere the political care of religion is not a nominal more than a real aid. If the spirit of armies be devout, the spirit out of the armies will never be less so; and a failure of religious instruction & exhortation from a voluntary source within or without, will rarely happen: and if such be not the spirit of armies, the official services of their Teachers are not likely to produce it. It is more likely to flow from the labours of a spontaneous zeal. The armies of the Puritans had their appointed Chaplains; but without these there would have been no lack of public devotion in that devout age.

The case of navies with insulated crews may be less within the scope of these reflections. But it is not entirely so. The chance of a devout officer, might be of as much worth to religion, as the service of an ordinary chaplain. [were it admitted that religion has a real interest in the latter.] But we are always to keep in mind that it is safer to trust the consequences of a right principle, than reasonings in support of a bad one.

Religious proclamations by the Executive recommending thanksgivings & fasts are shoots from the same root with the legislative acts reviewed.

Altho' recommendations only, they imply a religious agency, making no part of the trust delegated to political rulers.

The objections to them are 1. that Govts ought not to interpose in relation to those subject to their authority but in cases where they can do it with effect. An advisory Govt is a contradiction in terms. 2. The members of a Govt as such can in no sense, be regarded as possessing an advisory trust from their Constituents in their religious capacities. They cannot form an ecclesiastical Assembly, Convocation, Council, or Synod, and as such issue decrees or injunctions addressed to the faith or the Consciences of the people. In their individual capacities, as distinct from their official station, they might unite in recommendations of any sort whatever, in the same manner as any other individuals might do. But then their recommendations ought to express the true character from which they emanate. 3. They seem to imply and certainly nourish the erronious idea of a *national* religion. The idea just as it related to the Jewish nation under a theocracy, having been improperly adopted by so many nations which have embraced Xnity, is too apt to lurk in the bosoms even of Americans, who in general are aware of the distinction between religious & political societies. The idea also of a union of all to form one nation under one Govt in acts of devotion to the God of all is an imposing idea.

But reason and the principles of the Xn religion require that all the individuals composing a nation even of the same precise creed & wished to unite in a universal act of religion at the same time, the union ought to be effected thro' the intervention of their religious not of their political representatives. In a nation composed of various sects, some alienated widely from others, and where no agreement could take place thro' the former, the interposition of the latter is doubly wrong: 4. The tendency of the practice, to narrow the recommendation to the standard of the predominant sect. The Ist proclamation of Genl Washington dated Jany 1. 1795 (see if this was the 1st) recommending a day of thanksgiving, embraced all who believed in a supreme ruler of the Universe." That of Mr Adams called for a Xn worship. Many private letters reproached the Proclamations issued by J. M. for using general terms, used in that of Presit W—n; and some of them for not inserting particulars according with the faith of certain Xn sects. The practice if not strictly guarded naturally terminates in a conformity to the creed of the majority and a single sect, if amounting to a majority. 5. The last & not the least objection is the liability of the practice to a subserviency to political views; to the scandal of religion, as well as the increase of party animosities. Candid or incautious politicians will not always disown such views. In truth it is difficult to frame such a religious Proclamation generally suggested by a political State of things, without referring to them in terms having some bearing on party questions. The Proclamation of Pres: W. which was issued just after the suppression of the Insurrection in Penna and at a time when the public mind was divided on several topics, was so construed by many. Of this the Secretary of State himself, E. Randolph seems to have had an anticipation.

The oriinal draught of that Instrument filed in the Dept. of State . . . in the hand writing of Mr Hamilton the Secretary of the Treasury. It appears that several slight alterations only had been made at the suggestion of the Secretary of State; and in a marginal note in his hand, it is remarked that "In short this proclamation ought to savour as much as possible of religion, & not too much of having a political object." In a subjoined note in the hand of Mr. Hamilton, this remark is answered by the counter-remark that "A proclamation of a Government which is a national act, naturally embraces objects which are political" so *naturally*, is the idea of policy associated with religion, whatever be the mode or the occasion, when a function of the latter is assumed by those in power.

During the administration of Mr Jefferson no religious proclamation was issued. It being understood that his successor was disinclined to such interpositions of the Executive and by some supposed moreover that they might originate with more propriety with the Legislative Body, a resolution was passed requesting him to issue a proclamation.

It was thought not proper to refuse a compliance altogether; but a form & language were employed, which were meant to deaden as much as possible any claim of political right to enjoin religious observances by resting these expressly on the voluntary compliance of individuals, and even by limiting the recommendation to such as wished simultaneous as well as voluntary performance of a religious act on the occasion.

Source: Madison: Writings, *pp. 759–766.*

20. Amendment XIV, sec. 1, U.S. Constitution, (1868)

All persons born or naturalized in the United States and subject to the jurisdiction thereof, are citizens of the United States and of the State wherein they reside. No State shall make or enforce any law which shall abridge the privileges or immunities of citizens of the United States; nor shall any State deprive any person of life, liberty, or property, without due process of law; nor deny to any person within its jurisdiction the equal protection of the laws.

Source: Available online at URL: http://www.law. cornell.edu/constitution/constitution.amendmentxiv. html. Accessed on November 15, 2006.

21. The Blaine Amendment (proposed 1875)

No State shall make any law respecting an establishment of religion or prohibiting the free exercise thereof; and no money raised by taxation in any State, for the support of public schools, or derived from any public fund therefor, nor any public lands devoted thereto, shall ever be under the control of any religious sect, nor shall any money so raised, or lands so devoted be divided between religious sects or denominations.

Source: Available online at URL: http://www3. baylor.edu/Church_State/Blaine_Amendment.html. Accessed on January 19, 2006.

22. Preamble to the Constitution of the Jewish Theological Seminary (1886)

The necessity having been made manifest for associated and organized effort on the part of the Jews of America faithful to Mosaic Law and ancestral traditions, for the purpose of keeping alive the true Judaic spirit; in particular by the establishment of a seminary where the Bible shall be impartially taught, and rabbinical literature faithfully expounded, and more especially where youths, desirous of entering the ministry, may be thoroughly grounded in Jewish knowledge and inspired by the precept and the example of their instructors with the love of the Hebrew language, and a spirit of fidelity and devotion to the Jewish law, the subscribers have, in accordance with a resolution adopted at a meeting of ministers held Shebat 25, 5646 (January 31, 1886), at the synagogue Shearith Israel, New York, agreed to organize The Jewish Theological Seminary Association. . . .

Source: Marcus, The Jew in the American World: A Sourcebook, *p. 243.*

23. Charter of the Kehillah (Jewish Community) of New York City, April 5, 1914

The People of the State of New York, represented in Senate and Assembly, do enact as follows: . . . .

Sec. 2. The objects of said corporation shall be, to stimulate and encourage the instruction of the Jews residing in the city of New York in the tenets of their religion and in the history, language, literature, institutions and traditions of their people; to conduct, support and maintain schools and classes for that purpose; to publish and distribute text-books, maps, charts, and illustrations to facilitate such instruction; to conduct lectures and classes in civics and other kindred subjects; to establish an educational bureau to further the foregoing purposes; to conduct religious services and support, maintain and establish temporary as well as permanent synagogues; to adjust differences among Jewish residents or organizations located in said city, whenever thereunto requested by the parties thereto, by arbitration or by means of boards of mediation and conciliation; to maintain an employment bureau; to collate and publish statistical and other information concerning the Jewish inhabitants of said city and their activities; to study and ameliorate their social, moral and economic conditions, and to cooperate with the various charitable, philanthropic, educational and religious organizations and bodies of said city for the promotion of their common welfare . . .

Source: Marcus, The Jew in the American World: A Sourcebook, *pp. 334–335.*

24. Amendment XVIII, U.S. Constitution (1919)

Section 1. After one year from the ratification of this article the manufacture, sale, or transportation of intoxicating liquors within, the importation thereof into, or the exportation thereof from the United States and all territory subject to the jurisdiction thereof for beverage purposes is hereby prohibited.

Section 2. The Congress and the several States shall have concurrent power to enforce this article by appropriate legislation.

Section 3. This article shall be inoperative unless it shall have been ratified as an amendment to the Constitution by the legislatures of the several States, as provided in the Constitution, within seven years from the date of the submission hereof to the States by the Congress.

Source: Available online at URL: http://www.law.cornell.edu/constitution/constitution.amendmentxiv.html. Accessed on January 19, 2006.

25. Amendment XXI, U.S. Constitution (1933)

Section 1. The eighteenth article of amendment to the Constitution of the United States is hereby repealed.

Section 2. The transportation or importation into any State, Territory, or possession of the United States for delivery or use therein of intoxicating liquors, in violation of the laws thereof, is hereby prohibited.

Section 3. This article shall be inoperative unless it shall have been ratified as an amendment to the Constitution by conventions in the several States, as provided in the Constitution, within seven years from the date of the submission hereof to the States by the Congress.

Source: Available online at URL: http://www.law.cornell.edu/constitution/constitutionamendmentxiv.html. Accessed on January 19, 2006.

26. Student Non-Violent Coordinating Committee (SNCC) Founding Statement (1960)

We affirm the philosophical or religious ideal of nonviolence as the foundation of our purpose, the presupposition of our faith, and the manner of our action. Nonviolence as it grows from Judaic-Christian tradition seeks a social order of justice permeated by love. Integration of human endeavor represents the crucial first step toward such a society.

Through nonviolence, courage displaces fear; love transforms hate. Acceptance dissipates prejudice; hope ends despair. Peace dominates war; faith reconciles doubt. Mutual regard cancels enmity. Justice for all overthrows injustice. The redemptive community supersedes systems of gross social immorality.

Love is the central motif of nonviolence. Love is the force by which God binds man to Himself and man to man. Such love goes to the extreme; it remains loving and forgiving even in the midst of hostility. It matches the capacity of evil to inflict suffering with an even more enduring capacity to absorb evil, all the while persisting in love.

By appealing to conscience and standing on the moral nature of human existence, nonviolence nurtures the atmosphere in which reconciliation and justice become actual possibilities.

Source: Available online at URL: http://lists.village.virginia.edu/sixties/HTML_docs/Resources/Primary/Manifestos/SNCC_found ing.html. Accessed on January 19, 2006.

27. From the opinion of Justice Hugo Black for the U.S. Supreme Court in *Engel v. Vitale* (1963)

Mr. Justice BLACK delivered the opinion of the Court.

The respondent Board of Education of Union Free School District No. 9, New Hyde Park, New York, acting in its official capacity under state law, directed the School District's principal to cause the following prayer to be said aloud by each class in the presence of a teacher at the beginning of each school day:

"Almighty God, we acknowledge our dependence upon Thee, and we beg Thy blessings upon us, our parents, our teachers and our Country."

This daily procedure was adopted on the recommendation of the State Board of Regents, a governmental agency created by the State Constitution to which the New York Legislature has granted broad supervisory, executive, and legislative powers over the State's public school system. . . .

Shortly after the practice of reciting the Regents' prayer was adopted by the School District, the parents of ten pupils brought this action in a New York State Court insisting that use of this official prayer in the public schools was contrary to the beliefs, religions, or religious practices of both themselves and their children. . . .

We think that by using its public school system to encourage recitation of the Regents' prayer, the State of New York has adopted a practice wholly inconsistent with the Establishment Clause. There can, of course, be no doubt that New York's program of daily classroom invocation of God's blessings as prescribed in the Regents' prayer is a religious activity. It is a solemn avowal of divine faith and supplication for the blessings of the Almighty. The nature of such a prayer has always been religious. . . .

[W]e think that the constitutional prohibition against laws respecting an establishment of religion must at least mean that in this country it is no part of the business of government to compose official prayers for any group of the American people to recite as a part of a religious program carried on by government.

It is a matter of history that this very practice of establishing governmentally composed prayers for religious services was one of the reasons which caused many of our early colonists to leave England and seek religious freedom in America. The Book of Common Prayer, which was created under governmental direction and which was approved by Acts of Parliament in 1548 and 1549, set out in minute detail the accepted form and content of prayer and other religious ceremonies to be used in the established, tax-supported Church of England. The controversies over the Book and what should be its content repeatedly threatened to disrupt the peace of that country as the accepted forms of prayer in the established church changed with the views of the particular ruler that happened to be in control at the time. Powerful groups representing some of the varying religious views of the people struggled among themselves to impress their particular views upon the Government and obtain amendments of the Book more suitable to their respective notions of how religious services should be conducted in order that the official religious estab-

lishment would advance their particular religious beliefs. Other groups, lacking the necessary political power to influence the Government on the matter, decided to leave England and its established church and seek freedom in America from England's governmentally ordained and supported religion.

It is an unfortunate fact of history that when some of the very groups which had most strenuously opposed the established Church of England found themselves sufficiently in control of colonial governments in this country to write their own prayers into law, they passed laws making their own religion the official religion of their respective colonies. Indeed, as late as the time of the Revolutionary War, there were established churches in at least eight of the thirteen former colonies and established religions in at least four of the other five. But the successful Revolution against English political domination was shortly followed by intense opposition to the practice of establishing religion by law. This opposition crystallized rapidly into an effective political force in Virginia where the minority religious groups such as Presbyterians, Lutherans, Quakers and Baptists had gained such strength that the adherents to the established Episcopal Church were actually a minority themselves. In 1785–1786, those opposed to the established Church, led by James Madison and Thomas Jefferson, who, though themselves not members of any of these dissenting religious groups, opposed all religious establishments by law on grounds of principle, obtained the enactment of the famous 'Virginia Bill for Religious Liberty' by which all religious groups were placed on an equal footing so far as the State was concerned. Similar though less far-reaching legislation was being considered and passed in other States.

By the time of the adoption of the Constitution, our history shows that there was a widespread awareness among many Americans of the dangers of a union of Church and State. These people knew, some of them from bitter personal experience, that one of the greatest dangers to the freedom of the individual to worship in his own way lay in the Government's placing its official stamp of approval upon one particular kind of prayer or one particular form of religious services. They knew the anguish, hardship and bitter strife that could come when zealous religious groups struggled with one another to obtain the Government's stamp of approval from each King, Queen, or Protector that came to temporary power. The Constitution was intended to avert a part of this danger by leaving the government of this country in the hands of the people rather than in the hands of any monarch. But this safeguard was not enough. Our Founders were no more willing to let the content of their prayers and their privilege of praying whenever they pleased be influenced by the ballot box than they were to let these vital matters of personal conscience depend upon the succession of monarchs. The First Amendment was added to the Constitution to stand as a guarantee that neither the power nor the prestige of the Federal Government would be used to control, support or influence the kinds of prayer the American people can say—that the people's religions must not be subjected to the pressures of government for change each time a new political administration is elected to office. Under that Amendment's prohibition against governmental establishment of religion, as reinforced by the provisions of the Fourteenth Amendment, government in this country, be it state or federal, is without power to prescribe by law any particular form of prayer which is to be used as an official prayer in carrying on any program of governmentally sponsored religious activity.

There can be no doubt that New York's state prayer program officially establishes the religious beliefs embodied in the Regents' prayer. The respondents' argument to the contrary, which is largely based upon the contention that the Regents' prayer is 'nondenominational' and the fact that the program, as modified and approved by state courts, does not require all pupils to recite the prayer but permits those who wish to do so to remain silent or be excused from the room, ignores the essential nature of the program's constitutional defects. Neither the fact that the prayer may be denominationally neutral nor the fact that its observance on the part of the students is voluntary can serve to free it from the limitations of the Establishment Clause, as it might from the Free Exercise Clause, of the First Amendment, both of which are operative against the States by virtue of the Fourteenth Amendment. Although these two clauses may in certain instances overlap, they forbid two quite different kinds of governmental encroachment upon religious freedom. The Establishment Clause, unlike the Free Exercise Clause, does not depend upon any showing of direct governmental compulsion and is violated by the enactment of laws which establish an official religion whether those laws operate directly to coerce nonobserving individuals or not. This is not to say, of course, that laws officially prescribing a particular form of religious worship do not involve coercion of such individuals. When the power, prestige and financial support of gov-

ernment is placed behind a particular religious belief, the indirect coercive pressure upon religious minorities to conform to the prevailing officially approved religion is plain. But the purposes underlying the Establishment Clause go much further than that. Its first and most immediate purpose rested on the belief that a union of government and religion tends to destroy government and to degrade religion. The history of governmentally established rligion, both in England and in this country, showed that whenever government had allied itself with one particular form of religion, the inevitable result had been that it had incurred the hatred, disrespect and even contempt of those who held contrary beliefs. That same history showed that many people had lost their respect for any religion that had relied upon the support for government to spread its faith. The Establishment Clause thus stands as an expression of principle on the part of the Founders of our Constitution that religion is too personal, too sacred, too holy, to permit its 'unhallowed perversion' by a civil magistrate. Another purpose of the Establishment Clause rested upon an awareness of the historical fact that governmentally established religions and religious persecutions go hand in hand. The Founders knew that only a few years after the Book of Common Prayer became the only accepted form of religious services in the established Church of England, an Act of Uniformity was passed to compel all Englishmen to attend those services and to make it a criminal offense to conduct or attend religious gatherings of any other kind—a law which was consistently flouted by dissenting religious groups in England and which contributed to widespread persecutions of people like John Bunyan who persisted in holding 'unlawful (religious) meetings . . . to the great disturbance and distraction of the good subjects of this kingdom . . . .' And they knew that similar persecutions had received the sanction of law in several of the colonies in this country soon after the establishment of official religions in those colonies. It was in large part to get completely away from this sort of systematic religious persecution that the Founders brought into being our Nation, our Constitution, and our Bill of Rights with its prohibition against any governmental establishment of religion. The New York laws officially prescribing the Regents' prayer are inconsistent both with the purposes of the Establishment Clause and with the Establishment Clause itself.

It has been argued that to apply the Constitution in such a way as to prohibit state laws respecting an establishment of religious services in public schools is to indicate a hostility toward religion or toward prayer. Nothing, of course, could be more wrong. The history of man is inseparable from the history of religion. And perhaps it is not too much to say that since the beginning of that history many people have devoutly believed that 'More things are wrought by prayer than this world dreams of.' It was doubtless largely due to men who believed this that there grew up a sentiment that caused men to leave the cross-currents of officially established state religions and religious persecution in Europe and come to this country filled with the hope that they could find a place in which they could pray when they pleased to the God of their faith in the language they chose. And there were men of this same faith in the power of prayer who led the fight for adoption of our Constitution and also for our Bill of Rights with the very guarantees of religious freedom that forbid the sort of governmental activity which New York has attempted here. These men knew that the First Amendment, which tried to put an end to governmental control of religion and of prayer, was not written to destroy either. They knew rather that it was written to quiet well-justified fears which nearly all of them felt arising out of an awareness that governments of the past had shackled men's tongues to make them speak only the religious thoughts that government wanted them to speak and to pray only to the God that government wanted them to pray to. It is neither sacrilegious nor antireligious to say that each separate government in this country should stay out of the business of writing or sanctioning official prayers and leave that purely religious function to the people themselves and to those the people choose to look to for religious guidance.

It is true that New York's establishment of its Regents' prayer as an officially approved religious doctrine of that State does not amount to a total establishment of one particular religious sect to the exclusion of all others—that, indeed, the governmental endorsement of that prayer seems relatively insignificant when compared to the governmental encroachments upon religion which were commonplace 200 years ago. To those who may subscribe to the view that because the Regents' official prayer is so brief and general there can be no danger to religious freedom in its governmental establishment, however, it may be appropriate to say in the words of James Madison, the author of the First Amendment:

'(I)t is proper to take alarm at the first experiment on our liberties. . . . Who does not see that the same authority which can establish Christianity, in exclusion of all other Religions, may establish with the same ease any particular sect of Christians, in exclusion of all other Sects? That the same authority which can force a citizen to contribute three pence only of his property for the support of any one establishment, may force him to conform to any other establishment in all cases whatsoever?'

The judgment of the Court of Appeals of New York is reversed and the cause remanded for further proceedings not inconsistent with this opinion.

Reversed and remanded.

Source: 370 U.S. 421, 422–36 (1962)

28. Civil Rights Act of 1964

SEC. 201. (a) All persons shall be entitled to the full and equal enjoyment of the goods, services, facilities, and privileges, advantages, and accommodations of any place of public accommodation, as defined in this section, without discrimination or segregation on the ground of race, color, religion, or national origin. . . .

SEC. 703. (a) It shall be an unlawful employment practice for an employer—

(1) to fail or refuse to hire or to discharge any individual, or otherwise to discriminate against any individual with respect to his compensation, terms, conditions, or privileges of employment, because of such individual's race, color, religion, sex, or national origin; or

(2) to limit, segregate, or classify his employees in any way which would deprive or tend to deprive any individual of employment opportunities or otherwise adversely affect his status as an employee, because of such individual's race, color, religion, sex, or national origin.

Source: Available online at URL: http://usinfostate. gov/usa/infousa/laws/majorlaw/civil/r/9.htm. Accessed on January 19, 2006.

29. Declaration on the Relation of the Church to Non-Christian Religions, *Nostra Aetate*, Proclaimed by Pope Paul VI, October 28, 1965.

1. In our time, when day by day mankind is being drawn closer together, and the ties between different peoples are becoming stronger, the Church examines more closely the relationship to non-Christian religions. In her task of promoting unity and love among men, indeed among nations, she considers above all in

this declaration what men have in common and what draws them to fellowship.

One is the community of all peoples, one their origin, for God made the whole human race to live over the face of the earth. One also is their final goal, God. His providence, His manifestations of goodness, His saving design extend to all men, until that time when the elect will be united in the Holy City, the city ablaze with the glory of God, where the nations will walk in His light.

Men expect from the various religions answers to the unsolved riddles of the human condition, which today, even as in former times, deeply stir the hearts of men: What is man? What is the meaning, the aim of our life? What is moral good, what sin? Whence suffering and what purpose does it serve? Which is the road to true happiness? What are death, judgment and retribution after death? What, finally, is that ultimate inexpressible mystery which encompasses our existence: whence do we come, and where are we going?

2. From ancient times down to the present, there is found among various peoples a certain perception of that hidden power which hovers over the course of things and over the events of human history; at times some indeed have come to the recognition of a Supreme Being, or even of a Father. This perception and recognition penetrates their lives with a profound religious sense.

Religions, however, that are bound up with an advanced culture have struggled to answer the same questions by means of more refined concepts and a more developed language. Thus in Hinduism, men contemplate the divine mystery and express it through an inexhaustible abundance of myths and through searching philosophical inquiry. They seek freedom from the anguish of our human condition either through ascetical practices or profound meditation or a flight to God with love and trust. Again, Buddhism, in its various forms, realizes the radical insufficiency of this changeable world; it teaches a way by which men, in a devout and confident spirit, may be able either to acquire the state of perfect liberation, or attain, by their own efforts or through higher help, supreme illumination. Likewise, other religions found everywhere try to counter the restlessness of the human heart, each in its own manner, by proposing "ways," comprising teachings, rules of life, and sacred rites. The Catholic Church rejects nothing that is true and holy in these religions. She regards with sincere reverence those ways of conduct and of life, those precepts and teachings which, though differing in many aspects from the ones she holds and sets forth, nonetheless often reflect a ray of that Truth which enlightens all men. Indeed, she proclaims, and ever must proclaim Christ "the way, the truth, and the life" (John 14:6), in whom men may find the fullness of religious life, in whom God has reconciled all things to Himself.

The Church, therefore, exhorts her sons, that through dialogue and collaboration with the followers of other religions, carried out with prudence and love and in witness to the Christian faith and life, they recognize, preserve and promote the good things, spiritual and moral, as well as the socio-cultural values found among these men.

3. The Church regards with esteem also the Moslems. They adore the one God, living and subsisting in Himself; merciful and all-powerful, the Creator of heaven and earth, who has spoken to men; they take pains to submit wholeheartedly to even His inscrutable decrees, just as Abraham, with whom the faith of Islam takes pleasure in linking itself, submitted to God. Though they do not acknowledge Jesus as God, they revere Him as a prophet. They also honor Mary, His virgin Mother; at times they even call on her with devotion. In addition, they await the day of judgment when God will render their deserts to all those who have been raised up from the dead. Finally, they value the moral life and worship God especially through prayer, almsgiving and fasting.

Since in the course of centuries not a few quarrels and hostilities have arisen between Christians and Moslems, this sacred synod urges all to forget the past and to work sincerely for mutual understanding and to preserve as well as to promote together for the benefit of all mankind social justice and moral welfare, as well as peace and freedom.

4. As the sacred synod searches into the mystery of the Church, it remembers the bond that spiritually ties the people of the New Covenant to Abraham's stock.

Thus the Church of Christ acknowledges that, according to God's saving design, the beginnings of her faith and her election are found already among the Patriarchs, Moses and the prophets. She professes that all who believe in Christ—Abraham's sons according to faith—are included in the same Patriarch's call, and likewise that the salvation of the Church is mysteriously foreshadowed by the chosen people's exodus from the land of bondage. The Church, therefore, cannot forget that she received the revelation of the Old Testament through the people with whom God in His inexpressible mercy concluded the Ancient Covenant. Nor can she forget that she draws sustenance from the root of that well-cultivated olive tree onto which have been grafted the wild shoots, the Gentiles. Indeed, the Church believes that by His cross Christ, Our Peace, reconciled Jews and Gentiles. making both one in Himself.

The Church keeps ever in mind the words of the Apostle about his kinsmen: "theirs is the sonship and the glory and the covenants and the law and the worship and the promises; theirs are the fathers and from them is the Christ according to the flesh" (Rom. 9:4–5), the Son of the Virgin Mary. She also recalls that the Apostles, the Church's main-stay and pillars, as well as most of the early disciples who proclaimed Christ's Gospel to the world, sprang from the Jewish people.

As Holy Scripture testifies, Jerusalem did not recognize the time of her visitation, nor did the Jews in large number accept the Gospel; indeed not a few opposed its spreading. Nevertheless, God holds the Jews most dear for the sake of their Fathers; He does not repent of the gifts He makes or of the calls He issues—such is the witness of the Apostle. In company with the Prophets and the same Apostle, the Church awaits that day, known to God alone, on which all peoples will address the Lord in a single voice and "serve him shoulder to shoulder" (Soph. 3:9).

Since the spiritual patrimony common to Christians and Jews is thus so great, this sacred synod wants to foster and recommend that mutual understanding and respect which is the fruit, above all, of biblical and theological studies as well as of fraternal dialogues.

True, the Jewish authorities and those who followed their lead pressed for the death of Christ; still, what happened in His passion cannot be charged against all the Jews, without distinction, then alive, nor against the Jews of today. Although the Church is the new people of God, the Jews should not be presented as rejected or accursed by God, as if this followed from the Holy Scriptures. All should see to it, then, that in catechetical work or in the preaching of the word of God they do not teach anything that does not conform to the truth of the Gospel and the spirit of Christ.

Furthermore, in her rejection of every persecution against any man, the Church, mindful of the patrimony she shares with the Jews and moved not by political reasons but by the Gospel's spiritual love, decries hatred, persecutions, displays of anti-Semitism, directed against Jews at any time and by anyone.

Besides, as the Church has always held and holds now, Christ underwent His passion and death freely, because of the sins of men and out of infinite love, in order that all may reach salvation. It is, therefore, the burden of the Church's preaching to proclaim the cross of Christ as the sign of God's all-embracing love and as the fountain from which every grace flows.

5. We cannot truly call on God, the Father of all, if we refuse to treat in a brotherly way any man, created as he is in the image of God. Man's relation to God the Father and his relation to men his brothers are so linked together that Scripture says: "He who does not love does not know God" (1 John 4:8).

No foundation therefore remains for any theory or practice that leads to discrimination between man and man or people and people, so far as their human dignity and the rights flowing from it are concerned.

The Church reproves, as foreign to the mind of Christ, any discrimination against men or harassment of them because of their race, color, condition of life, or religion. On the contrary, following in the footsteps of the holy Apostles Peter and Paul, this sacred synod ardently implores the Christian faithful to "maintain good fellowship among the nations" (1 Peter 2:12), and, if possible, to live for their part in peace with all men, so that they may truly be sons of the Father who is in heaven.

Source: Available online at URL: www.vatican. va/archive/hist_councils/ii_vatican_council/ documents/vat-ii_dec/_19651028_nos tra-aetate_ en.html. Accessed on January 19, 2006.

30. From *Black Manifesto* (1969), adopted by the Black National Economic Conference

We the black people assembled in Detroit, Michigan for the National Black Economic Development Conference are fully aware that we have been forced to come together because racist white America has exploited our resources, our minds, our bodies, our labor. For centuries we have been forced to live as colonized people inside the United States, victimized by the most vicious, racist system in the world. We have helped to build the most industrial country in the world.

We are therefore demanding of the white Christian churches and Jewish synagogues which are part and parcel of the system of capitalism, that they begin to pay reparations to black people in this country. We are demanding $500,000,000 from the Christian white churches and the Jewish synagogues. This total comes to 15 dollars per nigger. This is a low estimate for we maintain there are probably more than 30,000,000 black people in this country. $15 a nigger is not a large sum of money and we know that the churches and synagogues have a tremendous wealth and its membership, white America, has profited and still exploits black people. We are also not unaware that the exploitation of colored peoples around the world is aided and abetted by the white Christian churches and synagogues. This demand for $500,000,000 is not an idle resolution or empty words. Fifteen dollars for every black brother and sister in the United States is only a beginning of the reparations due us as people who have been exploited and degraded, brutalized, killed and persecuted. Underneath all of this exploitation, the racism of this country has produced a psychological effect upon us that we are beginning to shake off. We are no longer afraid to demand our full rights as a people in this decadent society. . . .

Brothers and sisters, we no longer are shuffling our feet and scratching our heads. We are tall, black and proud.

And we say to the white Christian churches and Jewish synagogues, to the government of this country and to all the white racist imperialists who compose it, there is only one thing left that you can do to further degrade black people and that is to kill us. But we have been dying too long for this country. We have died in every war. We are dying in Vietnam today fighting the wrong enemy.

The new black man wants to live and to live means that we must not become static or merely believe in self-defense. We must boldly go out and attack the white Western world at its power centers. The white Christian churches are another form of government in this country and they are used by the government of this country to exploit the people of Latin America, Asia and Africa, but the day is soon coming to an end. Therefore, brothers and sisters, the demands we make upon the white Christian churches and the Jewish synagogues are small demands. They represent 15 dollars per black person in these United States. We can legitimately demand this from the church power structure. We must demand more from the United States Government.

But to win our demands from the church which is linked up with the United States Government, we must not forget that it will ultimately be by force and power that we will win.

We are not threatening the churches. We are saying that we know the churches came with the military might of the colonizers and have been sustained by the military might of the colonizers. Hence, if the churches in colonial territories were established by military might, we know deep within our hearts that we must be prepared to use force to get our demands. We are not saying that this is the road we want to take. It is not, but let us be very clear that we are not opposed to force and we are not opposed to violence. We were captured in Africa by violence. We were kept in bondage and political servitude and forced to work as slaves by the military machinery and the Christian church working hand in hand.

We recognize that in issuing this manifesto we must prepare for a long range educational campaign in all communities of this country, but we know that the Christian churches have contributed to our oppression in white America. We do not intend to abuse our black brothers and sisters in black churches who have uncritically accepted Christianity. We want them to understand how the racist white Christian church with its hypocritical declarations and doctrines of brotherhood has abused our trust and faith. An attack on the religious beliefs of black people is not our major objective, even though we know that we were not Christians, when we were brought to this country, but that Christianity was used to help enslave us. Our objective in issuing this Manifesto is to force the racist white Christian Church to begin the payment of reparations which are due to all black people, not only by the Church but also by private business and the U.S. government. We see this focus on the Christian Church as an effort around which all black people can unite.

Source: Available online at URL: http://www.nybooks. com/articles/11267. Accessed on January 28, 2006.

31. From *The Williamsburg Charter* (1988)

The Charter sets forth a renewed national compact, in the sense of a solemn mutual agreement between parties, on how we view the place of religion in American life and how we should contend with each other's deepest differences in the public sphere. It is a call to a vision of public life that will allow conflict to lead to consensus, religious commitment to reinforce political civility. In this way, diversity is not a point of weakness but a source of strength. . . .

We who live in the third century of the American republic can learn well from the past as we look to the future. Our Founders were both idealists and realists. Their confidence in human abilities was tempered by their skepticism about human nature. Aware of what was new in their times, they also knew the need for renewal in times after theirs. "No free government, or the blessings of liberty," wrote George Mason in 1776, "can be preserved to any people, but by a firm adherence to justice, moderation, temperance, frugality, and virtue, and by frequent recurrence to fundamental principles."

True to the ideals and realism of that vision, we who sign this Charter, people of many and various beliefs, pledge ourselves to the enduring precepts of the First Amendment as the cornerstone of the American experiment in liberty under law.

We address ourselves to our fellow citizens, daring to hope that the strongest desire of the greatest number is for the common good. We are firmly persuaded that the principles asserted here require a fresh consideration, and that the renewal of religious liberty is crucial to sustain a free people that would remain free. We therefore commit ourselves to speak, write and act according to this vision and these principles. We urge our fellow citizens to do the same.

To agree on such guiding principles and to achieve such a compact will not be easy. Whereas a law is a command directed to us, a compact is a promise that must proceed freely from us. To achieve it demands a measure of the vision, sacrifice and perseverance shown by our Founders. Their task was to defy the past, seeing and securing religious liberty against the terrible precedents of history. Ours is to challenge the future, sustaining vigilance and broadening protections against every new menace, including that of our own complacency. Knowing the unquenchable desire for freedom, they lit a beacon. It is for us who know its blessings to keep it burning brightly.

Source: Hunter and Guiness, Articles of Faith, Articles of Peace, *pp. 128, 144–145.*

Appendix B
Biographies of Major Personalities

Abbott, Lyman (1835–1922) *Congregationalist minister, magazine editor*

Although Lyman Abbott was admitted to the New York bar in 1856, the influence of Henry Ward Beecher, pastor of the Congregationalist Plymouth Church in Brooklyn, ultimately caused Abbott to change careers. After a period of private theological study, he became pastor of a Congregational church in Terre Haute, Indiana, in 1860. At the end of the Civil War, he directed the American Freedman's Union Commission, but toward the end of the 1860s he became a full-time writer. Initially Abbott edited the *Illustrated Christian Weekly*, but Henry Ward Beecher invited him to become associate editor of the *Christian Union* (later renamed *Outlook*) in 1876. Five years later, when Beecher resigned as editor in chief, Abbott became the periodical's senior editor. After Beecher's death in 1887, Plymouth Church called Abbott to become its new pastor, and for the next three decades Lyman Abbott served as both editor and pastor, championing a progressive form of Protestant Christianity.

Adler, Cyrus (1863–1940) *Semitic scholar, lay Jewish leader*

One of the foremost Semitic scholars at the turn of the 20th century, Cyrus Adler was also an influential lay leader among American Jews. He received the first doctorate awarded in Semitic studies in America from the University of Pennsylvania in 1887 and eventually became the librarian for the Smithsonian Institute and then in 1905 the Smithsonian's assistant secretary. While associated with the Smithsonian, Adler discovered and published the *Jefferson Bible*, a version of the New Testament gospels prepared by Thomas Jefferson to highlight the moral content of Jesus' teaching while eliminating mi-

raculous elements recorded in the New Testament. Also an active participant in Jewish affairs, Adler helped organize the Jewish Publication Society of America in 1888, the American Jewish Historical Society in 1892, and the American Jewish Committee in 1906. He served as president of the Jewish Publication Society from 1898 to 1921 and of the American Jewish Committee from 1929 to 1940. Toward the end of the 20th century's first decade, Adler returned to academic life, assuming the presidency in 1908 of the Dropsie College for Hebrew and Cognate Learning in Philadelphia. Still later, in 1915, he added to this responsibility the presidency of the Jewish Theological Seminary of America. He occupied both posts until his death.

Adler, Felix (1851–1933) *founder of Ethical Culture*

Although he was the son of a Jewish rabbi and seemed at first poised to become a rabbi within the Reform tradition of Judaism, Felix Adler migrated away from theism while he was a graduate student. After earning a Ph.D. from the University of Heidelberg in Germany in 1873, Adler returned to the United States, where his family had immigrated when he was six years old, and began teaching Hebrew and Oriental literature at Cornell University. But history remembers Adler less for this teaching career than for a series of meetings he began holding in 1876 that formed the genesis of the Society for Ethical Culture. Under Adler's leadership this society emphasized moral conduct rather than theology, becoming a kind of secular religion for its adherents. Adler's first book, *Creed and Deed* (1877), contrasted the concerns of traditional religions with those of his society. And the morality to which Ethical Culture aspired was not a mere abstract program but a concrete call for its members to engage in social action, leading, for example, to the society's establishing the first free kindergarten in the United States. Though Adler subsequently joined the faculty of Columbia University as a professor of political and social ethics, he continued to lead the Society for Ethical Culture throughout his life.

Alexander, Archibald (1772–1851) *Presbyterian theologian*

Archibald Alexander experienced a Christian conversion at a Baptist revival in the 1780s. Subsequently, he was licensed a Presbyterian minister in 1791 and pastored two churches in Charlotte County, Virginia. Toward the end of the decade he assumed the presidency of Hampden-Sydney College for nine years, then returned to full time pastoral work until chosen to serve as a professor and first president of Princeton Theological Seminary in 1812. During the early decades of the 19th century, Presbyterianism divided itself between Old School and New School, with Old School Presbyterians emphasizing the importance of traditional statements of Presbyterian orthodoxy such as the Westminster Confession and opposing the strong support of New School Presbyterians for revivalism. Alexander counted himself among the Old School and trained a generation of Presbyterian ministers to revere the orthodoxy of creed over the enthusiasms of revivalism. His influence extended even beyond his life through the teaching of his protégé Charles Hodge, who attended Princeton Theological Seminary and joined its faculty in 1822 as professor of Oriental and biblical literature.

Allen, Richard (1760–1831) *founder and first bishop of the African Methodist Episcopal Church*

Born a slave, Richard Allen was converted to Christianity and Methodism while a teenager. Allowed to purchase his freedom soon afterward, Allen used his liberty to become an itinerant Methodist minister beginning in 1780, preaching in Delaware, Maryland, New Jersey, and Pennsylvania. Eventually he became associated with St. George's Methodist Church in Philadelphia, but he and other black members of the church separated from this congregation in 1787, the same year Allen helped establish the Free African Society, a benevolent organization. Seven years later Allen joined with other African Americans to convert a former blacksmith shop into a church, dedicated on June 29, 1794, as the Bethel African Methodist Episcopal Church of Philadelphia. Five years later Francis Asbury ordained Allen the first African-American deacon in the Methodist Episcopal Church. In 1816 Allen led other black Methodists to form a separate denomination, the African Methodist Episcopal Church (or AME Church), of which Allen was ordained the first bishop.

Asbury, Francis (1745–1816) *Methodist bishop*

After being converted to Methodism in his teens, Francis Asbury was an itinerant Methodist minister in England from 1767 to 1771. At a conference of Methodist ministers in 1771, John Wesley called for ministers to go to America, and Asbury accepted this challenge and arrived in Philadelphia the same year. When the Revolutionary War began, most of the other Methodist ministers from England left America, but Asbury remained, though his refusal to forswear allegiance to the British Crown forced him to live in Delaware for a time. After the war in 1784, Wesley ordained Asbury and Thomas Coke joint superintendents of the Methodist Church in America, but Coke did not permanently remain in America, so Asbury became the de facto head of Methodists in the new nation.

Avery, Martha Gallison Moore (1851–1929) *Catholic lay preacher*

Toward the end of the 19th century, Martha Gallison Moore Avery was a Unitarian and a socialist, joining the Social Labor Party in 1891 and from 1892 to 1895 serving on the party's State Central Committee. In 1896 she established the Karl Marx Class, through which she lectured and led discussions concerning Marx's works. Through this class she met David Goldstein, who became a close friend and coworker for the rest of her life. After sending her daughter to a Catholic school in 1899, Avery became interested in Catholicism herself and eventually joined the Catholic Church in 1904. During this period she became increasingly critical of socialism. In the years that followed she became ever more conservative, opposing feminism and women's suffrage as threats to family life. In 1917 she and David Goldstein organized a street preaching project called the Catholic Truth Guild, which attempted to persuade those who would listen of the merits of Catholicism.

Backus, Isaac (1724–1806) *Baptist minister*

Converted during the Great Awakening, Isaac Backus joined the many others who separated from their Congregational churches in the wake of the revival. He served briefly as an itinerant preacher before being ordained a minister for a separate church near Middleborough, Massachusetts. Like many other such separatist believers after the Great Awakening, Backus eventually came to oppose the practice of infant baptism and thus became a Baptist, believing that the ordinance of baptism was properly reserved for those who had a personal conversion experience. Backus reorganized his church in 1756 as the First Baptist Church of Middleborough. He subsequently became an influential advocate for religious liberty and in 1773 published an important tract titled *An Appeal to the Public for Religious Liberty*. In the 1780s Backus conducted a preaching tour through Virginia and North Carolina sometimes credited with contributing to the beginning of the Second Great Awakening.

Ballou, Hosea (1771–1852) *Universalist minister*
The son of a Baptist minister, Ballou became the most important figure in the second generation of the Universalist movement in America. He became a Universalist in his teens, preached his first sermon in 1791, and was ordained a Universalist minister three years later. Soon afterward he rejected the doctrine of the Trinity, thus modeling the hospitableness of Universalists to Unitarianism that would eventually cause these two religious traditions to merge in the 20th century. But Ballou's most important contribution to the history of Universalism in America was his rejection of more traditional views of the atonement, according to which Christians have typically believed that Christ's death on the cross acted as a substitute for the eternal death deserved by sinful humanity. According to this view, Christ's death provided for a reconciliation between God and humanity. In 1804, however, Ballou published *A Treatise on Atonement*, which argued that God was infinitely loving and therefore needed no reconciliation. Christ's death, Ballou insisted, simply demonstrated this love and thus revealed to humanity the possibility of being reconciled with God.

Beecher, Henry Ward (1813–1887) *Congregationalist minister*
American writer Sinclair Lewis called Henry Ward Beecher "the archbishop of American liberal Protestantism." It was not enough that Beecher was part of an illustrious family, the son of famous Congregationalist minister and scholar Lyman Beecher and the brother of influential author Harriet Beecher Stowe. Beginning in the late 1840s he also preached from one of the most famous pulpits in the country, that of Plymouth Church in Brooklyn, New York, where he was minister for 40 years. Added to these distinctions was his impact as editor of two prominent periodicals, the *Independent* from 1861 to 1863 and still later the *Christian Union* from 1870 to 1881. The most significant blemish on an otherwise stellar ministerial career occurred beginning in 1872, when he was accused of committing adultery with the wife of a friend. Though exonerated by his church of this charge in 1874, a civil suit tried the next year resulted in a hung jury, thus not wholly cleansing the stain his reputation had suffered.

Beecher, Lyman (1775–1863) *Congregationalist minister, seminary professor*
One of the most prominent Protestant ministers of the middle decades of the 19th century, Lyman Beecher experienced conversion while a student at Yale College in the last decade of the 18th century. He was greatly influenced by Yale's president, Timothy Dwight, and after studying theology with Dwight following graduation, Beecher was licensed to preach in 1798. The next year he was ordained the minister of a Presbyterian church in East Hampton, Long Island. Subsequently he served as pastor of the Congregational church in Litchfield, Connecticut, and the Hanover Street Church in Boston. Early in the next decade, however, Beecher migrated west to Cincinnati, Ohio, where he became the first president of and a professor of theology at Lane Theological Seminary. Controversy stalked his years in Cincinnati, however. When he refused to align the seminary with abolitionist sentiments, many of his students left and enrolled in Oberlin Collegiate Institute (later Oberlin College). His sympathies for revivalism also placed him at odds with Old School Presbyterians, who unsuccessfully attempted to try him for heresy in 1835. Beecher was prominent in his own right but also because of the prominence of his children, including author Harriet Beecher Stowe and preacher Henry Ward Beecher. Lyman Beecher's contemporaries joked that the country was "inhabited by saints, sinners, and Beechers."

Beissel, Johann Conrad (1692–1768) *founder of the Ephrata commune of Seventh Day Baptists*
While a teenager and a baker's apprentice in Germany, Johann Conrad Beissel became a Pietist, that is, a Protestant believer who left the state church in a quest for personal holiness and religious devotion. Leaving the state church ultimately forced Beissel to leave his home and immigrate to America in 1720. There he settled in Pennsylvania and joined a group of German Baptists led by Peter Becker. He soon left this group, however, and lived for a time as a hermit until other German Baptists found him and convinced him to become their leader. This new

group eventually settled by the early 1730s on the Cocalico Creek in a community called Ephrata. Beissel and his followers were Sabbatarians, believing the appropriate day for Christian worship and rest was Saturday, the Old Testament Sabbath, a belief Beissel defended in *Mysterium Anomias* (1728), or *The Mystery of Lawlessness*. The Ephrata community was known for the works that flowed from its printing press and the celibacy practiced by both unmarried and married members of the community.

Bellows, Henry Whitney (1814–1882) *Unitarian minister*

A dominant figure among Unitarians during the second half of the 19th century, Henry Whitney Bellows graduated from Harvard Divinity School in 1837 and was subsequently ordained as minister of the First Unitarian Church in New York City. In the years that followed he established a reputation as a gifted preacher and a prolific writer. After the Civil War began Bellows served as the first president of the U.S. Sanitary Commission, an organization devoted to relief work among Union soldiers and Confederate prisoners. But Bellow's most significant labor lay in his work organizing the National Conference of Unitarian Churches in 1865. He adhered to a theological path that rejected Trinitarianism but nevertheless remained committed to other aspects of Christian orthodoxy. Moreover, he believed that Unitarian churches needed the support of religious rituals and ceremonies. More liberal Unitarians disagreed, however. Because Bellows was able to steer the National Conference of Unitarian Churches toward a relatively conservative theological orientation, liberal Unitarians split away from this venture and established the Free Religious Association.

Black Elk (1863–1950) *Lakota Sioux holy man*

As a nine-year-old boy, Black Elk experienced a religious vision that eventually made him a holy man among the Oglala tribe of the Lakota Sioux. He revealed this vision to the elders of his tribe when he was 17 and subsequently became a medicine man. In his 20s, Black Elk traveled widely in the United States and Europe with Buffalo Bill's Wild West Show. When he returned to South Dakota in 1889, he participated in the Ghost Dance movement. In the years following, which he spent on the Pine Ridge Reservation, Black Elk was exposed to Catholic missionaries and ultimately converted to Catholicism in 1904, at which time he assumed the name of Nicholas Black Elk. More than 25 years later the poet John G. Neihardt visited Black Elk and subsequently published an account of his interview with him in 1932 as *Black Elk Speaks*. When reprinted in 1961, this book played an important role in arousing interest in American Indian culture and religion.

Blackwell, Antoinette Louisa Brown (1825–1921) *Unitarian minister*

The first woman ordained as a minister in a major denomination, Antoinette Louisa Brown Blackwell grew up in the home of Congregationalist parents. She earned her undergraduate degree from Oberlin College, but after a further few years of theological study at this institution, she was refused a theology degree because she was a woman. Following a period of lecturing and occasional preaching, however, Blackwell was ordained the minister of a Congregational church in South Butler, New York, in 1853. By the next year, Blackwell's disagreements with orthodox Christian doctrines caused her to resign her position in the South Butler church. The following years saw her actively engaged in various reformist causes, especially those associated with women's rights. She also wrote avidly. Blackwell eventually became a Unitarian minister in 1878 and later helped establish All Souls Unitarian Church in Elizabeth, New Jersey.

Blavatsky, Helena Petrovna (1831–1891) *Theosophical Society cofounder*

The daughter of Russian aristocrats, Helena Petrovna Blavatsky came to the United States in 1871 after spending more than two decades traveling widely in Asia, Europe, and the Middle East, during which travels she studied the occult extensively. While investigating spiritualist phenomena at a farm in Vermont in 1874, Blavatsky met Henry Steele Olcott, who was also visiting the farm for the same purpose. The next year the two cofounded the Theosophical Society, which blended an interest in spiritualism with Eastern religious teaching. Over the coming years Olcott served as the organization's president, while Blavatsky articulated its religious beliefs and teachings, the first of which appeared in Blavatsky's 1877 book, *Isis Unveiled*. The following year Blavatsky and Olcott traveled to India, where they established chapters of the Theosophical Society and also pursued their interest in Eastern religious practices. They both subsequently became Buddhists while still leading the Theosophical Society, for which they established a world headquarters in 1882 in Adyar, where they had purchased an estate. After a psychic investigator from England accused Blavatsky of fraud in 1885, she left Adyar and eventually settled in

London, where she completed a second major book, *The Secret Doctrine* (1888).

Bradford, William (1590–1657) *governor of the Plymouth Colony*

As a young man William Bradford became associated with separatist Puritans who believed the Church of England was so contaminated with spiritual error that it had ceased to be a true church and that separation from it was the only acceptable course. He joined those who migrated to Holland in 1609 looking for a venue in which they could freely practice their faith. When a group of these religious dissenters, which history knows as the Pilgrims, traveled to the New World on the *Mayflower* in 1620, Bradford was among their number and helped to establish the Plymouth Colony. Subsequently, after the death of the colony's first governor, John Carver, the following year, Bradford became governor and served in this capacity for most of the remainder of his life. His *History of Plimoth Plantation*, published in 1856, nearly two centuries after his death, is a crucial source of information about the Pilgrims.

Brainerd, David (1718–1747) *Presbyterian missionary*

An early death from tuberculosis robbed David Brainerd of the opportunity for significant impact as a missionary to American Indians. Nevertheless, he became closely associated with Jonathan Edwards at the end of his life, and Edwards, well-known as a theologian and revival preacher during the Great Awakening, subsequently published Brainerd's diary. This work became one of the most influential devotional writings in the history of American Protestantism. Brainerd studied for a time at Yale before being expelled for criticizing members of the Yale faculty for lack of authentic saving faith. Subsequently he was ordained a Presbyterian minister and pursued an itinerant ministry as a missionary among the Seneca and Delaware Indians until 1747, when ill health forced him to abandon this ministry and retire to the home of Jonathan Edwards. There he edited his diary and prepared an account of his early life, published posthumously by Edwards in 1749 as *An Account of the Life of the Late Reverend Mr. David Brainerd.*

Brébeuf, Jean de (1593–1649) *Jesuit missionary to the Huron Indians in present-day Canada*

Jean de Brébeuf made his first trip to New France (present-day Canada) in 1625, where he began missionary activity among the Huron Indians. After several years he was recalled to France, but then he returned again to Huron territory in 1635 and began to establish missionary posts among the Huron. Though these were at first successful, the French traders and missionaries among the Huron spread epidemics that eventually turned the Huron against the missionaries. To this setback was added growing hostility of the Iroquois Indians, who allied themselves with Dutch traders against the Huron and the French. In 1649 an Iroquois war party took Jean de Brébeuf and his fellow missionary Gabriel Lallemant captive and tortured them to death. Brébeuf was declared a saint by Pope Pius XI in 1930.

Breck, James Lloyd (1818–1876) *Episcopalian missionary*

While a teenager, James Lloyd Breck determined to become an Episcopalian priest and came into contact with the Oxford Movement, which emphasized liturgical renewal. As a student at the General Theological Seminary in New York City, from which he graduated with his divinity degree in 1841, Breck committed himself to becoming a missionary and chose as his field of activity the western United States. He and other classmates from the seminary established an associate mission in Nashotah Lakes, Wisconsin. This form of missionary community involved several missionaries living and working together in a semimonastic order. At Nashotah Lakes Breck and his colleagues established several churches, as well as a school that became Racine College and a school of theology that became Nashotah House. In subsequent years Breck labored to establish additional missions in Minnesota and California.

Bresee, Phineas Franklin (1838–1915) *Church of the Nazarene founder*

Converted at a Methodist meeting in 1856, Phineas Bresee was soon a circuit-riding Methodist preacher. For the next three decades Bresee assumed increasing responsibility within the Methodist Church and eventually migrated to California. In 1891 he was appointed presiding elder of the Los Angeles district. During the same period, however, Bresee became ever more closely aligned with the Holiness movement, whose theology emphasized the possibility of Christians receiving the experience of a "second blessing" and of achieving perfection in the present life. In 1894 Bresee sought permission from Methodist authorities to work with the Peniel Mission in Los Angeles, a Holiness mission. When denied this permission, he abandoned the Methodist ministry, and the following year he and Joseph Pomeroy Widney established the

First Church of the Nazarene in Los Angeles. Widney soon returned to the Methodist Church, leaving Bresee to guide the early years of the growing number of congregations that eventually became the Church of the Nazarene denomination.

Briggs, Charles Augustus (1841–1913) *seminary professor*

After serving briefly in the Union army, Charles Augustus Briggs entered Union Theological Seminary in 1861 to prepare for the ministry. Following a break from the seminary to care for his family's business, he completed his theological studies at the University of Berlin, where he came in contact with higher criticism of the biblical texts. When he returned to the United States in 1869, he became the pastor of the First Presbyterian Church of Roselle, New Jersey, and then subsequently joined the faculty of Union Theological Seminary in 1874, where he pursued scholarship that alarmed more conservative Presbyterians. In 1891 the seminary appointed Briggs to the Edward Robinson Chair of Biblical Theology, and he delivered an inaugural lecture that denied the inerrancy of the Bible and the traditional authorships ascribed to Old Testament books. This lecture prompted the New York presbytery to initiate heresy proceedings against him. Though the presbytery ultimately cleared him of heresy charges, the general assembly of the Presbyterian Church suspended him as a minister in May 1893. Thereafter Briggs became an Episcopalian and was ordained a priest in 1899, while he remained on the faculty of Union Theological Seminary until his death.

Brooks, Phillips (1835–1893) *Episcopalian preacher, bishop*

After receiving his undergraduate degree from Harvard College in 1856 and graduating from Virginia Theological Seminary in 1859, Phillips Brooks was ordained a minister in the Episcopal Church and became the rector first of the Church of the Advent in Philadelphia, then of Philadelphia's Holy Trinity Church, and in 1869 of Boston's Trinity Church. From the pulpit of Trinity Church, Brooks became one of the most prominent preachers of his day. He also penned the lyrics to the Christmas hymn "O Little Town of Bethlehem." Harvard College tried to tempt him to accept a position on its faculty, but he chose to remain a preacher. Toward the end of his life, he finally surrendered his pulpit at Trinity Church to accept ordination as an Episcopalian bishop.

Brownson, Orestes Augustus (1803–1876) *Catholic journalist*

One of the foremost Catholic apologists of the 19th century, Orestes Augustus Brownson began his spiritual migration by joining a Presbyterian church when he was a teenager. By the mid-1820s he had rejected Calvinism, however, and become a Universalist minister. Toward the end of the decade, he worked for a time as a journalist, but in 1831 Brownson returned to preaching, first as a nondenominational minister and then in 1832 as a Unitarian minister. In 1844 Brownson made one further spiritual migration by converting to Catholicism. That same year he began publishing *Brownson's Quarterly Review*, which he used as a vehicle for defending Catholicism and commenting on social issues for the better part of three decades.

Bushnell, Horace (1802–1876) *Congregationalist minister*

In 1829 while studying to become a lawyer, Horace Bushnell experienced a religious conversion. Thereafter he determined to become a minister and graduated from Yale Divinity School in 1833, becoming the minister that year of Hartford's North Church. Both in his preaching and in writing Bushnell distanced himself from the revivalism then prominent on the American religious landscape. He argued in *Discourses on Christian Nurture* (1847) that Christian nurture rather than conversion was the ideal—children should be raised in such a way that they essentially grew up Christian. At the same time Bushnell charted a middle course between Unitarianism, which denied the Trinity, and more orthodox Protestants. He argued in *God in Christ* (1849) that the Trinity was the form in which God revealed himself to the world but not necessarily a feature of God's internal reality. This view almost led to Bushnell's being tried for heresy by the Hartford North Consociation of Congregationalist churches. After one attempt failed, however, Bushnell's church withdrew from the consociation in 1852.

Cabrini, Francesca Xavier (1850–1917) *Catholic missionary*

The first American citizen to be canonized as a saint by the Roman Catholic Church, Francesca Xavier Cabrini in 1880 founded the Missionaries of the Sacred Heart in Italy. Although she aspired to become a missionary to the Orient, she was dispatched in 1889 to the United States to minister to Italian immigrants there. Beginning in New York, where she arrived in America, Cabrini devoted nearly three decades to the work of establishing orphanages, schools, and hospitals. Her ministry took her to cities all across the United States including New Orleans, Chicago, Denver, Los Angeles, and Seattle. She also found time and energy to establish institutions in Europe, Central America, and South America. She was proclaimed a saint by Pope Pius XII on July 7, 1946.

Campbell, Alexander (1788–1866) *Disciples of Christ founder*

Born in Ireland, Alexander Campbell's father, Thomas, was a Presbyterian minister who immigrated to the United States in 1807. Alexander and the rest of the family followed two years later, after he studied a year at the University of Glasgow. When he arrived in America Alexander joined the Christian Association of Washington, Pennsylvania, which his father had organized that year. By 1810 Alexander Campbell was licensed to preach, and the next year he and his father organized the Christian Association into the Brush Run Church. Alexander was ordained minister of this church in 1812, and the members of this and other congregations associated with the Campbells came to be known as Disciples of Christ. For a time after Campbell became convinced that baptism was properly reserved for adult believers, the Brush Run Church associated itself with the Redstone Baptist Association beginning in 1815. But disagreement with the Baptists ultimately caused this association to collapse. In the 1830s the Disciples of Christ merged with Barton Stone and the believers associated with him, called the Christian Connexion. Under the leadership of Campbell and Stone, the Disciples of Christ rejected the accumulated creeds and traditions of organized Christianity in favor of a return to what they proclaimed to be the primitive beliefs and practices of the New Testament church. Campbell in 1840 led in establishing Bethany College. At the end of that decade the various Disciples of Christ churches joined together to form a general convention and chose Campbell as their president.

Carroll, John (1736–1815) *Catholic archbishop*

The first Catholic bishop in the United States, John Carroll joined the Jesuits in 1753. After studying philosophy and theology at Liège (present-day Belgium), he was ordained a priest in 1769. Several years later, however, in 1773 Pope Clement XIV dissolved the Jesuits, and Carroll was left for a time studying privately and conducting Mass for Catholics in a private chapel on his mother's estate in Maryland. During these years Carroll met Benjamin Franklin and joined with him in an unsuccessful attempt to persuade Canada to remain neutral during the Revolutionary War. In 1784 at Franklin's suggestion, the pope appointed Carroll director of Catholic missionary efforts in the United States. The same year Carroll published the first book written in America by a Roman Catholic, *Address to the Roman Catholics of the United States of America,* in which he defended freedom of religion. Later that decade American priests petitioned the pope to ordain an American bishop, and when this plan was approved Carroll was elected by his fellow priests and ordained bishop of the diocese of Baltimore in November 1789. The following decade he was named archbishop.

Cartwright, Peter (1785–1872) *Methodist minister*

Famous for playing the part of a backwoods preacher, Peter Cartwright grew up in Kentucky and had a conversion experience in 1801. Subsequently he joined the Methodist Church and became first an exhorter and then in 1804 an itinerant minister. No friend of slavery, Cartwright eventually migrated north to Illinois in 1824. There he was twice elected to the state legislature, defeating Abraham Lincoln in one contest. But in 1846, when he and Lincoln squared off in a race for the U.S. Congress, Lincoln won the election. Cartwright's political aspirations did not cause him to abandon ministry as a Methodist preacher. He served more than half a century as a presiding elder and in the decade before the Civil War published *Autobiography of Peter Cartwright, the Backwoods Preacher,* emphasizing the centrality of preaching to his life's story.

Cary, Lott (1780–1828) *Baptist missionary*

Born a slave on a plantation in Virginia, Lott Cary ultimately became the governor of the colony of Liberia. As a young man Cary learned to read and was able to use this skill to obtain a position as clerk in a tobacco warehouse. This position allowed Cary to sell small amounts of tobacco, the profits from which he ultimately applied to purchase freedom for himself and two of his children. He was subsequently licensed a minister by the First Baptist Church in Richmond, Virginia, where he eventually became interested in missions and in 1815 helped establish the Richmond African Baptist Missionary Society. In 1821 with the support of the Baptist Board of Foreign Missions and the American Colonization Society, he traveled to Liberia with his family as a missionary. He eventually served in the colonial government of Liberia and in 1828, before an untimely death in an explosion, served briefly as governor of Liberia.

Cayce, Edgar (1877–1945) *psychic*
Spiritualism has been a less peopled though quite prominent tributary of American religious experience, and Edgar Cayce was perhaps its most influential representative. As a young man he claimed to have obtained the ability to enter a trance and diagnose various illnesses. By the 1920s he had added to these diagnoses more general "life readings," which announced both past and future lives of subjects. That decade a wealthy patron paid for the construction of Cayce Hospital and Atlantic University in Virginia Beach. Although this institution closed during the Great Depression, Cayce's friends and associates eventually supported the founding of the Association for Research and Enlightenment.

Channing, William Ellery (1780–1842) *Unitarian minister*
Licensed to preach by Congregationalists in 1802, William Ellery Channing eventually became the most prominent Unitarian leader during the early 19th century, allowing history to know him as the "apostle of American Unitarianism." In 1803 he became the pastor of the Federal Street Church in Boston, where he served for the rest of his life. Already Channing had moved far in his theological thinking from orthodox Congregationalism—he believed neither in the Trinity nor in the deity of Jesus. In 1819, however, at an ordination sermon for a young minister at the First Independent Church in Baltimore, Channing articulated the core principles of what came to be known as Unitarianism. The sermon, "Unitarian Christianity," became something of a benchmark for the new theological movement. The following year Channing helped establish the Berry Street Conference, a forerunner of the American Unitarian Association, which was organized in 1825.

Chase, Philander (1775–1852) *Episcopal bishop, educator*
Philander Chase, who converted to Episcopalianism from Congregationalism while a student at Dartmouth College, helped to plant his denomination in the Midwest. Ordained a deacon in 1798 and then a priest the following year, Chase moved with his wife early in his ministerial career to New Orleans, where he established Christ Church in 1805. There for six years in hopes that the climate would help his wife's tuberculosis, the couple eventually returned to New England. In 1817, however, Chase migrated west to Worthington, Ohio, where he accepted a position as principal of the Worthington Academy. By 1819 he had been consecrated bishop of Ohio. Convinced of the need to establish a seminary in the west to train future Episcopalian ministers, Chase was able to raise money in England for this venture and founded Kenyon College and Gambier Theological Seminary in 1824. Ultimately forced to choose between his responsibilities as bishop and as an academic administrator, Chase surrendered his position as bishop in 1831. Four years later, however, he was elected bishop of Illinois, where he moved and subsequently founded Jubilee College in 1839.

Chauncy, Charles (1705–1787) *Congregationalist minister*
Known as "the Great Opposer of the Great Awakening," Charles Chauncy was minister of Boston's First Church, the city's oldest and most prestigious church, for nearly 60 years. He publicly criticized the tendency of revivalism to divide Christian believers and congregations. Less publicly, he turned away from the Calvinism espoused by preachers such as Jonathan Edwards, who emphasized that those who remained unconverted would suffer the torments of an everlasting hell. Chauncy instead came to believe in universal salvation—that Christ's sacrifice for sin would ultimately result in the salvation of everyone. Though he remained circumspect about announcing this belief for most of his life, he eventually published a defense of universalism in 1784 titled *The Mystery Hid from Ages and Generations, Made Manifest by the Gospel-Revelation.*

Clarke, John (1609–1676) *Baptist minister, colonial leader*
John Clark immigrated with his wife from England to Boston in 1637, but he found Puritan orthodoxy unpalatable and relocated to the Providence Colony. There he helped establish the towns of Portsmouth and Newport and became pastor of the church in Newport. During the mid-1640s he came to believe that the practice of infant baptism was not warranted by Scripture and eventually led his church to becoming a Baptist congregation in 1648. After his missionary activities in the Massachusetts Bay Colony landed him in jail, he wrote an important defense of religious liberty titled *Ill Newes from New-England: or a Narative of New-Englands Persecution. Wherein Is declared That While Old England Is Becoming New, New-England is Become Old*, published in London in 1652. The Providence Colony made Clarke its English agent, and after the restoration of the monarchy he worked with Roger Williams to obtain a new charter for Providence, which was granted in 1663. Clarke subsequently returned to Newport, where

he preached and participated in civil affairs, serving as deputy governor from 1669 to 1672.

Coffin, Henry Sloan (1877–1954) *Presbyterian minister, seminary professor*

Henry Sloan Coffin was a leading liberal Protestant minister and academic of the first half of the 20th century. After graduating from Yale in 1897, Coffin undertook theological studies first in Europe and subsequently at Union Theological Seminary in New York, from which he received his bachelor of divinity degree in 1900. Upon graduation from seminary he was ordained minister of the Bedford Park Presbyterian Church in the Bronx, New York. In 1904 he joined the faculty of Union Theological Seminary, and for the next 21 years he was both pastor and professor, though in 1905 he became minister of Madison Avenue Presbyterian Church. He became president of Union Theological Seminary in 1926, a position he held until his retirement in 1945, and was influential in persuading theologians Paul Tillich and Reinhold Niebuhr to join the seminary's faculty.

Coke, Thomas (1747–1814) *Methodist bishop*

Together with Francis Asbury, Thomas Coke served as one of the first two bishops of the Methodist Episcopal Church in America. Prior to becoming a Methodist minister he was ordained a priest in the Church of England and served first as deacon and then priest of a church in South Petherton, Somerset, from 1871 to 1877. He became a Methodist, however, after meeting John Wesley in 1876, and when he was dismissed from his parish the following year he became a trusted assistant to Wesley. Wesley subsequently dispatched Coke across the Atlantic in 1784 as a superintendent of Methodist activity in America. Coke attended the Christmas Conference held in Baltimore, Maryland, in December 1784, at which the Methodist Episcopal Church was established. There he and Francis Asbury were formally recognized as superintendents of the church (a title Asbury subsequently exchanged for bishop). In the years that followed Coke traveled back and forth across the Atlantic several times, acting as an emissary between Wesley and American Methodism. Asbury, who remained in America, consequently came to play a more prominent role in the early life of Methodism in the United States. Coke, for his part, ultimately devoted himself to Methodist missions in the Caribbean, Nova Scotia, the Channel Islands, Scotland, Ireland, Wales, and the West Indies. For this reason he is sometimes referred to as the "father of Methodist missions."

Conwell, Russell Herman (1843–1925) *Baptist minister, author*

Famous for insisting that God intended Christians to be wealthy, Russell Herman Conwell experienced conversion during the Civil War. He graduated from Albany Law School in 1865 and practiced law until 1879, when the experience of preaching for a church on a temporary basis caused him to abandon the practice of law to become a minister. In 1881 he became the pastor of Grace Baptist Church in Philadelphia, and under his leadership and charismatic preaching the church grew rapidly and substantially. Conwell led Grace Baptist Church to serve a variety of the needs of the community. In pursuit of this mission the church established Temple College (present-day Temple University) to provide education for church members and other residents of Philadelphia. In the early years of the 20th century, Conwell gained prominence as a lecturer, and one lecture, published in 1915 as *Acres of Diamonds*, became the characteristic statement of Conwell's belief in a gospel of prosperity.

Coppin, Fanny Jackson (1837–1913) *educator, religious leader*

Although she was born a slave, one of Fanny Coppin's aunts purchased her freedom when she was 10 years old. By 1851 she had moved with another aunt to Newport, Rhode Island, where she worked as a domestic for George Henry Calvert, the great grandson of Lord Baltimore. In Newport she used the money she earned to hire a tutor to give her private instruction. Thereafter she attended Rhode Island State Normal School and, more importantly, Oberlin Collegiate Institute (later Oberlin College), from which she graduated in 1865. Upon graduation she became principal of the female division of the Institute for Colored Youth in Philadelphia and in 1869 principal of both male and female divisions. She led the institute for more than 30 years, until her retirement in 1902, and was active throughout this period as a lay leader in the affairs of the AME Church.

Corrigan, Michael Augustine (1839–1902) *Catholic archbishop*

After receiving his doctorate of divinity in theology at the North American College in Rome, Michael Corrigan returned to the United States, where he served as a professor and later president of Seton Hall College from 1864 to 1876. During this period he became bishop of Newark in 1873 and then in 1880 coadjutor of the archdiocese of New York. Five years later he became archbishop of

New York, a position in which he would become known not only as a skilled ecclesiastical administrator but as a conservative opponent of Catholic assimilation to American values such as materialism and secularism. His clash with more progressive Catholic leaders came to be known as the Americanist controversy, an important episode of which involved a socially progressive priest in New York named Edward McGlynn whom Corrigan eventually suspended. Corrigan's efforts to persuade church authorities in Rome of the dangers of America's progressive Catholics ultimately saw Pope Leo XIII issue in 1899 the encyclical *Testem Benevolentiae*, which condemned Americanism as a heresy.

Cotton, John (1584–1652) *Puritan minister*

Before John Cotton immigrated to the Massachusetts Bay Colony in 1633, he was a well-known Puritan preacher in England. Once in America he became perhaps the most famous preacher of his generation and served as a teacher in the Congregationalist church in Boston. He became involved in controversy early in his tenure in Boston when Anne Hutchinson insisted that his theological views—which she characterized as teaching a "covenant of grace"—were superior to those of the Boston church's other minister, John Wilson. She was eventually excommunicated from the church and banished from the colony for views colonial leaders concluded were *Antinomian*, and Cotton himself was briefly implicated in the controversy surrounding these views. He was eventually exonerated and went on to become a prominent defender of the colony's close association between church and state. He defended the colony in print from the rhetorical attacks of Roger Williams, who insisted that church and state in Massachusetts practiced *The Bloody Tenet of Persecution*, as he titled his first major defense of religious liberty. Cotton responded with a work of his own, titled *The Bloody Tenet, Washed, and Made White in the Blood of the Lamb*.

Coughlin, Charles Edward (1891–1979) *Catholic priest, radio personality*

Ordained a priest in 1916, Charles Coughlin eventually settled in 1926 into the parish of Royal Oak, Michigan, in a church named Shrine of the Little Flower. Here he began radio broadcasts that CBS picked up and aired as the program *The Golden Hour of the Little Flower* in 1930. Coughlin became nationally prominent for rallying against "predatory capitalists" during the Great Depression. He initially supported and then later opposed the policies of President Franklin D. Roosevelt and helped to form the Union Party, which he disbanded after its presidential candidate performed poorly in the 1936 election. Subsequently his broadcast identified Jews—especially communist Jews—as national enemies and portrayed Adolf Hitler in a relatively positive light. As a result, in 1942 Catholic authorities compelled him to retire from broadcasting. Coughlin spent the rest of his life tending to parish affairs.

Damien, Father (1840–1889) *Catholic missionary*

Inspired by the example of his brother, a Catholic priest, Joseph de Veuster took vows as a brother of the Sacred Hearts of Jesus and Mary in 1860 and assumed the name Damien. When the same brother had to abandon plans to go to Hawaii as a missionary after contracting typhus, Damien went in his stead and upon his arrival in 1864 was ordained a priest. In 1873 he learned of the pitiful condition of lepers consigned to the island of Molokai and moved there. On Molokai he tended to both the spiritual and physical needs of the lepers and soon contracted leprosy himself, from which he eventually died.

Davies, Samuel (1723–1761) *Presbyterian minister*

In 1746 Samuel Davies was licensed a Presbyterian minister by the New Castle presbytery, a union of Presbyterian churches on friendly terms with the Great Awakening and revivalism. The next year the presbytery commissioned him to serve as an itinerant preacher in Virginia. There he established seven churches and helped to organize a presbytery for Virginia. In 1759 he accepted the presidency of the College of New Jersey (present-day Princeton University), though he died of pneumonia soon after moving to New Jersey.

Davis, Andrew Jackson (1826–1910) *spiritualist*

Called the Seer of Poughkeepsie, Andrew Jackson Davis was the most prominent American spiritualist of the 19th century. While still a teenager Davis claimed to have recognized his gift of being able to diagnose medical conditions while in a trance and to have met famous people from history in visionary journeys. He earned prominence as a spiritualist after the publication in 1847 of lectures delivered while in a trance, titled *The Principles of Nature, Her Divine Revelations, and a Voice to Mankind*. The following decade he published his principal work, a five-volume treatise titled *The Great Harmonia*, which appeared from 1850 to 1855 and which elaborated his "Harmonial Philosophy," which suggested the existence of successive spheres of existence through which souls passed after death.

Day, Dorothy (1897–1980) *cofounder of the Catholic Worker movement*

While in college Dorothy Day became a socialist and dropped out to begin writing for radical newspapers. In 1927 she became a Catholic, but she brought to her newfound faith the same commitment to social justice that had animated her previous life. After meeting Peter Maurin in 1932, the two began publication of the *Catholic Worker*, a magazine that prompted the creation of the Catholic Worker movement. Day and Maurin oversaw the creation of numerous hospitality houses and communal farms in which principles of social justice might be expressed through Christian community.

De, Abhay Charan (A. C. Prabhupāda Bhaktivedanta) (1896–1977) *founder of the International Society for Krishna Consciousness*

Abhay Charan De helped import Hinduism to the United States during the second half of the 20th century. Born in Calcutta, India, De became associated with a movement within Hinduism devoted to the worship of Krishna. In the 1950s he undertook *sannyāsa*, a life spent in renunciation of the world, and assumed the name Abhay Caranaravinda Prabhupāda Bhaktivedanta Swami. Subsequently, in 1965 he immigrated to the United States and founded the following year the International Society for Krishna Consciousness (ISKCON). The group is also known colloquially as the Hare Krishnas for their regular chanting of the mantra "Hare Krishna Hare Krishna Krishna Krishna Hare Hare Hare Rama Hare Rama Rama Rama Hare Hare." De led the group until illness prompted him to return to India, where he died in 1977.

De Smet, Pierre-Jean (1801–1873) *Catholic missionary*

After immigrating to the United States from Belgium, Pierre-Jean De Smet was ordained a Catholic priest in 1827. Sickness forced him to return to Europe to recuperate in 1833, but he arrived back in the United States by 1837 and soon set about founding St. Joseph's Mission at Council Bluffs, Iowa, among the Potawatomi. The following years saw him engaged in a variety of missionary activities among the American Indians of the Pacific Northwest, among whom he came to be known as Black Robe. In the 1850s the federal government turned to him as a mediator with Native American tribes. The following decade he performed his most well-known service to federal authorities by traveling alone into the camp of Sitting Bull and helping to negotiate the treaty of 1868 with the Sioux.

Divine, Major J. (Father Divine) (ca. 1879–1965) *Peace Movement founder*

After exposure to a variety of religious traditions, including attendance at the Azusa Street Revival in the early 20th century, George Baker, Jr., came to believe around 1912 while living in Baltimore that he was actually God. Known by the followers he soon collected as Major Jealous Divine or Father Divine, he made a practice of presiding over elaborate banquets for his followers. After settling for a time in Valdosta, Georgia, Father Divine defeated attempts of local authorities to have him committed as insane, and relocated first to Brooklyn, New York, then to Sayville on Long Island, where he and his wife purchased a home in 1919. Here Father Divine taught his followers to be hard working and self-reliant and continued to host banquets that by 1931 attracted as many as a thousand people to his house each weekend. This traffic annoyed neighbors, whose complaints eventually saw Divine charged and convicted of disturbing the peace. This conviction was reversed on appeal, but Divine left Sayville for Harlem, where he named his religious group the Peace Movement and led it to establish a variety of businesses intended to provide social services at a modest cost to the poor. Eventually he moved to the suburbs of Philadelphia, but not before the Peace Movement spread from Harlem to other cities.

Dixon, Amzi Clarence (1854–1925) *Baptist minister*

Amzi Dixon was an influential Baptist minister who preached from two of the world's most famous Protestant pulpits of his day, the Chicago Avenue Church in Chicago and the Metropolitan Tabernacle in London, which had been founded by Charles Hadden Spurgeon. He is remembered even more for serving as editor of a collection of conservative theological essays called *The Fundamentals*, published in 12 volumes from 1910 to 1915. Financed by two California businessmen, the collection was intended to defend orthodox beliefs such as the Virgin birth and the resurrection of Christ. Dixon edited the first five volumes of the series.

Drexel, Katherine (1858–1955) *Catholic missionary*

Katherine Drexel was an heiress who devoted her significant wealth to Catholic missions to American Indians and African Americans. After an audience with the pope in 1887 during which he suggested she become a missionary, Drexel became a nun and in 1891 established the Sisters of the Blessed Sacrament for Indians and Colored People. Over the following years Drexel used her wealth to help establish a variety of missionary institutions for Native Americans and African Americans, beginning with St. Catherine's School in Santa Fe, New Mexico, a school for Native-American children. Perhaps the most important institution she founded was Xavier College (present-day Xavier University) in New Orleans, a Catholic institution for African-American students established in 1925. In 2000 Pope John Paul II declared Katherine Drexel a saint.

Dunster, Henry (1609–1659) *college president*
A Cambridge educated Puritan minister, Henry Dunster immigrated to America in 1640 and was almost immediately invited to become president of newly established Harvard College. He served energetically and ably in the position for 14 years until he gradually developed theological ideas about baptism that placed him in conflict with the Puritans of Massachusetts Bay. Dunster came to hold Baptist beliefs—that is, he viewed baptism as inappropriate for infants since he concluded that the ordinance was reserved for those old enough to possess personal faith in Christ. He resigned as president of Harvard in 1654 and moved to the Plymouth Colony, where he died four years later.

Dwight, Timothy (1752–1817) *Congregationalist minister, educator*
Matriculated at Yale College when he was 13 years old, Timothy Dwight obtained first a bachelors degree and then a masters in 1771. After receiving these degrees he remained for a time at Yale as a tutor, began studying for the ministry in 1776, and was licensed to preach the following year. Apart from service as a chaplain during the Revolutionary War, the following years saw Dwight serve variously as a minister, a farmer, a state legislator, an educator, and a poet. In 1783 he accepted the offer to become minister of the church in Greenfield, Connecticut, where he also established a highly regarded school. After the death of Ezra Stiles in 1795, Dwight was invited to assume the presidency of Yale College, where he was also a professor of divinity for the remainder of his life.

Dyer, Mary (unknown–1660) *Quaker martyr*
Born Mary Barrett and married to William Dyer in 1633, Mary Dyer migrated with her husband to New England in 1635. There she became a friend and follower of Anne Hutchinson. In the wake of Hutchinson's banishment from the colony, Dyer and her family settled along with Hutchinson in Providence Colony. She traveled with her family to England in 1652, and during her five-year stay there she became a Quaker. On her way home to Providence in 1657 via Boston, she was arrested as a Quaker. Though released on bond on this occasion, when she returned to Massachusetts two years later she was sentenced to banishment. She defied this order later the same year and together with two other Quakers, William Robinson and Marmaduke Stevenson, was sentenced to be executed. Though Massachusetts authorities hanged the two men, they released Dyer and ordered her not to return to the colony. When she did so in the spring of 1660, she was arrested and executed by hanging on the Boston Commons.

Eddy, Mary Baker (1821–1910) *Christian Science founder*
The founder of one of America's indigenous religious traditions, Christian Science, Mary Baker Eddy spent much of her youth and early adulthood suffering from various physical ailments. In 1862 she met and experienced healing with Phineas Parkhurst Quimby, a mesmeric healer with whom she began to study. After Quimby's death in 1866, Eddy suffered a serious fall and subsequently, while reading the New Testament, had a healing experience that she attributed to the realization of her essential spiritual nature and her connection to the Divine Mind. This discovery became the basis for her subsequent teaching, and in 1875 she published the first of many editions of *Science and Health*, later expanded to include her notes on the Scripture and titled *Science and Health: With Key to the Scriptures*. Four years later she founded the Church of Christ, Scientist, for which her book was the central religious text, and guided the growth of this church over its initial decades.

Edwards, Jonathan (1703–1758) *Congregationalist minister, theologian*
Educated at Yale, in 1726 Jonathan Edwards became junior minister at the church of Northampton where his grandfather, Solomon Stoddard, was senior minister. As a result of his preaching, the Northampton church, which had seen several periods of revival during his grandfather's tenure as minister, also experienced revivals in 1734 and 1735 under Edwards's preaching. These revivals prefaced the more general revival, referred to

as the Great Awakening, sparked by the preaching of George Whitefield in the American colonies in 1740. Edwards, in fact, became a prominent defender of the Great Awakening, publishing *Some Thoughts Concerning the Present Revival of Religion* (1742), which vindicated main aspects of the awakening from its critics. The year before this publication, he preached one of America's most famous sermons, "Sinners in the Hands of an Angry God." Subsequently his insistence that participation in the Lord's Supper be reserved for those who had experienced conversion and his repudiation of the Half-Way Covenant resulted in his being forced out of the Northampton church in 1751. Edwards relocated to Stockbridge, Massachusetts, where he pastored a small church and served as a missionary to local American Indians. In 1758 he was installed as president of the College of New Jersey (later Princeton University), but after being inoculated for smallpox he contracted the disease and died slightly more than a month after assuming this post.

Einhorn, David (1809–1879) *Reform rabbi*

Beginning in 1842 David Einhorn served in rabbinical posts first in Germany and then briefly in Budapest before immigrating to the United States in 1855. By the time he arrived in America, he was clearly attached to the progressive theological principles characteristic of Reform Judaism, to which he had already given expression in *The Principles of Mosaic Religion* (1854). In the United States Einhorn became rabbi for the Har Sinai congregation in Baltimore, Maryland. His antipathy toward slavery, however, forced him to leave Baltimore for Philadelphia, where he served as rabbi of the Kenesseth Israel congregation from 1861 to 1866. Beginning in 1866 Einhorn served 13 years as rabbi of Adath Jeshurun in New York (later named Temple Beth-El). The same year he undertook this final post he also participated in the Philadelphia Conference of rabbis and was influential in producing the conference's statement of principles, which were a vigorous statement of Reform beliefs.

Eliot, John (1604–1690) *Puritan minister, missionary*

Though ordained a minister in the Church of England, John Eliot's Puritan views eventually led him to immigrate to New England in 1631. He was soon invited to assume the position of teacher in the church at Roxbury alongside the church's senior minister, Thomas Weld. A decade later Weld returned to England, and Eliot became senior minister, a position he would hold for nearly 50 years. History remembers him most for his energetic missionary efforts to American Indians, which began with his study of the Algonquian language in the early 1640s and with a preaching ministry in this language later in the decade. He eventually raised money to establish towns for Native American converts to Christianity, who came to be known as "praying Indians." His efforts to learn Algonquian allowed him to publish a New Testament in that language in 1661 and a translation of the Old Testament in 1663. Together these translations became the first complete Bible printed in North America.

England, John (1786–1842) *Catholic bishop*

Ordained a priest in Ireland in 1808, John England immigrated to the United States in 1820, where he was ordained the first bishop of Charleston, South Carolina. There he demonstrated a great enthusiasm for American democracy and transplanted some of the principles of American constitutionalism to the governance of his diocese. He drafted a *Constitution for the Diocese of Charleston* that provided a pattern for the participation of both the laity and the clergy in the supervision of church affairs. In view of these sympathies it was not unusual that he would become the first Catholic to address the U.S. Congress in 1826. He subsequently served as a negotiator on behalf of the Catholic Church with the government of Haiti.

Falwell, Jerry (1933–) *Baptist minister, television personality*

After earning his undergraduate degree from Lynchburg College in Virginia and a graduate theology degree from Baptist Bible College in Springfield, Missouri, Jerry Falwell returned to Lynchburg in 1958. There he established a Baptist church, later named Thomas Road Baptist Church, and almost immediately began broadcasting a radio program and soon afterward, a television program called the *Old-Time Gospel Hour.* Membership at Thomas Road Baptist Church grew swiftly, eventually reaching some 22,000 members by the 21st century. Falwell also established Lynchburg (later Liberty) Baptist College in 1971. During the Civil Rights era Falwell insisted that Christian ministers had no business engaging in social reform activities. Nevertheless, by the end of the 1970s he had reconsidered this view, and in 1979 he established an influential conservative political action group called the Moral Majority. Although the organization is often credited with helping Ronald Reagan win the presidency in 1980, it was disbanded later in the decade. In subsequent years, however, Falwell remained a prominent leader of what came to be known as the Christian right.

Farrakhan, Louis Abdul (1933–) *Nation of Islam leader*

After a brief career as a singer, Louis Eugene Walcott joined the Nation of Islam in 1955, changing his name first to Louis X and later to Louis Abdul Farrakhan. Following the teaching of Elijah Muhammad, Farrakhan believed that whites were devils whose tyrannical rule would eventually be displaced. Farrakhan was first an assistant to Malcolm X at the Nation of Islam's Boston temple and then senior minister of the Boston temple after Malcolm X assumed leadership of the Harlem temple. After Malcolm X left the Nation of Islam in 1963, Farrakhan assumed a prominent position both as leader of the Harlem temple and as Elijah Muhammad's national representative. With the death of Muhammad in 1975, Muhammad's son, W. Deen Muhammad, first attempted to steer the Nation of Islam toward more orthodox Islam and then disbanded the organization entirely. In the meantime, however, Farrakhan led a separate group to revitalize the Nation of Islam, and he remained the new organization's leader into the 21st century. Though he gained notoriety for frequent racist comments, especially aimed at Jews, Farrakhan also gained prominence in 1995 by organizing the Million Man March for African-American men.

Finney, Charles Grandison (1792–1875) *revivalist*

The most prominent revivalist of the mid-19th century, Charles G. Finney experienced a religious conversion at the age of 29 while apprenticed to a lawyer and immediately determined to become a preacher. He was licensed a Presbyterian minister in 1823 and spent the following years as an itinerant preacher. He gained prominence in 1830 and 1831 while conducting an extended series of revival services in Rochester, New York. Beginning in 1832 he served as minister of a church he established at Chathan Street Theater in New York City until he accepted a position on the faculty of Oberlin Collegiate Institute (later Oberlin College) on the condition that he be permitted to return to New York City each winter to preach at Broadway Tabernacle. In 1835, however, he resigned this pastorate to become minister of First Church in Oberlin in addition to his position as professor at Oberlin Collegiate Institute. Finney's emphasis on the ability of his hearers to receive salvation led him to abandon Presbyterianism in 1836 and become a Congregationalist. From 1851 to 1865 he also served as president of the Oberlin Collegiate Institute.

Fosdick, Harry Emerson (1878–1969) *Baptist minister*

In the furious theological battles between fundamentalism and modernism in the early 20th century, Harry Emerson Fosdick cast himself firmly on the side of modernism. He graduated from Union Theological Seminary in 1904 and accepted a position as minister of the First Baptist Church in Montclair, New Jersey. During the years he served at Montclair, he also earned an M.A. degree in political science from Columbia and taught part time at Union Theological Seminary. In 1915 he joined the seminary faculty full time, although three years later he accepted a position preaching at the First Presbyterian Church of New York City while continuing in his post at Union Theological Seminary. History remembers him most for a sermon preached to his congregation in 1922, titled "Shall the Fundamentalists Win?," which a wealthy friend, John D. Rockefeller, saw distributed to every minister in America. Eventually Rockefeller financed the construction of Riverside Church in New York, where Fosdick preached from 1931 until he retired in 1946.

Frelinghuysen, Theodorus Jacobus (1691– ca. 1747) *Dutch Reformed minister*

An advance herald of the Great Awakening, Theodorus Frelinghuysen was ordained a Dutch Reformed minister in Germany before immigrating to the United States in 1719, where he settled in central New Jersey's Raritan Valley. There he rejected formalisms such as recitation of the Lord's Prayer during church services and preached sermons emphasizing the necessity for personal conversion, even among his regular church members. During the course of his pastoral career, he became friends with Presbyterian minister Gilbert Tennent, and the two shared a common theological perspective and revivalistic preaching style that anticipated two more well-known preachers of the Great Awakening—George Whitefield and Jonathan Edwards.

Fuller, Charles Edward (1887–1968) *radio preacher*

After experiencing a conversion in 1916, Charles Fuller left his job at a packing plant for orange growers to become a preacher by studying at the fundamentalist Bible Institute of Los Angeles. Working first as president of the Orange County Christian Endeavor, Fuller established his own congregation, Calvary Church, in 1924.

By 1930 he was broadcasting a radio program from the church, and in 1933 he left the church to establish the Gospel Broadcasting Association. The next year he began airing the program that would make him nationally prominent over the following decades, the *Old Fashioned Revival Hour.* The success of this program ultimately allowed Fuller to establish Fuller Theological Seminary in 1947.

Garnet, Henry Highland (1815–1882) *Presbyterian minister, abolitionist*
A former slave who became a minister and an abolitionist, Henry Highland Garnet's family escaped from slavery on the underground railroad when he was a child. He studied at a variety of schools during his childhood and young adult years, graduating eventually from an abolitionist school in Whitesboro, New York, in 1839. Two years later he was ordained a Presbyterian minister and subsequently assumed the pastorate of the Liberty Street Presbyterian Church in Troy, New York. In 1843 he achieved prominence when he delivered a speech titled "Call to Rebellion" to the National Negro Convention in Buffalo, New York. After the Civil War he became pastor of the Fifteenth Street Presbyterian Church and in 1865 became the first African-American minister invited to address Congress. Toward the end of his life he undertook service as U.S. minister to Liberia, where he died.

Gibbons, James (1834–1921) *Catholic cardinal*
Ordained a priest in 1861, James Gibbons became secretary to Archbishop Martin Spalding in 1865. He was closely involved in the archbishop's preparations for the Second Plenary Council of Baltimore, and when this council recommended the creation of a new diocese for North Carolina, Spalding recommended that Gibbons be appointed bishop. Gibbons was thus ordained a bishop in 1868. He was an influential apologist for Catholicism, publishing *Faith of Our Fathers* in 1876. He received an appointment as bishop of Richmond in 1872 and in 1877 became archbishop of Baltimore. Chosen by Pope Leo XIII in 1844 to preside over the Third Plenary Council of Baltimore, Gibbons was appointed to the rank of cardinal in 1887. In the struggle between progressive and conservative Catholic leaders during the late 19th century, Gibbons aligned himself with the progressives. He persuaded the pope not to condemn the Knights of Labor and led in the founding of Catholic University in Washington, D.C.

Gladden, Solomon Washington (1836–1918)
Congregationalist minister, leader of the Social Gospel movement
Sometimes called the father of the Social Gospel movement, Washington Gladden was a Congregationalist minister whose most significant pastoral position was in a church in Columbus, Ohio. While in this pastorate Gladden became acquainted with and an ally of the labor movement. He became a prominent advocate of Christian engagement with the social ills of society not simply through individual acts of benevolence but through concrete efforts to secure social justice. Though not a socialist, he argued in *Applied Christianity: Moral Aspects of Social Questions* (1886) that Christian principles mandated an equitable distribution of the wealth created by the industrial revolution. In the early years of the 20th century, he labored to bring practical energy to his zeal for reform by serving briefly as an alderman for the city of Columbus, Ohio.

Grace, Charles Manuel (Sweet Daddy Grace) (1881–1960) *founder of the United House of Prayer for All People*
Born Marceline Manoel da Graca in Brava, Cape Verde Islands, Charles Manuel Grace immigrated to the United States about the turn of the 20th century and became a Holiness preacher. In the 1920s he appears to have established the first United House of Prayer either in North Carolina or in Washington, D.C. Toward the end of the decade he incorporated the United House of Prayer for All People on the Rock of the Apostolic Faith in Washington, D.C. More Houses of Prayer soon followed in other urban areas. Sweet Daddy Grace or Daddy Grace, as he was called, led his followers in Pentecostal-style ecstatic worship and urged them, in Holiness fashion, to abstain from alcohol and tobacco. From donations he collected from followers he financed projects such as apartment buildings and food kitchens for the poor and also a lavish life style for himself. The latter drew the attention of the Internal Revenue Service, which ultimately collected nearly $2 million from Grace's estate.

Graham, Billy (William Franklin Graham) (1918–) *revivalist*
The 20th century's most famous evangelist, Billy Graham was converted while a teenager and subsequently attended first Bob Jones University, then Florida Bible Institute, and finally Wheaton College to prepare for a ministry as a preacher. He was ordained a Southern Baptist minister in 1939, and after World War II he served as an evangelist

for "Youth for Christ." He came to national prominence in 1949 after a successful series of revival services in Los Angeles. The following decade saw him expand the range of his ministry under the umbrella of the Billy Graham Evangelistic Association (BGEA). These ministries included a radio broadcast called the *Hour of Decision*, the magazine *Christianity Today*, published beginning in 1955, and World Wide Pictures, which released its first feature film, *Mr. Texas*, in 1951. Graham's prominence gave him access to a number of American presidents—especially Richard Nixon—during the last half of the 20th century. At the beginning of the 21st century, however, he had finally neared the end of his public ministry and had left leadership of his evangelistic association in the hands of his son, Franklin Graham.

Gratz, Rebecca (1781–1869) *Jewish lay leader*

At the turn of the 19th century, Rebecca Gratz began a long career as a leader in various Jewish philanthropic associations, beginning with the Female Association for the Relief of Women and Children in Reduced Circumstances, which she helped found in 1801 and for which she was the secretary. She played a similar role in the establishment of the Philadelphia Orphan Asylum in 1815 and the Female Hebrew Benevolent Society (FHBS) in 1819. Later in life she persuaded the FHBS to open a Hebrew Sunday school in 1838 and served as its first superintendent. Even later she helped establish the Jewish Foster Home in 1855 and served as its secretary.

Handsome Lake (ca. 1735–1815) *Iroquois prophet*

Little is known concerning the early life of Handsome Lake, the half-brother of Iroquois leader Cornplanter. In 1799, at a period when Handsome Lake was struggling with alcoholism, he experienced a series of visions that stressed the need to abstain from alcohol and witchcraft and practice traditional sacred ceremonies. Handsome Lake attributed the sins of alcoholism and gambling to the baleful influence of Europeans acting under the influence of the Evil One. Those who refused to follow the injunctions Handsome Lake announced would be denied entrance into heaven. These counsels and his further admonition to avoid additional sales of land to whites helped stabilize and revitalize Iroquois culture after the devastations experienced during the Revolutionary War.

Haygood, Atticus Greene (1839–1896) *Methodist bishop, educator*

In contrast with southerners who after the Civil War pined for a "lost cause," Atticus Haygood emphasized the necessity for envisioning a "new South." He experienced a religious conversion in his teen-age years and subsequently attended Emory College (later Emory University), deciding before he graduated to become a Methodist minister. After being licensed to preach in 1858, Haygood served as a military chaplain during the Civil War, a pastor briefly afterward, and then an officer in various denominational concerns. He was named president of Emory in 1875. During his years there Haygood employed pen and voice to urge the equal treatment of African Americans and the provision to them of educational opportunities consistent with their position as fellow citizens. He wrote *Our Brother in Black* in 1881 and subsequently became an agent for the John F. Slater Fund, which promoted the cause of education among African Americans. In 1884 he surrendered his administrative post at Emory to work full time for the Slater Fund. Toward the end of his life he was elected and served for three years as a bishop of the Methodist Episcopal Church, South.

Heck, Barbara Ruckle (1734–1804) *Methodist lay leader*

Called the mother of Methodism in America, Barbara Heck immigrated to the United States from Ireland in 1760 with her family and several relatives, including her cousin Philip Embury. Tradition has it that she persuaded Embury to begin preaching in 1766 after discovering her brother and others playing cards. She is also credited with suggesting to Embury and other men in the newly founded Methodist society that they build a stone chapel on John Street in New York. The chapel opened on October 30, 1768, and may have been the first Methodist church building in America. During the Revolutionary War the loyalist sympathies of Heck and her family forced them to move to Canada, where they settled outside of Montreal at first and then later relocated to an area that is now Ontario.

Hedge, Frederic Henry (1805–1890) *Transcendentalist leader, Unitarian minister, educator*

Graduated from Harvard Divinity School in 1829, Frederic Hedge was ordained that year a minister of the Congregational church in West Cambridge (later Arlington), Massachusetts. He became involved in the activities of the Transcendentalist movement, helping to found the Transcendental Club in 1836 and leading the club to begin publishing the movement's chief periodical, the *Dial*, in 1840. During the 1850s he drifted into Unitarian pulpits and served four years as president of the American Unitarian Association beginning in 1859. At the end of his career he spent a dozen years as a professor of German at Harvard.

Heschel, Abraham Joshua (1907–1972) *Jewish theologian*

A social activist in his time, Abraham Heschel participated in the Civil Rights movement and in protests of the Vietnam War. Born in Poland, he received his Ph.D. from the University of Berlin in 1933, but after the Nazis came to power he had to leave Germany. He subsequently escaped from Poland just before it was invaded by Germany and immigrated to the United States, where he joined the faculty of Hebrew Union College in Cincinnati, Ohio. In 1945 he relocated to New York's Jewish Theological Seminary. He joined with Martin Luther King, Jr., in civil rights protests conducted in Selma, Alabama, in 1965 and subsequently cofounded Clergy Concerned about Vietnam. He also negotiated with Roman Catholic authorities in preparation for Vatican II, and his influence is thought to have helped remove anti-Semitic references from liturgical and educational materials of the Catholic Church.

Hodge, Charles (1797–1878) *Presbyterian theologian*

Charles Hodge joined the faculty of Princeton Theological Seminary as a young man in 1820. Apart from a brief period when he took a leave from the seminary to study abroad in Europe later that decade, Hodge remained at Princeton, devoting more than a half century to the defense of Calvinistic orthodoxy from the threats posed by theological liberalism on one hand and urban revivalism on the other. As well as being a gifted teacher, Hodge was a prolific writer, using the *Princeton Review*, which he established in the 1820s, as a vehicle for conveying his prodigious theological work. He penned a number of books as well, none more important than *Systematic Theology* (1871–72).

Hooker, Thomas (1586–1647) *Puritan minister*

A graduate of Emmanuel College at Cambridge, Thomas Hooker immigrated to Boston in 1633 after being forced to leave England because of his Puritan views. After his arrival he became the minister of the church in Newton. He served important roles in the Massachusetts Bay Colony's early encounters with religious dissenters, debating Roger Williams in 1635 and presiding over a synod that dealt with Anne Hutchinson's views in 1637. The year before this synod Hooker moved to Connecticut, where he and others established the town of Hartford. He is credited with encouraging the colony to adopt what became America's earliest constitution. Equally as important, he penned an important defense of Congregational Church structure titled *A Survey of the Summe of Church-Discipline*, which was itself influential in the development of the Cambridge Platform of 1648, a statement of governing principles adopted by New England's Congregational churches.

Hubbard, L. Ron (1911–1986) *founder of Scientology*

Prior to World War II L. Ron Hubbard fashioned a career as a writer of science fiction and adventure stories. During the war he served for a time in the navy. Afterward, he published *Dianetics: The Modern Science of Mental Health* (1950), the book around which Scientology took shape. Two years later he founded the Hubbard Association of Scientologists International, which led in 1954 to the establishment of the Church of Scientology in Los Angeles, California. In 1955 Hubbard moved to Washington, D.C., where he established the Founding Church of Scientology. At the end of that decade he relocated to England, where he established a Scientology school. He eventually returned to the United States in 1975 and returned to the work of writing science fiction as well by publishing *Battlefield Earth* in 1982 and a series called *Mission Earth* from 1985 to 1987.

Hutchinson, Anne Marbury (ca. 1591–1643) *Puritan lay leader*

Anne Hutchinson immigrated with her family to the Massachusetts Bay Colony in 1634 chiefly out of a desire to hear the preaching of Puritan minister John Cotton, who had himself moved to Boston the previous year and had been the family's minister in England. She began to hold religious meetings in her home at which she praised the preaching of Cotton for his focus on God's gracious gift of salvation in contrast with that of the Boston church's other minister, John Wilson. She criticized Wilson for placing too much emphasis on religious works as evidence that one was among God's elect. Although she attracted the support of Sir Henry Vane, the colony's governor, the majority of the colony's civil and religious leaders found her ideas alarming. Consequently she was tried for heresy by the colony's highest court in November of 1637 and banished from the colony. Subsequently she and her family relocated to what is present-day Rhode Island. After the death of her husband in 1642, she moved with her children to the Dutch colony of New Netherland and was killed soon afterward in an Indian raid.

Ireland, John (1838–1918) *Catholic archbishop*

A leader among 19th-century Catholics who supported the assimilation of Catholic immigrants into American society, John Ireland was consecrated archbishop of St. Paul in 1888. He became involved in the Americanist controversy toward the end of the century. This controversy pitted Ireland and other progressive Catholic leaders against conservatives such as New York's archbishop Michael Corrigan, who opposed Catholic assimilation to American values such as materialism and secularism. In 1899 Pope Leo XIII sided with the conservatives by naming Americanism a heresy in his encyclical letter *Testem benevolentiae*. In addition to his role in the Americanism controversy, Ireland is known for founding St. Paul Seminary and guiding the construction of the Cathedral of St. Paul and the Basilica of St. Mary in Minneapolis.

Jackson, Jesse (1941–) *Baptist minister, civil rights leader*

The most prominent African-American leader of the late 20th and early 21st centuries, Jesse Jackson became involved in the Civil Rights movement in the early 1960s. Though briefly enrolled in Chicago Theological Seminary, he left school to work for the Southern Christian Leadership Conference (SCLC) and was appointed in 1966 to head the Chicago branch of Operation Breadbasket. After Martin Luther King, Jr.'s, assassination in 1968, Jackson failed to assume the leadership of SCLC and in 1971 left the organization to establish Operation PUSH (People United to Serve Humanity) in Chicago. He announced his candidacy for the Democratic nomination for president of the United States 12 years later and won significant support for this nomination, although it ultimately went to Walter Mondale. Four year later he made an even stronger challenge for the Democratic nomination, eventually losing to Michael Dukakis. Toward the end of the 20th century he gained prominence by helping to negotiate the release of foreign hostages taken by Saddam Hussein and three U.S. servicemen taken prisoner by Yugoslav president Slobodan Milošević during the war in Kosovo.

Kaplan, Mordecai Menahem (1881–1983) *Jewish rabbi, founder of Reconstructionism*

Mordecai Kaplan founded a branch of American Judaism known as Reconstructionism. After receiving his rab-binate from the Jewish Theological Seminary in 1902, he served as rabbi for an Orthodox synagogue in New York known as Kehilath Jeshurun. He later became associated with the Jewish Theological Seminary in New York, which itself came to be a leading institution for Conservative Judaism in America. But as Kaplan had migrated earlier away from Orthodox Judaism, by the late 1920s he had moved away from Conservative Judaism as well and in 1927 left the seminary to assume a teaching position at the Jewish Institute of Religion. Even before this he had established the Society for the Advancement of Judaism in 1922, and this institution is frequently thought to be the birthplace of Reconstructionist Judaism.

Keith, George (1638–1716) *Quaker theologian, Anglican priest*

Born in Scotland, George Keith converted from Presbyterianism to Quakerism sometime after 1658. He soon became an influential Scottish apologist for Quakerism and, like many Quakers, spent time in jail for his beliefs. He eventually moved to America in 1684 and settled first in New Jersey and then later in Philadelphia. After the death of George Fox in 1691, Keith became embroiled in internal Quaker disagreements, erupting in a split between Keith and his followers, called Keithians or Christian Quakers, and other American Quakers. He found time during the controversy to pen the first American antislavery tract in 1693, titled *An Exhortation to Friends Concerning Buying or Keeping of Negroes*. That year he also traveled to England but found himself at odds with Quakers there as well. He ultimately abandoned Quakerism for the Anglican Church, being ordained an Anglican priest in 1700 and returning to America in 1702 as an Anglican missionary under the auspices of the Society for the Propagation of the Gospel.

King, Martin Luther, Jr. (1929–1968) *Baptist minister, civil rights leader*

After completing the dissertation for his Ph.D. from Boston University, ultimately received in 1955, Martin Luther King, Jr., became the pastor of the Dexter Avenue Baptist Church in Montgomery, Alabama, in 1954. The next year, when Rosa Parks was arrested for refusing to surrender her seat on a bus to a white person, King was elected president of the Montgomery Improvement Association, organized to protest racial segregation. In this position he won national attention for his efforts to coordinate a boycott of Montgomery's bus system, a boycott eventually vindicated when the U.S. Supreme Court struck down Alabama's bus segregation law. After this success King organized the Southern Christian Leadership Conference (SCLC) in 1957 and became its first president. Three years later he moved to Atlanta, where he joined his father as copastor of the Ebenezer Church, a position that allowed him to devote most of his energy to continued work on behalf of civil rights. This work reached a climax in 1963, when he helped organize civil demonstrations in Birmingham, Alabama, during the course of which he was arrested and penned one of the Civil Rights movement's most famous tracts, his "Letter from a Birmingham Jail." That year he also participated in the March on Washington and delivered perhaps his most famous speech, "I Have a Dream." As a culmination of King's efforts on behalf of civil rights, he received the Nobel Peace Prize in 1964. In 1968, however, while in Memphis to deliver a speech he was assassinated by James Earl Ray.

Kino, Eusebio Francisco (1645–1711) *Catholic missionary, explorer*

Ordained a Jesuit priest in 1676, Eusebio Kino coupled his missionary calling with an interest in cartography to become an explorer of and Catholic evangelist to the region that is the present-day southwestern United States. As a young man he had hoped to serve as a missionary in China or the Indies or "some other difficult one in nature," but his superiors dispatched him to Mexico, where he arrived in 1681. Two years later he founded the first mission in what is present-day California, and this would be only one of the many missionary outposts he established across his long career. His importance to the southwestern United States is not limited to his spiritual influence, however. As he established missions he also introduced farming and cattle raising to the areas in which he ministered, thus laying the basis for the future economic livelihood of these regions.

Las Casas, Bartolomé de (1474–1566) *advocate for the rights of American Indians*

The son of a father who had accompanied Columbus on his second voyage to the New World, Las Casas joined his first expedition to the Americas in 1502. Subsequently ordained a deacon in the Catholic Church, he traveled to Cuba, where his services won for him the rights of an *encomendero*. Under the *encomienda* system this meant that he was given the right to compel labor from Native Americans in a particular geographic area. His own experience as an *encomendero* and his observation of the mistreatment visited upon Indians by other *encomenderos* eventually turned him into an implacable foe of the *eoncomienda* system. He spent the rest of his life railing against the injustices and cruelties visited upon American Indians by Spanish conquistadores and colonists. He wrote two influential works, *Apologetic Historias de Las Indies* and *Historia de Las Indies*, which were published after he died. His criticism of the *encomienda* system helped persuade Spanish authorities to ameliorate at least some of its harsher aspects.

Lee, Ann (Mother Ann Lee) (1736–1784) *founder of the Shakers*

Born in Manchester, England, Ann Lee joined a religious group in 1761 of which she soon became the leader and which was known as the Shaking Quakers. After repeated clashes with English authorities and time in jail on two occasions, Mother Ann Lee (as her followers called her) migrated with her husband and some of the members of her group to America in 1774. After a few years Lee's husband left her, and she spent time again in jail in 1780 for refusing to support the war for independence from Britain. After her release she made a 28-month tour of New England, where she gained new converts to the Shakers. Lee created controversy as she traveled, since she believed that she was a second Christ, come to the world to announce the imminent arrival of a millennial kingdom. She died soon after completing this tour, but the Shakers continued to grow, with the first Shaker community formally established in New Lebanon, New York, in 1785, the year after Lee's death.

Leeser, Isaac (1806–1868) *Jewish teacher*

Born in Westphalia, Isaac Leeser immigrated to the United States when he was 18 years old and settled in Richmond, Virginia, where he worked in a general store owned by his uncle. In 1829 Congregation Mikveh Israel in Philadelphia invited Leeser to become its *hazzan*, or religious leader. Leeser labored for many years to make Jewish teaching and tradition accessible to English-speaking Jews. In Philadelphia he introduced the practice of preaching his sermons in English. Even more importantly, he produced an English translation of the Torah in 1845 and also English translations of the prayers and rituals of both Sephardic and Ashkenazic Judaism. Toward the end of his life he made one further significant contribution to American Judaism by establishing in Philadelphia the first rabbinical school, Maimonides College.

Machen, J. Gresham (1881–1937) *Presbyterian theologian*

A prominent opponent of theological liberalism in the early 20th century, J. Gresham Machen was ordained a minister in the Presbyterian Church (USA) and joined the regular faculty of Princeton Theological Seminary in 1914. Here he defended a conservative orthodoxy against the encroachments of modernism until his denomination and his seminary began to drift toward liberal stances on issues such as the divinity of Christ, his Virgin birth, and his bodily resurrection from the dead. Gresham achieved prominence with the publication of *Christianity and Liberalism* (1923), which argued that theological liberalism was not really a species of Christianity at all. In 1929 he left Princeton to help establish Westminster Theological Seminary as a more conservative center of Presbyterian learning. Machen subsequently joined in creating the Independent Board for Presbyterian Foreign Missions in 1933, and when ordered by the general assembly of the Presbyterian Church (USA) the next year to cease his association with this organization, he refused to do so and was subsequently stripped of his ordination in 1935. He and other conservatives then established the Presbyterian Church in America (subsequently renamed the Orthodox Presbyterian Church).

Makemie, Francis (ca. 1658–ca. 1708) *Presbyterian minister*

Known as the father of American Presbyterianism, Makemie immigrated to North America from Ireland in 1683. He was an itinerant preacher in Maryland, North Carolina, Virginia, and Barbados before he finally settled in Virginia after his wife inherited land there from her father. In the face of the aggressive activities of the Church of England's Society for the Propagation of the Gospel in Foreign Parts, founded in 1701, Makemie encouraged other Presbyterian ministers to establish the first American presbytery in 1706. Late in his life Makemie famously clashed with New York's autocratic governor by preaching without a license there. He was ultimately acquitted by a jury after being arrested and imprisoned, and he died soon after returning home.

Malcolm X (Malcolm Little) (1925–1965) *Nation of Islam leader*

Converted to the Nation of Islam while in prison, Malcolm Little changed his name to Malcolm X upon his parole in 1952. Elijah Muhammad, the leader of the Black Muslims, soon appointed Malcolm X head of the temple in Harlem, New York, and in 1962 his national representative. The next year, however, the two men became estranged after Malcolm X commented on the assassination of President John F. Kennedy that Kennedy "never foresaw that the chickens would come home to roost so soon." Muhammad soon suspended Malcolm X from his leadership positions within the Nation of Islam, and in the spring of 1964 Malcolm X withdrew from the Nation of Islam and founded Muslim Mosque, Inc. Soon afterward he made a pilgrimage to Mecca and subsequently announced that he had adopted a new name, el-Hajj Malik el-Shabazz, and established the Organization of Afro-American Unity. He was assassinated by members of the Nation of Islam on February 21, 1965, while making a speech in New York City.

Martin, Marie Guyart (Marie de l'Incarnation) (1599–1672) *Ursuline nun, missionary to American Indians in New France*

Known by Canadian Catholics as Marie de l'Incarnation (Marie of the Incarnation) Marie Guyart Martin grew up in Tours, France, and was briefly married to Claude Martin until his death two years after their marriage. Subsequently Martin entered the Ursuline convent in Tours in 1631. In 1639 she immigrated to Quebec in New France and founded the Ursuline order there and in 1642 a school for Huron and Algonquian Indian girls who were converts to Christianity. She lived and worked in Quebec for the remainder of her life. Although she published nothing during her life, she wrote two spiritual autobiographies, one of which survives, along with nearly 20,000 letters, of which 278 survive. These writings are valuable sources of information and perspective about the religious life of New France during the 17th century.

Mather, Cotton (1663–1728) *Puritan minister*

The last of a line of Puritan ministers that included his father, Increase, and his grandfather, Richard, Cotton Mather is known as a Puritan historian as well as a preacher. He served as junior minister alongside his father at the North Church in Boston for 40 years. While in this church both he and his father had occasion to observe the witchcraft proceedings at Salem in 1692 and 1693. Father and son, however, came to different conclusions about the legitimacy of these proceedings. Cotton wrote a defense of the Salem witchcraft trials titled *Wonders of the Invisible World*. His father, however, wrote a contrary evaluation that critiqued the proceedings, especially their reliance on so-called spectral evidence, evidence of witnesses who claimed to have seen the spectral images of alleged witches engaged in various devilish activities. History remembers Cotton Mather also as a historian of the early American Puritans based on his important work on this subject, *Magnalia Christi Americana.*

Mather, Increase (1639–1723) *Puritan minister*

One of the most prominent ministers of New England's second generation, Increase Mather was one of three great Puritan preachers from the family that included his father, Richard, and his son, Cotton. In 1664 he became the minister of Boston's North Church, where he served for 60 years. He was closely involved in both the political and theological affairs of the Massachusetts Bay Colony. In 1662 he participated in the synod that approved the Half-Way Covenant, although he disagreed with both his father and most of the other ministers by opposing the proposal to allow the baptism of children of parents who had been baptized but had not become church members. Later he joined in the Reforming Synod of 1679, at which he opposed the practice recommended by Solomon Stoddard of allowing individuals who led godly lives and professed belief in the essential doctrines of Christian faith to participate in the Lord's Supper even if they had not been converted. During the mid-1680s Mather traveled to England on behalf of Massachusetts to obtain a new colonial charter and returned home the next decade in time to criticize the witchcraft proceedings at Salem.

McPherson, Aimee Semple (1890–1944) *Pentecostal preacher*

After a brief tenure of service as a missionary to China with her husband, Robert Semple, Aimee Semple was forced to return to the United States after his sudden death in 1910. She subsequently married Harold ("Mack") McPherson, though she left him to become an itinerant preacher in 1915. By 1919 she had settled in Los Angeles, where she preached downtown at Victoria Hall. In 1921 she was able to begin construction on Angelus Temple, located near Echo Park. After the temple opened in 1923, McPherson attracted large audiences through dynamic preaching and a reputation as a faith healer. In 1927 she founded the Church of the Foursquare Gospel, a Pentecostal denomination. Even before this she had attracted controversy when she disappeared for a time and then returned, claiming to have been kidnapped.

Mendes, Henry Pereira (1852–1937) *Orthodox rabbi*

Born in England, Henry Mendes came to America in 1877 after serving as a rabbi in Manchester, England. He accepted a position as rabbi of Congregation Shearith Israel in New York City, where he served for more than 40 years. He sided with Orthodox Judaism against Reform Judaism, and together with Rabbi Sabato Morais of the Mikveh Israel congregation in Philadelphia, he helped found the Jewish Theological Seminary in New York in 1887. He served as president of the seminary from 1897 to 1902, leaving this post after the seminary came to embrace the views of Conservative Judaism.

Merton, Thomas (1915–1968) *Trappist monk*

The 20th century's most famous Catholic writer, Thomas Merton converted to Catholicism in 1938 while a graduate student. Following this conversion he entered the Trappist order and became a Trappist priest in 1949. Soon after joining the order his superiors recognized his talent as a writer and encouraged him in this vocation. He published *Thirty Poems* in 1944 and more important a best-selling spiritual autobiography titled *The Seven Storey Mountain* in 1947. Over the following years he continued to write prodigiously. Late in his life he became interested in comparisons between Western and Eastern mystical traditions and made a trip to India and Thailand to explore the connections between these traditions. While in Bangkok, Thailand, however, he died as a result of an accidental electrocution.

Miller, William (1782–1849) *founder of the Adventist movement*

Miller earned an important place in American religious history due to his predictions concerning the imminent appearance of Christ. After his conversion in a revival meeting Miller became a serious Bible student and eventually concluded that Christ would soon return to the Earth and establish his millennial kingdom. He initially predicted that Christ's appearance would occur sometime between March 21, 1843, and March 21, 1844. When this period passed he revised his prediction by declaring that Christ would return on October 22, 1844. When this date also passed without any evidence that Christ had returned, most of Miller's disciples—Millerites, as they were known—experienced "the Great Disappointment." Some, however, led by Ellen Gould Harmon White, continued to believe in Christ's imminent appearance and established Adventist churches.

Moody, Dwight Lyman (1837–1899) *revivalist*
The 19th century's most famous evangelist, Dwight L. Moody exchanged a career as a shoe salesman for full-time Christian ministry in 1858. After working for the U.S. Christian Commission during the Civil War, Moody became president of the Chicago YMCA after the war. While visiting England on YMCA business in 1872, he gained an invitation to return for a series of revival meetings, and when he did so took singer Ira Sankey along for what became a successful two-year series of revival meetings in Great Britain. In 1875 Moody and Sankey returned to the United States and launched revival campaigns in one after another of the nation's great cities. Toward the end of the decade Moody established schools for boys and girls in his hometown of Northfield, Massachusetts, and in 1880 founded the Northfield Conference, an annual meeting for students. In 1887 he established a school for Bible study called the Chicago Evangelization Society, renamed after his death the Moody Bible Institute.

Moon, Sun Myung (1920–   ) *founder of the Unification Church*
While still a teenager Korean-born Sun Myung Moon became convinced that Jesus had appeared to him and had commissioned him to divine service. By the mid-1940s Moon began teaching that the human race had been corrupted by Satan's physical seduction of Eve and awaited a new messiah who would provide physical salvation by marrying a perfect woman. After Moon moved to North Korea he was imprisoned for a time and upon his release in 1950 began writing what would eventually be published as the *Divine Principle*. In 1954 he founded the Holy Spirit Association for the Unification of World Christianity, commonly known as the Unification Church. The church's missionaries brought its teaching to the United States in the 1960s, and Moon himself visited America in the early 1970s and published an English translation of the *Divine Principle* in 1973. He spent time in an American prison for tax evasion. He announced formally in 1993 that he was the messiah.

Morais, Sabato (1823–1897) *Jewish rabbi*
One of Orthodox Judaism's most important American leaders during the 19th century, Sabato Morais was born in Italy and received his rabbinical education there, being ordained a rabbi in 1845. He subsequently migrated first to London and then in 1851 to Philadelphia, where he assumed the position of *hazan* at Congregation Mikveh Israel in Philadelphia, where he served until his death, more than 45 years later. In 1875 he joined with Isaac Mayer Wise in helping to establish the Hebrew Union College in Cincinnati, Ohio, but controversy over dietary issues at the college's first graduation ceremony prompted the more Orthodox Morais to separate from Wise, Reform Judaism's most important leader of the time. He subsequently joined in establishing the Jewish Theological Seminary in New York in 1886 as a more conservative alternative to Hebrew Union College. Morais served as president and professor at the new institution from 1887 until his death.

Muhammad, Elijah (1897–1975) *Nation of Islam leader*
An automobile factory worker when he met Wallace Fard in 1931, Robert Poole soon joined Fard's Lost-Found Nation of Islam and changed his name to Elijah Muhammad. When Fard disappeared mysteriously in 1934, Muhammad relocated to Chicago, where he soon established the headquarters of the Nation of Islam, proclaiming that Fard had been an incarnation of Allah and that Muhammad was his prophet. Muhammad refused to serve in the military during World War II and consequently spent four years in prison beginning in 1942. After his release, however, the Nation of Islam experienced rapid growth. During the later part of the 1940s, he gained an important disciple with the conversion of Malcolm Little (later renamed Malcolm X) while Little was serving a prison sentence. After the release of Malcolm X on parole in 1952, he soon became Muhammad's most important deputy, eventually serving as Muhammad's national representative beginning in 1962. The two men had a falling out toward the end of the next year, however, and Malcolm X subsequently left the Nation of Islam. Louis Farrakhan subsequently assumed Malcolm X's role within the Nation of Islam until Muhammad's death in 1975.

Murray, John Courtney (1904–1967) *Catholic priest, theologian*
One of the 20th century's most important Catholic theologian's, John Courtney Murray played an influential role in the Catholic Church's statements concerning religious liberty in connection with Vatican II. He was ordained a Catholic priest in 1933 and received his doctorate in sacred theology in 1936 from Gregorian University in Rome. Murray subsequently joined the faculty of Woodstock College in Maryland, where he taught for the remainder of his life and where he gradually earned the

reputation as the foremost Catholic theologian in America. During the 1950s he came into conflict with Catholic authorities over his church-state views. Official Catholic teaching of the time insisted that the ideal arrangement in societies was for the Catholic Church to be the officially established religion. Religious liberty and disestablishment were, under this view, mere accommodations to the reality that Catholics were not a majority in many places. Murray, however, viewed religious liberty and religious disestablishment as good in themselves. Ultimately he served as an adviser to the U.S. delegation to Vatican II in 1962 and helped draft the council's statement concerning religious liberty, titled *Dignitatis humanae personae,* which adopted many of his views.

Niebuhr, Helmut Richard (1894–1962) *theologian*

Though one of 20th-century America's most influential theologians, H. Richard Niebuhr never quite escaped the shadow of his more illustrious theologian brother, Reinhold Niebuhr. The father of both brothers was a minister in the German Evangelical Synod of North America, and each of the two initially served as ministers in this denomination. In 1919 H. Richard Niebuhr joined the faculty of Eden Theological Seminary, from which he and his brother had both graduated. He eventually earned a Ph.D. from Yale and joined the faculty of Yale Divinity School. Influenced like his brother by neo-orthodox theology, H. Richard Niebuhr's important works included *The Social Sources of Denominationalism* (1929) and *Christ and Culture* (1951).

Niebuhr, Reinhold (1892–1971) *theologian*

One of the 20th century's most influential American theologians, Reinhold Niebuhr was the minister of the Bethel Evangelical Church in Detroit, Michigan, from 1915 to 1928. In 1928 he joined the faculty of Union Theological Seminary and also the Socialist Party, of which he would remain a member and sometimes political candidate until 1940. Influenced by the neo-orthodox theology of Karl Barth and others, Niebuhr earned a reputation for realistic appraisals of the place of power in political and social processes. His book *Moral Man and Immoral Society* (1932) specifically rejected the idea that individual virtues could necessarily be practiced by societies. In this and other works he argued that the reality of sin justified the exercise of political power to achieve justice.

Noyes, John Humphrey (1811–1886) *Utopian leader*

The founder of the Oneida community, one of the 19th century's most famous utopian groups, John Humphrey Noyes experienced a revivalistic conversion shortly after he completed college at Dartmouth in 1830. He studied to become a minister at Andover Theological Seminary and Yale Divinity School, but by 1834 he had become convinced that Christ had returned to the earth in A.D. 70 and had made human perfection possible. Soon he gathered a group of disciples around him in Putney, Vermont, whom he taught that marriage should not be confined to one man and one woman but should involve multiple sexual relationships. Neighbors looked on the practice of complex marriage by Noyes and his followers with great suspicion, prompting Noyes to be charged with adultery in 1847. He and his followers responded by relocating to Oneida, New York, where he began to dictate the sexual couplings that would be allowed among the community. Eventually many of his followers drifted away, and the remainder reorganized their communal relationship in the form of a joint stock company in 1881.

Olcott, Henry Steel (1832–1907) *Theosophical Society cofounder*

The founder with Helena Petrovna Blavatsky of the Theosophical Society, Henry Steel Olcott served in the Civil War and worked subsequently as a journalist and then a lawyer. He met Blavatsky in the course of investigating psychic phenomena at a farm in Chittenden, Vermont. The following year, in 1875, the two established the Theosophical Society, a religious movement that mingled Western spiritualism with aspects of Eastern religion. Olcott served as the organization's president, while Blavatsky produced the group's main religious teachings, beginning with those announced in *Isis Unveiled* (1877). In 1878 Blavatsky and Olcott traveled to India, where they lectured widely and where in 1882 they established the world headquarters of the Theosophical Society on an estate they had purchased at Adyar. Both became increasingly interested in Eastern religious practices, and this interest led to their becoming Buddhists in 1880. Olcott published a *Buddhist Catechism* in 1885. He parted ways with Blavatsky around this time after an investigator sent to India by the Society for Psychical Research in England accused her of fraud. For the remainder of his life he served as president of the Theosophical Society.

Palmer, Phoebe Worrall (1807–1874) *Holiness preacher*

An important leader in the early Holiness movement, Phoebe Worrall Palmer became a lay revival preacher after she experienced what Holiness theology characterizes as entire sanctification in 1837. She preached widely in the United States, Canada, and Great Britain. She published her first book, *The Way of Holiness*, in 1845 and after the Civil War edited the magazine *Guide to Holiness* from 1862 to 1874. For roughly four decades she conducted regular weekly meetings called the Tuesday Meeting for the Promotion of Holiness. In addition to these activities Palmer devoted substantial energy to establishing rescue missions for the poor, including the Five Points Mission in New York City.

Parker, Quanah (ca. 1852–1911) *Native American political and religious leader*
Born the son of a Comanche warrior and a white mother, Quanah Parker became a leader among the Comanche after his tribe was consigned to a reservation in Oklahoma. He proved successful at negotiating with whites seeking to obtain grazing rights from his people and still later negotiated with the federal government on behalf of the Comanche. Parker also supported the growth of peyote religion among the Comanche. Peyoteism involved the ritual consumption of peyote buttons, a hallucinogen, and reflected a marriage of traditional Native American and Christian religious ideas. In the 20th century various practitioners of peyoteism organized themselves officially as the Native American Church.

Peale, Norman Vincent (1898–1993) *Methodist minister, author*
The popular author of *The Power of Positive Thinking* (1952), Norman Vincent Peale was a principal exemplar of the prosperity gospel during the middle years of the 20th century. Pastor initially of a small Methodist church in Brooklyn, New York, and then of a Dutch Reformed congregation in New York City called the Marble Collegiate Church, Peale began a radio broadcast called *The Art of Living* in 1933, which gained a wide audience. This program and his best-selling book *The Power of Positive Thinking* made Peale one of the most popular Christian preachers and writers of the 20th century.

Penn, William (1644–1718) *Quaker leader, founder of Pennsylvania*
Born into a wealthy family, William Penn became a Quaker while on a business trip for his father in Ireland in 1667. He subsequently became an influential apologist for Quakerism and for religious liberty, publishing the *Great Case for Liberty of Conscience* (1670) after he spent time in jail for his faith. In 1681 King Charles II granted Penn a charter to land in America as a way of repaying a debt to Penn's father. Penn seized this opportunity to establish a colony in America characterized by its significant respect for religious freedom. Personal financial difficulties ultimately forced Penn to spend time in debtors prison, however, after which he eventually returned to England. He spent the rest of his life in England tending by long distance the affairs of the colony that bore his name—Pennsylvania.

Rauschenbusch, Walter (1861–1918) *Baptist theologian, social reformer*
One of the main leaders in what came to be known as the Social Gospel movement, Walter Rauschenbusch received his undergraduate and theological degrees from the University of Rochester in the 1880s. After seminary he served as pastor of the Second German Baptist Church in the part of New York City known as Hell's Kitchen. When he joined the faculty of Rochester Seminary in 1897, he brought to his academic career a firm conviction that the Christian gospel could not ignore social circumstances and that Christians were obligated to bring gospel principles to bear upon the social structures and problems of the modern industrial world. In 1907 he published *Christianity and the Social Crisis* and in 1913, *Christianizing the Social Order*, both central texts of the Social Gospel movement.

Robertson, Pat (1930–) *television personality*
The son of a U.S. senator, Pat Robertson served in the marines during the Korean War and on his return graduated from Yale University Law School in 1955. After he failed to pass the bar, Robertson worked for a few years in business before experiencing a religious conversion and determining to become a minister. Following his graduation from New York Theological Seminary in 1959, Robertson moved to Virginia, where he bought a television station and founded the Christian Broadcast Network (CBN) in 1960. The network aired its first program in 1961, and Robertson was ordained a Southern Baptist minister the same year. In the early 1960s he solicited 700 viewers to support CBN as partners, and from this venture developed the *700 Club*, which adopted the format of a Christian talk show and was widely viewed. The success of his television network allowed Robertson to found CBN University (later Regent University) in 1978. A decade later he tried to use his national prominence to secure the Republican nomination for president of the United States. When he was unsuccessful he founded the

Christian Coalition in 1989, which engaged in a variety of political activities in support of conservative causes. Both this organization and Robertson's television program remained active into the 21st century.

Rowlandson, Mary (ca. 1637–1711) *Puritan author*
Famous for writing a narrative about her captivity for a time among American Indians of New England, the details of Rowlandson's early life are obscure. In 1656 she married Joseph Rowlandson, Puritan minister of the town of Lancaster, Massachusetts. She was taken captive along with three of her children and other relatives and neighbors in a raid on the town by Narragansett Indians in 1676 during King Philip's War. During her 11 weeks in captivity one of the children captured with her, six-year-old daughter Sarah, died, and she was separated from her other two children. Eventually she was ransomed and returned home, and subsequently the two children who survived captivity also were restored to her. Her husband died shortly after this incident, and she then remarried and wrote what became a best-selling account of her ordeal, *A Narrative of the Captivity and Restoration of Mrs. Mary Rowlandson*, published in 1682.

Russell, Charles Taze (1852–1916) *founder of the Watch Tower Bible and Tract Society (later the Jehovah's Witnesses)*
After exposure to Presbyterianism and Congregationalism, Charles Taze Russell eventually migrated to Adventism. In the early 1870s he led a Bible study group and began predicting that Jesus would spiritually return to the earth in 1874 and establish his millennial kingdom in 1914. Russell established the Watch Tower Bible and Tract Society in the early 1880s and incorporated the organization in 1884. Beginning in 1906 through to his death, Russell penned a series of Bible studies articulating his views eventually published as *Studies in Scripture* in 1917. These studies included a denial that Jesus was God, a theological position that placed him at odds with orthodox Christianity and distinguished his group from other strands of Adventist belief.

Rutherford, Joseph Franklin (Judge Rutherford) (1869–1942) *Jehovah's Witnesses leader*
A lawyer in his early adult life and briefly a specially appointed state judge, Judge Rutherford, as he preferred to be called, joined the Watch Tower Bible and Tract Society in 1906 and became one of the group's legal advisers. After the death of the group's founder, Charles Taze

Russell, in 1916, Rutherford was able to gain control of its various satellite organizations. From this position he led the society into a program of aggressive evangelism and to a stance of conscientious objection during World War I. For this stance Rutherford and other members of the society were imprisoned for a time. For the aggressive evangelism into which he led the society in the 1930s the Witnesses experienced recurring conflicts with local communities, which used a variety of legal devices to discourage witnessing and solicitation by the Jehovah's Witnesses. In 1920 he predicted that the end of the world would occur in 1925, and the uneventful passage of this date caused some Witnesses to drift away from the group.

Ryan, John Augustine (1869–1945) *Catholic priest, social reformer*
Nicknamed by one critic the Right Reverend New Dealer for his support of the progressive policies of President Franklin D. Roosevelt, John Ryan was a leading Catholic voice in support of social reform during the first half of the 20th century. Beginning with the publication of his dissertation in 1906, *A Living Wage: Its Ethical and Economic Aspects*, Ryan took an active part in advocating such reforms as progressive taxation and the minimum wage from his position as a member of the faculty of Catholic University. He drafted the influential statement adopted by the National Catholic Welfare Conference in 1920, titled *The Bishops' Program of Social Reconstruction*. His support for President Roosevelt ultimately caused him to become the first Catholic to deliver a benediction at a presidential inauguration at the beginning of Roosevelt's second term in office and won him appointment to the Industrial Appeals Board of the National Recovery Administration in 1934.

Sankey, Ira David (1840–1908) *revival singer, hymn composer*
After serving in the Union army during the Civil War, Ira Sankey worked as a tax collector while regularly singing at revivals and churches in Pennsylvania, where he lived. As president of a local chapter of the YMCA, Sankey attended the international meeting of the YMCA held in Indianapolis in 1870. There he met revivalist Dwight L. Moody, and the two formed an association that made them the most well-known revival team in the 19th century. They became internationally prominent after a successful series of revival meetings in Great Britain from 1873 to 1875 and returned to America to equal success. During a long career as a revival singer, Sankey also wrote

songs, perhaps the most famous of which was the gospel hymn "The Ninety and Nine."

Scofield, Cyrus Ingerson (1843–1921) *Congregationalist-Presbyterian minister, author of the Scofield Reference Bible*

Admitted to practice law in Kansas in 1869 and twice elected to the Kansas legislature in the early 1870s, C. I. Scofield attracted an unsavory reputation for dishonesty until he experienced a religious conversion in 1877. He subsequently became a Congregationalist minister, serving churches in St. Louis, Missouri, and Dallas, Texas, until 1895, when Dwight L. Moody, the 19th-century revivalist, invited Scofield to become the minister of the Trinitarian Congregationalist Church of East Northfield, Massachusetts, Moody's home church, and to become president of the Northfield Bible Training School. While in Northfield Scofield undertook the task of preparing an elaborate collection of Bible notes that offered a guide to dispensationalist premillennialism, a theological view that asserts that Christ will soon return to the Earth and establish his millennial kingdom. Published in 1909 by Oxford University Press, the Scofield Reference Bible helped popularize and defend the views of fundamentalism in general and dispensationalist premillennialism in particular. About the time of this publication, Scofield migrated from Congregationalism to Presbyterianism, the latter being more hospitable to his conservative theology.

Seabury, Samuel (1729–1796) *Episcopal bishop*

The son of a Congregational minister who converted to Anglicanism about the time he was born, Samuel Seabury pursued a career as a minister and a physician. After graduating from Yale he studied medicine at the University of Edinburgh and was ordained an Anglican priest in 1753. When he returned to America he served parishes in New Jersey and New York. During the revolutionary period Seabury was sufficiently vocal in his opposition to independence that he eventually had to take refuge on Long Island behind British lines after war began. Subsequently, though, he adjusted to the new political reality and became a leading force among those who labored to see an Episcopal bishop appointed for America. In November 1784 Seabury was, in fact, appointed to this position himself and consecrated bishop of Connecticut.

Sheen, Fulton John (1895–1979) *Catholic bishop, radio and television personality*

Ordained a Catholic priest in 1919, Fulton Sheen became one of America's most prominent 20th-century Catholic leaders. He joined the faculty of the Catholic University of America in 1926 and spent almost a quarter of a century there teaching philosophy and theology and writing prolifically. His most famous book was *Peace of Soul* (1949), which continued an ongoing debate he had with modern psychology. Leaving his university post in 1950, he became the national director for the Society for the Propagation of Faith and the following year was ordained titular bishop of Caesariana and auxiliary bishop of the archdiocese of New York. Even before the publication of *Peace with Soul*, Sheen had become famous as host of a radio program called *The Catholic Hour*, which began broadcasting in 1930. In the 1950s he shifted to television, airing the *Life Is Worth Living* program from 1951 to 1957 and *The Bishop Sheen Program* from 1961 to 1968.

Sheldon, Charles Monroe (1857–1946) *Congregationalist minister, author*

Among the many books espousing the tenets of the Social Gospel movement, the one with the widest popular influence was not a work of expository prose but of fiction. *In His Steps*, published by Charles Sheldon in 1897, offered a fictional account of a community in which Christians attempt to weigh their courses of action by asking "What would Jesus do?" Minister of the Central Congregational Church in Topeka, Kansas, beginning in 1888, Sheldon emphasized a Christ "for the common people" and led his church to engage in a variety of social services to the common people of Topeka, including the residents of Tennesseetown, a black ghetto near Sheldon's church. Begun as a series of stories Sheldon read to his congregation on Sunday evenings starting in 1891, *In His Steps* eventually sold millions of copies and became the most popular work produced by the Social Gospel movement.

Silver, Abba Hillel (1893–1963) *Reform rabbi, Zionist leader*

Though he grew up within the tradition of Reform Judaism and became a Reform rabbi, Abba Hillel Silver possessed a commitment to Zionism not normally shared by Reform Jews of the early 20th century. He started a Zionist club while still a boy and spoke at the 10th annual convention of the Federation of American Zionists when he was 14 years old. He graduated from Hebrew Union College in 1915 and eventually became the rabbi for a prominent Reform congregation, Tifereth Israel, in Cleveland, Ohio. Though he remained associated with this congregation for the rest of his life, his energies were directed most vigorously toward the cause of Zionism.

Together with Rabbi Stephen S. Wise, he served as co-chair of the American Zionist Emergency Council beginning in 1943 and lived to see the recognition of Israel as an independent nation in 1948.

Smith, Hannah Whitall (1832–1911) *Holiness preacher, author*

Though formally Quakers, both Hannah Whitall Smith and her husband, Robert Pearsall Smith, experienced revivalistic conversions in 1858. Toward the end of the next decade, they also experienced what Holiness groups refer to as the second blessing or entire sanctification. They subsequently traveled widely in both American and England preaching at Holiness conferences and gatherings. In 1875 Hannah Whitall Smith published one of the enduring classics of what came to be known as the Higher Life movement, *The Christian's Secret of a Happy Life*. Though she and her husband were present as speakers at the Brighton Conventions for the Promotion of Holiness in the spring of 1875, a precursor of the Keswick Convention launched that summer, they returned to America under a cloud of suspicion relating to supposed sexual immorality on the part of Robert. This experience distanced Smith from further activity in the Higher Life movement, and she turned her energies instead to the temperance movement in America until she and her husband relocated to England in 1887, a few years before her death.

Smith, Joseph (1805–1844) *founder of the Church of Jesus Christ of Latter-day Saints*

Founder of the Church of Jesus Christ of Latter-day Saints, commonly referred to as the Mormon Church, Joseph Smith claimed to have received a visit from the angel Moroni in the fall of 1823, who told him where to find golden plates inscribed in an ancient language accompanied by two stones needed to translate the plates. Four years later Smith claimed to retrieve the plates and set about translating them, finally publishing this translation in 1830 as the *Book of Mormon*, which recounted a history of America in which Christ had appeared before his crucifiction. That year he also founded the Church of Jesus Christ, later renamed the Church of Jesus Christ of Latter-day Saints. By 1831 Smith had moved with his followers to Kirtland, Ohio. They were eventually forced to move again, however, to Missouri, although their clashes with local residents ultimately prompted the governor of the state to threaten the Mormons with annihilation if they did not leave the state. By the end of 1839 Smith had established a new community named Nauvoo in Illinois on the Mississippi River. Two years later he began encouraging a circle of Mormon leaders to join him in the practice of polygamy. After Smith declared his candidacy for U.S. president in 1844, a local newspaper published a critique of Mormonism, and Smith ordered it shut down. For this he was arrested and jailed in Carthage, Illinois. While in jail he and his brother Hyrum were killed by a mob.

Smohalla (1815–1895) *American Indian prophet*

Smohalla was a medicine man and later prophet of the Wanapum tribe in the Pacific Northwest. In the late 1850s he was nearly killed in a fight with Chief Moses of the Sinkiuse tribe. By some accounts Smohalla escaped for a time to Mexico and later returned to Washington via Utah, where he came into contact with Mormons. In any event, he began to teach that a millennial kingdom was imminent in which American Indians would be resurrected and whites would disappear. His teaching led to a revitalization of the Washani, or Longhouse, religion.

Stoddard, Solomon (1643–1729) *Puritan minister*

Stoddard became the minister for the church in Northampton, Massachusetts, in 1669. He gained notoriety over the next two decades by altering significantly the terms of membership for his church. At the time he became a minister, most New England churches required evidence of an individual's conversion as a basis for church membership. Stoddard changed this requirement in two ways. First, he admitted as full church members so-called Half-Way members, that is, children of baptized but unconverted parents who had themselves been baptized as infants. Second, and even more controversially, Stoddard opened membership in his church—in particular, the right to participate in the ordinance of the Lord's Supper—to those who affirmed basic Christian doctrines and led morally upright lives, even if they could not give evidence that they had been converted. Stoddardism, as his position came to be called, was enormously influential in western Massachusetts and Connecticut.

Stone, Barton Warren (1772–1844) *leader in the Christian Restorationist movement*

Ordained a Presbyterian minister in 1797 after experiencing a revival conversion, Barton Stone participated with other preachers in the Cane Ridge Revival of 1801, often identified as the beginning of the Second Great Awakening. By 1803, however, his disagreements with other Presbyterians led to his being expelled from the Transylvania presbytery, of which he had been a member. Though he and other like-minded ministers organized the Springfield presbytery, they soon moved outside the bounds of Presbyterianism altogether by disbanding this ecclesiastical association and publishing "The Last Will and Testament of the Springfield Presbytery." Subsequently, claiming the Bible as their only source of spiritual authority, Stone and others named themselves simply Christians. Stone began publishing the *Christian Messenger* in 1826, which argued for an end to the various denominations that divided Christians. The resulting Christian movement ultimately joined with the Disciples of Christ, led by Alexander Campbell, in the early 1830s, thus combining the two most important branches of what is now known as the Restorationist movement in Protestant Christianity.

Strong, Josiah (1847–1916) *Congregationalist minister, social reformer*
One of the architects of the Social Gospel movement, Josiah Strong, a Congregationalist minister and denominational leader, earned national recognition with the publication of his first book, *Our Country: Its Possible Future and Its Present Crisis*, in 1885. Appointed general secretary of the Evangelical Alliance in 1886, he used this position to foster Christian engagement in the work of social reform. Though he was considered a progressive voice at the time, later critics have condemned the anti-Catholicism present in his first book as well as his panegyric to the superiority of the Anglo-Saxon race in *The New Era: or the Coming Kingdom* (1893). Like many other adherents of the Social Gospel in the late 19th and early 20th centuries, Strong was an early ally of the ecumenical movement.

Sunday, Billy (William Ashley Sunday) (1862–1935) *revivalist*
A baseball player who eventually became the most prominent evangelist of the early 20th century, Billy Sunday played successively with the Chicago White Stockings, the Pittsburgh Alleghenies, and finally the Philadelphia Phillies. He experienced conversion at a mission in Chicago in the mid-1880s and eventually surrendered his baseball glove in 1891 to work full time for the Chicago YMCA. Subsequently he worked briefly as an advance agent for revivalist J. Wilbur Chapman and then after Chapman retired to a stationary pastorate became a revival preacher himself beginning in 1896. For nearly two

decades his career of revival preaching made him the most well-known evangelist in America, although it did not assure him nomination as the Republican candidate for president of the United States when he ran for this office in 1920.

Suzuki, Daisetz Teitaro (1870–1966) *Buddhist teacher*
A Japanese Buddhist who studied at Engakuji, a Zen Buddhist temple in Kamakura, Japan, Suzuki came to the United States in 1897, where he worked with Paul Caros on the magazine *Open Court*. He subsequently helped Caros translate the *Tao te ching* into English and in 1907 published a survey of Buddhist teaching titled *Outlines of Mahayana Buddhism*. Two years later he returned to Japan, where he remained during the first half of the 20th century, holding various academic posts and continuing his work of making Buddhist teaching accessible to readers of English. After World War II, however, he returned again to America, where he taught first at the University of Hawaii and then in 1951 at Columbia University. After his retirement from academic life in 1957, he helped establish the Cambridge Buddhist Society in Cambridge, Massachusetts.

Szold, Henrietta (1860–1945) *Zionist leader, founder of Hadassah*
The daughter of a rabbi, Henrietta Szold showed an early aptitude that would have made her a rabbi had this been possible for a woman of her time. Instead she became a teacher, a writer, and then the literary secretary of the Jewish Publication Society of America in 1893. After she moved to Baltimore to care for her father, she joined the Zionist Association of Baltimore in 1897 and then in 1899 became a member of the executive council of the Federation of American Zionists. When her father died in 1902, she moved to New York and became the first female student of the Jewish Theological Seminary. She also joined a women's group devoted to Zionism known as the Hadassah Study Circle. In 1912 this group became the nucleus of a new women's organization called the Daughters of Zion, later renamed Hadassah, and Szold was elected its president. She served in this position until 1926, when she became more active in Palestinian affairs. With the rise of Nazism she helped organize a project called *Jugendaliyah*, the "coming out of the youths," designed to rescue European Jewish youths and relocate them to Palestine. This work occupied most of the remaining years of her life.

Tekakwitha, Kateri (1656–1680) *Catholic lay leader*
Kateri Tekakwitha was an American Indian convert to Catholicism, the daughter of a Mohawk chief and an Algonquian mother who was converted to Christianity. Father James de Lamberville visited her village when she was a young adult; under his teaching Tekakwitha became a Christian and was baptized in 1676. Ostracized thereafter by her village, Tekakwitha eventually made an arduous journey to the French mission of St. Francis Xavier at Sault St. Louis on the St. Lawrence River, near Montreal, Canada. There she took a vow of chastity, for which she became known as the Lily of the Mohawks, and practiced a vigorous asceticism that led to her death in 1680 at the age of 24. She eventually became the first American Indian proposed for sainthood by the Catholic church and was beatified by Pope John Paul II in 1980.

Tennent, Gilbert (1705–1764) *Presbyterian minister*
After graduating from Yale in 1725, Gilbert Tennent was licensed to preach by the Philadelphia presbytery. He was ordained the pastor of a church in New Brunswick, New Jersey, and there he formed an important friendship with the Dutch Reformed minister Theodorus Jacobus Frelinghuysen. Under the influence of Frelinghuysen, Tennent developed a revivalist preaching style that would anticipate the more prominent preaching of George Whitefield. Whitefield's preaching tour of the American colonies in 1740 sparked the Great Awakening, and Tennent accompanied Whitefield on this historic tour. Following the beginning of the Great Awakening, Presbyterians split between those ministers who supported this revival and those who opposed it. Tennent, not surprisingly, was among the supporters and participated in the formation of the New York synod, an association of like-minded ministers and their churches. In 1758, however, Tennent led in reconciling the New York and Philadelphia presbyteries and served as the first moderator of the reunited Presbyterians.

Tenskwatawa (the Shawnee Prophet) (1775–1836) *Native American religious leader*
Known as the Shawnee Prophet, Tenskwatawa helped revitalize American Indian religion in the early 19th century. He was born Lalawethika (the Noisemaker), the son of a Shawnee war chief in Ohio and the brother of the Shawnee leader Tecumseh. After an unsuccessful career as a medicine man, he experienced visions in 1805 that caused him to change his name to Tenskwa-

tawa and to vow not to drink alcohol. Three years later he and his brother Tecumseh relocated to Prophetstown in Indiana, where Tenskwatawa's influence and the still greater influence of his brother attracted many followers to Tenskwatawa's teachings. William Henry Harrison, then the governor of the Indiana Territory, led a military force against those gathered at Prophetstown in 1811. Though Tenskwatawa assured his followers that the weapons of the white soldiers would not hurt them, Harrison destroyed Prophetstown and killed many of the Native Americans there. He and his brother subsequently sided with the British during the War of 1812, and after Tecumseh's death in battle in 1813 Tenskwatawa fled to Canada, where he remained until he returned to the United States late in life and helped relocate the Shawnee in Ohio to a reservation in Kansas.

Tillich, Paul (1886–1965) *theologian*
Ordained a minister in the Evangelical Lutheran Church in 1912, after World War I Paul Tillich held a variety of academic posts in German universities. When the Nazis came to power in 1933, he was dismissed from his position at the University of Frankfurt for having publicly defended the cause of Jewish students. With the assistance of American theologian Reinhold Niebuhr, however, he came to the United States and joined the faculty of Union Theological Seminary in New York. In this position he gained increasing prominence for theological reflection aimed at engaging the anxieties of the age. He joined the faculty of Harvard University in 1955 and in 1962 was appointed the Nuveen Professor of Theology at the University of Chicago Divinity School.

Turner, Henry McNeal (1834–1915) *bishop of the African Methodist Episcopal Church*
Licensed a minister for the Methodist Episcopal Church, South in 1853 when he was 19, Henry McNeal Turner subsequently joined the African Methodist Episcopal (AME) church and served as minister to congregations in Baltimore and Washington, D.C. He was the first African American commissioned as a chaplain during the Civil War, and he served a regiment of black soldiers he helped organize called the First U.S. Colored Troops. After the war he worked as a missionary for the AME Church in the states of the former Confederacy. In the 1860s and 1870s he served for brief periods in the Georgia legislature before he was elected a bishop of the AME Church in 1880 and settled in Savannah. In the latter years of his life he warred against racist assumptions often implicit in

American Christianity, gaining notoriety for claiming in 1895 that "God is a Negro."

Webb, Muhammad Alexander Russell (1846–1916) *convert to Islam*

Raised in a Presbyterian family, Webb rejected Christianity by the time of his early adulthood. After working as a journalist and a magazine editor, he was appointed consul general for Manila, the Philippines, in 1887. While in Manila Webb converted to Islam, and he is thought to be the first white American convert to this religion. After several years Webb resigned his appointment and made a lecture tour of India before returning to the United States in 1893. He settled in New York, where he established the Oriental Publishing Company and began publishing *Moslem World.* The year he returned to the United States he also attended the World's Parliament of Religions in Chicago, where he gained prominence as an advocate of Islam.

White, Ellen Gould Harmon (1827–1915) *founder of the Seventh-Day Adventist Church*

After William Miller predicted that Christ would return to the Earth in 1844, many of his disciples experienced the Great Disappointment when the date predicted passed without the appearance of Christ. Ellen Gould Harmon White, however, experienced the first of many visions that year that confirmed her faith in Christ's imminent appearance. Along with her husband, James S. White, another former Millerite, she began an itinerant preaching ministry that year. She taught that Christians should worship on Saturday, the day of the Jewish Sabbath, and she also guided her disciples toward a focus on issues of health, including avoiding alcohol and tobacco and relying on natural remedies rather than physicians. Eventually she and her husband organized the believers who followed her teachings into churches named Seventh-Day Adventist in 1860 and into a formal denomination in 1863.

Whitefield, George (1714–1770) *revivalist*

Ordained an Anglican minister, George Whitefield was associated for a time with John and Charles Wesley's Holy Club at Oxford University, from which Methodism would spring. Whitefield, who was a Calvinist, eventually drifted out of the Methodist orbit and became famous in both England and America as a revival preacher. He visited America for the first time in 1738 and conceived the idea of establishing an orphanage in Georgia. He

traveled back to England to raise funds for this project, returned to the American colonies in 1739, and the next year began a preaching tour along the Atlantic seaboard that was instrumental in igniting the Great Awakening. He generally preached outdoors because no building could accommodate the thousands of listeners who flocked to hear him wherever he stopped to preach. On this visit he also established the orphanage he had dreamed of in Georgia and named it Bethesda. For the remainder of his life he traveled back and forth across the Atlantic numerous times, forging a model of revivalism that would play a dominant part in the religious life of America.

Willard, Francis Elizabeth Caroline (1839–1898) *social reformer*

After graduating from college, Francis Willard held a number of teaching positions before being named president of the Evanston College for Ladies in 1871 and then dean of women at Northwestern University in 1873. With the founding of the Women's Christian Temperance Union in 1874, Willard became first its corresponding secretary and then in 1879 its president for the remainder of her life. Although the union's first president focused the organization's efforts solely on temperance activities, Willard expanded its agenda to include a variety of social reforms, including women's suffrage and prison reform. She remained a Methodist all her life, though she became a socialist in 1889 and thereafter lobbied for public ownership of railroads, utilities, and factories.

Williams, Roger (ca. 1603–1683) *founder of the Providence Colony, advocate for religious liberty*

Roger Williams was banished from the Massachusetts Bay Colony in 1635 for his outspoken criticisms of the colony's government. Among his more significant charges against the colony were his complaints against the lack of religious liberty there and his insistence that King Charles I of England had no business giving away land in the New World and that colonists should have purchased their land from the American Indians who occupied it prior to the European arrivals. After leaving Massachusetts Williams helped establish the Providence Colony in what is now Rhode Island and secure official recognition of the colony from the English government. Though he served for a time as pastor of the Congregational church in Salem and later helped establish the first Baptist church in America, he eventually became a Seeker, believing that no true church existed any longer in the world. He is famous for his lively defenses of religious liberty in print, especially his book *The Bloody Tenet of Persecution*.

Winthrop, John (1588–1649) *early governor of the Massachusetts Bay Colony*

A member of the original Massachusetts Bay Company, John Winthrop was a wealthy Puritan layman who arrived with other colonists in Massachusetts in 1630 on board the *Arabella*. While onboard ship he delivered a famous sermon titled "A Model of Christian Charity" that articulated a vision of establishing a City upon a Hill in Massachusetts and counseled his fellow travelers on how they might achieve this ideal. Once arrived, he served as governor of the colony for most of the rest of his life and helped to superintend the close alliance between church and state that existed in the Massachusetts Bay Colony. His journal, *The History of New England from 1630 to 1649*, is a crucial source of information about early New England life.

Wise, Isaac Mayer (1819–1900) *Reform rabbi*

Called the father of Reform Judaism in the United States, Isaac Mayer Wise immigrated to America with his family from Bohemia in 1846. He served initially as rabbi of Congregation Beth-El in Albany, New York, but after conflict in this congregation over his Reform Judaism views, he left and established the Anshe Emeth congregation. Within several years, however, Wise accepted a position as rabbi of Congregation B'nai Yeshrun in Cincinnati, Ohio, where he remained the rest of his life. There he set about strengthening Reform Judaism in the United States. He published a Reform prayer book, *Minhag America*, in 1857 and helped establish institutions that would lie at the center of American Reform Judaism—the Union of American Hebrew Congregations in 1873, Hebrew Union College in Cincinnati in 1875, and the Central Conference of American Rabbis in 1883. Wise served as president of the Hebrew Union College and the Central Conference for the remainder of his life.

Wise, Stephen S. (1874–1949) *Reform rabbi, Zionist leader*

While Reform Jews in the early 20th century were generally unenthusiastic about the creation of a Jewish homeland in Palestine, Stephen Wise devoted himself to this cause. Initially rabbi of a Reform congregation in Portland, Oregon, Wise relocated to New York City in 1906, where he established an independent congregation called the Free Synagogue, which he led for almost four decades. History remembers him more, however, for his devotion to the cause of Zionism. He was a founding member of the Federation of American Zionists in 1898 and helped to create the American Jewish Congress in 1916. He worked closely with Louis Brandeis, associate justice of the U.S. Supreme Court, to further the cause of Zionism. Dissatisfied with Reform Judaism's lack of enthusiasm for a Jewish homeland, in 1922 he also helped to establish the Jewish Institute of Religion in New York as an alternative to Hebrew Union College in Cincinnati, Ohio, the premier educational institution of Reform Judaism in the United States.

Woodworth-Etter, Maria Beulah (1844–1924) *Holiness and Pentecostal evangelist*

Undertaking the ministry of an itinerant evangelist around 1880, Woodworth-Etter became one of the most prominent preachers of the late 19th and early 20th centuries. She did not attach herself to any particular denomination but was generally aligned with the Holiness movement until around 1912, when she became a Pentecostal. Known for standing with her hands outstretched for long periods during her services, Woodworth-Etter's popularity as a revival preacher suffered decline after she predicted in 1890 that an earthquake and a tidal wave would destroy Alameda, Oakland, and San Francisco on April 14 of that year. Even so, she remained active as an evangelist well into the 20th century.

Wovoka (Jack Wilson) (ca. 1856–1932) *Native American religious leader*

The son of American Indian shaman Tavibo, Wovoka was a leading figure in the Ghost Dance movement of 1890. Though raised by white parents after his father died, Wovoka acquired a reputation as a medicine man among his people. In the late 1880s he claimed to have received a revelation that a messiah would soon appear who could oversee the resurrection of all the dead Native Americans and the disappearance of whites. Wovoka taught his followers that participation in the Ghost Dance would hasten these events. Though he himself seems to have advised peaceful relations between American Indians and whites, Sioux who adopted the Ghost Dance interpreted it as a charter for militancy against whites. U.S. authorities subsequently came to distrust the movement, and this distrust partially fueled the massacre by U.S. troops of more than 200 Sioux men, women, and children at Wounded Knee on the Pine Ridge Indian Reservation in South Dakota on December 29, 1890. Wovoka eventually disassociated himself from the Ghost Dance movement until the early years of the 20th century, when he again helped stimulate a revival of the Ghost Dance.

Young, Brigham (1801–1877) *president of the Church of Jesus Christ of Latter-day Saints*
Brigham Young was the second president of the Church of Jesus Christ of Latter-day Saints, commonly known as the Mormons. He converted from Methodism to Mormonism in 1832 and soon joined Joseph Smith in Kirtland, Ohio, where the Mormon leader had set up headquarters. By 1835 Young had been appointed one of 12 apostles who assisted Smith in leadership of the church. After the Mormons relocated to Nauvoo, Illinois, and Smith was eventually killed by a mob, Young assumed leadership of the Mormons. He led the group in a migration west and in 1847 declared Salt Lake, Utah, their new home. After Congress declared Utah a territory, he served as first territorial governor from 1850 to 1857. Though conflict with federal authorities forced him to relinquish this post in 1857, he continued to lead the Mormons for another two decades.

Zinzendorf, Nicolaus Ludwig von (1700–1760) *Moravian leader*
Born into Austrian nobility, Nicolaus Ludwig von Zinzendorf was a leader within the German Pietism movement of the 18th century. This reform movement within German Lutheranism emphasized the importance of personal piety and holiness, its adherents believing that mainstream Lutheranism had improperly elevated formal assent to creed and participation in the sacraments over individual piety. Zinzendorf gave shelter to a group of Pietist refugees from Moravia who settled on his estate in Saxony and established a village called Herrnhut. With these Pietistic believers he helped establish the Church of the Brethren, also known as the Renewed Moravian Church, in 1727. After being temporarily exiled from Saxony, Zinzendorf traveled to America for 18 months beginning in 1741, where he attempted unsuccessfully to unite the various German Protestant groups and helped to establish a Moravian community in Bethlehem, Pennsylvania. While in America he also undertook missionary activities among American Indians in Pennsylvania.

Appendix C
Maps

Maps

1. Major societies of North and Central America, ca. 1500
2. Indian villages established by Puritan missionary John Elliot, to 1674
3. George Whitefield's tour of America, 1739–41
4. Anglican Church in Colonial America, to 1758

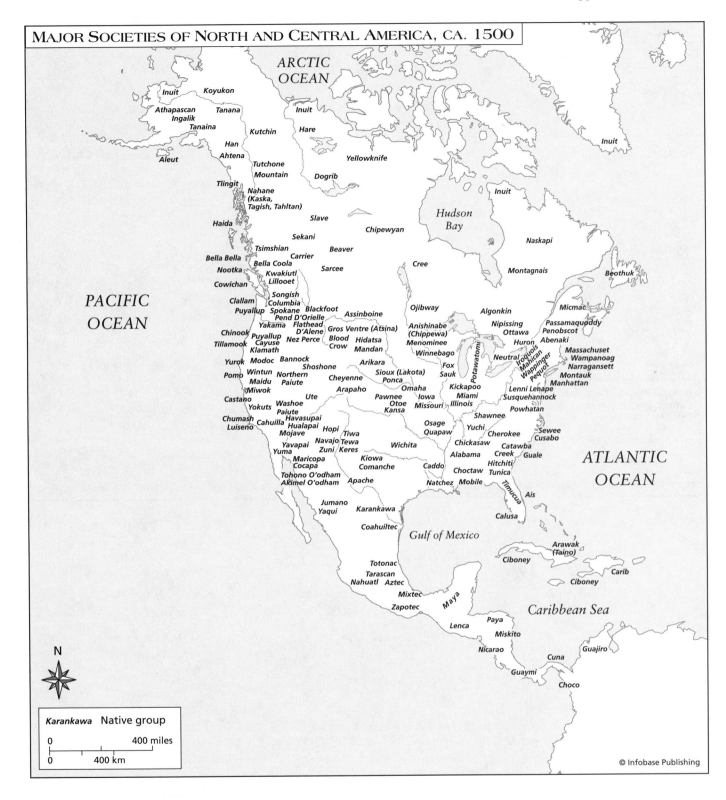

MAJOR SOCIETIES OF NORTH AND CENTRAL AMERICA, CA. 1500

ARCTIC OCEAN

Inuit

Koyukon

Inuit

Athapascan
Ingalik

Tanana

Inuit

Tanaina

Kutchin

Hare

Han

Ahtena

Yellowknife

Aleut

Tutchone
Mountain

Dogrib

Tlingit

Nahane
(Kaska,
Tagish, Tahltan)

Slave

Hudson
Bay

Inuit

Haida

Sekani

Chipewyan

Naskapi

Tsimshian

Beaver

Cree

Montagnais

Bella Bella

Carrier

Sarcee

Beothuk

Nootka

Bella Coola

Kwakiutl

Cowichan

Lillooet

Songish

Ojibway

Algonkin

Micmac

PACIFIC
OCEAN

Clallam

Columbia

Blackfoot

Assinboine

Nipissing

Passamaquoddy

Puyallup

Spokane
Pend D'Orielle

Anishinabe
(Chippewa)

Ottawa

Penobscot

Yakama

Flathead
D'Alene

Gros Ventre (Atsina)

Huron

Abenaki

Chinook

Puyallup
Cayuse

Nez Perce

Blood
Crow

Hidatsa

Menominee

Neutral

Iroquois

Massachuset

Tillamook

Klamath

Mandan

Winnebago

Mahican

Wampanoag

Wappinger

Narragansett

Yurok

Modoc

Bannock

Arikara

Fox

Pequot

Montauk

Pomo

Wintun

Shoshone

Sioux (Lakota)

Sauk

Manhattan

Northern
Paiute

Cheyenne

Ponca

Kickapoo

Lenni Lenape

Maidu

Omaha

Miami

Susquehannock

Miwok

Arapaho

Pawnee

Iowa

Illinois

Castano

Ute

Otoe

Missouri

Powhatan

Yokuts

Washoe
Paiute

Kansas

Osage

Shawnee

Yuchi

Chumash

Havasupai

Cahuilla

Hualapai

Hopi

Quapaw

Cherokee

Sewee

Luiseno

Mojave

Tiwa

Wichita

Chickasaw

Catawba

Cusabo

Yavapai

Navajo
Zuni

Tewa
Keres

Alabama

Creek

Guale

Yuma

Kiowa

Caddo

Choctaw

Hitchiti

ATLANTIC
OCEAN

Maricopa
Cocapa

Comanche

Tunica

Tohono O'odham

Apache

Natchez

Mobile

Akimel O'odham

Timucua

Ais

Jumano
Yaqui

Karankawa

Calusa

Coahuiltec

Gulf of Mexico

Arawak
(Taino)

Totonac

Ciboney

Carib

Tarascan
Nahuatl

Aztec

Ciboney

Mixtec

Maya

Caribbean Sea

Zapotec

Lenca

Paya

Nicarao

Miskito

Guajiro

Cuna

Guaymi

Choco

N

Karankawa   Native group

0   400 miles

0   400 km

© Infobase Publishing

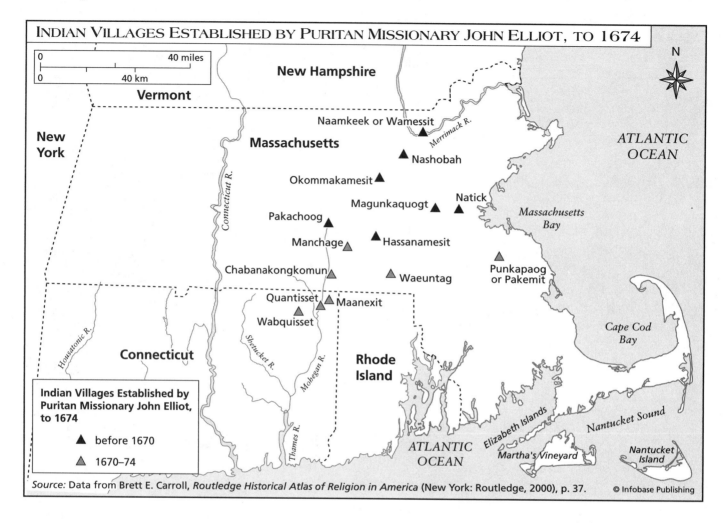

INDIAN VILLAGES ESTABLISHED BY PURITAN MISSIONARY JOHN ELLIOT, TO 1674

Source: Data from Brett E. Carroll, *Routledge Historical Atlas of Religion in America* (New York: Routledge, 2000), p. 37.   © Infobase Publishing

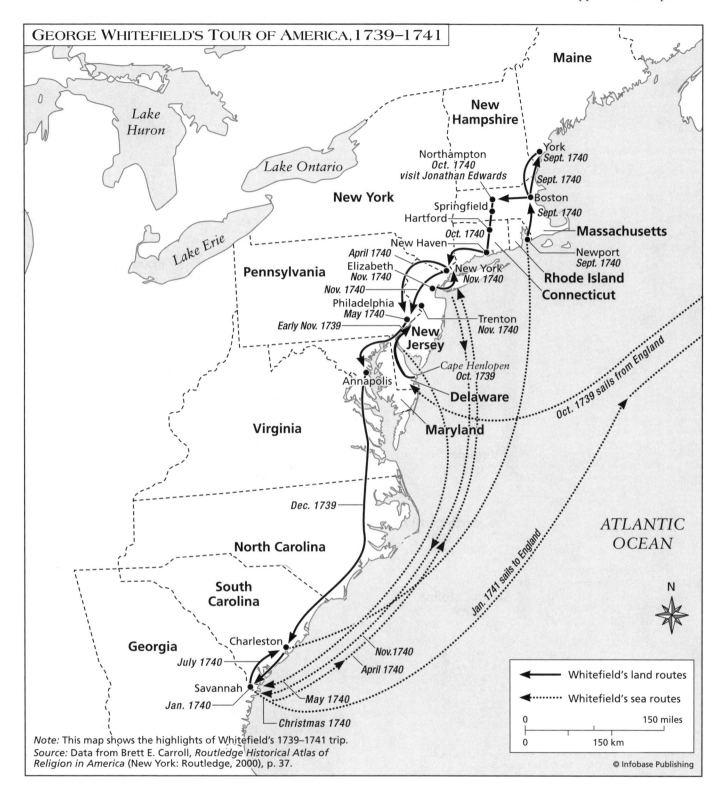

GEORGE WHITEFIELD'S TOUR OF AMERICA, 1739–1741

Maine

New Hampshire

Lake Huron

Lake Ontario

New York

Lake Erie

Pennsylvania

Northampton
*Oct. 1740
visit Jonathan Edwards*

York
Sept. 1740

Sept. 1740

Springfield
Hartford

Boston
Sept. 1740

Oct. 1740

New Haven

Massachusetts

April 1740
Elizabeth
Nov. 1740

New York
Nov. 1740

Newport
Sept. 1740

Rhode Island
Connecticut

Nov. 1740

Philadelphia
May 1740

Early Nov. 1739

New Jersey

Trenton
Nov. 1740

*Cape Henlopen
Oct. 1739*

Oct. 1739 sails from England

Annapolis

Delaware

Maryland

Virginia

Dec. 1739

ATLANTIC
OCEAN

North Carolina

Jan. 1741 sails to England

South
Carolina

N

Georgia

Charleston

Nov. 1740

July 1740

April 1740

Savannah

May 1740

Jan. 1740

Christmas 1740

	Whitefield's land routes
	Whitefield's sea routes

0 — 150 miles

0 — 150 km

Note: This map shows the highlights of Whitefield's 1739–1741 trip.
Source: Data from Brett E. Carroll, *Routledge Historical Atlas of Religion in America* (New York: Routledge, 2000), p. 37.

© Infobase Publishing

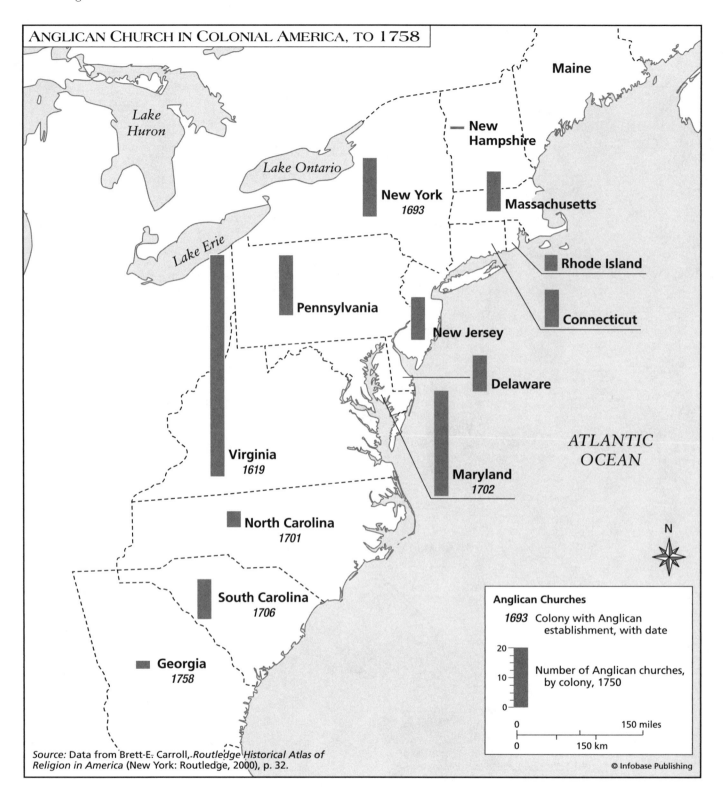

ANGLICAN CHURCH IN COLONIAL AMERICA, TO 1758

Maine

Lake Huron

Lake Ontario

New York
1693

New Hampshire

Massachusetts

Lake Erie

Pennsylvania

Rhode Island

Connecticut

New Jersey

Delaware

Virginia
1619

Maryland
1702

ATLANTIC OCEAN

North Carolina
1701

South Carolina
1706

N

Georgia
1758

Anglican Churches

1693 Colony with Anglican
establishment, with date

20 —
10 —
0 —

Number of Anglican churches,
by colony, 1750

0   150 miles
0   150 km

Source: Data from Brett-E. Carroll, *Routledge Historical Atlas of Religion in America* (New York: Routledge, 2000), p. 32.

© Infobase Publishing

Appendix D
Graphs and Tables

Graphs

1. Percentage of religious adherents among Americans, 1776–2000
2. Religious adherents by denomination, 1776 and 1850
3. Methodist and Baptist denominational family adherents, 1776–1980
4. Religious adherents per 1,000 population, 1850
5. Total adherents by denomination, 1850–1890
6. Shares of select religious groups, 1940–2000

Tables

1. Number of congregations per denomination, 1776
2. Market shares of religious denominations per 1,000 church members, 1940–2000

PERCENTAGE OF RELIGIOUS ADHERENTS AMONG AMERICANS, 1776–2000

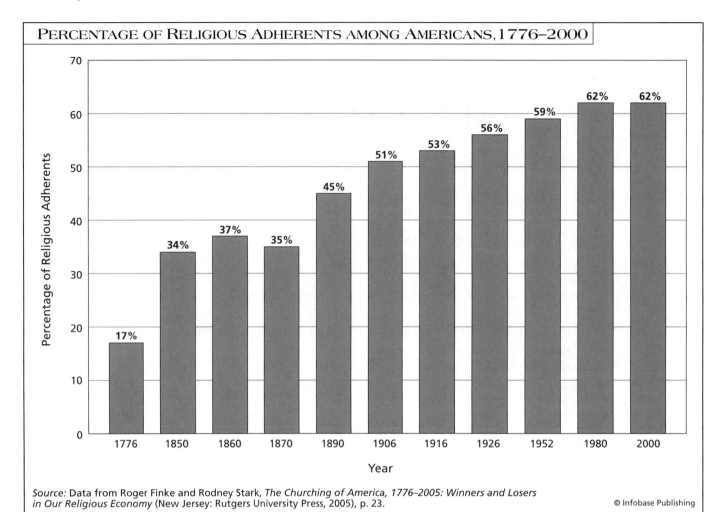

Source: Data from Roger Finke and Rodney Stark, *The Churching of America, 1776–2005: Winners and Losers in Our Religious Economy* (New Jersey: Rutgers University Press, 2005), p. 23.

© Infobase Publishing

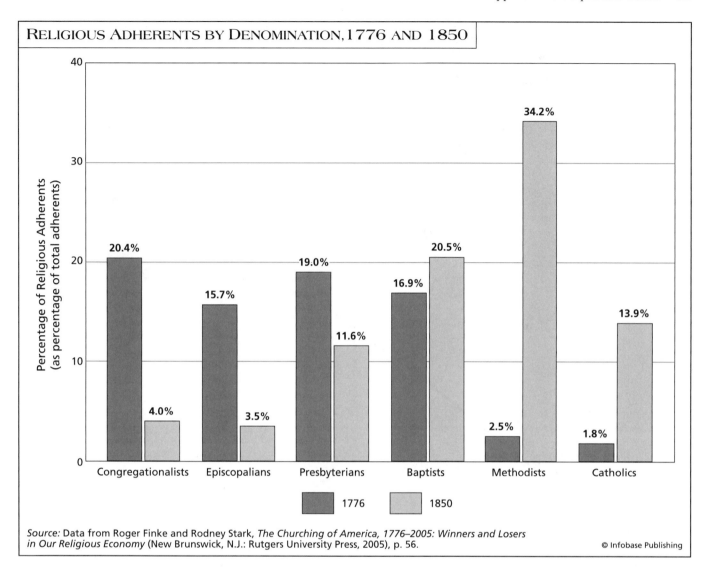

RELIGIOUS ADHERENTS BY DENOMINATION, 1776 AND 1850

Source: Data from Roger Finke and Rodney Stark, *The Churching of America, 1776–2005: Winners and Losers in Our Religious Economy* (New Brunswick, N.J.: Rutgers University Press, 2005), p. 56.

© Infobase Publishing

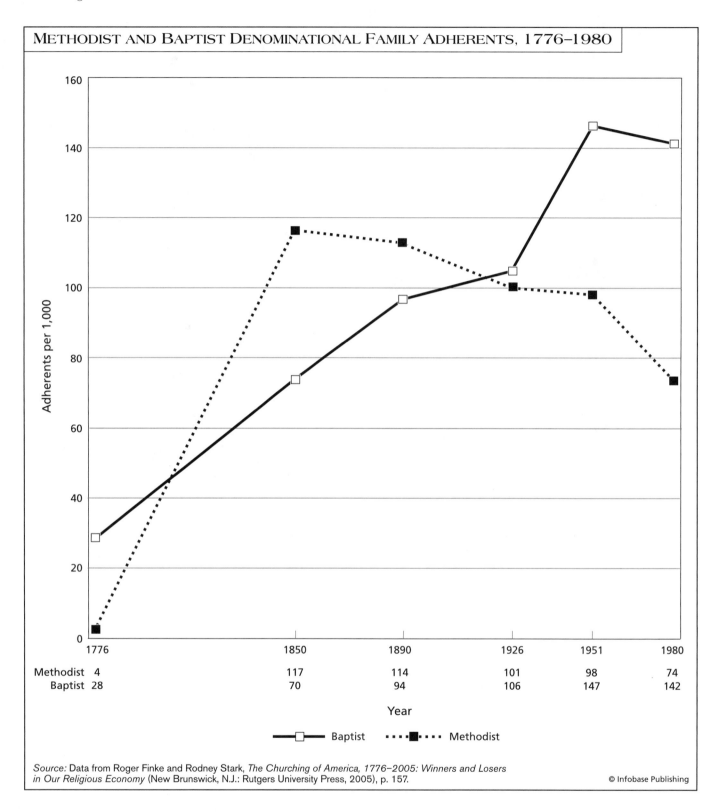

METHODIST AND BAPTIST DENOMINATIONAL FAMILY ADHERENTS, 1776–1980

	1776	1850	1890	1926	1951	1980
Methodist	4	117	114	101	98	74
Baptist	28	70	94	106	147	142

Year

□ Baptist ■ Methodist

Source: Data from Roger Finke and Rodney Stark, *The Churching of America, 1776–2005: Winners and Losers in Our Religious Economy* (New Brunswick, N.J.: Rutgers University Press, 2005), p. 157.

© Infobase Publishing

RELIGIOUS ADHERENTS, 1850

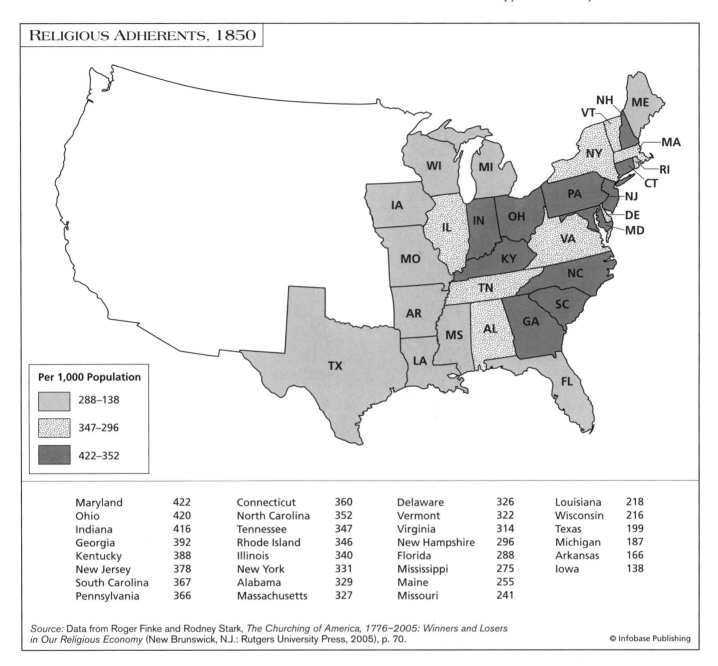

Per 1,000 Population

	288–138
	347–296
	422–352

Maryland	422	Connecticut	360	Delaware	326	Louisiana	218
Ohio	420	North Carolina	352	Vermont	322	Wisconsin	216
Indiana	416	Tennessee	347	Virginia	314	Texas	199
Georgia	392	Rhode Island	346	New Hampshire	296	Michigan	187
Kentucky	388	Illinois	340	Florida	288	Arkansas	166
New Jersey	378	New York	331	Mississippi	275	Iowa	138
South Carolina	367	Alabama	329	Maine	255		
Pennsylvania	366	Massachusetts	327	Missouri	241		

Source: Data from Roger Finke and Rodney Stark, *The Churching of America, 1776–2005: Winners and Losers in Our Religious Economy* (New Brunswick, N.J.: Rutgers University Press, 2005), p. 70.

TOTAL ADHERENTS BY DENOMINATION, 1850–1890

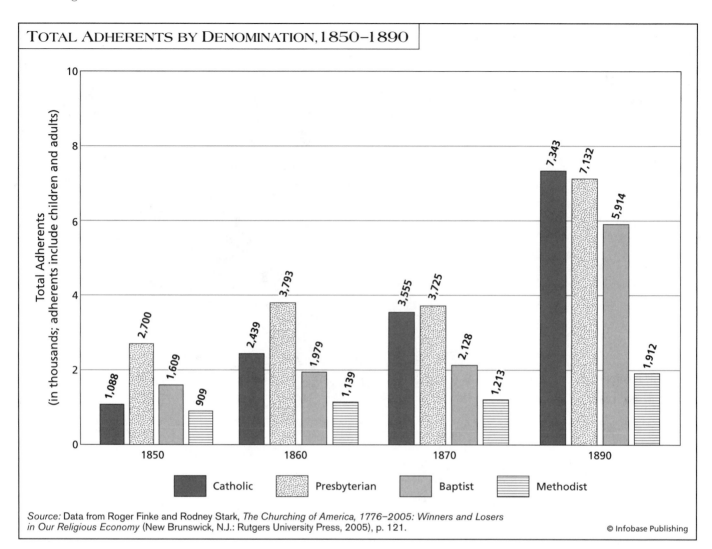

Total Adherents
(in thousands; adherents include children and adults)

Catholic   Presbyterian   Baptist   Methodist

Source: Data from Roger Finke and Rodney Stark, *The Churching of America, 1776–2005: Winners and Losers in Our Religious Economy* (New Brunswick, N.J.: Rutgers University Press, 2005), p. 121.

© Infobase Publishing

Shares of Select Religious Groups, 1940–2000

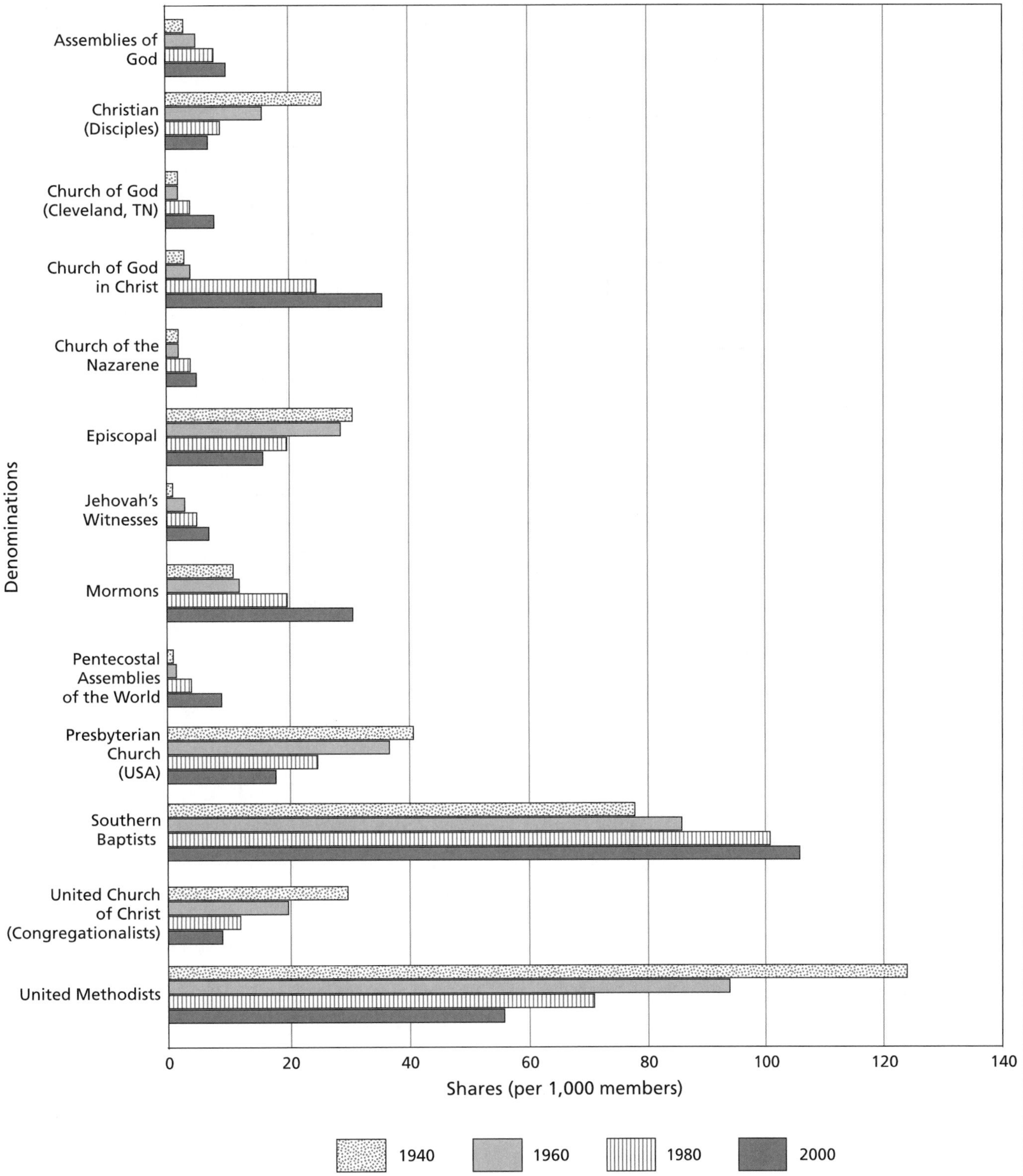
Assemblies of God
Christian (Disciples)
Church of God (Cleveland, TN)
Church of God in Christ
Church of the Nazarene
Episcopal
Jehovah's Witnesses
Mormons
Pentecostal Assemblies of the World
Presbyterian Church (USA)
Southern Baptists
United Church of Christ (Congregationalists)
United Methodists
Denominations
0
20
40
60
80
100
120
140
Shares (per 1,000 members)
1940
1960
1980
2000

Source: Data from Roger Finke and Rodney Stark, *The Churching of America, 1776–2005: Winners and Losers in Our Religious Economy* (New Brunswick, N.J.: Rutgers University Press, 2005), p. 121.

© Infobase Publishing

Number of Congregations per Denomination, 1776

Denomination	Number of Congregations
Congregational	668
Presbyterian*	588
Baptist†	497
Episcopal	495
Quakers	310
German Reformed	159
Lutheran§	150
Dutch Reformed	120
Methodist	65
Catholic	56
Moravian	31
Separatist and Independent	27
Dunker	24
Mennonite	16
Huguenot	7
Sandemaniah	6
Jewish	5
TOTAL	3,228

Source: Paullin (1932).
*Includes all divisions such as New Light, Old Light, Associate Reformed, etc.
†Includes all divisions such as Separate, Six Principle, Seventh Day, Rogerene, etc.
§Includes all synods.

Market Shares of Religious Denominations per 1,000 Church Members, 1940–2000

Religious Denomination	1940	1960	1980	2000	1940–2000 Percentage Loss or Gain
MAINLINE					
United Methodists	124.7	93.0	70.6	54.8	−56%
Presbyterian Church (USA)	41.7	36.4	24.3	16.6	−60%
Episcopal	31.4	28.6	20.7	15.3	−51%
Christian (Disciples)	25.7	15.7	8.7	5.4	−79%
United Church of Christ (Congregationalists)	26.5	19.6	12.9	9.1	−66%
EVANGELICALS					
Southern Baptists	76.7	85.0	100.9	104.9	+37%
Church of God in Christ	2.6	3.4	24.7	36.2	+1292%
Assemblies of God	3.1	4.4	7.8	9.9	+221%
Pentecostal Assemblies of the World	NA	0.4	3.7	9.9	+2375%
Church of God (Cleveland, Tenn.)	1.0	1.5	3.2	5.9	+501%
Church of the Nazarene	2.6	2.7	3.6	4.2	+63%
OTHER COSTLY RELIGIONS					
Mormons	12.0	13.0	20.9	30.8	+157%
Jehovah's Witnesses	NA	2.2	4.2	6.6	+200%

Source: Calculated from multiple editions of the *Yearbook of American and Canadian Churches.* "Inclusive membership" estimates are used for all denominations except the Assemblies of God and the Presbyterian Church (USA). Due to a lack of "inclusive" estimates for earlier years, their rates are based on the smaller totals known as "full member" estimates. The 2000 rate for the Church of God in Christ is based on a 1991 membership estimate.

Glossary

advent The calendar period during which Christians celebrate the birth of Jesus.

agnosticism The belief that it is not possible to know whether God exists.

altar call The event in some evangelical Protestant services when individuals are requested to make a public profession of their faith in Christ.

Anabaptists Protestant groups during the Reformation who insisted that the ordinance of baptism was not appropriate for infants but only for those old enough to have personal faith in Christ.

Anglican Relating to the Church of England. Outside England this religious tradition is referred to as Episcopalianism.

Antichrist According to Christian teaching, a diabolical opponent of Christ during the end times.

antinomianism For New England Puritans, the spiritual error of denying the importance of moral rules of conduct, the allegation of which against Anne Hutchinson led to her being banished.

anti-Semitism An attitude reflecting hostility to Jews or Judaism.

apocalypse A revelation, ordinarily relating to the end of time.

apologist Someone who defends or otherwise offers explanations in support of a particular faith.

apostolic succession The idea within the Christian tradition that certain religious leaders such as the pope derive their authority from a line of succession that reaches back to the original apostles of Jesus.

archdiocese In Catholicism, the chief diocese, led by an archbishop, who oversees a collection of dioceses.

Arianism Theological beliefs inconsistent with orthodox Christian belief in the Trinity, inherited from Arius, an Alexandrian priest of the fourth century A.D., who denied that Jesus was God.

Arminianism Theological views named for 16th-century Dutch Protestant theologian Jacobus Arminius that emphasize the free will of individuals and the ability of each individual to receive salvation as a matter of choice, in contrast with Calvinism.

Ashkenazic Jews Jews practicing traditions originating from Germanic lands.

atonement The means according to which God and sinners are reconciled, particularly in Judaism and Christianity. Prior to the destruction of the Jewish temple in Jerusalem in A.D. 70, atonement for Judaism involved sacrifices offered to God. Subsequently Judaism emphasized the practice of various religious observances as accomplishing atonement. Christians have seen atonement accomplished in the death of Christ on the cross but have differed in their understandings of how his death accomplishes atonement.

Azusa Street Revival The evangelical Christian awakening that occurred in Los Angeles in 1906 prompted by the preaching of African-American minister William Seymour and that was the precursor of the charismatic movement.

Calvinism The strand of Protestant Christianity, also referred to as the Reformed tradition, that emphasizes the sovereignty of God, the total depravity of humankind, and the election of particular individuals by God for salvation.

camp meetings Originating at the beginning of the 19th century, religious encampments at which families participated in multiple revival services each day.

catechism A summary of Christian doctrine, traditionally posed in the form of questions and answers.

charismatic movement A movement within Christianity that emphasizes miraculous gifts of the Holy Spirit, such as prophecy, healing, and speaking in tongues (glossolalia).

circuit riding   The practice, especially among early Methodists, of an itinerant minister serving several congregations rather than being settled with a single congregation.

convent   A communal residence for nuns.

conversion   The experience of adopting a new religious faith, or, in evangelical Christianity, of receiving salvation through personal faith in Christ.

cosmology   A theory or understanding concerning the nature of the universe.

creationism   Views relating to the origins of the world and humankind, often opposed to Darwinism, that emphasize the divine role in creation rather than natural explanations for the world's existence.

diocese   In Catholicism, the jurisdiction governed by a bishop.

ecclesiology   The study of the church.

encyclical   A letter addressed by the Catholic pope to the entire church.

Eucharist   The celebration in Christian churches of the death of Christ, also known as the Lord's Supper and Communion.

evangelical   A term derived from a Greek word meaning "gospel," or "good news," used to describe Christian believers—generally Protestants—who emphasize the importance of a personal conversion experience.

excommunication   The process by which a member is removed from the activities and life of a church.

Ghost Dance   A ritual practiced by certain American Indians that emphasizes the imminent return of the dead to join with the living in a new world.

glossolalia   Speaking in tongues, considered by certain Pentecostal and charismatic Christian groups as a miraculous gift of the Holy Spirit.

Great Awakening   A sustained and widespread revival movement experienced by the American colonies around the 1740s.

Half-Way Covenant   A compromise established by Congregational churches in the 17th century according to which the children of parents who had themselves been baptized but never obtained church membership might be baptized, although the children thus baptized were generally not considered church members or permitted to participate in the ordinance of the Lord's Supper until they had given evidence of a conversion experience.

homily   A sermon.

hush harbor   A secret location to which southern slaves gathered to worship privately.

liturgy   The official prayers, readings, and other events in a religious service.

Mass   In Catholicism, the celebration of the Eucharist, in which a priest presides and the laity participate.

mesmerism   The practice of inducing trancelike states as a means of acquiring healing or other spiritual powers.

Messiah   The anointed messenger of God, whom some Jews believe is still to come and whom Christians believe was Jesus.

monotheism   A belief that there is only one God.

original sin   The inherent capacity for sinful conduct believed by many Christians to have been communicated to the human race through the original sin of Adam and Eve.

Oxford Movement   A reform movement within the Church of England during the first half of the 19th century that emphasized the importance of ritual and liturgy.

Pietism   A strand of Protestant Christianity that emphasizes good works and personal holiness rather than doctrinal correctness.

pope   The title given to the head of the Roman Catholic Church.

Presbyterianism   A form of church government whose name is derived from the Greek *presbyteros*, meaning "elder." A branch of the Reformed tradition stemming from the theology of John Calvin, Presbyterianism embraces a hierarchical form of church government in which clergy and laity participate at several distinct levels: individual congregations, presbyteries, synods, and the general assembly. This form of church government is distinguished especially from Congregational structures, which locate church authority primarily in relatively autonomous individual congregations.

rector   A parish priest in Anglican churches or the priest in charge of a school or house for Roman Catholics.

Reformed tradition   The name given to Protestant theology originating with John Calvin, which emphasizes God's sovereignty and his election of particular individuals for salvation.

Restorationism   The theological impulse illustrated especially in the Disciples of Christ that seeks to restore the primitive purity and power of early Christianity unadorned by creeds and traditions.

Rogerenes   Followers of John Rogers, who split away from Rhode Island Baptist congregations to form new churches that worshiped on Saturday and rejected the use of medicine.

sacrament   One of the central rites of the Christian church.

Second Great Awakening   A revival that flourished in America during the 1780s and 1790s.

Sephardic Judaism   Jews and Jewish practices descended from Jews who originally lived in Spain or Portugal but were expelled from those countries in the 1490s.

session   In the organizational structure of Presbyterian churches, the group of elders elected by the congregation to oversee the church's affairs.

Social Gospel   Social reform movement associated with generally liberal Protestant churches at the end of the 19th century and the beginning of the 20th century.

Stoddardism   Late 17th- and early 18th-century Puritan practices named for Solomon Stoddard that liberalized the requirements for church membership and participation in the ordinance of the Lord's Supper.

theism   Belief in a transcendent personal God.

Theosophy   Religious movement combining elements of Western and Eastern traditions founded in the 19th century by Helena Petrovna Blavatsky and Henry Steel Olcott.

Trinitarianism   The orthodox Christian belief that God exists in three persons: the Father, the Son, and the Holy Spirit.

Unitarianism   A movement descended originally from the Christian tradition that rejected the orthodox Christian belief in the Trinity, that is, the belief that God exists in the persons of the Father, the Son, and the Holy Spirit.

Universalism   The belief that all individuals will eventually obtain salvation.

Vatican   The central administration of the Roman Catholic Church.

Westminster Confession   A 17th-century statement of faith of English Presbyterianism.

Notes

Introduction

1. Will Herberg, *Protestant, Catholic, Jew: An Essay in American Religious Sociology* (Garden City, N.Y.: Doubleday, 1955).
2. Diana L. Eck, *A New Religious America: How a "Christian Country" Has Become the World's Most Religiously Diverse Nation* (San Francisco: HarperSanFrancisco, 2001), 2–3.
3. Isaac Kramnick and R. Laurence Moore, *The Godless Constitution: The Case against Religious Correctness* (New York: Norton, 1996).
4. Harvey Cox, *The Secular City: Secularization and Urbanization in Theological Perspective* (New York: Macmillan, 1965).
5. Quoted in Rodney Stark and Roger Finke, *Acts of Faith: Explaining the Human Side of Religion* (Berkeley: University of California Press, 2000), 58.
6. Charles M. Sheldon, *In His Steps* (New York: [n.p.], 1899).

1. Migrations and Meetings: 1500–1620

1. Jake Page, *In the Hands of the Great Spirit: The 20,000 Year History of American Indians* (New York: Free Press, 2003), 28; Jon Butler, Grant Wacker, and Randall Balmer, *Religion in American Life* (Oxford: Oxford University Press, 2000), 19.
2. Joel W. Martin, *The Land Looks After Us: A History of Native American Religion* (Oxford: Oxford University Press, 2001), 15.
3. David E. Stannard, *American Holocaust: Columbus and the Conquest of the New World* (New York: Oxford University Press, 1992), 32, 41.
4. Charles H. Lippy, Robert Choquette, and Stafford Poole, *Christianity Comes to the Americas, 1492–1776* (New York: Paragon House, 1992), 29.
5. Page, *In the Hands of the Great Spirit*, 13.

6. William A Young, *Quest for Harmony: Native American Spiritual Traditions* (New York: Seven Bridges Press, 2002), 14–15.
7. Richard Erdoes and Alfonso Orti, eds., *American Indian Myths and Legends* (New York: Pantheon Books, 1984), 83, quoted in John Corrigan and Winthrop S. Hudson, *Religion in America: An Historical Account of the Development of American Religious Life,* 7th ed. (Upper Saddle River, N.J.: Pearson/Prentice Hall, 2004), 15.
8. Mircea Eliade, *The Sacred and the Profane: The Nature of Religion,* trans. by Willard R. Trask (New York: Harcourt, Brace, 1959).
9. Brian Moynahan, *The Faith: A History of Christianity* (New York: Doubleday, 2002), 506.
10. Edwin S. Gaustad and Leigh E. Schmidt, *The Religious History of America.* rev. ed. (San Francisco: HarperSanFrancisco, 2002), 17.
11. Ibid., 19.
12. Ibid., 37.
13. Ibid., 38.

2. The City on a Hill and Its Detractors and Alternatives: (1621–1659)

1. John Winthrop, "A Modell of Christian Charity," in *The Puritans: A Sourcebook of Their Writings,* edited by Perry Miller and Thomas H. Johnson, vol. 1 (New York: Harper & Row, 1963), 199.
2. Nathaniel Ward, *The Simple Cobler of Aggawam in America,* edited by P. M. Zall (Lincoln: University of Nebraska Press, 1969), 6.
3. John Cotton, *An Exposition upon the Thirteenth Chapter of the Revelation* (London, 1656), reprinted in part in *The Puritans: A Sourcebook of Their Writings,* vol. 1, 213.
4. Nathaniel B. Shurtleff, ed. *Records of the Governor and Company of the Massachusetts Bay in New England (1628–86),* vol. 1 (Boston: William White, 1853), 88.

5. Timothy L. Hall, *Separating Church and State: Roger Williams and Religious Liberty* (Urbana: University of Illinois Press, 1998), 38.

6. Cotton Mather, *Magnalia Christi Americana* (London: Printed for T. Parkhurst, 1702; New York: Arno Press, 1972), 430.

7. John R. Bartlett, ed., *Records of the Colony of Rhode Island and Providence Plantations, in New England*, vol. 1 (Providence: A. Crawford Greene & Brother, 1856), 14.

8. Richard L. Perry, ed., *Sources of Our Liberties: Documentary Origins of Individual Liberties in the United States Constitution and Bill of Rights* (Chicago: American Bar Foundation, rev. ed. 1978), 170.

9. Roger Williams, *The Bloudy Tenent Yet More Bloody*, in *The Complete Writings of Roger Williams*, vol. 4 (New York: Russell & Russell, 1963), 5.

10. Thomas J. Curry, *The First Freedoms: Church and State in America to the Passage of the First Amendment* (New York: Oxford University Press, 1986), 39.

11. Ibid.

12. Martin E. Marty, *Pilgrims in Their Own Land: 500 Years of Religion in America* (Boston: Little, Brown, 1984), 69.

13. Jonathan D. Sarna, *American Judaism: A History* (New Haven, Conn.: Yale University Press, 2004), 2.

3. New Anxieties: 1660–1699

1. Butler, et al., *Religion in American Life*, 63.

2. John Cotton, *The Bloody Tenent, Washed, and Made White in the Bloud of the Lambe* (1624), in Mark Douglas McGarvie, *One Nation Under Law: America's Early National Struggles to Separate Church and State* (Dekalb: Northern Illinois University Press, 2004), 21.

3. Anson Phelps Stokes, *Church and State in the United States*, vol. 1 (New York: Harper & Brothers, 1950), 206.

4. Richard W. Cogley, *John Eliot's Mission to the Indians before King Philip's War* (Cambridge, Mass.: Harvard University Press, 1999), 1.

5. Ibid., 2.

6. *The Laws and Liberties of Massachusetts* (Birmingham: The Legal Classics Library, 1982), 5.

7. Henry Wadsworth Longfellow, *Giles Corey of Salem Farms*. Available online at URL: http://etext.lib.virginia.edu/toc/modeng/public/LonCore.html. Accessed on August 29, 2005.

8. Peter Charles Hoffer, *The Salem Witchcraft Trials: A Legal History* (Lawrence: University Press of Kansas, 1997), 144.

9. Ibid., 2.

4. Awakenings: 1700–1740

1. Curry, *The First Freedoms*, 82.

2. Milton J. Coalter, *Gilbert Tennent, Son of Thunder: A Case Study of Continental Pietism's Impact on the First Great Awakening in the Middle Colonies* (New York: Greenwood Press, 1986), 14.

3. James Tanis, *Dutch Calvinistic Pietism in the Middle Colonies: A Study in the Life and Theology of Theodorus Jacobus Frelinghuysen* (The Hague: Martinus Nijhoff, 1967), 55–56.

4. Quoted ibid., 82.

5. Roy Hattersley, *The Life of John Wesley: A Brand from the Burning* (New York: Doubleday, 2003), 136.

6. Coalter, *Gilbert Tennent, Son of Thunder*, 43.

7. Jonathan Edwards, "Sinners in the Hands of an Angry God," in *American Sermons: The Pilgrims to Martin Luther King, Jr.*, edited by Michael Warner (New York: Library of America, 1999), 353.

8. Ibid., 356.

9. Ibid., 361.

10. Ibid., 362.

11. *American Sermons*, 900.

5. Revolutionary Religion: 1741–1780

1. G. K. Chesterton, *What I Saw in America* (New York: Dodd, Mead & Co., 1922), 18.

2. Corrigan and Hudson, *Religion in America*, 95.

3. John Cotton, *An Exposition upon the 13th Chapter of the Revelation* (London, 1656), reprinted in part in *The Puritans: A Sourcebook of Their Writings*, edited by Perry Miller and Thomas H. Johnson, vol. 1 (New York: Harper & Row, 1963), 213.

4. Harry S. Stout, *The New England Soul: Preaching and Religious Culture in Colonial New England* (New York: Oxford University Press, 1986), 194–195.

5. Quoted in Philip Davidson, *Propaganda and the American Revolution, 1763–1783* (Chapel Hill: University of North Carolina Press, 1941), 285.

6. The Constitution of Virginia—1776, Bill of Rights, sec. 1 & 16, reprinted in *The Federal and State Constitu-*

tions, edited by F. Thorpe, vol. 7 (Washington, D.C.: Government Printing Office, 1909), 3,813–3,814.

7. Constitution of New York—1777, art. XXXVIII, reprinted in *The Federal and State Constitutions,* vol. 5, 2,637.

8. Delaware Declaration of Rights—1776, reprinted in Philip B. Kurland and Ralph Lerner, *The Founders' Constitution* (Chicago: University of Chicago Press, 1987), vol. 5, p. 70; Constitution of Maryland—1776, Declaration of Rights, § 33, reprinted in *Federal and State Constitutions,* vol. 3, 1,689.

9. Constitution or Form of Government for the Commonwealth of Massachusetts—1780, Part the First, art. III, reprinted in *Federal and State Constitutions,* vol. 3, p. 1,890; Constitution of New Hampshire—1776, Part I, art. VI, reprinted in *Federal and State Constitutions,* vol. 4, 2,454.

10. Constitution of Connecticut—1818, art. I, § 4, reprinted in *Federal and State Constitutions,* vol. 1, 537.

11. South Carolina Constitution—1778, art. XXXVIII, reprinted in *Federal and State Constitutions,* vol. 6, 3,255–3,256.

12. Constitution of Delaware—1792, art. I, sec. 1, reprinted in *Federal and State Constitutions,* vol. 1, 568.

13. Constitution of South Carolina—1790, art. VIII, reprinted in *Federal and State Constitutions,* vol. 6, 326.

6. Religion and the New Nation: 1781–1819

1. Madison to William Bradford, January 24, 1774, in *James Madison on Religious Liberty,* 48.

2. James Madison, "Memorial and Remonstrance Against Religious Assessments," in *James Madison: Writings* (New York: Library of America, 1999), 30.

3. Ryhs Isaac, "The Rage of Malice of the Old Serpent Devil," in *The Virginia Statute for Religious Freedom: Its Evolution and Consequences in American History,* edited by Merrill D. Peterson and Robert C. Vaughan (Cambridge: Cambridge University Press, 1988), 151.

4. Thomas Jefferson, "A Bill for Establishing Religious Freedom," in *Thomas Jefferson: Writings* (New York: Library of America, 1984), 346.

5. Virginia Constitution of 1776, Declaration of Rights, art. 16, reprinted in *Federal and State Constitutions,* vol. 7, 3,814; New Jersey Constitution of 1776, art. XVIII, reprinted in *Federal and State Constitutions,* vol. 5, 2,597.

6. *The Articles of Confederation,* reprinted in Samuel A. Pleasants, *The Articles of Confederation* (Columbus, Ohio: C. E. Merrill, 1968), 60.

7. Stokes, *Church and State in the United States,* vol. 1, 486.

8. Thomas Jefferson to Messrs. Nehemiah Dodge and Others, a Committee of the Danbury Baptist Association, in the State of Connecticut, January 1, 1802, in *Thomas Jefferson: Writings,* 510.

9. Albert J. Raboteau, *Canaan Land: A Religious History of African Americans* (Oxford: Oxford University Press, 2001), 21.

10. Albert J. Raboteu, "Black Christianity in North America," in *Encyclopedia of American Religious Experience: Studies of Traditions and Movements,* ed. by Charles H. Lippy and Peter W. Williams (New York: Charles Scribner's Sons, 1988), vol. 1, 637.

11. Roger L. Nichols, *Indians in the United States and Canada: A Comparative History* (Lincoln: University of Nebraska Press, 1998), 156.

7. Reason and Revivalism: 1820–1840

1. Peter Williams, "Unitarianism and Universalism," in *Encyclopedia of the American Religious Experience: Studies of Traditions and Movements,* vol. 1 (New York: Charles Scribner's Sons, 1988), 579.

2. Charles Grandison Finney, *Lectures on Revivals,* available online at URL: http://xroads.virginia.edu/~HYPER/DETOC/religion/finney1.html. Accessed on August 29, 2005.

3. Corrigan and Hudson, *Religion in America,* 158–159.

4. Quoted in Sidney E. Ahlstrom, *A Religious History of the American People* (New Haven, Conn.: Yale University Press, 1972), 491.

5. Quoted in Black Touchstone, "Planters and Slave Religion in the Deep South," in *Masters & Slaves in the House of the Lord: Race and Religion in the American South—1740–1870,* ed. by John B. Boles (Lexington: University Press of Kentucky, 1988), 103.

6. Raboteau, *Canaan Land: A Religious History of African Americans,* 16.

7. Quoted in Black Touchstone, "Planters and Slave Religion in the Deep South," in *Masters & Slaves in the House of the Lord,* 104–105.

8. David W. Stowe, *How Sweet the Sound: Music in the Spiritual Lives of Americans* (Cambridge, Mass.: Harvard University Press, 2004), 106–107.

8. Expansion and Fractures: 1841–1860

1. Lyman Beecher, *A Plea for the West* (Cincinnati: Truman & Smith, 1835), 12.
2. Quoted in William Alexander Linn, "The Story of the Mormons from the Date of Their Origin to the Year 1901." Available online at URL: http://www.globusz.com/ebooks/Mormons/00000078.htm. Accessed on June 17, 2005.
3. Genesis 9:25–27.
4. Frederick Douglass, *Narrative of the Life of Frederick Douglass, An American Slave*, in *Frederick Douglass: Autobiographies* (New York: Library of America, 1994), 99.
5. Corrigan and Hudson, *Religion in America*, 192.

9. War and Reconstruction: 1861–1880

1. Available online at URL: http://www.law.ou.edu/hist/bathymn.html. Accessed on June 15, 2005.
2. Ahlstrom, *A Religious History of the American People*, 671.
3. Ibid., 670.
4. Abraham Lincoln, "Second Inaugural Address," in *Abraham Lincoln: Writings* (New York: Library of America, 1989), 687.
5. Ibid.
6. For this term, see Paul M. Sniderman and Thomas Piazza, *The Scar of Race* (Cambridge, Mass.: Harvard University Press, 1990).
7. D. Sullins, *Recollections of an Old Man: Seventy Years in Dixie, 1827–1897* (Bristol, Tenn., 1910), p. 327, quoted in Black Touchstone, "Planters and Slave Religion in the Deep South," in *Masters & Slaves in the House of the Lord*, 181.
8. Corrigan and Hudson, *Religion in America*, 242.
9. Leo Pfeffer, *Church State and Freedom* (Boston: Beacon Press, rev. ed. 1967), 241.

10. Immigrants, Industry, and the Social Gospel: 1881–1899

1. Quoted in George W. Ewing, ed., *The Well-Tempered Lyre: Songs & Verse of the Temperance Movement* (Dallas: SMU Press, 1977), 93.
2. Jack S. Blocker, Jr., *American Temperance Movements: Cycles of Reform* (Boston: Twayne Publishers, 1989), 61–64.
3. Quoted ibid., 83.
4. J. S. Slotkin, *The Peyote Religion: A Study in Indian-White Relations* (Glencoe, Ill.: Free Press, 1956), 19.
5. Omer C. Stewart. *Peyote Religion: A History* (Norman: University of Oklahoma Press, 1987), 50–51.
6. John Henry Barrows, "Words of Welcome," in Thomas A. Tweed and Stephen Prothero, *Asian Religions in America: A Documentary History* (New York: Oxford University Press, 1999), 128.
7. By the early 1880s more than 3 million immigrants had reached American shores from China, and Congress attempted to forestall further immigration by passing in 1882 the Chinese Exclusion Act, which suspended immigration from China for a decade. The act was extended in 1892 and then made permanent in 1904 until Congress finally repealed the exclusion policy in 1943.

11. Modernity and Its Critics: 1900–1920

1. Shailer Mathews, *The Faith of Modernism* (New York: Macmillan, 1924), 10.
2. Ibid., 115.
3. Quoted in A. N. Wilson, *God's Funeral* (New York: W. W. Norton & Co., 1999), 184.
4. Quoted in Brasher, *Encyclopedia of Fundamentalism*, 186.
5. Quoted ibid., 187.
6. ""Shall the Fundamentalists Win?": Defending Liberal Protestantism in the 1920s," Available online at URL: http://historymatters.gmu.edu/d/5070/. Accessed on July 4, 2005.
7. Ibid.
8. J. Gresham Machen, *Christianity & Liberalism* (New York: Macmillan, 1923), 8.
9. Allan Anderson, *An Introduction to Pentecostalism: Global Charismatic Christianity* (Cambrige: Cambridge University Press, 2004), 29.
10. Ibid., 29–30.
11. Grant Wacker, *Heaven Below: Early Pentecostals and American Culture* (Cambridge, Mass.: Harvard University Press, 2001), 2.
12. Acts 2:1–12.
13. For the restorationist aspect of Pentecostalism, see Edith L. Blumhofer, *Restoring the Faith: The Assemblies of*

God, Pentecostalism, and American Culture (Urbana: University of Illinois Press, 1993).

14. Anderson, *Introduction to Pentecostalism*, 34.
15. Wacker, *Heaven Below*, 5.
16. Anderson, *Introduction to Pentecostalism*, 39.
17. Quoted in Grant Wacker, "Pentecostalism," in *Encyclopedia of the American Religious Experience: Studies of Traditions and Movements*, edited by Charles H. Lippy and Peter W. Williams (New York: Charles Scribner's Sons, 1988), vol. 2, 933.
18. Anderson, *Introduction to Pentecostalism*, 40.

12. Under the Shadows of World Wars: 1921–1950

1. Available online at URL: http://www.law.umkc.edu/faculty/projects/ftrials/scopes/tennstat.htm. Accessed on July 4, 2005.
2. Quoted in Edward J. Larson, *Summer for the Gods: The Scopes Trial and America's Continuing Debate Over Science and Religion* (Cambridge, Mass.: Harvard University Press, 1997), 54–55.
3. *The World's Most Famous Court Trial: Tennessee Evolution Case* (Cincinnati: National Book Co., 3d ed. 1925; Birmingham: Legal Classics Library, 1984), 293, 302. Available online at URL: http://www.law.umkc.edu/faculty/projects/ftrials/scopes/day7.htm. Accessed on July 4, 2005.
4. Jay P. Dolan, *The American Catholic Experience: A History from Colonial Times to the Present* (Garden City, N.Y.: Doubleday, 1985), 332–333.
5. Shawn Francis Peters, *Judging Jehovah's Witnesses: Religious Persecution and the Dawn of the Rights Revolution* (Lawrence: University Press of Kansas, 2000), 1.
6. 319 U.S. 624, 642 (1943).
7. The Pittsburgh Liberal Religious Platform, November 16–18, 1885, in *The Jew in the American World: A Source Book*, ed. Jacob Rader Marcus (Detroit: Wayne State University Press, 1996), 242.
8. Ibid., 284.
9. Eck, *A New Religious America*, 239–240.
10. Quoted ibid., 234.
11. Arthur Huff Fauset, *Black Gods of the Metropolis: Negro Religious Cults of the Urban North* (Philadelphia: University of Pennsylvania Press, 1941, 2001), 26.

13. Equality and Explorations: 1951–1979

1. Martin Luther King, Jr., *I Have a Dream: Writings and Speeches That Changed the World*, edited by James M. Washington (San Francisco: HarperSanFrancisco, 1992), 104–105.
2. Patrick Allit, *Religion in America since 1945: A History* (New York: Columbia University Press, 2003), 48–49.
3. Malcolm X, *Malcolm X Speaks: Selected Speeches and Statements*, edited by George Breitman (New York: Grove Weidenfeld, 1965), 12–13.
4. Frances Fitzgerald, "A Reporter at Large: A Disciplined, Changing Army," *New Yorker*, May 18, 1981, 53, 60–63.
5. Thomas Jefferson, Letter to Messrs. Nehemiah Dodge and Others, a Committee of the Danbury Baptist Association, in the State of Connecticut, January 1, 1802, in *Thomas Jefferson: Writings*, 510.
6. Corrigan and Hudson, *Religion in America*, 417.
7. Tona J. Hangen, *Redeeming the Dial: Radio, Religion, & Popular Culture in America* (Chapel Hill: University of North Carolina Press, 2002), 68.
8. Dennis J. Bennett, *Nine O'Clock in the Morning* (Plainfield, N.J.: Logos International, 1970).
9. Dolan, *The American Catholic Experience*, 435.
10. Ibid., 436–438.

14. Religion and Politics Redux: 1980–present

1. Richard John Neuhaus, *The Naked Public Square: Religion and Democracy in America* (Grand Rapids, Mich.: Eerdmans, 1984).
2. For the religious element of antiabortion protests, see Dallas A. Blanchard, *The Anti-Abortion Movement and the Rise of the Religious Right: From Polite to Fiery Protest* (New York: Twayne Publishers, 1994), 38–39.
3. Carol J. C. Maxwell, *Pro-Life Activists in America: Meaning, Motivation, and Direct Action* (Cambridge: Cambridge University Press, 2002), 72.
4. Quoted in Allit, *Religion in America since 1945*, 175–176.
5. Quoted ibid., 253.
6. James Davison Hunter, *Culture Wars: The Struggle to Define America* (New York: BasicBooks, 1991).
7. *Hustler Magazine v. Falwell*, 485 U.S. 46 (1988).

8. Allit, *Religion in America since 1945*, 191–194.

9. *See* Lawrence Wright, *Saints & Sinners: Walker Railey, Jimmy Swaggert, Madalyn Murray O'Hair, Anton LaVey, Will Campbell, Matthew Fox* (New York: Knopf, 1993).

10. *Church of the Lukumi Babalu Aye v. City of Hialeah*, 508 U.S. 520 (1993).

11. *Sherbert v. Verner*, 374 U.S. 398 (1963).

12. *City of Boerne v. Flores*, 521 U.S. 507 (1997).

13. *Good News Club v. Milford Central School*, 533 U.S. 98 (2001).

14. The Court held graduation prayers unconstitutional in *Lee v. Weisman*, 505 U.S. 575 (1992) and prayers at football games unconstitutional in *Sante Fe Independent School District v. Doe*, 530 U.S. 290 (2000).

15. Jane I. Smith, *Islam in America* (New York: Columbia University Press, 1999), xii.

16. Eck, *A New Religious America*, 269.

Bibliography

Aberle, David. *The Peyote Religion among the Navaho*. Chicago: Aldine, 1966.

Abzug, Robert H. *Cosmos Crumbling: American Reform and the Religious Imagination*. New York: Oxford University Press, 1994.

Adams, Samuel. *The Writings of Samuel Adams*. Edited by Harry Alonzo Cushing. 4 vols. New York: G. P. Putnam's Sons, 1904–08.

Ahlstrom, Sydney E. *A Religious History of the American People*. New Haven, Conn.: Yale University Press, 1972.

Albanese, Catherine L. *America: Religion and Religions*, 2d ed. Belmont: Wadsworth, 1992.

————. *Nature Religion in America: From the Algonquin Indians to the New Age*. Chicago: University of Chicago Press, 1990.

Alexander, Hartley Burr. *The World's Rim: Great Mysteries of the North American Indians*. Lincoln: University of Nebraska Press, 1953.

Alexander, Jon. *American Personal Religious Accounts, 1600–1980: Toward an Inner History of America's Faiths*. New York: Edwin Mellen Press, 1983.

Allen, Richard. *The Life Experience and Gospel Labors of the Rt. Rev. Richard Allen*. Nashville: Abingdon Press, 1983.

Alley, Robert S., ed. *James Madison on Religious Liberty*. Buffalo, N.Y.: Prometheus Books, 1985.

Allit, Patrick. *Religion in America since 1945: A History*. New York: Columbia University Press, 2003.

American Sermons: The Pilgrims to Martin Luther King, Jr. Edited by Michael Warner. New York: Library of America, 1999.

Ammerman, Nancy Tatom. *Baptist Battles: Social Change and Religious Conflict in the Southern Baptist Convention*. New Brunswick, N.J.: Rutgers University Press, 1990.

Anderson, Allan. *An Introduction to Pentecostalism*. Cambridge: Cambridge University Press, 2004.

Anderson, Edward. *Peyote: The Divine Cactus*. Tucson: University of Arizona Press, 1980.

Anderson, H. George. *Lutheranism in the Southeastern States, 1860–1866: A Social History*. The Hague: Mouton, 1969.

Anderson, Robert Mapes. *Vision of the Disinherited: The Making of American Pentecostalism*. Peabody, Mass.: Hendrickson, 1992.

Anderson, Victor. *Pragmatic Theology: Negotiating the Intersections of an American Philosophy of Religion and Public Theology*. Albany: State University of New York Press, 1998.

Andrews, William L., ed. *Sisters of the Spirit: Three Black Women's Autobiographies of the Nineteenth Century*. Bloomington: Indiana University Press, 1986.

Antler, Joyce. *The Journey Home: Jewish Women and the American Century*. New York: Free Press, 1997.

Aptheker, Herbert, ed. *A Documentary History of the Negro People in the United States.* New York: Citadel Press, 1951.

Armstrong, Maurice W., Lefferts A. Loetscher, and Charles A. Anderson, eds. *The Presbyterian Enterprise: Sources of American Presbyterian History.* Philadelphia: Westminster, 1956.

Arrington, Leonard J., and Davis Bitton. *The Mormon Experience: A History of the Latter-Day Saints,* 2d ed. Urbana: University of Illinois Press, 1992.

The Articles of Confederation. Edited by Samuel A. Pleasants. Columbus, Ohio: C. E. Merrill, 1968.

Austin, Allan. *African Muslims in Antebellum America.* New York: Garland, 1984.

Backus, Isaac. *The Diary of Isaac Backus.* Edited by William G. McLoughlin. 3 vols. Providence: Brown University Press, 1979.

Baker, Frank. *From Wesley to Asbury: Studies in Early American Methodism.* Durham, N.C.: Duke University Press, 1976.

Barlow, Philip L. *Mormons and the Bible: The Place of the Latter-day Saints in American Religion.* New York: Oxford University Press, 1991.

Baum, Charlotte, Paula Hyman, and Sonya Michel. *The Jewish Woman in America.* New York: Dial Press, 1976.

Bellah, Robert N. *The Broken Covenant: American Civil Religion in a Time of Trial.* 2d ed. Chicago: University of Chicago Press, 1992.

———. "Civil Religion in America." *Daedalus* (winter 1967): 1–21.

Bellah, Robert N., and Fredrick E. Greenspahn. *Uncivil Religion: Interreligious Hostility in America.* New York: Crossroads, 1987.

Bennett, Dennis J. *Nine O'Clock in the Morning.* Plainfield, N.J.: Logos International, 1970.

Bercovitch, Sacvan. *The Puritan Origins of the American Self.* New Haven, Conn.: Yale University Press, 1975.

Berens, John F. *Providence and Patriotism in Early America 1640–1815.* Charlottesville: University Press of Virginia, 1978.

Berger, Peter L. *The Sacred Canopy: Elements of a Sociological Theory of Religion.* New York: Anchor, 1990.

Berkhofer, Robert F., Jr. *Salvation and the Savage: An Analysis of Protestant Missions and American Indian Response, 1787–1862.* Westport, Conn.: Greenwood, 1977.

Berkin, Carol, and Leslie Horowitz, eds. *Women's Voices, Women's Lives: Documents in Early American History.* Boston: Northeastern University Press, 1998.

Beversluis, Joel D., ed. *A Sourcebook for the Community of Religions.* Chicago: Council for a Parliament of the World's Religions, 1993.

Bierhorst, John, ed. *Myths and Tales of the American Indian.* New York: Indian Head Books, 1976.

———. *The Sacred Path: Spells, Prayers, & Power Songs of the American Indians.* New York: William Morrow, 1983.

Billington, Ray Allen. *The Protestant Crusade, 1800–1860: A Study of the Origins of American Nativism.* New York: Macmillan, 1938.

Black Elk. *Black Elk Speaks: Being the Life Story of a Holy Man of the Oglala Sioux, as Told through John G. Neihardt (Flaming Rainbow).* New York: Pocket Books, 1972.

Blanchard, Dallas A. *The Anti-Abortion Movement and the Rise of the Religious Right: From Polite to Fiery Protest.* New York: Twayne, 1994.

Blau, Joseph L. *Judaism in America: From Curiosity to Third Faith.* Chicago: University of Chicago Press, 1976.

Blaustein, Albert P., and Robert L. Zangrando, eds. *Civil Rights and African Americans: A Documentary History.* Evanston, Ill.: Northwestern University Press, 1991.

Blavatsky, H. P. *The Secret Doctrine: The Synthesis of Science, Religion, and Philosophy.* 4 vols., 3d ed. London: Theosophical Society, 1893.

Bloch, Ruth H. *Visionary Republic: Millennial Themes in American Thought, 1756–1800.* New York: Cambridge University Press, 1985.

Blocker, Jack S., Jr. *American Temperance Movements: Cycles of Reform.* Boston: Twayne, 1989.

Blumhofer, Edith L. *Restoring the Faith: The Assemblies of God, Pentecostalism, and American Culture.* Urbana: University of Illinois Press, 1993.

Bode, Carl, ed. *American Life in the 1840s.* New York: New York University Press, 1967.

Boles, George A. *The Great Revival, 1787–1805: The Origins of the Southern Evangelical Mind.* Lexington: University of Kentucky Press, 1972.

Boles, John B., ed. *Masters & Slaves in the House of the Lord: Race and Religion in the American South—1740–1870.* Lexington: University Press of Kentucky, 1988.

Bolton, Sidney. *Southern Anglicanism: The Church of England in Colonial South Carolina.* Westport, Conn.: Greenwood Press, 1982.

Bonomi, Patricia U. *Under the Cope of Heaven: Religion, Society, and Politics in Colonial America.* New York: Oxford University Press, 1986.

Boorstin, Daniel J. *An American Primer.* Chicago: University of Chicago Press, 1966.

Bourne, Russell. *Gods of War, Gods of Peace: How the Meeting of Native and Colonial Religions Shaped Early America.* New York: Harcourt, 2002.

Bowden, Henry Warner. *Native Americans and Christian Missions: Studies in Cultural Conflict.* Chicago: University of Chicago Press, 1981.

Boyer, Paul. *When Time Shall Be No More: Prophecy Belief in Modern American Culture.* Cambridge, Mass.: Belknap Press of Harvard University Press, 1992.

Boylan, Anne M. *Sunday School: The Formation of an American Institution, 1790–1880.* New Haven, Conn.: Yale University Press, 1988.

Bozeman, Theodore Dwight. *Protestants in an Age of Science: The Baconian Ideal and Antebellum American Religious Thought.* Chapel Hill: University of North Carolina Press, 1977.

Braden, Charles S. *Spirits in Rebellion: The Rise and Development of New Thought.* Dallas: Southern Methodist University Press, 1963.

———. *These Also Believe: A Study of Modern American Cults & Minority Religious Movements.* New York: Macmillan, 1949.

Bradford, William. *Of Plymouth Plantation.* Edited by Harvey Wish. New York: Capricorn Books, 1962.

Brasher, Brenda E., ed. *Encyclopedia of Fundamentalism.* New York: Routledge, 2001.

Braude, Ann. *Radical Spirits: Spiritualism and Women's Rights in Nineteenth-Century America.* 2d ed. Bloomington: Indiana University Press, 2001.

Breslaw, Elaine G. *Tituba, Reluctant Witch of Salem: Devilish Indians and Puritan Fantasies.* New York: New York University Press, 1996.

Brickley, Donald P. *Man of the Morning: The Life and Work of Phineas F. Bresee.* Kansas City, Mo.: Nazarene Publishing House, 1960.

Bristol, Frank Milton. *The Life of Chaplain McCabe: Bishop of the Methodist Episcopal Church.* New York: F. H. Revell, 1908.

Broches, Samuel. *Jews in New England.* 2 vols. New York: Bloch, 1942.

Bromley, David G., and Anson D. Shupe, Jr. *Strange Gods: The Great American Cult Scare.* Boston: Beacon, 1981.

Brooke, John L. *The Refiner's Fire: The Making of Mormon Cosmology, 1644–1844.* Cambridge: Cambridge University Press, 1994.

Brooks, Joanna. *American Lazarus: Religion and the Rise of African-American and Native American Literatures.* Oxford: Oxford University Press, 2003.

Brooks, Phillips. *The Life and Death of Abraham Lincoln: A Sermon Preached at the Church of the Holy Trinity, Philadelphia, Sunday Morning, April 23, 1865, by the Rev. Phillips Brooks.* Philadelphia: H. B. Ashmead, 1865.

Brown, Joseph Epes, ed. *The Sacred Pipe: Black Elk's Account of the Seven Rites of the Oglala Sioux.* Norman: University of Oklahoma Press, 1953.

Browne, Henry J. *The Catholic Church and the Knights of Labor.* Washington, D.C.: Catholic University of America Press, 1949.

Bruce, Steve. *Religion in the Modern World: From Cathedrals to Cults.* New York: Oxford University Press, 1996.

Buechner, Frederick. *The Sacred Journey.* New York: Harper & Row, 1982.

Bushman, Richard L. *Joseph Smith and the Beginnings of Mormonism.* Urbana: University of Illinois Press, 1984.

Butler, Jon. *Awash in a Sea of Faith: Christianizing the American People.* Cambridge, Mass.: Harvard University Press, 1990.

Butler, Jon, Grant Wacker, and Randall Balmer, *Religion in American Life: A Short History.* Oxford: Oxford University Press, 2003.

Byrd, William. *The Secret Diary of William Byrd of Westover, 1709–1712.* Edited by Louis B. Wright and Marion Tinling. Richmond, Va.: Dietz Press, 1941.

Campbell, Alexander. *The Christian System in Reference to the Union of Christians, and a Restoration of Primitive Christianity, as Plead in the Current Reformation.* Cincinnati: Standard, 1839.

Campbell, Bruce F. *Ancient Wisdom Revived: A History of the Theosophical Movement.* Berkeley: University of California Press, 1980.

Canavarro, Marie de S. *Insight into the Far East.* Los Angeles: Wetzel, 1925.

Carmody, Denise L. *The Republic of Many Mansions: Foundations of American Religion.* New York: Paragon House, 1990.

Carmody, Denise L., and John T. Carmody. *Exploring American Religion.* Mountain View, Calif.: Mayfield, 1990.

Carpenter, Joel A. *Revive Us Again: The Reawakening of American Fundamentalists.* New York: Oxford University Press, 1997.

Carter, Stephen. *The Culture of Disbelief: How American Law and Politics Trivialize Religious Devotion.* New York: BasicBooks, 1993.

Cartwright, Peter. *Autobiography of Peter Cartwright, The Backwoods Preacher.* Edited by W. P. Strickland. New York: Carlton & Porter, 1856.

Carwardine, Richard. *Evangelicals and Politics in Antebellum America.* New Haven, Conn.: Yale University Press, 1993.

Chesterton, G. K. *What I Saw in America.* New York: Dodd, Mead, 1922.

Choquette, Diane. *New Religious Movements in the United States and Canada: A Critical Assessment and Annotated Bibliography.* Westport, Conn.: Greenwood Press, 1985.

Chu, Jonathan M. *Neighbors, Friends, or Madmen: The Puritan Adjustment to Quakerism in Seventeenth-Century Massachusetts Bay.* Westport, Conn.: Greenwood Press, 1985.

Cimino, Richard, and Don Lattin. *Shopping for Faith: American Religion in the New Millennium.* San Francisco: Jossey-Bass, 1998.

Coalter, Milton J. *Gilbert Tennent, Son of Thunder: A Case Study of Continental Pietism's Impact on the First Great Awakening in the Middle Colonies.* New York: Greenwood Press, 1986.

Coffman, Ralph J. *Solomon Stoddard.* Boston: Twayne Publishers, 1978.

Cogley, Richard W. *John Eliot's Mission to the Indians Before King Philip's War.* Cambridge, Mass.: Harvard University Press, 1999.

Cohen, Charles Lloyd. *God's Caress: The Psychology of Puritan Religious Experience.* New York: Oxford University Press, 1986.

Cohen, Naomi Wiener. *Jews in Christian America: The Pursuit of Religious Equality.* New York: Oxford University Press, 1992.

Colbert, David, ed. *Eyewitness to America: 5000 Years of America in the Words of Those Who Saw It Happen.* New York: Pantheon Books, 1997.

Colden, Cadwallader. *The History of the Five Indian Nations of Canada which are Dependent on the Province of New York, and Are a Barrier Between the English and the French in that Part of the World.* 2 vols. New York: A. S. Barnes, 1904.

Collier-Thomas, Bettye. *Daughters of Thunder: Black Women Preachers and Their Sermons, 1850–1979.* San Francisco: Jossey-Bass, 1998.

Collins, John James. *Native American Religions: A Geographical Survey.* Lewiston, N.Y.: Edwin Mellen Press, 1991.

Colson, Charles W. *Born Again.* Old Tappan, N.J.: Chosen Books, 1976.

Commager, Henry Steele, ed. *Documents of American History.* 9th ed. New York: Appleton-Century-Crofts, 1973.

Conlin, Paul K. *Cane Ridge, America's Pentecost.* Madison: University of Wisconsin Press, 1990.

Conway, Jill K., Linda Kealey, and Janet E. Schulte. *The Female Experience in Eighteenth- and Nineteenth-Century America: A Guide to the History of American Women.* New York: Garland, 1982.

Conwell, Russell Herman. *Acres of Diamonds.* New York: Harper & Brothers, 1915; Old Tappan, N.J.: Fleming H. Revell, 1960.

Coppin, Fanny Jackson. *Reminiscences of School Life and Hints on Teaching.* New York: G. K. Hall, 1995.

Corrigan, John, and Winthrop S. Hudson. *Religion in America: An Historical Account of the Development of American Religious Life.* 7th ed. Upper Saddle River, N.J.: Pearson/Prentice Hall, 2004.

Cousins, Norman, ed. *"In God We Trust": The Religious Beliefs and Ideas of the American Founding Fathers.* New York: Harper & Brothers, 1958.

Cox, Harvey. *Fire from Heaven: The Rise of Pentecostal Spirituality and the Reshaping of Religion in the Twenty-first Century.* Reading, Mass.: Addison-Welsey, 1995.

———. *The Secular City: Secularization and Urbanization in Theological Perspective.* New York: Macmillan, 1965.

———. *Turning East.* New York: Simon & Schuster, 1977.

Cross, F. L., ed. *The Oxford Dictionary of the Christian Church.* 2d ed. London: Oxford University Press, 1984.

Cross, Whitney R. *The Burned Over District: The Social and Intellectual History of Enthusiastic Religion in Western New York, 1800–1850.* New York: Harper & Row, 1950.

Crowe, Charles, ed. *A Documentary History of American Thought and Society.* Boston: Allyn & Bacon, 1965.

Curry, Thomas J. *The First Freedoms: Church and State in America to the Passage of the First Amendment.* New York: Oxford University Press, 1986.

Curtis, Edward E. *Islam in Black America: Identity, Liberation, and Difference in African-American Islamic Thought.* Albany: State University of New York Press, 2002.

Davidson, Philip. *Propaganda and the American Revolution, 1763–1783.* Chapel Hill: University of North Carolina Press, 1941.

Dayton, Donald W. *Discovering an Evangelical Heritage.* New York: Harper & Row, 1976.

Deloria, Vine, Jr. *God Is Red: A Native View of Religion.* Rev. ed. Golden, Colo.: Fulcrum, 2003.

DeMellie, Raymond J., and Douglas R. Parks, eds. *Sioux Indian Religion.* Norman: University of Oklahoma Press, 1987.

De Vaca, Alvar Núñez Cabez. *Chronicle of the Narváez Expedition.* Trans. by Fanny Bandelier, rev. trans. by Harold Augenbraum. New York: Penguin, 2002.

Dickinson, Emily. *The Complete Poems of Emily Dickinson.* Edited by Thomas H. Johnson. Boston: Little, Brown, 1960.

Dillard, Annie. *Holy the Firm.* New York: Harper & Row, 1977.

———. *Teaching a Stone to Talk.* New York: Harper & Row, 1982.

Dinnerstein, Leonard. *Anti-Semitism in America.* Oxford: Oxford University Press, 1994.

Dolan, Jay P. *The American Catholic Experience: A History from Colonial Times to the Present.* Garden City, N.Y.: Doubleday, 1985.

———. *Catholic Revivalism: The American Experience, 1830–1900.* Notre Dame, Ind.: University of Notre Dame Press, 1978.

———. *The Immigrant Church: New York's Irish and German Catholics, 1815–1865.* Notre Dame, Ind.: University of Notre Dame Press, 1975.

Donin, Hayim Halevy. *To Be a Jew: A Guide to Jewish Observance in Contemporary Life.* New York: HarperCollins, 1972.

Dooling, D. M., and Paul Jordan-Smith. *I Become Part of It: Sacred Dimensions in Native American Life.* New York: Parabola, 1989.

DuBois, W. E. B. *W. E. B. DuBois: Writings.* New York: Library of America, 1986.

Duffield, Holley Gene. *Historical Dictionary of the Shakers.* Lanham, Md.: Scarecrow Press, 2000.

Dwight, Timothy. *The Major Poems of Timothy Dwight, 1752–1817, with a Dissertation on the History, Eloquence, and Poetry of the Bible.* Gainsville, Fla.: Scholars' Facsimiles & Reprints, 1969.

Eck, Diana L. *Encountering God: A Spiritual Journey from Bozeman to Banaras.* Boston: Beacon Press, 1993.

———. *A New Religious America: How a "Christian Country" Has Now Become the World's Most Religiously Diverse Nation.* San Francisco: HarperSanFrancisco, 2001.

Eddy, Mary Baker. *Science and Health: With Key to the Scriptures.* Boston: First Church of Christ, Scientist, 1994.

Edwards, Jonathan. *The Life of David Brainerd.* Edited by Norman Pettit. New Haven, Conn.: Yale University Press, 1985.

———. *The Works of Jonathan Edwards.* 2 vols. Peabody, Mass.: Hendrickson, 1998.

Eerdmans' Handbook to Christianity in America. Grand Rapids, Mich.: William B. Eerdmans, 1983.

Einhorn, Lois J. *The Native American Oral Tradition: Voices of the Spirit and the Soul.* Westport, Conn.: Praeger, 2000.

Eliade, Mircea. *Myth and Reality.* Translated by Willard R. Trask. New York: Harper & Row, 1975.

———. *The Quest: History and Meaning in Religion.* Chicago: University of Chicago Press, 1969.

———. *The Sacred and the Profane: The Nature of Religion.* Translated by Willard R. Trask. New York: Harcourt, Brace, 1959.

———, et al., eds. *The Encyclopedia of Religion.* New York: Macmillan, 1987.

Elliot, Jim. *The Journals of Jim Elliot.* Edited by Elisabeth Eliot. Old Tappan, N.J.: Fleming H. Revell, 1978.

Ellis, John Tracy. *American Catholicism.* Chicago: University of Chicago Press, 1969.

———, ed. *Documents of American Catholic History.* Milwaukee: Bruce, 1956.

Ellwood, Robert S., Jr. *Alternative Altars.* Chicago: University of Chicago Press, 1979.

———. *The Eagle and the Rising Sun: Americans and the New Religions of Japan.* Philadelphia: Westminster, 1974.

———. *Religious and Spiritual Groups in Modern America.* Englewood Cliffs, N.J.: Prentice Hall, 1973.

Erdoes, Richard, and Alfonso Ortiz, eds. *American Indian Myths & Legends.* Westminster, Md.: Pantheon, 1984.

Ewing, George W., ed. *The Well-Tempered Lyre: Songs & Verse of the Temperance Movement.* Dallas: SMU Press, 1977.

Fauset, Arthur Huff. *Black Gods of the Metropolis: Negro Religious Cults of the Urban North.* Philadelphia: University of Pennsylvania Press, 2001.

Fein, Leonard. *Where Are We? The Inner Life of America's Jews.* New York: Harper & Row, 1988.

Feingold, Henry L., ed. *The Jewish People in America.* 5 vols. Baltimore: Johns Hopkins University Press, 1992.

Fields, Rick. *How the Swans Came to the Lake: A Narrative History of Buddhism in America.* Boston: Shambhala, 1992.

Finke, Roger, and Rodney Stark. *The Churching of America, 1776–1990: Winners and Losers in Our Religious Economy.* New Brunswick, N.J.: Rutgers University Press, 1992.

Finkelstein, Louis. *American Spiritual Autobiographies: Fifteen Self-Portraits.* New York: Harper, 1948.

Finney, Charles. *The Memoirs of Charles G. Finney: The Complete Restored Text.* Grand Rapids, Mich.: Academie, 1989.

Fisher, Miles Mark. "Lott Cary, the Colonizing Missionary." *Journal of Negro History* 7 (Oct. 1922): 380–418.

Fleming, Walter L. *Documentary History of Reconstruction: Political, Military, Social, Religious, Educational & Industrial, 1865 to the Present Time.* Cleveland: A. H. Clark, 1906–07.

Floyd, Samuel A., Jr. *The Power of Black Music.* Oxford: Oxford University Press, 1995.

Foster, Lawrence. *Religion and Sexuality: Three American Communal Experiments of the Nineteenth Century.* New York: Oxford University Press, 1981.

Fox, Richard Wightman. *Jesus in America: Personal Savior, Cultural Hero, National Obsession.* San Francisco: HarperSanFrancisco, 2004.

Franklin, Benjamin. *The Works of Benjamin Franklin.* Edited by John Bigelow. New York: Putnam's, 1904.

Frazier, Franklin. *The Negro Church in America.* New York: Schocken, 1964.

Friess, Horace L. *Felix Adler and Ethical Culture: Memories and Studies.* Edited by Fannia Weingartner. New York: Columbia University Press, 1981.

Fu, Charles W., ed. *Religious Issues and Interreligious Dialogues: An Analysis and Sourcebook of Developments since 1945.* New York: Greenwood Press, 1989.

Gallagher, Edward J. *Early Puritan Writers, A Reference Guide: William Bradford, John Cotton, Thomas Hooker, Edward Johnson, Richard Mather, Thomas Shepard.* Boston: G. K. Hall, 1976.

Garretson, Freeborn. *American Methodist Pioneer: The Life and Journals of the Rev. Freeborn Garretson, 1752–1827.* Edited by Robert Drew Simpson. Rutland, Vt.: Academy Books, 1984.

Garrison, Winfred E., and Alfred T. DeGroot. *The Disciples of Christ: A History.* St. Louis: Bethany, 1958.

Gates, Henry Louis, Jr. *The Norton Anthology of African American Literature.* New York: Norton, 1996.

Gaustad, Edwin S. *A Documentary History of Religion in America since 1865.* 2d ed. Grand Rapids, Mich.: Eerdmans, 1993.

———. *A Documentary History of Religion in America to the Civil War.* 2d ed. Grand Rapids, Mich.: Eerdmans, 1993.

———. *Faith of Our Fathers: Religion and the New Nation.* San Francisco: Harper & Row, 1987.

———. *The Great Awakening in New England.* New York: Harper & Row, 1957.

———. *Neither King nor Prelate: Religion and the New Nation, 1776–1826.* Rev. ed. Grand Rapids, Mich.: Eerdmans, 1993.

Gaustad, Edwin S., and Leigh E. Schmidt. *The Religious History of America.* Rev. ed. San Francisco: HarperSanFrancisco, 2002.

Gedge, Karin E. *Without Benefit of Clergy: Women and the Pastoral Relationship in Nineteenth-Century American Culture.* Oxford: Oxford University Press, 2003.

Gibbons, James Cardinal. *A Retrospective of Fifty Years.* New York: Arno Press, 1972.

Gill, Sam D. *Native American Religions: An Introduction.* Belmont, Calif.: Wadsworth, 1982.

Gillis, Chester. *Roman Catholicism in America.* New York: Columbia University Press, 1999.

Glazer, Nathan. *American Judaism.* 2d ed. Chicago: University of Chicago Press, 1988.

Glazier, Stephen D., ed. *The Encyclopedia of African and African-American Religions.* New York: Routledge, 2001.

Goodman, Paul. *Towards a Christian Republic: Antimasonry and the Great Transition in New England, 1826–1836.* New York: Oxford University Press, 1988.

Gordis, Lisa M. *Opening Scripture: Bible Reading and Interpretive Authority in Puritan New England.* Chicago: University of Chicago Press, 2003.

Gordon, Milton. *Assimilation in American Life: The Role of Race, Religion, and National Origins.* New York: Oxford University Press, 1964.

Gort, Jerald D., et al., eds. *On Sharing Religious Experience: Possibilities of Interfaith Mutuality.* Grand Rapids, Mich.: Eerdmans, 1992.

Gottschalk, Stephen. *The Emergence of Christian Science in American Religious Life.* Berkeley: University of California Press, 1973.

Graham, Billy. *Just as I Am: The Autobiography of Billy Graham.* San Francisco: HarperSanFrancisco, 1997.

Greeley, Andrew M. *The Catholic Experience: An Interpretation of the History of American Catholicism.* Garden City, N.Y.: Doubleday, 1967.

Gribbin, William. *The Churches Militant: The War of 1812 and American Religion.* New Haven, Conn.: Yale University Press, 1973.

Griffin, Edward M. *Old Brick: Charles Chauncy of Boston, 1705–1787.* Minneapolis: University of Minnesota Press, 1980.

Guillermo, Artemio R. *Churches Aflame: Asian Americans and United Methodism.* Nashville: Abingdon Press, 1991.

Hackett, David G. *Religion and American Culture: A Reader.* 2d ed. New York: Routledge, 2003.

Haddad, Yvonne Yazbeck, ed. *The Muslims of America.* New York: Oxford University Press, 1993.

———, and Adair T. Lummis. *Islamic Values in the United States.* New York: Oxford University Press, 1987.

———, and John Esposito, eds. *Muslims on the Americanization Path?* Atlanta, Ga.: Scholars Press, 1998.

Hall, David D., ed. *The Antinomian Controversy, 1636–1638: A Documentary History.* Middletown, Conn.: Wesleyan University Press, 1968.

———. *The Faithful Shepherd: A History of the New England Ministry in the Seventeenth Century.* Chapel Hill: published for the Institute of Early American History and Culture, Williamsburg, Va., by the University of North Carolina Press, 1972.

———, ed. *Lived Religion in America.* Princeton, N.J.: Princeton University Press, 1997.

———. *World of Wonders, Days of Judgment: Popular Religious Belief in Early New England.* New York: Knopf, 1989.

Hall, Robert L. *An Archaeology of the Soul: North American Indian Belief and Ritual.* Urbana: University of Illinois Press, 1997.

Hall, Timothy L. *Separating Church and State: Roger Williams and Religious Liberty.* Urbana: University of Illinois Press, 1998.

Haller, William. *The Rise of Puritanism: The Way to the New Jerusalem as Set Forth in Pulpit and Press from Thomas Cartwright to John Lilburne and John Milton, 1570–1643.* New York: Harper, 1957.

Halvorson, Peter L., and William M. Newman. *Atlas of Religious Change in America, 1952–1990.* Atlanta, Ga.: Glenmary Research Center, 1994.

Hamm, Thomas D. *The Quakers in America.* New York: Columbia University Press, 2003.

Handy, Robert T. *A Christian America: Protestant Hopes and Historical Realities.* 2d ed. New York: New York University Press, 1984.

———. *A History of the Churches in the United States and Canada.* New York: Oxford University Press, 1977.

Hangen, Tona J. *Redeeming the Dial: Radio, Religion, & Popular Culture in America.* Chapel Hill: University of North Carolina Press, 2002.

Hanke, Lewis, ed. *History of Latin American Civilization: Sources and Interpretation.* 2 vols. Boston: Little, Brown, 1967.

Hankins, Barry. *The Second Great Awakening and the Trancendentalists.* Westport, Conn.: Greenwood Press, 2004.

Hanley, Mark Y. *Beyond a Christian Commonwealth: The Protestant Quarrel with the American Republic, 1830–1860.* Chapel Hill: University of North Carolina Press, 1994.

Harrison, Barbara Grizzuti. *Visions of Glory: A History and a Memory of Jehovah's Witnesses.* New York: Simon & Schuster, 1978.

Hart, Albert Bushnell, ed. *American History Told by Contemporaries.* 4 vols. New York: Macmillan, 1908.

Hart, D. G. *That Old-Time Religion in Modern America: Evangelical Protestantism in the Twentieth Century.* Chicago: Ivan R. Dee, 2002.

Harvey, Paul, and Philip Goff, eds. *The Columbia Documentary History of Religion in America since 1945.* New York: Columbia University Press, 2005.

Hasan, Asma Gull. *American Muslims: The New Generation.* New York: Continuum, 2000.

Hatch, Nathan O. *The Democratization of American Christianity.* Reprint ed. New Haven, Conn.: Yale University Press, 1991.

Hatchett, Marion J. *The Making of the First American Book of Common Prayer, 1776–1789.* New York: Seabury, 1982.

Hattersley, Roy. *The Life of John Wesley: A Brand from the Burning.* New York: Doubleday, 2003.

Haynes, Stephen R. *Noah's Curse: The Biblical Justification of American Slavery.* Oxford: Oxford University Press, 2002.

Heard, Alex. *Apocalypse Pretty Soon: Travels in End-time America.* New York: Norton, 1999.

Heimert, Alan E. *Religion and the American Mind from the Great Awakening to the Revolution.* Cambridge, Mass.: Harvard University Press, 1966.

Hening, William Waller, ed. *The Statutes at Large; Being a Collection of All the Laws of Virginia, from the First Session of the Legislature in the Year 1619.* Charlottesville: published for the Jamestown Foundation of the Commonwealth of Virginia by the University Press of Virginia, 1969.

Hennesey, James J. *American Catholics: A History of the Roman Catholic Community in the United States.* New York: Oxford University Press, 1982.

Herberg, Will. *Protestant–Catholic–Jew: An Essay in American Religious Sociology.* Rev. ed. Garden City, N.Y.: Anchor Books, 1960.

Hertzberg, Arthur. *The Jews in America, Four Centuries of an Uneasy Encounter: A History.* New York: Simon & Schuster, 1989.

Hewitt, Glenn Alden. *Regeneration and Morality: A Study of Charles Finney, Charles Hodge, John W. Nevin, and Horace Bushnell.* Brooklyn: Carlson, 1991.

Hill, Samuel S. *Encyclopedia of Religion in the South.* Macon, Ga.: Mercer, 1984.

Hillman, Eugene. *Many Paths: A Catholic Approach to Religious Pluralism.* New York: Orbis Books, 1989.

Hirschfelder, Arlene B. *The Encyclopedia of Native American Religions: An Introduction.* New York: Facts On File, 1992.

Hoffecker, W. Andrew. *Piety and the Princeton Theologians: Archibald Alexander, Charles Hodge, and Benjamin Warfield.* Grand Rapids, Mich.: Baker Book House, 1981.

Hoffer, Peter Charles. *The Devil's Disciples: Makers of the Salem Witchcraft Trials.* Baltimore: Johns Hopkins University Press, 1996.

————. *The Salem Witchcraft Trials: A Legal History.* Lawrence: University Press of Kansas, 1997.

Holifield, E. Brooks. *The Gentlemen Theologians: American Theology in Southern Culture, 1795–1860.* Durham, N.C.: Duke University Press, 1978.

————. *Theology in America: Christian Thought from the Age of the Puritans to the Civil War.* New Haven, Conn.: Yale University Press, 2003.

Holmes, David L. *A Brief History of the Episcopal Church.* Valley Forge, Pa.: Trinity Press International, 1993.

Holsey, Lucius Henry. *Autobiography, Sermons, Addresses, and Essays of Bishop L. H. Holsey, D. D.* Atlanta, Ga.: Franklin Print, 1898.

Hopkins, Dwight N., and George C. L. Cummings, eds. *Cut Loose Your Stammering Tongue: Black Theology in the Slave Narratives.* 2d ed. Louisville, Ky.: Westminster John Knox Press, 2003.

Howard, Thomas. *Christ the Tiger.* Philadelphia: J. B. Lippincott, 1967.

Hudson, Winthrop S., and John Corrigan. *Religion in America.* 5th ed. New York: Prentice Hall, 1992.

Hughes, Richard T., ed. *The American Quest for the Primitive Church.* Urbana: University of Illinois Press, 1988.

Hughes, Richard T., and C. Leonard Allen. *Illusions of Innocence: Protestant Primitivism in America, 1630–1875.* Chicago: University of Chicago Press, 1988.

Hultkrantz, Ake. *Native Religions of North America: The Power of Visions and Fertility.* San Francisco: Harper & Row, 1987.

Hunter, James Davison. *Culture Wars: The Struggle to Define America.* New York: Basic Books, 1991.

Hutcheson, Richard G., Jr. *God in the White House: How Religion Has Changed the Modern Presidency.* New York: Macmillan, 1988.

Hutchison, William R., ed. *Between the Times: The Travail of the Protestant Establishment in America 1900–1960.* Cambridge: Cambridge University Press, 1989.

————. *The Modernist Impulse in American Protestantism.* Cambridge, Mass.: Harvard University Press, 1976.

Hyman, Paula E., and Deborah Dash Moore, eds. *Jewish Women in America: An Historical Encyclopedia.* 2 vols. New York: Routledge, 1997.

Idleman, Finis S. *Peter Ainslie: Ambassador of Good Will.* Chicago: Willett, Clark, 1941.

Isherwood, Christopher, ed. *Vedanta for the Western World.* Hollywood, Calif.: Marcel Rodd, 1945.

Jackson, Carl T. *Vedanta for the West: The Ramakrishna Movement in the United States.* Bloomington: Indiana University Press, 1994.

Jackson, Phil. *Sacred Hoops: Spiritual Lessons of a Hardwood Warrior.* New York: Hyperion, 1995.

Jackson, S. Trevena. *Fanny Crosby's Story of Ninety-four Years.* New York: Fleming H. Revell, 1945.

James, William. *William James: Writings, 1878–1899.* New York: Library of America, 1992.

Jefferson, Thomas. *The Jefferson Bible: The Life and Morals of Jesus of Nazareth.* New York: Holt, 1995.

————. *The Papers of Thomas Jefferson.* Edited by Julian P. Boyd. 31 vols. Princeton, N.J.: Princeton University Press, 1950.

————. *Thomas Jefferson: Writings.* Edited by Merrill D. Peterson. New York: Library of America, 1984.

————. *The Writings of Thomas Jefferson: Being His Autobiography, Correspondence, Reports, Messages, Addresses, and Other Writings, Official and Private.* Edited by H. A. Washington. 9 vols. Washington, D.C.: Taylor & Maury, 1853–1854.

Jenkins, Philip. *Mystics and Messiahs: Cults and New Religions in American History.* New York: Oxford University Press, 2000.

————. *The Next Christendom: The Coming of Global Christianity.* New York: Oxford University Press, 2002.

Johnson, Edward. *Wonder-Working Providence of Sion's Saviour in New-England.* Delmar, N.Y.: Scholars' Facsimiles and Reprints, 1974.

Johnson, Paul E. *A Shopkeeper's Millennium: Society and Revivals in Rochester, New York, 1815–1837.* New York: Hill & Wang, 1978.

Jones, Charles Edwin. *Black Holiness.* Metuchen, N.J.: Scarecrow Press, 1987.

Jones, E. Stanley. *The Christ of the Indian Road.* 6th ed. New York: Abingdon Press, 1925.

Jordan, L. G. *Up the Ladder in Foreign Missions.* Nashville: National Baptist Publishing Board, 1903.

Jorgensen, Joseph G. *The Sun Dance Religion: Power for the Powerless.* Chicago: University of Chicago Press, 1974.

Joselit, Jenna Weissman. *The Wonders of America: Reinventing Jewish Culture 1880–1950.* New York: Hill & Wang, 1994.

Juster, Susan. *Disorderly Women: Sexual Politics & Evangelicalism in Revolutionary New England.* Ithaca, N.Y.: Cornell University Press, 1994.

Kamenetz, Rodger. *The Jew in the Lotus: A Poet's Rediscovery of Jewish Identity in Buddhist India.* San Francisco: HarperSanFrancisco, 1994.

Kammen, Michael. *Colonial New York: A History.* New York: Charles Scribner's Sons, 1975.

Kashima, Tetsuden. *Buddhism in America: The Social Organization of an Ethnic Religious Institution.* Westport, Conn.: Greenwood Press, 1977.

Kelley, Karla Bonsack, and Harris Francis. *Navajo Sacred Places.* Bloomington: Indiana University Press, 1994.

Kelly, Dean. *Why Conservative Churches Are Growing.* New York: Harper & Row, 1972.

Kerouac, Jack. *The Dharma Bums.* New York: Penguin Books, 1958.

King, Martin Luther, Jr. *I Have a Dream: Writings and Speeches That Changed the World.* Edited by James M. Washington. San Francisco: HarperSanFrancisco, 1992.

Kino, Eusebio. *Kino's Historical Memoir of Pimería Alta.* Edited by Herbert Eugene Bolton. 2 vols. Cleveland: Arthur H. Clark, 1919.

Kling, David W. *A Field of Divine Wonders: The New Divinity and Village Revivals in Northwestern Connecticut, 1792–1822.* University Park: Pennsylvania State University Press, 1993.

Knight, Janice. *Orthodoxies in Massachusetts: Rereading American Puritanism.* Cambridge, Mass.: Harvard University Press, 1994.

Knitter, Paul. *No Other Name? A Critical Survey of Christian Attitudes toward the World Religions.* Maryknoll, N.Y.: Orbis Books, 1985.

Knoppers, Laura Lunger, ed. *Puritanism and Its Discontents.* Newark: University of Delaware Press, 2003.

Kosmin, Barry A., and Seymour P. Lachman. *One Nation Under God: Religion in Contemporary American Society.* New York: Harmony Books, 1993.

Koszegi, Michael A., and J. Gordon Melton. *Islam in North America: A Sourcebook.* New York: Garland, 1992.

Kramnick, Isaac, and R. Laurence Moore. *The Godless Constitution: The Case Against Religious Correctness.* New York: Norton, 1996.

Krieger, David J. *The New Universalism: Foundations for a Global Theology.* Maryknoll, N.Y.: Orbis Books, 1991.

Kurland, Philip B., and Ralph Lerner. *The Founders' Constitution.* 5 vols. Chicago: University of Chicago Press, 1987.

Kwon, Ho-Youn, Kwang Chung Kim, and Stephan Warner, eds. *Korean-Americans and Their Religions: Pilgrims and Missionaries from a Different Shore.* University Park: Pennsylvania State University Press, 2001.

LaBarre, Weston. *The Ghost Dance-Origins of Religion.* Garden City, N.Y.: Doubleday, 1970.

Laderman, Gary, ed. *Religions of Atlanta: Religious Diversity in the Centennial Olympic City.* Atlanta: Scholars Press, 1996.

LaFantasie, Glen W., ed. *The Correspondence of Roger Williams.* 2 vols. Providence: Brown University Press, 1988.

Landing, James E. *Black Judaism: Story of an American Movement.* Durham, N.C.: Carolina Academic Press, 2002.

Lane, Isaac. *Autobiography of Bishop Isaac Lane, LL.D. with a Short History of the C.M.E. Church in America and of Methodism.* Nashville: Publishing House of the ME Church, South, 1916.

Langley, Winston E., and Vivian C. Fox, eds. *Women's Rights in the United States: A Documentary History.* Westport, Conn.: Greenwood Press, 1994.

Larson, Edward J. *Summer for the Gods: The Scopes Trial and America's Continuing Debate over Science and Religion.* Cambridge, Mass.: Harvard University Press, 1997.

Lawrence, Bruce B. *New Faiths, Old Fears: Muslims and Other Asian Immigrants in American Religious Life.* New York: Columbia University Press, 2002.

Laws and Liberties of Massachusetts. Birmingham, Ala.: Legal Classics Library, 1982.

Lawson, Ellen NicKenzie. *The Three Sarahs: Documents of Antebellum Black College Women.* New York: Edwin Mellen Press, 1984.

Leary, Timothy. *The Politics of Ecstasy.* New York: Putnam, 1968.

Lebeson, Anita Libman. *Recall to Life: The Jewish Woman in America.* South Brunswick, N.J.: Yoseloff, 1970.

Leone, Mark P. *Roots of Modern Mormonism.* Cambridge, Mass.: Harvard University Press, 1979.

Lincoln, Abraham. *Abraham Lincoln: Speeches and Writings.* 2 vols. New York: Library of America, 1989.

Lincoln, C. Eric, ed. *The Black Experience in Religion.* Garden City, N.Y.: Anchor Press, 1974.

———, and Lawrence H. Mamiya. *The Black Church in the African American Experience.* Durham, N.C.: Duke University Press, 1990.

Lindley, Susan Hill. *"You Have Stept Out of Your Place": A History of Women and Religion in America.* Louisville, Ky.: Westminster John Knox, 1996.

Lippy, Charles H. *Being Religious, American Style: A History of Popular Religiosity in the United States.* Westport, Conn.: Praeger, 1994.

———, Robert Choquette, and Stafford Poole. *Christianity Comes to the Americas, 1492–1776.* New York: Paragon House, 1992.

———, and Peter W. Williams, eds. *Encyclopedia of the American Religious Experience.* 3 vols. New York: Charles Scribner's Sons, 1988.

Livingston, James C. *Anatomy of the Sacred: An Introduction to Religion.* Upper Saddle River, N.J.: Prentice Hall, 1998.

Lochhead, David. *The Dialogical Imperative: A Christian Reflection on Interfaith Encounter.* Maryknoll, N.Y.: Orbis Books, 1988.

Loew, Cornelius R. *Myth, Sacred History and Philosophy: The Pre-Christian Religious Heritage of the West.* New York: Harcourt, Brace & World, 1967.

Loftin, John D. *Religion and Hopi Life in the Twentieth Century.* Bloomington: Indiana University Press, 1991.

Long, Charles H. *Significations: Signs, Symbols, and Images in the Interpretation of Religion.* Aurora, Colo.: Davies Group, 1999.

Long, Kathryn Teresa. *The Revival of 1857–58: Interpreting an American Religious Awakening.* New York: Oxford University Press, 1998.

Lossky, Nicholas, et. al., eds. *Dictionary of the Ecumenical Movement.* Geneva: World Council of Churches, 1991.

Loveland, Anne C. *Southern Evangelicals and the Social Order, 1800–1860.* Baton Rouge: Louisiana State University Press, 1980.

Lubarsky, Sandra B. *Tolerance and Transformation: Jewish Approaches to Religious Pluralism.* West Orange, N.J.: Cincinnati Hebrew Union College Press, 1990.

Ludlow, Daniel H., ed. *Encyclopedia of Mormonism.* 5 vols. New York: Macmillan, 1992.

Lundin, Roger, and Mark A. Noll, eds. *Voices from the Heart: Four Centuries of American Piety.* Grand Rapids, Mich.: Eerdmans, 1987.

Machen, J. Gresham. *Christianity and Liberalism.* Grand Rapids, Mich.: Eerdmans, 1946.

Mallon, Elias D. *Neighbors: Muslims in North America.* New York: Friendship Press, 1989.

Mandelker, Amy, and Elizabeth Powers, eds. *Pilgrim Souls: A Collection of Spiritual Autobiographies.* New York: Simon & Schuster, 1999.

Mandelker, Ira L. *Religion, Society, and Utopia in Nineteenth-Century America.* Amherst: University of Massachusetts Press, 1984.

Mann, Barbara Alice, ed. *Native American Speakers of the Eastern Woodlands: Selected Speeches and Critical Analysis.* Westport, Conn.: Greenwood Press, 2001.

Marcus, Jacob R. *The American Jewish Woman: A Documentary History.* Cincinnati: American Jewish Archives, 1981.

———. *Early American Jewry.* 2 vols. Philadelphia: Jewish Publication Society of America, 1951.

———, ed. *The Jew in the American World: A Source Book.* Detroit: Wayne State University Press, 1996.

Marsden, George M. *The Evangelical Mind and the New School Presbyterian Experience: A Case Study of Thought and Theology in Nineteenth-Century America.* New Haven, Conn.: Yale University Press, 1970.

———. *Fundamentalism and American Culture.* New York: Oxford University Press, 1982.

———. *Reforming Fundamentalism: Fuller Seminary and the New Evangelism.* Grand Rapids, Mich.: Eerdmans, 1987.

———. *Religion and American Culture.* San Diego: Harcourt, Brace, Jovanovich, 1990.

Martin, Joel W. *The Land Looks After Us: A History of Native American Religion.* Oxford: Oxford University Press, 2001.

Martin, William. *With God on Our Side: The Rise of the Religious Right in America.* New York: Broadway Books, 1996.

Marty, Martin. *Modern American Religion.* 3 vols. Chicago: University of Chicago Press, 1970–1996.

―――. *The One and the Many.* Cambridge, Mass.: Harvard University Press, 1997.

―――. *Pilgrims in Their Own Land: Five Hundred Years of Religion in America.* New York: Viking Penguin, 1985.

―――, and R. Scott Appleby. *The Glory and the Power: The Fundamentalist Challenge to the Modern World.* Boston: Beacon Press, 1992.

Mather, Cotton. *Magnalia Christi Americana.* New York: Arno Press, 1972.

―――. *The Wonders of the Invisible World: Being an Account of the Tryals of Several Witches Lately Executed in New-England.* London: John Russell Smith, 1862.

Mathews, Donald G. *Religion in the Old South.* Chicago: University of Chicago Press, 1977.

―――. *Slavery and Methodism: A Chapter in American Morality, 1780–1845.* Princeton, N.J.: Princeton University Press, 1965.

Matlins, Stuart M. *How to Be a Perfect Stranger: A Guide to Etiquette in Other People's Religious Ceremonies.* 2 vols. Woodstock, Vt.: Jewish Lights Publishing, 1997.

Matsuoka, Fumitaka. *Out of Silence: Emerging Themes in Asian American Churches.* Cleveland: United Church Press, 1995.

Maxwell, Carol J. C. *Pro-Life Activists in America: Meaning, Motivation, and Direct Action.* Cambridge: Cambridge University Press, 2002.

Mbiti, John. *African Religions and Philosophy.* Portsmouth, N.H.: Heinemann, 1990.

McCauley, Deborah Vansau. *Appalachian Mountain Religion: A History.* Urbana: University of Illinois Press, 1995.

McCloud, Sean. *Making the American Religious Fringe: Exotics, Subversives, & Journalists: 1955–1993.* Chapel Hill: University of North Carolina Press, 2004.

McDannell, Colleen, ed. *Religions of the United States in Practice.* 2 vols. Princeton, N.J.: Princeton University Press, 2001.

McGarvie, Mark Douglas. *One Nation Under Law: America's Early National Struggles to Separate Church and State.* Dekalb: Northern Illinois University Press, 2004.

McKivigan, John R. *The War Against Proslavery Religion: Abolitionism and the Northern Churches, 1830–1865.* Ithaca, N.Y.: Cornell University Press, 1984.

McLoughlin, William G. *Isaac Backus and the American Pietist Tradition.* Boston: Little, Brown, 1967.

―――. *Modern Revivalism: Charles Grandison Finney to Billy Graham.* New York: Ronald Press, 1959.

―――. *New England Dissent, 1630–1833: The Baptists and the Separation of Church and State.* 2 vols. Cambridge, Mass.: Harvard University Press, 1971.

―――. *Soul Liberty: The Baptists' Struggle in New England, 1630–1833.* Hanover, N.H.: University Press of New England for Brown University Press, 1991.

McPherson, Aimee Semple. *This Is That: Personal Experiences, Sermons, and Writings.* New York: Garland, 1985.

Mead, Sidney E. *The Lively Experiment: The Shaping of Christianity in America.* New York: Harper & Row, 1963.

―――. *The Nation with the Soul of a Church.* New York: Harper & Row, 1975.

Melton, J. Gordon. *Religious Bodies in the United States, A Directory.* New York: Garland, 1992.

Melton, Julius. *Presbyterian Worship in America: Changing Patterns since 1787.* Richmond, Va.: John Knox, 1967.

Mencken, H. L. *The Impossible Mencken: A Selection of His Best Newspaper Stories.* Edited by Marion Elizabeth Rodgers. New York: Doubleday, 1991.

Merton, Thomas. *The Seven Storey Mountain.* San Diego: Harcourt, Brace, Jovanovich, 1976.

Metcalf, Barbara. *Making Muslim Space in North America and Europe.* Berkeley: University of California Press, 1996.

Meyer, Donald B. *The Positive Thinkers.* New York: Doubleday, 1965.

Miller, Perry. *Roger Williams: His Contribution to the American Tradition.* New York: Atheneum, 1966.

Miller, Perry, and Thomas H. Johnson. *The Puritans: A Sourcebook of Their Writings.* Vol. 1, rev. ed. New York: Harper & Row, 1963.

Miller, William Lee. *The First Liberty: Religion and the American Republic.* New York: Knopf, 1987.

Moen, Matthew J. *The Transformation of the Christian Right.* Tuscaloosa: University of Alabama Press, 1992.

Mooney, James. *The Ghost-Dance Religion and the Sioux Outbreak of 1890.* Edited by Anthony F. C. Wallace. Chicago: University of Chicago Press, 1965.

Moore, R. Laurence. *Religious Outsiders and the Making of Americans.* New York: Oxford University Press, 1986.

Moore, Rebecca, Anthony B. Pinn, and Mary R. Sawyer, eds. *Peoples Temple and Black Religion in America.* Bloomington: Indiana University Press, 2004.

Moquin, Wayne, ed. *Great Documents in American Indian History.* New York: Da Capo Press, 1995.

Morgan, Edmund S. *The Gentle Puritan: A Life of Ezra Stiles.* New Haven, Conn.: Yale University Press, 1962.

————. *The Puritan Dilemma: The Story of John Winthrop.* 2d ed. New York: Longman, 1999.

Morris, Charles R. *American Catholic: The Saints and Sinners Who Built America's Most Powerful Church.* New York: Times Books, 1997.

Morrison, Samuel Eliot. *Builders of the Bay Colony.* Boston: Houghton Mifflin, 1930.

Moynahan, Brian. *The Faith: A History of Christianity.* New York: Doubleday, 2002.

Muck, Terry. *Those Other Religions in Your Neighborhood: Loving Your Neighbor When You Don't Know How.* Grand Rapids, Mich.: Zondervan, 1992.

Mulford, Carla, ed. *Early American Writings.* Oxford: Oxford University Press, 2002.

Murphy, Larry G., J. Gordon Melton, and Gary L. Ward, eds. *Encyclopedia of African American Religions.* New York: Garland, 1993.

Murray, John Courtney. *We Hold These Truths: Catholic Reflections on the American Proposition.* New York: Sheed & Ward, 1960.

Neihardt, John G. *Black Elk Speaks.* New York: MJF, 1996.

Neuhaus, Richard J. *The Naked Public Square: Religion and Democracy in America.* Grand Rapids, Mich.: Eerdmans, 1984.

Neusner, Jacob. *American Judaism: Adventure in Modernity.* Englewood Cliffs, N.J.: Prentice Hall, 1972.

Nichols, Roger L. *Indians in the United States and Canada: A Comparative History.* Lincoln: University of Nebraska Press, 1998.

Niebuhr, Reinhold. *Leaves from the Notebook of a Tamed Cynic.* Hamden, Conn.: Shoe String Press, 1956.

Noley, Homer. *First White Frost: Native Americans and United Methodism.* Nashville: Abingdon Press, 1991.

Noll, Mark A. *America's God: From Jonathan Edwards to Abraham Lincoln.* Oxford: Oxford University Press, 2002.

————. *A History of Christianity in the United States and Canada.* Grand Rapids, Mich.: Eerdmans, 1992.

————. *The Old Religion in a New World: The History of North American Christianity.* Grand Rapids, Mich.: Eerdmans, 2002.

————. *Princeton and the Republic, 1768–1822: The Search for a Christian Enlightenment in the Era of Samuel Stanhope Smith.* Princeton, N.J.: Princeton University Press, 1989.

————, ed. *The Princeton Theology, 1812–1921: Scripture, Science, Theological Method from Archibald Alexander to Benjamin Breckinridge Warfield.* Grand Rapids, Mich.: Baker Book House, 1983.

————, ed. *Religion and American Politics: From the Colonial Period to the 1980s.* New York: Oxford University Press, 1990.

Noonan, John T., Jr. *The Lustre of Our Country: The American Experience of Religious Freedom.* Berkeley: University of California Press, 1998.

Nouwen, Henri J. M. *Sabbatical Journey: The Diary of His Final Year.* New York: Crossroad, 1998.

Numbers, Ronald L. *Prophetess of Health: A Study of Ellen G. White.* New York: Harper & Row, 1976.

————, and Jonathan M. Butler, eds. *The Disappointed: Millerism and Millenarianism in the Nineteenth Century.* Bloomington: Indiana University Press, 1987.

Nyang, Sulayman S. *Islam in the United States of America.* Chicago: ABC International Group, 1999.

Obo, Franklin, ed. *The Columbia Documentary History of the Asian American Experience.* New York: Columbia University Press, 2002.

O'Brien, David J. *The Renewal of American Catholicism.* New York: Oxford University Press, 1972.

O'Connor, Flannery. *The Habit of Being: Letters.* Edited by Sally Fitzgerald. New York: Farrar, Straus & Giroux, 1979.

O'Neil, Maura. *Women Speaking, Women Listening: Women in Interreligious Dialogue.* Maryknoll, N.Y.: Orbis Books, 1990.

Oppenhiemer, Mark. *Knocking on Heaven's Door: American Religion in the Age of Counterculture.* New Haven, Conn.: Yale University Press, 2003.

Oren, Dan A. *Joining the Club: A History of Jews and Yale.* New Haven, Conn.: Yale University Press, 1985.

Orsi, Robert Anthony, ed. *Gods of the City.* Bloomington: Indiana University Press, 1999.

————. *The Madonna of 115th Street: Faith and Community in Italian Harlem, 1880–1950.* New York: Yale University Press, 1985.

Oxnam, G. Bromley. *I Protest.* New York: Harper & Brothers, 1954.

Page, Jake. *In the Hands of the Great Spirit: The 20,000 Year History of American Indians.* New York: Free Press, 2003.

Palóu's Life of Fray Junípero Serra. Translated by Maynard J. Geiger. Washington, D.C.: Academy of American Franciscan History, 1955.

Pals, Daniel J. *Seven Theories of Religion.* New York: Oxford University Press, 1996.

Parker, Arthur C. *Seneca Myths and Folk Tales.* Buffalo, N.Y.: Buffalo Historical Society, 1923.

Pears, Thomas Clinton, Jr. *Documentary History of William Tennent and the Log College.* Philadelphia: Presbyterian Historical Society, 1940.

Peden, Creighton. *The Chicago School: Voices in Liberal Religious Thought.* Bristol, Ind.: Wyndham Hall Press, 1987.

Penn, William. *The Witness of William Penn.* Edited by Frederick B. Tolles and E. Gordon Alderfer. New York: Macmillan Co., 1957.

Percy, Walker. *Lost in the Cosmos: The Last Self-Help Book.* New York: Farrar, Straus & Giroux, 1983.

Perry, Michael J. *Love and Power: The Role of Morality and Religion in American Politics.* New York: Oxford University Press, 1991.

Perry, Richard L., ed. *Sources of Our Liberties: Documentary Origins of Individual Liberties in the United States Constitution and Bill of Rights.* Rev. ed. Chicago: American Bar Foundation, 1978.

Peters, John L. *Christian Perfection and American Methodism.* Grand Rapids, Mich.: Zondervan, 1985.

Peters, Shawn Francis. *Judging Jehovah's Witnesses: Religious Persecution and the Dawn of the Rights Revolution.* Lawrence: University Press of Kansas, 2000.

Peyer, Bernd, ed. *The Elders Wrote: An Anthology of Early Prose by North American Indians, 1768–1931.* Berlin: Dietrich Reimer, 1982.

Pilmore, Joseph. *The Journal of Joseph Pilmore, Methodist Itinerant, for the Years August 1, 1769, to January 2, 1774.* Edited by Frederick E. Maser and Howard T. Maag. Philadelphia: Printed by Message Pub. Co. for the Historical Society of the Philadelphia Annual Conference of the United Methodist Church, 1969.

Pinn, Anne H., and Anthony B. Pinn. *Fortress Introduction to Black Church History.* Minneapolis: Fortress Press, 2001.

Pipes, Daniel. *Militant Islam Reaches America.* New York: Norton, 2002.

Pointer, Richard W. *Protestant Pluralism and the New York Experience: A Study of Eighteenth-Century Religious Diversity.* Bloomington: Indiana University Press, 1988.

Porterfield, Amanda. *The Transformation of American Religion.* New York: Oxford University Press, 2001.

Powers, William K. *Oglala Religion.* Lincoln: University of Nebraska Press, 1975.

Prebisch, Charles S. *American Buddhism.* North Scituate, Mass.: Duxbury, 1979.

———, and Kenneth Tanaka. *The Faces of Buddhism in America.* Berkeley: University of California Press, 1998.

Quebedeaux, Richard. *The New Charismatics: The Origins, Development, and Significance of Neo-Pentecostalism.* New York: Doubleday, 1975.

———. *The Worldly Evangelicals.* San Francisco: Harper & Row, 1978.

Queen, Edward L., Stephen R. Prothero, and Gardiner H. Shattuck, Jr. *The Encyclopedia of American Religious History.* New York: Facts On File, 1996.

Quinn, David B. *New American World: A Documentary History of North America to 1612.* 5 vols. New York: Arno Press, 1979.

Raboteau, Albert J. *A Fire in the Bones: Reflections on African-American Religious History.* Boston: Beacon Press, 1995.

———. *Slave Religion: "The Invisible Institution" in the Antebellum South.* New York: Oxford University Press, 1978.

Race, Alan. *Christians and Religious Pluralism.* Maryknoll, N.Y.: Orbis Books, 1982.

Raider, Mark. A., Jonathan D. Sarna, and Ronald W. Zweig, eds. *Abba Hillel Silver and American Zionism.* London: Frank Cass, 1997.

Raphael, Marc Lee. *Judaism in America.* New York: Columbia University Press, 2003.

Rauschenbusch, Walter. *Christianizing the Social Order.* New York: Macmillan, 1921.

Reagon, Bernice Johnson, ed. *We'll Understand It Better, By and By.* New York: Harper & Row, 1988.

Records of Salem Witchcraft: Copied from the Original Documents. 2 vols. New York: B. Franklin, 1972.

Reid, Daniel G., ed. *Dictionary of Christianity in America.* Downers Grove, Ill.: Inter-Varsity, 1990.

Rev. Thomas Bray: His Life and Selected Works Relating to Maryland. Edited by Bernard C. Steiner. New York: Arno Press, 1972.

Richardson, E. Allen. *East Comes West.* New York: Pilgrim Press, 1985.

———. *Strangers in This Land: Pluralism and the Response to Diversity in the United States.* New York: Pilgrim Press, 1988.

Richardson, Harry V. *Dark Salvation: The Story of Methodism As It Developed among Blacks in America.* Garden City, N.Y.: Doubleday, 1976.

Richey, Russell E. *Early American Methodism.* Bloomington: Indiana University Press, 1991.

Riggs, Marcia Y., ed. *Can I Get a Witness?: Prophetic Religious Voices of African American Women: An Anthology.* Maryknoll, N.Y.: Orbis Books, 1997.

Rivera N., Luis. *A Violent Evangelism: The Political and Religious Conquest of the Americas.* Louisville, Ky.: Westminster/John Knox Press, 1992.

Rochford, E. Burke, Jr. *Hare Krishna in America.* New Brunswick, N.J.: Rutgers University Press, 1985.

Roof, Wade Clark. *Contemporary American Religion.* 2 vols. New York: Macmillan, 2000.

Rosenwaike, Ira. *On the Edge of Greatness: A Portrait of American Jewry in the Early National Period.* Cincinnati: American Jewish Archives, 1985.

Roth, Randolph A. *The Democratic Dilemma: Religion, Reform, and the Social Order in the Connecticut River Valley of Vermont, 1791–1850.* New York: Cambridge University Press, 1987.

Rubin, Jerry. *Growing (Up) at Thirty-Seven.* New York: M. Evans, 1976.

Sale, Kirkpatrick. *The Conquest of Paradise: Christopher Columbus and the Columbian Legacy.* New York: Knopf, 1990.

Sarna, Jonathan D., *American Judaism: A History.* New Haven, Conn.: Yale University Press, 2004.

———, ed. *The Jews of Boston.* Boston: American Jewish Historical Society, 1996.

Sassi, Jonathan D. *A Republic of Righteousness: The Public Christianity of the Post-Revolutionary New England Clergy.* Oxford: Oxford University Press, 2001.

Schappes, Morris U. *A Documentary History of the Jews in the United States: 1654–1875.* New York: Citadel Press, 1950.

Schechter, Solomon. *Seminary Addresses & Other Papers.* New York: Arno Press, 1969.

Schmidt, Leigh Eric. "The Easter Parade: Piety, Fashion, and Display." In *Religion and American Culture: A Reader.* Edited by David G. Hackett. 2d ed. New York: Routledge, 2003.

Schultz, Jeffrey D., John G. West, and Iain S. MacLean. *Encyclopedia of Religion in American Politics.* Phoenix, Ariz.: Oryx Press, 1999.

Schwartz, Sally. *"A Mixed Multitude": The Struggle for Toleration in Colonial Pennsylvania.* New York: New York University Press, 1987.

Scott, Donald M. *From Office to Profession: The New England Ministry, 1750–1850.* Philadelphia: University of Pennsylvania Press, 1978.

Seager, Richard Hughes. *Buddhism in America.* New York: Columbia University Press, 1999.

Seltzer, Robert M., and Norman J. Cohen, eds. *The Americanization of the Jews.* New York: New York University Press, 1995.

Serafim, Archimandrite. *The Quest for Orthodox Unity in America.* New York: Saints Boris & Gleb, 1973.

Sernett, Milton C. *African American Religious History: A Documentary Witness.* 2d ed. Durham, N.C.: Duke University Press, 1999.

Sewell, William. *The History of the Rise, Increase, and Progress, of the Christian People Called Quakers.* Philadelphia: Uriah Hunt, 1832.

Sheen, Fulton J. *Treasure in Clay: The Autobiography of Fulton J. Sheen.* Garden City, N.Y.: Doubleday, 1980.

Shipps, Jan. *Mormonism: The Story of a New Religious Tradition.* Urbana: University of Illinois Press, 1984.

Shulman, Albert M. *The Religious Heritage of America.* San Diego: A. S. Barnes, 1981.

Silberman, Charles E. *A Certain People: American Jews and Their Lives Today.* New York: Summit, 1985.

Simpson, George Eaton. *Black Religions in the New World.* New York: Columbia University Press, 1978.

Skerrett, Ellen, Edward B. Kantowicz, and Steven V. Avella. *Catholicism Chicago Style.* Chicago: Loyola University Press, 1993.

Slave Narratives. New York: Library of America, 2002.

Slotkin, J. S. *The Peyote Religion: A Study in Indian-White Relations.* Glencoe, Ill.: Free Press, 1956.

Smith, Hannah Whitall. *The Christian's Secret of a Happy Life.* Westwood, N.J.: Revell, 1952.

Smith, H. Shelton. *"In His Image But . . .": Racism in Southern Religion, 1780–1910.* Durham, N.C.: Duke University Press, 1972.

Smith, Jane E. *Islam in America.* New York: Columbia University Press, 1999.

Smith, Jonathan Z. *Map Is Not Territory: Studies in the History of Religions.* Chicago: University of Chicago Press, 1993.

Smith, Timothy Lawrence. *Called unto Holiness: The Story of the Nazarenes.* Kansas City, Mo.: Nazarene, 1962.

Smith, Wilfred C. *The Meaning and End of Religion.* Minneapolis: Fortress Press, 1990.

———. *Religious Diversity.* New York: Crossroads, 1981.

Spalding, Thomas W. *The Premier See: A History of the Archdiocese of Baltimore, 1789–1989.* Baltimore: Johns Hopkins University Press, 1989.

Spencer, Jon Michael. *Black Hymnody: A Hymnological History of the African-American Church.* Knoxville: University of Tennessee Press, 1992.

Sproul, Barbara C. *Primal Myths: Creating the World.* New York: Harper & Row, 1979.

Stannard, David E. *American Holocaust: Columbus and the Conquest of the New World.* New York: Oxford University Press, 1992.

Stein, Stephen J. *Communities of Dissent: A History of Alternative Religions in America.* New York: Oxford University Press, 2002.

———. *The Shaker Experience in America: A History of the United Society of Believers.* New Haven, Conn.: Yale University Press, 1992.

Stevens, Charles Emery. *Anthony Burns: A History.* New York: Negro Universities Press, 1969.

Stewart, Omer C. *Peyote Religion, A History.* Norman: University of Oklahoma Press, 1987.

Stewart, Richard. *Leper Priest of Molokai: The Father Damien Story.* Honolulu: University of Hawaii Press, 2000.

St. John de Crevecoeur, J. Hector. *Letters from an American Farmer.* New York: Fox, Duffield, 1904.

Stokes, Anton Phelps. *Church and State in the United States.* 3 vols. New York: Harper & Bros., 1950.

Stout, Harry S. *The New England Soul: Preaching and Religious Culture in Colonial New England.* New York: Oxford University Press, 1986.

Stowe, David W. *How Sweet the Sound: Music in the Spiritual Lives of Americans.* Cambridge, Mass.: Harvard University Press, 2004.

Streng, Frederick J. *Understanding Religious Life.* Belmont, Calif.: Wadsworth, 1985.

Sullivan, Lawrence E., ed. *Native American Religions: North America.* New York: Macmillan, 1989.

Swann, Brian, ed. *Coming to Light: Contemporary Translations of the Native Literatures of North America.* New York: Vintage, 1994.

Sweeney, Douglas A. *Nathaniel Taylor, New Haven Theology, and the Legacy of Jonathan Edwards.* Oxford: Oxford University Press, 2003.

Sweet, William W. *Makers of Christianity: From John Cotton to Lyman Abbott.* New York: Macmillan, 1921.

——. *Religion in the Development of American Culture, 1765–1840.* New York: Charles Scribner's Sons, 1952.

——. *Religion on the American Frontier, 1783–1850.* 4 vols. New York: Cooper Square, 1964.

Synan, Vinson. *The Holiness-Pentecostal Movement in the United States.* Grand Rapids, Mich.: Eerdmans, 1971.

Tanis, James. *Dutch Calvinistic Pietism in the Middle Colonies: A Study in the Life and Theology of Theodorus Jacobus Frelinghuysen.* The Hague: Martinus Nijhoff, 1967.

Tappert, Theodore G., ed. *Lutheran Confessional Theology in America, 1840–1880.* New York: Oxford University Press, 1972.

Taylor, James Barnett. *Biography of Elder Lott Cary, Late Missionary to Africa.* Baltimore: Armstrong & Berry, 1837.

Tedlock, Dennis, and Barbara Tedlock. *Teachings from the American Earth: Indian Religion and Philosophy.* New York: Liveright, 1975.

Thiemann, Ronald F. *Religion in Public Life: A Dilemma for Democracy.* Washington, D.C.: Georgetown University Press, 1996.

Thomas, David Hurst, et al. *The Native Americans: An Illustrated History.* Atlanta, Ga: Turner Publishing, 1993.

Thomas, Herman Edward. *James W. C. Pennington: African American Churchman and Abolitionist.* New York: Garland, 1995.

Thompson, Norma H., ed. *Religious Pluralism and Religious Education.* Birmingham, Ala.: Religious Education Press, 1988.

Thompson, Rhodes, ed. *Voices from Cane Ridge.* St. Louis, Mo.: Bethany Press, 1954.

Thoreau, Henry David. *Henry David Thoreau.* New York: Library of America, 1985.

Three Prophets of Religious Liberalism: Channing, Emerson, Parker. Boston: Beacon Press, 1961.

Tillich, Paul. *Systematic Theology.* Chicago: University of Chicago Press, 1951.

Torbet, Robert G. *A History of the Baptists.* Valley Forge, Pa.: Judson, 1973.

Traboulay, David M. *Columbus and Las Casas: The Conquest and Christianization of America, 1492–1566.* Lanham, Md.: University Press of America, 1994.

Trinterud, Leonard J. *The Forming of an American Tradition: A Re-Examination of Colonial Presbyterianism.* Philadelphia: Westminster, 1949.

Trueblood, G. Elton. *The People Called Quakers.* New York: Harper & Row, 1966.

———. *While It Is Day: An Autobiography.* New York: Harper & Row, 1974.

Tucker, Karen B. Westerfield. *American Methodist Worship.* Oxford: Oxford University Press, 2001.

Turner, Richard Brent. *Islam in the African American Experience.* Bloomington: Indiana University Press, 1977.

Tuveson, Ernest L. *Redeemer Nation: The Idea of America's Millennial Role.* Chicago: University of Chicago Press, 1968.

Tweed, Thomas A. *The American Encounter with Buddhism, 1844–1912: Victorian Culture and the Limits of Dissent.* Bloomington: Indiana University Press, 1992.

Tweed, Thomas A., and Stephen Prothero, eds. *Asian Religions in America: A Documentary History.* New York: Oxford University Press, 1999.

Twentieth-Century Shapers of American Popular Religion. Edited by Charles H. Lippy. New York: Greenwood Press, 1989.

Underhill, Ruth M. *Red Man's Religion.* Chicago: University of Chicago Press, 1965.

Upham, Charles W. *Salem Witchcraft: With an Account of Salem Village and a History of Opinions on Witchcraft and Kindred Subjects.* 2 vols. New York: Frederick Ungar, 1959.

Urban, Linwood. *A Short History of Christian Thought.* New York: Oxford University Press, 1995.

Vanauken, Sheldon. *A Severe Mercy.* San Francisco: Harper & Row, 1977.

Vásquez, Mark G. *Authority and Reform: Religious and Educational Discourses in Nineteenth-century New England Literature.* Knoxville: University of Tennessee Press, 2003.

Vecsey, Christopher. *Imagine Ourselves Richly: Mythic Narratives of North American Indians.* New York: HarperCollins, 1991.

———, ed. *Religion in Native North America.* Moscow: University of Idaho Press, 1990.

Versluis, Arthur. *American Transcendentalism and Asian Religions.* Oxford: Oxford University Press, 1993.

Villafane, Eldin. *The Liberating Spirit: Toward an Hispanic American Pentecostal Social Ethic.* Grand Rapids, Mich.: Eerdmans, 1993.

Vining, Elizabeth Gray. *Friend of Life: The Biography of Rufus M. Jones.* Philadelphia: J. B. Lippincott, 1958.

Wacker, Grant. *Heaven Below: Early Pentecostals and American Culture.* Cambridge, Mass.: Harvard University Press, 2001.

Wagenknecht, Edward. *Daughters of the Covenant: Portraits of Six Jewish Women.* Amherst: University of Massachusetts Press, 1983.

Wald, Kenneth D. *Religion and Politics in the United States.* 3d ed. Washington, D.C.: CQ Press, 1997.

Walker, James R. *Lakota Belief and Ritual.* Edited by Raymond J. DeMallie and Elaine A. Jahner. Lincoln: University of Nebraska Press, 1980.

Walker, Wyatt Tee. *Somebody's Calling My Name: Black Sacred Music and Social Change.* Valley Forge, Pa.: Judson Press, 1979.

Wall, Steve. *Shadowcatchers: A Journey in Search of the Teachings of Native American Healers.* New York: HarperCollins, 1994.

Wallace, Anthony F. C. *The Death and Rebirth of the Seneca.* New York: Knopf, 1970.

Wallis, Jim. *God's Politics: Why the Right Gets It Wrong and the Left Doesn't Get It.* San Francisco: HarperSanFrancisco, 2005.

Ward, Nathaniel. *The Simple Cobler of Aggawam in America.* Edited by P. M. Zall. Lincoln: University of Nebraska Press, 1969.

Washington, James Melvin. *Conversations with God: Two Centuries of Prayers by African Americans.* New York: HarperCollins, 1994.

Washington, Joseph R., Jr. *Black Religion: The Negro and Christianity in the United States.* Lanham, Md.: University Press of America, 1984.

———. *Black Sects and Cults.* Garden City, N.Y.: Doubleday, 1973.

Watts, Alan. *In My Own Way: An Autobiography, 1915–1965.* New York: Vintage Books, 1972.

Weber, Paul J., and W. Landis Jones. *U.S. Religious Interest Groups: Institutional Profiles.* Westport, Conn.: Greenwood Press, 1994.

Weber, Timothy P. *Living in the Shadow of the Second Coming: American Pre-Millennialism, 1875–1982.* New York: Oxford University Press, 1982.

Weinberg, Sydney Stahl. *The World of Our Mothers: The Lives of Jewish Immigrant Women.* Chapel Hill: University of North Carolina Press, 1988.

Weisberger, Bernard A. *They Gathered at the River: The Story of the Great Revivalists and Their Impact upon Religion in America.* New York: Octagon, 1979.

Wells, David F., and John D. Woodridge. *The Evangelicals.* Nashville: Abingdon, 1975.

Wentz, Abdel Ross. *A Basic History of Lutheranism in America.* Philadelphia: Fortress Press, 1964.

Wentz, Richard E. *The Culture of Religious Pluralism.* Boulder, Colo.: Westview Press, 1998.

———. *Religion in the New World: The Shaping of Religious Traditions in the United States.* Minneapolis: Fortress Press, 1990.

Werblowsky, R. J. Zwi, and Geoffrey Wigoder, eds. *The Encyclopedia of the Jewish Religion.* New York: Holt, Rinehart & Winston, 1966.

West, Jessamyn, ed. *The Quaker Reader.* New York: Viking Press, 1962.

White, Richard. *The Middle Ground: Indians, Empires, and Republics in the Great Lakes Region.* Cambridge: Cambridge University Press, 1991.

White, Ronald C., Jr., and C. Howard Hopkins. *The Social Gospel: Religion and Reform in Changing America.* Philadelphia: Temple University Press, 1976.

Whitefield, George. *George Whitefield's Journals, 1737–41, to Which Is Prefixed His "Short Account" (1746) and "Further Account" (1747).* Edited by William W. Davis. Gainesville, Fla.: Scholars' Facsimiles & Reprints, 1969.

Wigger, John H. *Taking Heaven by Storm: Methodism and the Rise of Popular Christianity in America.* New York: Oxford University Press, 1998.

Wilcox, Clyde. *God's Warriors: The Christian Right in the Twentieth-Century.* Baltimore: Johns Hopkins University Press, 1991.

Willard, Frances E. *Writing Out My Heart: Selections from the Journal of Francis E. Willard, 1855–96.* Edited by Carolyn De Swarte Gifford. Urbana: University of Illinois Press, 1995.

Williams, Peter W. *America's Religions: From Their Origins to the Twenty-first Century.* Urbana: University of Illinois Press, 2002.

———. *Popular Religion in America Symbolic Change and the Modernization Process in Historical Perspective.* Englewood Cliffs, N.J.: Prentice Hall, 1980.

Williams, Raymond Brady. *Religions of Immigrants from India and Pakistan: New Threads in the American Tapestry.* Cambridge: Cambridge University Press, 1988.

Williamson, William B., ed. *An Encyclopedia of Religions in the United States: One Hundred Religious Groups Speak for Themselves.* New York: Crossroads, 1992.

Wills, Gary. *Under God: Religion and American Politics.* New York: Simon & Schuster, 1990.

Wilmore, Gayraud S. *Black Religion and Black Radicalism: An Interpretation of the Religious History of the Afro-American People.* 2d ed. Maryknoll, N.Y.: Orbis Books, 1983.

Wilson, A. N. *God's Funeral.* New York: Norton, 1999.

Wilson, John F., ed. *Church and State in America: A Bibliographical Guide.* New York: Greenwood Press, 1986.

Wilson, John F., and Donald L. Drakeman, eds. *Church and State in American History: Key Documents, Decisions, and Commentary From the Past Three Centuries.* 3d ed. Boulder, Colo.: Westview, 2003.

Wind, James P., and James W., Lewis, eds. *American Congregations.* 2 vols. Chicago: University of Chicago Press, 1994.

Winthrop, John. *The Journal of John Winthrop, 1630–1649.* Edited by Richard S. Dunn, James Savage, and Laetitia Yeandle. Cambridge, Mass.: Belknap Press of Harvard University Press, 1996.

Wise, Isaac M. *Reminiscences.* Translated by David Philopson. New York: Arno Press, 1973.

Wolf, William J. *Freedom's Holy Light: American Identity and the Future of Theology.* Wakefield, Mass.: Parameter, 1977.

Woodmason, Charles. *The Carolina Backcountry on the Eve of the Revolution: The Journal and Other Writings of Charles Woodmason, Anglican Itinerant.* Edited by Richard J. Hooker. Chapel Hill: published for the Institute of Early American History and Culture at Williamsburg, Va., by the University of North Carolina Press, 1953.

Woodson, Carter G. *The History of the Negro Church.* Washington, D.C.: Associated Publishers, 1992.

Wright, Francis. *Views of Society and Manners in America.* Edited by Paul R. Baker. Cambridge, Mass.: Belknap Press of Harvard University Press, 1963.

Wright, Lawrence. *Saints & Sinners: Walker Railey, Jimmy Swaggert, Madalyn Murray O'Hair, Anton LaVey, Will Campbell, Matthew Fox.* New York: Knopf, 1993.

Wuthnow, Robert. *After Heaven: Spirituality in America since the 1950s.* Berkeley: University of California Press, 1998.

———. *The Restructuring of American Religion: Society and Faith since World War II.* Princeton, N.J.: Princeton University Press, 1988.

X, Malcolm. *The Autobiography of Malcolm X.* With the assistance of Alex Haley. New York: Grove Press, 1966.

Yogananda, Paramahansa. *Autobiography of a Yogi.* 11th ed. Los Angeles: Self-Realization Fellowship, 1971.

Yoo, David, ed. *New Spiritual Homes: Religion and Asian Americans.* Honolulu: University of Hawaii Press, 1999.

Young, William A. *Quest for Harmony: Native American Spiritual Traditions.* New York: Seven Bridges Press, 2002.

Ziolkowski, Eric J., ed. *A Museum of Faiths: Histories and Legacies of the 1893 World's Parliament of Religions.* Atlanta, Ga.: Scholar's Press, 1993.

Zwaanstra, Henry. *Reformed Thought and Experience in a New World: A Study of the Christian Reformed Church and Its American Environment.* Grand Rapids, Mich.: Eerdmans, 1974.

Index

Locators in *italics* indicate illustrations. Locators in **boldface** indicate main entries/topics and biographies. Locators followed by *m* indicate maps. Locators followed by *t* indicate graphs and tables. Locators followed by *g* indicate glossary entries. Locators followed by *c* indicate chronology entries.

A

Abba Hillel Silver and American Zionism (Raider) 296
Abbott, Lyman 239, *240*, 289, **384**
Abdullah, Muhammad Nur 351
Abington Township v. Schempp 313*c*
abolitionism 154*c*, 171–172
abortion 299, 315*c*, 328, 329, 340*c*, 341*c*
Abraham Lincoln: Speeches and Writings (Lincoln) 207, 209–210
Abyssinian Baptist Church 131*c*, 251*c*, 287*c*
Acres of Diamonds (Conwell) 260
Act Concerning Religion 31, 38*c*
Act of Toleration x, 75, 76
Act to Prevent the Growth of Popery 83*c*
Adams, Samuel 115
Adler, Cyrus 226*c*, 227*c*, **384**
Adler, Felix 198, 204*c*, **384–385**
adoptions 342*c*
advent 430*g*
Adventist 176*c*
Africa, John 315*c*
African American(s). *See also* Civil Rights movement; Nation of Islam; slavery and slaves; *specific headings, e.g.:* King, Martin Luther, Jr.
   Baptist 149–150
   camp meeting *188*
   Lott Cary 109*c*, 132*c*, 153*c*, 390
   and Christianity **122–124,** 149–151, 193–196
   church services *294*
   conversion of 122, 149–151
   Alexander Crummell 176*c*
   Father Divine 254*c*, 267, 279–280, 394
   ecumenical movement 304
   emancipation and black churches 189
   expansion of Christianity of 193–196
   first known baptism of 37*c*
   Henry Highland Garnet 172, 176*c*, 202*c*, 398
   Sweet Daddy Grace 267, 279–281, 283*c*, 398
   Wilton Gregory 341*c*
   Atticus Greene Haygood and 226*c*

Islam, beginnings of 277–279
   Absalom Jones 123, 128*c*, 130*c*
   George Liele 109*c*
   Methodists 149–150, 192
   Mormon Church 317*c*
   National Baptist Convention 196, 253*c*
   nuns *195*
   Oblate Sisters of Providence 153*c*
   as partners in American life 192
   Thomas Paul 131*c*
   Providence Baptist Association 154*c*
   religious beliefs of slaves 149
   and revivalism *247*, 262–263
   Tougaloo University 193
   Charles Randolf Uncles 228*c*
African American Religious History (Sernett) 206–207
African Baptist church 128*c*
African Episcopal Church of St. Thomas 129*c*
African Meeting House 131*c*
African Methodist Episcopal Church (AME Church) 108*c*, 124, 132*c*, 177*c*, 202*c*
African Methodist Episcopal Zion Church 152*c*, 228*c*
African Union First Colored Methodist Protestant Church of America 202*c*
agnosticism 430*g*
Alaska 156*c*
alcohol 147. *See also* Prohibition
Alcoholics Anonymous 284*c*, 285*c*
Aleksy II (Russian Orthodox patriarch) 340*c*
Alexander, Archibald 129*c*, 131*c*, **385**
Alexander, Jon 158
Alexander VI (pope) 2, 11*c*
Algonquian Indians 37*c*, 54
Allen, Richard 123, **385**
   African Methodist Episcopal Church 124, 132*c*
   birth of 108*c*
   on church experience 160–161
   First National Negro Convention 153*c*
   Free African Society 123, 128*c*
   joins Methodist Church 109*c*
   licensed as preacher 128*c*
   ordained 108*c*, 130*c*, 132*c*
   St. George's Methodist Church 122–123
Allis, Oswald T. 283*c*
Al Qaeda. *See under* Q
altar call 430*g*
AMA. *See* American Missionary Association
AME Church. *See* African Methodist Episcopal Church
American Baptist Home Mission Society 154*c*
American Bible Society 132*c*, 147, 314*c*

American Board of Commissioners for Foreign Missions 131*c*, 147
American Buddhist Congress 340*c*
The American Catholic Experience (Dolan) 289
American Christian Movement for Life 315*c*
American Colonization Society 132*c*, 171–172
American Federation of Catholic Societies 251*c*
The American Friend (magazine) 228*c*
American Friends Service Committee 254*c*
American History Told by Contemporaries (Hart) 63–64, 235–236
American identity **98–102**
American Indian(s) 313*c*. *See also* Ghost Dance; peyoteism; *specific tribes*
   in 19th century 215
   Black Elk 201*c*, 251*c*, 283*c*, 387
   Jean de Brébeuf and 34*c*, 36*c*
   Catherine Brown 152*c*
   Canada 312*c*
   Cayuse mission 155*c*, 177*c*
   in colonial period **53–54**
   constitution of Iroquois Federation 11*c*
   Creek creation story 5
   cultural groups in 11*c*
   disease among 36*c*
   Jonathan Edwards and 107*c*
   John Eliot and 37*c*, 38*c*, 418*m*
   Juan de Escalona and 13*c*
   Fairgrounds Circle 3
   French Jesuits and 39*c*
   Guale Indians revolt 13*c*
   Marie Guyart and 30, 37*c*
   Handsome Lake 86*c*, 124, 130*c*, 399
   Hopewellians 3
   Anne Marbury Hutchinson and 37*c*
   Jicarilla Apache creation story 5
   and Junta of Valladolid 12*c*
   King Philip's War 54, 59*c*, 65
   Laws of Burgos 11*c*
   Longhouse religion 124
   Manhattan Island purchased from 34*c*
   Moors Indian Charity 107*c*
   New York Missionary Society 147
   Samson Occom and 108*c*
   Okanagon creation story 15
   ordination prohibited 13*c*
   Quanah Parker 178*c*, *220*, 407
   Paul II (pope) and 12*c*
   Praying Indians (converts to Christianity) 38*c*
   precolonial religious beliefs 2, 4–5
   pre-Columbian **2–5**
   Prophetstown destroyed 131*c*

C

S